k_{SIMPLE}	Nominal risk-free rate of interest; also referred to as i_{SIMPLE}
k_{ps}	Cost of preferred stock
k_{RF}	Rate of return on a risk-free security
k_s	(1) Cost of retained earnings
	(2) Required return on a stock
M	Maturity value of a bond
M/B	Market-to-book ratio
MCC	Marginal cost of capital
MIRR	Modified internal rate of return
N	Calculator key denoting number of periods
n	Life of a project
NPV	Net present value
NWC	Net working capital
P_o	Price of the stock today
P	Sales price per unit of product sold
P/E	Price/earnings ratio
PMT	Periodic level payment of an annuity
PV	Present value
PVA_n	Present value of an annuity for n years
PVIF	Present value interest factor for a lump sum
PVIFA	Present value interest factor for an annuity
Q	Quantity produced or sold
r	Correlation coefficient
ROA	Return on assets
ROE	Return on equity
RP	Risk premium
RP_M	Market risk premium
S	Sales in dollars
SML	Security Market Line
Σ	Summation sign (capital sigma)
σ	Standard deviation (lowercase sigma)
σ^2	Variance
t	Time period
T	Marginal income tax rate
TIE	Times interest earned
v	Variable cost as a percent of selling price
V	Variable cost per unit
V_d	Bond value
V_{ps}	Preferred stock value
VC	Total variable costs
WACC	Weighted average cost of capital
YTC	Yield to call
YTM	Yield to maturity

Essentials of
Managerial Finance

TWELFTH EDITION

Essentials of
Managerial Finance

TWELFTH EDITION

SCOTT BESLEY

University of South Florida

EUGENE F. BRIGHAM

University of Florida

THE DRYDEN PRESS
A DIVISION OF HARCOURT COLLEGE PUBLISHERS

Fort Worth   Philadelphia   San Diego   New York   Orlando   Austin   San Antonio
Toronto   Montreal   London   Sydney   Tokyo

PUBLISHER	Mike Roche
EXECUTIVE EDITOR	Mike Reynolds
MARKET STRATEGIST	Charles Watson
DEVELOPMENTAL EDITOR	Terri House
PROJECT EDITOR	Rebecca Dodson
ART DIRECTOR	April Eubanks
PRODUCTION MANAGER	Lois West

ISBN: 0-03-025872-3
Library of Congress Catalog Card Number: 99-76978

Address for Domestic Orders
The Dryden Press, 6277 Sea Harbor Drive, Orlando, FL 32887–6777
800-782-4479

Address for International Orders
International Customer Service
The Dryden Press, 6277 Sea Harbor Drive, Orlando, FL 32887–6777
407-345-3800
(fax) 407-345-4060
(e-mail) hbintl@harcourtbrace.com

Address for Editorial Correspondence
The Dryden Press, 301 Commerce Street, Suite 3700, Fort Worth, TX 76102

Web Site Address
http://www.harcourtcollege.com

THE DRYDEN PRESS, DRYDEN, and the DP LOGO are registered trademarks of Harcourt, Inc.

Printed in the United States of America

9 0 1 2 3 4 5 6 7 8   048   9 8 7 6 5 4 3 2 1

The Dryden Press
Harcourt College Publishers

THE DRYDEN PRESS SERIES IN FINANCE

Amling and Droms
Investment Fundamentals

Berry and Young
Managing Investments:
A Case Approach

Besley and Brigham
Essentials of Managerial Finance
Twelfth Edition

Besley and Brigham
Principles of Finance

Boone, Kurtz, and Hearth
Planning Your Financial Future
Second Edition

Brigham, Gapenski, and Daves
Intermediate Financial Management
Sixth Edition

Brigham, Gapenski, and Ehrhardt
Financial Management: Theory
and Practice
Ninth Edition

Brigham, Gapenski, and Klein
2000 Cases in Financial Management:
Dryden Request

Brigham and Houston
Fundamentals of Financial Management
Eighth Edition

Brigham and Houston
Fundamentals of Financial
Management: Concise
Second Edition

Chance
An Introduction to Derivatives
Fourth Edition

Clark, Gerlach, and Olson
Restructuring Corporate America

Conroy
Finance Interactive

Cooley
Advances in Business Financial
Management: A Collection of Readings
Second Edition

Dickerson, Campsey, and Brigham
Introduction to Financial Management
Fourth Edition

Eaker, Fabozzi, and Grant
International Corporate Finance

Gardner, Mills, and Cooperman
Managing Financial Institutions: An
Asset/Liability Approach
Fourth Edition

Gitman and Joehnk
Personal Financial Planning
Eighth Edition

Hall
Effective Use of a Financial Calculator

Harrington and Eades
Case Studies in Financial
Decision Making
Third Edition

Hayes and Meerschwam
Financial Institutions: Contemporary
Cases in the Financial Services Industry

Hearth and Zaima
Contemporary Investments: Security
and Portfolio Analyst's
Second Edition

Johnson
Issues and Readings in
Managerial Finance
Fourth Edition

Kidwell, Peterson, and Blackwell
Financial Institutions, Markets,
and Money
Seventh Edition

Koch and MacDonald
Bank Management
Fourth Edition

Leahigh
Pocket Guide to Finance

Maness and Zietlow
Short-Term Financial Management

Mayes and Shank
Financial Analysis with Lotus 1-2-3
for Windows

Mayes and Shank
Financial Analysis with Microsoft Excel

Mayo
Financial Institutions, Investments,
and Management: An Introduction
Sixth Edition

Mayo
Investments: An Introduction
Sixth Edition

Osteryoung, Newman, and Davies
Small Firm Finance: An
Entrepreneurial Analysis

Reilly and Brown
Investment Analysis and
Portfolio Management
Fifth Edition

Reilly and Norton
Investments
Fifth Edition

Sandburg
Discovering Your Finance Career

Seitz and Ellison
Capital Budgeting and Long-Term
Financing Decisions
Third Edition

Siegel and Siegel
Futures Markets

Smith and Spudeck
Interest Rates: Principles
and Applications

Stickney and Brown
Financial Reporting and Statement
Analysis: A Strategic Perspective
Fourth Edition

Essentials of Managerial Finance is intended for use in introductory finance courses. The book begins with a discussion of basic concepts, including accounting statements, security markets, interest rates, taxes, risk analysis, time value of money, and the basics of security valuation. Subsequent chapters explain how financial managers can help maximize their firms' values by improving decisions in such areas as capital budgeting, choice of capital structure, and working capital management. This organization has three important advantages:

1. Early in the book we explain how accounting data are used, how financial markets operate, and how security prices are determined. This shows students how managerial finance can affect the value of the firm. Also, early coverage of such key concepts as risk analysis, time value, and valuation techniques permits their use and reinforcement throughout the remainder of the book.
2. The book is structured around markets and valuation, which helps students see how the various topics relate to one another.
3. Most students—even those who do not plan to major in finance—are interested in stock and bond valuation, rates of return, and other similar topics. Because learning is a function of interest and motivation, and because *Essentials* begins by showing the relationships between security markets, stock values, and managerial finance, this organization is good from a pedagogic standpoint.

Now in its twelfth edition, *Essentials* has grown over the course of time, especially with respect to the long list of practical and theoretical developments it covers. On the recommendations of reviewers, we have restructured the discussion of a few topics that have been melded into *Essentials* that, because of level or simply the primary objectives of an introductory course in managerial finance, might be considered more appropriate for a more advanced book. We did not categorically omit these topics; rather, we placed some of them—such as modified internal rate of return—in appendices to offer instructors the option of covering the topics in the course.

Relationship with Our Other Books

As the body of knowledge expanded, it first became difficult, then impossible, to provide everything one needs to know about managerial finance in one text, especially an introductory text. This recognition has led us to limit the scope of this book and also to write other texts to deal with the materials that cannot be included in *Essentials*. *Principles of Finance* provides a more general coverage of the subject of finance than *Essentials*. *Principles of Finance* gives a survey of finance as a field of study by covering three major subject areas: (1) financial markets and institutions; (2) investments; and (3) managerial finance. Also, Louis Gapenski, Eugene Brigham, and Phillip Daves have coauthored an intermediate undergraduate text (*Intermediate Financial Management, Sixth Edition*), and Louis Gapenski, Eugene Brigham, and Michael Ehrhardt have coauthored a comprehensive book aimed primarily at MBAs (*Financial Management: Theory and Practice, Ninth Edition*).

The relationship between *Essentials* and the more advanced books deserves special comment. First, we recognize that the advanced books are often used by students who have also used *Essentials* in the introductory finance course, so we have avoided excessive overlap while exposing students to alternative points of view on controversial subjects. We should note, though, that students in advanced courses invariably tell us that they find it helpful to have the more difficult materials repeated—they need the review. Students also find that the style and notation used in our upper-level books are consistent with those in the introductory text—this makes learning easier. Regarding alternative points of view, we take a moderate, middle-of-the-road approach, and where serious controversy exists, we present the alternative points of view. Reviewers were asked to consider this point, and their comments have helped us eliminate potential biases.

Intended Market and Use

As noted previously, *Essentials* is intended for use as an introductory textbook. The key chapters can be covered in a one-term course; and, supplemented with cases and some outside readings, the book can also be used in a two-term course. If it is used in a one-term course, the instructor probably will cover only selected chapters, leaving the others for students either to examine on their own or to use as references in conjunction with work in later courses. Also, we wrote the chapters in a flexible, modular format to help instructors cover the material in a different sequence should they choose to do so.

Major Changes in the Twelfth Edition

The theory and practice of finance are dynamic, and as new developments occur, they should be incorporated into a textbook such as this one. Also, working with a team of reviewers, we are constantly looking for ways to improve the book in terms of clarity and student understanding. As a result, some important changes appear in this edition, the most important of which are discussed here.

Working Capital Management

Based on feedback from adopters of the book, we reduced the number of chapters used to cover working capital management. In addition, the working capital chapters now appear later in the book. Chapter 13, "Working Capital Policy," covers the general concepts of working capital management. Chapter 14, "Managing Short-Term Assets," and Chapter 15, "Managing Short-Term Liabilities (Financing)," provide discussions of techniques used to manage accounts and operations related to working capital. This modification has allowed us to cover essentially the same material as in previous editions, but in a more concise manner.

Capital Budgeting, Cost of Capital, and Capital Structure

The coverage of these important topics now occurs earlier in the book. Capital budgeting is discussed immediately following Part III, "Essential Concepts in Managerial Finance," which includes coverage of time value of money, risk, and valuation concepts. Positioning capital budgeting at this point in the book adds to the continuity of the overall presentation—capital budgeting is simply the application of the topics discussed in Part III. It is natural to follow capital budgeting with coverage of cost of capital and capital structure concepts, because such knowledge is needed to understand the meaning of the required rate of return used in capital budgeting decision making.

Multinational Finance Coverage

Our reviewers suggested that we meld coverage of multinational finance into the chapters where the specific topics are covered rather than have a separate chapter devoted to multinational managerial finance. Thus, we have included coverage of multinational finance throughout the book where appropriate.

Online Essentials

Clearly, the Internet has become a significant tool for both business and education. Therefore, we felt it was important to provide students information regarding use of the Internet in finance. For that reason, we have included a box at the end of each chapter called "Online Essentials" that provides addresses of Web sites that contain information about the topics covered in the chapter. The boxes also give brief descriptions of the Web sites. Because of the transitory nature of the Web, some of the addresses listed might change. We will attempt to update any changes on our book's Web site at www. harcourtcollege.com.

A Managerial Perspective, Industry Practice, and Ethical Dilemma

Although boxed business anecdotes are not new to this edition of *Essentials*, we want to draw attention to them because each is either new to this edition or updated since the previous edition. Each chapter leads off with "A Managerial Perspective," which can be used for student reading, for class lecture, or for both. The "Industry Practice" boxes show the application of the concepts in real-world situations. In addition, the "Ethical Dilemmas" expose students to the relationship between ethics and business, promote critical thinking and decision-making skills, and provide interesting vehicles for class discussion.

Number of Chapters

The consolidation of some of the working capital chapters and the integration of international financial management throughout the book have permitted us to reduce the number of chapters from the 21 contained in the previous edition to 18 in this edition.

Ancillary Materials

A number of items are available free of charge to adopting instructors:

1. **Instructor's Manual.** The comprehensive manual contains answers to all text questions and problems, a detailed set of lecture notes, detailed solutions to integrative problems, sample exams, and suggested course outlines.
2. **Lecture Presentation Software.** To facilitate classroom presentations, a computer graphics slide show written in Microsoft PowerPoint is available. The slides feature the essential topics presented in each chapter.

3. **Test Bank.** The Test Bank contains more than 1,000 class-tested questions and problems. True/false questions, multiple choice conceptual questions, multiple choice problems (that can be easily modified to short-answer problems by removing the answer choices), and financial calculator problems are included for every chapter. The Test Bank is available in computerized format, featuring the computerized test bank program EXAMaster+. EXAMaster+ has many features that allow the instructor to modify test questions, select items by key words, scramble tests for multiple sections, and test completely on the computer. The Test Bank is also available in WordPerfect format.

4. **Problem Diskette.** A diskette containing models for the computer-related end-of-chapter problems is also available.

5. **Web Site.** A book-designated Web site with numerous resources for instructors and students can be accessed through www.harcourtcollege.com.

6. **Transparencies.** A comprehensive set of transparency masters and acetates of exhibits and tables is available.

A number of additional items are available for purchase by students:

1. **Study Guide.** This supplement outlines the key sections of each chapter, provides students with self-test questions, and also provides a set of problems and solutions similar to those in the text and in the Test Bank. Because many instructors use multiple-choice exams, we include coverage of exam-type questions and problems in the Study Guide.

2. **Cases.** *Cases in Financial Management, Dryden Request,* by Eugene F. Brigham and Lin Klein is well suited for use with *Essentials.* The cases provide real-world applications of the methodologies and concepts developed in this book. In addition, all of the cases are available in a customized format, so that students pay only for the cases the instructor decides to use.

3. **Readings Books.** One readings book, *Issues and Readings in Managerial Finance, Fourth Edition,* edited by Ramon E. Johnson, provides an excellent mix of theoretical and practical articles that can be used to supplement the text. Another supplemental reader, *Advances in Business Financial Management: A Collection of Readings, Second Edition,* edited by Philip L. Cooley, provides a broader selection of articles from which to choose.

4. **Spreadsheet Analysis Books.** *Financial Analysis with Microsoft Excel* and *Financial Analysis with Lotus for Windows,* by Timothy Mayes and Todd Shank, fully integrate the teaching of spreadsheet analysis with the basic finance concepts. These books make good companions to *Essentials* in courses where computer work is highly emphasized.

5. **Blueprints.** This supplement consists of the Lecture Presentation Software slides in a printed format in order to facilitate notetaking in the classroom.

Harcourt College Publishers will provide complimentary supplements or supplement packages to those adopters qualified under our adoption policy. Please contact your sales representative to learn how you can qualify. If you receive supplements you do not need, please return them to your sales representative or send them to:

Attn: Returns Department
Troy Warehouse
465 South Lincoln Drive
Troy, MO 63379

Acknowledgments

This book reflects the efforts of a great many people over a number of years. For the twelfth edition, we are indebted to the following professors who provided their input for improving the book:

William Baker, *Stockton State College*
Yvett M. Bendeck, *University of Houston–Clear Lake*
Douglas Bible, *Louisiana State University–Shreveport*
Stephen Caples, *McNeese State University*
Shin-Herng Michelle Chu, *California State Polytechnic University–Pomona*
Paul F. Conway, *University of Notre Dame*
Ed Daley, *Virginia Military Institute*
Gordon Foster, *Metropolitan State University–Minneapolis*
V. Sivarama Krishnan, *Cameron University*
Douglas Leary, *St. John's University*
Iqbal Mansur, *Widener University*
Massoud Metghalchi, *University of Houston–Victoria*
Charlie Narron, *Mars Hill College*
Gladson Nwanna, *Morgan State University*
Phil Pennell, *Guilford College*
Glenn Petry, *Washington State University*
Ralph Pope, *California State University–Sacramento*
Murli Rajan, *University of Scranton*
Jim Reinemann, *College of Lake County*
Robert Ritzcovan, *Mercy College*
John D. Schatzberg, *University of New Mexico*
Ramesh Shah, *Widener University*
John Teall, *Pace University*
Randy Trostle, *Elizabethtown College*
Gautam Vora, *University of New Mexico*
Sally Jo Wright, *Sangamon State University*

Next, we would like to thank the following professors, whose reviews and comments have helped prior editions and our companion books:
Mike Adler, Syed Ahmad, Ed Altman, Bruce Anderson, Ron Anderson, Bob Angell, Vince Apilado, Henry Arnold, Bob Aubey, Gil Babcock, Peter Bacon, Kent Baker, Robert Balik, Tom Bankston, Les Barenbaum, Charles Barngrover, Bill Beedles, Moshe Ben-Horim, Bill Beranek, Tom Berry, Will Bertin, Dan Best, Roger Bey, Dalton Bigbee, John Bildersee, Russ Boisjoly, Keith Boles, Geof Booth, Jerry Boswell, Kenneth Boudreaux, Helen Bowers, Oswald Bowlin, Don Boyd, G. Michael Boyd, Pat Boyer, Joe Brandt, Elizabeth Brannigan, Greg Brauer, Mary Broske, Dave Brown, Kate Brown, Bill Brueggeman, Stephen G. Buell, Ted Byrley

Bill Campsey, Bob Carlson, Severin Carlson, David Cary, Steve Celec, Don Chance, Antony Chang, Susan Chaplinsky, Jay Choi, S. K. Choudhary, Lal Chugh, Maclyn Clouse, Margaret Considine, Phil Cooley, Joe Copeland, David Cordell, Marcia Cornett, M. P. Corrigan, John Cotner, Charles Cox, David Crary, John Crockett, Jr., Roy Crum, Brent Dalrymple, Bodie Dickerson, Bernard Dill, J. David Diltz, Gregg Dimkoff, Les Dlabay, Mark Dorfman, Gene Drzycimski, Dean Dudley, David Durst, Ed Dyl, Richard Edelman, Charles Edwards, John Ellis, Dave Ewert,

John Ezell, Michael Ferri, Jim Filkins, John Finnerty, Susan Fischer, Steven Flint, Russ Fogler, Dan French

Michael Garlington, David Garraty, Jim Garven, Adam Gehr, Jr., Jim Gentry, Philip Glasgo, Rudyard Goode, Walt Goulet, Bernie Grablowsky, Theoharry Grammatikos, Reynold Griffith, Ed Grossnickle, John Groth, Alan Grunewald, Manak Gupta, Sam Hadaway, Don Hakala, Paul Halpern, Gerald Hamsmith, William Hardin, John Harris, Paul Hastings, Bob Haugen, Steve Hawke, Del Hawley, Robert Hehre, George Hettenhouse, Hans Heymann, Kendall Hill, Roger Hill, Tom Hindelang, Linda Hittle, Ralph Hocking, J. Ronald Hoffmeister, Robert Hollinger, Jim Horrigan, John Houston, John Howe, Keith Howe

Steve Isberg, Jim Jackson, Kose John, Craig Johnson, Keith Johnson, Ramon Johnson, Ray Jones, Frank Jordan, Manual Jose, Alfred Kahl, Gus Kalogeras, Mike Keenan, Bill Kennedy, James Keys, Carol Kiefer, Joe Kiernan, Rick Kish, Don Knight, Dorothy Koehl, Jaroslaw Komarynsky, Duncan Kretovich, Harold Krogh, Charles Kroncke, Don Kummer, Joan Lamm, Larry Lang, P. Lange, Howard Lanser, John Lasik, Edward Lawrence, Martin Lawrence, Wayne Lee, Jim LePage, Jules Levine, John Lewis, Jason Lin, Chuck Linke, Bill Lloyd, Susan Long

Judy Maese, Bob Magee, Ileen Malitz, Phil Malone, Lewis Mandell, Terry Maness, Chris Manning, S. K. Mansinghka, Terry Martell, D. J. Masson, John Mathys, John McAlhany, Andy McCollough, Ambrose McCoy, Thomas McCue, Bill McDaniel, John McDowell, Charles McKinney, Robyn McLaughlin, Jamshid Mehran, Larry Merville, Rick Meyer, Jim Millar, Ed Miller, John Mitchell, Carol Moerdyk, Bob Moore, Barry Morris, Gene Morris, Fred Morrissey, Chris Muscarella, David Nachman, Tim Nantell, Don Nast, Bill Nelson, Bob Nelson, Bob Niendorf

Tom O'Brien, Dennis O'Connor, John O'Donnell, Jim Olsen, Robert Olsen, Jim Pappas, Stephen Parrish, Glenn Petry , Jim Pettijohn, Rich Pettit, Dick Pettway, Hugo Phillips, H. R. Pickett, John Pinkerton, Gerald Pogue, Eugene Poindexter, R. Potter, Franklin Potts, R. Powell, Chris Prestopino, Jerry Prock, Howard Puckett, Herbert Quigley, George Racette, Bob Radcliffe, Bill Rentz, Ken Riener, Charles Rini, John Ritchie, Pietra Rivoli, Antonio Rodriguez, James Rosenfeld, E. N. Roussakis, Dexter Rowell

Jim Sachlis, Abdul Sadik, Thomas Scampini, Kevin Scanlon, Frederick Schadler, Mary Jane Scheuer, Carl Schweser, David Scott, John Settle, Alan Severn, Sol Shalit, Frederic Shipley, Dilip Shome, Ron Shrieves, Neil Sicherman, J. B. Silvers, Clay Singleton, Joe Sinkey, Stacy Sirmans, Jaye Smith, Patricia Smith, Steve Smith, Don Sorensen, David Speairs, Ken Stanly, Ed Stendardi, Alan Stephens, Don Stevens, Jerry Stevens, Glen Strasburg, Philip Swensen, Ernest Swift, Paul Swink, Gary Tallman, Dular Talukdar, Dennis Tanner, Craig Tapley, Russ Taussig, Richard Teweles, Ted Teweles

Francis C. Thomas, Andrew Thompson, John Thompson, Dogan Tirtiroglu, Marco Tonietti, William Tozer, George Trivoli, George Tsetsekos, Ricardo Ulivi, David Upton, Howard Van Auken, Pretorious Van den Dool, Pieter Vandenberg, Paul Vanderheiden, JoAnn Vaughan, Jim Verbrugge, Patrick Vincent, Steve Vinson, Susan Visscher, John Wachowicz, Mike Walker, Sam Weaver, Kuo-Chiang Wei, Bill Welch, Robert J. Wiley, Norm Williams, Tony Wingler, Ed Wolfe, Don Woods, Michael Yonan, Dennis Zocco, and Kent Zumwalt.

Special thanks are due to Chris Barry, Texas Christian University, who wrote many of the original small business sections; to Dilip Shome, Virginia Polytechnic Institute, who helped greatly with the capital structure chapter; and to Roy Crum, University of

Florida, who provided input to the multinational finance material. Dana Aberwald Clark worked closely with us at every stage of the revision; her assistance was absolutely invaluable. Also, Louis Gapenski helped develop the integrative problems and offered advice on many other parts of the book. In addition, in previous editions, Steve Bouchard and Chad Hamilton worked through and/or discussed with us all or major parts of the book and supplements to help eliminate errors and confusing sections—this has helped us improve this edition.

Errors in the Text

At this point, most authors make a statement like this: "We appreciate all the help we received from the people listed above, but any remaining errors are, of course, our own responsibility." And generally there are more than enough remaining errors. Having experienced difficulty with errors ourselves, both as students and as instructors, we resolved to avoid this problem in *Essentials*. As a result of our error-detection procedures, we are convinced that it is relatively free of mistakes.

Partly due to our confidence that there are few errors in this book, but primarily because we want to correct any errors that might exist in this printing of the book, we are offering a reward of $10 per error to the first person who reports it to us. For purposes of this reward, errors are defined as spelling errors, errors in finance content and facts, and other errors that inhibit comprehension. Typesetting errors, such as spacing, or differences in opinion concerning grammatical or punctuation convention do not qualify for the reward. Finally, any qualifying error that has a follow-through effect is counted as two errors only. Errors should be reported to Scott Besley at the address given below.

Conclusion

Finance is, in a real sense, the cornerstone of the enterprise system—good financial management is vitally important to the economic health of business firms, and hence to the nation and the world. Because of its importance, finance should be widely and thoroughly understood, but this is easier said than done. The field is relatively complex, and it is undergoing constant change in response to shifts in economic conditions. All of this makes finance stimulating and exciting but also challenging and sometimes perplexing. We sincerely hope that *Essentials* will meet its own challenge by contributing to a better understanding of our financial system.

Scott Besley
College of Business Administration, BSN 3403
University of South Florida
4202 E. Fowler Avenue
Tampa, FL 33620-5500

Eugene F. Brigham
College of Business
University of Florida
Gainesville, FL 32611-7160

✳ BRIEF CONTENTS

CONTENTS

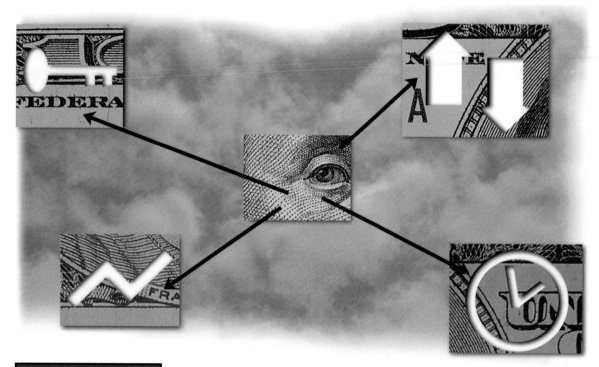

✳ PART I

Introduction to
Managerial Finance

CHAPTER 1

An Overview of Managerial Finance

CHAPTER 2

The Financial Environment: Markets, Institutions, Interest Rates, and Taxes

An Overview of Managerial Finance

A MANAGERIAL PERSPECTIVE

For two decades, William Bennett headed Circus Circus Enterprises, which he and cofounder William Pennington built into a major gaming organization through their vision that gambling could be mass-marketed with the allure of cheap travel junkets and low-stakes games. But on July 8, 1994, relenting to pressure from stockholders, Bennett resigned from his powerful position as chairman of the board of directors. A primary reason the stockholders forced Bennett out was because they saw the price of Circus Circus stock drop by almost 60 percent during the previous six months, and much of the blame for this devaluation was attributed to the fact that Bennett ruled the firm much like a dictator with his own agenda. The bottom line was that stockholders believed the value of their investment suffered under Bennett's administration—in their minds, the stockholders' best interests were not being served. For the same reason, Maurice Saatchi, chairman and cofounder of Saatchi & Saatchi PLC, a worldwide advertising agency with accounts such as Procter & Gamble and Hewlett-Packard, was forced to resign in December 1994. More recently, in June 1998, "Chainsaw Al" Dunlap was fired as CEO of Sunbeam, a small appliance manufacturer. Dunlap got his moniker because he became famous as a "turn-around artist" who would breathe life into a floundering business by paring down its operations through sales of inefficient divisions and lay-offs of large numbers of employees—he would bring his "chainsaw" to the corporate table to save the business. Unfortunately, Dunlap could not work miracles at Sunbeam. Just before he was fired, the price of Sunbeam's stock had dropped to $14 per share, which represented nearly a 73 percent loss in value from its 1997 high of $51. One of Sunbeam's biggest shareholders saw his nearly $1 billion investment decrease to less than $300 million. That stockholder, as well as the others, believed Dunlap was not acting in the best interests of the owners; otherwise, the stock value would not have decreased so significantly. In each of these instances, stockholders sent clear messages to management—it is the stockholders who are the owners of the firms, and, as such, top management should strive to achieve the stockholders' primary goal of value maximization.

When conflicts occur between managements' goals (e.g., job security, substantial compensation, and so on) and owners' goals (increased value), management should "do what is right for the company and its owners." To reduce the chances of conflicts in goals and ensure the goals of stockholders are pursued, many firms now require their senior managers to own stock in the companies they run. Firms such as Eastman Kodak, Xerox, Union Carbide, and Hershey Foods, to name a few, have policies that force those who are in top management positions to also be owners of the firms. It is believed that if managers also are owners, they will be more "in tune" with the other stockholders' interests and less inclined to pursue

continues

activities harmful to the stock's value. There is evidence that supports this contention—firms with executives that own substantial amounts of stock do very well.

As you read this chapter, think about some of the issues raised above: As a stockholder in a company, what goal (or set of goals) would you like to see pursued? To what extent should top managers let their own personal goals influence the decisions they make concerning how the firm is run? Would you, as an outside stockholder, feel more comfortable that your interests were being represented better if the firm's top managers also owned large amounts of the firm's stock? What factors should management consider when trying to boost the value of the firm's stock? ■

"Why should I study finance?" As a student, you might be asking yourself this question right now. To answer this question, we need to ask: What role does finance play in the successful operation of a firm? As we will see in this chapter and in the chapters that follow, proper financial management will help any business provide better products to its customers at lower prices, pay higher salaries to its employees, and still provide greater returns to investors who put up the funds needed to form and operate the business. Because the economy—both national and worldwide—consists of customers, employees, and investors, sound financial management contributes to the well-being of both individuals and the general population.

The purpose of this chapter is to provide an overview of managerial finance. After you finish the chapter, you should have a reasonably good idea of how finance knowledge is used in business. You should also have a better understanding of (1) some of the forces that will affect managerial finance in the future; (2) the way businesses are organized; (3) where finance fits in a firm's organizational structure relative to areas such as accounting, marketing, production, and personnel; (4) the goals of a firm and the way financial managers can contribute to the achieving these goals; and, (5) how U.S. firms differ from their foreign counterparts.

Career Opportunities in Finance

The study of finance consists of three interrelated areas: (1) *financial markets and institutions*, which deals with many of the topics covered in macroeconomics; (2) *investments*, which focuses on the decisions of individuals and financial and other institutions as they choose securities for their investment portfolios; and (3) *managerial finance*, or "business finance," which involves the actual management of the firm. Although our concern in the book is primarily with managerial finance, each of these areas is related to the other, so an individual who works in any one of the areas should have a good understanding of the other areas as well. The career opportunities within each field are many and varied. The purpose of this section is to give you a general idea of the areas in which finance graduates can expect to work.

Financial Markets and Institutions

Many finance majors go to work for financial institutions, including banks, insurance companies, savings and loans, and credit unions, which are an integral part of the financial marketplace. For success in the financial services industry, one needs a knowledge of the factors that cause interest rates to rise and fall, the regulations to which financial institutions are subject, and the various types of financial instruments (mortgages, auto loans, certificates of deposit, and so on). One also needs a general knowledge of all aspects of business administration, because the management of a financial institution involves accounting, marketing, personnel, and computer systems, as well as managerial finance.

Investments

Finance graduates who go into investments generally work for stock brokerage firms, banks, investment companies, or insurance companies. The three main functions in the investments area are (1) sales, (2) the analysis of individual securities, and (3) determining the optimal mix of securities for a given investor. As a finance graduate, you might get a job performing any one or some combination of these tasks. Even if you do not go into a career that has a direct link to finance, a basic understanding of the subject is necessary to be able to evaluate the performance of your personal investments, such as retirement funds in which you have a choice about where your contributions are invested.

Managerial Finance

Managerial finance is the broadest of the three areas and the one with the greatest number of job opportunities. Managerial finance is important in all types of businesses, whether they are public or private, deal with financial services, or are manufacturers. The types of tasks one encounters in managerial finance jobs range from making decisions regarding plant expansions to choosing what types of securities to issue to finance expansion. Financial managers also have the responsibility for deciding the credit terms under which customers can buy, how much inventory the firm should carry, how much cash to keep on hand, whether to acquire other firms (merger analysis), and how much of the firm's earnings to plow back into the business versus pay out as dividends.

Regardless of which area you go into, you will need a knowledge of all three areas. For example, a banker lending to businesses cannot do his or her job well without a good understanding of managerial finance because he or she must be able to judge how well a business is operated. The same thing holds for one of Merrill Lynch's security analysts, and even stockbrokers must have an understanding of general financial principles if they are to give intelligent advice to their customers. At the same time, corporate financial managers need to know what their bankers are thinking about and how investors are likely to judge their corporations' performances and thus determine their stock prices. So if you decide to make finance your career, you will need to know something about all three areas.

Self-Test Questions

What are the three main areas of finance?

If you have definite plans to go into one area, why is it necessary that you know something about the other areas?

Managerial Finance in the 20th Century[1]

When managerial finance emerged as a separate field of study in the early 1900s, the emphasis was on the legal aspects of mergers, the formation of new firms, and the various types of securities firms could issue to raise funds. This was a time when industrialization was sweeping the country; "big" was considered "powerful," so many takeovers and mergers were used to create large corporations. During the Depression era of the 1930s, however, an unprecedented number of business failures caused the emphasis in finance to shift to bankruptcy and reorganization, to corporate liquidity, and to regulation of security markets. During the 1940s and early 1950s, finance continued to be taught as a descriptive, institutional subject, viewed more from the standpoint of an outsider rather than from that of management. But with the advent of the computer for general business use, the focus began to shift more to the insider's point of view and the importance of financial decision making to the firm. A movement toward theoretical analysis began during the 1960s, and the focus of managerial finance shifted to decisions regarding the choice of assets and liabilities necessary to maximize the value of the firm. The focus on valuation continued through the 1980s, but the analysis was expanded to include (1) inflation and its effects on business decisions; (2) deregulation of financial institutions and the resulting trend toward large, broadly diversified financial services companies; (3) the dramatic increase in both the use of computers for analysis and the electronic transfer of information; (4) the increased importance of global markets and business operations; and (5) innovations in the financial products offered to investors. For example, during the 1980s there was a substantial increase in the popularity of leveraged buyouts, or LBOs, which are transactions to purchase a company with huge amounts of debt to form a new privately owned, highly leveraged company. And, in the 1990s, managerial finance was greatly influenced by fast-paced technological innovation and continued deregulation and globalization of businesses and financial markets.

As we head into a new century, mergers and acquisitions are still an important part of the financial world. But the most important trends that are expected to continue during the next decade or so are (1) the continued globalization of business, (2) a further increase in the use of electronic technology, especially technology dealing with the generation and movement of information, and (3) the regulatory attitude of the government.

The Globalization of Business

Four factors have made the trend toward globalization mandatory for many businesses:

1. Improvements in transportation and communications have lowered shipping costs and made international trade more feasible.
2. The political clout of consumers who desire low-cost, high-quality products has helped lower trade barriers designed to protect inefficient, high-cost domestic manufacturers.

---

[1] For an excellent discussion of the evolution of finance in the 20th century, see J. Fred Weston, "A (Relatively) Brief History of Finance Ideas," *Financial Practice and Education* (Spring/Summer 1994), 7–26.

3. As technology has become more advanced, the cost of developing new products has increased, and, as development costs rise, so must unit sales if the firm is to be competitive.

4. In a world populated with multinational firms able to shift production to wherever costs are lowest, a firm whose manufacturing operations are restricted to one country cannot compete unless costs in its home country happen to be low, a condition that does not necessarily exist for many U.S. corporations.

As a result of these four factors, survival requires that most manufacturers produce and sell globally. Later in this chapter we discuss international business and financial management in greater detail.

Service companies, including banks, advertising agencies, and accounting firms, also are being forced to "go global," because such firms can better serve their multinational clients if they have worldwide operations. There will, of course, always be some purely domestic companies, but you should keep in mind that the most dynamic growth, and the best opportunities, are often with companies that operate worldwide. Recent events in eastern Asia illustrate the interrelationship of the world's marketplaces—in 1998, economic catastrophes in Japan and southeast Asia caused American investors to become skittish and the financial markets in the United States to become more uncertain than previously.

Information Technology

Most large companies have networks of personal computers linked to one another, to the firm's own central computers, and to their customers' and suppliers' computers. Some companies, like General Motors, require their suppliers to be linked electronically so that orders and payments can be made via the computer. As we enter the next millennium, we will see continued advances in the use of electronic technology in managerial finance, and this technology will revolutionize the way financial decisions are made, just as it has in the past. One result of this "electronic revolution" that we have seen during the past couple of decades is the increased use of quantitative analysis via computer models for financial decision making. Therefore, it is clear that the next generation of financial managers will need stronger computer and quantitative skills than were required in the past.

Regulatory Attitude of the Government

In the past 20 years, the government has taken fairly friendly positions with respect to legislative enactments and regulatory enforcements affecting businesses. Much of the legislation has focused on deregulation of highly regulated industries. Industries that have been deregulated include financial services, transportation, communications, and utilities. In addition, for the most part, the government has not discouraged mergers and acquisitions—since 1985 record numbers of mergers at historically high values have taken place. During this period, economic conditions generally were very favorable, as evidenced by record levels posted by the stocks markets. In the future, if economic conditions sour, causing decreases in the securities markets, you can bet legislators will favor re-regulation if they believe deregulation contributed to the economic woes of the country. Historically, after the country has experienced economic tragedy, cries for new, tougher regulations have been abundant, and, for the most part, Congress has obliged.

Self-Test Question

How has managerial finance changed from the early 1900s through the 1990s?

Increasing Importance of Managerial Finance

The historical trends discussed in the previous section have greatly increased the importance of managerial finance. In earlier times the marketing manager would project sales, the engineering and production staffs would determine the assets necessary to meet those demands, and the financial manager's job was simply to raise the money needed to purchase the required plant, equipment, and inventories. That situation no longer exists; decisions now are made in a much more coordinated manner, and the financial manager generally has direct responsibility for the control process.

Eastern Airlines and Delta Airlines can be used to illustrate both the importance of managerial finance and the effects of financial decisions. In the 1960s, Eastern's stock sold for more than $60 per share while Delta's sold for just $10. By the end of the 1990s, Delta had become one of the world's strongest airlines, and its stock was selling for more than $60 per share. Eastern, on the other hand, had gone bankrupt and was no longer in existence. Although many factors combined to produce these divergent results, financial decisions exerted a major influence. Because Eastern had traditionally used a great deal of debt while Delta had not, Eastern's costs increased significantly, and its profits were lowered, when interest rates rose during the late 1970s and the early 1980s. Rising rates had only a minor effect on Delta. Further, when fuel price increases made it imperative for the airlines to buy new, fuel-efficient planes, Delta was able to do so, but Eastern was not. Finally, when the airlines were deregulated, Delta was strong enough to expand into developing markets and to cut prices as necessary to attract business, but Eastern was not.

The Delta-Eastern story, and others like it, illustrates how important proper financial planning is to long-run corporate survival; such awareness has increased the emphasis placed on the managerial finance function. Indeed, the value of managerial finance is reflected in the fact that more chief executive officers (CEOs) in the top 1,000 U.S. companies started their careers in finance than in any other functional area.

It also is becoming increasingly important for people in marketing, accounting, production, personnel, and other areas to understand finance in order to do a good job in their own fields. People in marketing, for instance, must understand how marketing decisions affect and are affected by funds availability, by inventory levels, by excess plant capacity, and so on. Similarly, accountants must understand how accounting data are used in corporate planning and are viewed by investors. As well, financial managers must have an understanding of marketing, accounting, and so forth to make more informed decisions about replacement or expansion of plant and equipment and how to best finance their firms.

Thus, *there are financial implications in virtually all business decisions, and nonfinancial executives simply must know enough finance to work these implications into their own specialized analyses.*[2] Because of this, every student of business, regardless of major, should be concerned with finance.

---

[2]It is an interesting fact that the course "Managerial Finance for Nonfinancial Executives" has the highest enrollment in most executive development programs.

Self-Test Questions

Why is financial planning important to today's chief executives?

Why do marketing people need to know something about managerial finance?

The Financial Manager's Responsibilities

The financial manager's task is to make decisions concerning the acquisition and use of funds for the greatest benefit of the firm. Here are some specific activities that are involved:

1. **Forecasting and planning.** The financial manager must interact with other executives as they look ahead and lay the plans that will shape the firm's future position.
2. **Major investment and financing decisions.** A successful firm generally has rapid growth in sales, which requires investments in plant, equipment, and inventory. The financial manager must help determine the optimal sales growth rate, and he or she must help decide on the specific assets to acquire and the best way to finance those assets. For example, should the firm raise funds by borrowing (debt) or by selling stock (equity)? If the firm uses debt (borrows), should it be long term or short term?
3. **Coordination and control.** The financial manager must interact with other executives to ensure that the firm is operated as efficiently as possible. All business decisions have financial implications, and all managers—financial and otherwise—need to take this into account. For example, marketing decisions affect sales growth, which, in turn, influences investment requirements. Thus, marketing decision makers must consider how their actions affect (and are affected by) such factors as the availability of funds, inventory policies, and plant capacity utilization.
4. **Dealing with the financial markets.** The financial manager must deal with the money and capital markets. As we will see in Chapter 2, each firm affects and is affected by the general financial markets where funds are raised, where the firm's securities are traded, and where its investors are either rewarded or penalized.

In summary, *financial managers make decisions regarding which assets their firms should acquire, how those assets should be financed, and how to manage their firms' existing resources.* If these responsibilities are performed optimally, financial managers will help to maximize the values of their firms, and this will also maximize the long-term welfare of those who buy from or work for the company, as well as the community where the firm is located.

Self-Test Question

What are four specific activities with which financial managers are involved?

Alternative Forms of Business Organization

There are three main forms of business organization: (1) proprietorships, (2) partnerships, and (3) corporations. In terms of numbers, about 75 percent of businesses are operated as proprietorships, nearly seven percent are partnerships, and the remaining 18 percent are corporations. Based on dollar value of sales, however, almost 90 percent of all business is conducted by corporations, while the remaining ten percent is generated by both proprietorships and partnerships.[3] Because most business is conducted by corporations, we will concentrate on them in this book. However, it is important to understand the differences among the three forms.

Proprietorship

PROPRIETORSHIP
An unincorporated business owned by one individual.

A **proprietorship** is an unincorporated business owned by one individual. Starting a proprietorship is fairly easy—just begin business operations. However, in most cases, even the smallest business must be licensed by the municipality (city, county, or state) in which it operates.

The proprietorship has three important *advantages:*

1. It is easily and inexpensively formed.
2. It is subject to few government regulations
3. It is taxed like an individual, not a corporation.

The proprietorship also has four important *limitations:*

1. The proprietor has *unlimited personal liability* for business debts, which can result in losses that exceed the money he or she has invested in the company.
2. The life of a business organized as a proprietorship is limited to the life of the individual who created it.
3. Transferring ownership is somewhat difficult—disposing of the business is similar to selling a house in that the proprietor has to seek out and negotiate with a potential buyer.
4. It is difficult for a proprietorship to obtain large sums of capital, because the firm's financial strength generally is based on the financial strength of the sole owner.

For these reasons, individual proprietorships are confined primarily to small business operations. In fact, only about one percent of all proprietorships have assets that are valued at $1 million or greater, while nearly 90 percent have assets valued at $100,000 or less. However, businesses frequently are started as proprietorships and then converted to corporations when their growth causes the disadvantages of being a proprietorship to outweigh the advantages.

---

[3]The statistics provided in this section are based on business tax filings reported by the Internal Revenue Service (IRS). Additional statistics can be found on the IRS Web site at http://www.irs.ustreas.gov/tax_stats.

Partnership

A **partnership** is like a proprietorship, except there are two or more owners. Partnerships can operate under different degrees of formality, ranging from informal, oral understandings to formal agreements filed with the secretary of the state in which the partnership does business. Most legal experts would recommend the partnership agreement be put in writing.

The *advantages* of a partnership are the same as for a proprietorship:

1. Formation is easy and relatively inexpensive.
2. It is subject to few government regulations.
3. It is taxed like an individual, not a corporation.

The *disadvantages* are also similar to those associated with proprietorships:

1. Unlimited liability.
2. Limited life of the organization.
3. Difficulty of transferring ownership.
4. Difficulty of raising large amounts of capital.

Regarding liability, the partners can potentially lose all of their personal assets, even those assets not invested in the business, because under partnership law each partner is liable for the business's debts. Therefore, if any partner is unable to meet his or her pro rata claim in the event the partnership goes bankrupt, the remaining partners must make good on the unsatisfied claims, drawing on their personal assets if necessary. Thus, the business-related activities of any of the firm's partners can bring ruin to the other partners, even though those partners were not a direct party to such activities. For example, the partners of the national accounting firm Laventhol and Horwath, a huge partnership that went bankrupt at the end of 1992 as a result of suits filed by investors who relied on faulty audit statements, learned all about the perils of doing business as a partnership—they discovered that a Texas partner who audits a savings and loan that goes under can bring ruin to a millionaire New York partner who never went near the S&L.[4]

The first three disadvantages—unlimited liability, impermanence of the organization, and difficulty of transferring ownership—lead to the fourth, the difficulty partnerships have in attracting substantial amounts of funds. This is no particular problem for a slow-growing business, but if a business's products really catch on, and if it needs to raise large amounts of funds to capitalize on its opportunities, the difficulty in attracting funds becomes a real drawback. Thus, growth companies such as Microsoft and Dell Computer generally begin life as a proprietorship or partnership, but at some point they find it necessary to convert to a corporation.

---

[4]However, it is possible to limit the liabilities of some of the partners by establishing a *limited partnership*, wherein one (or more) partner is designated the *general partner* and the others *limited partners*. Limited partnerships are quite common in the area of real estate investment, but they do not work well with most types of businesses, including accounting firms, because one partner rarely is willing to assume all of the business's risk. Not long ago, the national accounting firms reorganized themselves as limited liability partnerships, which are partnerships in which only the assets of the partnership and the "engagement" partner (partner in charge of the situation) are at risk.

Corporation

CORPORATION
A legal entity created by a state, separate and distinct from its owners and managers, having unlimited life, easy transferability of ownership, and limited liability.

A **corporation** is a legal entity created by a state. It is separate and distinct from its owners and managers. This separateness gives the corporation three major *advantages:*

1. A corporation can continue after its original owners and managers are deceased; thus it is said to have *unlimited life.*
2. Ownership interests can be divided into shares of stock, which in turn can be *transferred far more easily* than can proprietorship or partnership interests.
3. A corporation offers its owners *limited liability.* To illustrate the concept of limited liability, suppose you invested $10,000 to become a partner in a business that subsequently went bankrupt, owing creditors $1 million. Because the owners are liable for the debts of a partnership, you could be assessed for a share of the company's debt, and you could be held liable for the entire $1 million if your partners could not pay their shares—this is what we mean by unlimited liability. On the other hand, if you invested $10,000 in the stock of a corporation that then went bankrupt, your potential loss on the investment would be limited to your $10,000 investment.[5]

These three factors—unlimited life, easy transferability of ownership interest, and limited liability—make it much easier for corporations than for proprietorships or partnerships to raise money in the financial markets.

The corporate form of business offers significant advantages over proprietorships and partnerships, but it does have two primary disadvantages:

1. Corporate *earnings are subject to double taxation*—the earnings of the corporation are taxed, and then any earnings paid out as dividends are taxed again as income to the stockholders.
2. Setting up a corporation, and filing required state and federal reports, is more complex and time-consuming than for a proprietorship or a partnership.

CORPORATE CHARTER
A document filed with the secretary of the state in which the firm is incorporated that provides information about the company, including its name, address, directors, and amount of capital stock.

Although a proprietorship or a partnership can commence operations without much paperwork, setting up a corporation requires that the incorporators hire a lawyer to prepare a charter and a set of bylaws. The **corporate charter** includes the (1) name of the proposed corporation, (2) types of activities it will pursue, (3) amount of capital stock, (4) number of directors, and (5) names and addresses of directors. The charter is filed with the secretary of the state in which the firm will be incorporated, and, when it is approved, the corporation is officially in existence.[6] Then, after the corporation is in operation, quarterly and annual financial statements and tax reports must be filed with state and federal authorities.

BYLAWS
A set of rules drawn up by the founders of the corporation that indicate how the company is to be governed; includes procedures for electing directors, whether the common stock has a preemptive right, and how to change the bylaws when necessary.

The **bylaws** are a set of rules drawn up by the founders of the corporation to aid in governing the internal management of the company. Included are such points as (1)

---

[5]In the case of small corporations, the limited liability feature is often a fiction, because bankers and credit managers frequently require personal guarantees from the stockholders of small, weak businesses.

[6]A majority of major U.S. corporations are chartered in Delaware, which has, over the years, provided a favorable legal environment for corporations. It is not necessary for a firm to be headquartered, or even to conduct operations, in its state of incorporation.

would maximize the value of the stock you own, including dividends. We know, however, that because the stock of most large corporations is widely held, the managers of such organizations have a great deal of latitude in making business decisions. This being the case, might not managers pursue goals other than stock price maximization? For example, some have argued that the managers of a large, well-entrenched corporation could work just hard enough to keep stockholder returns at a "reasonable" level and then devote the remainder of their efforts and resources to public service activities, to employee benefits, to higher executive salaries, or to golf.

It is almost impossible to determine whether a particular management team is trying to maximize shareholder wealth or is merely attempting to keep stockholders satisfied while pursuing other goals. For example, how can we tell whether employee or community benefit programs are in the long-run best interests of the stockholders? Similarly, are relatively high executive salaries really necessary to attract and retain excellent managers, or are they just another example of managers taking advantage of stockholders?

It is impossible to give definitive answers to these questions. However, we do know that the managers of a firm operating in a competitive market will be forced to undertake actions that are reasonably consistent with shareholder wealth maximization. If they depart from this goal, they run the risk of being removed from their jobs. We will have more to say about the conflict between managers and shareholders later in the chapter.

Social Responsibility

SOCIAL RESPONSIBILITY
The concept that businesses should be actively concerned with the welfare of society at large.

Another issue that deserves consideration is **social responsibility:** Should businesses operate strictly in their stockholders' best interests, or are firms also responsible for the welfare of their employees, customers, and the communities in which they operate? Certainly firms have an ethical responsibility to provide a safe working environment, to avoid polluting the air or water, and to produce safe products. However, socially responsible actions have costs, and it is questionable whether businesses would incur these costs voluntarily. If some firms do act in a socially responsible manner while others do not, then the socially responsible firms will be at a disadvantage in attracting funds. To illustrate, suppose the firms in a given industry have **profits** and

NORMAL PROFITS/ RATES OF RETURN
Those profits and rates of return that are close to the average for all firms and are just sufficient to attract capital.

rates of return on investment that are close to **normal**—that is, close to the average for all firms and just sufficient to attract capital. If one company attempts to exercise social responsibility, it will have to raise prices to cover the added costs. If the other businesses in its industry do not follow suit, their costs and prices will be lower. The socially responsible firm will not be able to compete, and it will be forced to abandon its efforts. Thus, any voluntary socially responsible acts that raise costs will be difficult, if not impossible, in industries that are subject to keen competition.

What about oligopolistic firms with profits above normal levels? Cannot such firms devote resources to social projects? Undoubtedly they can, and many large, successful firms do engage in community projects, employee benefit programs, and the like, to a greater degree than would appear to be called for by pure profit or wealth maximization goals.[8] Still, publicly owned firms are constrained in such actions by capital market factors. To illustrate, suppose a saver who has funds to invest is considering two

---

[8]Even firms like these often find it necessary to justify such projects at stockholder meetings by stating that these programs will contribute to long-run profit maximization.

The Shareholders Meeting—Is It Just a Ritual?

Each year, nearly every American company that is publicly traded holds a shareholders meeting (1) to provide information concerning the previous year's performance, (2) to fill vacancies on the board of directors, and (3) to make decisions about major issues facing the firm.

A century ago, when a firm was owned by a few shareholders who typically lived close to the main factory or headquarters, the annual meeting was used to communicate with the owners and reach a consensus concerning matters affecting the future of the firm's operations. Today, the shareholders of most large American firms are scattered around the world, making it difficult to schedule a single meeting that all shareholders can attend. Further, disclosure laws that have been enacted in the 20th century require that publicly traded firms inform *all* shareholders of major developments via periodic financial reports, proxy statements, and other published reports, and the technology used to communicate this information has improved significantly, especially in the past two decades. So the annual meeting is no longer seen as the most important means to communicate with stockholders. Instead, the shareholders meeting has become an expensive ritual for many large corporations—for some firms the cost exceeds $1 million.

Will shareholders meetings of large corporations become a thing of the past? Perhaps. Consider the fact that most of the largest corporations in the United States are owned by institutional investors, such as mutual funds, insurance companies, and pension funds. If these investors want to know anything about the actions of a company, they simply call or fax the company's top management—they do not wait until the annual shareholders meeting to find out the answers to important questions they have today. In addition, companies are now required to provide shareholders with proxy statements that include much greater and more simplified financial information than ever before. The proxy statement, which must be mailed to shareholders prior to the shareholders meeting, includes information concerning the major issues that will be addressed at the annual meeting, and it provides a medium by which shareholders can

vote on the issues without actually attending the meeting. Most investors who own small amounts of large companies do not attend the annual meeting, so they rely on proxy voting to convey their feelings about the major issues facing the firms they own. The new disclosure rules require that proxy statements include information about executive compensation and firm performance, both in the current year and for the past five years. The financial data, including changes in the firm's stock price and the dividends paid, must be presented in graphical form along with comparative data of similar companies and some market index like the New York Stock Exchange Composite Index. The Securities and Exchange Commission (SEC) has mandated these new disclosure rules to help *all* investors become better informed about how executives are paid relative to the performance of their firms.

Modern technology and existing disclosure requirements have helped to decrease the role of the annual shareholders meeting—much of the business that used to take place at the shareholders meeting now is performed at other times, using modern communications media. So it seems the shareholders meeting as we know it today is more of a ritual than a functional activity. Consequently, in the future, we probably will see shareholders meetings change significantly, perhaps even disappear. Some suggestions are the following: (1) If shareholders meetings must be held, get them over with as quickly as possible. (2) Rather than hold a single, centrally located meeting, have a series of regional seminars to keep stockholders informed. (3) Eliminate shareholders meetings altogether—use proxy voting and surveys to conduct business and to determine stockholders' opinions.

It is clear that, as communication technology improves and disclosure requirements become more stringent, shareholders' relationships with companies will continue to change.

SOURCE: "Stop Us Before We Meet Again," *The Wall Street Journal*, March 18, 1994, A10, and "Your Money Matters: Weekend Report; Revolutionary Proxies: Read Them and Reap," *The Wall Street Journal*, January 29, 1994, C1.

alternative firms. One firm devotes a substantial part of its resources to social actions, while the other concentrates on profits and stock prices. Most investors are likely to shun the socially oriented firm, thus putting it at a disadvantage in the capital market. After all, why should the stockholders of one corporation subsidize society to a greater extent than those of other businesses? For this reason, even highly profitable firms (unless they are closely held rather than publicly owned) generally are constrained against taking unilateral cost-increasing social actions.

Does all this mean that firms should not exercise social responsibility? Not at all, but it does mean that most significant cost-increasing actions associated with social responsibility will have to be put on a *mandatory* rather than a voluntary basis, at least initially, to ensure that the burden falls uniformly on all businesses.

Stock Price Maximization and Social Welfare

If a firm attempts to maximize its stock price, is this good or bad for society? In general, it is good. Aside from such illegal actions as attempting to form monopolies, violating safety codes, and failing to meet pollution control requirements, *the same actions that maximize stock prices also benefit society.* First, note that stock price maximization requires efficient, low-cost plants that produce high-quality goods and services at the lowest possible cost. Second, stock price maximization requires the development of products that consumers want and need, so the profit motive leads to new technology, to new products, and to new jobs. Finally, stock price maximization necessitates efficient and courteous service, adequate stocks of merchandise, and well-located business establishments—these factors all are necessary to maintain a customer base that is necessary for producing sales, and thus profits. Therefore, actions that help a firm increase the price of its stock also are beneficial to society at large. This is why profit-motivated, free-enterprise economies have been so much more successful than socialistic and communistic economic systems. Because managerial finance plays a crucial role in the operation of successful firms, and because successful firms are absolutely necessary for a healthy, productive economy, it is easy to see why finance is important from a social standpoint.[9]

Self-Test Questions

What is management's primary goal?

What would happen if one firm attempted to exercise costly social responsibility, while its competitors did not exercise social responsibility?

How does the goal of stock price maximization benefit society at large?

---

[9]People sometimes argue that firms, in their efforts to raise profits and stock prices, increase product prices and gouge the public. In a reasonably competitive economy, which we have, prices are constrained by competition and consumer resistance. If a firm raises its prices beyond reasonable levels, it will simply lose its market share. Even giant firms like General Motors lose business to the Japanese and Germans, as well as to Ford and Chrysler, if they set prices above levels necessary to cover production costs plus a "normal" profit. Of course, firms want to earn more, and they constantly try to cut costs, to develop new products, and so on, and thereby to earn above-normal profits. Note, though, that if they are indeed successful and do earn above-normal profits, those very profits will attract competition that will eventually drive prices down, so again the main long-term beneficiary is the consumer.

Managerial Actions to Maximize Shareholder Wealth

**PROFIT
MAXIMIZATION**
The maximization of the
firm's net income.

**EARNINGS PER
SHARE (EPS)**
Net income divided by the
number of shares of
common stock
outstanding.

To maximize the price of a firm's stock, what types of actions should its management take? First, consider the question of stock prices versus profits: Will **profit maximization** also result in stock price maximization? In answering this question, we must consider the matter of total corporate profits versus **earnings per share (EPS).**

For example, suppose Xerox had 300 million shares outstanding and earned $1,200 million, or $4 per share. If you owned 100 shares of the stock, your share of the total profits would be $400. Now suppose Xerox sold another 300 million shares and invested the funds received in assets that produced $300 million of income. Total income would rise to $1,500 million, but earnings per share would decline from $4 to $2.50 = $1,500/600. Now your share of the firm's earnings would be only $250, down from $400. You (and other existing stockholders) would have suffered an earnings dilution, even though total corporate profits had risen. Therefore, other things held constant, *if management is interested in the well-being of its current stockholders, it should concentrate on earnings per share rather than on total corporate profits.*

Will maximization of expected earnings per share always maximize stockholder welfare, or should other factors be considered? Think about the *timing of the earnings.* Suppose Xerox had one project that would cause earnings per share to rise by $0.20 per year for five years, or $1 in total, while another project would have no effect on earnings for four years but would increase earnings by $1.25 in the fifth year. Which project is better—in other words, is $0.20 per year for five years better or worse than $1.25 in Year 5? The answer depends on which project adds the most to the value of the stock, which in turn depends on the time value of money to investors. Thus, timing is an important reason to concentrate on wealth as measured by the price of the stock rather than on earnings alone.

Another issue relates to *risk.* Suppose one project is expected to increase earnings per share by $1, while another is expected to raise earnings by $1.20 per share. The first project is not very risky—if it is undertaken, earnings will almost certainly rise by about $1 per share. However, the other project is quite risky, so, although our best guess is that earnings will rise by $1.20 per share, we must recognize the possibility that there might be no increase whatsoever, or even a loss. Depending on how averse stockholders are to risk, the first project might be preferable to the second.

The riskiness inherent in projected earnings per share (EPS) also depends on *how the firm is financed.* As we shall see, many firms go bankrupt every year, and the greater the use of debt, the greater the threat of bankruptcy. *Consequently, while the use of debt financing might increase projected EPS, debt also increases the riskiness of projected future earnings.*

Another issue is the matter of paying dividends to stockholders versus retaining earnings and reinvesting them in the firm, thereby causing the earnings stream to grow over time. Stockholders like cash dividends, but they also like the growth in EPS that results from plowing earnings back into the business. The financial manager must decide exactly how much of the current earnings to pay out as dividends rather than to retain and reinvest—this is called the **dividend policy decision.** The optimal dividend policy is the one that maximizes the firm's stock price.

**DIVIDEND POLICY
DECISION**
The decision as to how
much of current earnings
to pay out as dividends
rather than to retain for
reinvestment in the firm.

We see, then, that the firm's stock price is dependent on the following factors:

1. Projected earnings per share.
2. Timing of the earnings stream.

3. Riskiness of the projected earnings.
4. Use of debt.
5. Dividend policy.

Every significant corporate decision should be analyzed in terms of its effect on these factors and hence on the price of the firm's stock. For example, suppose Occidental Petroleum's coal division is considering opening a new mine. If this is done, can it be expected to increase EPS? Is there a chance that costs will exceed estimates, that prices and output will fall below projections, and that EPS will be reduced because the new mine was opened? How long will it take for the new mine to show a profit? How should the capital required to open the mine be raised? If debt is used, by how much will this increase Occidental's riskiness? Should Occidental reduce its current dividends and use the cash thus saved to finance the project, or should it maintain its dividends and finance the mine with external capital? Managerial finance is designed to help answer questions like these, plus many more.

Self-Test Questions

Will profit maximization always result in stock price maximization?

Identify five factors that affect the firm's stock price, and explain the effects of each of them.

Agency Relationships

An *agency relationship* exists when one or more people (the principals) hire another person (the agent) to perform a service and then delegate decision-making authority to that agent. Important agency relationships exist (1) between stockholders and managers and (2) between stockholders and creditors (debtholders).

Stockholders versus Managers

AGENCY PROBLEM
A potential conflict of interest between (1) the principals (outside shareholders) and the agent (manager) or (2) stockholders and creditors (debtholders).

A potential **agency problem** arises whenever the manager of a firm owns less than 100 percent of the firm's common stock. If a firm is a proprietorship managed by the owner, the owner-manager will presumably operate the business in a fashion that will improve his or her own welfare, with welfare measured in the form of increased personal wealth, more leisure, or perquisites.[10] However, if the owner-manager incorporates and sells some of the firm's stock to outsiders, a potential conflict of interests immediately arises. For example, the owner-manager might now decide not to work as hard to maximize shareholder wealth because less of this wealth will go to him or her, or decide to take a higher salary or enjoy more perquisites because part of those costs will fall on the outside stockholders. This potential conflict between two parties, the principals (outside shareholders) and the agent (manager), is an agency problem.

In general, if a conflict of interest exists, what can be done to ensure that management treats the outside stockholders fairly? Several mechanisms are used to motivate

---

[10]Perquisites are executive fringe benefits such as luxurious offices, use of corporate planes and yachts, personal assistants, and general use of business assets for personal purposes.

managers to act in the shareholders' best interests. These include (1) the threat of firing, (2) the threat of takeover, and (3) managerial compensation.

1. **The threat of firing.** It wasn't long ago that the management teams of large firms felt secure in their positions, because the chances of being ousted by stockholders were so remote that managers rarely felt their jobs were in jeopardy. This situation existed because ownership of most firms was so widely distributed, and management's control over the proxy (voting) mechanism was so strong, that it was almost impossible for dissident stockholders to gain enough votes to overthrow the managers. However, today much of the stock of an average large corporation is owned by a relatively few large institutions rather than by thousands of individual investors, and the institutional money managers have the clout to influence a firm's operations. Examples of major corporations whose managements have been ousted include United Airlines, Disney, and IBM.

HOSTILE TAKEOVER
The acquisition of a company over the opposition of its management.

2. **The threat of takeover. Hostile takeovers** (instances in which management does not want the firm to be taken over) are most likely to occur when a firm's stock is undervalued relative to its potential. In a hostile takeover, the managers of the acquired firm generally are fired, and any who are able to stay on lose the power they had prior to the acquisition. Thus, managers have a strong incentive to take actions that maximize stock prices. In the words of one company president, "If you want to keep control, don't let your company's stock sell at a bargain price."

Actions to increase the firm's stock price and to keep it from being a bargain obviously are good from the standpoint of the stockholders, but other tactics that managers can use to ward off a hostile takeover might not be. Two examples of questionable tactics are *poison pills* and *greenmail*. A **poison pill** is an action a firm can take that practically kills it and thus makes it unattractive to potential suitors. Examples include Disney's plan to sell large blocks of its stock at low prices to "friendly" parties, Scott Industries' decision to make all of its debt immediately payable if its management changed, and Carleton Corporation's decision to give huge retirement bonuses, which represented a large part of the company's wealth, to its managers if the firm was taken over (such payments are called *golden parachutes*). **Greenmail,** which is like blackmail, occurs when (a) a potential acquirer (firm or individual) buys a block of stock in a company, (b) the target company's management becomes frightened that the acquirer will make a tender offer and gain control of the company, and (c) to head off a possible takeover, management offers to pay greenmail, buying the stock owned by the potential raider at a price above the existing market price without offering the same deal to other stockholders. A good example of greenmail was Disney's buyback of 11.1 percent of its stock from Saul Steinberg's Reliance Group in 1984, which gave Steinberg a quick $60 million profit (he held the stock only a few months). The day the buyback was announced, the price of Disney's stock dropped approximately ten percent. A group of stockholders sued, and Steinberg and the Disney directors were forced to pay $45 million to Disney stockholders.

POISON PILL
An action taken by management to make a firm unattractive to potential buyers and thus to avoid a hostile takeover.

GREENMAIL
A situation in which a firm, trying to avoid a takeover, buys back stock at a price above the existing market price from the person(s) trying to gain control of the firm.

3. **Structuring managerial incentives.** Increasingly, firms are tying managers' compensation to the company's performance, and this motivates managers to operate in a manner consistent with stock price maximization.

In the 1950s and 1960s, most performance-based incentive plans involved **executive stock options,** which allowed managers to purchase stock at some

EXECUTIVE STOCK OPTION
A type of incentive plan that allows managers to purchase stock at some future time at a given price.

future time at a given price. Because the value of the options was tied directly to the price of the stock, it was assumed that granting options would provide an incentive for managers to take actions that would maximize the stock's price. This type of managerial incentive lost favor in the 1970s, however, because the general stock market declined, and stock prices did not necessarily reflect companies' earnings growth. Incentive plans should be based on those factors over which managers have control, and because they cannot control the general stock market, stock option plans were not good incentive devices. Therefore, while 61 of the 100 largest U.S. firms used stock options as their sole incentive compensation in 1970, not even one of the largest 100 companies relied exclusively on such plans in 1999.

An important incentive plan now is **performance shares,** which are shares of stock given to executives on the basis of performance as measured by earnings per share, return on assets, return on equity, and so on. For example, Honeywell uses growth in earnings per share as its primary performance measure. If the company achieves a targeted average growth in earnings per share, the managers will earn 100 percent of their shares. If the corporate performance is above the target, Honeywell's managers can earn even more shares. But if growth is below the target, they get less than 100 percent of the shares.

All incentive compensation plans—executive stock options, performance shares, profit-based bonuses, and so forth—are designed to accomplish two things. First, these plans provide inducements to executives to act on those factors under their control in a manner that will contribute to stock price maximization. Second, the existence of such performance plans helps companies attract and retain top-level executives. Well-designed plans can accomplish both goals.

PERFORMANCE SHARES
A type of incentive plan in which managers are awarded shares of stock on the basis of the firm's performance over given intervals with respect to earnings per share or other measures.

Stockholders versus Creditors

A second agency problem involves conflicts between stockholders and creditors (debtholders). Creditors lend funds to the firm at rates that are based on (1) the riskiness of the firm's existing assets, (2) expectations concerning the riskiness of future asset additions, (3) the firm's existing capital structure (that is, the amount of debt financing it uses), and (4) expectations concerning future capital structure changes. These are the factors that determine the riskiness of the firm's debt, so creditors base the interest rate they charge on expectations regarding these factors.

Now suppose the stockholders, acting through management, cause the firm to take on new ventures that have much greater risk than was anticipated by the creditors. This increased risk will cause the value of the outstanding debt to fall. If the risky ventures turn out to be successful, all of the benefits will go to the stockholders because the creditors only get a fixed return. However, if things go sour, the bondholders will have to share the losses. What this amounts to, from the stockholders' point of view, is a game of "heads I win, tails you lose," which obviously is not a good game for the bondholders.

Similarly, if the firm increases its use of debt in an effort to boost the return to stockholders, the value of the old debt will decrease, so we have another "heads I win, tails you lose" situation. To illustrate, consider what happened to RJR Nabisco's bondholders when, in 1988, RJR's chief executive officer announced his plan to take the company private with funds the company would borrow (termed a *leverage buyout*). Stockholders saw their shares jump in value from $56 to over $90 in just a few days, but RJR's bondholders suffered losses of approximately 20 percent. Investors immediately realized that taking RJR Nabisco private would cause the amount of its debt to rise dramatically, and thus its riskiness would soar. This, in turn, led to a huge decline in the price of RJR's outstanding bonds. Ultimately, RJR's management was not successful in its buyout attempt. But Nabisco was purchased by another company for more than $100 per share—what a gain for the stockholders!

Can and should stockholders, through their managers/agents, try to expropriate wealth from the firm's creditors? In general, the answer is no. First, because such attempts have been made in the past, creditors today protect themselves reasonably well against stockholder actions through restrictions in credit agreements. Second, if potential creditors perceive that a firm will try to take advantage of them in unethical ways, they will either refuse to deal with the firm or else will require a much higher than normal rate of interest to compensate for the risks of such "sneaky" actions. Thus, firms that try to deal unfairly with creditors either lose access to the debt markets or are saddled with higher interest rates, both of which decrease the long-run value of the stock.

In view of these constraints, it follows that the goal of maximizing shareholder wealth requires fair play with creditors: Stockholder wealth depends on continued access to capital markets, and access depends on fair play and abiding by both the letter and the spirit of credit agreements. Managers, as agents of both the creditors and the stockholders, must act in a manner that is fairly balanced between the interests of these two classes of security holders. Similarly, because of other constraints and sanctions, management actions that would expropriate wealth from any of the firm's **stakeholders** (employees, customers, suppliers, and so on) will ultimately be to the detriment of shareholders. Therefore, maximizing shareholder wealth requires the fair treatment of all stakeholders.

STAKEHOLDERS
Individuals or entities that have an interest in the well-being of a firm—stockholders, creditors, employees, customers, suppliers, and so on.

Self-Test Questions

What is an agency relationship, and what two major agency relationships affect managerial finance?

Give some examples of potential agency problems between stockholders and managers.

List several factors that motivate managers to act in the shareholders' interests.

Give an example of how an agency problem might arise between stockholders and creditors.

The External Environment

Although managerial actions affect the value of a firm's stock, external factors also influence stock prices. Included among these factors are legal constraints, the general level of economic activity, the tax laws, and conditions in the stock market. Figure 1–2 diagrams these general relationships. Working within the set of external constraints shown in the box at the extreme left, management makes a set of long-run strategic policy decisions that chart a future course for the firm. These policy decisions, along with the general level of economic activity and the level of corporate income taxes, influence the firm's expected profitability, the timing of its cash flows, their eventual transfer to stockholders in the form of dividends, and the degree of risk inherent in

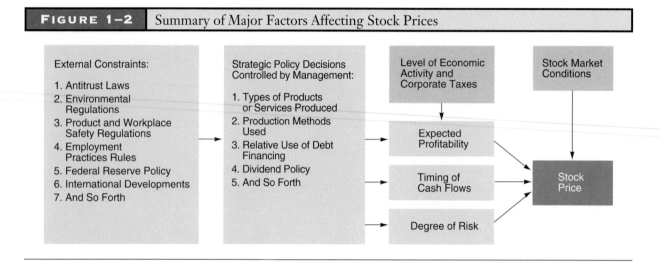

FIGURE 1–2 | Summary of Major Factors Affecting Stock Prices

projected earnings and dividends. Profitability, timing, and risk all affect the price of the firm's stock, but so does another factor, conditions in the stock market as a whole, because all stock prices tend to move up and down together to some extent.

Self-Test Question

Identify some factors beyond a firm's control that influence its stock price.

Business Ethics

The word *ethics* is defined in Webster's dictionary as "standards of conduct or moral behavior." Business ethics can be thought of as a company's attitude and conduct toward its employees, customers, community, and stockholders. High standards of ethical behavior demand that a firm treat each party it deals with in a fair and honest manner. A firm's commitment to business ethics can be measured by the tendency of the firm and its employees to adhere to laws and regulations relating to such factors as product safety and quality, fair employment practices, fair marketing and selling practices, the use of confidential information for personal gain, community involvement, bribery, and illegal payments to foreign governments to obtain business.

There are many instances of firms engaging in unethical behavior. For example, since 1985, the employees of several prominent Wall Street investment banking houses have been sentenced to prison for illegally using insider information on proposed mergers for their own personal gain, and E. F. Hutton, a large brokerage firm, lost its independence through a forced merger after it was convicted of cheating its banks out of millions of dollars in a check kiting scheme. Drexel Burnham Lambert, one of the largest investment banking firms, went bankrupt, and its "junk bond king," Michael Milken, who had earned $550 million in just one year, was sentenced to ten years in prison plus charged a huge fine for securities-law violations. Even more recently, Salomon Brothers Inc. was implicated in a Treasury-auction bidding scandal that resulted in the removal of key officers and a significant reorganization of the firm.

In spite of all this, the results of a recent study indicate that the executives of most major firms in the United States believe their firms should, and do, try to maintain high ethical standards in all of their business dealings. Further, most executives believe that there is a positive correlation between ethics and long-run profitability because ethical behavior (1) avoids fines and legal expenses, (2) builds public trust, (3) attracts business from customers who appreciate and support its policies, (4) attracts and keeps employees of the highest caliber, and (5) supports the economic viability of the communities in which it operates.

Most firms today have in place strong codes of ethical behavior, and they conduct training programs designed to ensure that all employees understand the correct behavior in different business situations. However, it is imperative that top management—the chairman, president, and vice presidents—be openly committed to ethical behavior and that they communicate this commitment through their own personal actions as well as through company policies, directives, and punishment/reward systems.

Self-Test Questions

How would you define "business ethics"?

Is "being ethical" good for profits in the long run? In the short run?

Forms of Businesses in Other Countries

Large corporations in the United States can best be described as "open" companies because they are publicly traded organizations that, for the most part, are independent of each other as well as the government. And, as we described in previous sections, such companies offer limited liability to owners who usually do not participate in the day-to-day operations and who can easily transfer ownership by trading stock in the financial markets. While most developed countries with free economies have business organizations that are similar to U.S. corporations, some differences exist relating to ownership structure and management of operations. Though a comprehensive discussion is beyond the scope of this book, in this section, we provide some examples of differences between U.S. companies and non-U.S. companies.

Firms in most developed economies, such as corporations in the United States, offer equities with limited liability to stockholders that can be traded in domestic financial markets. Such firms are not always called corporations, though. For instance, a comparable firm in England is called a "public limited company," or PLC, while in Germany it is known as an *Aktiengesellschaft*, or AG, and in Mexico, Spain, and Latin America it is called a *Sociedad Anónima*, or SA. Some of these firms are publicly traded, while others are privately held.

Like corporations in the United States, most of the large companies in England and Canada are "open" and the stock is widely dispersed among a number of different investors. Of note, though, is that about two-thirds of the traded stocks of English companies are owned by institutional investors rather than individuals. On the other hand, in much of continental Europe, stock ownership is more concentrated; major investor groups include families, banks, and other corporations. In Germany and France, for instance, corporations represent the primary group of shareholders, followed by families. Although banks do not hold a large number of shares of stock, they can greatly influence companies because many shareholders assign banks their proxy votes. Also, often the family unit has concentrated ownership and thus is a major influence in many of the large companies in developed countries such as these. The ownership structures of these firms and many other non-U.S. companies, including very large organizations, often are concentrated in the hands of a relatively few investors or investment groups. Such firms are considered "closed" because shares of stock are not publicly traded, there are relatively few individuals or groups that own the stock, and major stockholders often are involved in the daily operations of the firms.

The primary reason non-U.S. firms are likely to be more "closed," and thus have more concentrated ownership, than U.S. firms results from the "universal" banking relationships that exist outside the United States. Financial institutions in other countries generally are less regulated than in the United States, which means foreign banks, for instance, can provide businesses a greater variety of services, including short-term loans, long-term financing, investment banking services, and even stock ownership. And these services are available at many locations, or branches, throughout the country. Thus, non-U.S. firms tend to have close relationships with individual banking organizations, which also might have ownership positions in the firms. What this means is that banks in countries like Germany can meet the financing needs of family-owned businesses, even if they are very large, so such companies do not have to "go public," and thus relinquish some control, to finance additional growth. Consider the fact that in both France and Germany about 75 percent of the gross domestic product (GDP) comes from firms not publicly traded, that is, "closed" businesses. The opposite is true in the United States, because large firms do not have "one-stop" financing outlets; thus, growth generally has to be financed by bringing in outside owners, which results in more widely dispersed ownership.

INDUSTRIAL GROUPS
Organizations comprised of companies in different industries with common ownership interests, which include firms necessary to manufacture and sell products—a network of manufacturers, suppliers, marketing organizations, distributors, retailers, and creditors.

In some parts of the world, firms are part of **industrial groups,** which are organizations comprised of companies in different industries with common ownership interests and, in some instances, shared management. Firms in the industrial group are "tied" by a major lender, typically a bank, which often also has a significant ownership interest along with other firms in the group. The objective of an industrial group is to include firms that provide materials and services required to manufacture and sell products—that is, to create an organization that ties together all the functions of production and sales from start to finish. Thus, an industrial group includes firms involved in manufacturing, financing, marketing, and distribution of products, which includes suppliers of raw materials, production organizations, retail stores, and creditors. A portion of the stocks of firms that are members of an industrial group might be traded publicly, but the "lead" company, which is typically a major creditor, controls the management of the entire group. Industrial groups are most prominent in Asian countries. In Japan, an industrial group is called a *keiretsu,* and it is called a *chaebol* in Korea. Well-known *keiretsu* groups include Mitsubishi, Toshiba, and Toyota, while the best-known *chaebol* probably is Hyundai. The success of industrial groups in Japan and Korea has resulted in the establishment of similar organizations in developing countries located in Latin America, Asia, and Africa.

The differences in ownership concentration of non-U.S. firms might cause the behavior of managers, thus the goals they pursue, to differ. For instance, often it is argued that the greater concentration of ownership of non-U.S. firms permits managers to focus more on long-term objectives, especially wealth maximization, than short-term earnings, because firms have easier access to credit in times of financial difficulty—creditors who also are owners generally have greater interest in supporting short-term survival. On the other hand, it also has been argued that the ownership structures of non-U.S. firms create an environment where it is difficult to change managers, especially if they are significant stockholders. Such "entrenchment" could be very detrimental to firms if management is extremely inefficient. Consider, for example, firms in Japan that generally are very reluctant to fire employees, because losing your job is a disgrace in the Japanese culture. Whether the ownership structure of non-U.S. firms is an advantage or a disadvantage is debatable. But we do know that the greater concentration of ownership in non-U.S. firms permits greater control by individuals or groups than the more dispersed ownership structures of U.S. firms.

Self-Test Questions

What is the primary difference between U.S. corporations and non-U.S. firms?

What is an industrial group?

What are some of the names given to firms in other countries?

Multinational Corporations

Large firms, both U.S. and non-U.S., generally do not operate in a single country; rather they conduct business throughout the world. In fact, the largest firms in the world truly are "multinational" rather than "domestic" operations. Managers of such multinational companies face a wide range of issues that are not present when a company operates in a single country. In this section, we highlight the key differences between multinational and domestic corporations, and we discuss the impact of these differences on managerial finance for U.S. businesses.

MULTINATIONAL CORPORATION
A firm that operates in two or more countries.

The term **multinational corporation** is used to describe a firm that operates in two or more countries. Since World War II, a new and fundamentally different form of international commercial activity has developed, and it has increased greatly worldwide economic and political interdependence. Rather than merely buying resources from foreign concerns, multinational firms now make direct investments in fully integrated operations, with worldwide entities controlling all phases of the production process—from extraction of raw materials, through the manufacturing process, to distribution to consumers throughout the world. Today, multinational corporate networks control a large and growing share of the world's technological, marketing, and productive resources.

There are five principal reasons companies, both U.S. and foreign, go "international":

1. **To seek new markets.** After a company has saturated its home market, growth opportunities often are better in foreign markets. Thus, such homegrown firms as Coca-Cola and McDonald's have aggressively expanded into overseas markets, and foreign firms such as Sony and Toshiba are major competitors in the U.S. consumer electronics market.

2. **To seek raw materials.** It is not surprising that many U.S. oil companies, such as Exxon, have major subsidiaries around the world to ensure access to the basic resources needed to sustain the company's primary business line.

3. **To seek new technology.** No single nation holds a commanding advantage in all technologies, so companies scour the globe for leading scientific and design ideas. For example, Xerox has introduced more than 80 different office copiers in the United States that were engineered and built by its Japanese joint venture, Fuji Xerox.

4. **To seek production efficiency.** Companies in high production cost countries are shifting production to low-cost countries. For example, General Motors has production and assembly plants in Mexico and Brazil, and even Japanese manufacturers have shifted some of their production to lower-cost countries in the Pacific Rim. The ability to shift production from country to country has important implications for labor costs in all countries. For example, when Xerox threatened to move its copier rebuilding work to Mexico, its union in Rochester, New York, agreed to work rule and productivity improvements that kept the operation in the United States.

5. **To avoid political and regulatory hurdles.** The primary reason for Japanese auto companies to move production to the United States was to get around U.S. import quotas. Now, Honda, Nissan, and Toyota all assemble automobiles or trucks in the United States. Similarly, one of the factors that prompted U.S. pharmaceutical maker SmithKline and Britain's Beecham to merge was that they wanted to avoid licensing and regulatory delays in their largest markets, Western Europe and the United States. Now, SmithKline Beecham can identify itself as an inside player in both Europe and the United States.

During the 1980s and the 1990s, investments in the United States by foreign corporations increased significantly. This "reverse" investment is of increasing concern to U.S. government officials because of its implication for eroding the traditional doctrine of independence and self-reliance that always has been a hallmark of U.S. policy. Just as U.S. corporations with extensive overseas operations are said to use their economic power to exert substantial economic and political influence over host governments around the world, it is feared that foreign corporations might gain similar sway over U.S. policy. However, these developments suggest an increasing degree of mutual influence and interdependence among business enterprises and nations, to which the United States is not immune.

During the past couple of decades, some dramatic international changes have taken place, including the breakup, both politically and economically, of the former Soviet Union, the collapse of communism in many Eastern European countries, the reunification of Germany, the political revolution in South Africa, and economic disasters in Japan and Southeast Asia. Future events will include the continued phasing in of the European Economic Community with one Eurocurrency and the determination of how to help the cash-starved Eastern bloc nations. Also, there has been a war with Iraq and continuing turbulence in the Middle East and Eastern Europe. These events, and others that surely will occur, have an impact on the world economy.

Self-Test Questions

What is a multinational corporation?

Why do companies "go international"?

Multinational versus Domestic Managerial Finance

In theory, the concepts and procedures we will discuss in the remaining chapters of the text are valid for both domestic and multinational operations. However, several problems uniquely associated with the international environment increase the complexity of the manager's task in a multinational corporation, and they often force the manager to alter the way alternative courses of action are evaluated and compared. Six major factors distinguish managerial finance as practiced by firms operating entirely within a single country from management by firms that operate in several different countries:

1. **Different currency denominations.** Cash flows in various parts of a multinational corporate system generally are denominated in different currencies. Hence, an analysis of exchange rates, and the effects of fluctuating currency values, must be included in all financial analyses.

2. **Economic and legal ramifications.** Each country in which the firm operates has its own unique political and economic institutions, and institutional differences among countries can cause significant problems when a firm tries to coordinate and control the worldwide operations of its subsidiaries. For example, differences in tax laws among countries can cause a particular transaction to have strikingly dissimilar after-tax consequences, depending on where the transaction occurred. Similarly, differences in legal systems of host nations complicate many matters, from the simple recording of a business transaction to the role played by the judiciary in resolving conflicts. Such differences can restrict multinational corporations' flexibility to deploy resources as they wish and can even make procedures illegal in one part of the company that are required in another part. These differences also make it difficult for executives trained in one country to operate effectively in another.

3. **Language differences.** The ability to communicate is critical in all business transactions, and here persons who are American born and raised often are at a disadvantage because they generally are fluent only in English, whereas European and Japanese businesspeople usually are fluent in several languages, including English. Thus, it is easier for internationals to invade U.S. markets than it is for Americans to penetrate international markets.

4. **Cultural differences.** Even within geographic regions long considered fairly homogeneous, different countries have unique cultural heritages that shape values and influence the role of business in the society. Multinational corporations find that such matters as defining the appropriate goals of the firm, attitudes toward risk taking, dealings with employees, the ability to curtail unprofitable operations, and so on, can vary dramatically from one country to the next.

5. **Role of governments.** Most traditional models in finance assume the existence of a competitive marketplace in which the terms of trade are determined by the participants. The government, through its power to establish basic ground rules, is involved in this process, but its participation is minimal. Thus, the market provides both the primary barometer of success and the indicator of the actions that must be taken to remain competitive. This view of the process is reasonably correct for the United States and a few other major industrialized nations, but it does not accurately describe the situation in most of the world. Frequently, the terms under which companies compete, the actions that must be taken or avoided, and the terms of trade on various transactions are determined not in the marketplace but by direct negotiation between the host government and the multinational corporation. This is essentially a political process, and it must be treated as such.

6. **Political risk.** The distinguishing characteristic of a nation that differentiates it from a multinational corporation is that the nation exercises sovereignty over the people and property in its territory. Hence, a nation is free to place constraints on

the transfer of corporate resources and even to expropriate (take for public use) the assets of a firm without compensation. This is political risk, and it tends to be largely a given rather than a variable that can be changed by negotiation. Political risk varies from country to country, and it must be addressed explicitly in any financial analysis. Another aspect of political risk is terrorism against U.S. firms or executives abroad. For example, U.S. executives have been captured and held for ransom in several South American and Middle Eastern countries.

These six factors complicate managerial finance within multinational firms, and they increase the risks faced by the firms involved. However, prospects for high profits often make it worthwhile for firms to accept these risks and to learn how to minimize or at least live with them.

Self-Test Question

Identify and briefly explain six major factors that complicate managerial finance within multinational firms.

Organization of the Book

Part I consists of two background chapters. In this chapter, we have discussed the goals of the firm and the "philosophy" of managerial finance. Chapter 2 describes how financial markets operate, how interest rates are determined, and how our tax system affects both stock prices and managerial decisions.

Part II deals with forecasting and control. First, Chapter 3 describes the key financial statements, shows how analysts appraise a firm's performance, and explains how the various aspects of managerial finance relate to one another. Then, in Chapter 4, we focus on projecting future financial statements under different strategic plans and operating conditions.

Part III includes topics related to the theory of valuation. First, in Chapter 5, we see how risk is measured and how it affects security prices and rates of return. Then, Chapter 6 discusses the time value of money and its effects on asset values and rates of return. Finally, Chapter 7 explains how risk and time value determine asset values in the marketplace.

Part IV applies the concepts covered in Parts I through III to long-term, fixed asset decisions. Here we move into the execution phase of the long-range strategic planning process, considering the vital subject of capital budgeting. Because major capital expenditures take years to plan and implement, and because decisions in this area are generally not reversible and hence affect the firm's operations for many years, their effect on the firm's value is significant.

Part V focuses on long-term financial decisions: How do we determine the cost of each type of capital, and how does the method of financing affect the value of the firm? This section uses most of the valuation concepts developed in the previous two sections of the book, and here we analyze such key issues as the optimal debt/equity mix and dividend policy.

In Part VI, we examine short-term, day-to-day operating decisions. From accounting, we know that assets that are expected to be converted to cash within a year, such as inventories and accounts receivable, are called *current assets*, and that liabilities that must be paid off within a year are called *current liabilities*. The management of current assets and current liabilities is known as *working capital management*. In Chapters 13 through 15, we see how the proper amounts of cash, inventories, and accounts receivable are determined and how these current assets should be financed.

Finally, Part VII integrates the long-term strategic aspects of the book and shows how the parts fit together. In this section, we describe the principal sources and forms of capital, as well as the process used by a firm to raise capital for its growth needs. We also examine issues such as leasing and reorganizations.

As we have mentioned, the importance of the globalization of businesses has increased and will continue to increase significantly. Thus, we have included discussions of international financial management throughout the book—where appropriate, we discuss the implications of international finance after we first explain the fundamental concepts.

It is worth noting that some instructors may choose to cover the chapters in a different sequence from their order in the book. The chapters are written in a modular, self-contained manner, so such a reordering will present no major difficulties.

✴ SMALL BUSINESS

Goals and Resources in the Small Firm

Although small business is a vital contributor to the financial health of our economy, the businesses themselves often are fragile and susceptible to failure because of poor management, particularly financial management.

Significant differences exist between small and big businesses regarding the way they are owned, the way they are managed, and the financial and managerial resources at their disposal. These differences make it necessary to modify managerial finance principles for application in the small business area. Two especially important differences are resource shortages and goal conflicts.

RESOURCE SHORTAGES

It is not unusual for the founders of a small business to have full responsibility for all phases of the firm's operations. In fact, in many cases, these individuals are reluctant to relinquish any responsibilities even when the firm grows significantly. So management in small firms often is spread very thin, with one or two key individuals taking on far more responsibility than they can handle properly. If you talk to small business operators, you often will hear "this is my business, and I need to keep active in every aspect of the operations in order to monitor its pulse—no one can do

this for me." Unfortunately, it is this attitude that keeps most small businesses small.

Not only is management often spread thin in small firms, but such firms have great difficulty acquiring the new funds needed for expansion. Until a firm achieves a fairly substantial size, say, $15 million or so in sales, it cannot sell stock or bonds to the general public. Further, if the company does have a public stock offering at the first opportunity, its costs will be quite high in comparison to larger firms' costs of issuing stock. For example, it took Richard Smyth four tries and substantial expense to find a company that was willing to underwrite a $5.5 million initial public offering for Vista 2000 Inc., a small firm that develops and markets home safety devices in Roswell, Georgia. In general, small firms have very limited access to public capital markets. Access to nonpublic markets also is limited. For instance, banks sometimes are reluctant to lend substantial amounts to small firms that lack of financial history, and relatives' resources only extend so far.

Small firms thus have constraints both on their managerial talent and on their ability to obtain adequate capital. It is no wonder small firms often fail, given their poor (or overworked) management and lack of capital.

continues

GOAL CONFLICTS

Small businesses also differ from large firms with regard to corporate goals. Earlier in the chapter we pointed out that share price maximization is taken to be the goal of all firms. For a small firm, often the owner's livelihood is the business, because a substantial portion of the owner's wealth is bet on the success of the business. Generally, the small business owner is not diversified at all—every bit of wealth is invested in the business. Given this level of commitment and lack of a fallback position, small business owners take a very different posture toward risk taking than would a typical investor in a public company. Most public investors hold well-diversified portfolios of assets, and their employment incomes generally come from jobs in altogether separate industries. On the other hand, both the salary and investment income of a small business owner generally are dependent on the success of one company. This makes the risk exposure of the small business owner quite high.

The owner-managers of small firms are keenly interested in the value of their firms, even if this value cannot be observed in the market. But the motives of small business owners are complex. Some owners are motivated primarily by such considerations as the desire to be their "own boss," even if this means not letting the firm grow at the fastest rate possible or be as profitable as it could be. In other words, there is value to being in control, and that value is not easily measurable. As a result, we often observe small businesses taking actions, such as refusing to bring in new stockholders even when they badly need new capital, that do not make sense when judged on the basis of value maximization but that do make sense when seen in the light of the personal objectives of the owners.

To the extent that the goals of the small firm differ from value maximization, some of the prescriptions in this text might not be entirely applicable. However, most of the tools we develop will be useful for small businesses, even though the tools might have to be modified somewhat. In any event, brief "Small Business" sections in various chapters will serve as our vehicle for discussing issues of special importance to small firms.

✳ ETHICAL DILEMMA

Chances Are What They Don't Know Won't Hurt Them!

Futuristic Electronic Technologies (FET) recently released a new advanced electronic micro system to be used by financial institutions, large corporations, and governments to process and store financial data, including taxes, automatic payroll payments, and so on. Even though the technology used in the creation of the product was developed by FET, it is expected FET's competitors will soon possess similar technology. So to beat the competition to the market, FET introduced its new micro system a little earlier than originally planned. In fact, laboratory testing had not been fully completed before the product reached the market. The tests are complete now, and the final results suggest the micro system might be flawed with respect to how some data are retrieved and processed. The tests are not conclusive, though, and even if additional testing proves a flaw does exist, according to FET, it is of minuscule importance because the problem seems to occur for only one out of 100 million retrieval and processing attempts. The financial ramifications associated with the flaw are unknown at this time.

Assume you are one of FET's senior executives whose annual salary is based on the performance of the firm's common stock. You realize that if FET recalls the affected micro system the stock price will suffer; thus your salary for the year will be less than you expected. To complicate matters, you just purchased a very expensive house based on your salary expectations for the next few years—those expectations will not come true unless the new micro system is a success for FET. As one of the senior executives, you will help determine what course of action FET will follow with respect to the micro system. What should you do? Should you encourage FET to recall the micro system until further testing is completed? Or is there another course of action you can suggest?

Summary

This chapter has provided an overview of managerial finance. The key concepts covered are listed here:

- Finance consists of three interrelated areas: (1) **financial markets and institutions,** (2) **investments,** and (3) **managerial finance.**
- Managerial finance has undergone significant changes over time, but four issues have received the most emphasis in recent years: (1) **inflation** and its effects on interest rates, (2) **deregulation** of financial institutions, (3) a dramatic increase in **technology,** such as the use of telecommunications for transmitting information and the use of computers for analyzing the effects of alternative financial decisions, and (4) the increased importance of **global financial markets and business operations.**
- **Financial managers** are responsible for obtaining and using funds in a way that will **maximize the value of their firms.**
- The three main forms of business organization are the **proprietorship,** the **partnership,** and the **corporation.**
- Although each form of organization offers some advantages and disadvantages, **most business is conducted by corporations because this organizational form maximizes most firms' values.**
- The **primary goal** of management should be to **maximize stockholders' wealth,** and this means **maximizing the price of the firm's stock.** Further, actions that maximize stock prices also increase social welfare.
- An **agency problem** is a potential conflict of interests that can arise between (1) the owners of the firm and its management or (2) the stockholders and the creditors (debtholders).
- There are a number of ways to **motivate managers to act in the best interests of stockholders,** including (1) the **threat of firing,** (2) the **threat of takeovers,** and (3) properly structured **managerial incentives.**
- The **price of the firm's stock** depends on the firm's **projected earnings per share,** the **timing of its earnings,** the **riskiness of the projected earnings,** its **use of debt,** and its **dividend policy.**
- **Non-U.S. firms** generally have more concentrated ownership than U.S. firms. In some cases, firms in other countries are part of an **industrial group,** which is a network of firms with common ownership ties that provides the different functions required to manufacture and sell a product from start to finish. Examples of industrial groups include the *keiretsu* in Japan and the *chaebol* in Korea.
- **International operations** have become increasingly important to individual firms and to the national economy. A **multinational corporation** is a firm that operates in two or more nations.
- Companies go "international" for five primary reasons: (1) to **seek new markets,** (2) to **seek raw materials,** (3) to **seek new technology,** (4) to **seek production efficiency,** and (5) to **avoid trade barriers.**
- Six major factors distinguish managerial finance as practiced by domestic firms from that of multinational corporations: (1) **different currency denominations,** (2) **economic and legal ramifications,** (3) **languages,** (4) **cultural differences,** (5) **role of governments,** and (6) **political risk.**
- **Small businesses** are quite important in the aggregate, so we shall discuss small business issues throughout the text.

Questions

1–1 What are the three principal forms of business organization? What are the advantages and disadvantages of each?

1–2 Would the "normal" rate of return on investment be the same in all industries? Would "normal" rates of return change over time? Explain.

1–3 Would the role of the financial manager be likely to increase or decrease in importance relative to other executives if the rate of inflation increased? Explain.

1–4 Should stockholder wealth maximization be thought of as a long-term or a short-term goal? For example, if one action would probably increase the firm's stock price from a current level of $20 to $25 in six months and then to $30 in five years, but another action would probably keep the stock at $20 for several years but then increase it to $40 in five years, which action would be better? Can you think of some specific corporate actions that might have these general tendencies?

1–5 Drawing on your background in accounting, can you think of any accounting procedure differences that might make it difficult to compare the relative performance of different firms?

1–6 Would the management of a firm in an oligopolistic or in a competitive industry be more likely to engage in what might be called "socially conscious" practices? Explain your reasoning.

1–7 What is the difference between stock price maximization and profit maximization? Under what conditions might profit maximization not lead to stock price maximization?

1–8 If you were the president of a large, publicly owned corporation, would you make decisions to maximize stockholders' welfare or your own personal interests? What are some actions stockholders could take to ensure that management's interests and those of stockholders coincided? What are some other factors that might influence management's actions?

1–9 The president of United Semiconductor Corporation made this statement in the company's annual report: "United's primary goal is to increase the value of the common stockholders' equity over time." Later on in the report, the following announcements were made:

a. The company contributed $1.5 million to the symphony orchestra in San Francisco, its headquarters city.

b. The company is spending $500 million to open a new plant in Mexico. No revenues will be produced by the plant for four years, so earnings will be depressed during this period versus what they would have been had the decision not been made to open the new plant.

c. The company is increasing its relative use of debt. Whereas assets were formerly financed with 35 percent debt and 65 percent equity, henceforth the financing mix will be 50-50.

d. The company uses a great deal of electricity in its manufacturing operations, and it generates most of this power itself. Plans are to utilize nuclear fuel rather than coal to produce electricity in the future.

e. The company has been paying out half of its earnings as dividends and retaining the other half. Henceforth, it will pay out only 30 percent as dividends.

Discuss how each of these actions would be reacted to by United's stockholders, customers, and labor force, and then how each action might affect United's stock price.

1–10 Why do U.S. corporations build manufacturing plants abroad when they could build them at home?

1–11 Compared to the ownership structure of U.S. firms, which are "open" companies, what are some advantages of the ownership structure of non-U.S. firms, many of which are "closed" companies? Can you think of any disadvantages?

Self-Test Problem

Solution appears in Appendix B.

key terms   **ST–1** Define each of the following terms:

    a. Proprietorship; partnership; corporation
    b. Stockholder wealth maximization
    c. Hostile takeover
    d. Social responsibility; business ethics
    e. Normal profits; normal rate of return
    f. Agency problem; agency costs
    g. Poison pill; greenmail
    h. Performance shares; executive stock option
    i. Profit maximization
    j. Earnings per share
    k. Dividend policy decision
    l. Multinational corporation
    m. Political risk
    n. Industrial group; *chaebol; keiretsu*
    o. Small business versus large business

ONLINE ESSENTIALS

http://www.careers.wsj.com/   Careers.wsj.com
Provides information about various type of jobs in all areas of business and their availability, advice about job hunting, salary profiles for various jobs, and much more.

http://www.bloomberg.com/fun/jobs.html   Bloomberg PERSONAL
Provides a search for career opportunities in banking and finance.

http://www.cob.ohio-state.edu/~fin/osujobs.htm   Business Job Finder
Provides an indication of the skills and requirements needed for various careers in finance; also has links to related sites and information about other business areas.

http://www.nationjob.com/financial   NationJob Network
Lists job openings in the finance area with information about how to apply.

CHAPTER 2

The Financial Environment: Markets, Institutions, Interest Rates, and Taxes

A MANAGERIAL PERSPECTIVE

After reaching record highs during the first half of 1998, the stock market declined by nearly 20 percent in less than two months, from the end of July to mid-September. And, although the market once again reached record levels in March 1999, the path it took to get there could best be described as extremely precarious—the market lunged forward, then just as quickly it pulled back. Forecasters blamed the roller coaster ride that the market took on uncertainty generated by news that a global economic crisis was eminent—since the latter half of 1997, it was revealed that Japan and much of southeast Asia were in the grips of financial turmoil, attempts to develop a free economy in Russia seemed to be failing, and the economies of Brazil and many other countries appeared to be headed toward recessions. Given the global nature of many large U.S. companies and the fear that low-cost-labor countries such as Indonesia would "dump" cheap products in the international markets, experts predicted that the earnings growths of U.S. businesses would slow significantly in the near-term, and perhaps even in the longer-term. Even though interest rates on U.S. Treasury securities dropped to historically low levels in October 1998—30-year Treasuries were yielding less than

five percent because the Federal Reserve (Fed) cut interest rates in both September and October— the Fed was poised to cut rates even further to support the liquidity of the financial markets and to help prop up a U.S. economy that seemed to be slowing.

Five months later in March 1999, the economic outlook was much improved—the growth in the economy in the fourth quarter of 1998 reached a staggering 5.6 percent and the premier stock market measure, the Dow Jones Industrial Average (DJIA), topped 10,000 points for the first time in history. Many experts predicted that the Fed would change its tenor and favor increases in interest rates in an effort to keep the economy from "overheating," that is, to slow the economy to a manageable pace of two to three percent growth. If investors reached similar conclusions, they certainly would act on their expectations and begin selling bonds, which would increase interest rates; and higher interest rates probably would cause investors to sell stock in an effort to capture higher returns in the bond markets. Clearly, then, changing interest rates affect stock markets as well as bond, or debt, markets.

Whether a business or an individual, when we borrow we would like interest rates to be low.

continues

When rates are low, like they have been recently, many firms and individuals refinance to replace higher interest debt with lower interest debt. But, when interest rates are low, those who depend on the income from their investments suffer. Clearly, interest rates affect all of us. Thus, as you read this chapter, think about (1) all the factors the Fed must consider before attempting to change interest rates and (2) the effects of interest rate changes on inflation, on the financial markets, on you as an individual (student), and on the economy as a whole. ■

Financial managers must understand the environment and markets within which businesses operate. Therefore, in this chapter, we examine the markets where firms raise funds, securities are traded, and stock prices are established, as well as the institutions that operate in these markets. In the process, we will explore the principal factors that determine money costs in the economy. In addition, because taxes are critically important in financial decisions, we discuss some key features of the U.S. tax laws.

The Financial Markets

Businesses, individuals, and government units often need to raise capital to fund investments. For example, suppose Carolina Power & Light (CP&L) forecasts an increase in the demand for electricity in North Carolina, and the company decides to build a new power plant. Because CP&L almost certainly will not have the hundreds of millions or billions of dollars needed to pay for the plant, the company will have to raise these funds in the financial markets. Or suppose you want to buy a home that costs $100,000, but you only have $20,000 in savings. How can you raise the additional $80,000? At the same time, some individuals and firms have incomes that are greater than their current expenditures, so they have funds available to invest. For example, Carol Hawk has an income of $36,000, but her expenses are only $30,000, while Reliant Energy recently agreed to invest nearly $2.5 billion over the next seven years to purchase power companies in Europe.

People and organizations wanting to borrow money are brought together with those having surplus funds in the *financial markets*. Unlike *physical (real) asset markets*, which are those for such products as wheat, autos, real estate, computers, and machinery, *financial asset markets* deal with stocks, bonds, mortgages, and other *claims on real assets* with respect to the distribution of future cash flows.

FINANCIAL MARKETS
"Mechanisms" by which borrowers and lenders get together.

In a general sense, the term financial market refers to a conceptual "mechanism" rather than a physical location or a specific type of organization or structure. We usually describe the **financial markets** as being a system comprised of individuals and institutions, instruments, and procedures that bring together borrowers and savers, no matter the location. Note that "markets" is plural—there are a great many different financial markets, each one consisting of many institutions, in a developed economy such as ours. Each market deals with a somewhat different type of instrument in terms of the instrument's maturity and the assets backing it. Also, different markets serve different types of customers, or operate in different parts of the country. Here are some of the major types of markets:

✳ **INDUSTRY PRACTICE**

I'd Like to Apply for a Loan—By the Way, How Much Is the Broccoli Today?

To become more competitive with other financial institutions, banks are moving away from traditional banking practices. More and more, banks have become aggressive competitors for customers. For example, in their effort to get close to customers, some banks have located limited branch operations in local supermarkets. There were approximately 900 branches in supermarkets in 1990; in 1994, the number was about 2,100; and, by the end of 1998, the number had grown to nearly 8,000. In addition, branch banking operations have recently begun to appear in Wal-Mart stores. The fast-paced growth of shopping market branches is expected to continue because these operations are less expensive than free-standing branches and because store branches reach many customers that might not otherwise use the bank's services. For example, it is estimated that between 20,000 and 30,000 potential customers go to supermarkets and discount stores each week. These nontraditional branch banks are viewed as a means to reach a large group of potential customers that might not otherwise use banking services. Unfortunately, there is disagreement about the viability of such operations because: (1) it seems the customers who use store branches generally keep low balances in their accounts, and such accounts are not profitable for the bank; (2) most customers who need loans, such as mortgages and automobile financing, take their business to other, more traditional banking locations and often to other banks—such loan activity is the greatest profit generator of a bank; and, (3) it is difficult to maintain a steady workforce because store branches generally are open some nights, on Saturday, and perhaps even some Sundays. Even though much of a store banking operation is automated, a minimal staff is needed to monitor operations and help customers with questions and any difficulties that cannot be handled by a machine. In the future, you might be able to get an automobile loan at 2 A.M. in a Wal-Mart that is open 24 hours a day, seven days a week.

One of the fastest-growing areas of banking is electronic, or Internet, banking, which is commonly called either E-banking or virtual banking. One of the leaders in this arena is Net.B@nk, Inc., which opened its virtual doors in October 1996. In June 1999, the bank had nearly 40,000 customers with more than $415 million in deposits, more than $513 million in loans, and total assets that exceeded $817 million. Compared with operations at the same time a year earlier, Net.B@nk experienced substantial growth—assets grew by more than 230 percent and its dollar deposits increased by nearly 125 percent. Net.B@nk offers a full line of financial services, including checking accounts, certificates of deposit, loans, and so forth, and deposits are insured just like in traditional banks. Because the main office is a computer system, costs, especially overhead expenses, are lower than for traditional banks; thus, deposits can be paid higher rates, while loans can be offered at lower rates.

E-banking has not yet become a widespread phenomenon because it is struggling to win the trust of the masses—(1) many people still mistrust electronics and (2) E-banking has not attained the same level of trust that is associated with large, more traditional banks with physical locations. Even so, clearly, such nontraditional banking as described here is going to become more prevalent as banking organizations continue to change their operations to better compete with other financial institutions. It won't be long before you can get the mortgage for your house at the same place you buy IBM's common stock, which might also be the place you shop for your grocery or household needs—that location could either be a brick-and-mortar store or an electronic store.

FINANCIAL INTERMEDIARIES
Specialized financial firms that facilitate the transfer of funds from savers to borrowers.

The **financial intermediaries** shown in the third section of Figure 2–1 do more than simply transfer money and securities between borrowers and savers—they literally create new financial products. Because the intermediaries generally are large, they gain economies of scale in analyzing the creditworthiness of potential borrowers, in processing and collecting loans, in pooling risks, and thus helping individual savers diversify—that is, "not put all their financial eggs in one basket." Further, a system of specialized intermediaries can enable savings to do more than just draw interest. For example, individuals can put money into banks and get both interest income and a convenient way of making payments (checking), or put money into life insurance companies and get both interest income and financial protection for their beneficiaries.

In the United States and other developed nations, a large set of specialized, highly efficient financial intermediaries has evolved. Competition and government policy have created a rapidly changing arena, however, such that different types of institutions currently perform services that formerly were reserved for others. This trend, which most certainly will continue into the future, has caused institutional distinctions to become blurred. Still, there remains a degree of institutional identity, and here are the major classes of financial intermediaries:

1. *Commercial banks*, which are the traditional "department stores of finance," serve a wide variety of customers. Historically, the commercial banks were the major institutions that handled checking accounts and through which the Federal Reserve System expanded or contracted the money supply. Today, however, other institutions also provide checking services and significantly influence the effective money supply. Conversely, commercial banking organizations provide an ever-widening range of services, including trust operations, stock brokerage services, and insurance.

   Note that commercial banking organizations are quite different from investment banks. Commercial banks lend money, whereas investment banks help companies raise capital from other parties.[3]

2. *Savings and loan associations (S&Ls)*, which have traditionally served individual savers and residential and commercial mortgage borrowers, take the funds of many small savers and then lend this money to home buyers and other types of borrowers. Because the savers obtain a degree of liquidity that would be absent if they bought the mortgages or other securities directly, perhaps the most significant economic function of the S&Ls is to "create liquidity" that otherwise would be lacking. Savers benefit by being able to invest their savings in more liquid, better managed, and less risky accounts (investments), whereas borrowers benefit from the economies of scale that allow them to obtain more capital at lower costs than would otherwise be possible.[4]

3. *Credit unions* are cooperative associations whose members have a common bond, such as being employees of the same occupation or firm. Members'

---

[3]Prior to 1933, commercial banks offered investment banking services, but the Glass-Steagall Act, which was passed in that year, prohibited commercial banks from engaging in investment banking. Thus, the Morgan Bank was broken up into two separate organizations, one of which is now the Morgan Guaranty Trust Company, a commercial bank, while the other is Morgan Stanley, a major investment banking house, which is not considered a financial intermediary. Note also that Japanese and European banks can offer both commercial and investment banking services. This severely hinders U.S. banks in global competition, so recent legislative efforts have been aimed at improving the international competitiveness of U.S. banks.

[4]*Mutual savings banks*, which are similar to S&Ls, operate primarily in the northeastern states, accept savings primarily from individuals, and lend mainly on a long-term basis to home buyers and consumers.

savings are loaned only to other members, generally for auto purchases, home improvements, and the like. Credit unions often are the cheapest source of funds available to individual borrowers.

4. *Pension funds* are retirement plans funded by corporations or government agencies for their workers and administered primarily by the trust departments of commercial banks or by life insurance companies. Pension funds invest primarily in long-term financial instruments, such as bonds, stocks, mortgages, and real estate.

5. *Life insurance companies* take savings in the form of annual premiums, then invest these funds in stocks, bonds, real estate, and mortgages, and finally make payments to the beneficiaries of the insured parties. In recent years life insurance companies have also offered a variety of tax-deferred savings plans designed to provide benefits to the participants when they retire.

6. *Mutual funds* are investment companies that accept money from savers and then use these funds to buy various types of financial assets such as stocks, long-term bonds, short-term debt instruments, and so on. These organizations pool funds and thus reduce risks through diversification. Different funds are designed to meet the objectives of different types of savers. Hence, there are income funds for those who prefer current income, growth funds for savers who are willing to accept significant risks in the hopes of higher returns, and still other funds that are used as interest-bearing checking accounts (**money market funds**). There are literally hundreds of different types of mutual funds with dozens of different goals and purposes.

MONEY MARKET MUTUAL FUND
A mutual fund that invests in short-term, low-risk securities and allows investors to write checks against their accounts.

Financial institutions historically have been heavily regulated in the United States, with the primary purpose of this regulation being to ensure the safety of the institutions and thus to protect depositors. However, these regulations—which have taken the form of prohibitions on nationwide branch banking, restrictions on the types of assets the institutions can buy and sell, ceilings on the interest rates they can pay, and limitations on the types of services they can provide—have tended to impede the free flow of funds from surplus to deficit areas and thus have hurt the efficiency of our financial markets. Also, for the most part, U.S. financial institutions are at a competitive disadvantage in the international financial markets because most foreign financial institutions, including banks, are not as restricted with respect to organizational structure, ability to branch, nonbanking activities, and so forth. Recognizing this fact, Congress has authorized some major changes recently, and more will be forthcoming.

The result of the ongoing regulatory changes has been a blurring of the distinctions among the different types of institutions. Indeed, the trend in the United States today is toward huge financial service organizations, which own banks, S&Ls, investment banking houses, insurance companies, pension plan operations, and mutual funds, and which have branches across the country and even around the world. In recent years, for example, Citigroup was formed by combining (1) Travelers Group, which included an insurance company (Travelers) and an investment organization (Smith Barney); (2) Salomon Brothers, which was an investment organization that included an investment banking operation; and (3) Citicorp, which was one of the largest banking organizations in the United States. During the same period, BankAmerica Corporation and NationsBank Corporation combined forces to form the nation's largest bank, Bank of America, which boasts that it serves about one-third of U.S. households and that two-thirds of large U.S. corporations use its cash management services. In general, the direction of recent mergers and acquisitions in the financial services industry is to form larger, more diversified companies that can better compete internationally.

Self-Test Questions

Identify the three different ways capital is transferred between savers and borrowers.

Distinguish between investment banking houses and financial intermediaries, especially a commercial bank.

List the major types of intermediaries and briefly describe each one's function.

What effect do you think regulatory changes and competitive pressures will have on financial institutions in the future?

The Stock Market

As noted earlier, secondary markets are those in which outstanding, previously issued securities are traded. By far the most active secondary market, and the most important one to financial managers, is the stock market. It is here that the prices of firms' stocks are established, and, because the primary goal of managerial finance is to maximize the firm's stock price, a knowledge of this market is essential for anyone involved in managing a business.

When we differentiate stock markets, we have traditionally divided them into two basic types: (1) *organized exchanges*, which include the New York Stock Exchange (NYSE), the American Stock Exchange (AMEX), and several regional exchanges and (2) the less formal *over-the-counter market*. But, as we shall see shortly, these lines of demarcation are much less precise today than in past years due to market mergers. Because the organized exchanges have actual physical market locations and are easier to describe and understand, we will consider them first.

The Stock Exchanges

ORGANIZED SECURITY EXCHANGES
Formal organizations with physical locations where auction markets are conducted in designated ("listed") securities. The two major U.S. stock exchanges are the New York Stock Exchange (NYSE) and the American Stock Exchange (AMEX).

The **organized security exchanges** are tangible physical entities. Each of the larger ones occupies its own building, has specifically designated members, and has an elected governing body—its board of governors. Members are said to have "seats" on the exchange, although everybody stands up. These seats, which are bought and sold, give the holder the right to trade on the exchange. For example, there are 1,366 seats on the New York Stock Exchange (NYSE); and, in August 1999, a seat on the NYSE sold for $2.65 million, which is an all-time high.[5]

Most of the larger investment banking houses operate *brokerage departments* that own seats on the exchanges and designate one or more of their officers as members.

---

[5]NYSE stocks were not traded continuously until 1871. Prior to that time, stocks were traded sequentially according to their position on a stock roll, or roster, sheet. Members were assigned chairs, or "seats," to sit in while the roll call of stocks proceeded.

Exchange members meet in a large room equipped with telephones and other electronic equipment that enable each member to communicate with his or her firm's offices throughout the country. Currently, U.S. exchanges are open during normal working hours; but as the investment arena becomes more globalized, there has been increased pressure for the exchanges to become globalized by expanding their trading hours. For example, Richard Grasso, chairman of the NYSE, recently announced plans to examine the benefits of expanding the exchange's trading hours from six and one-half hours (9:30 A.M. to 4:00 P.M. eastern time) to 20 to 24 hours because it is expected that about one-third of the trades will be large multinational corporations within five years.

Like other markets, security exchanges facilitate communication between buyers and sellers. For example, Merrill Lynch might receive an order in its Atlanta office from a customer who wants to buy 100 shares of IBM stock. Simultaneously, Morgan Stanley Dean Witter's Denver office might receive an order from a customer wishing to sell 100 shares of IBM. Each broker communicates by wire with the firm's representative on the NYSE. Other brokers throughout the country are also communicating with their own exchange members. The exchange members with *sell orders* offer the shares for sale, and they are bid for by the members with *buy orders*. Thus, the exchanges operate as *auction markets*.[6]

The Over-the-Counter (OTC) Market

OVER-THE-COUNTER MARKET
A large collection of brokers and dealers, connected electronically by telephones and computers, that provides for trading in securities not listed on the organized exchanges.

If a security is not traded on an organized exchange, it is customary to say it is traded *over the counter.* In contrast to the organized security exchanges, the **over-the-counter market** is an intangible organization that consists of a network of brokers and dealers around the country. An explanation of the term "over-the-counter" will help clarify exactly what this market is. The exchanges operate as auction markets—buy and sell orders come in more or less simultaneously, and exchange members match these orders. If a stock is traded less frequently, perhaps because it is the stock of a new or a small

---

[6]The NYSE actually is a modified auction market, wherein people (through their brokers) bid for stocks. Originally—about 200 years ago—brokers would literally shout, "I have 100 shares of Union Pacific for sale; how much am I offered?" and then sell to the highest bidder. If a broker had a buy order, he or she would shout, "I want to buy 100 shares of Union Pacific; who'll sell at the best price?" The same general situation still exists, although the exchanges now have members known as specialists who facilitate the trading process by keeping an inventory of shares of the stocks in which they specialize. If a buy order comes in at a time when no sell order arrives, the specialist will sell off some inventory. Similarly, if a sell order comes in, the specialist will buy and add to inventory. The specialist sets a *bid price* (the price the specialist will pay for the stock) and an *asked price* (the price at which shares will be sold out of inventory). The bid and asked prices are set at levels designed to keep the inventory in balance. If many buy orders start coming in because of favorable developments or sell orders come in because of unfavorable events, the specialist will raise or lower prices to keep supply and demand in balance. Bid prices are somewhat lower than asked prices, with the difference, or *spread*, representing the specialist's profit margin.

Special facilities are available to help institutional investors such as mutual funds or pension funds sell large blocks of stock without depressing their prices. In essence, brokerage houses that cater to institutional clients will purchase blocks (defined as 10,000 or more shares) and then resell the stock to other institutions or individuals. Also, when a firm has a major announcement that is likely to cause its stock price to change sharply, it will ask the exchanges to halt trading in its stock until the announcement has been made and digested by investors. Thus, when Texaco announced that it planned to acquire Getty Oil, trading was halted for one day in both Texaco and Getty stocks.

firm, few buy and sell orders come in, and matching them within a reasonable length of time would be difficult. To avoid this problem, some brokerage firms maintain an inventory of such stocks—they buy when individual investors want to sell and sell when investors want to buy. At one time the inventory of securities was kept in a safe, and the stocks, when bought and sold, literally were passed over the counter.

Traditionally the over-the-counter market has been defined to include all facilities that are needed to conduct security transactions not conducted on the organized exchanges. These facilities consist of (1) the relatively few *dealers* who hold inventories of over-the-counter securities and who are said to "make a market" in these securities, (2) the thousands of *brokers* who act as *agents* in bringing these dealers together with investors, and (3) the computers, terminals, and *electronic networks* that provide a communications link between dealers and brokers. Unlike the organized exchanges, the OTC does not operate as an auction market. The dealers who make a market in a particular stock continuously quote a price at which they are willing to buy the stock (the *bid price*) and a price at which they will sell shares (the *asked price*). Each dealer's prices, which are adjusted as supply and demand conditions change, can be read off computer screens all across the country. The spread between bid and asked prices represents the dealer's markup, or profit.

Most of the brokers and dealers who make up the over-the-counter market are members of a self-regulating body known as the *National Association of Security Dealers* (NASD), which licenses brokers and oversees trading practices. The computerized trading network used by NASD is known as the NASD Automated Quotation System (NASDAQ), and *The Wall Street Journal* and other newspapers contain information on NASDAQ transactions. Today, the NASDAQ is considered a sophisticated market of its own, separate from the OTC. In fact, unlike the OTC, the NASDAQ has *market makers* who continuously monitor activities in various stocks to ensure they are available to traders who want to buy or sell. And, in an effort to become more competitive with the NYSE and with international markets, the NASDAQ, the AMEX, and the Philadelphia Stock Exchange merged in 1998 to form the Nasdaq-Amex Market Group, which might best be referred to as an *organized investment network*. Increased competition among global stock markets assuredly will result in similar alliances among various exchanges/markets in the future.

In terms of numbers of issues, the majority of stocks are traded over the counter. However, because the stocks of larger companies are listed on the exchanges, about two-thirds of the dollar volume of stock trading takes place on the exchanges.

Self-Test Questions

What are the two basic types of stock markets, and how do they differ?

Where are the greatest number of stocks traded, over-the-counter market or the stock exchanges?

Explain why the NASDAQ, AMEX, and Philadelphia merged. Do you expect that similar mergers will take place in the future? Why?

The Cost of Money

In a free economy, funds are allocated through the price system. *The interest rate is the price paid to borrow funds, whereas in the case of equity capital, investors expect to receive dividends and capital gains.* The factors that affect the supply of and demand for investment capital, and hence the cost of money, are discussed in this section.

The four most fundamental factors affecting the cost of money are (1) **production opportunities,** (2) **time preferences for consumption,** (3) **risk,** and (4) **inflation.** To see how these factors operate, visualize an isolated island community where the people survive on fish. They have a stock of fishing gear that permits them to live reasonably well, but they would like to have more fish. Suppose one of the inhabitants, Mr. Crusoe, has a bright idea for a new type of fishnet that would enable him to double his daily catch. But it would take him a year to design and build his net and to learn how to use it efficiently, and Mr. Crusoe most certainly would starve before he could put his new net into operation. Therefore, he might suggest to Ms. Robinson, Mr. Friday, and several others that if they would give him one fish each day for a year, he would return two fish a day during all of the next year. If Ms. Robinson accepted the offer, then the fish she gave to Mr. Crusoe would constitute *savings;* these savings would be *invested* in the fishnet; and the extra fish the net produced in the following year would constitute a *return on the investment.*

Obviously, the more *productive* Mr. Crusoe thought the new fishnet would be, the higher his expected return on the investment would be and the more he could afford to offer potential investors for their savings. In this example we assume that Mr. Crusoe thinks he will be able to pay, and thus he has offered, a 100 percent rate of return—he has offered to give back two fish for every one he received. He might have tried to attract savings for less—for example, he might have decided to offer only 1.5 fish a day next year for every one he receives this year, which would represent a 50 percent rate of return to Ms. Robinson.

How attractive Mr. Crusoe's offer appears to a potential saver would depend in large part on the saver's *time preference for consumption.* For example, Ms. Robinson might be thinking of retirement, and she might be willing to trade fish today for fish in the future on a one-for-one basis. On the other hand, Mr. Friday might be unwilling to "lend" a fish today for anything less than three fish next year, because he has a wife and several young children to feed with his current fish. Mr. Friday would be said to have a high time preference for consumption and Ms. Robinson a low time preference. Note also that if the entire population is living right at the subsistence level, time preferences for current consumption would necessarily be high, aggregate savings would be low, interest rates would be high, and capital formation would be difficult.

The risk inherent in the fishnet project, and thus in Mr. Crusoe's ability to repay the loan, also affects the return investors require: The higher the perceived risk, the higher the required rate of return. Also, in a more complex society there are many businesses like Mr. Crusoe's, many goods other than fish, and many savers like Ms. Robinson and Mr. Friday. Further, people use money as a medium of exchange rather than barter with fish. When money is used, rather than fish, its value in the future, which is affected by inflation, comes into play: The higher the expected rate of inflation, the larger the required return.

Thus, we see that the interest rate paid to savers depends in a basic way on (1) the rate of return producers expect to earn on invested capital, (2) savers' time preferences for current versus future consumption, (3) the riskiness of the loan, and (4) the expected future rate of inflation. The returns borrowers expect to earn by investing the funds they borrow set an upper limit on how much they can pay for savings, while consumers' time preferences for consumption establish how much consumption they are willing to defer, hence how much they will save at different levels of interest offered by borrowers. Higher risk and higher inflation also lead to higher interest rates.

PRODUCTION OPPORTUNITIES The returns available within an economy from investment in productive (cash-generating) assets.

TIME PREFERENCES FOR CONSUMPTION The preferences of consumers for current consumption as opposed to saving for future consumption.

RISK In a financial market context, the chance that a financial asset will not earn the return promised.

INFLATION The tendency of prices to increase over time.

Self-Test Questions

What is the price paid to borrow money called?

What is the "price" of equity capital?

What four fundamental factors affect the cost of money?

Interest Rate Levels

Funds are allocated among borrowers by interest rates: Firms with the most profitable investment opportunities are willing and able to pay the most for capital, so they tend to attract it away from less efficient firms or from those whose products are not in demand. Of course, our economy is not completely free in the sense of being influenced only by market forces—the federal government has agencies that help designated individuals or groups obtain credit on favorable terms, including small businesses, certain minorities, and firms willing to build plants in areas with high unemployment. Still, most capital in the U.S. economy is allocated through the price system.

Figure 2–2 shows how supply and demand interact to determine interest rates in two capital markets. Markets A and B represent two of the many capital markets in existence. The going interest rate, which can be designated as either k or i, but for purposes of the discussion here is designated as k, initially is ten percent for the low-risk securities in Market A. Borrowers whose credit is strong enough to qualify for this market can obtain funds at a cost of ten percent, and investors who want to put their money to work without much risk can obtain a ten percent return. Riskier borrowers must obtain higher-cost funds in Market B. Investors who are more willing to take risks invest in Market B expecting to earn a 12 percent return but also realizing that they might actually receive much less (or much more).

FIGURE 2–2	Interest Rates as a Function of Supply and Demand

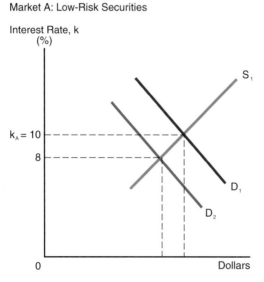

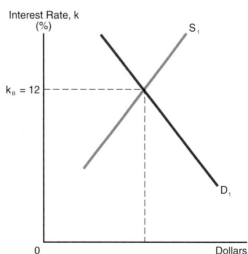

If the demand for funds declines, as it typically does during business recessions, the demand curves will shift to the left, as shown in curve D_2 in Market A. The market-clearing, or equilibrium, interest rate in this example declines to eight percent. Similarly, you should be able to visualize what would happen if the supply of funds tightens: The supply curve, S_1, would shift to the left, and this would raise interest rates and lower the level of borrowing in the economy.

Capital markets are interdependent. For example, if Markets A and B were in equilibrium before the demand shift to D_2 in Market A, this means that investors were willing to accept the higher risk in Market B in exchange for a risk premium of $12\% - 10\% = 2\%$. After the shift to D_2, the risk premium would initially increase to $12\% - 8\% = 4\%$. In all likelihood, this much larger premium would induce some of the lenders in Market A to shift to Market B; this, in turn, would cause the supply curve in Market A to shift to the left (or up) and that in Market B to shift to the right. The transfer of capital between markets would raise the interest rate in Market A and lower it in Market B, thus bringing the risk premium back closer to the original level, two percent. For example, when the rates on Treasury securities increase, the rates on corporate bonds and mortgages follow.

There are many capital markets in the United States. U.S. firms also invest and raise funds throughout the world, and foreigners both borrow and lend funds in the United States. There are markets in the United States for home loans, farm loans, business loans, government loans, and so forth. For each type of capital, there is a price, and these prices change over time as shifts occur in supply and demand conditions. Figure 2–3 shows how long- and short-term interest rates to business borrowers have varied since 1970. Notice that short-term interest rates are especially prone to rise during booms and then fall during recessions. (The shaded areas of the chart indicate recessions.) When the economy is expanding, firms need capital, and this demand for capital pushes rates up. Also, inflationary pressures are strongest during business booms, and that also exerts upward pressure on rates. Conditions are reversed during recessions such as the one in 1991 and 1992. Slack business reduces the demand for credit, the rate of inflation falls, and the result is a drop in interest rates.

These tendencies do not hold exactly—the period after 1984 is a case in point. The price of oil fell dramatically in 1985 and 1986, reducing inflationary pressures on other prices and easing fears of serious long-term inflation. Earlier, these fears had pushed interest rates to record levels. The economy from 1984 to 1987 was fairly strong, but the declining fears about inflation more than offset the normal tendency of interest rates to rise during good economic times, and the net result was lower interest rates.[7]

The relationship between inflation and long-term interest rates is highlighted in Figure 2–4, which plots rates of inflation along with long-term interest rates. Prior to 1965, when the average rate of inflation was about one percent, interest rates on the least risky bonds (AAA-rated) generally ranged from four percent to five percent. As the war in Vietnam accelerated in the late 1960s, the rate of inflation increased, and interest rates began to rise. The rate of inflation dropped after 1970 and so did long-term interest rates. However, the 1973 Arab oil embargo was followed by a quadrupling of oil prices in 1974, which caused a spurt in inflation, which in turn drove interest rates to new record highs in 1974 and 1975. Inflationary pressures eased in late 1975 and 1976

---

[7]Short-term rates are responsive to current economic conditions, whereas long-term rates primarily reflect long-run expectations for inflation. As a result, short-term rates are sometimes above and sometimes below long-term rates. The relationship between long-term and short-term rates is called the *term structure of interest rates*. This topic is discussed later in the chapter.

| FIGURE 2-3 | Long- and Short-Term Interest Rates, 1970–1988 |

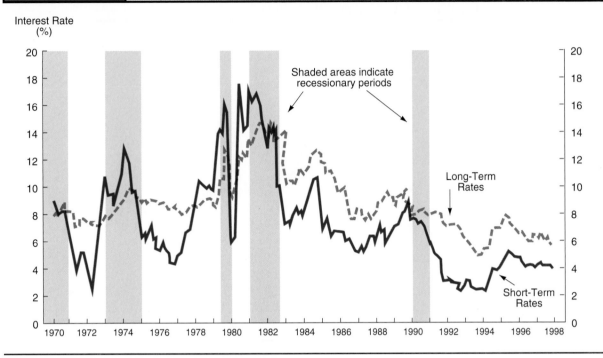

Interest Rate (%)

NOTES: (a) Short-term interest rates are measured by 3-month loans to very large, strong corporations, and long-term rates are measured by AAA corporate bonds.
(b) The tick marks on the x axis represent the middle of the year—that is, June.

SOURCE: Federal Reserve; http://www.bog.frb.fed.us/releases/

but then rose again after 1976. In 1980, inflation rates hit the highest level on record, and fears of continued double-digit inflation pushed interest rates up to historic highs. From 1981 through 1986, the inflation rate dropped sharply, and in 1986 inflation was only 1.1 percent, the lowest level in 25 years. In 1993, interest rates dropped to historical lows—the Treasury bill yield actually dropped below three percent. Currently (1999), there is a consensus among most economists, businesses, and consumers that we are in the midst of a very good economy—inflation has been around two percent or less for more than a year, Treasury bill rates are less than five percent, and the interest rate on long-term debt to strong corporations is about 6.5 percent.

Self-Test Questions

How are interest rates used to allocate capital among firms?

What happens to market-clearing, or equilibrium, interest rates in a capital market when the demand for funds declines? What happens when inflation increases or decreases?

Why does the price of capital change during booms and recessions?

How does risk affect interest rates?

How does a change in rates in one financial market affect the rates in other financial markets?

FIGURE 2–4	Relationship between Annual Inflation Rates and Long-Term Interest Rates, 1970–1998

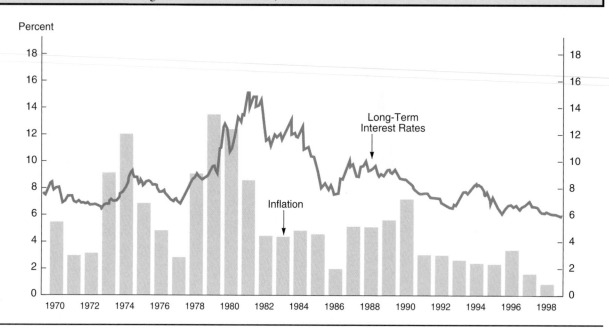

NOTES:

a. Interest rates are those for AAA long-term corporate bonds.

b. Inflation is measured as the annual rate of change in the Consumer Price Index (CPI).

SOURCE: Federal Reserve; http://www.bog.frb.fed.us/releases/

The Determinants of Market Interest Rates

In general, the quoted (or nominal) interest rate on a debt security, k, is composed of a real risk-free rate of interest, k*, plus several premiums that reflect inflation, the riskiness of the security, and the security's marketability (or liquidity). This relationship can be expressed as follows:

2–1	
	Quoted interest rate = $k = k^* + IP + DRP + LP + MRP$

In Equation 2–1, the variables are defined as follows:

k = the quoted, or *nominal*, rate of interest on a given security.[8] There are many different securities, hence many different quoted interest rates.

---

[8]The term *nominal* as it is used here means the *stated* rate as opposed to the *real* rate, which is adjusted to remove the effects of inflation. If you bought a ten-year Treasury bond in March 1999, the quoted, or nominal, rate would be about 5.6 percent, but if inflation was expected to average 2.1 percent over the next ten years, the real rate would be about 5.6% − 2.1% = 3.5%.

k* = the *real risk-free rate of interest;* k* is pronounced "k-star."

IP = inflation premium.

DRP = default risk premium.

LP = liquidity, or marketability, premium.

MRP = maturity risk premium.

We discuss the components whose sum makes up the quoted, or nominal, rate on a given security in the following sections.

The Real Risk-Free Rate of Interest, k*

REAL RISK-FREE RATE OF INTEREST, K*
The rate of interest that would exist on default-free U.S. Treasury securities if no inflation were expected.

The **real risk-free rate of interest, k*,** is defined as the interest rate that would exist on a security with a *guaranteed* payoff (termed a riskless, or risk-free, security) if inflation was expected to be zero during the investment period. It can be thought of as the rate of interest that would exist on short-term U.S. Treasury securities in an inflation-free world. The real risk-free rate changes over time depending on economic conditions, especially (1) on the rate of return corporations and other borrowers are willing to pay to borrow funds, and (2) on people's time preferences for current versus future consumption. It is difficult to measure the real risk-free rate precisely, but most experts think that k* has fluctuated in the range of one to four percent in the United States in recent years.

NOMINAL (QUOTED) RISK-FREE RATE, K$_{RF}$
The rate of interest on a security that is free of all risk; k$_{RF}$ is proxied by the T-bill rate or the T-bond rate. k$_{RF}$ includes an inflation premium.

The Nominal, or Quoted, Risk-Free Rate of Interest, k$_{RF}$

The **nominal,** or **quoted, risk-free rate, k$_{RF}$,** is the *real risk-free rate plus a premium for expected inflation:* $k_{RF} = k* + IP$. If we combine $k* + IP$ and let this sum equal k$_{RF}$, then Equation 2–1 becomes:

2–2	
	$$k = k_{RF} + DRP + LP + MRP$$

To be strictly correct, the risk-free rate should mean the interest rate on a security that has absolutely no risk at all—one that has no risk of default, no maturity risk, no liquidity risk, and no risk of loss if inflation increases. No such security exists in the real world; hence there is no observable truly risk-free rate. However, there is one security that is free of most risks—a U.S. Treasury bill (T-bill), which is a short-term security issued by the U.S. government. Treasury bonds (T-bonds), which are longer-term government securities, are free of default and liquidity risks, but T-bonds are exposed to some risk due to changes in the general level of interest rates.

If the term "risk-free rate" is used without either the term "real" or the term "nominal," people generally mean the quoted (nominal) rate, and we will follow that convention in this book. Therefore, when we use the term risk-free rate, we mean the nominal risk-free rate, k$_{RF}$, which includes an inflation premium equal to the average expected inflation rate over the life of the security. In general, we use the T-bill rate to approximate the short-term risk-free rate, and the T-bond rate to approximate the long-term risk-free rate. So, whenever you see the term "risk-free rate," assume that we are referring either to the quoted T-bill rate or to the quoted T-bond rate.

Inflation Premium (IP)

Inflation has a major impact on interest rates because it erodes the purchasing power of the dollar and lowers the real rate of return on investments. To illustrate, suppose you saved $1,000 and invested it in a certificate of deposit that matures in one year and pays five percent interest. At the end of the year you will receive $1,050—your original $1,000 plus $50 of interest. Now suppose the inflation rate during the year is ten percent, and it affects all items equally. If beer had cost $1 per bottle at the beginning of the year, it would cost $1.10 at the end of the year. Therefore, your $1,000 would have bought $1,000/$1 = 1,000 bottles at the beginning of the year but only $1,050/$1.10 = 955 bottles at year's end. *In real terms*, you would be worse off—you would receive $50 of interest, but it would not be sufficient to offset inflation. In this case, you would be better off buying 1,000 bottles of beer (or some other storable asset such as land, timber, apartment buildings, wheat, or gold) than investing in the certificate of deposit.

INFLATION PREMIUM (IP)
A premium for expected inflation that investors add to the real risk-free rate of return.

Investors are well aware of all this, so when they lend money, they build in an **inflation premium (IP)** equal to the *average inflation rate expected over the life of the security*. Therefore, if the real risk-free rate of interest, k*, is three percent, and if inflation is expected to be four percent (IP = 4%) during the next year, then the quoted rate of interest on one-year T-bills would be seven percent. In March of 1999, economists forecasted the one-year inflation rate to be between 1.5 percent and two percent, and, at the same time, the yield on one-year T-bills was about 4.7 percent. This implies that the real risk-free rate on short-term securities at that time was expected to be between 2.7 percent and 3.2 percent.

Default Risk Premium (DRP)

The risk that a borrower will *default* on a loan, which means not to pay the interest or the principal, also affects the market interest rate on a security: The greater the default risk, the higher the interest rate lenders charge (demand). Treasury securities have no default risk; thus, they generally carry the lowest interest rates on taxable securities in the United States. For corporate bonds, the better the bond's overall credit rating, the lower its default risk, and, consequently, the lower its interest rate.[9] Here are some representative interest rates on long-term bonds that existed in February 1999:

	RATE	DRP
U.S. Treasury	5.4%	—
AAA	6.4	1.0%
AA	6.7	1.3
A	6.9	1.5

[9]Bond ratings, and bonds' riskiness in general, will be discussed in detail in Chapter 17. For now, merely note that bonds rated AAA are judged to have less default risk than bonds rated AA, AA bonds are less risky than A bonds, and so on. Ratings might also be designated AAA or Aaa, AA or Aa, and so forth, depending on the rating agency. In this book the designations are used interchangeably.

The difference between the quoted interest rate on a T-bond and that on a corporate bond with similar maturity, liquidity, and other features is the **default risk premium (DRP).** Therefore, if the bonds listed previously were *otherwise similar*, the default risk premium would be $DRP = k - k_{RF}$, which are the values given above. Default risk premiums vary somewhat over time, but the February 1999 figures are representative of levels in recent years.

Liquidity Premium (LP)

Liquidity generally is defined as the ability to convert an asset to cash on short notice and "reasonably" capture the amount initially invested. Of course, the most liquid asset of all is cash, and the more easily an asset can be converted to cash at a price that substantially recovers the initial amount invested, the more liquid it is considered. Consequently, financial assets are considered more liquid than real assets, such as land and equipment, and short-term financial assets generally are more liquid than long-term financial assets. Because liquidity is important, investors evaluate and include **liquidity premiums (LP)** when interest rates are established. Although it is very difficult to accurately measure liquidity premiums, a differential of at least two and probably four or five percentage points exists between the least liquid and the most liquid financial assets of similar default risk and maturity.

Maturity Risk Premium (MRP)

The prices of bonds decline whenever interest rates rise, and because interest rates can and do occasionally rise, all bonds, even Treasury bonds, have an element of risk called **interest rate risk.** As a general rule, the bonds of any organization, from the U.S. government to General Motors, have more interest rate risk the longer the maturity of the bond.[10] Therefore, a **maturity risk premium (MRP),** which is higher the longer the years to maturity, must be included in the required interest rate. The effect of maturity risk premiums is to raise interest rates on long-term bonds relative to those on short-term bonds. This premium, like the others, is extremely difficult to measure, but (1) it seems to vary over time, rising when interest rates are more volatile and uncertain, then falling when interest rates are more stable, and (2) in recent years, the maturity risk premium on 30-year T-bonds appears to have generally been in the range of one or two percentage points.[11]

We should mention that although long-term bonds are heavily exposed to maturity risk, short-term investments are heavily exposed to **reinvestment rate risk.** When short-term investments mature and the proceeds are reinvested, or "rolled over," a decline in interest rates would necessitate reinvestment at a lower rate and hence would lead to a decline in interest income. Thus, although "investing short" preserves one's

DEFAULT RISK PREMIUM (DRP)
The difference between the interest rate on a U.S. Treasury bond and a corporate bond of equal maturity and marketability.

LIQUIDITY PREMIUM (LP)
A premium added to the rate on a security if the security cannot be converted to cash on short notice and at close to the original cost.

INTEREST RATE RISK
The risk of capital losses to which investors are exposed because of changing interest rates.

MATURITY RISK PREMIUM (MRP)
A premium that reflects interest rate risk; bonds with longer maturities have greater interest rate risk.

REINVESTMENT RATE RISK
The risk that a decline in interest rates will lead to lower income when bonds mature and funds are reinvested.

[10]For example, if someone had bought a 30-year Treasury bond for $1,000 in 1972, when the long-term interest rate was seven percent, and held it until 1981, when long-term T-bond rates were about 14.5 percent, the value of the bond would have declined to about $514. That would represent a loss of almost half the money, and it demonstrates that long-term bonds, even U.S. Treasury bonds, are not riskless. However, had the investor purchased short-term T-bills in 1972 and subsequently reinvested the principal each time the bills matured, he or she would still have had $1,000. This point will be discussed in detail in Chapter 7.

[11]The MRP has averaged 1.3 percentage points over the past 65 years. See *Stocks, Bonds, Bills, and Inflation: 1998 Yearbook* (Chicago: Ibbotson Associates, 1998).

principal, the interest income provided by short-term investments varies from year to year, depending on reinvestment rates.[12]

Self-Test Questions

Write out an equation for the nominal interest rate on any debt security.

Distinguish between the real risk-free rate of interest, k*, and the nominal, or quoted, risk-free rate of interest, k_{RF}.

How is inflation considered when interest rates are determined by investors in the financial markets? Explain.

Does the interest rate on a T-bond include a default risk premium? Explain.

Briefly explain the following statement: "Although long-term bonds are heavily exposed to maturity rate risk, short-term bills are heavily exposed to reinvestment rate risk."

The Term Structure of Interest Rates

TERM STRUCTURE OF INTEREST RATES
The relationship between yields and maturities of securities.

A study of Figure 2–3 reveals that at certain times, such as in 1998, short-term interest rates are lower than long-term rates, whereas at other times, such as in 1980 and 1981, short-term rates are higher than long-term rates. The relationship between long- and short-term rates, which is known as the **term structure of interest rates,** is important to corporate treasurers, who must decide whether to borrow by issuing long- or short-term debt, and to investors, who must decide whether to buy long- or short-term bonds. Thus, it is important to understand (1) how long- and short-term rates are related to each other and (2) what causes shifts in their relative positions.

YIELD CURVE
A graph showing the relationship between yields and maturities of securities.

To begin, we can find the interest rates on Treasury bonds of various maturities at a given point in time in a source such as *The Wall Street Journal* or the *Federal Reserve Bulletin.* For example, the tabular section of Figure 2–5 presents interest rates for different maturities on two different dates. The set of data for a given date, when plotted on a graph such as that in Figure 2–5, is called the **yield curve** for that date. The yield curve changes both in position and in slope over time. In March of 1980, all rates were relatively high, and short-term rates were higher than long-term rates, so the yield curve on that date was *downward sloping.* However, in March of 1999, all rates were much lower, and short-term rates were lower than long-term rates, so the yield curve at that time was *upward sloping.* Had we drawn the yield curve during January of 1982, it would have been essentially horizontal, because long- and short-term bonds on that date had about the same rate of interest (see Figure 2–3).

"NORMAL" YIELD CURVE
An upward-sloping yield curve.

Historically, in most years, long-term rates have been above short-term rates, so usually the yield curve has been upward sloping. For this reason, people often call an upward-sloping yield curve a **"normal" yield curve** and a yield curve that slopes

---

[12]Long-term bonds also have some reinvestment rate risk. To actually earn the quoted rate on a long-term bond, the interest payments must be reinvested at the quoted rate. However, if interest rates fall, the interest payments would be reinvested at a lower rate; thus, the realized return would be less than the quoted rate. Note, though, that the reinvestment rate risk is lower on a long-term bond than on a short-term bond because only the interest payments (rather than interest plus principal) on the long-term bond are exposed to reinvestment rate risk. Only zero coupon bonds, discussed in Chapters 7 and 17, are completely free of reinvestment rate risk.

| FIGURE 2–5 | U.S. Treasury Bond Interest Rates on Different Dates |

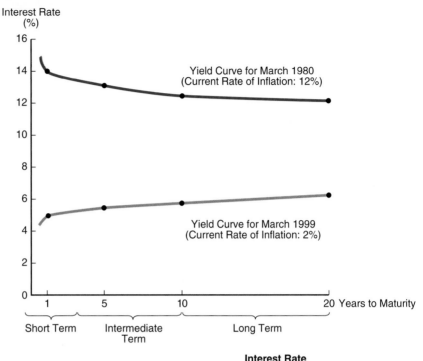

| | Interest Rate | |
Term to Maturity	March 1980	March 1999
6 months	15.0%	4.6%
1 year	14.0	4.9
5 years	13.5	5.2
10 years	12.8	5.5
20 years	12.5	5.9

INVERTED
("ABNORMAL") YIELD
CURVE
A downward-sloping yield
curve.

downward an **inverted,** or **"abnormal," yield curve.** Thus, in Figure 2–5, the yield curve for March 1980 was inverted, but the one for March 1999 was fairly normal.

Term Structure Theories (Explanations)

Several theories have been proposed to explain the shape of the yield curve. The three major ones are (1) the expectations theory, (2) the liquidity preference theory, and (3) the market segmentation theory.

EXPECTATIONS
THEORY
The theory that the shape
of the yield curve depends
on investors' expectations
about future inflation
rates.

Expectations Theory   The **expectations theory** states that the yield curve depends on *expectations* concerning future inflation rates. Specifically, $k_{RF,t}$, the nominal interest rate on a U.S. Treasury bond that matures in t years, is found as follows under the expectations theory:

$$k_{RF,t} = k^* + IP_t$$

Here k^* is the real risk-free interest rate, and IP_t is an inflation premium, which is equal to the *average expected rate of inflation* over the t years until the bond matures. Under the expectations theory, the maturity risk premium (MRP) is assumed to be zero, and, for Treasury securities, the default risk premium (DRP) and liquidity premium (LP) also are zero.

To illustrate, suppose that in late December of 1999 the real risk-free rate of interest was $k^* = 3\%$ and expected inflation rates for the next three years were as follows:[13]

YEAR	EXPECTED ANNUAL (1-YEAR) INFLATION RATE	EXPECTED AVERAGE INFLATION RATE FROM 2000 TO INDICATED YEAR (IP$_t$)
2000	2%	2% /1 = 2%
2001	4%	(2% + 4%) /2 = 3%
2002	9%	(2% + 4% + 9%) /3 = 5%

Given these expectations, the following interest rate pattern should exist:

BOND TYPE	REAL RISK-FREE RATE (k*)		INFLATION PREMIUM: AVERAGE EXPECTED RATE (IP$_t$)		NOMINAL TREASURY BOND RATE FOR EACH MATURITY (k$_{T\text{-bond}}$)
1-year bond	3%	+	2%	=	5%
2-year bond	3%	+	3%	=	6%
3-year bond	3%	+	5%	=	8%

If the yields on these hypothetical bonds were plotted, the yield curve would be upward sloping, similar to the March 1999 yield curve in Figure 2–5. Had the pattern of expected inflation rates been reversed, with inflation expected to fall from nine percent to two percent over the three-year period, the pattern of interest rates would produce an inverted yield curve like the March 1980 curve in Figure 2–5.

LIQUIDITY PREFERENCE THEORY
The theory that, all else equal, lenders prefer to make short-term loans rather than long-term loans; hence, they will lend short-term funds at lower rates than long-term funds.

Liquidity Preference Theory　The **liquidity preference theory** states that long-term bonds normally yield more than short-term bonds for two reasons: (1) All else equal, investors generally prefer to hold short-term securities, because such securities are more liquid in the sense that they can be converted to cash with little danger of loss of principal. Investors will, therefore, generally accept lower yields on short-term securities, and this leads to relatively low short-term rates. (2) Borrowers, on the other hand, generally prefer long-term debt, because short-term debt exposes them to the risk of having to repay the debt under adverse conditions. Accordingly, borrowers want to "lock into" long-term funds, which means they are willing to pay a higher rate, other things held constant, for long-term funds than for short-term funds—this also leads to relatively low short-term rates. Thus, lender and borrower preferences both operate to cause short-term rates to be lower than long-term rates. Taken together, these two sets of preferences—and hence the liquidity preference theory—imply that under normal conditions, a positive maturity risk premium (MRP) exists, and the MRP increases with years to maturity, causing the yield curve to be upward sloping.

---

[13]Technically, we should be using geometric averages rather than arithmetic averages, but the differences are not material in this example. For a discussion of this point, see Frank K. Reilly and Edgar A. Norton, *Investments*, 5th ed. (Fort Worth, TX: The Dryden Press, 1999), Chapter 1.

MARKET SEGMENTATION THEORY
The theory that each borrower and lender has a preferred maturity and that the slope of the yield curve depends on the supply of and demand for funds in the long-term market relative to the short-term market.

Market Segmentation Theory   Briefly, the **market segmentation theory** states that each lender and each borrower has a preferred maturity. For example, a person borrowing to buy a long-term asset like a house, or an electric utility borrowing to build a power plant, would want a long-term loan. However, a retailer borrowing in September to build its inventories for Christmas would prefer a short-term loan. Similar differences exist among savers—for example, a person saving up to take a vacation next summer would want to lend in the short-term market, but someone saving for retirement 20 years hence would probably buy long-term securities.

The thrust of the market segmentation theory is that the slope of the yield curve depends on supply/demand conditions in the long- and short-term markets. Thus, according to this theory, the yield curve could at any given time be either flat, upward sloping, or downward sloping. An upward-sloping yield curve would occur when there was a large supply of short-term funds relative to demand, but a shortage of long-term funds. Similarly, a downward-sloping curve would indicate relatively strong demand for funds in the short-term market compared to that in the long-term market. A flat curve would indicate balance between the two markets.

Various tests of the theories explaining the shape of the yield curve have been conducted, and these tests indicate that all three theories have some validity. Thus, the shape of the yield curve at any given time is affected (1) by expectations about future inflation, (2) by liquidity preferences, and (3) by supply/demand conditions in long- and short-term markets. One factor might dominate at one time, another at another time, but all three affect the term structure of interest rates.

Self-Test Questions

What is a yield curve, and what information would you need to draw this curve?

Discuss the validity of each of the three theories that have been proposed to explain the shape of the yield curve.

Distinguish between the shapes of a "normal" yield curve and an "inverted" yield curve, and explain when each might exist.

Other Factors That Influence Interest Rate Levels

Factors other than those discussed in the previous section also influence both the general level of interest rates and the shape of the yield curve. The four most important factors are (1) Federal Reserve policy, (2) the level of the federal budget deficit, (3) the foreign trade balance, and (4) the level of business activity.

Federal Reserve Policy

As you probably learned in your economics courses, (1) the money supply has a major effect on both the level of economic activity and the rate of inflation, and (2) in the United States, the Federal Reserve Board controls the money supply. If the Fed wants to control growth in the economy, it slows growth in the money supply. The initial effect of such an action is to cause interest rates to increase and inflation to stabilize. The reverse holds if the Fed loosens the money supply.

To illustrate, to support market liquidity and to encourage continued economic prosperity, the Federal Reserve took steps to reduce interest rates in three of the last four months in 1998. Because the Fed deals primarily in the short-term end of the market, these reductions had the direct effect of pushing short-term interest rates down. Long-run rates followed, but the very fact that the Fed was taking action to control adverse economic pressures affected investors' expectations concerning inflation, hence, interest rates.

During periods when the Fed is actively intervening in the markets, the yield curve will be distorted. Short-term rates will be temporarily "too low" if the Fed is easing credit, and "too high" if it is tightening credit. Long-term rates are not affected as much by Fed intervention because they represent averages of short-term expectations.

Federal Deficits

If the federal government spends more than it takes in from tax revenues, it runs a deficit, and that deficit must be covered either by borrowing or by printing money. If the government borrows, this added demand for funds pushes up interest rates. If it prints money, this increases expectations for future inflation, which also drives up interest rates. Thus, the larger the federal deficit, other things held constant, the higher the level of interest rates. Whether long- or short-term rates are more affected depends on how the deficit is financed, so we cannot state, in general, how deficits will affect the slope of the yield curve.

Foreign Trade Balance

Businesses and individuals in the United States buy from and sell to people and firms in other countries. If we buy more than we sell (that is, if we import more than we export), we are said to be running a foreign trade deficit. When trade deficits occur, they must be financed, and the main source of financing is debt.[14] Therefore, the larger our trade deficit, the more we must borrow, and as we increase our borrowing, this drives up interest rates. Also, foreigners are willing to hold U.S. debt only if the interest rate on this debt is competitive with interest rates in other countries. Therefore, if the Federal Reserve attempts to lower interest rates in the United States, causing our rates to fall below rates abroad, then foreigners will sell U.S. bonds, which will depress bond prices and cause U.S. interest rates to increase. Thus, the existence of a deficit trade balance hinders the Fed's ability to combat a recession by lowering interest rates.

The United States has been running annual trade deficits since the mid-1970s, and the cumulative effect of these deficits is that the United States is by far the largest debtor nation of all time. As a result, our interest rates are very much influenced by interest rate trends in other countries around the world (higher rates abroad lead to higher U.S. rates). Because of all this, U.S. corporate treasurers—and anyone else who is affected by interest rates—must keep up with developments in the world economy.

Business Activity

Figure 2–3, presented earlier, can be examined to see how business conditions influence interest rates. Here are the key points revealed by the graph:

---

[14]The deficit could also be financed by selling assets, including gold, corporate stocks, entire companies, and real estate. The United States has financed its massive trade deficits by all of these means at various times, but the primary method has been by borrowing.

1. Because inflation increased from the late 1960s to 1981, the general tendency during this period was toward higher interest rates. However, since the 1981 peak, the trend has generally been downward.
2. Until the mid-1960s, short-term rates were almost always below long-term rates. Thus, in those years the yield curve was almost always "normal" in the sense that it was upward sloping.
3. The shaded areas in the graph represent recessions, during which both the demand for money and the rate of inflation tend to fall, and, at the same time, the Federal Reserve tends to increase the money supply in an effort to stimulate the economy. As a result, there is a tendency for interest rates to decline during recessions. Currently, in early 1999, the economy is strong, so any actions taken by the Fed to change interest rates are efforts to keep inflation in check.
4. During recessions, short-term rates decline more sharply than long-term rates. This occurs because (a) the Fed operates mainly in the short-term sector, so its intervention has the strongest effect here, and (b) long-term rates reflect the average expected inflation rate over the next 20 to 30 years, and this expectation generally does not change much, even when the current rate of inflation is low (or high).

Self-Test Questions

Other than inflationary expectations, liquidity preferences, and normal supply/demand fluctuations, name four additional factors that influence interest rates and explain their effects.

How does the Fed stimulate the economy? How does the Fed affect interest rates?

Interest Rate Levels and Stock Prices

Interest rates have two effects on corporate profits. First, because interest is a cost, the higher the rate of interest, the lower a firm's profits, other things held constant. Second, interest rates affect the level of economic activity, and economic activity affects corporate profits. Interest rates obviously affect stock prices because of their effects on profits, but, perhaps even more important, they have an effect due to competition in the marketplace between stocks and bonds. If interest rates rise sharply, investors can get higher returns in the bond market, which induces them to sell stocks and to transfer funds from the stock market to the bond market. A massive sale of stocks in response to rising interest rates obviously would depress stock prices. Of course, the reverse occurs if interest rates decline. Indeed, the bull market of December 1991, when the Dow Jones Industrial Index rose ten percent in less than a month, was caused almost entirely by the sharp drop in long-term interest rates. On the other hand, the poor performance exhibited by the stock market in 1994—common stocks declined in average by more than three percent—resulted from sharp increase in interest rates during that year. For the past several years, as interest rates have declined and remained at historically low levels, the stock market has been the "hot" investment.

Self-Test Question

In what two ways do changes in interest rates affect stock prices?

Congress does not change the tax laws, changes still will occur because certain aspects of the tax calculation are tied to the rate of inflation. Thus, by the time you read this section, tax rates and other factors might be different from those we provide. Even so, this section should give you an understanding of the basics of our tax system.

Individual Income Taxes

PROGRESSIVE TAX
A tax that requires a higher percentage payment on higher incomes. The personal income tax in the U.S. is progressive.

Individuals pay taxes on wages and salaries, on investment income (dividends, interest, and profits from the sale of securities), and on the profits of *proprietorships and partnerships*. Our tax rates are **progressive**—that is, the higher one's income, the larger the percentage paid in taxes. The individual tax rates for 1999 are provided in the appendix, Table 2A–1. In this section, we discuss some of the general topics applicable to those who are affected by the individual tax code section.

TAXABLE INCOME
Gross income minus exemptions and allowable deductions as set forth in the tax code.

1. **Taxable income** is defined as gross income less a set of exemptions and deductions that are spelled out in the instructions to the tax forms individuals must file. When filing a tax return in 2000 for the tax year 1999, each taxpayer will receive an exemption of $2,750 for each dependent, including the taxpayer, which reduces taxable income. However, this exemption is indexed to rise with inflation, and the exemption is phased out for high-income taxpayers. Also, certain expenses, such as mortgage interest paid, state and local income taxes paid, and charitable contributions, can be deducted and thus can be used to reduce taxable income; but again, high-income taxpayers lose some of this benefit.

MARGINAL TAX RATE
The tax applicable to the last unit of income.

2. The **marginal tax rate** is defined as the tax on the last unit of income. The marginal tax rate is represented by the tax bracket you are in. For example, if you are single and your taxable income is $50,000, then your marginal tax rate is 28 percent. As Table 2A–1 shows, marginal rates begin at 15 percent, rise to 28, then to 31 percent, and so on.

AVERAGE TAX RATE
Taxes paid divided by taxable income.

3. One can calculate **average tax rates** from the data in Table 2A–1. The average tax rate equals the percent of taxable income that is paid in taxes. For example, if Jill Smith, a single individual, had taxable income of $35,000, her tax bill would be $3,862.50 + ($35,000 − $25,750)(0.28) = $6,452.50. Her average tax rate would be $6,452.50/$35,000 = 18.4% versus a marginal rate of 28 percent. If Jill received a raise of $1,000, bringing her income to $36,000, she would have to pay an additional $280 in taxes, so her after-tax raise would be $720. In addition, her social security taxes would increase.

Taxes on Dividend and Interest Income   Dividend and interest income received by individuals from corporate securities or other investments is added to other income and thus is taxed at the rates shown in Table 2A–1. Because corporations pay dividends out of earnings that already have been taxed, there is *double taxation* of corporate income.

It should be noted that under U.S. tax laws, interest on most state and local government bonds, called *municipals* or *munis*, is not subject to federal income taxes. Thus, investors get to keep all of the interest received from most municipal bonds but only a fraction of the interest received from bonds issued by corporations or by the U.S. government. This means that a lower-yielding muni can provide the same after-tax return as a higher-yielding corporate bond. For example, a taxpayer in the 31 percent marginal tax bracket who could buy a muni that yields six percent would have to receive a before-tax yield of 8.7 percent on a corporate or U.S. Treasury bond to have the same after-tax income:

$$\text{Equivalent pretax yield on a taxable investment} = \frac{\text{Yield on tax-free investment}}{1 - \text{Marginal tax rate}}$$

$$= \frac{6\%}{1 - 0.31} = 8.7\%$$

If we know the yield on the taxable bond (investment), we can use the following equation to find the equivalent yield on a muni (tax-free investment):

$$\text{Yield on tax-free investment} = \left(\begin{array}{c} \text{Pretax yield on} \\ \text{taxable investment} \end{array} \right) \times (1 - \text{Marginal tax rate})$$

$$= 8.7\% \times (1 - 0.31) = 6.0\%$$

The exemption from federal taxes stems from the separation of federal and state powers, and its primary effect is to help state and local governments borrow at lower rates than otherwise would be available to them.

Interest Paid by Individuals   For the most part, the interest paid by individuals on loans is *not* tax deductible. The principal exception to this is the interest paid on mortgage financing used to purchase a house for personal residence, which is tax deductible. The effect of tax deductible interest payments is to lower the actual cost of the mortgage to the taxpayer. For example, if Staci Jones has an eight percent mortgage on her house and she has a marginal tax rate equal to 36 percent, the after-tax cost of her mortgage is as follows:

$$\text{After-tax rate} = 8.0\%(1 - 0.36) = 5.1\%$$

Capital Gains versus Ordinary Income   Assets such as stocks, bonds, and real estate are defined as *capital assets*. If you buy a capital asset and later sell it for more than your

CAPITAL GAIN (LOSS)
The profit (loss) from the sale of a capital asset for more (less) than its purchase price.

purchase price, the profit is called a **capital gain;** if you suffer a loss, it is called a **capital loss.** An asset sold within one year of the time it was purchased produces a *short-term gain or loss*, whereas one held for more than one year produces a *long-term gain or loss*. If you sell a capital asset for exactly what you paid for it, you will have neither a gain nor a loss; you simply get back your original investment, and no tax is due.

There has been a great deal of controversy over the proper tax rate for capital gains. It has been argued that lower tax rates on capital gains (1) stimulate the flow of venture capital to new, start-up businesses, which generally provide capital gains as opposed to dividend income and (2) cause companies to retain and reinvest a high percentage of their earnings in an effort to provide their stockholders with lightly taxed capital gains as opposed to highly taxed dividend income. The proponents of preferential capital gains tax rates lost the argument in 1986, but in 1990 they did succeed in getting the rate for long-term capital gains capped at 28 percent and the cap was further lowered to 20 percent in 1998. In 1999, the tax rate applied to capital gains for assets held less than one year was the marginal tax rate of the taxpayer, and it was 20 percent for assets held longer than one year.

Business versus Personal Expenses *Individuals* pay taxes on the income generated by proprietorships and partnerships they own—the income *passes through* to the owners of these types of businesses. Therefore, we to need differentiate business expenses, which are tax deductible, from personal expenses, which are not tax deductible. Generally speaking, an allowable business expense is a cost incurred to generate business revenues. On the other hand, if the expense is incurred for personal benefit (use), it is considered a personal expense. For instance, Loretta Kay owns a house in which she lived until last month, at which time she moved and rented the house to a group of college students. Three months ago, the plumbing burst in the kitchen, and Loretta had to call the plumber for repairs. The repairs cost $1,000. Is this a tax deductible expense? No, because the house was Loretta's personal residence at the time. Last night, Loretta had to call the plumber again to fix pipes that had burst in the same house, which she now has rented to the students—the repairs cost $1,200. Is this a tax deductible expense? Yes, the expense was incurred for business purposes because the house now is rental property, which is considered a business operation.

Corporate Income Taxes

The corporate tax structure is shown in the appendix, Table 2–2A. The structure is similar to the individual rates. However, there are some areas where the corporate tax code and the individual tax code differ significantly. We discuss some of the differences in this section.

Interest and Dividend Income Received by a Corporation Interest income received by a corporation is taxed as ordinary income at regular corporate tax rates. However, 70 percent of the dividends received by one corporation from another corporation is excluded from taxable income, while the remaining 30 percent is taxed at the ordinary tax rate.[16] Thus, a corporation earning $12 million with a 35 percent marginal tax rate would pay only $(0.30)(0.35) = 0.105 = 10.5\%$ of its dividend income as taxes, so its effective tax rate on intercorporate dividends would be 10.5 percent. If this firm receives $10,000 in dividends from another corporation, its after-tax dividend income would be $8,950:

$$\text{After-tax income} = \text{Before-tax income} - \text{Taxes}$$
$$= \$10,000 - [\$10,000(0.30)](0.35)$$
$$= \$10,000(1 - 0.105) = \$10,000(.895) = \$8,950$$

If the corporation pays out its own after-tax income to its stockholders as dividends, the income ultimately is subjected to triple taxation: (1) the original corporation is taxed first, (2) then the second corporation is taxed on the dividends it receives, and (3) the individuals who receive the final dividends are taxed again. This is the reason for the 70 percent exclusion on intercorporate dividends.

---

[16]The size of the dividend exclusion actually depends on the degree of ownership. Corporations that own less than 20 percent of the stock of the dividend-paying company can exclude 70 percent of the dividends received; firms that own over 20 percent but less than 80 percent can exclude 80 percent of the dividends; and firms that own over 80 percent can exclude the entire dividend payment. Because most companies own less than 20 percent of other companies, we will assume a 70 percent dividend exclusion.

Interest and Dividends Paid by a Corporation   A firm's operations can be financed with either debt or equity capital. If it uses debt, it must pay interest on this debt (to banks and to bondholders), whereas if it uses equity, it will pay dividends to the stockholders. The interest paid by a corporation is deducted from its operating income to obtain its taxable income, but the dividends paid are not deductible. Therefore, a firm needs $1 of pretax income to pay $1 of interest, but if it is in the 35 percent bracket, it needs $1.54 of pretax income to pay $1 of dividends:

$$\text{Pretax income needed} \atop \text{to pay \$1 of dividends} = \frac{\$1}{1 - \text{Tax rate}} = \frac{\$1}{1 - 0.35} = \$1.54$$

Of course, it generally is not possible to finance exclusively with debt capital, and the risk of doing so would offset the benefits of the higher expected income. Still, *the fact that interest is a deductible expense has a profound effect on the way businesses are financed—our tax system favors debt financing over equity financing.* This point is discussed in more detail in Chapters 10 and 11.

Corporate Capital Gains   Before 1987, corporate long-term capital gains were taxed at lower rates than ordinary income, as was true for individuals. Under current law, however, corporations' capital gains are taxed at the same rates as their operating income.

Corporate Loss Carryback and Carryover   Ordinary corporate operating losses can be carried back **(carryback)** to each of the preceding two years and carried over **(carryover)** for the next 20 years to offset taxable income in those years. For example, an operating loss reported in 2000 could be carried back and used to reduce taxable income in 1998 and 1999, and carried forward, if necessary, and used in 2001, 2002, and so on, to the year 2020 to offset future taxable income. The loss is applied first to the earliest year, then to the next earliest year, and so on, until losses have been used up or the 20-year carryover limit has been reached.

To illustrate, partial income statements for Apex Corporation are given in Table 2–2. In 1998 and 1999, Apex produced positive taxable income amounts, and it paid the appropriate taxes in each of these years, which totaled $154 million. However, in 2000, Apex incurred a taxable loss equal to $700 million. The carryback feature allows Apex to write off this taxable loss against positive taxable income beginning in 1998. Note, the loss is large enough that the *adjusted* taxable incomes for 1998 and 1999 equal zero. Apex can amend the tax forms it filed in 1998 and 1999, and, thus, it would receive a tax refund equal to $154 million. After adjusting the previous two years' tax forms, Apex still would have $260 million of unrecovered loss from 2000 to carry over through the year 2020, if necessary. The purpose of permitting firms to treat losses like this is to avoid penalizing corporations whose incomes fluctuate substantially from year to year.

Accumulated Earnings Tax   Corporations could refrain from paying dividends to permit their stockholders to avoid personal income taxes on dividends. To prevent this, the tax code contains an **improper accumulation** provision, which states that earnings accumulated by a corporation are subject to penalty rates *if the purpose of the accumulation is to enable stockholders to avoid personal income taxes.* A cumulative total of $250,000 (the balance sheet item "retained earnings") is by law exempted from the accumulated

TAX LOSS CARRYBACK AND CARRYOVER
Losses that can be carried backward or forward in time to offset taxable income in a given year.

IMPROPER ACCUMULATION
Retention of earnings by a business for the purpose of enabling stockholders to avoid personal income taxes.

TABLE 2–2	Apex Corporation: Partial Income Statements for 1998–2000 (millions of dollars)		
	1998	**1999**	**2000**
Original Statement:			
Taxable income	$260	$180	($700)
Taxes (35%)	(91)	(63)	245
Net income	$169	$117	($455)
			TOTAL EFFECT OF CARRY-BACK
Adjusted Statement:			
Original taxable income	$260	$180	
Carry-back credit	(260)	(180)	$440
Adjusted taxable income	0	0	
Taxes (35%)	0	0	0
Adjusted net income	$ 0	$ 0	
Taxes originally paid	91	63	$154 = Tax refund
Loss available to carry forward in 2001–2020 = $700 − $440 = $260			

earnings tax for most corporations. This is a benefit primarily to small corporations. But, the improper accumulation penalty applies only if the retained earnings in excess of $250,000 are shown to be *unnecessary to meet the reasonable needs of the business.* A great many companies do indeed have legitimate reasons for retaining more than $250,000 of earnings. For example, earnings might be retained and used to pay off debt, to finance growth, or to provide the corporation with a cushion against possible cash drains caused by losses. How much a firm should properly accumulate for uncertain contingencies is a matter of judgment.

Consolidated Corporate Tax Returns   If a corporation owns 80 percent or more of another corporation's stock, it can aggregate income and file one consolidated tax return; thus, the losses of one company can be used to offset the profits of another. (Similarly, one division's losses can be used to offset another division's profits.) No business ever wants to incur losses—you can go broke losing $1 to save 34¢ in taxes— but tax offsets do make it more feasible for large, multidivisional corporations to undertake risky new ventures or ventures that will suffer losses during a developmental period and profits thereafter.

Taxation of Small Businesses: S Corporations   The Internal Revenue Code provides that small businesses (fewer than 75 stockholders) that meet certain restrictions as spelled out in the tax code can be set up as corporations and thus receive the benefits of the corporate form of organization—especially limited liability—yet still be taxed as proprietorships or partnerships rather than as corporations.

S CORPORATION
A small corporation which, under Subchapter S of the Internal Revenue Code, elects to be taxed as a proprietorship or a partnership yet retains limited liability and other benefits of the corporate form of organization.

These corporations are called **S corporations.** For a corporation that elects S corporation status for tax purposes, all of the income of the business is reported as personal income by the owners, and it is taxed at the rates that apply to individuals. This would be preferred by owners of small corporations in which all or most of the income earned each year is distributed as dividends because the income would be taxed only once at the individual level.

Depreciation   Depreciation plays an important role in income tax calculations. Congress specifies, in the tax code, the life over which assets can be depreciated for tax purposes and the methods of depreciation that can be used. Because these factors have a major influence on the amount of depreciation a firm can take in a given year, and thus on the firm's taxable income, depreciation has an important effect on taxes paid and cash flows from operations. We will discuss how depreciation is calculated and how it affects income and cash flows when we discuss the subject of capital budgeting in Chapters 8 and 9.

Self-Test Questions

Explain what is meant by the statement: "Our tax rates are progressive."

Are tax rates progressive for all income ranges?

Explain the difference between marginal tax rates and average tax rates.

What are capital gains and losses, and how are they differentiated from ordinary income?

How does the federal income tax system tax corporate dividends received by a corporation and those received by an individual? Why is this distinction made?

Briefly explain how tax loss carryback and carryover procedures work.

Summary

In this chapter we discussed the nature of financial markets, the types of institutions that operate in these markets, how interest rates are determined, some of the ways in which interest rates affect business decisions, and the federal income tax system. The key concepts covered are as follows:

- There are many different types of **financial markets.** Each market serves a different region or deals with a different type of security.
- Transfers of capital between borrowers and savers take place (1) by **direct transfers** of money and securities; (2) by transfers through **investment banking houses,** which act as middlemen; and (3) by transfers through **financial intermediaries,** which create new securities.
- The **stock market** is an especially important market because this is where stock prices (which are used to "grade" managers' performances) are established.
- There are two basic types of stock markets—the **organized exchanges** and the **over-the-counter market.**
- Capital is allocated through the price system—a price must be paid to "rent" money. Lenders charge **interest** on funds they lend, while equity investors receive **dividends and capital gains** in return for letting firms use their money.
- Four fundamental factors affect the cost of money: (1) **production opportunities,** (2) **time preferences for consumption,** (3) **risk,** and (4) **inflation.**

- The **risk-free rate of interest, k_{RF},** is defined as the real risk-free rate, k^*, plus an inflation premium (IP): $k_{RF} = k^* + IP$.
- The **nominal (or quoted) interest rate** on a debt security, k, is composed of the real risk-free rate, k^*, plus premiums that reflect **inflation (IP), default risk (DRP), liquidity (LP),** and **maturity risk (MRP):**

$$k = k^* + IP + DRP + LP + MRP.$$

- If the **real risk-free rate of interest and the various premiums were constant over time,** interest rates in the economy would be stable. However, both the real rate and the premiums—especially the premium for expected inflation—**do change over time, causing market interest rates to change.** Also, Federal Reserve intervention to increase or decrease the money supply (as well as international currency flows) leads to fluctuations in interest rates.
- The relationship between the yields on securities and the securities' maturities is known as the **term structure of interest rates,** and the **yield curve** is a graph of this relationship.
- The yield curve is normally **upward sloping**—this is called a **normal yield curve**—but the curve can **slope downward** (an **inverted yield curve**) if the demand for short-term funds is relatively strong or if the rate of inflation is expected to decline.
- **Interest rate levels have a profound effect on stock prices.** Higher interest rates (1) slow down the economy, (2) increase interest expenses and thus lower corporate profits, and (3) cause investors to sell stocks and transfer funds to the bond market. Each of these factors tends to depress stock prices.
- The value of any asset depends on the stream of **after-tax cash flows** it produces. Tax rates and other aspects of our tax system are changed by Congress every year or so.
- In the United States, income tax rates are **progressive**—the higher one's income, the larger the percentage paid in taxes, up to a point.
- Assets such as stocks, bonds, and real estate are defined as **capital assets.** If a capital asset is sold for more than the purchase price, the profit is called a **capital gain.** If the capital asset is sold for a loss, it is called a **capital loss.**
- **Interest income** received by a corporation is taxed as ordinary income; however, **70 percent of the dividends received by one corporation from another is excluded from taxable income.**
- Because **interest paid by a corporation is a deductible expense** while dividends are not, our tax system favors debt financing over equity financing.
- Ordinary corporate operating losses can be **carried back** to each of the preceding two years and carried over for the next 20 years to offset taxable income in those years.
- **S corporations** are small businesses that have the limited-liability benefits of the corporate form of organization yet obtain the benefits of being taxed as a partnership or a proprietorship.

Questions

2-1 What are financial intermediaries, and what economic functions do they perform?

2–2 Suppose interest rates on residential mortgages of equal risk were eight percent in California and ten percent in New York. Could this differential persist?

What forces might tend to equalize rates? Would differentials in borrowing costs for businesses of equal risk located in California and New York be more or less likely to exist than differentials in residential mortgage rates? Would differentials in the cost of money for New York and California firms be more likely to exist if the firms being compared were very large or if they were very small? What are the implications of all this for the pressure now being put on Congress to permit banks to engage in *unrestricted* nationwide branching?

2–3 What would happen to the standard of living in the United States if people lost faith in the safety of our financial institutions? Why?

2–4 How does a cost-efficient capital market help to reduce the prices of goods and services?

2–5 Which fluctuate more, long- or short-term interest rates? Why?

2–6 Suppose you believe that the economy is just entering a recession. Your firm must raise capital immediately, and debt will be used. Should you borrow on a long-term or a short-term basis? Why?

2–7 Suppose a new process was developed that could be used to make oil out of sea water. The equipment required is quite expensive, but it would, in time, lead to very low prices for gasoline, electricity, and other types of energy. What effect would this have on interest rates?

2–8 Suppose a new and much more liberal Congress and administration were elected and their first order of business was to take away the independence of the Federal Reserve System and to force the Fed to greatly expand the money supply. What effect would this have

    a. On the level and slope of the yield curve immediately after the announcement?

    b. On the level and slope of the yield curve that would exist two or three years in the future?

2–9 It is a fact that the federal government (1) encouraged the development of the savings and loan industry; (2) virtually forced the industry to make long-term, fixed-interest-rate mortgages; and (3) forced the savings and loans to obtain most of their capital as deposits that were withdrawable on demand.

    a. Would the savings and loan associations be better off in a world with a "normal" or an inverted yield curve?

    b. Would the savings and loan industry be better off if the individual institutions sold their mortgages to federal agencies and then collected servicing fees or if the institutions held the mortgages that they originated?

2–10 Suppose interest rates on Treasury bonds rose from six to twelve percent as a result of higher interest rates in Europe. What effect would this have on the price of an average company's common stock?

2–11 Suppose you owned 100 shares of General Motors stock and the company earned $6 per share during the last reporting period. Suppose further that GM could either pay all its earnings out as dividends (in which case you would receive $600) or retain the earnings in the business, buy more assets, and cause the price of the stock to go up by $6 per share (in which case the value of your stock would rise by $600).

    a. How would the tax laws influence what you, as a typical stockholder, would want the company to do?

    b. Would your choice be influenced by how much other income you had? Why might the desires of a 35-year-old doctor differ with respect to corporate dividend policy from those of a pension fund manager or a retiree living on a small income?

    c. How might the corporation's decision with regard to the dividends it pays influence the price of its stock?

2–12 What does *double taxation of corporate income* mean?

2–13 If you were starting a business, what tax considerations might cause you to prefer to set it up as a proprietorship or a partnership rather than as a corporation? Would you consider the average or the marginal tax rate more relevant?

2–14 Explain how the federal income tax structure affects the choice of financing (use of debt versus equity) of U.S. business firms.

Self-Test Problems

(Solutions appear in Appendix B)

key terms   **ST-1** Define each of the following terms:
    a. Money market; capital market
    b. Primary market; secondary market
    c. Investment banker; financial intermediary
    d. Mutual fund; money market fund
    e. Organized security exchanges; over-the-counter market
    f. Production opportunities; time preferences for consumption
    g. Real risk-free rate of interest, k^*; nominal risk-free rate of interest, k_{RF}
    h. Inflation premium (IP); default risk premium (DRP)
    i. Liquidity; liquidity premium (LP)
    j. Interest rate risk; maturity risk premium (MRP); reinvestment rate risk
    k. Term structure of interest rates; yield curve
    l. "Normal" yield curve; inverted ("abnormal") yield curve
    m. Market segmentation theory; liquidity preference theory; expectations theory
    n. Progressive tax
    o. Marginal and average tax rates
    p. Capital gain or loss
    q. Tax loss carryback and carryover
    r. S corporation

inflation rates   **ST-2** Assume that it is now January 1, 2000. The rate of inflation is expected to be six percent throughout 2000. However, increased government deficits and renewed vigor in the economy are then expected to push inflation rates higher. Investors expect the inflation rate to be seven percent in 2001, eight percent in 2002, and nine percent in 2003. The real risk-free rate, k^*, currently is three percent. Assume that no maturity risk premiums are required on bonds with five years or less to maturity. The current interest rate on five-year T-bonds is 11 percent.
    a. What is the average expected inflation rate over the next four years?
    b. What should be the prevailing interest rate on four-year T-bonds?
    c. What is the implied expected inflation rate in 2004, or Year 5, given that bonds that mature in that year yield 11 percent?

form of business and taxes   **ST-3** John Thompson is planning to start a new business, JT Enterprises, and he must decide whether to incorporate or to do business as a sole proprietorship. Under either form, Thompson will initially own 100 percent of the firm, and tax considerations are important to him. He plans to finance the firm's expected growth by drawing a salary just sufficient for his family's living expenses, which he estimates will be about $40,000, and by retaining all other income in the business. Assume that as a married man with one child, Thompson has income tax exemptions of 3 × $2,750 = $8,250 and he estimates that his itemized deductions for each of the three years will be $9,000. He expects JT Enterprises to grow and to earn income of $60,000 in 2000, $90,000 in 2001, and $110,000 in 2002. Which form of business organization will allow Thompson to pay the lowest taxes (and retain the most income) during the period from 2000 to 2002? Assume that the tax rates given in the appendix are applicable for all future years. (Social security taxes would also have to be paid, but ignore them.)

Problems

(Note: By the time this book is published, Congress may have changed rates or other provisions of current tax law; as noted in the chapter, such changes occur fairly often. Work all problems on the assumption that the information in the chapter is still current.)

yield curve   **2–1** Suppose you and most other investors expect the rate of inflation to be seven percent next year, to fall to five percent during the following year, and then to remain at a rate of three percent thereafter. Assume that the real risk-free rate, k^*, is two percent and that maturity risk premiums on Treasury securities rise from zero on very short-term bonds (those that mature in a few days) by 0.2 percentage points for each year to maturity, up to a limit of 1.0 percentage point on five-year or longer-term T-bonds.

    a. Calculate the interest rate on one-, two-, three-, four-, five-, ten-, and twenty-year Treasury securities, and plot the yield curve.

    b. Now suppose Exxon, an AAA-rated company, had bonds with the same maturities as the Treasury bonds. As an approximation, plot an Exxon yield curve on the same graph with the Treasury bond yield curve. (*Hint:* Think about the default risk premium on Exxon's long-term versus its short-term bonds.)

    c. Now plot the approximate yield curve of Long Island Lighting Company, a risky nuclear utility.

yield curves   **2–2** The following yields on U.S. Treasury securities were taken from *The Wall Street Journal* on March 15, 1999:

TERM	RATE
6 months	4.7%
1 year	4.9
2 years	5.1
3 years	5.1
4 years	5.2
5 years	5.2
10 years	5.6
20 years	6.0
30 years	5.8

Plot a yield curve based on these data. Discuss how each term structure theory can explain the shape of the yield curve you plot.

inflation and interest rates   **2–3** It is January 1, 2000. Inflation currently is about two percent; throughout 1999, the Fed took action to maintain inflation at this level. However, the economy has shown signs that it might be beginning to grow too quickly, and reports indicate that inflation is expected to increase during the next five years. Assume that *at the beginning of 2000*, the rate of inflation expected for 2000 is four percent; for 2001, it is *expected* to be five percent; for 2002, it is *expected* to be seven percent; and, for 2003 and every year thereafter, it is *expected* to settle at four percent.

a. What was the average expected inflation rate over the five-year period 2000-2004?

b. What average nominal interest rate would, over the five-year period, be expected to produce a two percent real risk-free rate of return on five-year Treasury securities?

c. Assuming a real risk-free rate of two percent and a maturity risk premium that starts at 0.1 percent and increases by 0.1 percent *each year*, estimate the interest rate in January 2000 on bonds that mature in one, two, five, ten, and twenty years, and draw a yield curve based on these data.

d. Describe the general economic conditions that could be expected to produce an upward-sloping yield curve.

e. If the consensus among investors in early 2000 had been that the expected rate of inflation for every future year was five percent (that is, $I_t = I_{t+1} = 5\%$ for t = 1 to ∞), what do you think the yield curve would have looked like? Consider all the factors that are likely to affect the curve. Does your answer here make you question the yield curve you drew in Part c?

loss carryback, carryover   **2–4** The Angell Company has made $150,000 before taxes during each of the past 15 years, and it expects to make $150,000 a year before taxes in the future. However, in 2000 the firm incurred a loss of $650,000. The firm will claim a tax credit at the time it files its 2000 income tax return, and it will receive a check from the U.S. Treasury. Show how it calculates this credit, and then indicate the firm's tax liability for each of the next five years. Assume a 30 percent tax rate on all income to ease the calculations.

loss carryback, carryover   **2–5** The projected taxable income of the Glasgo Corporation, formed in 1999, is indicated in the following table. (Losses are shown in parentheses.) What is the corporate tax liability for each year? Use tax rates as shown in the appendix.

YEAR	TAXABLE INCOME
1999	$ (95,000)
2000	70,000
2001	55,000
2002	80,000
2003	(150,000)

form of organization   **2–6** Kate Brown has operated her small repair shop as a sole proprietorship for several years, but projected changes in her business's income have led her to consider incorporating. Brown is married and has two children. Her family's only income, an annual salary of $45,000, is from operating the business. (The business actually earns more than $45,000, but Kate reinvests the additional earnings in the business.) She itemizes deductions, and she is able to deduct $8,000. These deductions, combined with her four personal exemptions for 4 × $2,750 = $11,000, give her a taxable income of $45,000 − $8,000 − $11,000. (Assume the personal exemption remains at $2,750.) Of course, her actual taxable income, if she does not incorporate, would be higher by the amount of reinvested income.

Brown estimates that her business earnings before salary and taxes for the period 2000 to 2002 will be as follows:

YEAR	EARNINGS BEFORE SALARY AND TAXES
2000	$65,000
2001	85,000
2002	95,000

a. What would her total taxes (corporate plus personal) be in each year under
 (1) A non-S corporate form of organization? (2000 tax = $6,900.00)
 (2) A proprietorship? (2000 tax = $7,283.50)
b. Should Brown incorporate? Discuss.

personal taxes   **2–7** Margaret Considine has this situation for the year 2000: salary of $60,000; dividend income of $10,000; interest on IBM bonds of $5,000; interest on state of Florida municipal bonds of $10,000; proceeds of $22,000 from the sale of IBM stock purchased in 1985 at a cost of $9,000; and proceeds of $22,000 from the November 2000 sale of IBM stock purchased in October 2000 at a cost of $21,000. Margaret gets one exemption ($2,750), and she has allowable itemized deductions of $5,000; these amounts will be deducted from her gross income to determine her taxable income.

a. What is Margaret's federal tax liability for 2000?
b. What are her marginal and average tax rates?
c. If she had some money to invest and was offered a choice of either state of Florida bonds with a yield of nine percent or more IBM bonds with a yield of 11 percent, which should she choose and why?
d. At what marginal tax rate would Margaret be indifferent in her choice between the Florida and IBM bonds?

tax liability   **2–8** Donald Jefferson and his wife Maryanne live in a modest house located in a Los Angeles suburb. Donald has a job at Pittsford CastIron that pays him $50,000 annually. In addition, he and Maryanne receive $2,500 interest from bonds they purchased ten years ago. To supplement his annual income, Donald bought rental property a few years ago. Every month he collects $3,500 rent from all the property he owns. Maryanne manages the rental property, and she is paid $15,000 annually for her work. During 2000, Donald had to have the plumbing fixed in the houses he rents and the house in which he and his wife live. The plumbing bill for the rented houses was $1,250, and it was $550 for the Jefferson's personal residence. In 2000, Donald paid $18,000 for mortgage interest and property taxes—$12,650 was for the rental houses, and the remaining $5,350 was for the house occupied by him and his wife. Donald and Maryanne have three children who have graduated from medical college and now are working as physicians in other states.

a. What is the Jefferson's tax liability for 2000?
b. What would the tax liability be if the Jeffersons did not have the rental property? (Assume Maryanne would not get another job if the Jeffersons did not own the rental property.)
c. Why is the plumbing expense a tax deduction for the rental property but not for the house in which the Jeffersons live?

Exam-Type Problems

The problems included in this section are set up in such a way that they could be used as multiple-choice exam problems.

expected rate of interest

2–9 Suppose the annual yield on a two-year Treasury bond is 11.5 percent, while that on a one-year bond is ten percent; k* is three percent, and the maturity risk premium is zero.

    a. Using the expectations theory, forecast the interest rate on a one-year bond during the second year. (Hint: Under the expectations theory, the yield on a two-year bond is equal to the average yield on one-year bonds in Years 1 and 2.)

    b. What is the expected inflation rate in Year 1? Year 2?

expected rate of interest

2–10 Assume that the real risk-free rate is four percent and that the maturity risk premium is zero. If the nominal rate of interest on one-year bonds is 11 percent and that on comparable-risk two-year bonds is 13 percent, what is the one-year interest rate that is expected for Year 2? What inflation rate is expected during Year 2? Comment on why the average interest rate during the two-year period differs from the one-year interest rate expected for Year 2.

corporate tax liability

2–11 The Ramjah Corporation had $200,000 of taxable income from operations in 2000.

    a. What is the company's federal income tax bill for the year?

    b. Assume the firm receives an additional $40,000 of interest income from some corporate bonds it owns. What is the tax on this interest income?

    c. Now assume that Ramjah does not receive the interest income, but does receive an additional $40,000 as dividends on some stock it owns. What is the tax on this dividend income?

corporate tax liability

2–12 The Zocco Corporation has a 2000 taxable income of $365,000 from operations after all operating costs, but before (1) interest charges of $50,000, (2) dividends received of $15,000, (3) dividends paid of $25,000, and (4) income taxes.

    a. What is the firm's income tax liability and its after-tax income?

    b. What are the company's marginal and average tax rates on taxable income?

capital gains tax liability

2–13 Compute the capital gains tax liability for each of the following:

    a. An individual sold a municipal bond for $1,150, two years after it was purchased for $950.

    b. An individual sold 100 shares of a stock for $12 per share, two years after it was purchased at a price equal to $10 per share.

    c. A corporation bought 100 shares of stock of another company for $55 per share, and then sold it for $57 per share two years later.

corporate tax liability

2–14 In 1999, Ibis International had a taxable income of $150,000 from operations. During the year, Ibis paid $45,000 interest on its outstanding debt (e.g., bank loans and bonds), and it paid its common stockholders $22,000 dividends. The company received $18,000 interest because it invested in the debt of other companies, and it also received $8,000 dividends from its investments in other companies' common stocks. What is the company's tax liability and its after-tax income?

interest rates

2–15 The rate of inflation for the coming year is expected to be three percent, and the rate of inflation in Year 2 and thereafter is expected to be constant at some level above three percent. Assume that the real risk-free rate is k* = 2% for all maturities and the expectations theory fully explains the yield curve, so there are no maturity premiums. If three-year Treasury bonds yield two percentage points more than one-year bonds, what rate of inflation is expected after Year 1?

after-tax returns   **2–16** Carver Corporation has $10,000 that it plans to invest. It is thinking of putting the funds in either AT&T bonds that yield 11 percent, state of Florida municipal bonds that yield eight percent, or AT&T preferred stock that has a dividend yield of nine percent. Carver's corporate tax rate is 20 percent. Assuming that Carver chooses strictly on the basis of after-tax returns, which security should be selected? What is the after-tax return on the security that should be selected?

Integrative Problem

financial markets and taxes   **2–17** Assume that you recently graduated with a degree in finance and have just reported to work as an investment advisor at the firm of Balik and Kiefer Inc. Your first assignment is to explain the nature of the U.S. financial markets and institutions to Michelle DeLatorre, a professional tennis player who has just come to the United States from Chile. DeLatorre is a highly ranked tennis player who expects to invest substantial amounts of money through Balik and Kiefer. She is also very bright and therefore she would like to understand in general terms what will happen to her money. Your boss has developed the following questions, which you must ask and answer to explain the U.S. financial system to DeLatorre.

  a. What is a *financial market?* How are financial markets differentiated from markets for *physical assets?*

  b. Differentiate between *money markets* and *capital markets.*

  c. Differentiate between a *primary market* and a *secondary market.* If Microsoft decided to issue additional common stock, and DeLatorre purchased 100 shares of this stock from Merrill Lynch, the underwriter, would this transaction be a primary market transaction or a secondary market transaction? Would it make a difference if DeLatorre purchased previously outstanding Microsoft stock in the over-the-counter market?

  d. Describe the three primary ways in which capital is transferred between savers and borrowers.

  e. Securities can be traded on *organized exchanges* or in the *over-the-counter market.* Define each of these markets, and describe how stocks are traded in each of them.

  f. What do we call the *price* that a borrower must pay for debt capital? What is the price of equity capital? What are the four most fundamental factors that affect the cost of money, or the general level of interest rates, in the economy?

  g. What is the *real risk-free rate of interest (k*)* and the *nominal risk-free rate (k_{RF})?* How are these two rates measured?

  h. Define the terms *inflation premium (IP), default risk premium (DRP), liquidity premium (LP),* and *maturity risk premium (MRP).* Which of these premiums is included when determining the interest rate on (1) short-term U.S. Treasury securities, (2) long-term U.S. Treasury securities, (3) short-term corporate securities, and (4) long-term corporate securities? Explain how the premiums would vary over time and among the different securities listed earlier.

  i. What is the *term structure* of interest rates? What is a *yield curve?* At any given time, how would the yield curve facing a given company such as

AT&T or Chrysler compare with the yield curve for U.S. Treasury securities? Draw a graph to illustrate your answer.

j. Several theories have been advanced to explain the shape of the yield curve. The three major ones are (1) the *market segmentation theory*, (2) the *liquidity preference theory*, and (3) the *expectations theory*. Briefly describe each of these theories. Do economists regard one as being "true"?

k. Suppose most investors expect the rate of inflation to be five percent next year, six percent the following year, and eight percent thereafter. The real risk-free rate is three percent. The maturity risk premium is zero for bonds that mature in one year or less, 0.1 percent for two-year bonds, and the MRP increases by 0.1 percent per year thereafter for 20 years, after which it is stable. What is the interest rate on one-, ten-, and twenty-year Treasury bonds? Draw a yield curve with these data. Is your yield curve consistent with the three term-structure theories?

l. Working with DeLatorre has required you to put in a lot of overtime, so you have had very little time to spend on your private finances. It's now April 1, and you have only two weeks left to file your income tax return. You have managed to get all the information together that you will need to complete your return. Balik and Kiefer Inc. paid you a salary of $45,000, and you received $3,000 in dividends from common stock that you own. You are single, so your personal exemption is $2,750 and your itemized deductions are $5,500.

   (1) On the basis of the information above and the 1999 individual tax rate schedule, what is your tax liability?

   (2) What are your marginal and average tax rates?

m. Assume that a corporation has $100,000 of taxable income from operations plus $5,000 of interest income and $10,000 of dividend income. What is the company's tax liability?

n. Assume that after paying your personal income tax, as calculated in part l, you have $5,000 to invest. You have narrowed your investment choices down to California municipal bonds with a yield of seven percent or IBM bonds with a yield of ten percent. Which one should you choose, and why? At what marginal tax rate would you be indifferent to the choice between California and IBM bonds?

Computer-Related Problem

Work this problem only if you are using the computer problem diskette.

effect of form of business on taxes

2–18 The problem requires you to rework Problem 2–6 using the following data. Use File C2 on the computer problem diskette.

a. Suppose Brown decides to pay out (1) 50 percent or (2) 100 percent of the after-salary corporate income in each year as dividends. Would such dividend policy changes affect her decision about whether to incorporate?

b. Suppose business improves so that actual earnings before salary and taxes in each year are twice the original estimate. Also assume that if Brown chooses to incorporate she will continue to receive a salary of $45,000 and to reinvest additional earnings in the business. (No dividends would be paid.) What would be the effect of this increase in business income on Brown's decision to incorporate?

> **ONLINE ESSENTIALS**
>
> **http://www.sec.gov**   Securities and Exchange Commission (SEC)
> Provides investment information, including the rules and regulations monitored by the SEC, investment data, and links to related sites.
>
> **http://nyse.com**   New York Stock Exchange
>
> **http://www.nasdaq.com**   NASDAQ
>
> **http://www.amex.com**   American Stock Exchange
> Information about stock markets and stock data can be obtained directly from these Web sites.
>
> **http://www.federalreserve.gov**   Federal Reserve and Banking Information
> Provides information about the U.S. banking system, economic and banking data, and links to the district Federal Reserve Banks, which have substantial amounts of economic data, including interest rates, inflation rates, and so on.
>
> **http://irs.ustreas.gov**   Internal Revenue Service
> The latest tax rates, information about impending tax legislation, and various data related to business tax filings can be obtained from this site.

APPENDIX 2A

1999 Tax Rate Schedules

Table 2A–1 gives the 1999 tax rates for individuals and Table 2A–2 gives the 1999 tax rates for corporations. Even though these rates probably have changed, they should be used for all of the problems in this chapter that require the computation of tax liabilities.

TABLE 2A–1	Individual Tax Rates for 1999

UNMARRIED TAXPAYERS, NOT HEADS OF HOUSEHOLDS

TAXABLE INCOME BRACKET	BASE TAX AMOUNT	PLUS THIS PERCENT OF THE AMOUNT OVER		AVERAGE TAX RATE AT THE TOP OF THE BRACKET
$ 1 – $ 25,750	$ 0.00	+ 15.0%	$ 0	15.0%
25,751 – 62,450	3,862.50	+ 28.0%	25,750	22.6
62,451 – 130,250	14,138.50	+ 31.0%	62,450	27.0
130,251 – 283,150	35,156.50	+ 36.0%	130,250	31.9
Above 283,150	90,200.50	+ 39.6%	283,150	≈40.0

MARRIED TAXPAYERS FILING JOINT RETURNS

TAXABLE INCOME BRACKET	BASE TAX AMOUNT	PLUS THIS PERCENT OF THE AMOUNT OVER		AVERAGE TAX RATE AT THE TOP OF THE BRACKET
$ 1 – $ 43,050	$ 0.00	+ 15.0%	$ 0	15.0%
43,051 – 104,050	6,457.50	+ 28.0%	43,050	22.6
104,051 – 158,550	23,537.50	+ 31.0%	104,050	25.5
158,551 – 283,150	40,432.50	+ 36.0%	158,550	30.1
Above 283,150	85,288.50	+ 39.6%	283,150	≈40.0

NOTES:

a. The personal exemption for 1999 was $2,750 per person or dependent. The total amount of this exemption can be deducted from income to compute taxable income. For example, for a family of four, the total personal exemption would be $11,000 = 4 × $2,750.

b. If the taxpayer does not want to itemize deductions such as interest payments made on mortgages, charitable contributions, and so on, the standard deduction can be taken. In 1999, the standard deduction for an unmarried taxpayer, not the head of a household, was $4,300, and it was $7,200 for married taxpayers filing joint returns.

c. The tax rate applied to capital gains for assets held less than 12 months (short term) was the marginal tax rate of the taxpayer, and 20 percent for assets held 12 months or more (long term).

TABLE 2A–2	Corporate Tax Rates for 1999

TAXABLE INCOME BRACKET	BASE TAX AMOUNT	PLUS THIS PERCENT OF THE AMOUNT OVER		AVERAGE TAX RATE AT THE TOP OF THE BRACKET
$ 0 – $ 50,000	$ 0	+ 15%	$ 0	15.0%
50,001 – 75,000	7,500	+ 25	50,000	18.3
75,001 – 100,000	13,750	+ 34	75,000	22.3
100,001 – 335,000	22,250	+ 39	100,000	34.0
335,001 – 10,000,000	113,900	+ 34	335,000	34.0
10,000,001 – 15,000,000	3,400,000	+ 35	10,000,000	34.3
15,000,001 – 18,333,333	5,150,000	+ 38	15,000,000	35.0
Above 18,333,333	6,416,667	+ 35	18,333,333	35.0

NOTE:

For taxable income above $335,000, there is a surtax, which could increase the marginal tax rate to about 40 percent.

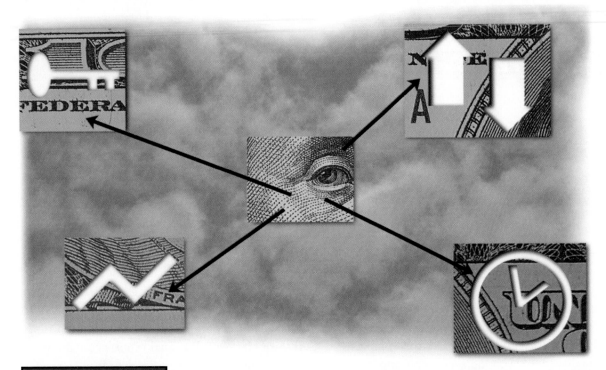

PART II

Forecasting, Planning, and Control

CHAPTER 3

Analysis of Financial Statements

A MANAGERIAL PERSPECTIVE

Corporations in the United States are required to make "full and fair" disclosure of their operations by publishing various financial statements and other reports required by the Securities and Exchange Commission (SEC), the Financial Accounting Standards Board (FASB), and the American Institute of Certified Public Accountants (AICPA). One such publication is the annual report, which is often used to convey more than financial results; in some cases, the annual report is viewed as an opportunity to showcase top management and sell the future of the company, without regard to the financial information. So it is not unusual for work on the annual report to begin as much as six months before its publication, and many firms hire professional designers and writers to ensure that the final product looks sharp and reads well. Some firms pride themselves in the unique packaging designs used. For example, since 1977, McCormick & Company has used one of the spices and seasonings it produces to scent the paper on which its annual report is printed—the scent for 1998 was vanilla.

In most instances, the puffery contained in annual reports detracts from the primary purpose to provide objective financial information about the firm. Of course, there are companies that use the annual report as originally intended—to communicate the financial position of the firm. One such firm is Berkshire Hathaway, whose legendary chairman Warren Buffett says, "I assume I have a very intelligent partner who has been away for a year and needs to be filled in on all that's happened." Consequently, in his letters he often admits mistakes and emphasizes the negative along with the positive. Buffett also uses his letters to educate his shareholders and to help them interpret the data presented in the rest of the report. Berkshire Hathaway's annual reports contain little, if any, puffery, freeing readers to focus on the company's financial statements and Buffett's interpretation of them. Some CEOs might contend that such a bare-bones approach is too dull for the average stockholder and, further, that some readers might actually be intimidated by the information overload. But the manner in which Chairman Buffett presents financial information for Berkshire Hathaway seems to work because the company's stockholders are considered more sophisticated than average investors. If you would like to examine some of the statements made by Warren Buffett, visit their Web site at http://berkshirehathaway.com.

More and more, firms are recognizing that the "slick" annual report has (1) lost its credibility with serious seekers of financial information and (2) become increasingly more expensive to produce. With the growth in electronic communications, the trend in recent years has been to post annual reports, devoid of the traditional "frills," on the company's Web site and refer stockholders to that location.

As you read this chapter, think about the kinds of information corporations provide their stock-

continues

holders. Do you think the basic financial statements provide adequate data for investment decisions? What other information might be helpful? Also, consider the pros and cons of Chairman Buffett's decision to include frank and frequently self-critical letters in his company's annual reports. Would you suggest that other companies follow suit? ■

Financial statement analysis involves a comparison of a firm's performance with that of other firms in the same line of business, which usually is identified by the firm's industry classification. Generally speaking, the analysis is used to determine the firm's financial position in order to identify its current strengths and weaknesses and to suggest actions the firm might enact to take advantage of the strengths and correct the weaknesses in the future.

Financial statement analysis is not only important for the firm's managers, it also is important for the firm's investors and creditors. Internally, financial managers use the information provided by financial analysis to help make financing and investment decisions to maximize the firm's value. Externally, stockholders and creditors use financial statement analysis to evaluate the attractiveness of the firm as an investment by examining its ability to meet its current and expected future financial obligations.

In this chapter, we discuss how to evaluate a firm's current financial position. For the most part, this chapter should be a review of what you learned in accounting. However, accounting focuses on how financial statements are made, whereas our focus is on how they are used by management to improve the firm's performance and by investors (either stockholders or creditors) to examine the firm's financial position when evaluating its attractiveness as an investment. Then, in the remaining chapters, we will examine the types of actions that a firm can take to improve its financial position in the future and thus to increase the price of its stock.

Financial Statements and Reports

ANNUAL REPORT
A report issued annually by a corporation to its stockholders. It contains basic financial statements, as well as management's opinion of the past year's operations, and the firm's future prospects.

Of the various reports corporations issue to their stockholders, the **annual report** probably is the most important. Two types of information are given in this report. First, there is a verbal section, often presented as a letter from the chairman, that describes the firm's operating results during the past year and then discusses new developments that will affect future operations. Second, the annual report presents four basic financial statements: the *income statement*, the *balance sheet*, the *statement of retained earnings*, and the *statement of cash flows*. Together, these statements give an accounting picture of the firm's operations and financial position. Detailed data are provided for the two most recent years, along with historical summaries of key operating statistics for the past five or ten years.[1]

---

[1]Firms also provide quarterly reports, but these are much less comprehensive than the annual reports. In addition, larger firms file even more detailed statements, giving breakdowns for each major division or subsidiary, with the Securities and Exchange Commission (SEC). These reports, called *10-K reports*, are made available to stockholders upon request to a company's corporate secretary. Finally, many larger firms also publish *statistical supplements*, which give financial statement data and key ratios going back ten to twenty years.

TABLE 3–1	Unilate Textiles: Comparative Income Statements for Years Ending December 31 (millions of dollars, except per share data)

	2000	1999
Net sales	$ 1,500.0	$ 1,435.0
Cost of goods sold	(1,230.0)[a]	(1,176.7)
Gross profit	$ 270.0	$ 258.3
Fixed operating expenses except depreciation	(90.0)	(85.0)
Depreciation	(50.0)	(40.0)
Earnings before interest and taxes (EBIT)	$ 130.0	$ 133.3
Interest	(40.0)	(35.0)
Earnings before taxes (EBT)	$ 90.0	$ 98.3
Taxes (40%)	(36.0)	(39.3)
Net income	$ 54.0	$ 59.0
Preferred dividends	0.0	0.0
Earnings available to common stockholders (EAC)	$ 54.0	$ 59.0
Common dividends	(29.0)	(27.0)
Addition to retained earnings	$ 25.0	$ 32.0
Per Share Data:		
Shares outstanding	25.00	25.00
Common stock price	$ 23.00	$ 23.00
Earnings per share	$ 2.16	$ 2.36
Dividends per share	$ 1.16	$ 1.08

[a]Here, and throughout the text, parentheses are used to denote negative numbers.

The quantitative and verbal information contained in the annual report are equally important. The financial statements report what actually has happened to the firm's financial position and to its earnings and dividends over the past few years, whereas the verbal statements attempt to explain why things turned out the way they did. For example, Table 3–1 shows that Unilate Textiles' earnings decreased by $5 million in 2000, to $54 million versus $59 million in 1999. In the annual report, management reported that the 8.5 percent earnings drop resulted from losses associated with a poor cotton crop and from increased costs due to a three-month strike and a retooling of the factory. However, management then went on to paint a more optimistic picture for the future, stating that full operations had been resumed, that several unprofitable businesses had been eliminated, and that 2001 profits were expected to rise sharply. Of course, an increase in profitability might not occur, and analysts should compare management's past statements with subsequent results to determine if management's optimism is justified. In any event, *the information contained in an annual report is used by investors to form expectations about future earnings and dividends.* Therefore, the annual report obviously is of great interest to investors.

For illustrative purposes, we will use data taken from Unilate Textiles, a manufacturer and distributor of a wide variety of textiles and clothing items. Formed in 1980 with the merger of three family-owned firms in North Carolina, Unilate has grown steadily and has earned a reputation for being one of the best firms in its industry.

The Income Statement

INCOME STATEMENT
A statement summarizing the firm's revenues and expenses over an accounting period, generally a quarter or a year.

The **income statement,** often referred to as the profit and loss statement, presents the results of business operations during a specified period of time such as a quarter or a year. The statement summarizes the revenues generated and the expenses incurred by the firm during the accounting period. Table 3–1 gives the 1999 and 2000 income statements for Unilate Textiles. Net sales are shown at the top of each statement, after which various costs, including income taxes, are subtracted to obtain the net income available to common stockholders. A report on earnings and dividends per share is given at the bottom of the statement. In managerial finance, earnings per share (EPS) is called "the bottom line," denoting that of all the items on the income statement, EPS is the most important. Unilate earned $2.16 per share in 2000, down from $2.36 in 1999, but it still raised the per share dividend from $1.08 to $1.16.

It is important to remember that not all of the amounts shown on the income statement represent cash flows. Recall from what you learned in accounting that, for most corporations, the income statement is generated using the accrual method of accounting. This means revenues are recognized when they are earned, not when the cash is received, and expenses are realized when they are incurred, not when the cash is paid. This point will be addressed further later in the chapter.

The Balance Sheet

BALANCE SHEET
A statement of the firm's financial position at a specific point in time.

The **balance sheet** shows the financial position of a firm at a specific point in time. This financial statement indicates the investments made by the firm in the form of assets and the means by which the assets were financed, whether the funds were raised by borrowing (liabilities) or by selling ownership shares (equity). Unilate's year-end 1999 and 2000 balance sheets are given in Table 3–2. The top portion of the balance sheet shows that on December 31, 2000, Unilate's assets totaled $845 million, while the bottom portion shows the liabilities and equity, or the claims against these assets. The assets are listed in order of their "liquidity," or the length of time it typically takes to convert them to cash. The claims are listed in the order in which they must be paid: Accounts payable generally must be paid within 30 to 45 days, accruals are payable within 60 to 90 days, and so on, down to the stockholders' equity accounts, which represent ownership and need never be "paid off."

Some additional points about the balance sheet are worth noting:

1. **Cash versus other assets.** Although the assets are all stated in terms of dollars, only cash represents actual money. Receivables are bills others owe Unilate; inventories show the dollars the company has invested in raw materials, work-in-process, and finished goods available for sale; and net fixed assets reflect the amount of money Unilate paid for its plant and equipment when it acquired those assets less the amount that has been written off (depreciated) since the acquisition of those assets. Unilate can write checks at present for a total of $15 million (versus current liabilities of $130 million due within a year). The noncash assets should produce cash over time, but they do not represent cash in hand, and the amount of cash they would bring if they were sold today could be higher or lower than the values at which they are carried on the books (their book values).

TABLE 3-2	Unilate Textiles: December 31 Comparative Balance Sheets (millions of dollars)			

		2000		1999
Assets				
Cash and marketable securities		$ 15.0		$ 40.0
Accounts receivable		180.0		160.0
Inventory		270.0		200.0
Total current assets		$465.0		$400.0
Gross plant and equipment	$680.0		$600.0	
Less: Accumulated depreciation	(300.0)		(250.0)	
Net plant and equipment		380.0		350.0
Total assets		$845.0		$750.0
Liabilities and Equity				
Accounts payable		$ 30.0		$ 15.0
Accruals		60.0		55.0
Notes payable		40.0		35.0
Total current liabilities		$130.0		$105.0
Long-term bonds		300.0		255.0
Total liabilities		$430.0		$360.0
Common stock		130.0		130.0
Retained earnings		285.0		260.0
Owners' equity		$415.0		$390.0
Total liabilities and equity		$845.0		$750.0

NOTE: Unilate has no preferred stock, so owners' equity includes common equity only.

COMMON STOCKHOLDERS' EQUITY (NET WORTH) The capital supplied by common stockholders—capital stock, paid-in capital, retained earnings, and, occasionally, certain reserves.

2. **Liabilities versus stockholders' equity.** The claims against assets are of two types—liabilities (or money the company owes) and the stockholders' ownership position.[2] The balance sheet must *balance*, so the **common stockholders' equity,** or **net worth,** is a residual which represents the amount stockholders would receive if all of the firm's assets could be sold at their book values and all of the liabilities could be paid at their book values. Unilate's 2000 net worth is

Assets − Liabilities = Stockholders' equity

$845 million − $430 million = $415 million

[2]One could divide liabilities into (1) debts owed to someone and (2) other items, such as deferred taxes, reserves, and so on. Because we do not make this distinction, the terms *debt* and *liabilities* are used synonymously. It should be noted that firms occasionally set up reserves for certain contingencies, such as the potential costs involved in a lawsuit currently in the courts. These reserves represent an accounting transfer from retained earnings to the reserve account. If the company wins the suit, retained earnings will be credited and the reserve will be eliminated. If it loses, a loss will be recorded, cash will be reduced, and the reserve will be eliminated.

Suppose assets decline in value—for example, suppose some of the accounts receivable are written off as bad debts. If liabilities remain constant, the value of the stockholders' equity must decline. Therefore, the risk of asset value fluctuations is borne by the stockholders. Note, however, that if asset values rise (perhaps because of inflation), these benefits will accrue exclusively to the stockholders. The change in the firm's net worth is reflected by changes in the retained earnings account; if bad debts are written off on the asset portion of the balance sheet, the retained earnings balance is reduced on the liabilities and equity portion.

3. **Preferred versus common stock.** Chapter 18 includes a detailed discussion of preferred stock and its use as a source of financing. As we will see, preferred stock is a hybrid, or a cross between common stock and debt. In the event of bankruptcy, the payoff to preferred stock ranks below debt but above common stock. Common stockholders, who are the "true" owners of the firm, often view preferred stock as another form of debt because, like debt, the payment to preferred stockholders (dividend) is fixed, so preferred stockholders do not benefit if the company's earnings grow. Also, most financial analysts combine preferred stock with debt when evaluating the financial position of a firm because, even though it is not a liability, the preferred dividend is considered a fixed obligation of the firm. Therefore, when the term "equity" is used in finance, we generally mean "common equity." Like most firms, Unilate Textiles does not currently use preferred stock financing.

4. **Breakdown of the common equity account.** A detailed discussion of the common equity accounts is given in Chapter 16. At this point, it is important to note that often the common equity section is divided into three accounts: common stock, paid-in capital, and retained earnings.

5. The **retained earnings** account is built up over time as the firm "saves," or reinvests, a part of its earnings rather than paying everything out as dividends. The other two common equity accounts arise from the issuance of stock to raise new capital.

   The breakdown of the common equity accounts shows whether the company actually earned the funds reported in its equity accounts or whether the funds came mainly from selling stock. This information is important both to creditors and to stockholders. For instance, a potential creditor would be interested in the amount of money the owners put up, while stockholders would want to know the form in which the money was put up. In the remainder of this chapter, we generally aggregate the three common equity accounts and call this sum common equity or net worth.

6. **Accounting alternatives.** Not every firm uses the same method to determine the account balances shown on the balance sheet. For instance, Unilate uses the FIFO (first-in, first-out) method to determine the inventory value shown on its balance sheet. It could have used the LIFO (last-in, first-out) method. During a period of rising prices, compared to LIFO, FIFO will produce a higher balance sheet inventory value but a lower cost of goods sold, thus a higher net income.

   In some cases, a company uses one accounting method to construct financial statements provided to stockholders and another accounting method for tax purposes, internal reports, and so on. For example, a company will use the most accelerated method permissible to calculate depreciation for tax purposes because accelerated methods lower the taxable income. At the same time, the company might use straight line depreciation for constructing financial statements

RETAINED EARNINGS
That portion of the firm's earnings that has been saved rather than paid out as dividends.

reported to stockholders, because a higher net income results. There is nothing illegal or unethical with this practice, but when evaluating firms, users of financial statements must be aware that more than one accounting alternative is available for constructing financial statements.

7. **The time dimension.** The balance sheet can be thought of as a snapshot of the firm's financial position *at a point in time*—for example, on December 31, 1999. Thus, on December 31, 1999, Unilate had $40 million of cash and marketable securities, but this account had been reduced to $15 million by the end of 2000. The income statement, on the other hand, reports on operations *over a period of time*—for example, during the calendar year 2000. Unilate's 2000 sales amounted to $1.5 billion, and its net income available to common stockholders was $54 million. The balance sheet changes every day as inventories are increased or decreased, as fixed assets are added or retired, as bank loans are increased or decreased, and so forth. Companies whose businesses are seasonal have especially large changes in their balance sheets during the year. For example, most retailers have large inventories just before Christmas but low inventories and high accounts receivable just after Christmas. Therefore, firms' balance sheets will change over the year, depending on the date on which the statement is constructed.

Statement of Retained Earnings

STATEMENT OF RETAINED EARNINGS
A statement reporting the change in the firm's retained earnings as a result of the income generated and retained during the year. The balance sheet figure for retained earnings is the sum of the earnings retained for each year the firm has been in business.

Changes in the common equity accounts between balance sheet dates are reported in the **statement of retained earnings.** Unilate's statement is shown in Table 3–3. The company earned $54 million during 2000, it paid out $29 million in common dividends, and it retained $25 million for reinvestment in the business. Thus, the balance sheet item "Retained Earnings" increased from $260 million at the end of 1999 to $285 million reported at the end of 2000. Note that the balance sheet account "Retained Earnings" represents a claim *against assets*, not assets per se. Further, firms retain earnings primarily to expand the business, and this means investing in plant and equipment, in inventories, and so on, *not* necessarily in a bank account. Changes in retained earnings represent the recognition that income generated by the firm during the accounting period has been reinvested in assets rather than paid out as dividends to stockholders. In other words, changes in retained earnings result because common stockholders allow the firm to reinvest in itself funds that otherwise could be distributed as dividends. *Thus, retained earnings as reported on the balance sheet do not represent cash and are not "available" for the payment of dividends or anything else.*[3]

---

[3]The amount reported in the retained earnings account is *not* an indication of the amount of cash the firm has. Cash (as of the balance sheet date) is found in the cash account—an asset account. A positive number in the retained earnings account indicates only that in the past, according to generally accepted accounting principles, the firm has earned an income, but its dividends have been less than its reported income. Even though a company reports record earnings and shows an increase in the retained earnings account, it still may be short of cash.

The same situation holds for individuals. You might own a new BMW (no loan), lots of clothes, and an expensive stereo, and, hence, have a high net worth, but if you had only 23 cents in your pocket plus $5 in your checking account, you would still be short of cash.

TABLE 3–3	Unilate Textiles: Statement of Retained Earnings for the Year Ending December 31, 2000 (millions of dollars)

Balance of retained earnings, December 31, 1999	$260
Add: 2000 net income	54
Less: 2000 dividends to stockholders	(29)
Balance of retained earnings, December 31, 2000	$285

Accounting Income versus Cash Flow

When you studied the construction of income statements in accounting, the emphasis probably was on determining the net income of the firm. In finance, however, we focus on *cash flows*. The value of an asset (or a whole firm) is determined by the cash flows it generates. The firm's net income is important, but cash flows are even more important, because cash is needed to continue normal business operations such as the payment of financial obligations, the purchase of assets, and the payment of dividends.

As we discussed in Chapter 1, the goal of the firm should be to maximize the price of its stock. Because the value of any asset, including a share of stock, depends on the cash flows produced by the asset, managers should strive to maximize cash flows available to investors over the long run. A business's **cash flows** include the cash receipts and the cash disbursements. The income statement contains revenues and expenses, some of which are cash items and some of which are noncash items. Generally the largest noncash item included on the income statement is depreciation, which is an operating cost. We need to understand the role of depreciation for the recognition of income, as well as the impact depreciation has on cash flows.

Depreciation results because we want to match revenues and expenses, not because we want to match cash inflows and cash outflows, to compute the income earned by the firm during a specific accounting period. When a firm purchases a long-term asset, it is intended to be used to produce revenues for multiple years in the future. The cash payment for the asset occurs on the date of purchase. But because the productive capacity of the asset is not used up in the year of purchase, its full cost is not recognized as an expense in that year. Rather, the value of the asset is expensed away over its lifetime, because, as it is used to generate revenues, the value of the asset declines. Depreciation is the means by which the reduction in the asset's value, which is an operating cost, is matched with the revenues the asset helps to produce. For example, if a machine with a life of five years and a zero expected salvage value was purchased in 1999 for $100,000, the total $100,000 cost is not expensed in 1999; instead, it is charged against production over the machine's five-year depreciable life. The annual depreciation charge is deducted from sales revenues, along with other operating costs such as labor and raw materials, to determine income. However, because funds were expended back in 1999, the depreciation charged against income in 2000 through 2003 is not a cash outlay, as are labor or raw materials charges. The bottom line is that *depreciation is a noncash charge used to compute net income, so if net income is used to obtain an estimate of the net cash flow from operations, the amount of depreciation must be added back to the income figure.*

CASH FLOWS
The cash receipts and the cash disbursements, as opposed to the revenues and expenses reported for the computation of net income, generated by a firm during some specified period.

To see how depreciation affects cash flows, consider the following simplified income statement (Column 1) and cash flow statement (Column 2). Here we assume that all sales revenues were received in cash during the year and that all costs except depreciation were paid in cash during the year. Cash flows are seen to equal net income plus depreciation:

	INCOME STATEMENT (1)		CASH FLOWS (2)	
Sales revenues		$750		$750
Cost, except depreciation	$(525)		$(525)	
Depreciation (DEP)	(75)		—	
Total operating costs		(600)		(525) (Cash costs)
Earnings before taxes		$150		$225 (Pretax cash flow)
Taxes (40%)		(60)		(60) (From Column 1)
Net income (NI)		$ 90		
Add back depreciation		75		
Net cash flow = NI + DEP		$165		$165

As we will see in Chapter 7, a stock's value is based on the cash flows that investors expect it to provide in the future. Although any individual investor could sell the stock and receive cash for it, the *cash flow* provided by the stock itself is the expected future dividend stream, and that expected dividend stream provides the fundamental basis for the stock's value.

Because dividends are paid in cash, a company's ability to pay dividends depends on its cash flows. Cash flows generally are related to **accounting profit,** which is simply net income reported on the income statement. Although companies with relatively high accounting profits generally have relatively high cash flows, the relationship is not precise. Therefore, investors are concerned with cash flow projections as well as profit projections.

Firms can be thought of as having two separate but related bases of value: *existing assets,* which provide profits and cash flows, and *growth opportunities,* which represent opportunities to make new investments that will increase future profits and cash flows. The ability to take advantage of growth opportunities often depends on the availability of the cash needed to buy new assets, and the cash flows from existing assets are often the primary source of the funds used to make profitable new investments. This is another reason why both investors and managers are concerned with cash flows as well as profits.

For our purposes, it is useful to divide cash flows into two classes: (1) *operating cash flows* and (2) *other cash flows.* **Operating cash flows** are those that arise from normal operations, and they are, in essence, the difference between cash collections and cash expenses, including taxes paid. Other cash flows arise from borrowing, from the sale of fixed assets, or from the repurchase of common stock. Our focus here is on operating cash flows.

Operating cash flows can differ from accounting profits (or net income) for two primary reasons:

1. All the taxes reported on the income statement might not have to be paid during the current year, or, under certain circumstances, the actual cash payments

ACCOUNTING PROFIT
A firm's net income as reported on its income statement.

OPERATING CASH FLOWS
Those cash flows that arise from normal operations; the difference between cash collections and cash expenses.

for taxes might exceed the tax figure deducted from sales to calculate net income. The reasons for these tax cash flow differentials are discussed in detail in accounting courses.

2. Sales might be on credit, hence not represent cash, and some of the expenses (or costs) deducted from sales to determine profits might not be cash costs. Most important, depreciation is not a cash cost.

Thus, operating cash flows could be larger or smaller than accounting profits during any given year. The effect of the major noncash expense, depreciation, was discussed earlier, and we will consider the cash flow implications of credit sales as opposed to cash sales in a later chapter.

The Cash Flow Cycle

As a company like Unilate goes about its business, it sells products. Sales lead (1) to a reduction of inventories, (2) to an increase in cash or accounts receivable, and (3) if the sales price exceeds the cost of the item sold, to a profit. So, when Unilate sells its products, both the income statement and the balance sheet are affected. It is critical that you understand (1) businesses deal with physical units like autos, computers, or aluminum; (2) physical transactions are translated into dollar terms through the accounting system; and (3) the purpose of financial analysis is to examine the accounting numbers in order to determine how efficiently the firm produces and sells physical goods and services and to evaluate the financial position of the firm.

Several factors make financial analysis difficult. One of them is the variations that exist in accounting methods among firms. As was discussed previously, different methods of inventory valuation and depreciation can lead to differences in reported profits for otherwise identical firms, and a good financial analyst must be able to adjust for these differences if he or she is to make valid comparisons among companies. Another factor involves timing—an action is taken at one point in time, but its full effects cannot be accurately measured until some later period.

CASH FLOW CYCLE
The way in which actual net cash, as opposed to accounting net income, flows into or out of the firm during some specified period.

To understand how timing influences the financial statements, we must understand the **cash flow cycle** as set forth in Figure 3–1. In the figure, rectangles represent balance sheet accounts—assets and claims against assets—whereas circles represent income items and cash flow activities that affect balance sheet accounts. Each rectangle can be thought of as a reservoir, and there is a certain amount of the asset or liability in the reservoir (account) on each balance sheet date. Various transactions cause changes in the accounts, just as adding or subtracting water changes the level in a reservoir. The direction of the change in each reservoir is indicated by the direction of the arrow(s) connected to that reservoir. For example, because collecting an account receivable reduces the receivables reservoir but increases the cash reservoir, an arrow goes *from* the accounts receivable reservoir *to* the collections circle, then *from* the collections circle *to* the cash and marketable securities reservoir.

The cash account is the focal point of the figure. Certain events, such as collecting accounts receivable or borrowing money from the bank, will cause the cash account to increase, while the payment of taxes, interest, dividends, and accounts payable will cause it to decline. Similar comments could be made about all the balance sheet accounts—their balances rise, fall, or remain constant depending on events that occur during the period under study, which for Unilate is January 1, 2000 through December 31, 2000.

FIGURE 3–1 Cash and Materials Flows within the Firm (millions of dollars)

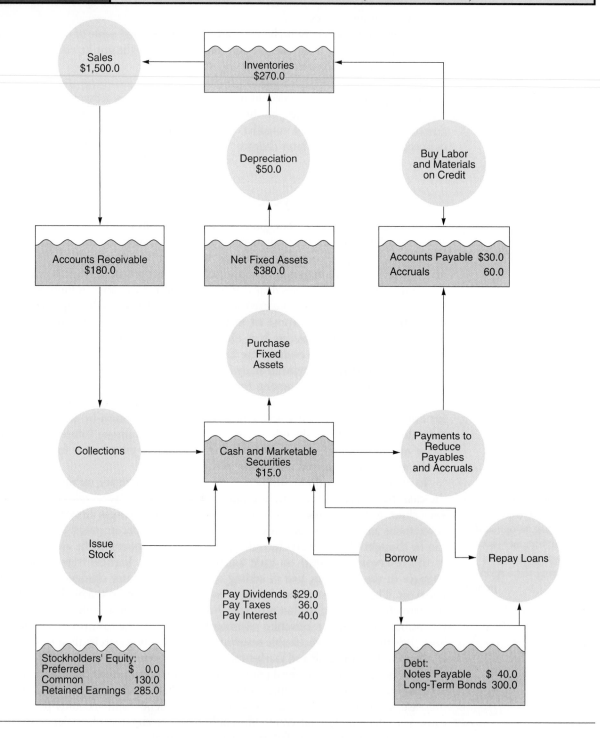

Projected increases in sales might require the firm to raise cash by borrowing from its bank or by selling new stock. For example, if Unilate anticipates an increase in sales, it will (1) expend cash to buy or build fixed assets; (2) step up purchases of raw materials, thereby increasing both raw materials inventories and accounts payable; (3) increase production, which will lead to an increase in both accrued wages and work-in-process; and (4) eventually build up its finished goods inventory. Some cash will have been expended and hence removed from the cash account, and the firm will have obligated itself to expend still more cash within a few weeks to pay off its accounts payable and its accrued wages. These cash-using events will have occurred before any new cash has been generated from sales. Even when the expected sales do occur, there will still be a lag in the generation of cash until receivables are collected—because Unilate grants credit for 30 days, it will have to wait 30 days (perhaps longer) after a sale is made before cash comes in. Depending on how much cash the firm had at the beginning of the buildup, on the length of its production-sales-collection cycle, and on how long it can delay payment of its own payables and accrued wages, Unilate might have to obtain substantial amounts of additional cash by selling stock or bonds or by borrowing from the bank.

If the firm is profitable, its sales revenues will exceed its costs, and its cash inflows eventually will exceed its cash outlays. However, even a profitable business can experience a cash shortage if it is growing rapidly. It might have to pay for plant, materials, and labor before cash from the expanded sales starts flowing in. For this reason, rapidly growing firms generally require large bank loans or capital from other sources.

An unprofitable firm, such as one headed for bankruptcy, will have larger cash outlays than inflows. This, in turn, will lower the cash account and also cause a slowdown in the payment of accrued wages and accounts payable, and it might also lead to heavy borrowings. Accordingly, liabilities rise to excessive levels in unprofitable firms. Similarly, an overly ambitious expansion plan will result in excessive inventories and fixed assets, while too lenient a credit/collection policy will result in high accounts receivable, which eventually will result in bad debts and reduced profits.

If a firm runs out of cash and cannot obtain enough to meet its obligations, then it cannot operate, and it will have to declare bankruptcy. In fact, thousands of companies have been forced to do just that. Therefore, an accurate cash flow forecast is a critical element in managerial finance.[4] Financial analysts are well aware of all this, and they use the analytical techniques discussed in the remainder of this chapter to help discover cash flow problems before they become serious.

Statement of Cash Flows

STATEMENT OF CASH FLOWS
A statement reporting the impact of a firm's operating, investing, and financing activities on cash flows over an accounting period.

The graphic cash flow analysis set forth in Figure 3–1 is converted into numerical form and reported in annual reports as the **statement of cash flows.** This statement is designed to show how the firm's operations have affected its cash position by examining the investment (uses of cash) and financing decisions (sources of cash) of the firm. The information contained in the statement of cash flows can help answer questions such as: Is the firm generating the cash needed to purchase additional fixed assets for growth? Does the firm have excess cash flows that can be used to repay debt or to

---

[4]The mechanics of a cash forecast are explained later in the book along with a more detailed discussion of cash management.

invest in new products? This information is useful both for financial managers and investors, so the statement of cash flows is an important part of the annual report.

Constructing a statement of cash flows is relatively easy. First, to some extent, the cash flow effects of a firm's operations are shown in its income statement. For example, Unilate reported its 2000 net income as $54 million, which we know includes a $50 million depreciation expense that is a noncash operating cost. So, if the $50 million depreciation expense is added back to the $54 million net income, we have an estimate of cash flows from normal operations equal to $104 million. For most firms, however, some of the reported revenues have not been collected and some of the reported expenses have not been paid at the time the income statement is constructed. To adjust the *estimate* of cash flows obtained from the income statement and to account for cash flows not reflected in the income statement, we need to examine the impact of changes in the balance sheet accounts during the year in question. Looking at the changes in the balance sheet accounts from the beginning to the end of the year, we want to identify which items provided cash (source) and which items used cash (use) during the year. To determine whether a change in a balance sheet account was a source or a use of cash, we can use the following simple rules:

SOURCES OF CASH	USES OF CASH
Increase in a Liability or Equity Account	***Decrease in a Liability or Equity Account***
Borrowing funds or selling stock provides the firm with cash.	Paying off a loan or buying back stock uses cash.
Decrease in an Asset Account	***Increase in an Asset Account***
Selling inventory or collecting receivables provides cash.	Buying fixed assets or buying more inventory uses cash.

Using these rules, we can identify which changes in Unilate's balance sheet accounts provided cash and which changes used cash during 2000. Table 3–4 shows the results of this identification. In addition, the table includes the cash flow information contained in Unilate's 2000 income statement.

The information contained in Table 3–4 can be used to construct the statement of cash flows shown in Table 3–5.[5] Each balance sheet change in Table 3–4 is classified as resulting from (1) operations, (2) long-term investments, or (3) financing activities. Operating cash flows are those associated with the production and sale of goods and services. The amount of net income plus depreciation is the primary operating cash flow, but changes in accounts payable, accounts receivable, inventories, and accruals are also classified as operating cash flows, because these accounts are directly affected by the firm's day-to-day operations. Investment cash flows arise from the purchase or sale of plant, property, and equipment. Financing cash inflows result from issuing debt or common stock, while financing outflows occur when the firm pays dividends or repays debt. The cash inflows and outflows from these three activities are summed to determine their impact on the firm's liquidity position, which is measured by the change in the cash and marketable securities accounts.

---

[5]There are two different formats for presenting the cash flow statement. The method we present here is called the *indirect method*. Cash flows from operations are calculated by starting with net income, adding back expenses not paid out of cash and subtracting revenues that do not provide cash. Using the *direct method*, operating cash flows are found by summing all revenues that provide cash and then subtracting all expenses that are paid in cash. Both formats produce the same result, and both are accepted by the Financial Accounting Standards Board.

TABLE 3-4	Unilate Textiles: Cash Sources and Uses during 2000 (millions of dollars)

	12/31/00	12/31/99	CHANGE SOURCES	USES
Balance Sheet Changes				
Cash and marketable securities	$ 15.0	$ 40.0	$ 25.0	
Accounts receivable	180.0	160.0		$ 20.0
Inventory	270.0	200.0		70.0
Gross plant and equipment	680.0	600.0		80.0
Accounts payable	30.0	15.0	15.0	
Accruals	60.0	55.0	5.0	
Notes payable	40.0	35.0	5.0	
Long-term bonds	300.0	255.0	45.0	
Common stock (25 million shares)	130.0	130.0		
Income Statement Information				
Net income		$ 54.0		
Add: Depreciation		50.0		
Gross cash flow from operations		$104.0	104.0	
Dividend payment		29.0	—	29.0
Totals			$199.0	$199.0

The top part of Table 3–5 shows cash flows generated by and used in operations—for Unilate, operations provided net cash flows of $34 million. The operating cash flows are generated principally from the day-to-day operations of the firm, and this amount can be determined by adjusting the net income figure to account for noncash items. The day-to-day operations of Unilate in 2000 provided $124 million of funds; however, the increases in inventories and investment in receivables during the year accounted for a combined use of funds equal to almost 73 percent of this amount, or $90 million. The second section shows long-term investing activities. Unilate purchased fixed assets totaling $80 million; this was its only investment activity during 2000. Unilate's financing activities, shown in the lower section of Table 3–5, included borrowing from banks (notes payable), selling new bonds, and paying dividends to its common stockholders. Unilate raised $50 million by borrowing, but it paid $29 million in dividends, so its net inflow of funds from financing activities during 2000 was $21 million.

When all of these sources and uses of cash are totaled, we see that Unilate had a $25 million cash shortfall during 2000. It met that shortfall by drawing down its cash and marketable securities holdings by $25 million, as shown in Table 3–2, the firm's balance sheet, and in Table 3–4.

Unilate's statement of cash flows should be of some concern to the financial manager and to outside analysts. The company generated $34 million cash from operations, it spent an additional $80 million on new fixed assets, and it paid out another $29 million in dividends. It covered these cash outlays by borrowing heavily, by selling off marketable securities, and by drawing down its bank account. Obviously, this

TABLE 3–5	Unilate Textiles: Statement of Cash Flows for the Period Ending December 31, 2000 (millions of dollars)

Cash Flows from Operating Activities

Net income	$ 54.0	
Additions to net income		
Depreciation[a]	50.0	
Increase in accounts payable	15.0	
Increase in accruals	5.0	
Subtractions from net income		
Increase in accounts receivable	(20.0)	
Increase in inventory	(70.0)	
Net cash flow from operations		$ 34.0

Cash Flows from Long-Term Investing Activities

Acquisition of fixed assets		$(80.0)

Cash Flows from Financing Activities

Increase in notes payable	$ 5.0	
Increase in bonds	45.0	
Dividend payment	(29.0)	
Net cash flow from financing		$ 21.0
Net change in cash		$(25.0)
Cash at the beginning of the year		40.0
Cash at the end of the year		$ 15.0

[a]Depreciation is a noncash expense that was deducted when calculating net income. It must be added back to show the correct cash flow from operations.

situation cannot continue year after year, so something will have to be done. We will consider some of the actions the financial manager might recommend, but first we must examine the financial statements in more depth.

Self-Test Questions

Identify the two types of information given in the annual report.

Describe these four basic financial statements: (1) the income statement, (2) the balance sheet, (3) the statement of retained earnings, and (4) the statement of cash flows.

Explain the following statement: "Retained earnings as reported on the balance sheet do not represent cash and are not 'available' for the payment of dividends or anything else."

Differentiate between operating cash flows and other cash flows.

List two reasons why operating cash flows can differ from net income.

In accounting, the emphasis is on the determination of net income. What is emphasized in finance, and why is this emphasis important?

Assuming that depreciation is the only noncash cost, how can someone calculate a business's cash flow?

Describe the general rules for identifying whether changes in balance sheet accounts represent sources or uses of cash.

Ratio Analysis

Financial statements provide information about a firm's position at a point in time as well as its operations over some past period. However, the real value of financial statements lies in the fact that they can be used to help predict a firm's financial position in the future and to determine expected earnings and dividends. From an investor's standpoint, *predicting the future is what financial statement analysis is all about*, while from management's standpoint, *financial statement analysis is useful both as a way to anticipate future conditions and, more important, as a starting point for planning actions that will influence the future course of events.*

An analysis of the firm's ratios generally is the first step in a financial analysis. The ratios are designed to show relationships between financial statement accounts *within* firms and *between* firms. Translating accounting numbers into relative values, or ratios, allows us to compare the financial position of one firm to another, even if their sizes are significantly different. For example, Firm A might have debt of $5,248,760 and interest charges of $419,900, while Firm B might have debt of $52,647,980 and interest charges of $3,948,600. Which company is stronger? The true burden of these debts, and the companies' ability to repay them, can be ascertained (1) by comparing each firm's debt to its assets and (2) by comparing the interest it must pay to the income it has available for payment of interest. Such comparisons are made by ratio analysis.

In the following paragraphs, we calculate the 2000 financial ratios for Unilate Textiles and then evaluate those ratios in relation to the industry averages.[6] Note that all dollar amounts in the ratio calculations are in millions, except where per share values are used.

Liquidity Ratios

LIQUID ASSET
An asset that can be easily converted into cash without significant loss of its original value.

A **liquid asset** is one that can be easily converted to cash without significant loss of its original value. Converting assets, especially current assets such as inventory and receivables, to cash is the primary means by which a firm obtains the funds needed to pay its current bills. Therefore, a firm's "liquid position" deals with the question of how well the firm is able to meet its current obligations. Short-term, or current, assets are more easily converted to cash (more liquid) than long-term assets. So, in general, one firm would be considered more liquid than another firm if it has a greater proportion of its total assets in the form of current assets.

Unilate has debts totaling $130 million that must be paid off within the coming year. Will it have trouble satisfying those obligations? A full liquidity analysis requires

---

[6]In addition to the ratios discussed in this section, financial analysts also employ a tool known as common size balance sheets and income statements. To form a *common size* balance sheet, one simply divides each asset and liability item by total assets and then expresses the result as a percentage. The resultant percentage statement can be compared with statements of larger or smaller firms, or with those of the same firm over time. To form a common size income statement, one simply divides each income statement item by sales.

LIQUIDITY RATIOS
Ratios that show the relationship of a firm's cash and other current assets to its current liabilities.

the use of cash budgets (described later in the book), but, by relating the amount of cash and other current assets to the firm's current obligations, ratio analysis provides a quick, easy-to-use measure of liquidity. Two commonly used **liquidity ratios** are discussed in this section.

Current Ratio   The **current ratio** is calculated by dividing current assets by current liabilities:

CURRENT RATIO
This ratio is calculated by dividing current assets by current liabilities. It indicates the extent to which current liabilities are covered by assets expected to be converted into cash in the near future.

$$\text{Current ratio} = \frac{\text{Current assets}}{\text{Current liabilities}}$$

$$= \frac{\$465.0}{\$130.0} = 3.6 \text{ times}$$

Industry average $= 4.1$ times

Current assets normally include cash, marketable securities, accounts receivable, and inventories. Current liabilities consist of accounts payable, short-term notes payable, current maturities of long-term debt, accrued income taxes, and other accrued expenses (principally wages).

If a company is getting into financial difficulty, it begins paying its bills (accounts payable) more slowly, borrowing more from its bank, and so on. If current liabilities are rising faster than current assets, the current ratio will fall, and this could spell trouble. Because the current ratio provides the best single indicator of the extent to which the claims of short-term creditors are covered by assets that are expected to be converted to cash fairly quickly, it is the most commonly used measure of short-term solvency. Care must be taken when examining the current ratio, just as it should be when examining any ratio individually. For example, just because a firm has a low current ratio, even one below 1.0, this does not mean the current obligations cannot be met.

Unilate's current ratio of 3.6 is below the average for its industry, 4.1, so its liquidity position is somewhat weak. Still, because current assets are scheduled to be converted to cash in the near future, it is highly probable that they could be liquidated at close to their stated value. With a current ratio of 3.6, Unilate could liquidate current assets at only 28 percent of book value and still pay off current creditors in full.[7]

Although industry average figures are discussed later in some detail, it should be noted at this point that an industry average is not a magic number that all firms should strive to maintain—in fact, some very well-managed firms will be above the average while other good firms will be below it. However, if a firm's ratios are far removed from the average for its industry, an analyst should be concerned about why this variance occurs. Thus, a significant deviation from the industry average should signal the analyst (or management) to *check further*, even if the deviation is considered to be in the "good" direction. For example, we know that Unilate's liquidity position currently is below average. But what would you conclude if Unilate's current ratio actually was nearly twice that of the industry, perhaps 8.0? Is this good? Maybe not. Because current assets, which are considered liquid, generally generate lower rates of return than long-term assets, it might be argued that firms with too much liquidity are not investing wisely.

---

[7]$1/3.6 = 0.28$, or 28 percent. Note that $0.28(\$465) = \$130$, which is the amount of current liabilities.

QUICK (ACID TEST)
RATIO
This ratio is calculated by
deducting inventories
from current assets and
dividing the remainder by
current liabilities. The
quick ratio is a variation of
the current ratio.

Quick, or Acid Test, Ratio   The **quick**, or **acid test, ratio** is calculated by deducting inventories from current assets and then dividing the remainder by current liabilities:

$$\text{Quick, or acid test, ratio} = \frac{\text{Current assets} - \text{Inventories}}{\text{Current liabilities}}$$

$$= \frac{\$465.0 - \$270.0}{\$130.0} = \frac{\$195.0}{\$130.0} = 1.5 \text{ times}$$

Industry average = 2.1 times

Inventories typically are the least liquid of a firm's current assets; hence, they are the assets on which losses are most likely to occur in the event of liquidation. Therefore, a measure of the firm's ability to pay off short-term obligations without relying on the sale of inventories is important.

The industry average quick ratio is 2.1, so Unilate's ratio value of 1.5 is low in comparison with the ratios of other firms in its industry. Still, if the accounts receivable can be collected, the company can pay off its current liabilities even without having to liquidate its inventory.

Our evaluation of the liquidity ratios suggests that Unilate's liquidity position currently is poor. To get a better idea of why Unilate is in this situation, we must examine its asset management ratios.

Asset Management Ratios

The second group of ratios, the **asset management ratios,** measures how effectively the firm is managing its assets. These ratios are designed to answer this question: Does the total amount of each type of asset as reported on the balance sheet seem reasonable, too high, or too low in view of current and projected sales levels? Firms invest in assets to generate revenues both in the current period and in future periods. To purchase their assets, Unilate and other companies must borrow or obtain funds from other sources. If they have too many assets, their interest expenses will be too high; hence, their profits will be depressed. On the other hand, because production is affected by the capacity of assets, if assets are too low, profitable sales might be lost because the firm is unable to manufacture enough products.

ASSET MANAGEMENT
RATIOS
A set of ratios that
measures how effectively a
firm is managing its assets.

Inventory Turnover   The **inventory turnover ratio** is defined as follows:[8]

INVENTORY
TURNOVER RATIO
The ratio calculated by
dividing cost of goods sold
by inventories.

$$\text{Inventory turnover ratio} = \frac{\text{Cost of goods sold}}{\text{Inventories}}$$

$$= \frac{\$1,230.0}{\$270.0} = 4.6 \text{ times}$$

Industry average = 7.4 times

---

[8]Some compilers of financial ratio statistics, such as Dun & Bradstreet, use the ratio of sales to inventories carried at cost to represent inventory turnover. If this form of the inventory turnover ratio is used, we must recognize that the true turnover will be overstated, because sales are stated at market prices while inventories are carried at cost.

As a rough approximation, each item of Unilate's inventory is sold out and re-stocked, or "turned over," 4.6 times per year, which is considerably lower than the in-dustry average of 7.4 times.[9] This suggests that Unilate is holding excessive stocks of inventory; excess stocks are, of course, unproductive and represent an investment with a low or zero rate of return. Unilate's low inventory turnover ratio makes us question the current ratio. With such a low turnover, we must wonder whether the firm is hold-ing damaged or obsolete goods (e.g., textile types and patterns from previous years) not actually worth their stated value.

Care must be used when calculating and using the inventory turnover ratio because purchases of inventory, thus the cost of goods sold figure, occur over the entire year, whereas the inventory figure is for one point in time. For this reason, it is better to use an average inventory measure.[10] If the firm's business is highly seasonal, or if there has been a strong upward or downward sales trend during the year, it is essential to make such an adjustment. To maintain comparability with industry averages, however, we did not use the average inventory figure in our computations.

DAYS SALES OUTSTANDING (DSO)
The ratio calculated by dividing accounts receivable by average sales per day; indicates the average length of time it takes the firm to collect for credit sales.

Day Sales Outstanding   Days sales outstanding (DSO), also called the "average collection period" (ACP), is used to evaluate the firm's ability to collect its credit sales in a timely manner. DSO is calculated as follows:[11]

$$\text{DSO} = \frac{\text{Day sales}}{\text{outstanding}} = \frac{\text{Receivables}}{\text{Average sales per day}} = \frac{\text{Receivables}}{\left[\frac{\text{Annual sales}}{360}\right]}$$

$$= \frac{\$180.0}{\left[\frac{\$1{,}500.0}{360}\right]} = \frac{\$180.0}{\$4.167} = 43.2 \text{ days}$$

$$\text{Industry average} = 32.1 \text{ days}$$

---

[9]"Turnover" is a term that originated many years ago with the old Yankee peddler who would load up his wagon with goods then go off on his route to peddle his wares. The merchandise was his "work-ing capital," because it was what he actually sold, or "turned over," to produce his profits, whereas his "turnover" was the number of trips he took each year. Annual sales divided by inventory equaled turnover, or trips per year.

[10]Preferably, the average inventory value should be calculated by summing the monthly figures dur-ing the year and dividing by 12. If monthly data are not available, one can add the beginning and end-ing figures and divide by two; this will adjust for growth but not for seasonal effects. Using this approach, Unilate's average inventory for 2000 would be $235 = ($200 + $270)/2, and its inventory turnover would be 5.2 = $1,230/$235, which is still well below the industry average given above.

[11]To compute DSO using this equation, we have to assume all of the firm's sales are credit. We usually compute DSO in this manner because information on credit sales generally is unavailable, so total sales must be used. Because all firms do not have the same percentage of credit sales, there is a chance that the days sales outstanding will be somewhat in error. Also, note that by convention the financial com-munity generally uses 360 rather than 365 as the number of days in the year for purposes such as this. Finally, it would be better to use average receivables, either an average of the monthly figures or (be-ginning receivables + ending receivables)/2 = ($160 + $180)/2 = $170 in the formula. Had the annual average receivables been used, Unilate's DSO would have been $170/$4.17 = 40.8 days. The 40.8-day figure is the more accurate one, but because the industry average was based on year-end receivables, we used 43.2 days for our comparison. The DSO is discussed further in Chapter 14.

The DSO represents the average length of time that the firm must wait after making a sale before receiving cash, which is the average collection period. Unilate has about 43 days' sales outstanding, well above the 32-day industry average. The DSO can also be evaluated by comparison with the terms on which the firm sells its goods. For example, Unilate's sales terms call for payment within 30 days, so the fact that 43 days' sales, not 30 days', are outstanding indicates that customers, on the average, are not paying their bills on time. If the trend in DSO over the past few years has been rising, but the credit policy has not been changed, this would be even stronger evidence that steps should be taken to improve the time it takes to collect accounts receivable. This seems to be the case for Unilate because its 1999 DSO was about 40 days.

**FIXED ASSETS
TURNOVER RATIO**
The ratio of sales to net
fixed assets.

Fixed Assets Turnover   The **fixed assets turnover ratio** measures how effectively the firm uses its plant and equipment to help generate sales. It is computed as follows:

$$\text{Fixed assets turnover ratio} = \frac{\text{Sales}}{\text{Net fixed assets}}$$

$$= \frac{\$1,500.0}{\$380.0} = 3.9 \text{ times}$$

$$\text{Industry average} = 4.0 \text{ times}$$

Unilate's ratio of 3.9 times is almost equal to the industry average, indicating that the firm is using its fixed assets about as intensively (efficiently) as are the other firms in the industry. Unilate seems to have neither too much nor too few fixed assets in relation to other firms.

Care should be taken when using the fixed assets turnover ratio to compare different firms. Recall from accounting that most balance sheet accounts are stated in terms of historical costs. Inflation might cause the value of many assets that were purchased in the past to be seriously understated. Therefore, if we were comparing an old firm that acquired its fixed assets years ago at low prices with a new company that acquired its fixed assets only recently, we probably would find that the old firm had a higher fixed assets turnover. Because financial analysts typically do not have the data necessary to make inflation adjustments, they must simply recognize that a problem exists and deal with it judgmentally. In Unilate's case, the issue is not a serious one because all firms in the industry are about the same age and have been expanding at about the same rate; thus, the balance sheets of the comparison firms are indeed comparable.

**TOTAL ASSETS
TURNOVER RATIO**
The ratio calculated by
dividing sales by total
assets.

Total Assets Turnover   The final asset management ratio, the **total assets turnover ratio,** measures the turnover of all of the firm's assets. It is calculated as follows:

$$\text{Total assets turnover ratio} = \frac{\text{Sales}}{\text{Total assets}}$$

$$= \frac{\$1,500.0}{\$845.0} = 1.8 \text{ times}$$

$$\text{Industry average} = 2.1 \text{ times}$$

Unilate's ratio is somewhat below the industry average, indicating that the company is not generating a sufficient volume of business given its investment in total assets. To become more efficient, sales should be increased, some assets should be disposed of, or a combination of these steps should be taken.

Our examination of Unilate's asset management ratios shows that its fixed assets turnover ratio is very close to the industry average, but its total assets turnover is below average. The fixed assets turnover ratio excludes current assets, while the total assets turnover ratio does not. Therefore, comparison of these ratios confirms our conclusion from the analysis of the liquidity ratios—Unilate seems to have a liquidity problem. The fact that the inventory turnover ratio and the average collection period are below average suggests, at least in part, the poor liquidity might be attributable to problems with inventory and receivables management. Slow sales and slow collections of credit sales suggest Unilate might rely more heavily on external funds, such as loans, than the industry to pay current obligations. Examining the debt management ratios will help us to determine if this actually is the case.

Debt Management Ratios

The extent to which a firm uses debt financing has three important implications: (1) By raising funds through debt, stockholder ownership is not diluted. (2) Creditors look to the equity, or owner-supplied funds, to provide a margin of safety; if the stockholders have provided only a small proportion of the total financing, the risks of the enterprise are borne mainly by its creditors. (3) If the firm earns more on investments financed with borrowed funds than it pays in interest, the return on the owners' capital is magnified, or "leveraged."

FINANCIAL LEVERAGE
The use of debt financing. **Financial leverage,** or borrowing, affects the expected rate of return realized by stockholders for two reasons: (1) the interest on debt is tax deductible while dividends are not, so paying interest lowers the firm's tax bill, all else equal; and (2) usually the rate a firm earns from its investments in assets is different from the rate at which it borrows. If the firm has healthy operations, it generally invests the funds it raises at a rate of return that is greater than the interest rate on its debt. In combination with the tax advantage debt has compared to stock, the higher investment rate of return produces a magnified positive return to the stockholders. Under these conditions, leverage works to the advantage of the firm and its stockholders. Unfortunately, financial leverage is a double-edged sword. When the firm experiences poor business conditions, typically sales are lower and costs are higher than expected, but the cost of borrowing still must be paid. The *costs* (interest payments) associated with borrowing are contractual and do not vary with sales, and they must be paid to keep the firm from potential bankruptcy. Therefore, the required interest payments might be a very significant burden for a firm that has liquidity problems. In fact, if the interest payments are high enough, a firm with a positive operating income actually could end up with a negative return to stockholders. Under these conditions, leverage works to the detriment of the firm and its stockholders.

A detailed discussion of financial leverage is given in the next chapter. For the purposes of ratio analysis, we need to understand that firms with relatively high debt ratios have higher expected returns when the business is normal or good, but they are exposed to risk of loss when the business is poor. Thus, firms with low debt ratios are less risky, but they also forgo the opportunity to leverage up their return on equity. The prospects of high returns are desirable, but investors are averse to risk. Therefore, decisions about the use of debt require firms to balance higher expected returns against increased risk. Determining the optimal amount of debt for a given firm is a complicated process, and we defer a discussion of this topic until Chapter 11. For now

✳ INDUSTRY PRACTICE

What Do Corporate Controllers Really Think about Financial Reporting Requirements?

How do you think the persons who construct financial statements feel about financial disclosure requirements? A recent study conducted by *CFO*, a publication whose readership consists primarily of financial executives, gives some indication of what it takes to construct financial statements and how corporate controllers feel about the process. In the study, *CFO* surveyed controllers from 500 large U.S. corporations and found some interesting results.

According to the controllers, an average of 1,011 hours are spent preparing annual reports. In addition, nearly three quarters of the respondents indicated that they have six or more employees involved in the preparation of the reports; about 40 percent have more than ten persons working on the reports. Thus, on average, it takes one full-time employee about 126 days to construct annual reports; six employees would need 21 days to complete the same task. Unfortunately, the future trend is not encouraging, because most of the controllers believe the time it takes to prepare the reports has increased by more than 25 percent during the past decade, primarily because the reporting requirements have become more rigorous. Costs seem to have increased comparably, but not many (less than 20 percent) of the controllers could provide an indication of how much is spent on financial disclosure. Those who could provide estimates said the costs range from $85,000 to nearly $5 million.

With all the time, effort, and costs required to prepare annual reports, you would expect that the end product would be very beneficial to the intended audiences, which we generally view as investors and creditors. But the study produced two interesting results. First, about 86 percent of the controllers that responded said that they believe their most important users, thus their intended audience, are either financial analysts (55 percent) or institutional investors (35 percent). Only 18 percent responded that they believe the intended audience is individual shareholders and 12 percent indicated the audience consists of the regulators who set the reporting standards. Second, it seems controllers do not believe the required reports provide very useful information. One half of the respondents indicated that they believe shareholders cannot easily understand the information included in their financial reports.

Recently, regulatory and standard-setting organizations, such as the American Institute of Certified Public Accounts (AICPA), the Financial Accounting Standards Board (FASB), and the Securities and Exchange Commission (SEC), proposed new financial reporting guidelines, including the disclosure of nonfinancial information, such as customer satisfaction, and forward-looking information, such as the strategies the firm intends to pursue in the future. One reason that was given for making such proposals was that financial information that is currently disclosed has become less useful to investors and creditors. When asked about the proposed changes, 84 percent of the controllers indicated that such information would not improve shareholders' understanding of their companies. In fact, 54 percent indicated that their reports already include nonfinancial information and 39 percent said that forward-looking information is included. Even so, a majority of the controllers opposed requirements to include either type of information in financial reporting in the future.

In general, the results of the *CFO* study show that controllers believe financial reporting is an onerous, but necessary task. It appears, however, that they do not believe the information provided is as useful to shareholders as regulators and those who set reporting standards think. Clearly, then, changes should be made. But what should those changes be? The answer is not clear, primarily because there is debate concerning whether those who set the standards for financial reporting are more concerned with the needs of the reports users or with trying to ensure that reporting systems are not abused either by management or by investors.

SOURCES: Lori Calabro, "The View from the Trenches," *CFO*, January 1997, 23; Randy Myers, "Indecent Disclosure," *CFO*, January 1997, 21–28.

we will simply look at two procedures analysts use to examine the firm's debt in a financial statement analysis: (1) they check balance sheet ratios to determine the extent to which borrowed funds have been used to finance assets, and (2) they review income statement ratios to determine how well operating profits can cover fixed charges such as interest. These two sets of ratios are complementary, so analysts use both types.

DEBT RATIO
The ratio of total debt to total assets. It is a measure of the percentage of funds provided by creditors.

Debt Ratio The **debt ratio** measures the percentage of the firm's assets financed by creditors (borrowing), and it is computed as follows:

$$\text{Debt ratio} = \frac{\text{Total debt}}{\text{Total assets}}$$

$$= \frac{\$130.0 + \$300.0}{\$845.0} = \frac{\$430.0}{\$845.0} = 0.509 = 50.9\%$$

$$\text{Industry average} = 45.0\%$$

Total debt includes both current liabilities and long-term debt. Creditors prefer low debt ratios, because the lower the ratio, the greater the cushion against creditors' losses in the event of liquidation. The owners, on the other hand, can benefit from leverage because it magnifies earnings, thus the return to stockholders. But too much debt often leads to financial difficulty, which eventually might cause bankruptcy.

Unilate's debt ratio is 50.9 percent; this means that its creditors have supplied about half the firm's total financing. Because the average debt ratio for this industry is 45 percent, Unilate might find it difficult to borrow additional funds without first raising more equity capital through a stock issue. Creditors might be reluctant to lend the firm more money, and management would be subjecting the firm to a greater chance of bankruptcy if it sought to increase the debt ratio much further by borrowing additional funds.[12]

TIMES-INTEREST-EARNED (TIE) RATIO
The TIE ratio is computed by dividing earnings before interest and taxes (EBIT) by interest charges; it measures the ability of the firm to meet its annual interest payments.

Times Interest Earned The **times-interest-earned (TIE) ratio** is defined as follows:

$$\text{Times-interest-earned (TIE) ratio} = \frac{\text{EBIT}}{\text{Interest charges}}$$

$$= \frac{\$130.0}{\$40.0} = 3.3 \text{ times}$$

$$\text{Industry average} = 6.5 \text{ times}$$

The TIE ratio measures the extent to which earnings before interest and taxes (EBIT), also called operating income, can decline before the firm is unable to meet its annual interest costs. Failure to meet this obligation can bring legal action by the firm's

---

[12]The ratio of debt to equity is also used in financial analysis. The debt-to-assets (D/A) and debt-to-equity (D/E) ratios are simply transformations of each other, because total debt plus total equity must equal total assets:

$$D/E = \frac{D/A}{1 - D/A}, \text{ and } D/A = \frac{D/E}{1 + D/E}$$

creditors, possibly resulting in bankruptcy. Note that earnings before interest and taxes, rather than net income, is used in the numerator. Because interest is paid with pretax dollars, the firm's ability to pay current interest is not affected by taxes.

Unilate's interest is covered 3.3 times. Because the industry average is 6.5 times, compared to firms in the same business, Unilate is covering its interest charges by a low margin of safety. Thus, the TIE ratio reinforces our conclusion based on the debt ratio that Unilate would face difficulties if it attempted to borrow additional funds.

FIXED CHARGE COVERAGE RATIO This ratio expands the TIE ratio to include the firm's annual long-term lease payments and sinking fund payments.

Fixed Charge Coverage   The **fixed charge coverage ratio** is similar to the times-interest-earned ratio, but it is more inclusive because it recognizes that many firms lease assets and also must make sinking fund payments.[13] Leasing has become widespread in certain industries in recent years, making this ratio preferable to the times-interest-earned ratio for many purposes. Unilate's annual long-term lease payments are $10 million, and it must make an annual $8 million sinking fund payment to help retire its debt. Because sinking fund payments must be paid with after-tax dollars, whereas interest and lease payments are paid with pretax dollars, the sinking fund payment must be divided by (1 − Tax rate) to find the before-tax income required to pay taxes and still have enough left to make the sinking fund payment.[14]

Fixed charges include interest, annual long-term lease obligations, and sinking fund payments, and the fixed charge coverage ratio is defined as follows:

$$\text{Fixed charge coverage ratio} = \frac{\text{EBIT} + \text{Lease payments}}{\text{Interest charges} + \text{Lease payments} + \left[\frac{\text{Sinking fund payments}}{(1 - \text{Tax rate})}\right]}$$

$$= \frac{\$130.0 + \$10.0}{\$40.0 + \$10.0 + \left[\frac{\$8.0}{(1 - 0.4)}\right]} = \frac{\$140}{\$63.33} = 2.2 \text{ times}$$

Industry average = 5.8 times

In the numerator of the fixed charge coverage ratio, the lease payments are added to EBIT because we want to determine the firm's ability to cover its fixed charges from the income generated before any fixed charges are deducted. The EBIT figure represents the firm's operating income, net of lease payments, so the lease payments must be added back.

Unilate's fixed charges are covered only 2.2 times, as opposed to an industry average of 5.8 times. Again, this indicates that the firm is weaker than average, and this points out the difficulties Unilate probably would encounter if it attempted to increase its debt.

---

[13]Generally, a long-term lease is defined as one that extends for more than one year. Thus, rent incurred under a six-month lease would not be included in the fixed charge coverage ratio, but rental payments under a one-year or longer lease would be defined as a fixed charge and would be included. A sinking fund is a required annual payment designed to reduce the balance of a bond or preferred stock issue. Sinking funds will be discussed in Chapter 17.

[14]Note that $8/(1 − 0.4) = $13.33. Therefore, if the company had pretax income of $13.33, it could pay taxes at a 40 percent rate and have exactly $8 left with which to make the sinking fund payment. Dividing by (1 − T) is called "grossing up" an after-tax value to find the corresponding pretax value.

Our examination of Unilate's debt management ratios indicates that the company has a debt ratio that is *above* the industry average, and it has coverage ratios that are significantly *below* the industry average. This suggests that Unilate is in a relatively dangerous position with respect to leverage (debt). In fact, Unilate might have great difficulty borrowing additional funds until its debt position improves. If Unilate cannot pay its current obligations as a result, it might be forced into bankruptcy. To see how Unilate's debt position has affected its profits, we next examine the profitability ratios.

Profitability Ratios

PROFITABILITY RATIOS
A group of ratios showing the effect of liquidity, asset management, and debt management on operating results.

Profitability is the net result of a number of policies and decisions. The ratios examined thus far provide some information about the way the firm is operating, but the **profitability ratios** show the combined effects of liquidity, asset management, and debt management on operating results.

NET PROFIT MARGIN ON SALES
This ratio measures net income per dollar of sales; it is calculated by dividing net income by sales.

Net Profit Margin on Sales   The **net profit margin on sales,** which gives the profit per dollar of sales, is calculated as follows:

$$\text{Profit margin on sales} = \frac{\text{Net Income}}{\text{Sales}}$$

$$= \frac{\$54.0}{\$1,500.0} = 0.036 = 3.6\%$$

Industry average = 4.7%

Unilate's profit margin is below the industry average of 4.7 percent, indicating that its sales are too low, its costs are too high, or both. Remember that, according to the debt ratio, Unilate has a greater proportion of debt than the industry average, and the times interest earned ratio shows that Unilate's interest payments on its debt are not covered as well as the rest of the industry. This is one of the reasons Unilate's profit margin is low. To see this, we can compute the ratio of EBIT (operating income) to sales, which is called the *operating profit margin.* Unilate's operating profit margin of 8.7 percent is about the same as the industry, so the cause of the low net profit margin is the relatively high interest attributable to the firm's above-average use of debt.

RETURN ON TOTAL ASSETS (ROA)
The ratio of net income to total assets; it provides an idea of the overall return on investment earned by the firm.

Return on Total Assets   The ratio of net income to total assets measures the **return on total assets (ROA)** after interest and taxes:

$$\text{Return on total assets (ROA)} = \frac{\text{Net Income}}{\text{Total assets}}$$

$$= \frac{\$54.0}{\$845.0} = 0.064 = 6.4\%$$

Industry average = 12.6%

Unilate's 6.4 percent return is well below the 12.6 percent average for the industry. This low return results from the company's above-average use of debt.

Return on Common Equity   The ratio of net income to common equity measures the **return on common equity (ROE),** or the *rate of return on stockholders' investment:*[15]

$$\text{Return on common equity (ROE)} = \frac{\text{Net income available to common stockholders}}{\text{Common equity}}$$

$$= \frac{\$54.0}{\$415.0} = 0.130 = 13.0\%$$

$$\text{Industry average} = 17.2\%$$

Unilate's 13.0 percent return is below the 17.2 percent industry average. This result is due to the company's greater use of debt (leverage), a point that is analyzed further later in this chapter.

Our examination of Unilate's profitability ratios shows that its operating results have suffered due to its poor liquidity position, its poor asset management, and its above-average debt. In the final group of ratios, we will examine Unilate's market value ratios to get an indication of how investors feel about the company's current financial position.

Market Value Ratios

The **market value ratios** represent a group of ratios that relate the firm's stock price to its earnings and book value per share. These ratios give management an indication of what investors think of the company's past performance and future prospects. If the firm's liquidity, asset management, debt management, and profitability ratios are all good, then its market value ratios will be high, and its stock price will probably be as high as can be expected. Of course, the opposite also is true.

Price/Earnings Ratio   The **price/earnings (P/E) ratio** shows how much investors are willing to pay per dollar of reported profits. To compute the P/E ratio, we need to know the firm's earnings per share (EPS):

$$\text{Earnings per share} = \frac{\text{Net income available to common stockholders}}{\text{Number of common shares outstanding}}$$

$$= \frac{\$54.0}{25.0} = \$2.16$$

Unilate's stock sells for $23, so with an EPS of $2.16 its P/E ratio is 10.6:

$$\text{Price/earnings (PE) ratio} = \frac{\text{Market price per share}}{\text{Earnings per share}}$$

$$= \frac{\$23.00}{\$2.16} = 10.6 \text{ times}$$

$$\text{Industry average} = 13.0 \text{ times}$$

---

[15]Net income to common stockholders is computed by subtracting preferred dividends from net income. Because Unilate has no preferred stock, the net income available to common stockholders is the same as the net income.

Other things held constant, P/E ratios are higher for firms with high growth prospects, but they are lower for riskier firms. Because Unilate's P/E ratio is below those of other textile manufacturers, this suggests that the company is regarded as being somewhat riskier than most, as having poorer growth prospects, or both. From our analysis of its debt management ratios, we know Unilate has above-average risk associated with leverage; but we do not know if its growth prospects are poor.

Market/Book Ratio   The ratio of a stock's market price to its book value gives another indication of how investors regard the company. Companies with relatively high rates of return on equity generally sell at higher multiples of book value than those with low returns. First, we find Unilate's book value per share:

$$\text{Book value per share} = \frac{\text{Common equity}}{\text{Number of common shares outstanding}}$$

$$= \frac{\$415.0}{25.0} = \$16.60$$

Now we divide the market value per share by the book value per share to get a **market/book (M/B) ratio** of 1.4 times for Unilate:

MARKET/BOOK (M/B) RATIO
The ratio of a stock's market price to its book value.

$$\text{Market/book ratio} = \frac{\text{Market price per share}}{\text{Book value per share}}$$

$$= \frac{\$23.00}{\$16.60} = 1.4 \text{ times}$$

$$\text{Industry average} = 2.0 \text{ times}$$

Investors are willing to pay less for Unilate's book value than for that of an average textile manufacturer. This should not be surprising, because, as we discovered previously, Unilate has generated below-average returns with respect to both total assets and common equity. Generally, the stocks of firms that earn high rates of return on their assets sell for prices well in excess of their book values. For very successful firms, the market/book ratio can be as much as ten to fifteen times.

Our examination of Unilate's market value ratios indicates that investors are not excited about the future prospects of its common stock as an investment. Perhaps investors believe Unilate is headed toward bankruptcy if actions are not taken to correct its liquidity and asset management problems and to improve its leverage position. A method used to get an indication of the direction a firm is headed is to evaluate the trends of the ratios over the past few years to answer the question: Is the firm's position improving or deteriorating?

Trend Analysis

The analysis of its ratios indicates that Unilate's current financial position is poor when compared to the industry norm. But this analysis does not tell us whether Unilate's financial position is better or worse than previous years. To determine in which direction the firm is headed, it is important to analyze trends in ratios. By examining the

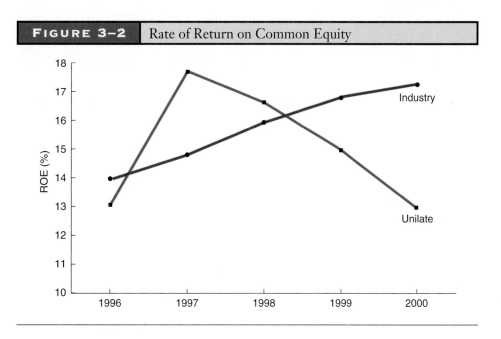

FIGURE 3–2   Rate of Return on Common Equity

paths taken in the past, **trend analysis** provides information about whether the firm's financial position is more likely to improve or deteriorate in the future. A simple approach to trend analysis is to construct graphs containing both the firm's ratios and the industry averages for the past five years. Using this approach, we can examine both the direction of the movement in, and the relationships between, the firm's ratios and the industry averages. Figure 3–2 shows that Unilate's return on equity has declined since 1996, even though the industry average has shown relatively stable growth. Other ratios could be analyzed similarly. If we were to compare Unilate's ratios from 2000 with those from 1999, we would discover Unilate's financial position has deteriorated, not strengthened—this is not a good trend.

Summary of Ratio Analysis: The DuPont Chart

Table 3–6 summarizes Unilate's ratios, and Figure 3–3, which is called a **DuPont chart** because that company's managers developed the general approach, shows the relationships between return on investment, asset turnover, and the profit margin. The left side of the chart develops the profit margin on sales. The various expense items are listed and then summed to obtain Unilate's total costs, which are subtracted from sales to obtain the company's net income. When we divide net income by sales, we find that 3.6 percent of each sales dollar is left over for stockholders. If the profit margin is low or trending down, one can examine the individual expense items to identify and then correct problems.

The right side of Figure 3–3 lists the various categories of assets, totals them, and then divides sales by total assets to find the number of times Unilate "turns its assets over" each year. The company's total assets turnover ratio is 1.8 times.

TABLE 3–6	Unilate Textiles: Summary of Financial Ratios (millions of dollars, except per share dollars)

RATIO	FORMULA FOR CALCULATION	CALCULATION	RATIO	INDUSTRY AVERAGE	COMMENT
Liquidity					
Current	$\dfrac{\text{Current assets}}{\text{Current liabilitites}}$	$\dfrac{\$465.0}{\$130.0}$	= 3.6×	4.1×	Low
Quick, or acid test	$\dfrac{\text{Current assets} - \text{Inventories}}{\text{Current liabilitites}}$	$\dfrac{\$195.0}{\$130.0}$	= 1.5×	2.1×	Low
Asset Management					
Inventory turnover	$\dfrac{\text{Cost of goods sold}}{\text{Inventories}}$	$\dfrac{\$1{,}230.0}{\$270.0}$	= 4.6×	7.4×	Low
Days sales outstanding (DSO)	$\dfrac{\text{Receivables}}{\left[\dfrac{\text{Annual sales}}{360}\right]}$	$\dfrac{\$180.0}{\$4.167}$	= 43.2 days	32.1 days	Poor
Fixed assets turnover	$\dfrac{\text{Sales}}{\text{Net fixed assets}}$	$\dfrac{\$1{,}500.0}{\$380.0}$	= 3.9×	4.0×	OK
Total assets turnover	$\dfrac{\text{Sales}}{\text{Total assets}}$	$\dfrac{\$1{,}500.0}{\$845.0}$	= 1.8×	2.1×	Low
Debt Management					
Debt ratio	$\dfrac{\text{Total debt}}{\text{Total assets}}$	$\dfrac{\$430.0}{\$845.0}$	= 50.9%	45.0%	Poor
Times interest earned (TIE)	$\dfrac{\text{EBIT}}{\text{Interest charges}}$	$\dfrac{\$130.0}{\$40.0}$	= 3.3×	6.5×	Low
Fixed charge coverage	$\dfrac{\text{EBIT} + \text{Lease payments}}{\text{Interest charges} + \text{Lease payments} + \left[\dfrac{\text{Sinking fund pmt}}{(1 - \text{Tax rate})}\right]}$	$\dfrac{\$140.0}{\$63.33}$	= 2.2×	5.8×	Low
Profitability					
Profit margin on sales	$\dfrac{\text{Net income}}{\text{Sales}}$	$\dfrac{\$54.0}{\$1{,}500.0}$	= 3.6%	4.7%	Poor
Return on total assets (ROA)	$\dfrac{\text{Net income}}{\text{Total assets}}$	$\dfrac{\$54.0}{\$845.0}$	= 6.4%	12.6%	Poor
Return on common equity (ROE)	$\dfrac{\text{Net income available to common stockholders}}{\text{Common equity}}$	$\dfrac{\$54.0}{\$415.0}$	= 13.0%	17.2%	Poor
Market Value					
Price/Earnings (P/E)	$\dfrac{\text{Market price per share}}{\text{Earnings per share}}$	$\dfrac{\$23.00}{\$2.16}$	= 10.6×	13.0×	Low
Market/Book	$\dfrac{\text{Market price per share}}{\text{Book value per share}}$	$\dfrac{\$23.00}{\$16.60}$	= 1.4×	2.0×	Low

| **FIGURE 3–3** | DuPont Chart Applied to Unilate Textiles (millions of dollars) |

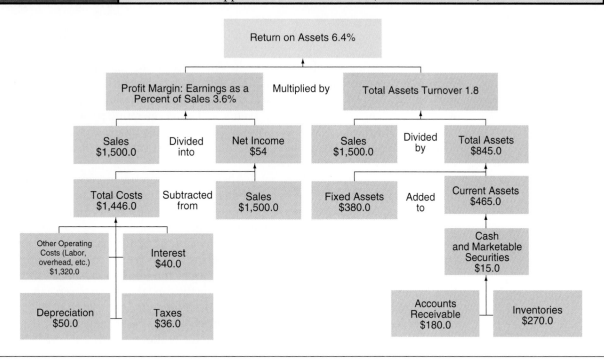

DUPONT EQUATION
A formula that gives the rate of return on assets by multiplying the profit margin by the total assets turnover.

The profit margin times the total assets turnover is called the **DuPont equation,** and it gives the rate of return on assets (ROA):[16]

$$
\boxed{
\begin{aligned}
\text{3-1} \quad
\text{ROA} &= \text{Net profit margin} \times \text{Total assets turnover} \\
&= \frac{\text{Net income}}{\text{Sales}} \times \frac{\text{Sales}}{\text{Total assets}}
\end{aligned}
}
$$

$$
= \frac{\$54.0}{\$1,500.0} \times \frac{\$1,500.0}{\$845.0}
$$

$$
= \quad 3.6\% \quad \times \quad 1.8 \quad \approx 6.4\%
$$

---

[16]The number reported here for the total assets turnover is rounded to the nearest decimal place, so the ROA does not equal 6.4 percent if the rounded result for the total assets turnover is used. If the ratios are carried to two decimal places, the DuPont computation would be ROA = 3.60% × 1.78 = 6.41%.

Unilate made 3.6 percent, or 3.6 cents, on each dollar of sales, and assets were "turned over" 1.8 times during the year, so the company earned a return of 6.4 percent on its assets.

Unilate's management can use the DuPont system to analyze ways of improving the firm's performance. Focusing on the left, or "profit margin," side of its DuPont chart, Unilate's marketing people can study the effects of raising sales prices (or lowering them to increase volume), of moving into new products or markets with higher margins, and so on. The company's cost accountants can study various expense items and, working with engineers, purchasing agents, and other operating personnel, seek ways of holding down costs. On the "turnover" side, Unilate's financial analysts, working with both production and marketing people, can investigate ways of minimizing the investment in various types of assets.

As a result of such an analysis, Sarah Allen, Unilate's president, recently announced a series of moves designed to cut operating costs by more than 20 percent per year. Allen also announced that the company intends to concentrate its capital in markets where profit margins are reasonably high, and that if competition increases in certain of its product markets (such as the low-price end of the textiles market), Unilate will withdraw from those markets. Unilate is seeking a high return on equity, and Allen recognizes that if competition drives profit margins too low in a particular market, it then becomes impossible to earn high returns on the capital invested to serve that market. Therefore, if it is to achieve a high ROE, Unilate might have to develop new products and shift capital into new areas. The company's future depends on this type of analysis, and if it succeeds in the future, then the DuPont system will have helped it achieve that success.

Self-Test Questions

Identify two ratios that are used to analyze a firm's liquidity position, and write out their equations.

Identify four ratios that are used to measure how effectively a firm is managing its assets, and write out their equations.

Identify three ratios that are used to measure the extent to which a firm uses debt financing, and write out their equations.

Identify three ratios that show the combined effects of liquidity, asset management, and debt management on profitability, and write out their equations.

Identify two ratios that relate a firm's stock price to its earnings and book value per share, and write out their equations.

Explain how the DuPont equation and chart combine several ratios to reveal the basic determinants of ROE.

Comparative Ratios

COMPARATIVE RATIO ANALYSIS
An analysis based on a comparison of a firm's ratios with those of other firms in the same industry.

The preceding analysis of Unilate Textiles involved a **comparative ratio analysis** because the ratios calculated for Unilate were compared with those of other firms in the same industry. Comparative ratios for a large number of industries are available from a number of sources, including Dun & Bradstreet (D&B), Robert Morris Associates, and the U.S. Commerce Department. Trade associations and individual firms' credit departments also compile industry average financial ratios. Finally, financial statement data for thousands of publicly owned corporations are available from various databases; and because brokerage houses, banks, and other financial institutions have access to these data, security analysts can and do generate comparative ratios tailored to their specific needs. Table 3–7 provides a sample of the ratios provided by the *Almanac of Business and Industrial Financial Ratios*.

Each of the data-supplying organizations uses a somewhat different set of ratios designed for its own purposes. For example, D&B deals mainly with small firms, many of which are proprietorships, and it sells its services primarily to banks and other lenders. Therefore, D&B is concerned largely with the creditor's viewpoint, and its ratios emphasize current assets and liabilities, not market value ratios. Thus, when you select a comparative data source, you should be sure that your emphasis is similar to that of the agency whose ratios you plan to use. Additionally, there are often definitional differences in the ratios presented by different sources, so before using a source, be sure to verify the exact definitions of the ratios to ensure consistency with your work.

Self-Test Questions

Differentiate between trend analysis and comparative ratio analysis.

Why is it necessary to conduct both trend and comparative ratio analyses?

Uses and Limitations of Ratio Analysis

As noted earlier, ratio analysis is used by three main groups: (1) *managers*, who employ ratios to help analyze, control, and thus improve the firm's operations; (2) *credit analysts*, such as bank loan officers or bond rating analysts, who analyze ratios to help ascertain a company's ability to pay its debts; and (3) *security analysts*, including both stock analysts, who are interested in a company's efficiency and growth prospects, and bond analysts, who are concerned with a company's ability to pay interest on its bonds as well as with the liquidating value of the assets in the event the company fails. In later chapters we will look more closely at the basic factors that underlie each ratio, and at that point you will get a better idea about how to interpret and use ratios.

While ratio analysis can provide useful information concerning a company's operations and financial condition, it does have inherent problems and limitations that necessitate care and judgment. Some potential problems are listed here:

1. Many large firms operate a number of different divisions in quite different industries, and in such cases it is difficult to develop a meaningful set of industry averages for comparative purposes. This tends to make ratio analysis more useful for small, narrowly focused firms than for large, multidivisional ones.
2. Most firms want to be better than average, so merely attaining average performance is not necessarily good. As a target for high-level performance, it is best to focus on the industry leaders' ratios.
3. Inflation might distort firms' balance sheets—if recorded values are historical, they could be substantially different from "true" values. Further, because inflation affects both depreciation charges and inventory costs, profits are also affected. Thus, a ratio analysis for one firm over time, or a comparative analysis of firms of different ages, must be interpreted with judgment.

| TABLE 3–7 | Ratios for Selected Industries |

SIC Code, Line of Business, (Number of Firms)	Type of Operations	Current Ratio	Quick Ratio	Debt Ratio	TIE Ratio	Days Sales Outstanding	Total Inventory Turnover	Asset Turnover	Profit Margin	Return on Assets	Return on Equity
		×	×	%	×	Days	×	×	%	%	%
2830 Drugs (1,456)	Manufacturing	1.1	0.8	61.7	5.2	133.3	4.1	0.6	10.6	11.1	15.0
3670 Electronic Components (12,173)	Manufacturing	1.9	1.1	51.4	6.6	59.1	6.1	1.2	5.4	11.6	13.5
5030 Lumber & Construction (9,118)	Wholesale	1.6	0.9	65.2	2.5	37.5	9.4	3.2	1.3	9.2	12.1
5170 Petroleum & Products (11,612)	Wholesale	1.1	0.4	87.9	1.4	56.3	4.3	0.7	1.2	4.4	6.9
5220 Building Materials Dealers (12,721)	Retail	2.1	0.8	45.9	4.8	25.5	5.2	2.4	3.3	12.9	14.2
5251 Hardware Stores (12,186)	Retail	2.0	0.6	67.4	1.0	28.7	3.3	2.2	1.6	3.2	5.1

SOURCE: *Almanac of Business and Industrial Financial Ratios, 1999 Edition*

SIC codes are "Standard Industrial Classification" codes used by the U.S. government to classify companies.

4. Seasonal factors can also distort a ratio analysis. For example, the inventory turnover ratio for a textile firm will be radically different if the balance sheet figure used for inventory is the one just before versus the one just after the close of the fall fashion season. This problem can be minimized by using monthly averages for inventory (and receivables) when calculating ratios such as turnover.

5. Firms can employ **"window dressing" techniques** to make their financial statements look stronger. To illustrate, a Chicago builder borrowed on a two-year basis on December 28, 2000, held the proceeds of the loan as cash for a few days, and then paid off the loan ahead of time on January 2, 2001. This improved the company's current and quick ratios, and made his year-end 2000 balance sheet look good. However, the improvement was strictly window dressing; a week later the balance sheet was back at the old level.

6. Different accounting practices can distort comparisons. As noted earlier, inventory valuation and depreciation methods can affect financial statements and thus make comparisons among firms difficult.

7. It is difficult to generalize about whether a particular ratio is "good" or "bad." For example, a high current ratio might indicate a strong liquidity position, which is good, or excessive cash, which is bad (because excess cash in the bank is a nonearning asset). Similarly, a high fixed assets turnover ratio may denote either a firm that uses its assets efficiently or one that is undercapitalized and cannot afford to buy enough assets.

8. A firm might have some ratios that look "good" and others that look "bad," making it difficult to tell whether the company is, on balance, strong or weak. However, statistical procedures can be used to analyze the net effects of a set of ratios. Many banks and other lending organizations use statistical procedures to analyze firms' financial ratios, and, on the basis of their analyses, classify companies according to their probability of getting into financial trouble.[17]

Ratio analysis is useful, but analysts should be aware of these problems and make adjustments as necessary. Ratio analysis conducted in a mechanical, unthinking manner is dangerous, but used intelligently and with good judgment, it can provide useful insights into a firm's operations. Probably *the most important and most difficult input to successful ratio analysis is the judgment used when interpreting the results to reach an overall conclusion about the firm's financial position.*

Self-Test Questions

Name three types of users of ratio analysis. What type of ratios does each group emphasize?

List several potential problems with ratio analysis.

---

[17]The technique used is discriminant analysis. For a discussion, see Edward I. Altman, "Financial Ratios, Discriminant Analysis, and the Prediction of Corporate Bankruptcy," *Journal of Finance* (September 1968), 589–609, or Eugene F. Brigham, Louis C. Gapenski, and Phillip R. Daves, *Intermediate Financial Management*, 6th ed. (Fort Worth, TX: The Dryden Press, 1999), Chapter 20.

✳ ETHICAL DILEMMA

Hocus-Pocus—Look, An Increase in Sales!

Dynamic Energy Wares (DEW) manufactures and distributes products that are used to save energy and to help reduce and reverse the harmful environmental effects of atmospheric pollutants. DEW relies on a relatively complex distribution system to get the products to its customers—large companies, which account for nearly 30 percent of total sales, purchase directly from DEW, while smaller companies and retailers that sell to individuals are required to purchase from one of the 50 independent distributors that are contractually obligated to *exclusively* sell DEW's products.

DEW's accountants have just finished the financial statements for the third quarter of the fiscal year, which ended three weeks ago. The results are terrible—profits are down 30 percent from this time last year when a downturn in sales began. Profits are depressed primarily because DEW continues to lose market share to a competitor that started business nearly two years ago.

Senior management has decided it needs to take action that will boost sales in the fourth quarter so that year-end profits are "more acceptable." So, starting immediately, DEW will (1) eliminate all direct sales, which means large companies now must purchase from DEW's distributors like the smaller companies and retailers, (2) require distributors to maintain certain minimum inventory levels, which are much higher than previous levels, and (3) form a task force to study and propose ways the firm can recapture lost market share.

The financial manager, who is your boss, has asked you to attend a hastily called meeting of DEW's distributors to announce the implementation of the changes in operations. At the meeting, the distributors will be informed that they must increase inventory to the required minimum level before the end of DEW's current fiscal year or face losing the distributorship. According to your boss, the reason for this requirement is to ensure that distributors can meet the increased demand they will gain because the large companies no longer will be allowed to purchase directly from DEW. But the sales forecast you have been working on for the past couple of months indicates distributors' sales are expected to decline by almost ten percent during the next year, thus the added inventories might be extremely burdensome to the distributors. When you approached your boss about this, she said: "Tell the distributors not to worry! We won't require payment for six months, and any of the additional inventory that remains unsold after nine months can be returned. But they *must* take delivery of the inventory within the next two months."

It appears the actions implemented by DEW will produce favorable year-end sales results for the current fiscal year. Do you agree with the decisions made by DEW's senior management? Will you be comfortable announcing the decisions to DEW's distributors? How would you respond to a distributor who says "DEW doesn't care about us, the company just wants to look good, no matter who gets hurt—that's unethical?" What are you going to say to your boss? Are you going to the distributors' meeting?

Summary

The primary purposes of this chapter were (1) to describe the basic financial statements and (2) to discuss techniques used by investors and managers to analyze the statements. The key concepts covered are listed here.

- The four basic statements contained in the annual report are the **balance sheet, the income statement, the statement of retained earnings,** and the **statement of cash flows.** Investors use the information provided in these statements to form expectations about the future levels of earnings and dividends, and about the firm's riskiness.

- **Operating cash flows** differ from reported **accounting income.** Investors should be more interested in a firm's projected cash flows than in reported earnings, because it is cash, not paper profits, that is paid out as dividends and plowed back into the business to produce growth.
- **Financial statement analysis** generally begins with the calculation of a set of **financial ratios** designed to reveal the relative strengths and weaknesses of a company as compared to other companies in the same industry and to show whether the firm's position has been improving or deteriorating over time.
- **Liquidity ratios** show the relationship of a firm's current assets to its current liabilities and thus indicate the firm's ability to meet its current obligations.
- **Asset management ratios** measure how effectively a firm is managing its assets.
- **Debt management ratios** reveal (1) the extent to which the firm is financed with debt and (2) its likelihood of defaulting on its debt obligations.
- **Profitability ratios** show the combined effects of liquidity, asset management, and debt management policies on operating results.
- **Market value ratios** relate the firm's stock price to its earnings and book value per share, providing an indication of how investors regard the firm's future prospects.
- **Trend analysis** is important because it reveals whether the firm's ratios are improving or deteriorating over time.
- The **DuPont chart** is designed to show how the profit margin on sales and the assets turnover ratio interact to determine the rate of return on equity.
- In analyzing a small firm's financial position, ratio analysis is a useful starting point. However, the analyst must also (1) examine the quality of the financial data, (2) ensure that the firm is sufficiently diversified to withstand shifts in customers' buying habits, and (3) ensure that the firm has a plan for the succession of its management.

Ratio analysis has limitations, but used with care and judgment, it can be very helpful. The interpretation of the computed ratio values is the most important ingredient for reaching a conclusion regarding both the existing and the prospective financial position of a firm.

Questions

3–1 What four statements are contained in most annual reports?

3–2 If a "typical" firm reports $20 million of retained earnings on its balance sheet, could its directors declare a $20 million cash dividend without any qualms whatsoever? Explain why or why not.

3–3 Describe the changes in balance sheet accounts that would constitute sources of funds. What changes would be considered uses of funds?

3–4 Financial ratio analysis is conducted by four groups of analysts: managers, equity investors, long-term creditors, and short-term creditors. What is the primary emphasis of each of these groups in evaluating ratios?

3–5 What are some cares that must be taken when using ratio analysis? What is the most important aspect of ratio analysis?

3–6 Profit margins and turnover ratios vary from one industry to another. What differences would you expect to find between a grocery chain like Safeway and a steel company? Think particularly about the turnover ratios and the profit margin, and think about the DuPont equation.

Financial Analysis in the Small Firm

Financial ratio analysis is especially useful for small businesses, and readily available sources provide comparative data by size of firm. For example, the *Almanac of Business and Industrial Financial Ratios* provides comparative ratios for a number of small-firm classes, including the size range of zero to $100,000 in assets. Nevertheless, analyzing a small firm's statements presents some unique problems. We examine here some of those problems from the standpoint of a bank loan officer, one of the most frequent users of ratio analysis.

When examining a small-business credit prospect, a banker is essentially making a prediction about the ability of the company to repay its debt. In making this prediction, the banker is concerned about indicators of liquidity and about continuing prospects for profitability, especially with respect to the firm's ability to generate cash flows. Bankers like to conduct business with a new customer if it appears that loans can be paid off on a timely basis and that the company will remain in business and therefore be a customer of the bank for some years to come. Thus, both short-run and long-run viability are of interest to the banker. At the same time, the banker's perceptions about the business are important to the owner-manager, because the bank probably will be the firm's primary source of funds.

The first problem the banker is likely to encounter is that, unlike the bank's bigger customers, the small firm might not have audited financial statements. Further, the statements that are available might have been produced on an irregular basis (e.g., in some months or quarters but not in others). If the firm is young, it might have historical financial statements for only one year, or perhaps none at all. Also, the financial statements might have been constructed by the owner's brother-in-law rather than by a reputable accounting firm.

The quality of its financial data could therefore be a problem for a small business that is attempting to establish a banking relationship. This could keep the firm from getting credit even though it is really on solid financial ground. Therefore, it is in the owner's interest to make sure that the firm's financial data are credible, even if it is more expensive to do so. Furthermore, if the banker is uncomfortable with the data, the firm's management should also be uncomfortable. Because many managerial decisions depend on the numbers in the firm's accounting statements, those numbers should be as accurate as possible.

For a given set of financial ratios, a small firm might be riskier than a larger one. Small firms often produce a single product or rely heavily on a single customer, or both. For example, several years ago a company called Yard Man Inc. manufactured and sold lawn equipment. Most of Yard Man's sales were attributable to the business relationship it had with Sears. When Sears decided to drop Yard Man as a supplier, the company was left without its most important customer. The original Yard Man company is no longer in business. Because large firms typically have a broad customer base, they do not rely as much on a single customer.

A similar danger applies to a single-product company. Just as the loss of a key customer can be disastrous for a small business, so can a shift in the tides of consumer interest in a particular fad. For example, not long ago, Coleco manufactured and sold the extremely popular Cabbage Patch dolls. The phenomenal popularity of the dolls was a great boon for Coleco, but the public is fickle. One can never predict when such a fad will die out, leaving the company with a great deal of capacity to make a product that no one will buy, and with a large amount of overvalued inventory. Exactly that situation hit Coleco, and it was forced into bankruptcy.

The extension of credit to a small company, and especially to a small owner-managed company, often involves yet another risk that is less of a problem for larger firms—namely, dependence on the leadership of a single key individual whose unexpected death could cause the company to fail. For such a firm, it is important to have a plan of management succession clearly specified so creditors are assured the business will continue without interruption if some sort of disaster befalls the "key" manager. In addition, the firm

continues

could carry "key person insurance," payable to the bank or other creditor for the purposes of retiring the loan in the event of the key person's death.

In summary, to determine the financial strength of a small firm, the financial analyst must "look beyond the ratios" and analyze the viability of the firm's products, customers, management, and market. Ratio analysis is only the first step in a sound evaluation of the firm's ability to repay its debt and meet its other financial obligations.

3–7 If a firm's ROE is low and management wants to improve it, explain how using more debt might help. Could using too much debt be a detriment?

3–8 How might (a) seasonal factors and (b) different growth rates distort a comparative ratio analysis? Give some examples. How might these problems be alleviated?

3–9 The following table shows the balance sheets for Batelan Corporation for the fiscal years 1999 and 2000. In the column to the right of the balance sheet amounts, indicate whether the change in the account balance represents a source or a use of cash for the firm. Place a (+) in the space provided to indicate a source of funds, a (−) to indicate a use of funds, and a (0) if it cannot be determined whether the change was a source or a use of cash.

	2000	1999	SOURCE (+) OR USE (−)?
Cash	$ 400	$ 500	_____
Accounts receivable	250	300	_____
Inventory	450	400	_____
Current assets	$1,100	$1,200	
Net property and equipment	1,000	950	_____
Total assets	$2,100	$2,150	
Accounts payable	$ 200	$ 400	_____
Accruals	300	250	_____
Notes payable	400	200	_____
Current liabilities	$ 900	$ 850	
Long-term debt	800	900	
Total liabilities	$1,700	$1,750	
Common stock	250	300	_____
Retained earnings	150	100	_____
Total equity	$ 400	$ 400	
Total liabilities and equity	$2,100	$2,150	

From these balance sheets, can you tell whether the Batelan generated a positive or negative net income during 2000? Can you tell if dividends were paid? Explain.

3–10 Indicate the effects of the transactions listed in the following table on total current assets, current ratio, and net income. Use (+) to indicate an increase, (−) to indicate a decrease, and (0) to indicate either no effect or an indeterminate effect. Be prepared to state any necessary assumptions, and assume an initial current ratio of more than 1.0. (Note: A good accounting background is necessary to answer some of these questions; if yours is not strong, just answer the questions you can handle.)

	TOTAL CURRENT ASSETS	CURRENT RATIO	EFFECT ON NET INCOME
a. Cash is acquired through issuance of additional common stock.	_____	_____	_____
b. Merchandise is sold for cash.	_____	_____	_____
c. Federal income tax due for the previous year is paid.	_____	_____	_____
d. A fixed asset is sold for less than book value.	_____	_____	_____
e. A fixed asset is sold for more than book value.	_____	_____	_____
f. Merchandise is sold on credit.	_____	_____	_____
g. Payment is made to trade creditors for previous purchases.	_____	_____	_____
h. A cash dividend is declared and paid.	_____	_____	_____
i. Cash is obtained through short-term bank loans.	_____	_____	_____
j. Short-term notes receivable are sold at a discount.	_____	_____	_____
k. Marketable securities are sold below cost.	_____	_____	_____
l. Advances are made to employees.	_____	_____	_____
m. Current operating expenses are paid.	_____	_____	_____
n. Short-term promissory notes are issued to trade creditors in exchange for past due accounts payable.	_____	_____	_____
o. 10-year notes are issued to pay accounts payable.	_____	_____	_____
p. A fully depreciated asset is retired.	_____	_____	_____
q. Accounts receivable are collected.	_____	_____	_____
r. Equipment is purchased with short-term notes.	_____	_____	_____
s. Merchandise is purchased on credit.	_____	_____	_____
t. The estimated taxes payable are increased.	_____	_____	_____

Self-Test Problems

(Solutions appear in Appendix B)

key terms   **ST–1**   Define each of the following terms:
   a. Annual report; income statement; balance sheet
   b. Equity, or net worth; paid-in capital; retained earnings
   c. Cash flow cycle
   d. Statement of retained earnings; statement of cash flows
   e. Depreciation; inventory valuation methods
   f. Liquidity ratios: current ratios; quick, or acid test, ratio
   g. Asset management ratios: inventory turnover ratio; days sales outstanding (DSO); fixed assets turnover ratio; total assets turnover ratio
   h. Financial leverage; debt ratio; times-interest-earned (TIE) ratio; fixed charge coverage ratio
   i. Profitability ratios: profit margin on sales; return on total assets (ROA); return on common equity (ROE)
   j. Market value ratios: price/earnings (P/E) ratio; market/book (M/B) ratio; book value per share
   k. Trend analysis; comparative ratio analysis
   l. DuPont chart; DuPont equation
   m. "Window dressing"; seasonal effects on ratios

ST–2   K. Billingsworth & Company had earnings per share of $4 last year, and it paid a $2 dividend. Total retained earnings increased by $12 million during the year, while book value per share at year-end was $40. Billingsworth has no preferred stock, and no new common stock was issued during the year. If Billingsworth's year-end debt (which equals its total liabilities) was $120 million, what was the company's year-end debt/assets ratio?

debt ratio   **ST–3**   The following data apply to A. L. Kaiser & Company (millions of dollars):

Cash and marketable securities	$ 100.00
Fixed assets	$ 283.50
Sales	$1,000.00
Net income	$ 50.00
Quick ratio	2.0×
Current ratio	3.0×
DSO	40.0 days
ROE	12.0%

Kaiser has no preferred stock—only common equity, current liabilities, and long-term debt.
   a. Find Kaiser's (1) accounts receivable (A/R), (2) current liabilities, (3) current assets, (4) total assets, (5) ROA, (6) common equity, and (7) long-term debt.
   b. In part a, you should have found Kaiser's accounts receivable (A/R) = $111.1 million. If Kaiser could reduce its DSO from 40 days to 30 days while holding other things constant, how much cash would it generate? If this cash were used to buy back common stock (at book value) and thus reduced the amount of common equity, how would this affect (1) the ROE, (2) the ROA, and (3) the total debt/total assets ratio?

Problems

ratio analysis   **3–1** Data for Unilate Textiles' 1999 financial statements are given in Table 3–1 and Table 3–2 in the chapter.

   a. Compute the 1999 values of the ratios indicated in the following table:

		1999 VALUES
RATIO	UNILATE	INDUSTRY
Current ratio	_____	3.9×
Days sales outstanding	_____	33.5 days
Inventory turnover	_____	7.2×
Fixed asset turnover	_____	4.1×
Debt ratio	_____	45.0%
Net profit margin	_____	4.6%
Return on assets	_____	11.8%

   b. Briefly comment on Unilate's 1999 financial position. Can you see any obvious strengths or weaknesses?
   c. Compare Unilate's 1999 ratios with its 2000 ratios, which are presented in Table 3–6 in the chapter. Comment on whether you believe Unilate's financial position improved or deteriorated during 2000.
   d. What other information would be useful for projecting whether Unilate's financial position is expected to get better or worse in the future?

ratio analysis   **3–2** Data for Campsey Computer Company and its industry averages follow.
   a. Calculate the indicated ratios for Campsey.
   b. Construct the DuPont equation for both Campsey and the industry.
   c. Outline Campsey's strengths and weaknesses as revealed by your analysis.
   d. Suppose Campsey had doubled its sales as well as its inventories, accounts receivable, and common equity during 2000. How would that information affect the validity of your ratio analysis? (Hint: Think about averages and the effects of rapid growth on ratios if averages are not used. No calculations are needed.)

Campsey Computer Company:
Balance Sheet as of December 31, 2000

Cash	$ 77,500	Accounts payable	$129,000
Receivables	336,000	Notes payable	84,000
Inventories	241,500	Other current liabilities	117,000
Total current assets	$655,000	Total current liabilities	$330,000
Net fixed assets	292,500	Long-term debt	256,500
		Common equity	361,000
Total assets	$947,500	Total liabilities and equity	$947,500

Campsey Computer Company:
Income Statement for Year Ended December 31, 2000

Sales	$ 1,607,500
Cost of goods sold	(1,353,000)
Gross profit	$ 254,500
Fixed operating expenses except depreciation	(143,000)
Depreciation	(41,500)
Earnings before interest and taxes	$ 70,000
Interest	(24,500)
Earnings before taxes	$ 45,500
Taxes (40%)	(18,200)
Net income	$ 27,300

RATIO	CAMPSEY	INDUSTRY AVERAGE
Current ratio	_____	2.0 ×
Days sales outstanding	_____	35 days
Inventory turnover	_____	5.6 ×
Total assets turnover	_____	3.0 ×
Profit margin on sales	_____	1.2%
Return on assets	_____	3.6%
Return on equity	_____	9.0%
Debt ratio	_____	60.0%

balance sheet analysis   **3–3** Complete the balance sheet and sales information in the table that follows for Isberg Industries using the following financial data:

Debt ratio: 50%
Quick ratio: 0.80 ×
Total assets turnover: 1.5 ×
Days sales outstanding: 36 days
Gross profit margin on sales: (Sales − Cost of goods sold)/Sales = 25%
Inventory turnover ratio: 5 ×

BALANCE SHEET

Cash	_____	Accounts payable	_____
Accounts receivable	_____	Long-term debt	$ 60,000
Inventories	_____	Common stock	_____
Fixed assets	_____	Retained earnings	$ 97,500
Total assets	$300,000	Total liabilities and equity	_____
Sales	_____	Cost of goods sold	_____

Taxes (40%)	(72,272)
Net income	$ 108,408
Number of shares outstanding	23,000
Per-Share Data	
EPS	$ 4.71
Cash dividends	$ 0.95
P/E ratio	5×
Market price (average)	$23.57

INDUSTRY FINANCIAL RATIOS (2001)[a]

Quick ratio	1.0×
Current ratio	2.7×
Inventory turnover[b]	5.8×
Days sales outstanding	32 days
Fixed assets turnover[b]	13.0×
Total assets turnover[b]	2.6×
Return on assets	9.1%
Return on equity	18.2%
Debt ratio	50.0%
Profit margin on sales	3.5%
P/E ratio	6.0×

[a]Industry average ratios have been constant for the past four years.
[b]Based on year-end balance sheet figures.

Exam-Type Problems

The problems included in this section are set up in such a way that they could be used as multiple-choice exam problems.

ratio calculation **3–6** Assume you are given the following relationships for the Zumwalt Corporation:

Sales/total assets	1.5×
Return on assets (ROA)	3%
Return on equity (ROE)	5%

Calculate Zumwalt's profit margin and debt ratio.

liquidity ratio **3–7** The Hindelang Corporation has $1,312,500 in current assets and $525,000 in current liabilities. Its initial inventory level is $375,000, and it will raise funds as additional notes payable and use them to increase inventory. How much can Hindelang's short-term debt (notes payable) increase without pushing its current ratio below 2.0? What will be the firm's quick ratio after Hindelang has raised the maximum amount of short-term funds?

ratio calculations **3–8** The W. F. Bailey Company had a quick ratio of 1.4, a current ratio of 3.0, and inventory turnover of 5 times, total current assets of $810,000, and cash and marketable securities of $120,000 in 2000. If the cost of goods sold equaled 86 percent of sales, what were Bailey's annual sales and its DSO for 2000?

times-interest-earned ratio   **3–9** Wolken Corporation had $500,000 of debt outstanding, and it pays an interest rate of ten percent annually. Wolken's annual sales are $2 million; its average tax rate is 20 percent; and its net profit margin on sales is five percent. If the company does not maintain a TIE ratio of at least five times, its bank will refuse to renew the loan, and bankruptcy will result. What is Wolken's TIE ratio?

return on equity   **3–10** Coastal Packaging's ROE last year was only three percent, but its management has developed a new operating plan designed to improve things. The new plan calls for a total debt ratio of 60 percent, which will result in interest charges of $300 per year. Management projects an EBIT of $1,000 on sales of $10,000, and it expects to have a total assets turnover ratio of 2.0. Under these conditions, the average tax rate will be 30 percent. If the changes are made, what return on equity will Coastal earn? What is the ROA?

return on equity   **3–11** Earth's Best Company has sales of $200,000, a net income of $15,000, and the following balance sheet:

Cash	$ 10,000	Accounts payable	$ 30,000
Receivables	50,000	Other current liabilities	20,000
Inventories	150,000	Long-term debt	50,000
Net fixed assets	90,000	Common equity	200,000
Total assets	$300,000	Total liabilities and equity	$300,000

a. The company's new owner thinks that inventories are excessive and can be lowered to the point where the current ratio is equal to the industry average, 2.5×, without affecting either sales or net income. If inventories are sold off and not replaced so as to reduce the current ratio to 2.5×, if the funds generated are used to reduce common equity (stock can be repurchased at book value), and if no other changes occur, by how much will the ROE change?

b. Now suppose we wanted to take this problem and modify it for use on an exam; that is, to create a new problem which you have not seen to test your knowledge of this type of problem. How would your answer change if (1)We doubled all of the dollar amounts? (2) We stated that the target current ratio was 3.0×? (3) We said that the company had 10,000 shares of stock outstanding, and we asked how much the change in part a would increase EDS? (4) What would your answer to (3) be if we changed the original problem to state that the stock was selling for twice book value, so common equity would not be reduced on a dollar-for-dollar basis?

c. Now explain how we could have set the problem up to have you focus on changing accounts receivable, or fixed assets, or using the funds generated to retire debt (we would give you the interest rate on outstanding debt), or how the original problem could have stated that the company needed *more* inventories and it would finance them with new common equity or with new debt.

statement of cash flows   **3–12** The consolidated balance sheets for the Lloyd Lumber Company at the beginning and end of 2000 follow. The company bought $50 million worth of fixed assets. The charge for depreciation in 2000 was $10 million. Net income was $33 million, and the company paid out $5 million in dividends.

STATEMENT OF CASH FLOWS (2000):

Operating Activities	
Net income	$ 44,220
Other additions (sources of cash):	
Depreciation	20,000
Increase in acccounts payable	29,600
Increase in accruals	4,000
Subtractions (uses of cash)	
Increases in accounts receivable	(50,800)
Increase in inventories	(120,800)
Net cash flow from operations	($ 73,780)
Long-Term Investing Activities	
Investment in fixed assets	($ 36,000)
Financing Activities	
Increase in notes payable	$ 25,000
Increase in long-term debt	101,180
Payment of cash dividends	(22,000)
Net cash flow from financing	104,180
Net reduction in cash account	($ 5,600)
Cash at beginning of year	57,600
Cash at end of year	$ 52,000

OTHER DATA	2000	1999
December 31 stock price	$ 6.00	$ 8.50
Number of shares	100,000	100,000
Dividends per share	$ 0.22	$ 0.22
Lease payments	$ 40,000	$ 40,000

Industry average data for 2000:

RATIO	INDUSTRY AVERAGE
Current	2.7×
Quick	1.0×
Inventory turnover	6.0×
Days sales outstanding (DSO)	32.0 days
Fixed assets turnover	10.7×
Total assets turnover	2.6×
Debt ratio	50.0%
TIE	2.5×
Fixed charge coverage	2.1×
Profit margin	3.5%
ROA	9.1%
ROE	18.2%
Price/earnings	14.2×
Market/book	1.4×

Assume that you are Donna Jamison's assistant and that she has asked you to help her prepare a report that evaluates the company's financial condition. Then answer the following questions:

a. What can you conclude about the company's financial condition from its statement of cash flows?

b. What is the purpose of financial ratio analysis, and what are the five major categories of ratios?

c. What are Computron's current and quick ratios? What do they tell you about the company's liquidity position?

d. What are Computron's inventory turnover, days sales outstanding, fixed assets turnover, and total assets turnover ratios? How does the firm's utilization of assets stack up against that of the industry?

e. What are the firm's debt, times-interest-earned, and fixed charge coverage ratios? How does Computron compare to the industry with respect to financial leverage? What conclusions can you draw from these ratios?

f. Calculate and discuss the firm's profitability ratios—that is, its profit margin, return on assets (ROA), and return on equity (ROE).

g. Calculate Computron's market value ratios—that is, its price/earnings ratio and its market/book ratio. What do these ratios tell you about investors' opinions of the company?

h. Use the DuPont equation to provide a summary and overview of Computron's financial condition. What are the firm's major strengths and weaknesses?

i. Use the following simplified 2000 balance sheet to show, in general terms, how an improvement in one of the ratios, say, the DSO, would affect the stock price. For example, if the company could improve its collection procedures and thereby lower the DSO from 37.6 days to 27.6 days, how would that change "ripple through" the financial statements (shown in thousands below) and influence the stock price?

Accounts receivable	$ 402	Debt	$ 965
Other current assets	888		
Net fixed assets	361	Equity	686
Total assets	$1,651	Total liabilities and equity	$1,651

j. Although financial statement analysis can provide useful information about a company's operations and its financial condition, this type of analysis does have some potential problems and limitations, and it must be used with care and judgment. What are some problems and limitations?

Computer-Related Problem

Work the problem in this section only if you are using the computer problem diskette.

ratio analysis   **3–15** Use the computerized model in the File C3 to solve this problem.

a. Refer to Problem 3–5. Suppose Cary Corporation is considering installing a new computer system that would provide tighter control of inventories, accounts receivable, and accounts payable. If the new system is installed, the following data are projected (rather than the data given in Problem 3–5) for the indicated balance sheet and income statement accounts:

Accounts receivable	$ 395,000
Inventories	700,000
Other fixed assets	150,000
Accounts and notes payable	275,000
Accruals	120,000
Cost of goods sold	3,450,000
Administrative and selling expenses	248,775
P/E ratio	6×

How do these changes affect the projected ratios and the comparison with the industry averages? (Note that any changes to the income statement will change the amount of retained earnings; therefore, the model is set up to calculate 2001 retained earnings as 2000 retained earnings plus net income minus dividends paid. The model also adjusts the cash balance so that the balance sheet balances.)

b. If the new computer were even more efficient than Cary's management had estimated and thus caused the cost of goods sold to decrease by $125,000 from the projections in part a, what effect would that have on the company's financial position?

c. If the new computer were less efficient than Cary's management had estimated and caused the cost of goods sold to increase by $125,000 from the projections in part a, what effect would that have on the company's financial position?

d. Change, one by one, the other items in part a to see how each change affects the ratio analysis. Then think about and write a paragraph describing how computer models like this one can be used to help make better decisions about the purchase of such things as a new computer system.

ONLINE ESSENTIALS

http://www.icbinc.com   Investor Communications Business, Inc.
Provides annual reports for companies listed in *The Wall Street Journal* that have the symbol ♣ next to their names. In addition, links to related sites are found here. Many reports are also available from the companies' Web sites.

http://www.wsj.com   Wall Street Journal
Various articles about businesses and the economy can be found here; there are also links to databases that include financial information from corporations and to related sites.

Chapter 4

Financial Planning and Control

A Managerial Perspective

In November 1994, Sony Corporation, the Japanese consumer electronics firm, wrote off more than $3.2 billion in assets, causing the book value of its assets to immediately decrease by about 30 percent and the market value of its stock to decrease by 13 percent within a one-week period. The write-off was directly attributed to Sony Pictures, the motion picture business that had been formed five years earlier with the $5 billion purchase of Columbia Pictures and TriStar Pictures from Coca-Cola Company. According to most analysts, the success of Sony's 1988 purchase of CBS Records, one of the world's largest record companies, teased the company into expanding its entertainment operations to the "Hollywood scene." Unfortunately, Sony did not follow the old adage "Look before you leap"— company executives seemingly did not have a formal financial plan or control mechanism for the movie business. Michael Schulhof, chairman of Sony Corporation of America, was put in charge of Sony Pictures, even though he was unknown in the motion picture industry. He hired two movie producers, neither of whom had previous experience running a movie studio, to head the production facilities. From 1989 to 1994 more than $1 billion was spent on refurbishing studio lots and on executive perquisites such as fresh flowers, antiques, private chefs, and lavish parties. But Sony Pictures' movie-production companies, Columbia and TriStar, were unable to consistently produce hit movies; in fact, most of the pictures were expensive flops, including *Last Action Hero*, *I'll Do Anything*, and *Mary Shelley's Frankenstein*. Was Sony Pictures just unlucky? Not according to Chuck Goto, an analyst with Smith Barney at the time, who noted that "[i]f you look at it very objectively, it's clear the company mismanaged shareholders' money" by not planning adequately. It seems the only plan Sony had was to pour money into movies, and this strategy was destined to fail because there was not adequate forecasting and control to head off any problems that arose.

Even though it replaced the management and reorganized the operational structure of its motion picture business at the end of 1994, Sony had additional write-offs in 1995. Since that time, however, Sony Pictures Entertainment (SPE) has produced some hit motion pictures that have helped SPE weather the rocky financial storm it inherited from the previous managers. In fact, in 1997, the Columbia TriStar Motion Picture Group (the moniker that was born with the reorganization) broke revenue records in the motion picture industry by grossing nearly $1.3 billion in U.S. theaters and more than $2.3 billion internationally. Some of the movies that helped SPE achieve this success included *Men in Black*, *My Best Friend's Wedding*, and *Air Force One*.

Many of the problems Sony Pictures originally experienced could have been avoided or reduced substantially if Sony Corporation had a financial plan in place before it entered the movie industry. Most analysts agree that the value of Sony

continues

Pictures had decreased by about 50 percent from 1989 to 1994 when Sony began "biting the bullet" and initiated efforts to turn around its motion picture business. At that time, Sony had to evaluate the effects on forecasted earnings and stock prices of cutting certain costs, writing off additional assets and controlling the finances associated with the motion picture businesses—a *plan* was devised to salvage Sony Pictures, which provided encouragement to Sony Corporation's investors and potential investors and proved successful, at least so far. ■

FINANCIAL PLANNING
The projection of sales, income, and assets based on alternative production and marketing strategies, as well as the determination of the resources needed to achieve these projections.

In the previous chapter, we focused on how to use financial statement analysis to evaluate the existing financial position of a firm. In this chapter, we will see how a financial manager can use some of the information obtained through financial statement analysis for financial planning and control of the firm's future operations. Well-run companies generally base their operating plans on a set of forecasted financial statements. The **financial planning** process begins with a sales forecast for the next few years. Then the assets required to meet the sales targets are determined, and a decision is made concerning how to finance the required assets. At that point, income statements and balance sheets can be projected, and earnings and dividends per share, as well as the key ratios, can be forecasted.

FINANCIAL CONTROL
The phase in which financial plans are implemented; control deals with the feedback and adjustment process required to ensure adherence to plans and modification of plans because of unforeseen changes.

Once the "base case" forecasted financial statements and ratios have been prepared, top managers want to know (1) how realistic the results are, (2) how to attain the results, and (3) what impact changes in operations would have on the forecasts. At this stage, which is the **financial control** phase, the firm is concerned with implementing the financial plans, or forecasts, and dealing with the feedback and adjustment process that is necessary to ensure the goals of the firm are pursued appropriately.

The first part of the chapter is devoted to financial planning using projected financial statements, or forecasts, and the second part of the chapter focuses on financial control using budgeting and the analysis of leverage to determine how changes in operations affect financial forecasts.

Sales Forecasts

SALES FORECAST
A forecast of a firm's unit and dollar sales for some future period; generally based on recent sales trends plus forecasts of the economic prospects for the nation, region, industry, and so forth.

Forecasting is an essential part of the planning process, and a **sales forecast** is the most important ingredient of financial forecasting. The sales forecast generally starts with a review of sales during the past five to ten years, which can be expressed in a graph such as that in Figure 4–1. The first part of the graph shows five years of historical sales for Unilate Textiles, the textile and clothing manufacturer we analyzed in the previous chapter. The graph could have contained ten years of sales data, but Unilate typically focuses on sales figures for the latest five years because the firm's studies have shown that future growth is more closely related to the recent than to the distant past.

Unilate had its ups and downs during the period from 1996 through 2000. In 1998, poor cotton production in the United States and diseased sheep in Australia resulted in low textile production, which caused sales to fall below the 1997 level. Then a significant increase in both the supply of cotton and the supply of wool in 1999 pushed sales up by 15 percent. Based on a regression analysis, Unilate's forecasters determined

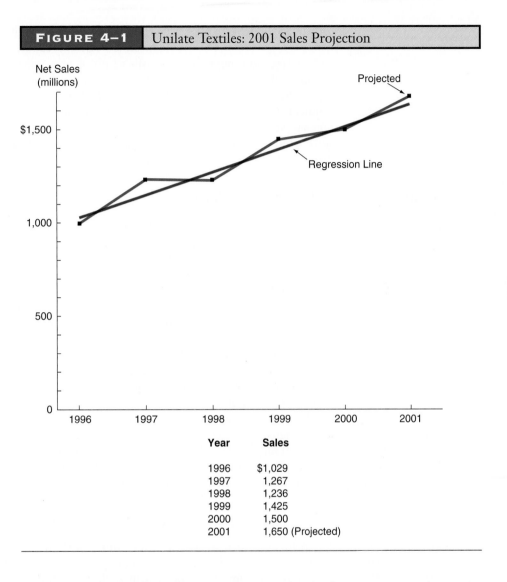

FIGURE 4–1 | Unilate Textiles: 2001 Sales Projection

Year	Sales
1996	$1,029
1997	1,267
1998	1,236
1999	1,425
2000	1,500
2001	1,650 (Projected)

that the average annual growth rate in sales over the past five years was nearly ten percent. To determine the forecasted sales growth for 2001, some of the factors that Unilate considered included projections of expected economic activity, competitive conditions, and product development and distribution both in the markets in which Unilate currently operates and in the markets it plans to enter into in the future. Often firms develop mathematical models such as regression equations to take into consideration such factors when forecasting future sales. Based on its historical sales trend, plans for new product and market introductions, and Unilate's forecast for the economy, the firm's planning committee has projected a ten percent growth rate for sales during 2001. So 2001 sales are expected to be $1,650 million, which is ten percent higher than 2000 sales of $1,500 million.

If the sales forecast is inaccurate, the consequences can be serious. First, if the market expands significantly *more* than Unilate has geared up for, the company probably will not be able to meet demand. Customers will buy competitors' products, and Unilate will lose market share, which will be hard to regain. On the other hand, if the projections are overly optimistic, Unilate could end up with too much plant, equipment, and inventory. This would mean low turnover ratios, high costs for depreciation and storage, and, possibly, write-offs of obsolete or unusable inventory. All of this would result in a low rate of return on equity, which in turn would depress the company's stock price. If Unilate had financed an unnecessary expansion with debt, its problems would, of course, be compounded. Remember from our analysis of its 2000 financial statements in the previous chapter that Unilate's current financial position is considered poor. Thus, an accurate sales forecast is critical to the well-being of the firm.[1]

Self-Test Questions

How do past trends affect a sales forecast?

Briefly explain why an accurate sales forecast is critical to profitability.

Projected (Pro Forma) Financial Statements

ADDITIONAL FUNDS NEEDED (AFN)
Funds that a firm must raise externally through borrowing or by selling new stock.

Any forecast of financial requirements involves (1) determining how much money the firm will need during a given period, (2) determining how much money the firm will generate internally during the same period, and (3) subtracting the funds generated from the funds required to determine the external financial requirements. One method used to estimate external requirements is the *projected, or pro forma, balance sheet method*, which is discussed in this section.

The projected balance sheet method is straightforward—simply project the asset requirements for the coming period, then project the liabilities and equity that will be generated under normal operations, and subtract the projected liabilities and equity from the required assets to estimate the **additional funds needed (AFN)** to support the level of forecasted operations. The steps in the procedure are explained next.

Step 1. Forecast the 2001 Income Statement

PROJECTED (PRO FORMA) BALANCE SHEET METHOD
A method of forecasting financial requirements based on forecasted financial statements.

The **projected (pro forma) balance sheet method** begins with a forecast of sales. Next, the income statement for the coming year is forecasted to obtain an initial estimate of the amount of retained earnings the company will generate during the year. This requires assumptions about the operating cost ratio, the tax rate, interest charges, and the dividends paid. In the simplest case, the assumption is made that costs will increase at the same rate as sales; in more complicated situations, cost changes are forecasted separately. Still, the objective of this part of the analysis is to determine how much income the company will earn and then retain for reinvestment in the business during the forecasted year.

Table 4–1 shows Unilate's actual 2000 income statement and the initial forecast of the 2001 income statement if the conditions just mentioned exist. To create the 2001

---

[1]A sales forecast is actually the *expected value of a probability distribution* with many possible levels of sales. Because any sales forecast is subject to a greater or lesser degree of uncertainty, for financial planning we are often just as interested in the degree of uncertainty inherent in the sales forecast (σ sales) as we are in the expected value of sales. The concepts of probability distribution measures as they apply to corporate finance are discussed in Chapter 5.

TABLE 4–1	Unilate Textiles: Actual 2000 and Projected 2001 Income Statements (millions of dollars, except per share data)		

	2000 RESULTS	2001 FORECAST BASIS[a]	INITIAL FORECAST
Net sales	$ 1,500.0	× 1.10	$ 1,650.0
Cost of goods sold	(1,230.0)	× 1.10	(1,353.0)
Gross profit	$ 270.0		$ 297.0
Fixed operating costs except depreciation	(90.0)	× 1.10	(99.0)
Depreciation	(50.0)	× 1.10	(55.0)
Earnings before interest and taxes (EBIT)	$ 130.0		143.0
Less interest	(40.0)		(40.0)[b]
Earnings before taxes (EBT)	$ 90.0		$ 103.0
Taxes (40%)	(36.0)		(41.2)
Net Income	$ 54.0		$ 61.8
Common dividends	(29.0)		(29.0)[b]
Addition to retained earnings	$ 25.0		$ 32.8
Earnings per share	$ 2.16		$ 2.47
Dividends per share	$ 1.16		$ 1.16
Number of common shares (millions)	25.00		25.00

[a]× 1.10 indicates "times (1 + g)"; used for items that grow proportionally with sales.

[b]Indicates a 2000 figure carried over for the preliminary forecast.

income forecast, we assume that sales and variable operating costs will be ten percent greater in 2001 than in 2000. In addition, it is assumed that Unilate currently operates at full capacity, so it will need to expand its plant capacity in 2001 to handle the additional operations. Therefore, in Table 4–1, the 2001 forecasts of sales, *all* operating costs, and depreciation are 10 percent greater than their 2000 levels. The result is that earnings before interest and taxes (EBIT) is forecasted to be $143 million in 2001.

To complete the initial forecast of 2001 income, we assume no change in the financing of the firm because, at this point, it is not known if additional financing is needed. But it is apparent that the 2001 interest expense will change if the amount of debt (borrowing) the firm needs to support the forecasted increase in operations changes. To forecast the 2001 dividends, we simply assume the dividend per share will be the same as it was in 2000, $1.16; so the total common dividends forecasted for 2001 would be $29.0 million if no additional common stock is issued. Like the interest expense amount, however, the amount of total dividends used to create this initial forecast will change if Unilate decides to sell new stock to raise any additional financing necessary to support the new operations or to raise the dividends per share paid to existing shareholders.

From the initial forecast of 2001 income contained in Table 4–1, we can see that $32.8 million dollars is expected to be added to retained earnings in 2001. As it turns out, this addition to retained earnings represents the amount Unilate is expected to invest in itself (internally generated funds) to support the increase in operations in 2001. So the next step is to determine what impact this level of investment will have on the Unilate's forecasted 2001 balance sheet.

Step 2. Forecast the 2001 Balance Sheet

If we assume the 2000 end-of-year asset levels were just sufficient to support 2000 operations, then in order for Unilate's sales to increase in 2001, its assets must also grow. Because the company was operating at full capacity in 2000, *each* asset account must increase if the higher sales level is to be attained: More cash will be needed for transactions, higher sales will lead to higher receivables, additional inventory will have to be stocked, and new plant and equipment must be added for production.

Further, if Unilate's assets are to increase, its liabilities and equity must also increase—the additional assets must be financed in some manner. Some liabilities will increase *spontaneously* due to normal business relationships. For example, as sales increase, so will Unilate's purchases of raw materials, and these larger purchases will spontaneously lead to higher levels of accounts payable. Similarly, a higher level of operations will require more labor, while higher sales will result in higher taxable income. Therefore, both accrued wages and accrued taxes will increase. In general, these current liability accounts, which provide **spontaneously generated funds,** will increase at the same rate as sales.

Notes payable, long-term bonds, and common stock will not rise spontaneously with sales—rather, the projected levels of these accounts will depend on conscious financing decisions that will be made later. Therefore, for the initial forecast, it is assumed these account balances remain unchanged from their 2000 levels.

Table 4–2 contains Unilate's 2000 actual balance sheet and an initial forecast of its 2001 balance sheet. The mechanics of the balance sheet forecast are similar to those used to develop the forecasted income statement. First, those balance sheet accounts that are expected to increase directly with sales are multiplied by 1.10 to obtain the initial 2001 forecasts. Thus, 2001 cash is projected to be $15.0 \times 1.10 = \$16.5$ million, accounts receivable are projected to be $180.0 \times 1.10 = \$198.0$ million, and so on. In our example, all assets increase with sales, so once the individual assets have been forecasted, they can be summed to complete the asset side of the forecasted balance sheet.

Next, the spontaneously increasing liabilities (accounts payable and accruals) are forecasted. Then those liability and equity accounts whose values reflect conscious management decisions—notes payable, long-term bonds, and stock—*initially are forecasted* to remain at their 2000 levels. Thus, the amount of 2001 notes payable initially is set at $40.0 million, the long-term bond account is forecasted at $300.0 million, and so forth. The forecasted 2001 level of retained earnings will be the 2000 level plus the forecasted addition to retained earnings, which was computed as $32.8 million in the projected income statement we created in Step 1 (Table 4–1).

The forecast of total assets in Table 4–2 is $929.5 million, which indicates that Unilate must add $84.5 million of new assets (compared to 2000 assets) to support the higher sales level expected in 2001. However, according to the initial forecast of the 2001 balance sheet, the total liabilities and equity sum to only $886.8 million, which is an increase of only $41.8 million. So the amount of total assets exceeds the amount of total liabilities and equity by $42.7 million = $929.5 million − $886.8 million. This indicates $42.7 million of the forecasted increase in total assets will not be financed by liabilities that spontaneously increase with sales (accounts payable and accruals) or by an increase in retained earnings. Unilate can raise the additional $42.7 million, which we designate *additional funds needed (AFN)*, by borrowing from the bank as notes

SPONTANEOUSLY GENERATED FUNDS Funds that are obtained from routine business transactions.

TABLE 4–2	Unilate Textiles: Actual 2000 and Projected 2001 Balance Sheets (millions of dollars)

	2000 BALANCES	**FORECAST BASIS[a]**	**2001 INITIAL FORECAST**
Cash	$ 15.0	× 1.10	$ 16.5
Accounts receivable	180.0	× 1.10	198.0
Inventories	270.0	× 1.10	297.0
Total current assets	$465.0		$511.5
Net plant and equipment	380.0	× 1.10	418.0
Total Assets	$845.0		$929.5
Accounts payable	$ 30.0	× 1.10	$ 33.0
Accruals	60.0	× 1.10	66.0
Notes payable	40.0		40.0[b]
Total current liabilities	$130.0		$139.0
Long-term bonds	300.0		300.0[b]
Total liabilities	$430.0		$439.0
Common stock	130.0		130.0[b]
Retained earnings	285.0	+$32.8[d]	317.8
Total owners' equity	$415.0		$447.8
Total Liabilities and Equity	$845.0		$886.8
Additional funds needed (AFN)			$ 42.7[c]

[a] × 1.10 indicates "times (1 + g)"; used for items which grow proportionally with sales.

[b] Indicates a 2000 figure carried over for the initial forecast.

[c] The "additional funds needed (AFN)" is computed by subtracting the amount of total liabilities and equity from the amount of total assets.

[d] The $32.8 million represents the "addition to retained earnings" from the 2001 Projected Income Statement given in Table 4–1.

payable, by issuing long-term bonds, by selling new common stock, or by some combination of these actions.

The initial forecast of Unilate's financial statements has shown us that (1) higher sales must be supported by higher asset levels, (2) some of the asset increases can be financed by spontaneous increases in accounts payable and accruals and by retained earnings, and (3) any shortfall must be financed from external sources, either by borrowing or by selling new stock.

Step 3. Raising the Additional Funds Needed

Unilate's financial manager will base the decision of exactly how to raise the $42.7 million additional funds needed on several factors, including its ability to handle additional debt, conditions in the financial markets, and restrictions imposed by existing

✳ INDUSTRY PRACTICE

What Is a "Good" Sales Forecast?

Managers know that sales forecasts are essential for effective planning and future survival of their businesses. In this chapter, we describe only one rather simple forecasting technique—pro forma forecasting.

There are numerous forecasting techniques that can be used to predict sales; some of the procedures are quantitative and very sophisticated, while others are rather subjective in nature. Many of the quantitative methods are inexpensive to apply, and they provide more accurate forecasts than the judgmental, "seat-of-the-pants" forecasting approaches. Given the current understanding of the quantitative models, many of which are covered in the curricula offered by business schools, and the proliferation of computer technology in business, you would expect most managers to use the more sophisticated sales forecasting methods. But a recent survey of 500 companies in the United States indicates that managers primarily rely on judgmental methods, including the manager's opinion, to formulate sales forecasts, not the more sophisticated, quantitative techniques. The managers surveyed indicated they possessed the knowledge and technology to apply the quantitative forecasting methods, but most preferred to trust their own or their colleagues' experiences when forecasting sales. Even those managers who use quantitative methods stated that they generally subjectively adjust the forecasts resulting from these models to incorporate qualitative factors, including knowledge of the operating environment, the product quality, and previous experience with the models. In fact, the results of the survey suggest that the primary reasons managers do not use sophisticated forecasting models is because they believe the data needed to use such models appropriately either are not relevant or are not available.

Consequently, for the most part, managers believe their judgments provide sales forecasts that are as "good" as sophisticated models. "Good" might not relate to forecast accuracy, though, because about 85 percent of the survey's respondents indicated that they would prefer to either underestimate or overestimate when forecasting sales. More than 70 percent said they "underforecast" sales because when the forecast is exceeded, an explanation is not needed and a reward might even be considered; but, when actual sales turn out to be less than forecasted, job security becomes tenuous. Interestingly, the respondents who said they "overforecast" indicated that the primary reason was because they could get more staff to support the higher amount of sales. So, to many managers, forecasting sales is more of an art than a science.

SOURCE: Nada R. Sanders and Karl B. Manrodt, "Forecasting Practices in U.S. Corporations: Survey Results," *Interfaces*, March–April 1994, 92(9).

debt agreements. The decisions concerning how to best finance the firm are discussed in Chapter 11. At this point, it is important to understand that, regardless of how Unilate raises the $42.7 million AFN, the initial forecasts of both the income statement and the balance sheet will be affected. If Unilate takes on new debt, its interest expenses will rise; and if additional shares of common stock are sold, *total* dividend payments will increase if the *same dividend per share* is paid to all common stockholders. Each of these changes, which we term financing feedbacks, will affect the amount of additional retained earnings originally forecasted, which in turn will affect the amount of additional funds needed.

Remember from our ratio analysis in the previous chapter that we concluded Unilate has a below-average debt position. Consequently, Unilate has decided any additional funds needed to support future operations will be raised mainly by issuing new common stock. Following this financing policy should help improve Unilate's debt position as well as its overall profitability.

Step 4. Financing Feedbacks

FINANCING FEEDBACKS
The effects on the income statement and balance sheet of actions taken to finance forecasted increases in assets.

As mentioned in Step 3, one complexity that arises in financial forecasting relates to **financing feedbacks.** The external funds raised to pay for new assets create additional expenses that must be reflected in the income statement and that lower the initially forecasted addition to retained earnings, which means more external funds are needed to make up for the lower amount added to retained earnings. In other words, if Unilate raised the $42.7 million AFN by issuing new debt and new common stock, it would find both the interest expense and the total dividend payments would be higher than the amounts contained in the forecasted income statement shown in Table 4–1. Consequently, after adjusting for the higher interest and dividend payments, the forecasted addition to retained earnings would be lower than the initial forecast of $32.8 million. Because the retained earnings will be lower than projected, a financing shortfall will exist even after the original AFN of $42.7 million is considered. So in reality, Unilate must raise more than $42.7 million to account for the financing feedbacks that affect the amount of internal financing expected to be generated from the increase in operations. To determine the amount of external financing actually needed, we have to adjust the initial forecasts of both the income statement (Step 1) and the balance sheet (Step 2) to reflect the impact of raising the additional external financing. This process has to be repeated until AFN = 0 in Table 4–2, which means Step 1 and Step 2 might have to be repeated several times to fully account for the financing feedbacks.

Table 4–3 contains the adjusted 2001 preliminary forecasts for the income statement and the balance sheet of Unilate Textiles after all of the financing effects are considered. To generate the adjusted forecasts, it is assumed that of the total external funds needed, 65 percent will be raised by selling new common stock at $23 per share, 15 percent will be borrowed from the bank at an interest rate of seven percent, and 20 percent will be raised by selling long-term bonds with a coupon interest of ten percent. Under these conditions, it can be seen from Table 4–3 that Unilate actually needs $45.0 million to support the forecasted increase in operations, not the $42.7 million contained in the initial forecast. The additional $2.3 million is needed because the added amounts of debt and common stock will cause interest and dividend payments to increase, which will decrease the contribution to retained earnings by $2.3 million.[2]

Analysis of the Forecast

The 2001 forecast as developed here represents a preliminary forecast, because we have completed only the first stage of the entire forecasting process. Next, the projected statements must be analyzed to determine whether the forecast meets the firm's financial targets. If the statements do not meet the targets, then elements of the forecast must be changed.

Table 4–4 shows Unilate's 2000 ratios as they were reported back in Table 3–6 in the previous chapter, plus the projected 2001 ratios based on the preliminary forecast and the industry average ratios. As we noted in Chapter 3, the firm's financial condition at the close of 2000 was weak, with many ratios being well below the industry averages. The preliminary final forecast for 2001 (after financing feedbacks are considered), which assumes that Unilate's past practices will continue into the future, shows an improved debt position. But the overall financial position still is somewhat weak, and this condition will persist unless management takes some actions to improve things.

---

[2]Appendix 4A gives a more detailed description of the iterations required to generate the final forecasts.

TABLE 4–3	Unilate Textiles: 2001 Adjusted Forecast of Financial Statements (millions of dollars)

INCOME STATEMENT

	INITIAL FORECAST	ADJUSTED FORECAST	FINANCING ADJUSTMENT
Net sales	$ 1,650.0	$ 1,650.0	
Cost of goods sold	(1,353.0)	(1,353.0)	
Gross profit	$ 297.0	$ 297.0	
Fixed operating costs except depreciation	(99.0)	(99.0)	
Depreciation	(55.0)	(55.0)	
Earnings before interest and taxes (EBIT)	$ 143.0	$ 143.0	
Less interest	(40.0)	(41.4)	(1.4)
Earnings before taxes (EBT)	$ 103.0	$ 101.6	(1.4)
Taxes (40%)	(41.2)	(40.7)	0.5
Net Income	$ 61.8	$ 61.0	(0.8)[b]
Common dividends	(29.0)	(30.5)	(1.5)
Addition to retained earnings	$ 32.8	$ 30.5	(2.3)[a]
Earnings per share	$ 2.47	$ 2.32	
Dividends per share	$ 1.16	$ 1.16	
Number of common shares (millions)	25.00	26.27	

BALANCE SHEET

Cash	$ 16.5	$ 16.5	
Accounts receivable	198.0	198.0	
Inventories	297.0	297.0	
Total current assets	$511.5	$ 511.5	
Net plant and equipment	418.0	418.0	
Total Assets	$929.5	$ 929.5	
Accounts payable	$ 33.0	$ 33.0	
Accruals	66.0	66.0	
Notes payable	40.0	46.8	$ 6.8
Total current liabilities	$139.0	$ 145.8	
Long-term bonds	300.0	309.0	$ 9.0
Total liabilities	$439.0	$ 454.8	

continues

TABLE 4-3	Concluded

BALANCE SHEET

	INITIAL FORECAST	ADJUSTED FORECAST	FINANCING ADJUSTMENT
Common stock	130.0	159.3	$ 29.3
Retained earnings	317.8	315.5	$ (2.3)[a]
Total owners' equity	$447.8	$ 474.8	
Total Liabilities and Equity	$886.8	$ 929.5	
Additional Funds Needed (AFN)	$ 42.7	$ 0.0	$ 42.8 [b,c]

[a] The financing adjustment for the addition to retained earnings in the income statement is the same as the financing adjustment for retained earnings in the balance sheet.

[b] Rounding difference.

[c] The total AFN, or external funding needs, equal $42.7 million plus the $2.3 million decrease in the change in retained earnings from the initial forecast; thus, total funds needed equal $45.0 million—$6.8 million will be from new bank notes, $9.0 million will come from issuing new bonds, and $29.3 million will be raised by issuing new common stock.

TABLE 4-4	Unilate Textiles: Key Ratios

	2000	ADJUSTED PRELIMINARY 2001	INDUSTRY AVERAGE
Current ratio	3.6×	3.5×	4.1×
Inventory turnover	4.6×	5.6×	7.4×
Days sales outstanding	43.2 days	43.2 days	32.1 days
Total assets turnover	1.8×	1.8×	2.1×
Debt ratio	50.9%	48.9%	45.0%
Times interest earned	3.3×	3.5×	6.5×
Profit margin	3.6%	3.7%	4.7%
Return on assets	6.4%	6.6%	12.6%
Return on equity	13.0%	12.8%	17.2%

Unilate's management actually plans to take steps to improve its financial condition. The plans are to (1) close down certain operations, (2) modify the credit policy to reduce the collection period for receivables, and (3) better manage inventory so that products are turned over more often. These proposed operational changes will affect both the income statement and the balance sheet, so the preliminary forecast will have to be revised again to reflect the impact of such changes. When this process is complete, management will have its final forecast. To keep things simple, we do not show the final forecast here; instead, for the remaining discussions we assume the preliminary forecast is not substantially different and use it as the final forecast for Unilate's 2001 operations.

As we have shown, forecasting is an iterative process, both in the way the financial statements are generated and in the way the financial plan is developed. For planning purposes, the financial staff develops a preliminary forecast based on a continuation of past policies and trends. This provides the executives with a starting point, or "straw man" forecast. Next, the model is modified to see what effects alternative operating plans would have on the firm's earnings and financial condition. This results in a revised forecast.

Self-Test Questions

What is the AFN, and how is the projected balance sheet method used to estimate it?

What is a financing feedback, and how do financing feedbacks affect the estimate of AFN?

Why is it necessary for the forecasting process to be iterative?

Other Considerations in Forecasting

We have presented a very simple method for constructing pro forma financial statements under rather restrictive conditions. In this section, we describe some other conditions that should be considered when creating forecasts.

Excess Capacity

The construction of the 2001 forecasts for Unilate was based on the assumption that the firm's 2000 operations were at full capacity, so any increase in sales would require additional assets, especially plant and equipment. If Unilate did *not* operate at full capacity in 2000, then plant and equipment would only have to be increased if the additional sales (operations) forecasted in 2001 exceeded the unused capacity of the existing assets. For example, if Unilate actually utilized only 80 percent of its fixed assets' capacity to produce 2000 sales of $1,500 million, then

$$\$1,500.0 \text{ million} = 0.80 \times (\text{Plant capacity})$$

$$\text{Plant capacity} = \frac{\$1,500.0 \text{ million}}{0.80} = \$1,875 \text{ million}$$

In this case, then, Unilate could increase sales to $1,875 million, or by 25 percent of 2000 sales, before full capacity is reached and plant and equipment would have to be increased. In general, we can compute the sales capacity of the firm if it is known what percent of assets are utilized to produce a particular level of sales:

$$\text{Full capacity sales} = \frac{\text{Sales level}}{\left(\begin{array}{c}\text{Percent of capacity used} \\ \text{to generate sales level}\end{array}\right)}$$

If Unilate does not have to increase plant and equipment, fixed assets would remain at the 2000 level of $380 million, so the amount of AFN would be $4.7 million, which is $38 million (ten percent of $380 million fixed assets) less than the initial forecast reported in Table 4–1.

In addition to the excess capacity of fixed assets, the firm could have excesses in other assets that can be used for increases in operations. For instance, in the previous chapter, we concluded that Unilate's inventory level at the end of 2000 probably was greater than it should have been. If true, some increase in 2001 forecasted sales can be absorbed by the above-normal inventory and production would not have to be increased until inventory levels are reduced to normal—this requires no additional financing.

In general, excess capacity means less external financing is required to support increases in operations than would be needed if the firm previously operated at full capacity.

Economies of Scale

There are economies of scale in the use of many types of assets, and when such economies occur, a firm's variable cost of goods sold ratio is likely to change as the size of the firm changes (either increases or decreases) substantially. Currently, Unilate's variable cost ratio is 82 percent of sales; but the ratio might decrease to 80 percent of sales if operations increase significantly. If everything else is the same, changes in the variable cost ratio affect the addition to retained earnings, which in turn affects the amount of AFN.

Lumpy Assets

LUMPY ASSETS
Assets that cannot be acquired in small increments; instead, they must be obtained in large, discrete amounts.

In many industries, technological considerations dictate that if a firm is to be competitive, it must add fixed assets in large, discrete units; such assets often are referred to as **lumpy assets.** For example, in the paper industry, there are strong economies of scale in basic paper mill equipment, so when a paper company expands capacity, it must do so in large, lumpy increments. Lumpy assets primarily affect the turnover of fixed assets and, consequently, the financial requirements associated with expanding. For instance, if instead of $38 million Unilate needed an additional $50 million in fixed assets to increase operations ten percent, the AFN would be much greater. With *lumpy assets*, it is possible that a small projected increase in sales would require a significant increase in plant and equipment, which would require a very large financial requirement.

Self-Test Question

Discuss three factors that might cause "spontaneous" assets and liabilities to change at a different rate than sales.

Financial Control—Budgeting and Leverage

In the previous section, we focused on financial forecasting, emphasizing how growth in sales requires additional investment in assets, which in turn generally requires the firm to raise new funds externally. In the sections that follow, we consider the planning and control systems used by financial managers when implementing the forecasts.

First, we look at the relationship between sales volume and profitability under different operating conditions. These relationships provide information that is used by managers to plan for changes in the firm's level of operations, financing needs, and profitability. Later, we examine the control phase of the planning and control process, because a good control system is essential both to ensure that plans are executed properly and to facilitate a timely modification of plans if the assumptions on which the initial plans were based turn out to be different than expected.

The planning process can be enhanced by examining the effects of changing operations on the firm's profitability, both from the standpoint of profits from operations and from the standpoint of profitability after financing effects are considered. When Jack Smith became CEO at General Motors in 1992, he and his management team examined the operations that existed at GM at that time. They found the company's performance to be dismal, especially in North America, which produced almost a $5 billion loss in earnings before interest and taxes. Part of the solution to GM's problems was to reduce operating and financing costs in order to create more efficient operations—the hope was to break even, or to bring operating income up to zero, by 1993. That goal was accomplished, and in 1998 operating income from North American operations was nearly $3 billion. To achieve this turnaround, Smith and his staff at GM had to evaluate the impact on sales and net income of reducing costs through layoffs, savings in materials purchases, lowering debt, and so forth. In the next few sections, we look at some of the areas Smith might have evaluated to provide information about the effects of changing GM's operations.

Self-Test Question

How can the planning process be enhanced with a good financial control system?

Operating Breakeven Analysis

**OPERATING
BREAKEVEN
ANALYSIS**
An analytical technique for studying the relationship between sales revenues, operating costs, and profits.

The relationship between sales volume and operating profitability is explored in cost-volume-profit planning, or operating breakeven analysis. **Operating breakeven analysis** is a method of determining the point at which sales will just cover operating costs—that is, the point at which the firm's operations will break even. It also shows the magnitude of the firm's operating profits or losses if sales exceed or fall below that point. Breakeven analysis is important in the planning and control process because the cost-volume-profit relationship can be influenced greatly by the proportion of the firm's investment in assets that are fixed. A sufficient volume of sales must be anticipated and achieved if fixed and variable costs are to be covered, or else the firm will incur losses from operations. In other words, if a firm is to avoid accounting losses, its sales must cover all costs—those that vary directly with production and those that remain constant even when production levels change. Costs that vary directly with the level of production generally include the labor and materials needed to produce and sell the product, while the fixed operating costs generally include costs such as depreciation, rent, and insurance expenses that are incurred regardless of the firm's production level.

Operating breakeven analysis deals only with the upper portion of the income statement—the portion from sales to net operating income (NOI), which is also termed

TABLE 4-5	Unilate Textiles: 2001 Forecasted Operating Income (millions of dollars)

Sales (S)	$ 1,650.0
Variable cost of goods sold (VC)	(1,353.0)
Gross profit (GP)	$ 297.0
Fixed operating costs (F)	(154.0)
Net operating income (NOI)	$ 143.0

NOTES:

Sales in units = 110 million units.

Selling price per unit = $15.00.

Variable costs per unit = $1,353/110 = $12.30

Fixed operating costs = $154 million, which includes $55 million depreciation and $99 million in other fixed costs such as rent, insurance, and general office expenses.

earnings before interest and taxes (EBIT). This portion generally is referred to as the *operating section*, because it contains only the revenues and expenses associated with the normal production and selling operations of the firm. Table 4–5 gives the operating section of Unilate's forecasted 2001 income statement, which was shown in Table 4–3. For the discussion that follows, we have assumed that all of Unilate's products sell for $15.00 each and the variable cost of goods sold per unit is $12.30, which is 82 percent of the selling price.

Breakeven Graph

Table 4–5 shows the net operating income for Unilate if 110 million products are produced and sold during the year. But what if Unilate doesn't sell 110 million products? Certainly, the firm's net operating income will be something other than $143 million. Figure 4–2 shows the total revenues and total operating costs for Unilate at various levels of sales, beginning with zero. According to the information given in Table 4–5, Unilate has fixed costs, which include depreciation, rent, insurance, and so on, equal to $154 million. This amount must be paid even if the firm produces and sells nothing, so the $154 million fixed cost is represented by a horizontal line. If Unilate produces and sells nothing, its sales revenues will be zero; but *for each unit sold*, the firm's sales will increase by $15. Therefore, the total revenue line starts at the origin of the X and Y axes, and it has a slope equal to $15.00 to account for the dollar increase in sales for each additional unit sold. On the other hand, the line representing the total operating costs intersects the Y axis at $154 million, which represents the fixed costs incurred even when no products are sold, and it has a slope equal to $12.30, which is the cost directly associated with the production of each additional unit sold. The point at which the total revenue line intersects the total cost line is the **operating breakeven point,** because this is where the revenues generated from sales just cover the *total operating costs* of the firm. Notice that prior to the breakeven point, the total cost line is above the total revenue line, which shows Unilate will suffer operating losses because the total costs cannot be covered by the sales revenues. And, after the breakeven point, the

OPERATING BREAKEVEN POINT Represents the level of production and sales at which operating income is zero; it is the point at which revenues from sales just equal total operating costs.

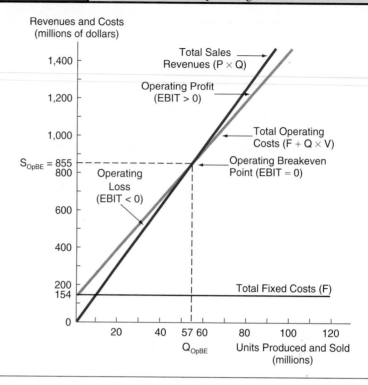

| FIGURE 4–2 | Unilate Textiles: Operating Breakeven Chart |

NOTES:

S_{OpBE} = operating breakeven in dollars

Q = sales in units: Q_{OpBE} = operating breakeven in units

F = fixed costs = $154 million

V = variable costs per unit = $12.30

P = price per unit = $15.00

total revenue line is above the total cost line because revenues are more than sufficient to cover total operating costs, so Unilate will realize operating profits.[3]

Breakeven Computation

Figure 4–2 shows that Unilate must sell 57 million units to be at the operating breakeven point. If Unilate sells 57 million products, it will generate $855 million in sales revenues, which will be just enough to cover the $855 million total operating costs—$154 million fixed costs and $701 million variable costs (57 million units at $12.30 per unit). If we do not have a graph like Figure 4–2, how can the operating

---

[3]In Figure 4–2, we assume the operating costs can be divided into two distinct groups—fixed costs and variable costs. It should be noted that there are costs that are considered semivariable (or semifixed). These costs are fixed for a certain range of operations but change if operations are either higher or lower. For the analysis that follows, we have assumed there are no semivariable costs, so that the operating costs can be separated into either a fixed component or a variable component.

breakeven point be computed? Actually, it is rather simple. Remember, the operating breakeven point is where the revenues generated from sales just cover the total operating costs, which include both the costs directly attributable to producing each unit and the fixed operating costs that remain constant regardless of the production level. As long as the selling price of each unit (the slope of the total revenue line) is greater than the variable operating cost of each unit (the slope of the total operating cost line), each unit sold will generate revenues that contribute to covering the fixed operating costs. For Unilate, this contribution (termed the *contribution margin*) is $2.70, which is the difference between the $15.00 selling price and the $12.30 variable cost of each unit. To compute the operating breakeven for Unilate then, we have to determine how many units need to be sold to cover the fixed operating cost of $154 million if each unit has a contribution margin equal to $2.70. Just divide the $154 million fixed cost by the $2.70 contribution margin and you will discover the breakeven point is 57 million units, which equates to $855 million in sales revenues.

More formally, the operating breakeven point can be found by setting the total revenues equal to the total operating costs so that net operating income (NOI) is zero. In equation form, NOI = 0 if

$$
\begin{array}{ccccc}
\dfrac{\text{Sales}}{\text{revenues}} & = & \dfrac{\text{Total operating}}{\text{costs}} & = & \dfrac{\text{Total}}{\text{variable costs}} + \dfrac{\text{Total}}{\text{fixed costs}} \\[2ex]
(P \times Q) = & & \text{TOC} & = & (V \times Q) \quad + \quad F
\end{array}
$$

where P is the sales price per unit, Q is the number of units produced and sold, V is the variable operating cost per unit, and F is the total fixed operating costs. Solving for the quantity that needs to be sold, Q, produces a formula that can be used to find the number of units that needs to be sold to achieve operating breakeven.

4–1

$$
Q_{\text{OpBE}} = \frac{F}{P - V} = \frac{F}{\text{Contribution margin}}
$$

Thus, the operating breakeven point for Unilate is

$$
Q_{\text{OpBE}} = \frac{\$154.0 \text{ million}}{\$15.00 - \$12.30} = \frac{\$154.0 \text{ million}}{\$2.70} = 57.0 \text{ million units.}
$$

In the remainder of the chapter, we omit the word *million* in the computations and include it only in the final answer.

From Equation 4–1, we can see that the operating breakeven point is lower (higher) if the numerator is lower (higher) or if the denominator is higher (lower). Therefore, all else equal, one firm will have a lower operating breakeven point than another firm if its fixed costs are lower, if selling price of its product is higher, if its variable operating cost per unit is lower, or if some combination of these exists. For instance, if Unilate could increase the sales price per unit from $15.00 to $15.80 without affecting either its fixed operating costs ($154 million) or its variable operating cost per unit ($12.30), then its operating breakeven point would fall to 44 million units.

The operating breakeven point also can be stated in terms of the total sales revenues needed to cover total operating costs. At this point, we just need to multiply the sales price per unit by the breakeven quantity we found using Equation 4–1, which yields $855 million for Unilate. Or we can restate the contribution margin as a percent of the sales price per unit (this is called the *gross profit margin*) and then apply Equation 4–1. In other words,

4–2

$$S_{OpBE} = \frac{F}{1 - \left(\dfrac{V}{P}\right)} = \frac{F}{\text{Gross profit margin}}$$

Solving Equation 4–2 for Unilate, the operating breakeven based on dollar sales is

$$S_{OpBE} = \frac{\$154.0}{1 - \left(\dfrac{\$12.30}{\$15.00}\right)} = \frac{\$154.0}{1 - 0.82} = \frac{\$154.0}{0.18} = \$855.6 \text{ million}$$

Equation 4–2 shows that 18¢ of every $1 sales revenues goes to cover the fixed operating costs, so about $855 million worth of the product must be sold to break even. (If we use Equation 4–1 to compute the operating breakeven rounded to two decimal places, the result is 57.04 million units; thus the dollar sales needed to break even is 57.04 × $15 = $855.6 million.)

Breakeven analysis based on dollar sales rather than on units of output is useful in determining the breakeven volume for a firm that sells many products at varying prices. This analysis requires only that total sales, total fixed costs, and total variable costs at a given level are known.

Using Operating Breakeven Analysis

Operating breakeven analysis can shed light on three important types of business decisions: (1) When making new product decisions, breakeven analysis can help determine how large the sales of a new product must be for the firm to achieve profitability. (2) Breakeven analysis can be used to study the effects of a general expansion in the level of the firm's operations; an expansion would cause the levels of both fixed and variable costs to rise, but it would also increase expected sales. (3) When considering modernization and automation projects, where the fixed investment in equipment is increased in order to lower variable costs, particularly the cost of labor, breakeven analysis can help management analyze the consequences of purchasing these projects.

However, care must be taken when using operating breakeven analysis. To apply breakeven analysis as we have discussed here requires that the sales price *per unit*, the variable cost *per unit*, and the *total* fixed operating costs do not change with the level of the firm's production and sales. Within a narrow range of production and sales, this assumption probably is not a major issue. But what if the firm expects either to produce a much greater (or fewer) number of products than normal or to expand (reduce) its plant and equipment significantly? Will the numbers change? Most likely the answer is yes. Therefore, use of a single breakeven chart like the one presented in Figure 4–2 is impractical—such a chart provides useful information, but the fact that it cannot deal with changes in the price of the product, with changing variable cost rates, and with changes in fixed cost levels suggests the need for a more flexible type of analysis. Today, such analysis is provided by computer simulation. Functions such as those expressed in Equations 4–1 and 4–2 (or more complicated versions of them) can be put into a spreadsheet or similarly modeled with other computer software, and then variables such as sales price, P, the variable cost per unit, V, and the level of fixed costs, F can be changed. The model can instantaneously produce new versions of Figure 4–2, or a whole set of such graphs, to show what the operating breakeven point would be under different production setups and price-cost situations.

Self-Test Questions

Is interest paid considered in operating breakeven analysis? Why or why not?

Give the equations used to calculate the operating breakeven point in units and in dollar sales.

Give some examples of business decisions for which operating breakeven analysis might be useful.

Identify some limitations to the use of a single operating breakeven chart.

Operating Leverage

OPERATING LEVERAGE
The existence of fixed operating costs, such that a change in sales will produce a larger change in operating income (EBIT).

If a high percentage of a firm's total operating costs are fixed, the firm is said to have a high degree of **operating leverage.** In physics, leverage implies the use of a lever to raise a heavy object with a small amount of force. In politics, people who have leverage can accomplish a great deal with their smallest word or action. *In business terminology, a high degree of operating leverage, other things held constant, means that a relatively small change in sales will result in a large change in operating income.*

Operating leverage arises because the firm has fixed operating costs that must be covered no matter the level of production. The impact of the leverage, however, depends on the actual operating level of the firm. For example, Unilate has $154.0 million in fixed operating costs, which are covered rather easily because the firm currently sells 110 million products; thus, it is well above its operating breakeven point of 57 million units. But what would happen to the operating income if Unilate sold more or less than forecasted? To answer this question we need to determine the **degree of operating leverage (DOL)** associated with Unilate's forecasted 2001 operations.

DEGREE OF OPERATING LEVERAGE
The percentage change in NOI (or EBIT) associated with a given percentage change in sales.

Operating leverage can be defined more precisely in terms of the way a given change in sales volume affects operating income (NOI). To measure the effect of a change in sales volume on NOI, we calculate the degree of operating leverage, which is defined as the percentage change in NOI (or EBIT) associated with a given percentage change in sales:

4–3

$$DOL = \frac{\text{Percentage change in NOI}}{\text{Percentage change in sales}} = \frac{\left(\dfrac{\Delta NOI}{NOI}\right)}{\left(\dfrac{\Delta Sales}{Sales}\right)} = \frac{\left(\dfrac{\Delta EBIT}{EBIT}\right)}{\left(\dfrac{\Delta Sales}{Sales}\right)} = \frac{\left(\dfrac{\Delta EBIT}{EBIT}\right)}{\left(\dfrac{\Delta Q}{Q}\right)}$$

In effect, the DOL is an index number that measures the effect of a change in sales on operating income or EBIT.

Table 4–5 shows that the NOI for Unilate is $143.0 million at production and sales equal to 110 million units. If the number of units produced and sold increases to 121 million, the operating income (in millions of dollars) would be

$$\text{NOI} = 121(\$15.00 - \$12.30) - \$154.0 = \$172.7$$

So the degree of operating leverage associated with this change is 2.08:

$$\text{DOL} = \frac{\left[\dfrac{\$172.7 - \$143.0}{\$143.0}\right]}{\left[\dfrac{\$15.00(121 - 110)}{\$15.00(110)}\right]} = \frac{\left(\dfrac{\$29.7}{\$143.0}\right)}{\left(\dfrac{11}{110}\right)} = \frac{0.208}{0.100} = \frac{20.8\%}{10.0\%} = 2.08\times$$

To interpret the meaning of the value of the degree of operating leverage, remember we computed the percent change in operating income and then divided the result by the percent change in sales. Taken literally then, Unilate's DOL of 2.08× indicates that the percent change in operating income will be 2.08 times the percent change in sales from the current 110 million units ($1,650.0 million). So if the number of units sold increases from 110 million to 121 million, or by 10 percent, Unilate's operating income should increase by 2.08 × 10% = 20.8%—at 121 million units, *operating income* should be 20.8 percent greater than the $143.0 million generated at 110 million units of sales; the new operating income should be $172.7 million = 1.208 × $143 million. Table 4–6 shows a comparison of the operating incomes generated at the two different sales levels.

The results contained in Table 4–6 show that Unilate's *gross profit* would increase by $29.7 million, or by ten percent, if sales increase ten percent. The fixed operating costs remain constant at $154.0 million, so EBIT also increases by $29.7 million, and the total impact of a ten percent increase in sales is a 20.8 percent increase in operating income. If the fixed operating costs were to increase in proportion to the increase in sales—that is ten percent—then the net operating income would also increase by

---

TABLE 4–6	Unilate Textiles: Operating Income at Sales Levels of 110 Million Units and 121 Million Units (millions of dollars)

	2001 FORECASTED OPERATIONS	SALES INCREASE	UNIT CHANGE	PERCENT CHANGE
Sales in units (millions)	110	121	11	+10.0%
Sales revenues	$1,650.0	$1,815.0	$165.0	+10.0%
Variable cost of goods sold	(1,353.0)	(1,488.3)	(135.3)	+10.0%
Gross profit	$ 297.0	$ 326.7	$ 29.7	+10.0%
Fixed operating costs	(154.0)	(154.0)	(0.0)	0.0%
Net operating income (EBIT)	$ 143.0	$ 172.7	$ 29.7	+20.8%

ten percent because all revenues and costs would have changed by the same proportion. But in reality, fixed operating costs will not change (a zero percent increase); thus, a ten percent increase in Unilate's forecasted 2001 sales will result in an *additional* 10.8 percent increase in operating income. The total increase is 20.8 percent, which results because operating leverage exists.

Equation 4–3 can be simplified so that the degree of operating leverage at a particular level of operations can be calculated as follows:[4]

> **4–4**
>
> $$DOL_Q = \frac{Q(P - V)}{Q(P - V) - F}$$

Or, rearranging the terms, DOL can be stated in terms of sales revenues as follows:

> **4–4a**
>
> $$DOL_S = \frac{(Q \times P) - (Q \times V)}{(Q \times P) - (Q \times V) - F} = \frac{S - VC}{S - VC - F} = \frac{\text{Gross profit}}{\text{EBIT}}$$

To solve Equation 4–4 or Equation 4–4a, we only need information from Unilate's forecasted operations; we do not need information about the possible change in forecasted operations. So Q represents the forecasted 2001 level of production and sales, and S and VC are the sales and variable operating costs, respectively, at that level of operations. For Unilate, the equation solution for DOL would be

$$DOL_{54} = \frac{110(\$15.00 - \$12.30)}{110(\$15.00 - \$12.30) - \$154} = \frac{\$1,650 - \$1,353}{\$1,650 - \$1,353 - \$154}$$

$$= \frac{\$297}{\$143} = 2.08\times$$

---

[4]Equation 4–4 can be derived by restating Equation 4–3 in terms of the variables we have defined previously, and then simplifying the result. Starting with Equation 4–3, we have

$$DOL = \frac{\text{Percentage change in NOI}}{\text{Percentage change in sales}} = \frac{\left(\dfrac{\Delta NOI}{NOI}\right)}{\left(\dfrac{\Delta Sales}{Sales}\right)} = \frac{\left(\dfrac{\Delta EBIT}{EBIT}\right)}{\left(\dfrac{\Delta Q}{Q}\right)} \qquad 4\text{–}3$$

EBIT can be stated as the gross profit, Q(P − V), minus the fixed operating costs, F. So, if we use Q to indicate the level of operations forecasted for 2001 and Q* to indicate the level of operations that would exist if operations were different, the percent change in EBIT is stated as

$$\%\Delta EBIT = \frac{[Q^*(P - V) - F] - [Q(P - V) - F]}{Q(P - V) - F} = \frac{(Q^* - Q)(P - V)}{Q(P - V) - F}$$

Substituting into Equation 4–3, restating the denominator, and solving, yields

$$DOL = \frac{\left[\dfrac{(Q^* - Q)(P - V)}{Q(P - V) - F}\right]}{\left[\dfrac{Q^* - Q}{Q}\right]} = \frac{(Q^* - Q)(P - V)}{Q(P - V) - F} \times \left(\frac{Q}{Q^* - Q}\right) = \frac{Q(P - V)}{Q(P - V) - F} \qquad 4\text{–}4$$

TABLE 4–7	Unilate Textiles: Operating Income at Sales Levels of 110 Million Units and 99 Million Units (millions of dollars)

	2001 FORECASTED OPERATIONS	SALES DECREASE	UNIT CHANGE	PERCENT CHANGE
Sales in units (millions)	110	99	(11)	−10.0%
Sales revenues	$1,650.0	$1,485.0	$(165.0)	−10.0%
Variable cost of goods sold	(1,353.0)	(1,217.7)	135.3	−10.0%
Gross profit	$ 297.0	$ 267.3	$(29.7)	−10.0%
Fixed operating costs	(154.0)	(154.0)	(0.0)	0.0%
Net operating income (EBIT)	$ 143.0	$ 113.3	$(29.7)	−20.8%

Equation 4–4 normally is used to analyze a single product, such as GM's Chevrolet Cavalier, whereas Equation 4–4a is used to evaluate an entire firm with many types of products and, hence, for which "quantity in units" and "sales price" are not meaningful.

The DOL of 2.08× indicates that *each* 1 percent *change* in sales will result in a 2.08 percent *change* in operating income. What would happen if Unilate's sales decrease, say, by ten percent? According to the interpretation of the DOL figure, Unilate's operating income would be expected to decrease by 20.8 percent. Table 4–7 shows that this actually would be the case. Therefore, the DOL value indicates the *change* (increase or decrease) in operating income resulting from a *change* (increase or decrease) in the level of operations. It should be apparent that the greater the DOL, the greater the impact of a change in operations on operating income, whether the change is an increase or a decrease.

The DOL value found by using Equation 4–5 is the degree of operating leverage only for a specific initial sales level. For Unilate, that sales level is 110 million units, or $1,650 million. The DOL value would differ if the initial (existing) level of operations differed. For example, if Unilate's operating cost structure was the same, but only 65 million units were produced and sold, the DOL would have been

$$DOL_{65} = \frac{(65)(\$15.00 - \$12.30)}{[(65)(\$15.00 - \$12.30)] - \$154.0} = \frac{\$175.5}{\$21.5} = 8.16\times$$

The DOL at 65 million units produced and sold is nearly four times greater than the DOL at 110 million units. Thus, from a base sales of 65 million units, a ten percent increase in sales, from 65 million units to 71.5 million units, would result in a 8.16 × 10% = 81.6% increase in operating income, from $21.5 million to $39.05 million. This shows that when Unilate's operations are closer to its operating breakeven point of 57 million units, its degree of operating leverage is higher.

In general, given the same operating cost structure, if a firm's level of operations is decreased, its DOL increases; or, stated differently, the closer a firm is to its operating breakeven point, the greater is its degree of operating leverage. This occurs because, as Figure 4–2 indicates, the closer a firm is to its operating breakeven point, the more likely it is to incur an operating loss due to a decrease in sales—there is not a very large buffer in operating income to absorb a decrease in sales and still be able to cover the fixed operating costs. Similarly, at the same level of production and sales, a firm's degree of operating leverage will be higher the lower the contribution margin for its products—the lower the contribution margin, the less each product sold is able to help cover the fixed operating costs, and the closer the firm is to its operating breakeven point. Therefore, the higher the DOL for a particular firm, it generally can be concluded the closer the firm is to its operating breakeven point, and the more sensitive its operating income is to a change in sales volume. *Greater sensitivity generally implies greater risk; thus, it can be stated that firms with higher DOLs generally are considered to have riskier operations than firms with lower DOLs.*

Operating Leverage and Operating Breakeven

The relationship between operating leverage and the operating breakeven point is illustrated in Figure 4–3, where various levels of operations are compared for Unilate and two other textile manufacturers. One firm has a higher contribution margin than Unilate and the other firm has lower fixed operating costs, so we know the other two firms have operating breakeven points that are less than Unilate's. Allied Cloth has the lowest operating breakeven point, because it has the highest contribution margin relative to its fixed costs. Unilate has the highest operating breakeven point because it uses the greatest relative amount of operating leverage of the three firms. Consequently, all else equal, of the three textile manufacturers, Unilate's operating income would be magnified the most if actual sales turned out to be greater than forecasted; but it also would experience the greatest decrease in operating income if actual sales turned out to be less than expected.

Self-Test Questions

What does the term "high degree of operating leverage" imply, and what are some implications of having a high degree of operating leverage?

What is the general equation used to calculate the degree of operating leverage?

What is the association between the concepts of operating breakeven and operating leverage?

Financial Breakeven Analysis

FINANCIAL BREAKEVEN ANALYSIS
Determining the operating income (EBIT) the firm needs to just cover all of its fixed financing costs and produce earnings per share equal to zero.

Operating breakeven analysis deals with evaluation of production and sales to determine at what level the firm's sales revenues will just cover its operating costs; the point where the operating income is zero. **Financial breakeven analysis** is a method of determining the operating income, or EBIT, the firm needs to just cover all of its *financing costs* and produce earnings per share equal to zero. Typically, the financing costs involved in financial breakeven analysis consist of the interest payments to bondholders and the dividend payments to preferred stockholders. Usually these financing costs are fixed, and, in every case, they must be paid before dividends can be paid to common stockholders.

Financial breakeven analysis deals with the lower portion of the income statement—the portion from operating income (EBIT) to earnings available to common

FIGURE 4-3	Operating Leverage

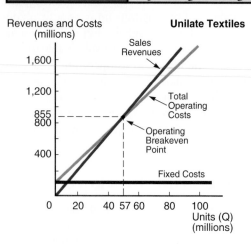

Selling price = $15.00
Variable cost per unit = $12.30
Fixed costs = $154 million
Operating breakeven = 57 million units
= $855 million

SALES LEVEL		TOTAL OPERATING COSTS	OPERATING PROFIT	
UNITS (Q)	REVENUES ($)		(EBIT)	DOL
30	$ 450	$ 523	$ (73)	
60	900	892	8	20.3
110	1,650	1,507	143	2.1
150	2,250	1,999	251	1.6

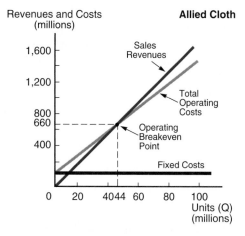

Selling price = $15.00
Variable cost per unit = $11.50
Fixed costs = $154 million
Operating breakeven = 44 million units
= $660 million

SALES LEVEL		TOTAL OPERATING COSTS	OPERATING PROFIT	
UNITS (Q)	REVENUES ($)		(EBIT)	DOL
30	$ 450	$ 499	$ (49)	
60	900	844	56	3.8
110	1,650	1,419	231	1.7
150	2,250	1,879	371	1.4

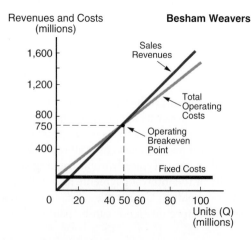

Selling price = $15.00
Variable cost per unit = $12.30
Fixed costs = $135 million
Operating breakeven = 50 million units
= $750 million

SALES LEVEL		TOTAL OPERATING COSTS	OPERATING PROFIT	
UNITS (Q)	REVENUES ($)		(EBIT)	DOL
30	$ 450	$ 504	$ (54)	
60	900	873	27	6.0
110	1,650	1,488	162	1.8
150	2,250	1,980	270	1.5

TABLE 4–8	Unilate Textiles: 2001 Forecasted Earnings per Share (millions of dollars)

Earnings before interest and taxes (EBIT)	$ 143.0
Interest	(41.4)
Earnings before taxes (EBT)	$ 101.6
Taxes (40%)	(40.6)
Net income	$ 61.0
Preferred dividends	(0.0)
Earnings available to common stockholders	$ 61.0

NOTES:

$Shrs_C$ = Number of common shares = 26.3 million

EPS = Earnings per share = $61.0/26.3 = $2.32

stockholders. This portion of the income statement generally is referred to as the *financing section*, because it contains the expenses associated with the financing arrangements of the firm. The financing section of Unilate's forecasted 2001 income statement is contained in Table 4–8.

Breakeven Graph

FINANCIAL
BREAKEVEN POINT
The level of EBIT at
which EPS equals zero.

Figure 4–4 shows the earnings per share (EPS) for Unilate at various levels of EBIT. The point at which EPS equals zero is referred to as the **financial breakeven point.** As the graph indicates, the financial breakeven point for Unilate is where EBIT equals $41.4 million. At this EBIT level, the income generated from operations is just sufficient to cover the financing costs, including income taxes; thus, EPS equals zero. To see this, we can compute the EPS when EBIT is $41.4 million:

Earnings before interest and taxes (EBIT)	$41.4
Interest	(41.4)
Earnings before taxes (EBT)	0.0
Taxes (40%)	(0.0)
Net income	0.0
Earnings available to common stockholders (EAC)	$ 0.0

EPS = $0/26.3 = $0

Breakeven Computation

The results obtained from Figure 4–4 can be translated algebraically to produce a relatively simple equation that can be used to compute the financial breakeven point of any firm. First, remember the financial breakeven point is defined as the level of EBIT that generates EPS equal to zero. Therefore, at the financial breakeven point,

Table 4–9 shows the results of increasing Unilate's EBIT 20.8 percent. The increase in EPS is 29.2 percent, which is 1.40 times the change in EBIT; so the DFL for Unilate equals 1.40.

The degree of financial leverage at a particular level of EBIT can be computed easily by using the following equation:[6]

4–8

$$DFL = \frac{EBIT}{EBIT - I} = \frac{EBIT}{EBIT - [Financial\ BEP]}$$

Using Equation 4–8, the DFL for Unilate Textiles at EBIT equal to $143.0 million (sales of 110 million units) is

$$DFL_{110} = \frac{\$143.0}{\$143.0 - \$41.4} = \frac{\$143.0}{\$101.6} = 1.40\times$$

The interpretation of the DFL value is the same as for the degree of operating leverage, except the starting point for evaluating financial leverage is the earnings

---

[6]Equation 4–8 can be derived easily by expanding Equation 4–7, rearranging the terms, and then simplifying the results. If we use EPS and EBIT to indicate the forecasted 2001 EPS and EBIT, respectively, and EPS* and EBIT* to indicate the EPS and EBIT that would exist after a change in sales volume, then

$$DFL = \frac{\left(\dfrac{\Delta EPS}{EPS}\right)}{\left(\dfrac{\Delta EBIT}{EBIT}\right)} = \frac{\left(\dfrac{EPS^* - EPS}{EPS}\right)}{\left(\dfrac{EBIT^* - EBIT}{EBIT}\right)}$$

The computation for 2001 forecasted earnings per share is

$$EPS = \frac{(EBIT - I)(1 - T)}{Shrs_c}$$

where $Shrs_C$ is the number of common shares outstanding. The percent change in EPS can be written and simplified as follows:

$$\Delta EPS = \frac{\left[\dfrac{(EBIT^* - I)(1 - T)}{Shrs_c}\right] - \left[\dfrac{(EBIT - I)(1 - T)}{Shrs_c}\right]}{\left[\dfrac{(EBIT - I)(1 - T)}{Shrs_c}\right]} = \frac{(EBIT^* - I)(1 - T) - (EBIT - I)(1 - T)}{(EBIT - I)(1 - T)}$$

$$= \frac{EBIT^* - EBIT}{(EBIT - I)}$$

Substituting this relationship into the computation of DFL, we have

$$DFL = \frac{\left[\dfrac{(EBIT^* - EBIT)}{EBIT - I}\right]}{\left[\dfrac{(EBIT^* - EBIT)}{EBIT}\right]} = \frac{(EBIT^* - EBIT)}{(EBIT - I)} \times \frac{EBIT}{(EBIT^* - EBIT)}$$

$$= \frac{EBIT}{EBIT - I} = \frac{EBIT}{EBIT - [Financial\ BEP]}$$

If a firm has preferred stock, the relationship given in Equation 4–6 can be substituted in the above equation for the financial breakeven point.

TABLE 4–9	Unilate Textiles: Earnings per Share at Sales Levels of 110 Million Units and 121 Million Units (millions of dollars, except per share data)[a]

	2001 FORECASTED OPERATIONS	SALES INCREASE	DOLLAR CHANGE	PERCENT CHANGE
Sales in units (millions)	110	121		+10.0%
Earnings before interest and taxes (EBIT)	$ 143.0	$ 172.7	$ 29.7	+20.8%
Interest (I)	(41.4)	(41.4)	(0.0)	+ 0.0%
Earnings before taxes (EBT)	$ 101.6	$ 131.3	$ 29.7	+29.2%
Taxes (40%)	(40.6)	(52.5)	(11.9)	+29.2%
Net income	$ 61.0	$ 78.8	$ 17.8	+29.2%
Earning per share (26.3 million shares)	$ 2.32	$ 3.00	$ 0.68	+29.2%

NOTE:

[a]A spreadsheet was used to generate the results in this table. Only the final results are rounded; thus, there might be some rounding differences if you rely on some of the values in the table, which are rounded to one decimal place, to compute the other values.

before interest and taxes (EBIT) and the ending point is earnings per share (EPS). So because the DFL for Unilate is 1.40×, the company can expect a 1.40 percent change in EPS for every one percent change in EBIT; a 20.8 percent increase in EBIT results in approximately a 29.2 percent (20.8 percent × 1.40) increase in earnings available to common stockholders, thus the same percent increase in EPS (the number of common shares outstanding does not change). Unfortunately, the opposite also is true—if Unilate's 2001 EBIT is 20.8 percent below expectations, its EPS will be 29.2 percent below the forecast of $2.32, or $1.64. To prove this result is correct, construct the financing section of Unilate's income statement when EBIT equals $113.3 million = (1 − 0.208) × $143.0 million.

The value of the degree of financial leverage found using Equation 4–8 pertains to one specific initial EBIT level. If the level of sales changes, and thus the EBIT changes, so does the value computed for DFL. For example, at sales equal to 80 million units, Unilate's EBIT would be $62 million = [80 million ($15.00 − $12.30)] − $154.0 million, and the DFL value would be

$$DFL_{80} = \frac{\$62.0}{\$62.0 - \$41.4} = \frac{\$62.0}{\$20.6} = 3.01\times$$

Compared to sales equal to 110 million units, at sales equal to 80 million units Unilate would have greater difficulty covering the fixed financing costs, so its DFL is much greater. At EBIT equal to $62.0 million, Unilate is close to its financial breakeven point—EBIT equal to $41.4 million—and its degree of financial leverage is high. So the more difficulty a firm has covering its fixed financing costs with operating income, the greater its degree of financial leverage. In general then, the higher the DFL for a particular firm, it generally can be concluded the closer the firm is to its financial breakeven point, and the more sensitive its earnings per share is to a change in operating income. *Greater sensitivity implies greater risk; thus it can be stated that firms with higher DFLs generally are considered to have greater financial risk than firms with lower DFLs.*

Self-Test Questions

What does the term "high degree of financial leverage" imply, and what are some implications of having a high degree of financial leverage?

Give the general equation used to calculate the degree of financial leverage. Compare the equation for DFL to the equation for times-interest-earned ratio given in Chapter 3.

Combining Operating and Financial Leverage (DTL)

Our analysis of operating leverage and financial leverage has shown that *(1) the greater the degree of operating leverage, or fixed operating costs for a particular level of operations, the more sensitive EBIT will be to changes in sales volume, and (2) the greater the degree of financial leverage, or fixed financial costs for a particular level of operations, the more sensitive EPS will be to changes in EBIT.* Therefore, if a firm has a considerable amount of both operating and financial leverage, then even small changes in sales will lead to wide fluctuations in EPS. Look at the impact leverage has on Unilate's forecasted 2001 operations. We found that if the sales volume increases by ten percent, Unilate's EBIT would increase by 20.8 percent; and if EBIT increases by 20.8 percent, its EPS would increase by 29.2 percent. So in combination, a ten percent increase in sales volume would result in a 29.2 percent increase in EPS. This shows the impact of total leverage, which is the combination of both operating leverage and financial leverage, with respect to Unilate's current operations.

The degree of total leverage (DTL) is defined as the percent change in EPS resulting from a change in sales volume. This relationship can be written as follows:

$$\text{4-9} \qquad \begin{array}{c}\text{Degree of}\\ \text{total leverage}\end{array} = \text{DTL} = \frac{\left(\dfrac{\Delta\text{EPS}}{\text{EPS}}\right)}{\left(\dfrac{\Delta\text{Sales}}{\text{Sales}}\right)} = \frac{\left(\dfrac{\Delta\text{EBIT}}{\text{EBIT}}\right)}{\left(\dfrac{\Delta\text{Sales}}{\text{Sales}}\right)} \times \frac{\left(\dfrac{\Delta\text{EPS}}{\text{EPS}}\right)}{\left(\dfrac{\Delta\text{EBIT}}{\text{EBIT}}\right)} = \text{DOL} \times \text{DFL}$$

Combining the equations for DOL (Equations 4–4 and 4–4a) and for DFL (Equation 4–8), Equation 4–9 can be restated as follows:

$$\text{4-10} \qquad \text{DTL} = \frac{\text{Gross profit}}{\text{EBIT}} \times \frac{\text{EBIT}}{\text{EBIT} - [\text{Financial BEP}]} = \frac{\text{Gross profit}}{\text{EBIT} - [\text{Financial BEP}]}$$

$$= \frac{S - VC}{\text{EBIT} - I} = \frac{Q(P - V)}{[Q(P - V) - F] - I}$$

Using Equation 4–10, the degree of total leverage for Unilate would be

$$\text{DTL}_{110} = \frac{110(\$15.00 - \$12.30)}{[110(\$15.00 - \$12.30) - \$154.0] - \$41.4}$$

$$= \frac{\$297.0}{\$143.0 - \$41.4} = \frac{\$297.0}{\$101.6}$$

$$= 2.92\times$$

According to Equation 4–9, we could have arrived at the same result for DTL by multiplying the degree of operating leverage by the degree of financial leverage, so the DTL for Unilate would be $2.08 \times 1.40 \approx 2.92$. This value indicates that for every one percent change in sales volume, Unilate's EPS will change by 2.92 percent; a ten percent increase in sales will result in a 29.2 percent increase in EPS. This is exactly the impact expected.

The value of DTL can be used to compute the new earnings per share (EPS*) after a change in sales volume. We already know that Unilate's EPS will change by 2.92 percent for every one percent change in sales. So EPS* resulting from a ten percent increase in sales can be computed as follows:

$$\text{EPS*} = \text{EPS}[1 + (.10)(2.92)] = \$2.32 \times (1 + 0.292) = \$3.00$$

which is the same result given in Table 4–9.

The degree of combined (total) leverage concept is useful primarily for the insights it provides regarding the joint effects of operating and financial leverage on earnings per share. The concept can be used to show management, for example, that a decision to automate a plant and to finance the new equipment with debt would result in a situation in which a ten percent decline in sales would result in a nearly 50 percent decline in earnings, whereas with a different operating and financial package, a ten percent sales decline would cause earnings to decline only by 15 percent. Having the alternatives stated in this manner gives decision makers a better idea of the ramifications of alternative actions with respect to the firm's level of operations and how those operations are financed.

Self-Test Questions

What information is provided by the degree of total (combined) leverage?

What does the term "high degree of total leverage" imply?

Using Leverage and Forecasting for Control

From the discussion in the previous sections, it should be clear what the impact on income would be if the 2001 sales forecast for Unilate Textiles is different than expected. If sales are greater than expected, both operating and financial leverage will magnify the "bottom line" impact on EPS (DTL = 2.92). But the opposite also holds. Consequently, if Unilate does not meet its forecasted sales level, leverage will result in a magnified loss in income compared to what is expected. This will occur because production facilities might have been expanded too greatly, inventories might be built up too quickly, and so on; the end result might be that the firm suffers a significant income loss. This loss will result in a lower than expected addition to retained earnings, which means the plans for additional external funds needed to support the firm's operations will be inadequate. Likewise, if the sales forecast is too low, then, if the firm is at full capacity, it will not be able to meet the additional demand, and sales opportunities will be lost—perhaps forever. In the previous sections, we showed only how changes in operations (2001 forecasts) affect the income generated by the firm; we did not continue the process to show the impact on the balance sheet and the financing needs of the firm. To determine the impact on the financial statements, the financial manager needs to repeat the steps discussed in the first part of this chapter. It is at this stage the financial manager needs to evaluate and act on the feedback received from the forecasting and budgeting processes. In effect, then, the forecasting (planning) and control of the firm is an ongoing activity, a vital function to the long-run survival of any firm.

The forecasting and control functions described in this chapter are important for several reasons. First, if the projected operating results are unsatisfactory, management can "go back to the drawing board," reformulate its plans, and develop more reasonable targets for the coming year. Second, it is possible that the funds required to meet the sales forecast simply cannot be obtained; if so, it obviously is better to know this in advance and to scale back the projected level of operations than to suddenly run out of cash and have operations grind to a halt. Third, even if the required funds can be raised, it is desirable to plan for their acquisition well in advance. Finally, any deviation from the projections needs to be dealt with to improve future forecasts and the predictability of the firm's operations to ensure the goals of the firm are being pursued appropriately.

Self-Test Question

Why is it important that the forecasting and control of the firm be an ongoing activity?

✳ ETHICAL DILEMMA

Competition-Based Planning—Promotion or Payoff?

A few months ago, Kim Darby, financial manager of Republic Communications Corporation (RCC), contacted you about a job opening in the financial planning division of the company. RCC is a well-established firm that has offered long-distance phone service in the United States for more than three decades. But recent deregulation in the telecommunications industry has RCC concerned, because competition has increased significantly—today there are many more firms offering long-distance services than

five years ago. In fact, RCC has seen its profits decline along with market share since deregulation began. Kim Darby indicated that RCC wants to reverse this trend by improving the company's planning function so that long-distance rates can be set to better attract and keep customers in the future. According to her, that is the reason she contacted you.

When she first called, Kim told you RCC would like to hire you because you are one of the "up-and-comers" in the telecommunications industry. You

continues

have worked at National Telecommunications, Inc. (NTI), one of RCC's fiercest competitors, since you graduated from college four years ago, helping to develop their rate-setting program, which many consider the best in the industry.

Taking the position at RCC would be comparable to a promotion with a $30,000 salary increase and provide greater chances for advancement than your current position at NTI. So, after interviewing with RCC and talking to friends and family, a couple of days ago you informally accepted the job at RCC—you have not yet notified NTI of your decision.

Earlier today, Kim called to see if you could start your new position in a couple of weeks. RCC would like you to start work as soon as possible because it wants to begin a redesign of its rate-setting plan in an effort to regain market share. During the conversation, Kim mentioned that it would be helpful if you could bring the rate-setting program and some rate-setting information with you to your new job—it will help RCC rewrite its rate-setting program. In an attempt to allay any reservations you might have, Kim told you that NTI sells its software to other companies and any rate setting information is available to the public through states' public service commissions, so everything you bring really is well known in the industry and should be considered in the public domain. And, according to Kim, RCC is not going to copy the rate-setting program—her attitude is "what is wrong with taking a look at it as long as we don't copy the program?" If you provide RCC with NTI's rate-setting program, you know it will help the company to plan better, and better planning will lead to increased market share and higher stock prices. An improved rate-setting plan might net RCC as much as $200 million each year, and RCC has a very generous bonus system to reward employees who help the company improve its market position. If you do not provide the software, you might start your new job "off on the wrong foot." What should you do?

Summary

The first part of this chapter described in broad outline how firms project their financial statements and determine their capital requirements. The second part of the chapter included a discussion of how we can evaluate the effects of changes in forecasts on the income of the firm. The key concepts covered in the chapter are listed here:

- **Financial planning** involves making projections of sales, income, and assets based on alternative production and marketing strategies and then deciding how to meet the forecasted financial requirements.
- **Financial control** deals with the feedback and adjustment process that is required (1) to ensure that plans are followed or (2) to modify existing plans in response to changes in the operating environment.
- Management establishes a **target balance sheet** on the basis of ratio analysis.
- The **projected, or pro forma, balance sheet method** is used to forecast financial requirements.
- A firm can determine the amount of **additional funds needed (AFN)** by estimating the amount of new assets necessary to support the forecasted level of sales and then subtracting from that amount the spontaneous funds that will be generated from operations. The firm can then plan to raise the AFN through bank borrowing, by issuing securities, or both.
- **Operating breakeven analysis** is a method of determining the point at which sales will just cover operating costs, and it shows the magnitude of the firm's operating profits or losses if sales exceed or fall below that point.

- The **operating breakeven point** is the sales volume at which total operating costs equal total revenues and operating income (EBIT) equals zero. The equation used to compute the operating breakeven point is

$$Q_{OpBE} = \frac{F}{P - V} = \frac{F}{\text{Contribution margin}}$$

- **Operating leverage** is a measure of the extent to which fixed costs are used in a firm's operations. A firm with a high percentage of fixed costs is said to have a **high** degree of operating leverage.
- The **degree of operating leverage (DOL)** shows how a change in sales will affect operating income. Whereas *breakeven analysis* emphasizes the volume of sales the firm needs to be profitable, the *degree of operating leverage* measures how sensitive the firm's profits are to changes in the volume of sales. The equation used to calculate the DOL is

$$DOL_Q = \frac{Q(P - V)}{Q(P - V) - F}$$

- **Financial breakeven analysis** is a method of determining the point at which EBIT will just cover financing costs, and it shows the magnitude of the firm's earnings per share (EPS) if EBIT exceeds or falls below that point.
- The **financial breakeven point** is the level of EBIT that produces EPS = 0. The equation used to compute the financial breakeven point is

$$EBIT_{FinBE} = I + \frac{D_{ps}}{(1 - T)}$$

- **Financial leverage** is a measure of the extent to which fixed financial costs exist in a firm's operations. A firm with a high percentage of fixed financial costs is said to have a **high** degree of financial leverage.
- The **degree of financial leverage (DFL)** shows how a change in EBIT will affect EPS. The equation used to calculate the DFL is

$$DFL = \frac{EBIT}{EBIT - I} = \frac{EBIT}{EBIT - [\text{Financial BEP}]}$$

- **Total (combined) leverage** is a measure of the extent to which total fixed costs (operating and financial) exist in a firm's operations. A firm with a high percentage of total fixed costs is said to have a **high** degree of total leverage.
- The **degree of total leverage (DTL)** shows how a change in sales will affect EPS. The equation used to calculate the DTL is

$$DTL = \frac{S - VC}{EBIT - I} = \frac{Q(P - V)}{Q(P - V) - F - I}$$

The forecasting and control functions require continuous attention to ensure that the goals of the firm are being met. Forecasting and control provide the foresight needed to implement adjustments to future operations so the firm moves in the intended direction and wealth maximization is achieved.

Questions

4–1 Certain liability and net worth items generally increase spontaneously with increases in sales. Put a checkmark (√) by those items that typically increase spontaneously:

Accounts payable	_____
Notes payable to banks	_____
Accrued wages	_____
Accrued taxes	_____
Mortgage bonds	_____
Common stock	_____
Retained earnings	_____

4–2 Suppose a firm makes the following policy changes. If the change means that external, nonspontaneous financial requirements (AFN) will increase, indicate this by a (+); indicate a decrease by a (−); and indicate indeterminate or no effect by a (0). Think in terms of the immediate, short-run effect on funds requirements.

a. The dividend payout ratio is increased. _____
b. The firm contracts to buy, rather than make, certain components used in its products. _____
c. The firm decides to pay all suppliers on delivery, rather than after a 30-day delay, to take advantage of discounts for rapid payment. _____
d. The firm begins to sell on credit (previously all sales had been on a cash basis). _____
e. The firm's profit margin is eroded by increased competition; sales are steady. _____
f. Advertising expenditures are stepped up. _____
g. A decision is made to substitute long-term mortgage bonds for short-term bank loans. _____
h. The firm begins to pay employees on a weekly basis (previously it had paid at the end of each month). _____

4–3 What benefits can be derived from breakeven analysis, both operating and financial? What are some problems with breakeven analysis?

4–4 Explain how profits or losses will be magnified for a firm with high operating leverage as opposed to a firm with lower operating leverage.

4–5 Explain how profits or losses will be magnified for a firm with high financial leverage as opposed to a firm with lower financial leverage.

4–6 What data are necessary to construct an operating breakeven chart?

4–7 What data are necessary to construct a financial breakeven chart?

4–8 What would be the effect of each of the following on a firm's operating and financial breakeven point? Indicate the effect in the space provided by placing a (+) for an increase, a (−) for a decrease, and a (0) for no effect. When answering this question, assume everything except the change indicated is held constant.

	OPERATING BREAKEVEN	FINANCIAL BREAKEVEN
a. An increase in the sales price	_____	_____
b. A reduction in variable labor costs	_____	_____
c. A decrease in fixed operating costs	_____	_____
d. Issuing new bonds	_____	_____
e. Issuing new preferred stock	_____	_____
f. Issuing new common stock	_____	_____

4–9 Assume that a firm is developing its long-run financial plan. What period should this plan cover—one month, six months, one year, three years, five years, or some other period? Justify your answer.

Self-Test Problems

(Solutions appear in Appendix B)

key terms **ST–1** Define each of the following terms:
  a. Sales forecast
  b. Projected balance sheet method
  c. Spontaneously generated funds
  d. Dividend payout ratio
  e. Pro forma financial statement
  f. Additional funds needed (AFN)
  g. Financing feedback
  h. Financial planning; financial control
  i. Operating breakeven analysis; operating breakeven point, Q_{OpBE}
  j. Financial breakeven analysis; financial breakeven point (EPS level)
  k. Operating leverage; degree of operating leverage (DOL)
  l. Financial leverage; degree of financial leverage (DFL)
  m. Combined (total) leverage; degree of total leverage (DTL)

operating leverage and breakeven analysis **ST–2** Olinde Electronics Inc. produces stereo components that sell for P = $100. Olinde's fixed costs are $200,000; 5,000 components are produced and sold each year; EBIT is currently $50,000; and Olinde's assets (all equity financed) are $500,000. Olinde estimates that it can change its production process, adding $400,000 to investment and $50,000 to fixed operating costs. This change will (1) reduce variable costs per unit by $10 and (2) increase output by 2,000 units, but (3) the sales price on all units will have to be lowered to $95 to permit sales of the additional output. Olinde has tax loss carryovers that cause its tax rate to be zero. Olinde uses no debt, and its average cost of capital is ten percent.
  a. Should Olinde make the change?
  b. Would Olinde's degree of operating leverage increase or decrease if it made the change? What about its operating breakeven point?
  c. Suppose Olinde were unable to raise additional equity financing and had to borrow the $400,000 to make the investment at an interest rate of eight percent. Use the DuPont equation to find the expected return on total assets (ROA) of the investment. Should Olinde make the change if debt financing must be used?
  d. What would Olinde's degree of financial leverage be if the $400,000 was borrowed at the eight percent interest rate?

Problems

4–1 Magee Computers makes bulk purchases of small computers, stocks them in conveniently located warehouses, and ships them to its chain of retail stores. Magee's balance sheet as of December 31, 2000, is shown here (in millions of dollars):

Cash	$ 3.5	Accounts payable	$ 9.0
Receivables	26.0	Notes payable	18.0
Inventories	58.0	Accruals	8.5
Current assets	$ 87.5	Current liabilities	$ 35.5
Net fixed assets	35.0	Long-term bonds	6.0
		Common stock	15.0
		Retained earnings	66.0
		Total liabilities	
Total assets	$122.5	and equity	$122.5

Sales for 2000 were $350 million, while net income for the year was $10.5 million. Magee paid dividends of $4.2 million to common stockholders. Sales are projected to increase by $70 million, or 20 percent, during 2001. The firm is operating at full capacity. Assume that all ratios remain constant.

a. Construct Magee's pro forma balance sheet for December 31, 2001. Assume that all external capital requirements are met by bank loans and are reflected in notes payable. Do not consider any financing feedback effects.

b. Now calculate the following ratios, based on your projected December 31, 2001, balance sheet. Magee's 2000 ratios and industry average ratios are shown here for comparison:

	MAGEE COMPUTERS		INDUSTRY AVERAGE
	12/31/01	12/31/00	12/31/00
Current ratio	_____	2.5	3.0
Debt/total assets	_____	33.9%	30.0%
Return on equity	_____	13.0%	12.0%

c. (1) Now assume that Magee grows by the same $70 million but that the growth is spread over five years—that is, that sales grow by $14 million each year. Do not consider any financing feedback effects.

   (2) Construct a pro forma balance sheet as of December 31, 2001, using notes payable as the balancing item.

   (3) Calculate the current ratio, debt/assets ratio, and rate of return on equity as of December 31, 2005. [*Hint:* Be sure to use total sales, which amount to $1,960 million, to calculate retained earnings but 2005 profits to calculate the rate of return on equity—that is, return on equity = (2005 profits)/(12/31/05 equity).]

d. Do the plans outlined in parts a or c seem feasible to you? That is, do you think Magee could borrow the required capital, and would the company be raising the odds on its bankruptcy to an excessive level in the event of some temporary misfortune?

concluded

Interest	(150)
Earnings before taxes	$ 400
Taxes (40%)	(160)
Net income	$ 240

Per Share Data

Common stock price	$16.96
Earnings per share (EPS)	$ 1.60
Dividends per share (DPS)	$ 1.04

a. The firm operated at full capacity in 2000. It expects sales to increase by 20 percent during 2001 and expects 2001 dividends per share to increase to $1.10. Use the projected balance sheet method to determine how much outside financing is required, developing the firm's pro forma balance sheet and income statement, and use AFN as the balancing item.

b. If the firm must maintain a current ratio of 2.3 and a debt ratio of 40 percent, how much financing, after the first pass, will be obtained using notes payable, long-term debt, and common stock?

c. Make the second pass financial statements incorporating financing feedbacks, using the ratios in part b. Assume that the interest rate on debt averages ten percent.

operating breakeven analysis

4–5 The Weaver Watch Company manufactures a line of ladies' watches, which is sold through discount houses. Each watch is sold for $25; the fixed costs are $140,000 for 30,000 watches or less; variable costs are $15 per watch.

a. What is the firm's gain or loss at sales of 8,000 watches? Of 18,000 watches?

b. What is the operating breakeven point? Illustrate by means of a chart.

c. What is Weaver's degree of operating leverage at sales of 8,000 units? Of 18,000 units? (*Hint:* Use Equation 4–4 to solve this problem.)

d. What happens to the operating breakeven point if the selling price rises to $31? What is the significance of the change to the financial manager?

e. What happens to the operating breakeven point if the selling price rises to $31 but variable costs rise to $23 a unit?

operating breakeven analysis

4–6 The following relationships exist for Dellva Industries, a manufacturer of electronic components. Each unit of output is sold for $45; the fixed costs are $175,000, of which $110,000 are annual depreciation charges; and variable costs are $20 per unit.

a. What is the firm's gain or loss at sales of 5,000 units? Of 12,000 units?

b. What is the operating income breakeven point?

c. Assume Dellva is operating at a level of 4,000 units. Are creditors likely to seek the liquidation of the company if it is slow in paying its bills?

financial leverage

4–7 Gordon's Plants has the following partial income statement for 2000:

Earnings before interest and taxes	$4,500
Interest	(2,000)
Earnings before taxes	$2,500
Taxes (40%)	(1,000)
Net income	$1,500
Number of common shares	1,000

a. If Gordon's has no preferred stock, what is its financial breakeven point? Show that the amount you come up with actually is the financial breakeven by recreating the portion of the income statement shown here for that amount.

b. What is the degree of financial leverage for Gordon's? What does this value mean?

c. If Gordon's actually has preferred stock that requires payment of dividends equal to $600, what would be the financial breakeven point? Show that the amount you compute is the financial breakeven by recreating the portion of the income statement shown here for that amount. What is the degree of financial leverage in this case?

Exam-Type Problems

The problems in this section are set up in such a way that they could be used as multiple-choice exam problems.

operating leverage   **4-8** The Niendorf Corporation produces tea kettles, which it sells for $15 each. Fixed costs are $700,000 for up to 400,000 units of output. Variable costs are $10 per kettle.

a. What is the firm's gain or loss at sales of 125,000 units? Of 175,000 units?

b. What is the operating breakeven point? Illustrate by means of a chart.

c. What is Niendorf's degree of operating leverage at sales of 125,000 units? Of 150,000 units? Of 175,000 units? (*Hint:* You may use either Equation 4–4 or 4–4a to solve this problem.)

degree of operating   **4-9** **a.** Given the following graphs, calculate the total fixed costs, variable costs per
leverage   unit, and sales price for Firm A. Firm B's fixed costs are $120,000, its variable costs per unit are $4, and its sales price is $8 per unit.

b. Which firm has the higher degree of operating leverage? Explain.

c. At what sales level, in units, do both firms earn the same profit?

Breakeven Charts for Problem 4–9

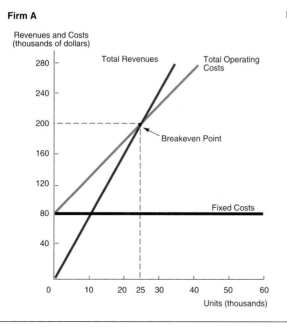

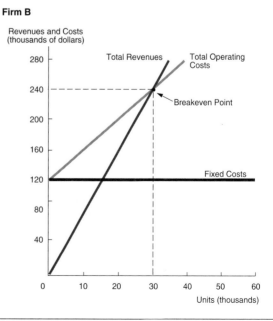

TABLE IP4–1	Financial Statements and Other Data on NWC (millions of dollars)

A. 2000 Balance Sheet

Cash and securities	$ 20	Accounts payable and accruals		$ 100
Accounts receivable	240	Notes payable		100
Inventories	240	Total current liabilities		$ 200
Total current assets	$ 500	Long-term debt		100
		Common stock		500
Net fixed assets	500	Retained earnings		200
Total assets	$1,000	Total liabilities and equity		$1,000

B. 2000 Income Statement

Sales	$ 2,000.00
Less: Variable costs	(1,200.00)
Fixed costs	(700.00)
Earnings before interest and taxes	$ 100.00
Interest	(16.00)
Earnings before taxes	$ 84.00
Taxes (40%)	(33.60)
Net income	$ 50.40
Dividends (30%)	(15.12)
Addition to retained earnings	$ 35.28

C. Key Ratios

	NWC	INDUSTRY	COMMENT
Profit margin	2.52	4.00	
Return on equity	7.20	15.60	
Days sales outstanding (360 days)	43.20 days	34.00 days	
Inventory turnover	5.00×	8.00×	
Fixed assets turnover	4.00×	5.00×	
Total assets turnover	2.00×	2.50×	
Total debt ratio	30.00%	36.00%	
Times interest earned	6.25×	9.40×	
Current ratio	2.50×	3.00×	
Payout ratio	30.00%	30.00%	

accounts receivable? If the company were able to bring these ratios into line with the industry averages, what effect would this have on its AFN and its financial ratios?

f. How would changes in these items affect the AFN? (1) The dividend payout ratio, (2) the profit margin, (3) the plant capacity, and (4) NWC begins buying from its suppliers on terms that permit it to pay after 60 days rather than after 30 days. (Consider each item separately and hold all other things constant.)

Part II. Breakeven Analysis and Leverage

One of NWC's employees recently submitted a proposal that NWC should expand its operations and sell its chemicals in retail establishments such as Home Depot, Lowe's, Scotty's, and so on. To determine the feasibility of the idea, Sue needs to perform a breakeven analysis. The fixed costs associated with producing and selling the chemicals to retail stores would be $60 million, the selling price per unit is expected to be $10, and the variable cost ratio would be the same as it is currently.

a. What is the operating breakeven point both in dollars and in number of units for the employee's proposal?

b. Draw the operating breakeven chart for the proposal. Should the employee's proposal be adopted if NWC can produce and sell 20 million units of the chemical?

c. If NWC can produce and sell 20 million units of its product to retail stores, what would be its degree of operating leverage? What would be NWC's percent increase in operating profits if sales actually were ten percent higher than expected?

d. Assume NWC has excess capacity, so it does not need to raise any additional external funds to implement the proposal—that is, its 2001 interest payments remain the same as 2000. What would be its degree of financial leverage and its degree of total leverage? If the actual sales turned out to be ten percent greater than expected, as a percent, how much greater would the earnings per share be?

e. Explain how breakeven analysis and leverage analysis can be used for planning the implementation of this proposal.

Computer-Related Problem

Work the problem in this section only if you are using the computer problem diskette.

forecasting   **4–14** Use the model in File C4 to solve this problem. Stendardi Industries' 2000 financial statements are shown in the following table:

STENDARDI INDUSTRIES:
BALANCE SHEET AS OF DECEMBER 31, 2000
(MILLIONS OF DOLLARS)

Cash	$ 4.0	Accounts payable	$ 8.0
Receivables	12.0	Notes payable	5.0
Inventories	16.0	Current liabilities	$13.0
Current assets	$32.0	Long-term debt	12.0
Net fixed assets	40.0	Common stock	20.0
		Retained earnings	27.0
Total assets	$72.0	Total liabilities and equity	$72.0

Stendardi Industries:
Income Statement for December 31, 2000
(Millions of Dollars)

Sales	$80.0
Operating costs	(71.3)
Earnings before interest and taxes	$ 8.7
Interest	(2.0)
Earnings before taxes	$ 6.7
Taxes (40%)	(2.7)
Net income	$ 4.0
Dividends (40%)	$1.60
Addition to retained earnings	$2.40

Assume that the firm has no excess capacity in fixed assets, that the average interest rate for debt is 12 percent, and that the projected annual sales growth rate for the next five years is 15 percent.

a. Stendardi plans to finance its additional funds needed with 50 percent short-term debt and 50 percent long-term debt. Using the projected balance sheet method, prepare the pro forma financial statements for 2001 through 2005, and then determine (1) additional funds needed, (2) the current ratio, (3) the debt ratio, and (4) the return on equity.

b. Sales growth could be five percentage points above or below the projected 15 percent. Determine the effect of such variances on AFN and the key ratios.

c. Perform an analysis to determine the sensitivity of AFN and the key ratios for 2005 to changes in the dividend payout ratio as specified in the following, assuming sales grow at a constant 15 percent. What happens to AFN if the dividend payout ratio (1) is raised from 40 to 70 percent or (2) is lowered from 40 to 20 percent?

ONLINE ESSENTIALS

http://www.toolkit.cch.com/text/P06_7530.asp   Business Owner's Toolkit
This is a tutorial for breakeven analysis, with links to definitions and analyses related to such analyses.

http://www.Cybersolve.com/breakeven.html   Breakeven Analysis: Tutorial
This is a breakeven analysis tutorial that provides the ability to fill in values and complete breakeven computations and then shows the results graphically.

http://www.cfopub.com   *CFO*
This is the Web page of *CFO*, a publication for financial executives. It provides interesting articles about budgeting and financial forecasting.

Projected Financial Statements, Including Financing Feedbacks

In the chapter, we discussed the procedure used to construct pro forma financial statements. The first step is to estimate the level of operations and then project the impact such operations will have on the financial statements of the firm. We found that when a firm needs additional external financing, its existing interest and dividend payments will change; thus, the values initially projected for the financial statements will be affected. Therefore, to recognize these *financing feedbacks*, the construction of projected financial statements needs to be an iterative process. In this appendix, we give an indication of the iterative process for constructing the pro forma statements for Unilate. Table 4A-1 contains the initial projected statements shown in Table 4–1 and Table 4–2 of the chapter; then some of the subsequent "passes" used to adjust the forecasted statements are given. According to the discussion given in the chapter, the forecasted statements first are constructed assuming only retained earnings and spontaneous financing are available to support the forecasted operations. This "first pass" is necessary to provide an indication of the additional external funds that are needed—Unilate needs $42.7 million. But if Unilate raises this additional amount by borrowing from the bank and by issuing new bonds and new common stock, then its interest and dividend payments will increase. This can be seen by examining the income statement, which was constructed in the second pass to show the effects of raising the $42.7 million additional funds needed. Because Unilate would have additional debt, it would have to pay $1.30 million more interest; and because it has more shares of common stock outstanding, it would have to pay $1.40 million more dividends. Consequently, as the second pass balance sheet shows, if Unilate only raises the $42.7 million AFN (additional funds needed) initially computed, it would find there still would be a need for funds—the AFN would be $2.18 million—because the addition to retained earnings would be lower than expected originally. As it turns out, Unilate actually would need to raise $45.0 million to support the forecasted 2001 operations—$6.75 million from notes, $9.0 million from bonds, and $29.25 million from stock.

TABLE 4A-1	Unilate Textiles: 2001 Forecast of Financial Statements (millions of dollars)

INCOME STATEMENT

	INITIAL PASS	FEED-BACK	SECOND PASS		FINAL PASS
Earnings before interest and taxes (EBIT)	$ 143.00		$ 143.00		$ 143.00
Less interest	(40.00)	+ 1.30	(41.30)	+0.07	(41.37)
Earnings before taxes (EBT)	$ 103.00		$ 101.70		$ 101.63
Taxes (40%)	(41.20)	− 0.52	(40.68)	−0.03	(40.65)
Net Income	$ 61.80		$ 61.02		$ 60.98
Common dividends	(29.00)	+ 1.40	(30.40)	+0.08	(30.48)
Addition to retained earnings	$ 32.80	− 2.18	$ 30.62	−0.12	$ 30.50
Earnings per share	$ 2.47		$ 2.33		$ 2.32
Dividends per share	$ 1.16		$ 1.16		$ 1.16
Number of common shares (millions)	25.00		26.21		26.27

BALANCE SHEET

	INITIAL PASS	FEED-BACK	SECOND PASS		FINAL PASS
Cash	$ 16.50		$ 16.50		$ 16.50
Accounts receivable	198.00		198.00		198.00
Inventories	297.00		297.00		297.00
Total current assets	$511.50		$511.50		$511.44
Net plant and equipment	418.00		418.00		418.00
Total Assets	$929.50		$929.50		$929.50
Accounts payable	$ 33.00		$ 33.00		$ 33.00
Accruals	66.00		66.00		66.00
Notes payable	40.00	+ 6.41	46.41	+0.34	46.75
Total current liabilities	$139.00		$145.41		$145.75
Long-term bonds	300.00	+ 8.54	308.54	+0.46	309.00
Total liabilities	$439.00		$453.95		$454.75
Common stock	130.00	+27.76	157.76	+1.49	159.25
Retained earnings	317.80	− 2.18	315.62	−0.12	315.50
Total owners' equity	$447.80		$473.37		$474.75
Total Liabilities and Equity	$886.80	+40.52	$927.32	+2.18	$929.50
Additional Funds Needed (AFN)	$ 42.70		$ 2.18		$ 0.00

NOTE:

The results in this table are carried to two decimal places to show some of the more subtle changes that occur. Even so, you will find some rounding differences when summing the feedback amounts.

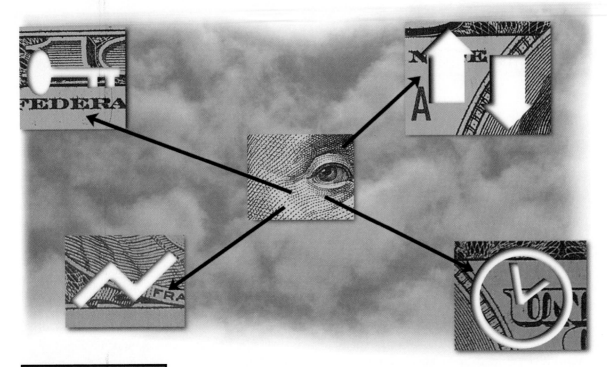

PART III

Essential Concepts in Managerial Finance

CHAPTER 5

Risk and Rates of Return

The performance of the major stock markets from 1995 through 1998 can best be described as remarkable—a period investors would love to repeat again and again. During this four-year period, stocks traded in U.S. stock markets earned an average return greater than 20 percent a year. In 1998, companies such as Microsoft and MCI WorldCom more than doubled in value. The value of other companies such as America Online, Amazon.com, and Yahoo!, which are Internet-based organizations, increased by more than 500 percent. Consider the return you would have earned in 1998 if you purchased Amazon.com at the beginning of the year for $30.13, and at the end of the year it was selling for $321.25—that's a one-year return of 966 percent. Even as these stocks experienced unbelievable gains, other stocks suffered debilitating losses. Financial difficulties at FPA Medical Management, a health care services company, caused the stock to decline from $18.63 at the beginning of the year to 13 cents by the end of the year—a return equal to a *loss* of 99.3 percent. At the same time, the price of CompUSA's stock declined by more than 58 percent and Disney was down more than nine percent. As these examples show, investors who "put all their eggs in one basket" faced considerable risk in the stock markets—they would have won big if the "basket" they chose was Amazon.com's stock, but they would have lost almost everything if the "basket" they chose was FPA Medical Management. Investors who diversified by spreading their investments among many

stocks, perhaps through mutual funds, would have earned a return somewhere between the extraordinary increases posted by Amazon.com, America Online, and Yahoo! and the extraordinary decreases posted by FPA Medical Management, CompUSA, and others—very large "baskets" of such diversified investments would have earned returns fairly close to the average of the stock markets.

Investing is risky! Although the stock markets performed well from 1995 through 1998, they also go through periods of decreasing prices, or average returns that are negative. For instance, in 1990 and 1994, the average stock listed on the New York Stock Exchange decreased in value. More recently, during a six-week period in the summer of 1998, the market tumbled nearly 20 percent, and more than half of the drop occurred within one week. In mid-July 1998, the Dow Jones Industrial Average (DJIA) reached 9338, a record high at the time; by the end of August the DJIA was at 7539, which was less than the 7908 level it began the year. And, in the first three months of 1999, the DJIA rose above 10,000, and then quickly retreated, in some cases to less than 9700. What a roller-coaster ride! What risk!

Who knows what the stock market will be doing when you read this book—it could be an up market, which is referred to as a *bull*, or it could be a down market, which is referred to as a *bear*. But we know that as times change, investment strategies and portfolio mixes need to be changed

continues

to meet new conditions. Thus, it is important to understand the basic concepts of risk and return and how diversification affects investment decisions. You will discover that investors can create portfolios of securities to reduce risk without reducing the average return on their investments. After reading this chapter, you should have a better understanding of how risk affects investment returns and how to evaluate risk when selecting investments such as those described here. ∎

In this chapter we take an in-depth look at how investment risk should be measured and how it affects assets' values and rates of return. Recall that in Chapter 2, when we examined the determinants of interest rates, we defined the real risk-free rate, k*, to be the rate of interest on a risk-free security in the absence of inflation. The actual interest rate on a particular debt security was shown to be equal to the real risk-free rate plus several premiums that reflect both inflation and the riskiness of the security in question. In this chapter we define more precisely what the term *risk* means as it relates to investments, we examine procedures used to measure risk, and we discuss the relationship between risk and return. It is important for both investors and financial managers to understand these concepts and use them when considering investment decisions, whether the decisions concern financial assets or real assets.

We will demonstrate in this chapter that each investment—each stock, bond, or physical asset—has two different types of risk: (1) diversifiable risk and (2) nondiversifiable risk. The sum of these two components is the investment's total risk. Diversifiable risk is not important to rational, informed investors because they will eliminate its effects by "diversifying" it away. The really significant risk is nondiversifiable risk—this risk is bad in the sense that it cannot be eliminated, and if you invest in anything other than riskless assets, such as short-term Treasury bills, you will be exposed to it. In the balance of the chapter we will explain these risk concepts and show you how risk enters into the investment decision process.

Defining and Measuring Risk

Risk is defined in *Webster's Collegiate Dictionary* as "possibility of loss or injury: *peril*." Thus, we generally use the term *risk* to refer to the chance that some unfavorable event will occur. For example, if you engage in skydiving, you are taking a chance with your life—skydiving is risky. If you bet on the horses, you are risking your money. If you invest in speculative stocks (or, really, *any* stock), you are taking a risk in the hope of making an appreciable return.

Most people view risk in the manner we just described—a chance of loss. But in reality, *risk* occurs when we cannot be certain about the outcome of a particular activity or event, so we are not sure what will occur in the future. Consequently, *risk* results from the fact that an action such as investing can produce more than one outcome in the future.

To illustrate the riskiness of financial assets, suppose you have a large amount of money to invest for one year. You could buy a Treasury security that has an expected return equal to six percent. The rate of return expected from this investment can be determined quite precisely because the chance of the government defaulting on Treasury securities is negligible; the outcome essentially is guaranteed, which means this is a risk-free investment. On the other hand, you could buy the common stock of a newly formed company that has developed technology that can be used to extract petroleum from the mountains in South America without defacing the landscape and without harming the ecology. The technology has yet to be proven economically feasible, so it is not known what returns the common stockholders will receive in the future. Experts who have analyzed the common stock of the company have determined that the *expected*, or average long-run, return for such an investment is 30 percent; each year the investment could yield a positive return as high as 900 percent, but there also is the possibility the company will not survive, in which case, the entire investment will be lost and the return will be −100 percent. The return investors receive each year cannot be determined precisely because more than one outcome is possible—this is a risky investment. Because there is a significant danger of actually earning considerably less than the expected return, investors probably would consider the stock to be quite risky. But there also is a very good chance the actual return will be greater than expected, which, of course, is an outcome we gladly accept. So, when we think of investment risk, along with the chance of actually receiving less than expected, we should consider the chance of actually receiving more than expected. If we consider investment risk from this perspective, we can define **risk** as the chance of receiving an actual return other than expected, which simply means there is *variability in the returns*, or outcomes, from the investment. Therefore, investment risk can be measured by the variability of the investment's returns.

Investment risk, then, is related to the possibility of actually earning a return other than expected—the greater the variability of the possible outcomes, the riskier the investment. And as we will soon discover, *the return expected from an investment is positively related to the investment's risk—a higher expected return represents an investor's compensation for taking on greater risk*. But this relationship is not quite as clear-cut as it sounds, because we generally define and evaluate risk on two different bases: (1) **stand-alone risk,** which is the risk associated with an investment when it is held by itself, not in combination with other assets, and (2) **portfolio risk,** which is the risk associated with an investment when it is held in combination with other assets, not by itself. In the remainder of the chapter, we define risk more precisely and differentiate between stand-alone risk and portfolio risk when determining the appropriate expected rate of return for an investment.

RISK
The chance that an outcome other than expected will occur.

STAND-ALONE RISK
The risk associated with an investment when it is held by itself, or in isolation, not in combination with other assets.

PORTFOLIO RISK
The risk associated with an investment when it is held in combination with other assets, not by itself.

PROBABILITY DISTRIBUTION
A listing of all possible outcomes, or events, with a probability (chance of occurrence) assigned to each outcome.

Probability Distributions

An event's *probability* is defined as the chance that the event will occur. For example, a weather forecaster might state, "There is a 40 percent chance of rain today and a 60 percent chance that it will not rain." If all possible events, or outcomes, are listed, and if a probability is assigned to each event, the listing is called a **probability distribution.** For our weather forecast, we could set up the following probability distribution:

OUTCOME (1)	PROBABILITY (2)
Rain	0.40 = 40%
No rain	0.60 = 60
	1.00 100%

The possible outcomes are listed in column 1, while the probabilities of these outcomes, expressed both as decimals and as percentages, are given in column 2. Notice that the probabilities must sum to 1.0, or 100 percent, to account for all the possible outcomes.

Probabilities can also be assigned to the possible outcomes (or returns) from an investment. If you buy a bond, you expect to receive interest on the bond, and those interest payments will provide you with a rate of return on your investment. The possible outcomes from this investment are (1) that the issuer will make the interest payments or (2) that the issuer will fail to make the interest payments. The higher the probability of default on the interest payments, the riskier the bond; and the higher the risk, the higher the rate of return you would require to invest in the bond. If instead of buying a bond you invest in a stock, you will again expect to earn a return on your money, which will come from dividends plus capital gains. Again, the riskier the stock—which means the greater the variability of the possible payoffs—the higher the stock's expected return must be to induce you to invest in it.

With this in mind, consider the possible rates of return that you might earn next year on a $10,000 investment in the stock of either Martin Products Inc. or U.S. Electric. Martin manufactures and distributes computer terminals and equipment for the rapidly growing data transmission industry. Because its sales are cyclical, its profits rise and fall with the business cycle. Further, its market is extremely competitive, and some new company could develop better products that could literally bankrupt Martin. U.S. Electric, on the other hand, supplies electricity, which is an essential service, and because it has city franchises that protect it from competition, its sales and profits are relatively stable and predictable.

The rate-of-return probability distributions for the two companies are shown in Table 5–1. Here we see that there is a 20 percent chance of a boom, in which case both companies will have high earnings, pay high dividends, and enjoy capital gains; there is a 50 percent probability of a normal economy and moderate returns; and there is a 30 percent probability of a recession, which will mean low earnings and dividends as well as capital losses. Notice, however, that Martin Products' rate of return could vary far more widely than that of U.S. Electric. There is a fairly high probability that the value of Martin's stock will vary substantially, resulting in a loss of 60 percent or a gain of 110 percent, while there is no chance of a loss for U.S. Electric and its maximum gain is 20 percent.[1]

Self-Test Questions

What does "investment risk" mean?

Set up illustrative probability distributions for (1) a bond investment and (2) a stock investment.

---

[1]It is, of course, completely unrealistic to think that any stock has no chance of a loss. Only in hypothetical examples could this occur. To illustrate, the price of Columbia Gas's stock dropped from $34.50 to $20.00 in just three hours on June 19, 1991. All investors were reminded that any stock is exposed to some risk of loss, and those investors who bought Columbia Gas learned this lesson the hard way.

TABLE 5-1	Probability Distributions for Martin Products and U.S. Electric

		RATE OF RETURN ON STOCK IF THIS STATE OCCURS	
STATE OF THE ECONOMY	PROBABILITY OF THIS STATE OCCURRING	MARTIN PRODUCTS	U.S. ELECTRIC
Boom	0.2	110%	20%
Normal	0.5	22	16
Recession	0.3	−60	10
	1.0		

Expected Rate of Return

Table 5–1 provides the probability distributions showing the possible outcomes for investing in Martin Products and U.S. Electric. We can see that the most likely outcome is for the economy to be normal, in which case Martin will return 22 percent and U.S. Electric will return 16 percent. But other outcomes are also possible, so we need to somehow summarize the information contained in the probability distributions into a single measure that considers all these possible outcomes—that measure is the expected value, or *expected rate of return*, for the investments.

Simply stated, the **expected rate of return (value)** is the *weighted average* of the outcomes, where the weights we use are the probabilities. Table 5–2 shows how the expected rates of return for Martin Products and U.S. Electric are computed—we multiply each possible outcome by the probability it will occur and then sum the results. We designate the expected rate of return, $\hat{k}$ which is termed "k-hat."[2]

The expected rate of return can be calculated using the following equation:

5-1	

$$\text{Expected rate of return} = \hat{k} = Pr_1k_1 + Pr_2k_2 + \ldots + P$$

$$= \sum_{i=1}^{n} Pr_ik_i$$

Here k_i is the ith possible outcome, Pr_i is the probability the ith outcome will occur, and n is the number of possible outcomes. Thus, $\hat{k}$ is a weighted average of the possible outcomes (the k_i values), with each outcome's weight being its probability of

---

[2]In Chapter 7, we use k_d to signify the return on a debt instrument and k_s to signify the return on a stock. In this section, however, we discuss only returns on stocks; thus, the subscript s is unnecessary, and we use the term $\hat{k}$ rather than $\hat{k}_s$.

TABLE 5–2	Calculation of Expected Rates of Return: Martin Products and U.S. Electric				
		MARTIN PRODUCTS		**U.S. ELECTRIC**	
STATE OF THE ECONOMY (1)	**PROBABILITY OF THIS STATE OCCURRING** (2)	**RETURN IF THIS STATE OCCURS** (3)	**PRODUCT:** (2) × (3) = (4)	**RETURN IF THIS STATE OCCURS** (5)	**PRODUCT:** (2) × (5) = (6)
Boom	0.2	110%	22%	20%	4%
Normal	0.5	22	11	16	8
Recession	0.3	−60	−18	10	3
	1.0		$\hat{k}_{Martin} = $ 15%		$\hat{k}_{US} = $ 15%

occurrence. Using the data for Martin Products, we obtain its expected rate of return as follows:

$$\hat{k} = Pr_1(k_1) + Pr_2(k_2) + Pr_3(k_3)$$

$$= 0.2(110\%) + 0.5(22\%) + 0.3(-60\%)$$

$$= 15.0\%$$

Notice the expected rate of return does not equal any of the possible payoffs for Martin Products given in Table 5–2. Stated simply, the expected rate of return represents the average payoff investors will receive from Martin Products if the probability distribution given in Table 5–2 does not change over a long period of time. For example, if the probability distribution for Martin Products is correct, then 20 percent of the time the future economic condition will be termed a boom and investors will earn a 110 percent rate of return; 50 percent of the time the economy should be normal and the investment payoff will be 22 percent; and 30 percent of the time the economy should be recessionary and the payoff will be a loss equal to 60 percent. On average then, Martin Products' investors will earn 15 percent.

We can graph the rates of return to obtain a picture of the variability of possible outcomes; this is shown in the Figure 5–1 bar charts. The height of each bar signifies the probability that a given outcome will occur. The range of probable returns for Martin Products is from +110 to −60 percent, with an expected return of 15 percent. The expected return for U.S. Electric also is 15 percent, but its range is much narrower.

Continuous versus Discrete Probability Distributions

DISCRETE PROBABILITY DISTRIBUTION
The number of possible outcomes is limited or finite.

Thus far we have assumed that only three states of the economy can exist: recession, normal, and boom. So the probability distributions given in Table 5–1 are called **discrete** because there is a finite, or limited, number of outcomes. Actually, of course, the state of the economy could range from a deep depression to a fantastic boom, and

| FIGURE 5–1 | Probability Distributions of Martin Products' and U.S. Electric's Rates of Return |

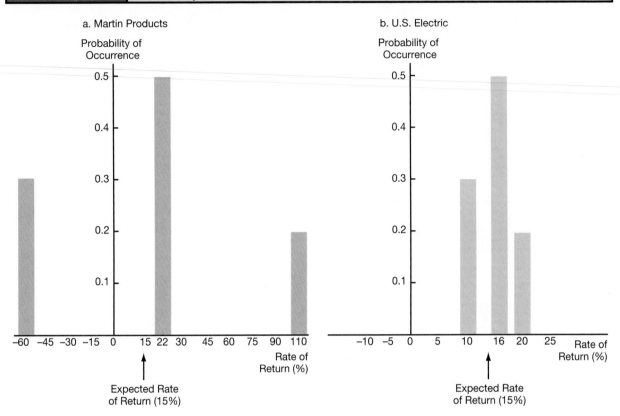

there are an unlimited number of possibilities in between. Suppose we had the time and patience to assign a probability to each possible state of the economy (with the sum of the probabilities still equaling 1.0), and to assign a rate of return to each stock for each state of the economy. We would have a table similar to Table 5–1, except that it would have many more entries in each column. This table could be used to calculate expected rates of return as shown previously, and the probabilities and outcomes could be approximated by continuous curves such as those presented in Figure 5–2. Here we have changed the assumptions so that there is essentially a zero probability that Martin Products' return will be less than −60 percent or more than 110 percent, or that U.S. Electric's return will be less than ten percent or more than 20 percent, but virtually any return within these limits is possible. These probability distributions are **continuous** because, in each case, the number of outcomes possible is unlimited—U.S. Electric's return could be 10.01 percent, 10.001 percent, and so on.

CONTINUOUS PROBABILITY DISTRIBUTION
The number of possible outcomes is unlimited or infinite.

The tighter the probability distribution, the less variability there is and the more likely it is that the actual outcome will be close to the expected value; consequently, the less likely it is that the actual return will be much different from the expected return. Thus, the tighter the probability distribution, the lower the risk assigned to a stock. Because U.S. Electric has a relatively tight probability distribution, *its actual* return is likely to be closer to its 15 percent expected return than is that of Martin Products.

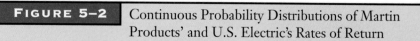

FIGURE 5-2	Continuous Probability Distributions of Martin Products' and U.S. Electric's Rates of Return

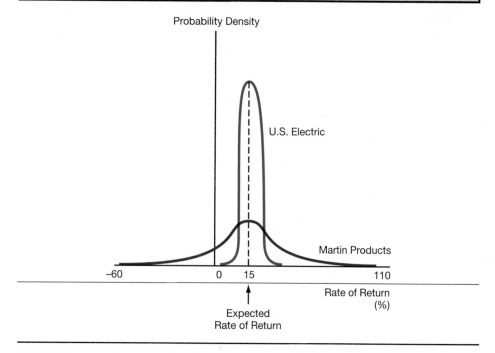

NOTE: The assumptions regarding the probabilities of various outcomes have been changed from those in Figure 5–1. There the probability of obtaining exactly 16 percent return for U.S. Electric was 50 percent; here it is *much smaller* because there are many possible outcomes instead of just three. With continuous distributions, it is more appropriate to ask what the probability is of obtaining at least some specified rate of return than to ask what the probability is of obtaining exactly that rate. This topic is covered in detail in statistics courses.

Measuring Stand-Alone Risk: The Standard Deviation

Because we have defined risk as the variability of returns, we can measure risk by examining the tightness of the probability distribution associated with the possible outcomes. In general, the width of a probability distribution indicates the amount of scatter, or variability, of the possible outcomes. Therefore, *the tighter the probability distribution of expected returns, the less its variability—thus the smaller the risk associated with the investment.* According to this definition, U.S. Electric is much less risky than Martin Products because the actual payoffs that are possible are closer to the expected return for U.S. Electric than for Martin Products.

To be most useful, any measure of risk should have a definite value—we need a measure of the tightness of the probability distribution. The measure we use most often is the **standard deviation,** the symbol for which is σ, pronounced "sigma." The smaller the standard deviation, the tighter the probability distribution, and, accordingly, the lower the riskiness of the investment. To calculate the standard deviation, we proceed as shown in Table 5–3, taking the following steps:

STANDARD DEVIATION, σ
A measure of the tightness, or variability, of a set of outcomes.

TABLE 5-3		Calculating Martin Products' Standard Deviation				

PAYOFF k_i (1)		EXPECTED RETURN $\hat{k}$ (2)		$k_i - \hat{k}$ (3)	$(k_i - \hat{k})^2$ (4)	PROBABILITY (5)	$(k_i - \hat{k})^2 PR_i$ (4) × (5) = (6)
110%	−	15%	=	95	9,025	0.2	(9,025)(0.2) = 1,805.0
22	−	15	=	7	49	0.5	(49)(0.5) = 24.5
(60)	−	15	=	−75	5,625	0.3	(5,625)(0.3) = 1,687.5

Variance = σ^2 = 3,517.0

Standard deviation = $\sigma = \sqrt{\sigma^2} = \sqrt{3,517.0}$ =   59.3%

1. We calculate the expected rate of return using Equation 5–1. For Martin, we previously found $\hat{k} = 15\%$.
2. Subtract the expected rate of return ($\hat{k}$) from each possible outcome (k_i) to obtain a set of deviations from $\hat{k}$:

$$\text{Deviation}_i = k_i - \hat{k}.$$

The deviations are shown in Column 3 of Table 5–3.
3. Square each deviation (shown in Column 4), multiply the result by the probability of occurrence for its related outcome (Column 5), and then sum these products to obtain the **variance** of the probability distribution, which is shown in Column 6. Thus, variance is defined as

VARIANCE, σ^2
The standard deviation squared.

5–2

$$\text{Variance} = \sigma^2 = \sum_{i=1}^{n} (k_i - \hat{k})^2 Pr_i$$

4. Finally, we take the square root of the variance to obtain the standard deviation shown at the bottom of Column 6:

5–3

$$\text{Standard deviation} = \sigma = \sqrt{\sigma^2} = \sqrt{\sum_{i=1}^{n} (k_i - \hat{k})^2 Pr_i}$$

Thus, the standard deviation is a weighted average deviation from the expected value, and it gives an idea of how far above or below the expected value the actual value is likely to be. Martin's standard deviation is seen in Table 5–3 to be 59.3 percent, and, using these same procedures, we find U.S. Electric's standard deviation to be 3.6 percent. The larger standard deviation of Martin Products indicates a greater variation of returns, thus a greater chance that the expected return will not be realized; therefore,

COEFFICIENT OF VARIATION (CV)
Standardized measure of the risk per unit of return; calculated as the standard deviation divided by the expected return.

Martin Products would be considered a riskier investment than U.S. Electric, according to this measure of risk.[3]

Coefficient of Variation

Another useful measure to evaluate risky investments is the **coefficient of variation (CV),** which is the standard deviation divided by the expected return:

> **5–4**
>
> $$\text{Coefficient of variation} = CV = \frac{\text{Risk}}{\text{Return}} = \frac{\sigma}{\hat{k}}$$

The coefficient of variation shows the risk per unit of return, and it provides a more meaningful basis for comparison when the expected returns on two alternatives are not the same. Because U.S. Electric and Martin Products have the *same expected return, it is not necessary to compute the coefficient of variation* to compare the two investments. In this case, most people would prefer to invest in U.S. Electric because it offers the same expected return with lower risk. The firm with the larger standard deviation, Martin, must have the larger coefficient of variation; in fact, the coefficient of variation for Martin is 59.3%/15% = 3.95 and that for U.S. Electric is 3.6%/15% = 0.24.

---

[3]In the example we described the procedure for finding the mean and standard deviation when the data are in the form of a known probability distribution. If only sample returns data over some *past period* are available, the standard deviation of returns can be estimated using this formula:

$$\text{Estimated } \sigma = S = \sqrt{\frac{\displaystyle\sum_{t=1}^{n}(\bar{k}_t - \bar{k}_{Avg})^2}{n-1}}$$

5–3a

Here $\bar{k}_t$ ("k bar t") denotes the past realized rate of return in Period t, and $\bar{k}_{Avg}$ is the average annual return earned during the last n years. Here is an example:

YEAR	$\bar{k}_t$
1998	15%
1999	−5
2000	20

$$\bar{k}_{Avg} = \frac{15 + (-5) + 20}{3} = 10\%$$

$$\text{Estimated } \sigma = S = \sqrt{\frac{(15-10)^2 + (-5-10)^2 + (20-10)^2}{3-1}}$$

$$= \sqrt{\frac{350}{2}} = 13.2\%$$

The historical σ often is used as an estimate of the future σ. Much less often, and generally incorrectly, $\bar{k}_{Avg}$ for some past period is used as an estimate of $\hat{k}$, the expected future return. Because past variability is likely to be repeated, s might be a good estimate of future risk, but it is much less reasonable to expect that the past *level* of return (which could have been as high as +100 percent or as low as −50 percent) is the best expectation of what investors think will happen in the future.

| FIGURE 5–3 | Comparison of Probability Distributions and Rates of Return for U.S. Electric and Biobotics Corporation |

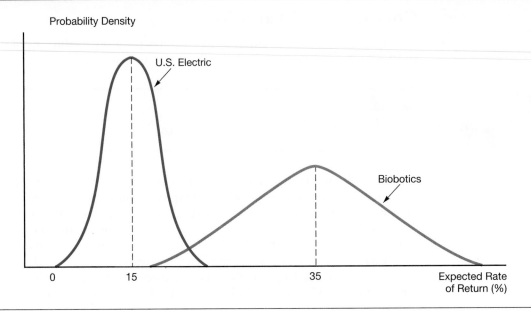

Thus, Martin is nearly 16.5 times riskier than U.S. Electric on the basis of this criterion.

The coefficient of variation is more useful when we consider investments that have different expected rates of return *and* different levels of risk. For example, Biobotics Corporation is a biological research and development firm that, according to stock analysts, offers investors an expected rate of return equal to 35 percent with a standard deviation of 7.5 percent. Biobotics offers a higher expected return than U.S. Electric, but it also is riskier. So, with respect to both risk and return, which is a better investment? If we calculate the coefficient of variation for Biobotics, we find it equals 7.5%/35% = 0.21, which is slightly less than U.S. Electric's coefficient of variation of 0.24. Consequently, Biobotics actually has less risk per unit of return than U.S. Electric, even though its standard deviation is higher. In this case, the additional expected return offered by the Biobotics investment is more than sufficient to compensate for the additional risk.

The probability distributions for U.S. Electric and Biobotics are graphed in Figure 5–3. U.S. Electric has the smaller standard deviation, hence the more peaked probability distribution. But it is clear from the graph that the chances of a really high return are higher for Biobotics than for U.S. Electric because Biobotics' expected return is so high. *Because the coefficient of variation captures the effects of both risk and return, it is a better measure for evaluating risk in situations where investments differ with respect to both their amounts of total risk and their expected returns.*

Risk Aversion and Required Returns

Suppose you have worked hard and saved $1 million, which you now plan to invest. You can buy a ten percent U.S. Treasury note, and at the end of one year you will have a sure $1.1 million, which is your original investment plus $100,000 in interest. Alternatively, you can buy stock in R&D Enterprises. If R&D's research programs are successful, your stock will increase in value to $2.2 million; however, if the research fails, the value of your stock will go to zero, and you will be penniless. You regard R&D's chances of success or failure as being 50-50, so the expected value of the stock investment is 0.5($0) + 0.5 ($2,200,000) = $1,100,000. Subtracting the $1 million cost of the stock leaves an expected profit of $100,000, or an expected (but risky) ten percent rate of return:

$$\text{Expected rate of return} = \frac{\text{Expected ending value} - \text{Beginning value}}{\text{Beginning value}}$$

$$= \frac{\$1,100,000 - \$1,000,000}{\$1,000,000}$$

$$= \frac{\$100,000}{\$1,000,000} = 0.10 = 10\%$$

Thus, you have a choice between a sure $100,000 profit (representing a ten percent rate of return) on the Treasury note and a risky expected $100,000 profit (also representing a ten percent expected rate of return) on the R&D Enterprises stock. Which one would you choose? *If you choose the less risky investment, you are risk averse. Most investors are indeed risk averse, and certainly the average investor is risk averse, at least with regard to his or her "serious money." Because this is a well-documented fact, we shall assume* **risk aversion** *throughout the remainder of the book.*

RISK AVERSION
Risk-averse investors require higher rates of return to invest in higher-risk securities.

What are the implications of risk aversion for security prices and rates of return? The answer is that, other things held constant, the higher a security's risk, the higher the return investors demand, thus the less they are willing to pay for the investment. To see how risk aversion affects security prices, we can analyze the situation with U.S. Electric and Martin Products stocks. Suppose each stock sold for $100 per share and each had an expected rate of return of 15 percent. Investors are averse to risk, so there would be a general preference for U.S. Electric because there is less variability in its payoffs (less uncertainty). People with money to invest would bid for U.S. Electric rather than Martin stock, and Martin's stockholders would start selling their stock and using the money to buy U.S. Electric stock. Buying pressure would drive up the price of U.S. Electric's stock, and selling pressure would simultaneously cause Martin's price to decline.

These price changes, in turn, would cause changes in the expected rates of return on the two securities. Suppose, for example, that the price of U.S. Electric stock was bid up from $100 to $150, whereas the price of Martin's stock declined from $100 to $75. This would cause U.S. Electric's expected return to fall to ten percent, while Martin's expected return would rise to 20 percent. The difference in returns, 20% − 10% = 10%, is a **risk premium, RP**, which represents the compensation investors require for assuming the *additional* risk of Martin stock.

RISK PREMIUM, RP
The portion of the expected return that can be attributed to the additional risk of an investment; it is the difference between the expected rate of return on a given risky asset and that on a less risky asset.

This example demonstrates a very important principle: In a market dominated by risk-averse investors, *riskier securities must have higher expected returns*, as estimated by the average investor, than less risky securities, because if this situation does not hold, investors will buy and sell investments and prices will continue to change until the higher risk investments have higher expected returns than the lower risk investments. We will consider the question of how much higher the returns on risky securities must

than the weighted average of the stocks' σ's. In fact, at least theoretically, it is possible to combine two stocks that by themselves are quite risky as measured by their standard deviations and to form a portfolio that is completely riskless, or risk-free, with $\sigma_P = 0$.

To illustrate the effect of combining securities, consider the situation in Figure 5–4. The bottom section gives data on rates of return for Stocks W and M individually, and also for a portfolio invested 50 percent in each stock. The three top graphs show the actual historical returns for each investment from 1996 through 2000, and the lower graphs show the probability distributions of returns, assuming that the future is expected to be like the past. The two stocks would be quite risky if they were held in isolation, but when they are combined to form Portfolio WM, they are not risky at all. (*Note:* These stocks are called W and M because their returns graphs in Figure 5–4 resemble a W and an M.)

The reason Stocks W and M can be combined to form a riskless portfolio is that their returns move opposite each other—when W's returns fall, those of M rise, and vice versa. The relationship between two variables is called *correlation*, and the **correlation coefficient, r,** measures the degree of the relationship between the variables.[5] In statistical terms, we say that the returns on Stocks W and M are perfectly negatively correlated, with $r = -1.0$.

The opposite of perfect negative correlation, with $r = -1.0$, is perfect positive correlation, with $r = +1.0$. Returns on two perfectly positively correlated stocks would move up and down together, and a portfolio consisting of two such stocks would be exactly as risky as the individual stocks. This point is illustrated in Figure 5–5, where we see that the portfolio's standard deviation is equal to that of the individual stocks. Thus, diversification does nothing to reduce risk if the portfolio consists of perfectly positively correlated stocks.

Figure 5–4 and Figure 5–5 demonstrate that when stocks are perfectly negatively correlated ($r = -1.0$), all risk can be diversified away, but when stocks are perfectly positively correlated ($r = +1.0$), diversification is ineffective. In reality, most stocks are positively correlated, but not perfectly so. On average, the correlation coefficient for the returns on two randomly selected stocks would be about $+0.5$, and for most pairs of stocks, r would lie in the range of $+0.4$ to $+0.6$. *Under such conditions, combining stocks into portfolios reduces risk but does not eliminate it completely.* Figure 5–6 illustrates this point with two stocks whose correlation coefficient is $r = +0.67$. The portfolio's average return is 15.0 percent, which is exactly the same as the average return for each of the two stocks, but its standard deviation is 20.6 percent, which is less than the standard deviation of either stock. Thus, the portfolio's risk is *not* an average of the risks of its individual stocks—diversification has reduced, but not eliminated, risk.

From these two-stock portfolio examples, we have seen that in one extreme case ($r = -1.0$), risk can be completely eliminated, while in the other extreme case ($r = +1.0$), diversification does no good. In between these extremes, combining two stocks into a portfolio reduces, but does not eliminate, the riskiness inherent in the individual stocks.

CORRELATION COEFFICIENT, r
A measure of the degree of relationship between two variables.

---

[5]The *correlation coefficient*, r, can range from $+1.0$, denoting that the two variables move in the same direction with exactly the same degree of synchronization every time movement occurs, to -1.0, denoting that the variables always move with the same degree of synchronization, but in opposite directions. A correlation coefficient of zero suggests that the two variables are not related to each other—that is, changes in one variable are *independent* of changes in the other.

FIGURE 5-4   Rate of Return Distributions for Two Perfectly Negatively Correlated Stocks (r = −1.0) and for Portfolio WM

a. Rates of Return

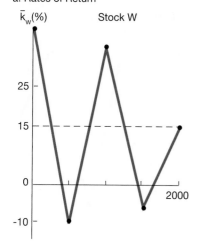

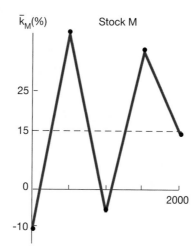

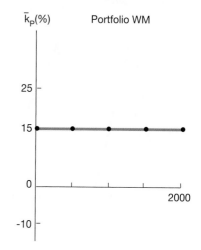

b. Probability Distributions of Returns

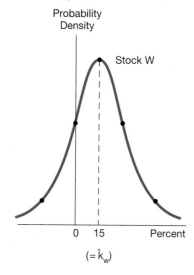

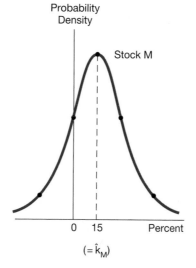

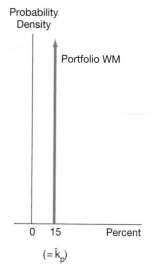

YEAR	STOCK W ($\bar{k}_W$)	STOCK M ($\bar{k}_M$)	PORTFOLIO WM ($\bar{k}_p$)
1996	40%	(10%)	15%
1997	(10)	40	15
1998	35	(5)	15
1999	(5)	35	15
2000	15	15	15
Average return	15%	15%	15%
Standard deviation	22.6%	22.6%	0.0%

FIGURE 5–5   Rate of Return Distributions for Two Perfectly Positively Correlated Stocks (r = + 1.0) and for Portfolio MM'

a. Rates of Return

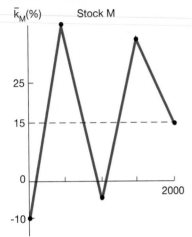
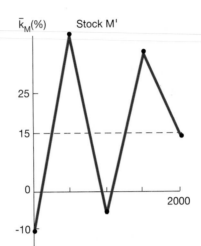
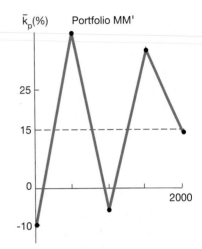

b. Probability Distributions of Returns

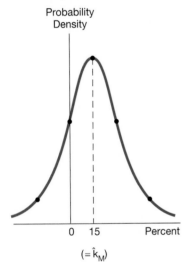
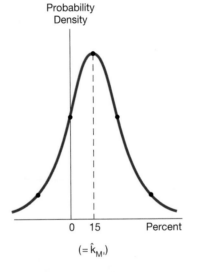
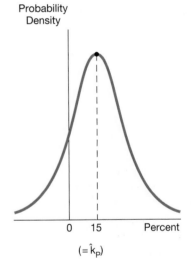

YEAR	STOCK M $(\bar{k}_M)$	STOCK M' $(\bar{k}_{M'})$	PORTFOLIO MM' $(\bar{k}_P)$
1996	(10%)	(10%)	(10%)
1997	40	40	40
1998	(5)	(5)	(5)
1999	35	35	35
2000	15	15	15
Average return	15%	15%	15%
Standard deviation	22.6%	22.6%	22.6%

FIGURE 5–6 Rate of Return Distributions for Two Partially Correlated Stocks (r = +0.67) and for Portfolio WY

a. Rates of Return

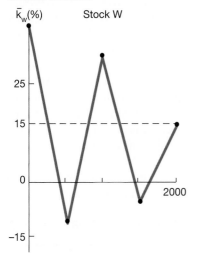
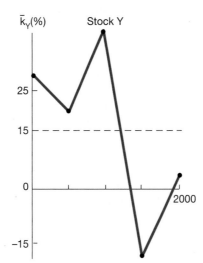
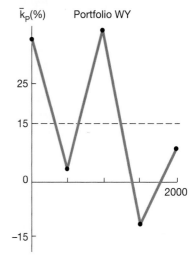

b. Probability Distribution of Returns

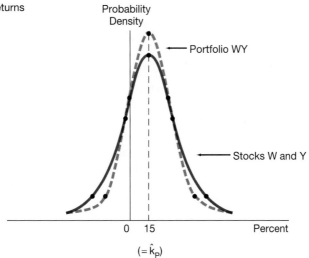

YEAR	STOCK W ($\bar{k}_w$)	STOCK Y ($\bar{k}_Y$)	PORTFOLIO WY ($\bar{k}_P$)
1996	40%	28%	34%
1997	(10)	20	5
1998	35	41	38
1999	(5)	(17)	(11)
2000	15	3	9
Average return	15%	15%	15%
Standard deviation	22.6%	22.6%	20.6%

What would happen if we included more than two stocks in the portfolio? *As a rule, the riskiness of a portfolio will be reduced as the number of stocks in the portfolio increases.* If we added enough stocks, could we completely eliminate risk? In general, the answer is no, but the extent to which adding stocks to a portfolio reduces its risk depends on the *degree of correlation* among the stocks: *The smaller the positive correlation coefficient, the greater the diversification effect of adding a stock to a portfolio.* If we could find a set of stocks whose correlations were negative, all risk could be eliminated. *In the typical case, where the correlations among the individual stocks are positive but less than +1.0, some, but not all, risk can be eliminated.*

To test your understanding, would you expect to find higher correlations between the returns on two companies in the same or in different industries? For example, would the correlation of returns on Ford's and General Motors' (GM) stocks be higher, or would the correlation coefficient be higher between either Ford or GM and Procter & Gamble (P&G), and how would those correlations affect the risk of portfolios containing them?

Answer: Ford's and GM's returns should have a correlation coefficient of about 0.9 with one another because both are affected by auto sales, but only about 0.4 with those of P&G.

Implications: A two-stock portfolio consisting of Ford and GM would be riskier than a two-stock portfolio consisting of Ford or GM, plus P&G. Thus, to minimize risk, portfolios should be diversified *across* industries.

Firm-Specific Risk versus Market Risk

As noted earlier, it is very difficult, if not impossible, to find stocks whose expected returns are not positively correlated—most stocks tend to do well when the economy is strong and do poorly when it is weak.[6] Thus, even very large portfolios end up with a substantial amount of risk, but the risk generally is less than if all of the money was invested in only one stock.

To see more precisely how portfolio size affects portfolio risk, consider Figure 5–7, which shows how portfolio risk is affected by forming larger and larger portfolios of randomly selected stocks listed on the New York Stock Exchange (NYSE). Standard deviations are plotted for an average one-stock portfolio, for a two-stock portfolio, and so on, up to a portfolio consisting of all 1,500-plus common stocks that were listed on the NYSE at the time the data were graphed. The graph illustrates that, in general, the riskiness of a portfolio consisting of average NYSE stocks tends to decline and to approach some minimum limit as the size of the portfolio increases. According to the data, σ_1, the standard deviation of a one-stock portfolio (or an average stock), is approximately 28 percent. A portfolio consisting of all of the stocks in the market, which is called the *market portfolio*, would have a standard deviation, σ_M, of about 15.1 percent, which is shown as the horizontal dashed line in Figure 5–7.

Figure 5–7 shows that almost half of the riskiness inherent in an average individual stock can be eliminated if the stock is held in a reasonably well-diversified portfolio,

---

[6]It is not too hard to find a few stocks that happened to rise because of a particular set of circumstances in the past while most other stocks were declining; it is much harder to find stocks that could logically be *expected* to go up in the future when other stocks are falling. Payco American, the collection agency discussed earlier, is one of those rare exceptions.

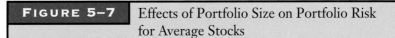

FIGURE 5–7 | Effects of Portfolio Size on Portfolio Risk for Average Stocks

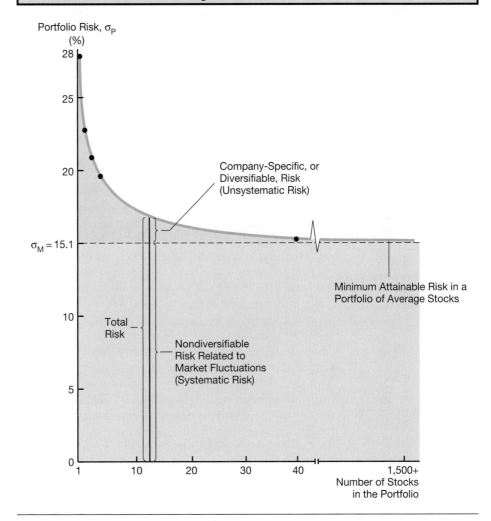

which is one containing approximately 40 or more stocks. Some risk always remains, however, so it is virtually impossible to diversify away the effects of broad stock market movements that affect almost all stocks.

The part of a stock's risk that can be eliminated is called *diversifiable*, or *firm-specific* or *unsystematic, risk*; the part that cannot be eliminated is called *nondiversifiable*, or *market* or *systematic, risk*. The name is not especially important, but the fact that a large part of the riskiness of any individual stock can be eliminated through portfolio diversification is vitally important.

Firm-specific, or **diversifiable, risk** is caused by such things as lawsuits, strikes, successful and unsuccessful marketing programs, the winning and losing of major contracts, and other events that are unique to a particular firm. Because the actual outcomes of these events are essentially random, their effects on a portfolio can be eliminated by diversification—bad events in one firm will be offset by good events in

FIRM-SPECIFIC, OR DIVERSIFIABLE, RISK
That part of a security's risk associated with random outcomes generated by events, or behaviors, specific to the firm; it *can* be eliminated by proper diversification.

another. **Market,** or **nondiversifiable, risk,** on the other hand, stems from factors that *systematically* affect most firms, such as war, inflation, recessions, and high interest rates. Because most stocks tend to be affected similarly (negatively) by these *market* conditions, systematic risk cannot be eliminated by portfolio diversification.

We know that investors demand a premium for bearing risk; that is, the higher the riskiness of a security, the higher the expected return required to induce investors to buy (or to hold) it. However, if investors are primarily concerned with *portfolio risk* rather than the risk of the individual securities in the portfolio, how should the riskiness of an individual stock be measured? The answer, as provided by the **Capital Asset Pricing Model (CAPM),** is this: *The relevant riskiness of an individual stock is its contribution to the riskiness of a well-diversified portfolio.* In other words, the riskiness of General Electric's stock to a doctor who has a portfolio of 40 stocks or to a trust officer managing a 150-stock portfolio is the contribution that the GE stock makes to the portfolio's riskiness. The stock might be quite risky if held by itself, but if most of this stand-alone risk can be eliminated by diversification, then its **relevant risk,** which is its *contribution to the portfolio's risk*, is much smaller than its total, or stand-alone, risk.

A simple example will help make this point clear. Suppose you are offered the chance to flip a coin once; if a head comes up, you win $20,000, but if it comes up tails, you lose $16,000. This is a good bet—the expected return is 0.5($20,000) + 0.5(−$16,000) = $2,000. However, it is a highly risky proposition because you have a 50 percent chance of losing $16,000. Thus, you might well refuse to make the bet. Alternatively, suppose you were offered the chance to flip a coin 100 times, and you would win $200 for each head but lose $160 for each tail. It is possible that you would flip all heads and win $20,000, and it is also possible that you would flip all tails and lose $16,000, but the chances are very high that you would actually flip about 50 heads and about 50 tails, winning a net of about $2,000. Although each individual flip is a risky bet, collectively you have a low-risk proposition because most of the risk has been diversified away. This is the idea behind holding portfolios of stocks rather than just one stock, except that with stocks all of the risk cannot be eliminated by diversification—those risks related to broad, systematic changes in the stock market will remain.

Are all stocks equally risky in the sense that adding them to a well-diversified portfolio would have the same effect on the portfolio's riskiness? The answer is no. Different stocks will affect the portfolio differently, so different securities have different degrees of relevant risk. How can the relevant risk of an individual stock be measured? As we have seen, all risk except that related to broad market movements can, and presumably will, be diversified away. After all, why accept risk that can be easily eliminated? *The risk that remains after diversifying is market risk, or risk that is inherent in the market, and it can be measured by evaluating the degree to which a given stock tends to move up and down with the market.* In the next section, we develop a measure of a stock's market risk, and then, in a later section, we introduce an equation for determining the required rate of return on a stock, given its market risk.

The Concept of Beta

Remember the relevant risk associated with an individual stock is based on its systematic risk, which depends on how sensitive the firm's operations are to economic events such as interest rate changes and inflationary pressures. Because the general movements in the financial markets reflect movements in the economy, the market risk of a stock can be measured by observing its tendency to move with the market, or with an average stock that has the same characteristics as the market. The measure of a stock's

BETA COEFFICIENT, β
A measure of the extent to which the returns on a given stock move with the stock market.

sensitivity to market fluctuations is called its **beta coefficient,** and it generally is designated with the Greek symbol for beta, β. Beta is a key element of the CAPM.

An *average-risk stock* is defined as one that tends to move up and down in step with the general market as measured by some index, such as the Dow Jones Industrial Index, the S&P 500 Index, or the New York Stock Exchange Composite Index. Such a stock will, *by definition,* have a beta, β, of 1.0, which indicates that, in general, if the market moves up by ten percent, the stock will also move up by ten percent, while if the market falls by ten percent, the stock likewise will fall by ten percent. A portfolio of such β = 1.0 stocks will move up and down with the broad market averages, and it will be just as risky as the averages. If β = 0.5, the stock is only half as volatile as the market—it will rise and fall only half as much—and a portfolio of such stocks will be half as risky as a portfolio of β = 1.0 stocks. On the other hand, if β = 2.0, the stock is twice as volatile as an average stock, so a portfolio of such stocks will be twice as risky as an average portfolio. The value of such a portfolio could double—or halve—in a short time, and if you held such a portfolio, you could quickly become a millionaire—or a pauper.

Figure 5–8 graphs the relative volatility of three stocks. The data below the graph assume that in 1998 the "market," defined as a portfolio consisting of all stocks, had a total return (dividend yield plus capital gains yield) of k_M = 14%, and Stocks H, A, and L (for High, Average, and Low risk) also had returns of 14 percent. In 1999 the market went up sharply, and the return on the market portfolio was k_M = 28%. Returns on the three stocks also went up: H soared to 42 percent; A went up to 28 percent, the same as the market; and L only went up to 21 percent. Now suppose that the market dropped in 2000, and the market return was k_M = −14%. The three stocks' returns also fell, H plunging to −42 percent, A falling to −14 percent, and L going down only to k_L = 0%. Thus, the three stocks all moved in the same direction as the market, but H was by far the most volatile; A was just as volatile as the market; and L was less volatile than the market.

Beta measures a stock's volatility relative to an average stock (or the market), which has β = 1.0, and a stock's beta can be calculated by plotting a line like those in Figure 5–8. The slopes of the lines show how each stock moves in response to a movement in the general market—indeed, *the slope coefficient of such a "regression line" is defined as a beta coefficient.* (Procedures for actually calculating betas are described in Appendix 5A.) Betas for literally thousands of companies are calculated and published by Merrill Lynch, *Value Line,* and numerous other organizations. The beta coefficients of some well-known companies are shown in Table 5–4. Most stocks have betas that range from 0.50 to 1.50, and the average for all stocks is 1.0 by definition.[7]

If a higher-than-average-beta stock (one whose beta is greater than 1.0) is added to an average-beta (β = 1.0) portfolio, then the beta, and consequently the riskiness, of the portfolio will increase. Conversely, if a lower-than-average-beta stock (one whose beta is less than 1.0) is added to an average-risk portfolio, the portfolio's beta and risk will decline. *Thus, because a stock's beta measures its contribution to the riskiness of a portfolio, theoretically beta is the correct measure of the stock's riskiness.*

---

[7] In theory, betas can be negative—if a stock's returns tend to rise when those of other stocks decline, and vice versa, then the regression line in a graph such as Figure 5–8 will have a downward slope, and the beta will be negative. Note, though, that *Value Line* follows nearly 1,800 stocks, and none has a negative beta. Payco American, the collection agency company, might have a negative beta, but it is too small to be followed by *Value Line* and most other services that calculate and report betas.

| FIGURE 5–8 | Relative Volatility of Stocks H, A, and L |

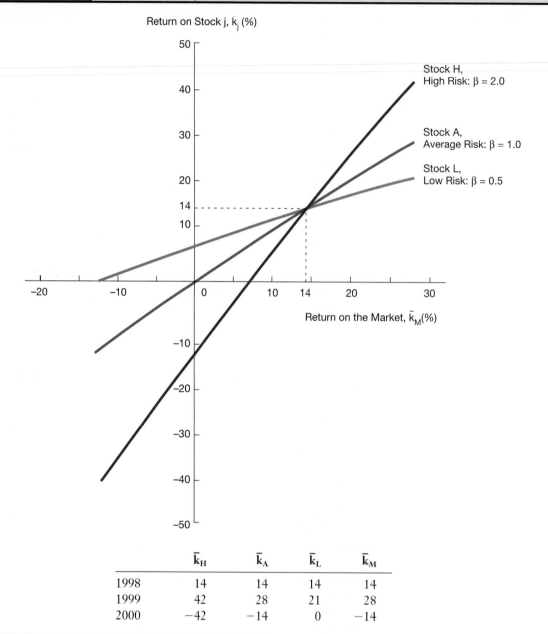

	$\bar{k}_H$	$\bar{k}_A$	$\bar{k}_L$	$\bar{k}_M$
1998	14	14	14	14
1999	42	28	21	28
2000	−42	−14	0	−14

The preceding analysis of risk in a portfolio setting is part of the Capital Asset Pricing Model (CAPM), and we can summarize our discussion to this point as follows:

1. A stock's risk consists of two components—*market risk* and *firm-specific risk*.
2. *Firm-specific risk* can be eliminated through diversification, and most investors do indeed diversify, either by holding large portfolios or by purchasing shares in a mutual fund. We are left, then, with *market risk*, which is caused by general

TABLE 5–4	Illustrative List of Beta Coefficients

COMPANY	BETA	INDUSTRY/PRODUCT
I. Above Average Market Risk: $\beta > 1.0$		
Merrill Lynch & Co	2.00	Investment/financial services
America Online	1.75	Online computer services
General Electric	1.20	Conglomerate: Various products
Microsoft	1.10	Computer software and programming
II. Average Market Risk: $\beta = 1.0$		
Intel Corporation	1.00	Semiconductors/computer components
Kmart	1.00	Retail discount store
Wal-Mart	1.00	Retail discount store
III. Below Average Market Risk: $\beta < 1.00$		
General Mills	0.65	Food processing
Anheuser Busch	0.70	Beverages (alcoholic)
Consolidated Edison	0.55	Electric utilities
Pacific Gas & Electric	0.50	Utilities

SOURCE: *Value Line*, March 19, 1999.

movements in the stock market and which reflects the fact that most stocks are systematically affected by certain overall economic events like changes in interest rates and inflation. Market risk is the only relevant risk to a rational, diversified investor, because he or she should have already eliminated firm-specific risk.

3. Investors must be compensated for bearing risk—*the greater the riskiness of a stock, the higher its required return.* However, compensation is required only for risk that cannot be eliminated by diversification. If risk premiums existed on stocks with high diversifiable risk, well-diversified investors would start buying these securities and bidding up their prices, and their final (equilibrium) expected returns would reflect only nondiversifiable market risk.

An example might help clarify this point. Suppose half of Stock A's risk is market risk (it occurs because Stock A moves up and down with the market). The other half of A's risk is diversifiable. You hold only Stock A, so you are exposed to all of its risk. As compensation for bearing so much risk, *you want* a risk premium of eight percent above the six percent Treasury bond rate. Thus, the return you demand from this investment is 14% = 6% + 8%. But suppose other investors, including your professor, are well diversified; they also hold Stock A, but they have eliminated its diversifiable risk and thus are exposed to only half as much risk as you. Therefore, their risk premium will be only half as large as yours, and they will *require* a return of only 10% = 6% + 4% to invest in the stock.

If the stock actually yielded more than 10 percent in the market, others, including your professor, would buy it. If it yielded the 14 percent you demand, you would be willing to buy the stock, but the well-diversified investors would compete with you to acquire it, thus bid its price up and its yield down, and this would keep you from getting the stock at the return you need to compensate you for taking on its *total risk.* In the end, you would have to accept a 10 percent return or else keep your money in the bank. Thus, risk premiums in a market populated with *rational* investors will reflect only market risk.

4. The market risk of a stock is measured by its *beta coefficient*, which is an index of the stock's relative volatility. Some benchmark values for beta are shown here:

$\beta = 0.5$: Stock is only half as volatile, or risky, as the average stock.

$\beta = 1.0$: Stock is of average risk.

$\beta = 2.0$: Stock is twice as risky as the average stock.

5. *Because a stock's beta coefficient determines how the stock affects the riskiness of a diversified portfolio, beta is the most relevant measure of a stock's risk.*

Portfolio Beta Coefficients

A portfolio consisting of low-beta securities will itself have a low beta because the beta of any set of securities is a weighted average of the individual securities' betas:

$$\boxed{\begin{array}{c} \text{5–6} \\ \\ \beta_P = w_1\beta_1 + w_2\beta_2 + \ldots + w_n\beta_n \\ \\ = \displaystyle\sum_{j=1}^{N} w_j\beta_j \end{array}}$$

Here β_P is the beta of the portfolio, and it reflects how volatile the portfolio is in relation to the market; w_j is the fraction of the portfolio invested in the jth stock; and β_j is the beta coefficient of the jth stock. For example, if an investor holds a \$105,000 portfolio consisting of \$35,000 invested in each of 3 stocks, and each of the stocks has a beta of 0.7, then the portfolio's beta will be $\beta_{P1} = 0.7$:

$$\beta_{P1} = 0.33(0.7) + 0.33(0.7) + 0.33(0.7) = 0.7$$

Such a portfolio will be less risky than the market: it should experience relatively narrow price swings and have relatively small rate-of-return fluctuations. In terms of Figure 5–8, the slope of its regression line would be 0.7, which is less than that for a portfolio of average stocks.

Now suppose one of the existing stocks is sold and replaced by a stock with $\beta_j = 2.5$. This action will increase the riskiness of the portfolio from $\beta_{P1} = 0.7$ to $\beta_{P2} = 1.3$:

$$\beta_{P2} = 0.33(0.7) + 0.33(0.7) + 0.33(2.5) = 1.3$$

Had a stock with $\beta_j = 0.2$ been added, the portfolio beta would have declined from 0.7 to 0.53. Adding a low-beta stock, therefore, would reduce the riskiness of the portfolio.

Self-Test Questions

Explain the following statement: "A stock held as part of a portfolio is generally less risky than the same stock held in isolation."

What is meant by perfect positive correlation, by perfect negative correlation, and by zero correlation?

INDUSTRY PRACTICE

The Three P's of Finance (Risk Management)

If you have taken a basic marketing course, you probably remember the four P's of marketing—product, price, promotion, and place. But have you heard about the three P's of finance?

In a recently published article, Andrew W. Lo describes how risk should be managed using the "3 P's of Total Risk Management"—probabilities, prices, and preferences.* Professor Lo proposes that, instead of relying entirely on statistical measures such as beta or standard deviation, risk management should include consideration of how much risk can be tolerated and how much diversification or hedging should be attempted. He contends this concept is based on the most basic of economic principles—the law of supply and demand. In essence, the *price* of any commodity is based on demand relative to supply; demand is a function of average *preferences* of individuals relative to their needs and constraints; and, preferences, in turn, are affected by the chances, or *probabilities*, certain events will occur in the future.

In the chapter, we show how probabilities and various outcomes can be combined to determine the expected value (return) of an investment. We also introduce the Capital Asset Pricing Model (CAPM) and show that total risk is not the appropriate risk to consider when evaluating an investment if it is going to be added to a diversified portfolio (see the discussion about firm-specific risk versus market risk in the chapter). These methods seem to be straight-forward, and both approaches either directly or indirectly incorporate knowledge of probabilities to determine prices (in percentage form). But neither method does a very good job of including preferences in risk evaluation, including the degree to which an individual is willing to take on additional risk and how the uncertainty of risk is viewed. To illustrate, consider two investments that have expected returns with the same

standard deviation and the same beta. According to our discussion in the chapter, both investments should be considered equally risky; thus, investors should be indifferent when selecting between them. But, realistically, an investor might prefer one of the investments because of his or her preferences concerning differences in specific characteristics associated with that investment versus the other investment (e.g., the investment is also owned by investment guru Warren Buffett). Even though these differences should be captured by the risk measures used, an investor might incorporate such knowledge in the final investment decision. Clearly, then, if many other investors act similarly, the prices of the two investments in our example would differ.

At this time, neither a model nor a procedure to incorporate the three P's into risk analysis exists. So, as Professor Lo notes:

> The challenge that lies ahead for risk-management practice is, of course, to integrate the three P's into a single and complete risk-management protocol. This daunting but essential process is a prerequisite to the growth and health of financial markets and institutions in the next century. The global financial system is becoming more complex each year, with links and interdependencies that develop and mutate day by day. Risk-management technologies must evolve in tandem.

In the future, look for TRM, total risk management, to become a common buzzword in finance, like TQM, total quality management, has in production and marketing management.

*Andrew W. Lo, "The Three P's of Total Risk Management," *Financial Analysts Journal*, January/February 1999, 13–26.

In general, can the riskiness of a portfolio be reduced to zero by increasing the number of stocks in the portfolio? Explain.

What is meant by diversifiable risk and nondiversifiable risk?

What is an average-risk stock?

Why is beta the theoretically correct measure of a stock's riskiness?

If you plotted the returns on a particular stock versus those on the Dow Jones Industrial Average index over the past five years, what would the slope of the line you obtained indicate about the stock's risk?

The Relationship between Risk and Rates of Return

In the preceding section we saw that under the CAPM theory, beta is the appropriate measure of a stock's relevant risk. Now we must specify the relationship between risk and return: For a given level of beta, what rate of return will investors require on a stock in order to compensate them for assuming the risk? To begin, let us define the following terms:

$$\hat{k}_j = \textit{Expected} \text{ rate of return on the } j^{th} \text{ stock.}$$

$$k_j = \textit{Required} \text{ rate of return on the } j^{th} \text{ stock. Note that if } \hat{k}_j \text{ is less}$$
than k_j, you would not purchase this stock, or you would sell it if you owned it. If $\hat{k}_j$ is greater than k_j, you would want to buy the stock, and you would be indifferent if $\hat{k}_j = k_j$.

$$k_{RF} = \text{Risk-free rate of return. In this context, } k_{RF} \text{ is generally}$$
measured by the return on long-term U.S. Treasury securities.

$$\beta_j = \text{Beta coefficient of the } j^{th} \text{ stock. The beta of an average}$$
stock is $\beta_A = 1.0$.

$$k_M = \text{Required rate of return on a portfolio consisting of all}$$
stocks, which is the market portfolio. k_M also is the required rate of return on an average, or $\beta_A = 1.0$, stock.

$$RP_M = (k_M - k_{RF}) = \text{Market risk premium. This is the additional return above}$$
the risk-free rate required to compensate an average investor for assuming an average amount of risk ($\beta_A = 1.0$).

$$RP_j = (k_M - k_{RF})\beta_j = \text{Risk premium on the } j^{th} \text{ stock. The stock's risk premium}$$
is less than, equal to, or greater than the premium on an average stock, depending on whether its beta is less than, equal to, or greater than 1.0. If $\beta_j = \beta_A = 1.0$, then $RP_j = RP_M$.

MARKET RISK PREMIUM, RP$_M$
The additional return over the risk-free rate needed to compensate investors for assuming an average amount of risk.

The **market risk premium, RP$_M$,** depends on the degree of aversion that investors on average have to risk.[8] Let us assume that at the current time, Treasury bonds yield

---

[8]This concept, as well as other aspects of CAPM, is discussed in more detail in Chapter 26 of Eugene F. Brigham, Louis C.Gapenski, and Phillip R Daves, *Intermediate Financial Management*, 6th ed. (Fort Worth, TX: The Dryden Press, 1999). It should be noted that the risk premium of an average stock, $k_M - k_{RF}$, cannot be measured with great precision because it is impossible to obtain precise values for the expected future return on the market, k_M. However, empirical studies suggest that where long-term U.S. Treasury bonds are used to measure k_{RF} and where k_M is an estimate of the expected return on the S&P 400 Industrial Stocks, the market risk premium varies somewhat from year to year, and it has generally ranged from four to eight percent during the past 20 years.

Chapter 3 of *Intermediate Financial Management* also discusses the assumptions embodied in the CAPM framework. Some of the assumptions of the CAPM theory are unrealistic, and because of this the theory does not hold exactly.

$k_{RF} = 6\%$ and an average share of stock has a required return of $k_M = 14\%$. Therefore, the market risk premium is 8 percent:

$$RP_M = k_M - k_{RF} = 14\% - 6\% = 8\%$$

It follows that if one stock is twice as risky as another, its risk premium would be twice as high, and, conversely, if its risk is only half as much, its risk premium would be half as large. Further, we can measure a stock's relative riskiness by its beta coefficient. Therefore, if we know the market risk premium, RP_M, and the stock's risk as measured by its beta coefficient, β_j, we can find its risk premium as the product $RP_M \times \beta_j$. For example, if $\beta_j = 0.5$ and $RP_M = 8\%$, then RP_j is 4 percent:

> **5–7**
>
> $$\text{Risk premium for Stock j} = RP_j = RP_M \times \beta_j$$

$$= 8\% \times 0.5$$
$$= 4.0\%$$

As the discussion in Chapter 2 implies, the required return for any investment can be expressed in general terms as

$$\text{Required return} = \text{Risk-free return} + \text{Premium for risk}$$
$$k_j = \qquad k_{RF} \qquad + \qquad RP_j$$

According to the discussion presented earlier, then, the required return for Stock j can be written as

> **5–8**
>
> $$k_j = k_{RF} + (RP_M)\beta_j$$
> $$= k_{RF} + (k_M - k_{RF})\beta_j$$

$$= 6\% + (14\% - 6\%)(0.5)$$
$$= 6\% + 8\%(0.5)$$
$$= 10\%$$

Equation 5–8 is the equation for CAPM equilibrium pricing, and it generally is called the **Security Market Line (SML).**

SECURITY MARKET LINE (SML)
The line that shows the relationship between risk as measured by beta and the required rate of return for individual securities. SML = Equation 5–8.

If some other stock was riskier than Stock j and had $\beta_{j2} = 2.0$, then its required rate of return would be 22 percent:

$$k_{j2} = 6\% + (8\%)2.0 = 22\%$$

An average stock, with $\beta = 1.0$, would have a required return of 14 percent, the same as the market return:

$$k_A = 6\% + (8\%)1.0 = 14\% = k_M$$

As we just noted, Equation 5–8 is called the Security Market Line (SML) equation, and it is often expressed in graph form, as in Figure 5–9, which shows the SML when $k_{RF} = 6\%$ and $k_M = 14\%$. Note the following points:

1. *Required rates of return* are shown on the vertical axis, while risk as measured by beta is shown on the horizontal axis. This graph is quite different from the one shown in Figure 5–8, where the returns on individual stocks were plotted on the vertical axis and returns on the market index were shown on the horizontal axis. The slopes of the three lines in Figure 5–8 represented the three stocks' betas, and these three betas are now plotted as points on the horizontal axis in Figure 5–9.
2. Riskless securities have $\beta_j = 0$; therefore, k_{RF} appears as the vertical axis intercept in Figure 5–9.
3. The slope of the SML reflects the degree of risk aversion in the economy; the greater the average investor's aversion to risk, (a) the steeper the slope of the line, (b) the greater the risk premium for any stock, and (c) the higher the required rate of return on stocks.[9] These points are discussed further in a later section.
4. The values we worked out for stocks with $\beta_j = 0.5$, $\beta_j = 1.0$, and $\beta_j = 2.0$ agree with the values shown on the graph for k_{Low}, k_A, and k_{High}.

Both the Security Market Line and a company's position on it change over time due to changes in interest rates, investors' risk aversion, and individual companies' betas. Such changes are discussed in the following sections.

The Impact of Inflation

As we learned in Chapter 2, interest amounts to "rent" on borrowed money, or the price of money; thus, k_{RF} is the price of money to a riskless borrower. We also learned that the risk-free rate as measured by the rate on U.S. Treasury securities is called the *nominal*, or *quoted*, rate, and it consists of two elements: (1) a *real inflation-free rate of return*, k^*, and (2) an *inflation premium*, IP, equal to the anticipated rate of inflation.[10] Thus, $k_{RF} = k^* + IP$.

If the expected rate of inflation rose by two percent, this would cause k_{RF} to increase two percent. Such a change is shown in Figure 5–10. Notice that under the CAPM, the increase in k_{RF} also causes an *equal* increase in the rate of return on all risky assets because the inflation premium is built into the required rate of return of both riskless

---

[9]Students sometimes confuse beta with the slope of the SML. This is a mistake. The slope of any line is equal to the "rise" divided by the "run," or $(Y_1 - Y_0)/(X_1 - X_0)$. Consider Figure 5–9. If we let $Y = k$ and $X = \beta$, and we go from the origin to $\beta = 1.0$, we see that the slope is $(k_M - k_{RF})/(\beta_M - \beta_{RF}) = (14 - 6)/(1 - 0) = 8$. Thus, the slope of the SML is equal to $(k_M - k_{RF})$, the market risk premium. In Figure 5–9, $k_j = 6\% + (8\%)\beta_j$, so a doubling of beta (for example, from 1.0 to 2.0) would produce an eight percentage point increase in k_j.

[10]Long-term Treasury bonds also contain a maturity risk premium, MRP. Here we include the MRP in k^* to simplify the discussion.

FIGURE 5–9	The Security Market Line (SML)

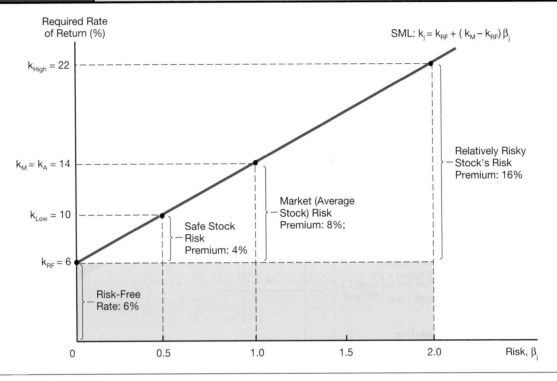

and risky assets.[11] For example, the risk-free return increases from six percent to eight percent, and the rate of return on an average stock, k_M, increases from 14 percent to 16 percent—all securities' returns increase by two percentage points.

Changes in Risk Aversion

The slope of the Security Market Line reflects the extent to which investors are averse to risk—the steeper the slope of the line, the greater the average investor's risk aversion. If investors were *indifferent* to risk, and if k_{RF} were six percent, then risky assets would also provide an expected return of six percent: If there was no risk aversion, there would be no risk premium, so the SML would be horizontal. *As risk aversion increases, so does the risk premium* and, thus, the slope of the SML.

---

[11]Recall that the inflation premium for any asset is equal to the average expected rate of inflation over the life of the asset. Thus, in this analysis we must assume either that all securities plotted on the SML graph have the same life or that the expected rate of future inflation is constant.

    It also should be noted that k_{RF} in a CAPM analysis can be proxied by either a long-term rate (the T-bond rate) or a short-term rate (the T-bill rate). Traditionally, the T-bill rate was used, but in recent years there has been a movement toward use of the T-bond rate because there is a closer relationship between T-bond yields and stocks than between T-bill yields and stocks. See *Stocks, Bonds, Bills, and Inflation; 1999 Yearbook* (Chicago: Ibbotson & Associates, 1999), for a discussion.

- The **expected return** on an investment is the mean value of its probability distribution of possible returns.
- The **higher the probability** that the actual return will be *significantly different* from the expected return, the **greater the risk** associated with owning an asset.
- The average investor is **risk averse,** which means that he or she must be compensated for holding risky securities; therefore, riskier securities must have higher expected returns than less risky securities.
- A stock's risk consists of (1) **company-specific risk,** which can be eliminated by diversification, plus (2) **market, or beta, risk,** which cannot be eliminated by diversification.
- The **relevant risk** of an individual security is its contribution to the riskiness of a well-diversified portfolio, which is the security's **market risk.** Because market risk cannot be eliminated by diversification, investors must be compensated for it.
- A stock's **beta coefficient,** β, is a measure of the stock's market risk. Beta measures the extent to which the stock's returns move with the market.
- A **high-beta stock** is more volatile than an average stock, while a **low-beta stock** is less volatile than an average stock. An **average stock** has $\beta = 1.0$.
- The **beta of a portfolio** is a **weighted average** of the betas of the individual securities in the portfolio.
- The **Security Market Line (SML)** equation shows the relationship between a security's risk and its required rate of return. The return required for any security j is equal to the **risk-free rate** plus the **market risk premium** times the **security's beta:** $k_j = k_{RF} + (k_M - k_{RF})\beta_j$.
- Even though the expected rate of return on a stock generally is equal to its required return, a number of things can happen to cause the required rate of return to change: (1) the **risk-free rate can change** because of changes in anticipated inflation, (2) a **stock's beta can change,** or (3) **investors' aversion to risk can change.**

In the next two chapters, we will see how a security's rate of return affects its value. Then, in the remainder of the book, we will examine the ways in which a firm's management can influence a stock's riskiness and hence its price.

Questions

5–1 The probability distribution of a less risky expected return is more peaked than that of a riskier return. What shape would the probability distribution have for (a) completely certain returns and (b) completely uncertain returns?

5–2 Security A has an expected return of seven percent, a standard deviation of expected returns of 35 percent, a correlation coefficient with the market of -0.3, and a beta coefficient of -0.5. Security B has an expected return of 12 percent, a standard deviation of returns of ten percent, a correlation with the market of 0.7, and a beta coefficient of 1.0. Which security is riskier? Why?

5–3 Suppose you owned a portfolio consisting of $250,000 worth of long-term U.S. government bonds.
   a. Would your portfolio be riskless?
   b. Now suppose you hold a portfolio consisting of $250,000 worth of 30-day Treasury bills. Every 30 days your bills mature and you reinvest the principal ($250,000) in a new batch of bills. Assume that you live on the investment income from your portfolio and that you want to maintain a constant standard of living. Is your portfolio *truly* riskless?

c. Can you think of any asset that would be completely riskless? Could someone develop such an asset? Explain.

5–4 A life insurance policy is a financial asset. The premiums paid represent the investment's cost.

  a. How would you calculate the expected return on a life insurance policy?

  b. Suppose the owner of a life insurance policy has no other financial assets—the person's only other asset is "human capital," or lifetime earnings capacity. What is the correlation coefficient between returns on the insurance policy and returns on the policyholder's human capital?

  c. Life insurance companies have to pay administrative costs and sales representatives' commissions; hence, the expected rate of return on insurance premiums is generally low, or even negative. Use the portfolio concept to explain why people buy life insurance in spite of negative expected returns.

5–5 If investors' aversion to risk increased, would the risk premium on a high-beta stock increase more or less than that on a low-beta stock? Explain.

Self-Test Problems

(Solutions appear in Appendix B)

key terms   **ST–1** Define the following terms, using graphs or equations to illustrate your answers wherever feasible:

  a. Risk; probability distribution

  b. Expected rate of return, $\hat{k}$; required rate of return, k

  c. Continuous probability distribution

  d. Standard deviation, σ; variance, σ^2; coefficient of variation, CV

  e. Risk aversion; realized rate of return

  f. Risk premium for Stock j, RP_j; market risk premium, RP_M

  g. Capital Asset Pricing Model (CAPM)

  h. Expected return on a portfolio, $\hat{k}_P$

  i. Correlation coefficient, r

  j. Market risk; company-specific risk; relevant risk

  k. Beta coefficient, β; average stock's beta, β_A

  l. Security Market Line (SML); SML equation

  m. Slope of SML as a measure of risk aversion

realized rates of return   **ST–2** Stocks A and B have the following historical returns:

YEAR	STOCK A'S RETURNS, k_A	STOCK B'S RETURNS, k_B
1996	−10.00%	−3.00%
1997	18.50	21.29
1998	38.67	44.25
1999	14.33	3.67
2000	33.00	28.30

  a. Calculate the average rate of return for each stock during the period 1996 through 2000. Assume that someone held a portfolio consisting of 50 percent of Stock A and 50 percent of Stock B. What would have been the realized rate of return on the portfolio in each year from 1996 through 2000? What would have been the average return on the portfolio during this period?

a. Calculate the expected rates of return for the market and Stock S.
b. Calculate the standard deviations for the market and Stock S.
c. Calculate the coefficients of variation for the market and Stock S.

expected returns   **5–5** Stocks X and Y have the following probability distributions of expected future returns:

PROBABILITY	X	Y
0.1	−10%	−35%
0.2	2	0
0.4	12	20
0.2	20	25
0.1	38	45

a. Calculate the expected rate of return, $\hat{k}$, for Stock Y. ($\hat{k}_X = 12\%$.)
b. Calculate the standard deviation of expected returns for Stock X. ($\sigma_Y = 20.35\%$.) Now calculate the coefficient of variation for Stock Y. Is it possible that most investors might regard Stock Y as being less risky than Stock X? Explain.

required rate of return   **5–6** Suppose $k_{RF} = 8\%$, $k_M = 11\%$, and $k_B = 14\%$.
a. Calculate Stock B's beta.
b. If Stock B's beta were 1.5, what would be B's new required rate of return?

required rate of return   **5–7** Suppose $k_{RF} = 9\%$, $k_M = 14\%$, and $\beta_X = 1.3$.
a. What is k_X, the required rate of return on Stock X?
b. Now suppose k_{RF} (1) increases to ten percent or (2) decreases to eight percent. The slope of the SML remains constant. How would this affect k_M and k_X?
c. Now assume k_{RF} remains at nine percent, but k_M (1) increases to 16 percent or (2) falls to 13 percent. The slope of the SML does not remain constant. How would these changes affect k_X?

portfolio beta   **5–8** Suppose you hold a diversified portfolio consisting of a $7,500 investment in each of 20 different common stocks. The portfolio beta is equal to 1.12. Now, suppose you have decided to sell one of the stocks in your portfolio with a beta equal to 1.0 for $7,500 and to use these proceeds to buy another stock for your portfolio. Assume the new stock's beta is equal to 1.75. Calculate your portfolio's new beta.

portfolio required return   **5–9** Suppose you are the money manager of a $4 million investment fund. The fund consists of four stocks with the following investments and betas:

STOCK	INVESTMENT	BETA
A	$ 400,000	1.50
B	600,000	−0.50
C	1,000,000	1.25
D	2,000,000	0.75

If the market required rate of return is 14 percent and the risk-free rate is six percent, what is the fund's required rate of return?

required rate of return   **5–10** Stock R has a beta of 1.5, Stock S has a beta of 0.75, the expected rate of return on an average stock is 15 percent, and the risk-free rate of return is nine percent. By how much does the required return on the riskier stock exceed the required return on the less risky stock?

Integrative Problem

risk and return   **5-11** Assume that you recently graduated with a major in finance, and you just landed a job in the trust department of a large regional bank. Your first assignment is to invest $100,000 from an estate for which the bank is trustee. Because the estate is expected to be distributed to the heirs in about one year, you have been instructed to plan for a one-year holding period. Further, your boss has restricted you to the following investment alternatives, shown with their probabilities and associated outcomes. (Disregard for now the items at the bottom of the data; you will fill in the blanks later.)

RETURNS ON ALTERNATIVE INVESTMENTS

ESTIMATED RATE OF RETURN

STATE OF THE ECONOMY	PROB.	T-BILLS	HIGH TECH	COLLECTIONS	U.S. RUBBER	MARKET PORTFOLIO	2-STOCK PORTFOLIO
Recession	0.1	8.0%	−22.0%	28.0%	10.0%	−13.0%	
Below Average	0.2	8.0	−2.0	14.7	−10.0	1.0	
Average	0.4	8.0	20.0	0.0	7.0	15.0	
Above Average	0.2	8.0	35.0	−10.0	45.0	29.0	
Boom	0.1	8.0	50.0	−20.0	30.0	43.0	
$\hat{k}$							
σ							
CV							
β							

The bank's economic forecasting staff has developed probability estimates for the state of the economy, and the trust department has a sophisticated computer program that was used to estimate the rate of return on each alternative under each state of the economy. High Tech Inc. is an electronics firm; Collections Inc. collects past-due debts; and U.S. Rubber manufactures tires and various other rubber and plastics products. The bank also maintains an "index fund," that owns a market-weighted fraction of all publicly traded stocks; you can invest in that fund and thus obtain average stock market results. Given the situation as described, answer the following questions:

a. (1) Why is the T-bill's return independent of the state of the economy? Do T-bills promise a completely risk-free return?

(2) Why are High Tech's returns expected to move with the economy whereas Collections' are expected to move counter to the economy?

b. Calculate the expected rate of return on each alternative and fill in the row for $\hat{k}$ in the preceding table.

c. You should recognize that basing a decision solely on expected returns is only appropriate for risk-neutral individuals. Because the beneficiaries of the trust, like virtually everyone, are risk averse, the riskiness of each alternative is an important aspect of the decision. One possible measure of risk is the *standard deviation* of returns.

(1) Calculate this value for each alternative, and fill in the row for σ in the preceding table.

(2) What type of risk is measured by the standard deviation?

(3) Draw a graph that shows *roughly* the shape of the probability distributions for High Tech, U.S. Rubber, and T-bills.

d. Suppose you suddenly remembered that the *coefficient of variation (CV)* is generally regarded as being a better measure of total risk than the standard deviation when the alternatives being considered have widely differing expected returns. Calculate the CVs for the different securities, and fill in the row for CV in the preceding table. Does the CV produce the same risk rankings as the standard deviation?

e. Suppose you created a two-stock portfolio by investing $50,000 in High Tech and $50,000 in Collections.
   (1) Calculate the expected return ($\hat{k}_P$), the standard deviation (σ_P), and the coefficient of variation (CV_P) for this portfolio and fill in the appropriate rows in the preceding table.
   (2) How does the riskiness of this two-stock portfolio compare to the riskiness of the individual stocks if they were held in isolation?

f. Suppose an investor starts with a portfolio consisting of one randomly selected stock. What would happen (1) to the riskiness and (2) to the expected return of the portfolio as more and more randomly selected stocks were added? What is the implication for investors? Draw two graphs to illustrate your answer.

g. (1) Should portfolio effects impact the way investors think about the riskiness of individual stocks?
   (2) If you chose to hold a one-stock portfolio and consequently were exposed to more risk than diversified investors, could you expect to be compensated for all of your risk; that is, could you earn a risk premium on that part of your risk that you could have eliminated by diversifying?

h. The expected rates of return and the beta coefficients of the alternatives as supplied by the bank's computer program are as follows:

SECURITY	RETURN ($\hat{k}$)	RISK (BETA)
High Tech	17.4%	1.29
Market	15.0	1.00
U.S. Rubber	13.8	0.68
T-bills	8.0	0.00
Collections	1.7	(0.86)

   (1) What is a *beta coefficient*, and how are betas used in risk analysis?
   (2) Do the expected returns appear to be related to each alternative's market risk?
   (3) Is it possible to choose among the alternatives on the basis of the information developed thus far?
   (4) Use the data given at the start of the problem to construct a graph that shows how the T-bill's, High Tech's, and Collections' beta coefficients are calculated. Then discuss what betas measure and how they are used in risk analysis.

i. (1) Write out the security market line (SML) equation, use it to calculate the required rate of return on each alternative, and then graph the relationship between the expected and required rates of return.

(2) How do the expected rates of return compare with the required rates of return?

(3) Does the fact that Collections has a negative beta make any sense? What is the implication of the negative beta?

(4) What would be the market risk and the required return of a 50-50 portfolio of High Tech and Collections? Of High Tech and U.S. Rubber?

j. (1) Suppose investors raised their inflation expectations by three percentage points over current estimates as reflected in the 8 percent T-bill rate. What effect would higher inflation have on the SML and on the returns required on high- and low-risk securities?

(2) Suppose instead that investors' risk aversion increased enough to cause the market risk premium to increase by three percentage points. (Inflation remains constant.) What effect would this have on the SML and on returns of high- and low-risk securities?

Computer-Related Problem

Work the problem in this section only if you are using the computer problem diskette.

realized rates of return   **5–12** Using the computerized model in File C5, rework Problem 5–3, assuming that a third stock, Stock C, is available for inclusion in the portfolio. Stock C has the following historical returns:

YEAR	STOCK C'S RETURN, k_C
1996	32.00%
1997	(11.75)
1998	10.75
1999	32.25
2000	(6.75)

a. Calculate (or read from the computer screen) the average return, standard deviation, and coefficient of variation for Stock C.

b. Assume that the portfolio now consists of 33.33 percent of Stock A, 33.33 percent of Stock B, and 33.33 percent of Stock C. How does this affect the portfolio return, standard deviation, and coefficient of variation versus when 50 percent was invested in A and in B?

c. Make some other changes in the portfolio, making sure that the percentages sum to 100 percent. For example, enter 25 percent for Stock A, 25 percent for Stock B, and 50 percent for Stock C. (Note that the program will not allow you to enter a zero percentage in Stock C.) Notice that k_p remains constant and that σ_p changes. Why do these results occur?

d. In Problem 5–3, the standard deviation of the portfolio decreased only slightly because Stocks A and B were highly positively correlated with one another. In this problem, the addition of Stock C causes the standard deviation of the portfolio to decline dramatically, even though $\sigma_C = \sigma_A = \sigma_B$. What does this indicate about the correlation between Stock C and Stocks A and B?

e. Would you prefer to hold the portfolio described in Problem 5–3 consisting only of Stocks A and B or a portfolio that also included Stock C? If others react similarly, how might this affect the stocks' prices and rates of return?

ONLINE ESSENTIALS

http://www.yahoo.com   Yahoo
Betas for various companies are available at this site. To get a company's beta (a) click on "Stock Quotes"; (b) insert the ticker symbol of the company in the appropriate box and click on "Get Quotes"; and (c) click on the "Profile" selection. Other investment information is also available.

http://quote.fool.com   The Motley Fool
Betas for various companies are available at this site. To get a company's beta, insert its symbol and click "go," and then click "Snapshot." The beta is given in the "Price and Volume" information. Other investment information is also available.

http://www.bloomberg.com   Bloomberg Personal Finance
A great deal of information about publicly traded companies is available here. You can get an indication of a company's risk by looking at its historical returns.

http://www.ibbotson.com   Ibbotson Associates
For a fee you can get betas and risk information for a large number of companies. There are also free research reports related to risk analysis available.

APPENDIX 5A

Calculating Beta Coefficients

The CAPM is an *ex ante* model, which means that all of the variables represent before-the-fact, *expected* values. In particular, the beta coefficient used in the SML equation should reflect the expected volatility of a given stock's return versus the return on the market during some *future* period. However, people generally calculate betas using data from some past period and then assume that the stock's relative volatility will be the same in the future as it was in the past.

To illustrate how betas are calculated, consider Figure 5A–1. The data at the bottom of the figure show the historical realized returns for Stock J and for the market over the past five years. The data points have been plotted on the scatter diagram, and a regression line has been drawn. If all the data points had fallen on a straight line, as they did in Figure 5–8 in the chapter, it would be easy to draw an accurate line. If they do not, as in Figure 5A–1, then you must fit the line either "by eye" as an approximation or with a calculator or a computer.

Recall what the term *regression line*, or *regression equation*, means: The equation $Y = \alpha + \beta X + \epsilon$ is the standard form of a simple linear regression. It states that the de-

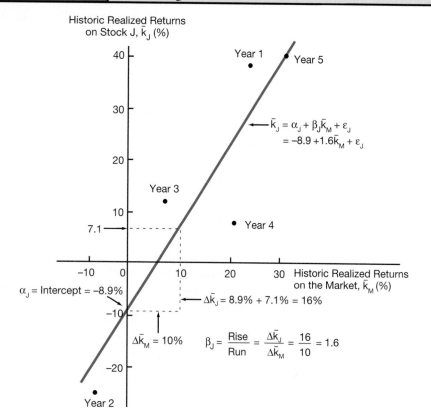

FIGURE 5A–1 | Calculating Beta Coefficients

YEAR	MARKET ($\bar{k}_M$)	STOCK J ($\bar{k}_J$)
1	23.8%	38.6%
2	−7.2	−24.7
3	6.6	12.3
4	20.5	8.2
5	30.6	40.1
Average $\bar{k}$	14.9%	14.9%
$\sigma_{\bar{k}}$	15.1%	26.5%

pendent variable, Y, is equal to a constant, α (the Y intercept), plus β times X, where β is the slope coefficient and X is the independent variable, plus an error term, ϵ. Thus, the rate of return on the stock during a given time period (Y) depends on what happens to the general stock market, which is measured by X = $\bar{k}_M$.

Once the data have been plotted and the regression line has been drawn on graph paper, we can estimate its intercept and slope, the α and β values in Y = α + βX. The intercept, α, simply is the point where the line cuts the vertical axis. The slope coefficient, β, can be estimated by the "rise over run" method. This involves calculating the amount by which $\bar{k}_J$ increases for a given increase in $\bar{k}_M$. For example, we observe in Figure 5A–1 that $\bar{k}_J$ increases from −8.9 percent to +7.1 percent (the rise) when $\bar{k}_M$ increases from 0 percent to 10.0 percent (the run). Thus β, the beta coefficient, can be measured as follows:

$$\text{beta} = \beta = \frac{\text{Rise}}{\text{Run}} = \frac{\Delta Y}{\Delta X} = \frac{7.1 - (-8.9)}{10.0 - 0.0} = \frac{16.0}{10.0} = 1.6$$

Note that rise over run is a ratio, and it would be the same if measured using any two arbitrarily selected points on the line.

The regression line equation enables us to predict a rate of return for Stock J, given a value of $\bar{k}_M$. For example, if $\bar{k}_M$ = 15%, we would predict $\bar{k}_J$ = −8.9% + 1.6(15%) = 15.1%. However, the actual return probably would differ from the predicted return. This deviation is the error term, ϵ_J, for the year, and it varies randomly from year to year depending on company-specific factors. Note, though, that the higher the correlation coefficient, the closer the points lie to the regression line, and the smaller the errors.

If you have taken a statistics course that covered regression analysis, you are aware that five observations are not sufficient to attain valid results. In actual practice, monthly (or daily) rather than annual returns are generally used for $\bar{k}_J$ and $\bar{k}_M$, and five years (or around 200 days) of data are often employed; thus, there would be 5 × 12 = 60 data points on the scatter diagram. Also, in practice one would use the *least squares method* for finding the regression coefficients α and β; this procedure minimizes the squared values of the error terms. It is discussed in statistics courses.

The least squares value of beta can be obtained quite easily with a financial calculator or a spreadsheet, such as Excel® or Lotus 1-2-3®.

CHAPTER 6

The Time Value of Money

A MANAGERIAL PERSPECTIVE

Even as a student, you should be thinking about retirement. Don't laugh—most experts would agree you should have some financial plan for achieving your retirement goals when you start your professional career, or very soon afterward, or you will find those goals difficult, if not impossible, to attain. Chances are that unless you create a savings plan for retirement as soon as you start your career, either you will have to work longer than you had planned to attain the retirement lifestyle you desire or you will have to live below the standard of living you planned for your retirement years. According to the experts, saving for retirement cannot begin too soon. Unfortunately, most Americans are professional procrastinators when it comes to saving and investing for retirement. The savings rate in the United States is the lowest of any developed country—currently it is only about four percent, down from nine percent at its peak in 1974. One reason many people give for their lack of savings is that they expect to receive social security benefits when they retire. But don't bet on it! The ratio of workers paying into social security to retirees receiving benefits, which was 16.5 in 1950, was down to 3.3 in 1998, and it is expected to be less than 2.0 by the year 2030. What does all this mean? Unless Congress takes some action and the funds going into social security are increased substantially relative to the benefits expected to be paid out in the future, it is estimated the government retirement system will go bankrupt sometime between 2020 and 2030. There are a number of reasons the future of social security is in doubt. First, the life expectancy of Americans has increased by more than 15 years, from 61 to over 76, since the inception of social security in 1935, and it is expected to increase further in the future. Second, the number of elderly as a percent of the American population has increased substantially. Consider the fact that the proportion of Americans 65 or older was only four percent in 1900, it was about 12.5 percent in 1998, and it is expected to be 25 percent by the year 2040. Third, more than 77 million "baby boomers" born between 1946 and 1964 are beginning to retire, which will add a tremendous burden to the system. At some point in the future, there might be more retirees receiving social security benefits than workers making contributions to the plan, because birthrates since the mid-1960s have fallen sharply—from 1946 to 1964 the average family had three children, but from 1970 to 1990 the average number of children dropped to two.

What does the retirement plight of the baby boomers (and their children) have to do with the time value of money? Actually, a great deal. According to a study published by the National Commission on Retirement Policy, social security currently is the primary source of retirement income for 66 percent of beneficiaries, and it represents the only income for 16 percent. And an earlier study conducted by *Money* magazine and

continues

225

Oppenheimer Management Corporation indicated that Americans do little more than talk about retirement plans until late in their professional careers; in many cases too late for their retirement goals to be achievable. To retire comfortably, ten to 20 percent of your income should be set aside each year. For example, it is estimated that a 35-year old who is earning $55,000 would need at least $1 million to retire at the current standard of living in 30 years. To achieve this goal, the individual would have to save about $10,500 each year at seven percent return, which represents nearly a 20 percent annual savings. The annual savings would have been about one-half this amount (just over $5,000) if the individual had begun saving for retirement at age 25.

The techniques and procedures covered in this chapter are exactly the ones used by experts to forecast the boomers' retirement needs, their probable wealth at retirement, and the resulting shortfall. If you study this chapter carefully, perhaps you can avoid the trap into which many people seem to be falling—spending today rather than saving for the future. ■

SOURCES: Penelope Wang, "How to Retire with Twice as Much Money," *Money* (October 1994), 76(10); "Can America Afford to Retire: The Retirement Security Challenge Facing You and the Nation," National Commission on Retirement Policy, Center for Strategic International Studies, 1998.

Financial decision making, whether from the perspective of firms or investors, is primarily concerned with determining how value will be affected by the expected outcomes (payoffs) associated with alternative choices. For example, if you have $5,500 to invest today, you must decide what to do with the money. If you have the opportunity to purchase an investment that will return $7,020 after five years or an investment that will return $8,126 after eight years, which should you choose? To answer this question, you must determine which investment alternative has greater value to you.

All else equal, a dollar received soon is worth more than a dollar expected in the distant future because the sooner a dollar is received the quicker it can be invested to earn a positive return. So does that mean the five-year investment is more valuable than the eight-year investment? Not necessarily, because the eight-year investment promises a higher dollar payoff than the five-year investment. To determine which investment is more valuable, the dollar payoffs for the investments need to be compared at the same point in time. Thus, for these two investments, we could determine the current values of both investments by restating, or revaluing, the payoffs expected at different times in the future (e.g., $7,020 in five years and $8,126 in eight years) in terms of current (today's) dollars. The concept used to revalue payoffs such as those associated with these investments is termed the *time value of money*. It is essential that both financial managers and investors have a clear understanding of the time value of money and its impact on the value of an asset. These concepts are discussed in this chapter, where we show how the timing of cash flows affects asset values and rates of return.

The principles of time value analysis that are developed in this chapter have many applications, ranging from setting up schedules for paying off loans to decisions about whether to acquire new equipment. *In fact, of all the techniques used in finance, none is more important than the concept of the time value of money (TVM)*. Because this concept is used throughout the remainder of the book, it is vital that you understand TVM before you move on to other topics.

Cash Flow Time Lines

CASH FLOW TIME LINE
An important tool used in time value of money analysis; it is a graphical representation used to show the timing of cash flows.

One of the most important tools in time value of money analysis is the **cash flow time line,** which is used to help us visualize when the cash flows associated with a particular situation occur. Constructing a cash flow time line will help you to solve problems related to the time value of money, because illustrating what happens in a particular situation generally makes it easier to set up the problem for solution. To illustrate the time line concept, consider the following diagram:

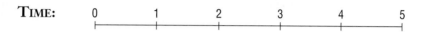

Time 0 is today; Time 1 is one period from today, or the end of Period 1; Time 2 is two periods from today, or the end of Period 2; and so on. Thus, the values on top of the tick marks represent end-of-period values. Often the periods are years, but other time intervals such as semiannual periods, quarters, months, or even days are also used. If each period on the time line represents a year, the interval from the tick mark corresponding to 0 to the tick mark corresponding to 1 would be Year 1, the interval from the tick mark corresponding to 1 to the tick mark corresponding to 2 would be Year 2, and so on. Note that each tick mark corresponds to the end of one period as well as the beginning of the next period. In other words, the tick mark at Time 1 represents the end of Year 1; it also represents the beginning of Year 2 because Year 1 has just passed.[1]

 Cash flows are placed directly below the tick marks, and interest rates are shown directly above the cash flow time line. Unknown cash flows, which we are trying to find in the analysis, are indicated by question marks. For example, consider the following time line:

OUTFLOW
A payment, or disbursement, of cash for expenses, investments, and so on.

Here the interest rate for each of the three periods is 5 percent; a single amount (or lump sum) cash **outflow** is made at Time 0; and the Time 3 value is an unknown **inflow.** Because the initial $100 is an outflow (an investment), it has a minus sign. Because the Period 3 amount is an inflow, it does not have a minus sign. Note that no cash flows occur at Time 1 and Time 2. Note also that we do not show dollar signs on time lines; this reduces clutter.

INFLOW
A receipt of cash from an investment, an employer, or other sources.

 The cash flow time line is an essential tool for better understanding time value of money concepts—even experts use cash flow time lines to analyze complex problems. We will be using cash flow time lines throughout the book, and you should get into the habit of using them when you work problems.

---

[1]For our discussions, the difference between the end of one period and the beginning of the next period is the same as one day ending and the next day beginning—it occurs in less than one second.

Self-Test Questions

Draw a three-year time line to illustrate the following situation: (1) an outflow of $5,000 occurs at Time 0; (2) inflows of $2,000 occur at the end of Years 1, 2, and 3; (3) the interest rate during the three years is 12 percent.

Future Value

COMPOUNDING
The process of determining the value of a cash flow or series of cash flows some time in the future when compound interest is applied.

A dollar in hand today is worth more than a dollar to be received in the future because, if you had it now, you could invest it, earn interest, and end up with more than one dollar in the future. The process of going from today's values, which are termed present values (PV), to future values (FV) is called **compounding.** To illustrate, suppose you deposited $100 in a bank account that paid five percent interest each year. How much would you have at the end of one year? To begin, we define the following terms:

PV = Present value, or beginning amount, in your account. Here PV = $100.

i = Interest rate the bank pays on the account per year. The interest earned is based on the balance in the account at the beginning of each year, and we assume that it is paid at the end of the year. Here i = 5%, or, expressed as a decimal, i = 0.05. Throughout this chapter, we designate the interest rate as i because that symbol is used on most financial calculators. Note, though, that in later chapters we use the symbol k to denote interest rates because k is used more often in the financial literature.

INT = Dollars of interest you earn during the year = (Beginning of year amount) × i. Here INT = $100 × 0.05 = $5 in the first year.

FV_n = Future value, or value of the account at the end of n periods (years in this case), after the interest earned has been added to the account.

n = Number of periods interest is earned. Here n = 1.

In our example, n = 1, so FV_n can be calculated as follows:

$$FV_n = FV_1 = PV + INT$$
$$= PV + (PV \times i)$$
$$= PV(1 + i)$$

$$= \$100(1 + 0.05) = \$100(1.05) = \$105.$$

FUTURE VALUE (FV)
The amount to which a cash flow or series of cash flows will grow over a given period of time when compounded at a given interest rate.

Thus, the **future value (FV)** at the end of one year, FV_1, equals the present value multiplied by 1.0 plus the interest rate. So you will have $105 in one year if you invest $100 today and five percent interest is paid at the end of the year.

What would you end up with if you left your $100 in the account for five years? Here is the cash flow time line set up to show the amount at the end of each year:

Time:	0	5%	1	2	3	4	5
Initial deposit:	−100		$FV_1 = ?$	$FV_2 = ?$	$FV_3 = ?$	$FV_4 = ?$	$FV_5 = ?$
Interest earned this year:			5.00	5.25	5.51	5.79	6.08
Interest from previous years:			0.00	5.00	10.25	15.76	21.55
Total amount at the end of each period:			105.00	110.25	115.76	121.55	**127.63**

Note the following points: (1) You start by depositing $100 in the account—this is shown as an outflow at time period 0. (2) You earn $100 × 0.05 = $5 of interest during the first year, so the amount at the end of Year 1 is $100 + $5 = $105. (3) You start the second year with $105, so, in the second year, you earn five percent interest both on the $100 you invested originally and on the $5 paid to you as interest in the first year; $5.25 interest is earned in the second year, so at the end of the second year you have $110.25. Your interest during Year 2, $5.25, is higher than the first year's interest of $5, because you earned $5 × 0.05 = $0.25 interest on the first year's interest. (4) This process continues, and because the beginning balance is higher in each succeeding year, the annual amount of interest earned increases. (5) The total interest earned, $27.63, is reflected in the final balance at the end of the fifth year, $127.63. As you can see, the total interest earned is greater than $5 per year, which is 5 percent of the original $100 investment, because each year the interest paid was left in the account to earn additional interest the next year. The total *additional* interest earned would be $2.63—this results because interest is earned on interest already paid, which means **compounded interest** is received.

COMPOUNDED INTEREST
Interest earned on interest.

Note that the value at the end of Year 2, $110.25, is equal to

$$FV_2 = FV_1(1 + i)$$
$$= [PV(1 + i)](1 + i)$$
$$= PV(1 + i)^2$$
$$= \$100(1.05)^2 = \$110.25$$

Continuing, the balance at the end of Year 3 is

$$FV_3 = FV_2(1 + i)$$
$$= [PV(1 + i)^2](1 + i)$$
$$= PV(1 + i)^3$$
$$= \$100(1.05)^3 = \$115.76$$

and

$$FV_5 = \$100(1.05)^5 = \$127.63$$

In general, the future value of an initial sum at the end of n years can be found by applying Equation 6–1:

6–1	
	$FV_n = PV(1 + i)^n$

Equation 6–1 and most other time value of money problems can be solved in three ways: numerically with a regular calculator, with interest tables, or with a financial calculator.

Numerical Solution

According to Equation 6–1, to compute the future value, FV, of an amount invested today (PV) we need to determine by what multiple the amount invested will increase in the future. As you can see, the multiple by which any amount will increase is based on the total dollar interest earned, which depends on both the interest rate and the length of time interest is earned. This multiple, termed the **future value interest factor for i and n (FVIF$_{i,n}$)**, is defined as $(1 + i)^n$.

FUTURE VALUE INTEREST FACTOR FOR I AND N (FVIF$_{i,n}$) The future value of $1 left on deposit for n periods at a rate of i percent per period—the multiple by which an initial investment grows because of the interest earned.

The value for FVIF$_{i,n}$ can be computed using a regular calculator either by (1) multiplying $(1 + i)$ by itself $n - 1$ times, or (2) using the exponential function to raise $(1 + i)$ to the nth power. For our example, you can enter $1 + i = 1.05$ into your calculator, and then multiply 1.05 by itself four times; or, using the exponential function key on your calculator, which generally is labeled y^x, you can enter 1.05 into your calculator, press the ▮y^x function key, enter 5, and then press the ▮=▮ key. In either case, your answer would be 1.276282, which you would multiply by $100 to get the final answer, $127.6282, which would be rounded to $127.63.

In certain time value of money problems, it is difficult to arrive at a solution using a regular calculator. We will tell you this when we have such a problem, and in these cases we will not show a numerical solution. Also, at times we show the numerical solution just below the time line, as a part of the diagram, rather than in a separate section.

Interest Tables (Tabular Solution)

As we showed in the previous section, computing the values for FVIF$_{i,n}$ is not a very difficult task if you have a calculator handy. Table 6–1 gives the future value interest factors for i values from 4% to 6% and n values from 1 to 6 periods, while Table A–3 in Appendix A at the back of the book contains FVIF$_{i,n}$ values for a wide range of i and n values.

Because $(1 + i)^n = FVIF_{i,n}$, Equation 6–1 can be rewritten as follows:

6–1a	
	$FV_n = PV(1 + i)^n = PV(FVIF_{i,n})$

To illustrate, the FVIF for our five-year, five percent interest problem can be found in Table 6–1 by looking down the first column to Period 5, and then looking across that row to the 5% column, where we see that FVIF$_{5\%,5}$ = 1.2763. Then, the value of $100 after five years is found as follows:

$$FV_n = PV(FVIF_{i,n})$$

$$= \$100(FVIF_{5\%,5})$$

TABLE 6-1	Future Value Interest Factors: $FVIF_{i,n} = (1 + i)^n$		
PERIOD (N)	4%	5%	6%
1	1.0400	1.0500	1.0600
2	1.0816	1.1025	1.1236
3	1.1249	1.1576	1.1910
4	1.1699	1.2155	1.2625
5	1.2167	**1.2763**	1.3382
6	1.2653	1.3401	1.4185

$$= \$100(1.2763)$$
$$= \$127.63$$

Financial Calculator Solution

Equation 6–1 and a number of other equations have been programmed directly into *financial calculators*, and such calculators can be used to find future values. Note that calculators have five keys that correspond to the five most commonly used time value of money variables:[2]

Here N = The number of periods; some calculators use n rather than N.

   I = Interest rate per period; some calculators use i, INT, or I/Y rather than I.

PV = Present value.

PMT = Annuity payment. This key is used only if the cash flows involve a series of equal, or constant, payments (an annuity). If there are no periodic payments in the particular problem, then PMT = 0. We will use this key later in the chapter.

FV = Future value.

   In this chapter, we will deal with equations that involve only four of the variables at any one time—three of the variables will be known and the calculator will then solve for the fourth (unknown) variable. In the next chapter, when we deal with bonds, we will use all five variables in the bond valuation equation.[3]

---

[2]On some financial calculators, these "keys" actually are buttons on the face of the calculator, while on others they are shown on a screen after the user goes into the time value of money (TVM) menu. The discussions in this chapter assume the appropriate keys are buttons on your calculator.

[3]The equation programmed into the calculators actually has five variables, one for each key. In this chapter, the value of one of the variables is always zero. It is a good idea to get into the habit of inputting a zero for the unused variable (whose value automatically is set equal to zero when you clear the calculator's memory); if you forget to clear your calculator, this procedure will help you avoid trouble.

To find the future value of $100 after five years at 5 percent interest using a financial calculator, note again that we are dealing with Equation 6–1:

$$FV_n = PV(1 + i)^n \qquad \qquad (6\text{--}1)$$

The equation has four variables, FV_n, PV, i, and n. If we know any three, we can solve for the fourth. In our example, we can enter PV = −100, I = 5, PMT = 0, and N = 5. Then, when we press the FV key, we will get the answer, FV = 127.6282 (rounded to four decimal places). Note that on some calculators you are required to press a "Compute" (sometimes labeled CPT or COMP) key before pressing the FV key to get the answer.

Most financial calculators require that all cash flows be designated as either inflows or outflows, because the computations are based on the fact that we generally pay (cash outflows) to receive benefits (cash inflows). For these calculators, you must enter cash outflows as negative numbers. In our illustration, you deposit, or put in, the initial amount (which is an outflow to you) and you take out, or receive, the ending amount (which is an inflow to you). If your calculator requires that you input outflows as negative numbers, the PV would be entered as −100. If you forget the negative sign and enter 100, then the calculator would assume you received $100 in the current period and that you must pay it back with interest in the future, so the FV would appear as −127.63, a cash outflow. Sometimes the convention of changing signs can be confusing, but, if you think about what you are doing, you should not have a problem with whether the calculator gives you a positive or a negative answer.

We also should note that financial calculators permit you to specify the number of decimal places that are displayed. For most calculators, at least 12 significant digits are used in the actual calculations. But, for the purposes of reporting the results of the computations, generally we use two places for answers when working with dollars or percentages and four places when working with decimals. *The nature of the problem dictates how many decimal places should be displayed*—to be safe, you might want to set your calculator so the floating decimal format is used and round the final results yourself.

Technology has progressed to the point where it is far more efficient to solve most time value of money problems with a financial calculator. *However, you must understand the concepts behind the calculations and know how to set up cash flow time lines in order to work complex problems.* This is true for stock and bond valuation, capital budgeting, and many other important types of problems such as retirement planning, mortgage payments, and other situations that affect you personally.

Problem Format

To help you understand the various types of time value problems, in most cases, we use a standard format in the book. First, we state the problem in words. Next, we diagram the problem using a cash flow time line. Then, beneath the time line, we show the equation that must be solved. Finally, we present the three alternative procedures for solving the equation to obtain the answer: (1) use a regular calculator, (2) use the tables, or (3) use a financial calculator.

To illustrate the format, we use the five-year, five percent example:

CASH FLOW TIME LINE:

EQUATION:

$$FV_n = PV(1 + i)^n = \$100(1.05)^5$$

1. NUMERICAL SOLUTION:

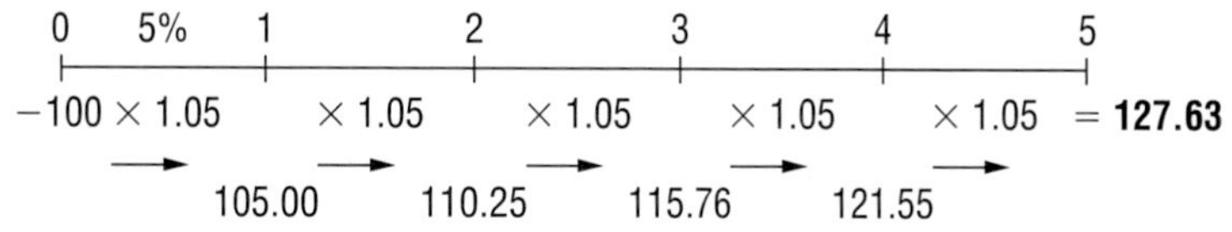

```
0      5%     1          2          3          4          5
├──────────┼──────────┼──────────┼──────────┼──────────┤
-100 × 1.05     × 1.05     × 1.05     × 1.05     × 1.05  = 127.63
              105.00     110.25     115.76     121.55
```

Using a regular calculator, raise 1.05 to the fifth power and multiply by $100 to get

$$FV_5 = \$100(1.05)^5$$
$$= \$100(1.2763)$$
$$= \$127.63$$

2. TABULAR SOLUTION:

Look up $FVIF_{5\%,5}$ in Table 6–1 or Table A–3 at the end of the book and then multiply by $100:

$$FV_5 = \$100(FVIF_{5\%,5})$$
$$= \$100(1.2763)$$
$$= \$127.63$$

3. FINANCIAL CALCULATOR SOLUTION:

Inputs:	5	5	−100	0	?
	N	**I**	**PV**	**PMT**	**FV**
Output:					= 127.63

Note that the calculator diagram tells you to input N = 5, I = 5, PV = −100, and PMT = 0, and then to press the FV key to get the answer, 127.63. Also, note that in this particular problem the PMT key does not really come into play, because no constant series of payments is involved.[4] Finally, you should recognize that small rounding differences often occur among the various solution methods because tables use fewer significant digits (4) than do calculators (12 to 14), and also because rounding sometimes is done at intermediate steps in long problems rather than only in the final solution.

Graphic View of the Compounding Process: Growth

Figure 6–1 shows how $1 (or any other sum) grows over time at various interest rates. The data used to plot the curves could be obtained from Table A–3, or it could be generated with a calculator. The higher the rate of interest, the faster the rate of growth. *The interest rate is, in fact, a growth rate:* If a sum is deposited and earns five percent

---

[4]We input PMT = 0, but if you cleared the calculator before you started, that already would have been done for you.

FIGURE 6–1	Relationships among Future Value, Growth, Interest Rates, and Time

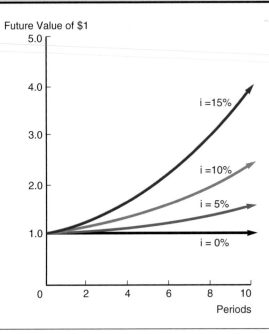

interest, then the funds on deposit will grow at a rate of five percent per period. Note also that TVM concepts can be applied to anything that is growing—sales, population, earnings per share, or whatever.

Self-Test Questions

Explain what is meant by the following statement: "A dollar in hand today is worth more than a dollar to be received next year."

What is compounding? What is "interest on interest"?

Explain the following equation: $FV_1 = PV + INT$.

Set up a cash flow time line that shows the following situation: (1) Your initial deposit is $100. (2) The account pays five percent interest annually. (3) You want to know how much money you will have at the end of three years.

What equation could you use to solve the preceding problem?

What are the five TVM (time value of money) input keys on a financial calculator?

Present Value

OPPORTUNITY COST RATE
The rate of return on the best available alternative investment of equal risk.

Suppose you have some extra cash, and you have a chance to buy a low-risk security that will pay $127.63 at the end of five years. Your local bank is currently offering five percent interest on five-year certificates of deposit, and you regard the security as being very safe. The five percent rate is called your **opportunity cost rate,** or the rate of return you could earn on alternative investments of *similar risk*. How much should you be willing to pay for the security?

From the future value example presented in the previous section, we saw that an initial amount of $100 invested at five percent per year would be worth $127.63 at the end of five years. As we will see in a moment, you should be indifferent to the choice between $100 today and $127.63 at the end of five years, and the $100 is defined as the **present value,** or **PV,** of $127.63 due in five years when the opportunity cost rate is five percent. If the price of the security is anything less than $100, you should definitely buy it because it would cost you exactly $100 to produce the $127.63 in five years if you earned a five percent return. Therefore, if you could find another investment with the same risk that would produce the same future amount ($127.63) but it cost less than $100 (say $95), then you could earn a return higher than five percent by purchasing that investment. Similarly, if the price of the security is greater than $100, you should not buy it because it would cost you only $100 to produce the same future amount at the given rate of return. If the price is exactly $100, then you could either buy it or turn it down because $100 is the security's fair value if it has a five percent expected return.

In general, *the present value of a cash flow due n years in the future is the amount that, if it were on hand today, would grow to equal the future amount.* Because $100 would grow to $127.63 in five years at a five percent interest rate, $100 is the present value of $127.63 due five years in the future when the opportunity cost rate is 5 percent. Finding present values is called **discounting,** and it simply is the reverse of compounding—if you know the PV, you can compound to find the FV, while if you know the FV, you can discount to find the PV. When discounting, you would follow these steps:

PRESENT VALUE (PV)
The value today of a future cash flow or series of cash flows.

DISCOUNTING
The process of finding the present value of a cash flow or a series of cash flows; the reverse of compounding.

CASH FLOW TIME LINE:

```
0    5%    1        2        3        4        5
├─────────┼────────┼────────┼────────┼────────┤
PV = ?                                      127.63
```

EQUATION:

To develop the present value, or discounting, equation, we begin with Equation 6–1:

$$FV_n = PV(1 + i)^n = PV(FVIF_{i,n})$$ **(6–1)**

and then solve for PV to yield

6–2

$$PV = \frac{FV_n}{(1 + i)^n} = FV_n\left[\frac{1}{(1 + i)^n}\right] = FV_n(PVIF_{i,n})$$

The middle form and the last form of Equation 6–2 recognizes that the interest factor $PVIF_{i,n}$ is equal to

6–2a

$$PVIF_{i,n} = \frac{1}{(1 + i)^n}$$

The term given in Equation 6–2a is called the **present value interest factor for i and n (PVIF$_{i,n}$).**

1. Numerical Solution:

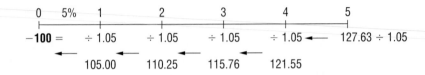

Using a regular calculator, raise 1.05 to the fifth power and divide $127.63 by the result, or divide $127.63 by 1.05 five times:

$$PV = \frac{\$127.63}{(1.05)^5}$$

$$= \frac{\$127.63}{1.2763} = \$127.63(0.7835)$$

$$= \$100$$

2. Tabular Solution:

Table A–1 in Appendix A contains present value interest factors for selected values of i and n, PVIF$_{i,n}$. The value of PVIF$_{i,n}$ for i = 5% and n = 5 periods is 0.7835, so the present value of $127.63 to be received after five years when the opportunity cost rate is five percent equals

$$PV = \$127.63(PVIF_{5\%,5})$$

$$= \$127.63(0.7835)$$

$$= \$100$$

3. Financial Calculator Solution:

Inputs:	5	5	?	0	127.63
	N	**I**	**PV**	**PMT**	**FV**
Output:			= −100		

Enter N = 5, I = 5, PMT = 0, and FV = 127.63, and then press PV to get PV = −100.

Graphic View of the Discounting Process

Figure 6–2 shows how the present value of $1 (or any other sum) to be received in the future diminishes as the time to receipt or the interest rate increases. Again, the data used to plot the curves could be obtained either with a calculator or from Table A–1, and the graph shows that (1) the present value of a sum to be received at some future date decreases and approaches zero as the payment date is extended further into the future and (2) the rate of decrease is greater the higher the interest (discount) rate. At relatively high interest rates, funds due in the future are worth very little today, and even at a relatively low discount rate, the present value of a sum due in the very distant future is quite small.

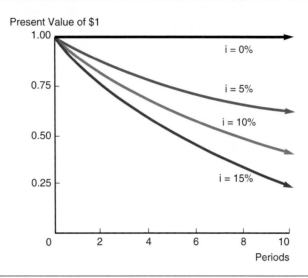

| FIGURE 6–2 | Relationships among Present Value, Interest Rates, and Time |

For example, at a 20 percent discount rate, $5 million due in 100 years is worth only about 6¢ today. (However, 6¢ would grow to $5 million in 100 years at 20 percent.)

Self-Test Questions

What is meant by the term "opportunity cost rate"?

What is discounting? How is it related to compounding?

How does the present value of an amount to be received in the future change as the time is extended and as the interest rate increases?

Solving for Time and Interest Rates

At this point, you should realize that the compounding and discounting processes are reciprocals, or inverses, of one another and that we have been dealing with one equation in two different forms:

FV FORM:

| 6–1 |

$$FV_n = PV(1 + i)^n = PV(FVIF_{i,n})$$

PV FORM:

| 6–2 |

$$PV = \frac{FV_n}{(1 + i)^n} = FV_n\left[\frac{1}{(1 + i)^n}\right] = FV_n(PVIF_{i,n})$$

There are four variables in these equations—PV, FV, i, and n—and if you know the values of any three, you (or your financial calculator) can find the value of the fourth. To this point, we have known the interest rate, i, and the number of years, n, plus either the PV or the FV. In many situations, though, you will need to solve for either i or n, as we discuss next.

Solving for i

Suppose you can buy a security at a price of $78.35 that will pay you $100 after five years. Here we know PV, FV, and n, but we do not know i, the interest rate you will earn on your investment. Problems such as this are solved as follows:

CASH FLOW TIME LINE:

EQUATION:

$$FV_n = PV(1 + i)^n \qquad (6-1)$$

$100 = $78.35(1 + i)^5$. Solve for i.

1. NUMERICAL SOLUTION:

One method of finding the value of i is to go through a trial-and-error process in which you insert different values of i into Equation 6–1 until you find a value that "works" in the sense that the right side of the equation equals $100. The solution value is $i = 0.05$, or five percent. This trial-and-error procedure is extremely tedious and inefficient for most time value problems, so it is rarely used in the real world. Alternatively, in this case, you could solve this problem by using relatively simple algebra to find i directly:

$$FV_n = PV (1 + i)^n = PV (FVIF_{i,n})$$
$$\$100 = \$78.35(1 + i)^5$$
$$(1 + i)^5 = \frac{100}{\$78.35} = 1.2763 = FVIF_{i,5}$$
$$(1 + i) = (1.273)^{\frac{1}{5}} = 1.05$$
$$i = 1.05 - 1 = 0.05 = 5.0\%$$

2. TABULAR SOLUTION:

As these computations show, $FVIF_{i,5} = 1.2763$. Using Table A–3, look across the Period 5 row until you find FVIF = 1.2763. This value is in the 5% column, so the interest rate at which $78.35 grows to $100 over five years is five percent.[5] This

---

[5]The solution could also be set up in present value format:
$$PV = FV_n(PVIF_{i,n})$$
$$\$78.35 = \$100(PVIF_{i,5})$$
$$PVIF_{i,5} = \$78.35/\$100 = 0.7835.$$
This value corresponds to $i = 5\%$ in Table A–1.

procedure can be used only if the interest rate is in the table; therefore, it will not work for fractional interest rates or where n is not a whole number. Approximation procedures can be used, but they can be laborious and inexact.

3. FINANCIAL CALCULATOR SOLUTION:

Inputs:	5	?	−78.35	0	100
	N	**I**	**PV**	**PMT**	**FV**
Output:		= 5.0			

Enter N = 5, PV = −78.35, PMT = 0, and FV = 100, and then press I to get I = 5. This procedure can be used for any interest rate or any value of n, including fractional values.

Solving for n

Suppose you know that the security will provide a return of ten percent per year, that it will cost $68.30, and that you will receive $100 at maturity, but you do not know when the security matures. Thus, you know PV, FV, and i, but you do not know n, the number of periods. Here is the situation:

CASH FLOW TIME LINE:

$$0 \quad 10\% \quad 1 \qquad 2 \qquad n-1 \qquad n = ?$$

−68.30 $\qquad\qquad\qquad\qquad\qquad\qquad\qquad$ 100.00

EQUATION:

$$FV_n = PV(1 + i)^n$$

$100 = \$68.30(1.10)^5$. Solve for n.

(6–1)

1. NUMERICAL SOLUTION:

Again, you could go through a trial-and-error process wherein you substitute different values for n into the equation. Eventually, you would find that n = 4 "works," so it takes four years for $68.30 to grow to $100 if the interest rate is 10 percent.[6]

---

[6]The value of n can also be found as follows:

$$\$100 = \$68.30(1.10)^n$$

$$(1.10)^n = \frac{\$100}{\$68.30} = 1.4641$$

$$\ln[(1.10)^n] = n[\ln(1.10)] = \ln(1.4641)$$

$$n = \frac{\ln(1.4641)}{\ln(1.10)} = \frac{0.3812}{0.0953} = 4.00$$

You can use your calculator to find ln, which is the natural logarithm. For most calculators, you insert the number, say, 1.4641, and then press the LN key (or its equivalent)—the result is 0.3812.

2. TABULAR SOLUTION:

$$FV_n = PV(1 + i)^n = PV(FVIF_{i,n})$$

$$\$100 = \$68.30(FVIF_{10\%,n})$$

$$FVIF_{10\%,n} = \frac{100}{\$68.30} = 1.4641$$

Now look down the 10% column in Table A–3 until you find FVIF = 1.4641. This value is in Row 4, which indicates that it takes four years for $68.30 to grow to $100 at a 10 percent interest rate.[7]

3. FINANCIAL CALCULATOR SOLUTION:

Inputs:	?	10	−68.30	0	100
	N	**I**	**PV**	**PMT**	**FV**
Output:	= 4.0				

Enter I = 10, PV = −68.30, PMT = 0, and FV = 100, and then press N to get N = 4.

Self-Test Questions

Assuming that you are given PV, FV, and the interest rate, i, write out an equation that can be used to determine the time period, n.

Assuming that you are given PV, FV, and the time period, n, write out an equation that can be used to determine the interest rate, i.

Explain how a financial calculator can be used to solve for i and for n.

Future Value of an Annuity

ANNUITY
A series of payments of an equal amount at fixed intervals for a specified number of periods.

ORDINARY (DEFERRED) ANNUITY
An annuity whose payments occur at the end of each period.

ANNUITY DUE
An annuity whose payments occur at the beginning of each period.

An **annuity** is a series of equal payments made at fixed intervals for a specified number of periods. For example, $100 at the end of each of the next three years is a three-year annuity. The payments are given the symbol PMT, and they can occur at either the beginning or the end of each period. If the payments occur at the end of each period, as they typically do in business transactions, the annuity is called an **ordinary**, or **deferred, annuity.** If payments are made at the *beginning* of each period, the annuity is an **annuity due.** Because ordinary annuities are more common in finance, when the term "annuity" is used in this book, you should assume that the payments occur at the end of each period unless otherwise noted.

---

[7]The problem could also be solved as follows:

$$PV = FV_n(PVIF_{i,n})$$

$$\$68.30 = \$100(PVIF_{10\%,n})$$

$$PVIF_{10\%,n} = \$68.30/\$100 = 0.6830.$$

This value corresponds to n = 4 in Table A–1.

Ordinary Annuities

If you deposit $100 at the end of each year for three years in a savings account that pays 5 percent interest per year, how much will you have at the end of three years? To answer this question, we must find the future value of an ordinary annuity, **FVA**ₙ. Each payment is compounded out to the end of Period n, and the sum of the compounded payments is the future value of the annuity.

CASH FLOW TIME LINE:

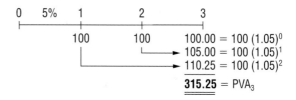

Here we show the regular cash flow time line as the top portion of the diagram, but we also show how each cash flow is processed to produce the value FVA_n in the lower portion of the diagram.

EQUATION:

The cash flow time line shows that we can compute the future value of the annuity simply by determining the future values of the individual payments and then summing the results. Thus, the equation for the future value of an ordinary annuity can be written as follows:

6–3

$$FVA_n = PMT(1 + i)^0 + PMT(1 + i)^1 + PMT(1 + i)^2$$
$$+ \ldots + PMT(1 + i)^{n-1}$$

$$= PMT \sum_{t=1}^{n} (1 + i)^{n-t} = PMT \sum_{t=0}^{n-1} (1 + i)^t$$

Note that the first line of Equation 6–3 presents the annuity payments in reverse order of payment, and the superscript in each term indicates the number of periods of interest each payment receives. In other words, because the first annuity payment was made at the end of Period 1, interest would be earned in Period 2 through Period n only; thus, compounding would be for $n - 1$ periods rather than n periods, compounding for the second annuity payment would be for Period 3 through Period n, or $n - 2$ periods, and so on. The last annuity payment is made at the same time the computation is made, so there is no time for interest to be earned; thus, the superscript 0 represents the fact that no interest is earned. Simplifying the first line produces the last line of Equation 6–3.

1. NUMERICAL SOLUTION:

The lower section of the cash flow time line shows the numerical solution. The future value, FV, of each cash flow is found, and those FVs are summed to find the FV of the annuity. This is a tedious process for long annuities.

The numerical solution is easier if we simplify Equation 6–3 as follows:[8]

6–3a

$$FVA_n = PMT\left[\sum_{t=1}^{n}(1+i)^{n-t}\right] = PMT\left[\frac{(1+i)^n - 1}{i}\right]$$

Using Equation 6–3a, the future value of a $100 deposited at the end of each year for three years in a savings account that earns five percent interest per year is:

$$FVA_3 = \$100\left[\frac{(1.05)^3 - 1}{0.05}\right]$$

$$= \$100(3.1525)$$

$$= \$315.25$$

2. TABULAR SOLUTION:

The summation term in the brackets in Equation 6–3a is called the **future value interest factor for an annuity of n payments at i interest (FVIFA$_{i,n}$):**

$$FVIFA_{i,n} = \sum_{t=1}^{n}(1+i)^{n-t} = \frac{(1+i)^n - 1}{i}$$

FUTURE VALUE INTEREST FACTOR FOR AN ANNUITY (FVIFA$_{i,n}$)
The future value interest factor for an annuity of n periods compounded at i percent.

FVIFAs have been calculated for various combinations of i and n; Table A–4 in Appendix A contains a set of FVIFA factors. To find the answer to the three-year, $100 annuity problem, first refer to Table A–4 and look down the 5% column to the third period; the FVIFA is 3.1525. Thus, the future value of the $100 annuity is $315.25:

$$FVA_n = PMT(FVIFA_{i,n})$$

$$FVA_3 = \$100(FVIFA_{5\%,3})$$

$$= \$100(3.1525)$$

$$= \$315.25.$$

3. FINANCIAL CALCULATOR SOLUTION:

Inputs:	3	5	0	−100	?
	N	**I**	**PV**	**PMT**	**FV**
Output:					= 315.25

Note that in annuity problems, the PMT key is used in conjunction with the N and I keys, plus either the PV or the FV key, depending on whether you are trying to find

---

[8]The simplification shown in Equation 6–3a is found by applying the algebra of geometric progressions. This equation is useful in situations in which the required values of i and n are not in the tables or when a financial calculator is not available.

the PV or the FV of the annuity. In our example, you want the FV, so press the FV key to get the answer, $315.25. Because there is no initial payment, we input PV = 0.

Annuities Due

Had the three $100 payments in the previous example been made at the *beginning* of each year, the annuity would have been an *annuity due*. In the cash flow time line, each payment would be shifted to the left one year; therefore, each payment would be *compounded for one extra year (period)*, which means each payment would earn interest for an additional year.

CASH FLOW TIME LINE:

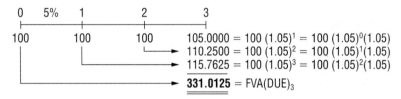

```
0     5%    1           2           3
├──────────┼───────────┼───────────┤
100        100         100         105.0000 = 100 (1.05)¹ = 100 (1.05)⁰(1.05)
│          │                  └──→  110.2500 = 100 (1.05)² = 100 (1.05)¹(1.05)
│          └────────────────────→  115.7625 = 100 (1.05)³ = 100 (1.05)²(1.05)
└───────────────────────────────→  331.0125 = FVA(DUE)₃
```

Again, the regular time line is shown at the top of the diagram, and the future value of each annuity payment at the end of Year 3 is shown in the Year 3 column, with the actual computations shown to the right.

1. NUMERICAL SOLUTION:

We can find the FV of each cash flow and then sum the results to find the FV of the annuity due, FVA(DUE)_n. This procedure is shown in the lower section of the cash flow time line. Note from the diagram that the difference between an ordinary annuity and an annuity due is that *each of the payments of the annuity due earns interest for one additional year.* So the numerical solution for an annuity due can also be found by adjusting Equations 6–3 and 6–3a to account for the fact that each annuity payment is able to earn an additional year's interest when compared to an ordinary annuity. The solution for FVA(DUE)_n is

6–3b

$$\text{FVA(DUE)}_n = \text{PMT}\left[\sum_{t=1}^{n}(1+i)^t\right] = \text{PMT}\left[\left\{\sum_{t=1}^{n}(1+i)^{n-t}\right\}\times(1+i)\right]$$

$$= \text{PMT}\left[\left\{\frac{(1+i)^n-1}{i}\right\}\times(1+i)\right]$$

The future value of the three $100 deposits made at the beginning of each year into a savings account that earns five percent annually is

$$\text{FVA(DUE)}_3 = \$100\left[\left\{\frac{(1.05)^3-1}{0.05}\right\}\times(1.05)\right]$$

$$= \$100[(3.1525)\times1.05]$$

$$= \$331.0125$$

2. Tabular Solution:

As we have shown, for an annuity due, each payment is compounded for one additional period, so the future value interest factor for an *annuity due*, **FVIFA(DUE)$_{i,n}$**, is equal to the FVIFA$_{i,n}$ for an ordinary annuity compounded for one additional period. In other words,

> **6–3c**
>
> $$FVIFA(DUE)_{i,n} = \left[\left\{\frac{(1 + i)^n - 1}{i}\right\} \times (1 + i)\right]$$
>
> $$= [(FVIFA_{i,n})(1 + i)]$$

FVIFA(DUE)$_{i,n}$
The future value interest factor for an annuity due—FVIFA(DUE)$_{i,n}$ = FVIFA$_{i,n}$ × (1 + i).

Here is the tabular solution for FVA(DUE)$_n$:

$$FVA(DUE)_n = PMT[FVIFA(DUE)_{i,n}]$$
$$= PMT[(FVIFA_{i,n})(1 + i)]$$
$$FVA(DUE)_3 = \$100[(3.1525)(1.05)]$$
$$= \$331.0125$$

The payments occur earlier than for the ordinary annuity, so more interest is earned. Therefore, the future value of the annuity due is larger—$331.01 versus $315.25 for the ordinary annuity.

3. Financial Calculator Solution:

Most financial calculators have a switch, or key, marked DUE or BEG that allows you to switch from end-of-period payments (ordinary annuity) to beginning-of-period payments (annuity due). When the beginning mode is activated, the display normally will show the word BEGIN, or the letters BGN. Thus, to deal with annuities due, switch your calculator to BEGIN and proceed as before:

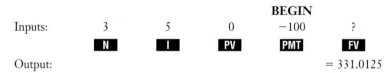

				BEGIN	
Inputs:	3	5	0	−100	?
	N	**I**	**PV**	**PMT**	**FV**
Output:					= 331.0125

Enter N = 3, I = 5, PV = 0, PMT = −100, and then press FV to get the answer, $331.01. Because most problems specify end-of-period cash flows, you should always switch your calculator back to END mode after you work an annuity due problem.

Self-Test Questions

What is the difference between an ordinary annuity and an annuity due?

How do you modify the FVIFA$_{i,n}$ for determining the value of an ordinary annuity in order to determine the value of an annuity due?

Which annuity has the greater future value: an ordinary annuity or an annuity due? Why?

Explain how financial calculators can be used to solve future value of annuity problems.

Present Value of an Annuity

Suppose you were offered the following alternatives: (1) a three-year annuity with payments of $100 at the end of each year or (2) a lump-sum payment today. You have no need for the money during the next three years, so if you accept the annuity, you would simply deposit the payments in a savings account that pays five percent interest per year. Similarly, the lump-sum payment would be deposited into the same account. How large must the lump-sum payment today be to make it equivalent to the annuity?

PVAₙ

The present value of an ordinary annuity with n payments.

To answer this question, we must find the present value of an ordinary annuity, **PVAₙ**. Each payment is discounted, and the sum of the discounted payments is the present value of the annuity.

CASH FLOW TIME LINE:

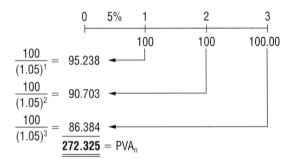

$$\frac{100}{(1.05)^1} = 95.238$$

$$\frac{100}{(1.05)^2} = 90.703$$

$$\frac{100}{(1.05)^3} = 86.384$$

$$\underline{\underline{272.325}} = PVA_n$$

The regular cash flow time line is shown at the top of the diagram, and the numerical solution values are on the left. The PV of the annuity, PVAₙ, is $272.325.

EQUATION:

As you can see from the cash flow time line, the present value of an annuity can be determined by computing the PV of the individual payments and summing the results. The general equation used to find the PV of an ordinary annuity is shown here:

6–4

$$PVA_n = PMT\left[\frac{1}{(1 + i)^1}\right] + PMT\left[\frac{1}{(1 + i)^2}\right] + \ldots + PMT\left[\frac{1}{(1 + i)^n}\right]$$

$$= PMT\left[\sum_{t=1}^{n}\frac{1}{(1 + i)^t}\right]$$

---

1. NUMERICAL SOLUTION:

One method of determining the present value of the annuity is to compute the present value of each cash flow and then sum the result. This procedure is shown in the lower left section of the cash flow time line diagram, where we see that the PV of the annuity is $272.325. This approach can be tedious if the number of annuity payments is large.

The numerical solution is easier if we simplify Equation 6–4:[9]

6–4a

$$PVA_n = PMT\left[\sum_{t=1}^{n}\frac{1}{(1+i)^t}\right] = PMT\left[\frac{1 - \frac{1}{(1+i)^n}}{i}\right]$$

Using Equation 6–4a, the PV of the three-year annuity with end-of-year payments of $100 is

$$PVA_n = \$100\left[\frac{1 - \frac{1}{(1.05)^3}}{0.05}\right]$$

$$= \$100(2.72325)$$

$$= \$272.325$$

2. Tabular Solution:

The summation term in the brackets in Equation 6–4 is called the **present value interest factor for an annuity of n payments at i interest (PVIFA$_{i,n}$):**[10]

$$PVIFA_{i,n} = \sum_{t=1}^{n}\frac{1}{(1+i)^t} = \left[\frac{1 - \frac{1}{(1+i)^n}}{i}\right]$$

The values for PVIFA at different values of i and n are shown in Table A–2 at the back of the book.

To find the answer to the three-year, $100 annuity problem, simply refer to Table A–2 and look down the 5% column to the third period. The PVIFA is 2.7232, so the present value of the $100 annuity is $272.32:

$$PVA_n = PMT(PVIFA_{i,n})$$

$$PVA_3 = \$100(PVIFA_{5\%,3})$$

$$= \$100(2.7232)$$

$$= \$272.32$$

3. Financial Calculator Solution:

Inputs:	3	5	?	−100	0
	N	**I**	**PV**	**PMT**	**FV**
Output:			= 272.325		

---

[9]Like Equation 6–3a, the simplification shown in Equation 6–4a is found by applying the algebra of geometric progressions. This equation is useful in situations in which the required values of i and n are not in the tables or when a financial calculator is not available.

[10]It should be apparent from Equation 6–4 that, unlike the interest factors for the FV and PV of a lump-sum amount (FVIF$_{i,n}$ and PVIF$_{i,n}$, respectively), the interest factors for the FV and PV of an annuity (FVIFA$_{i,n}$ and PVIFA$_{i,n}$, respectively) are not reciprocals of each other. In other words, the inverse of the sum of a series of values does not equal the sum of the inverses of those same values—that is, $1/(2 + 3 + 4) = 1/9 \neq 1/2 + 1/3 + 1/4 = 13/12$.

Enter N = 3, I = 5, PMT = −100, and FV = 0, and then press the PV key to find the PV, $272.32.

One especially important application of the annuity concept relates to loans with constant payments, such as mortgages and auto loans. With such loans, called amortized loans, *the amount borrowed is the present value of an ordinary annuity*, and the payments constitute the annuity stream. We will examine constant payment loans in more depth in a later section of this chapter.

Annuities Due

Had the three $100 payments in our earlier example been made at the *beginning* of each year, the annuity would have been an *annuity due*. On the cash flow time line, each payment would be shifted to the left one year, so each payment would be *discounted for one less year*. Here is the cash flow time line setup:

Cash Flow Time Line:

$$\frac{100}{(1.05)^1} \times (1.05) = \frac{100}{(1.05)^0} = 100.000$$

$$\frac{100}{(1.05)^2} \times (1.05) = \frac{100}{(1.05)^1} = 95.238$$

$$\frac{100}{(1.05)^3} \times (1.05) = \frac{100}{(1.05)^2} = 90.703$$

$$\underline{\underline{285.941}} = PVA_n$$

(Time line: 0 at 5%, 1, 2, 3; payments of 100 at times 0, 1, 2.)

1. Numerical Solution:

Again, we can find the PV of each cash flow and then sum these PVs to find the PV of the annuity due, PVA(DUE)$_n$. This procedure is illustrated in the lower section of the time line diagram. Because the cash flows occur sooner, the PV of the annuity due exceeds that of the ordinary annuity—$285.94 versus $272.32.

The cash flow time line shows that the difference between the PV of an annuity due and the PV of an ordinary annuity is that *each of the payments of the annuity due is discounted one less year*. So the numerical solution for an annuity due can also be found by adjusting Equations 6–4 and 6–4a to account for the fact each annuity payment will have the *opportunity* to earn an additional year's (period's) interest when compared with an ordinary annuity:

6–4b

$$PVA(DUE)_n = \left[\sum_{t=0}^{n-1} \frac{1}{(1+i)^t} \right] = PMT \left[\left\{ \sum_{t=1}^{n} \frac{1}{(1+i)^t} \right\} \times (1+i) \right]$$

$$= PMT \left[\left\{ \frac{1 - \frac{1}{(1+i)^n}}{i} \right\} \times (1+i) \right]$$

Therefore, if the three $100 payments were made at the beginning of the year, the PV of the annuity would be:

$$= \text{PVA(DUE)}_3 = \$100\left[\left\{\frac{1 - \frac{1}{(1.05)^3}}{0.05}\right\} \times (1.05)\right]$$

$$= \$100[(2.72325)(1.05)]$$

$$= \$100(2.85941)$$

$$= \$285.941$$

2. TABULAR SOLUTION:

We can use the PVIFAs given in Table A–2, which are computed for ordinary annuities, if we adjust these values to account for the fact that the payments associated with
an annuity due occur one period earlier than the payments associated with an ordinary
annuity. As the cash flow time line and the numerical solution indicate, the adjustment
is rather simple—just multiply the PVIFA for an ordinary annuity by $(1 + i)$. So, the
present value interest factor for an annuity due, **PVIFA(DUE)**$_{i,n}$, is:

> **6–4c**
>
> $$\text{PVIFA(DUE)}_{i,n} = \left[\left\{\frac{1 - \frac{1}{(1 + i)^n}}{i}\right\} \times (1 + i)\right]$$
>
> $$= [(\text{PVIFA}_{i,n})(1 + i)]$$

PVIFA(DUE)$_{i,n}$
The present value interest
factor for an annuity
due—PVIFA(DUE)$_{i,n}$ =
PVIFA$_{i,n}$ × $(1 + i)$.

The tabular solution for PVA(DUE)$_n$ is

$$\text{PVA(DUE)}_n = \text{PMT}[\text{PVIFA(DUE)}_{i,n}]$$

$$= \text{PMT}[(\text{PVIFA}_{i,n}) \times (1 + i)]$$

$$\text{PVA(DUE)}_3 = \$100[(2.7232)(1.05)]$$

$$= \$100(2.85941)$$

$$= \$285.941$$

3. FINANCIAL CALCULATOR SOLUTION:

				BEGIN	
Inputs:	3	5	?	−100	0
	N	**I**	**PV**	**PMT**	**FV**
Output:			= 285.94		

Switch to the beginning-of-period mode (BEGIN), and then enter N = 3, I = 5,
PMT = −100, and FV = 0, and then press PV to get the answer, $285.94. Again, *be-
cause most problems deal with end-of-period cash flows, don't forget to switch your calculator
back to the END mode.*

Self-Test Questions

Which annuity has the greater present value: an ordinary annuity or an annuity due?
Why?

Explain how financial calculators can be used to find present values of annuities.

Solving for Interest Rates with Annuities

Suppose you pay $846.80 for an investment that promises to pay you $250 per year for the next four years. If the payments are made at the end of each year, what interest rate (rate of return) will you earn on this investment? We can solve this problem as follows:

Cash Flow Time Line:

```
0   i = ?   1           2           3           4
|-----------|-----------|-----------|-----------|
-846.80    250         250         250         250
```

Equation:

$$PVA_n = PMT(PVIFA_{i,n})$$

$$\$846.80 = \$250(PVIFA_{i=?,4})$$

(6–4)

1. Numerical Solution:

To solve this problem numerically, you would have to use a trial-and-error process in which you plug different values for i into either Equation 6–4 or Equation 6–4a until you find the value for i where the present value of the four-year $250 annuity is equal to $846.80. The solution is i = 0.07, or 7%.

2. Tabular Solution:

If we solve the equation given above for the PVIFA, we find

$$PVIFA_{i=?,4} = \frac{\$846.80}{\$250} = 3.3872$$

Using Table A–2, look across the Period 4 row until you find PVIFA = 3.3872. This value is in the 7% column, so the interest rate at which a four-year $250 annuity has a present value equal to $846.80 is seven percent. This method cannot be used if the interest rate is not in the table; instead, you would have to use your financial calculator to solve the problem.

3. Financial Calculator Solution:

Inputs:	4	?	−846.80	250	0
	N	**I**	**PV**	**PMT**	**FV**
Output:		= 7.0			

Enter N = 4, PV = −846.80, PMT = 250, and FV = 0, and then press I to get the answer, 7.0%.

In the problem we just solved, the information that was given included the amount of the annuity payment, the *present value* of the annuity, and the number of years the annuity payment is received. If the *future value* of the annuity was given instead of the present value, to find i, we would follow the same procedures outlined here, but Equation 6–3 would be used because it applies to future values. For example, let's assume a financial institution has an investment that requires you to make annual payments equal to $250 starting at the end of this year, and in four years the financial institution will pay you $1,110. In this case, we know the amount of the annuity ($250), the length of the annuity (four years), and the future value of the annuity ($1,110). What interest rate would you earn on this investment? The procedure to solve this problem is the same as just outlined, except you use the FVA_n equation (Equation 6–3) instead of the PVA_n equation for the numerical and tabular solution, and the FV key ($1,110) instead of the PV key for the financial calculator solution. Try it—you should get i = 7%.

Self-Test Question

Describe how you would solve for interest rates with annuities using the numerical solution method.

Perpetuities

PERPETUITY
A stream of equal payments expected to continue forever.

Most annuities call for payments to be made over some finite period of time—for example, $100 per year for three years. However, some annuities go on indefinitely, or perpetually, and these annuities are called **perpetuities.** The present value of a perpetuity is found by applying Equation 6–5.[11]

6–5

$$PVP = \frac{\text{Payment}}{\text{Interest rate}} = \frac{PMT}{i}$$

Perpetuities can be illustrated by some British securities issued after the Napoleonic Wars. In 1815, the British government sold a huge bond issue and used the proceeds to pay off many smaller issues that had been floated in prior years to pay for the wars. Because the purpose of the bonds was to consolidate past debts, the bonds were called **consols.** Suppose each consol promised to pay $100 per year in perpetuity. (Actually, interest was stated in pounds.) What would each bond be worth if the opportunity cost rate, or discount rate, was five percent? The answer is $2,000:

CONSOL
A perpetual bond issued by the British government to consolidate past debts; in general, any perpetual bond.

$$PVP = \frac{\$100}{0.05} = \$2,000$$

Suppose the interest rate rose to ten percent; what would happen to the consol's value? The value would drop to $1,000:

$$PVP = \frac{\$100}{0.10} = \$1,000$$

---

[11]The derivation of Equation 6–5 is given in the Extension section of Chapter 28 in Eugene F. Brigham, Louis C. Gapenski, and Phillip R. Daves, *Intermediate Financial Management*, 6th ed. (Fort Worth, TX: Dryden Press, 1999).

We see that the value of a perpetuity changes dramatically when interest rates change. Perpetuities are discussed further in the next chapter, where procedures for finding the value of various types of securities are discussed.

Self-Test Questions

What happens to the value of a perpetuity when interest rates increase?

What happens when interest rates decrease? Why do these changes occur?

Uneven Cash Flow Streams

UNEVEN CASH FLOW STREAM
A series of cash flows in which the amount varies from one period to the next.

The definition of an annuity includes the words *constant amount*—in other words, annuities involve payments that are equal in every period. Although many financial decisions do involve constant payments, some important decisions involve uneven, or nonconstant, cash flows. For example, common stocks typically pay an increasing stream of dividends over time, and fixed asset investments such as new equipment normally do not generate constant cash flows. Consequently, it is necessary to extend our time value discussion to include **uneven cash flow streams.**

Throughout the book, we will follow convention and reserve the term **payment (PMT)** for annuity situations where the cash flows are constant, and we will use the term **cash flow (CF)** to denote cash flows in general, which includes uneven cash flows. Financial calculators are set up to follow this convention, so if you are using one and dealing with uneven cash flows, you will need to use the cash flow register.

PAYMENT (PMT)
This term designates constant cash flows.

CASH FLOW (CF)
This term designates cash flows in general, including uneven cash flows.

Present Value of an Uneven Cash Flow Stream

The PV of an uneven cash flow stream is found as the sum of the PVs of the individual cash flows of the stream. For example, suppose we must find the PV of the following cash flow stream, discounted at six percent:

```
 0     6%    1        2        3        4        5
 |-----------|--------|--------|--------|--------|
PV = ?      100      300      200      200     1,000
```

The PV is found by applying this general present value equation:

6-6

$$PV = CF_1\left[\frac{1}{(1+i)^1}\right] + CF_2\left[\frac{1}{(1+i)^2}\right] + \ldots + CF_n\left[\frac{1}{(1+i)^n}\right]$$

$$= \sum_{t=1}^{n}CF_t\left[\frac{1}{(1+i)^t}\right] = \sum_{t=1}^{n}CF_t\,(PVIF_{i,t})$$

We can find the PV of each individual cash flow (using the numerical, tabular, or financial calculator methods) and then sum these values to find the present value of the stream. Here is what the process would look like:

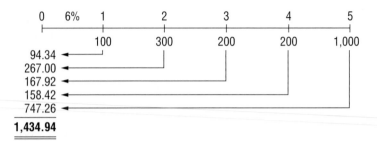

All we did was to apply Equation 6–6, show the individual PVs in the left column of the diagram, and then sum these individual PVs to find the PV of the entire stream.

The present value of any cash flow stream can always be found by summing the present values of the individual cash flows as shown here. However, when cash flows are constant, we can simplify our computations by applying the annuity solutions discussed earlier.

Problems involving uneven cash flows can be solved in one step with most financial calculators. First, you input the individual cash flows in chronological order into the cash flow register. Cash flows usually are designated CF_0, CF_1, CF_2, CF_3, and so on. Next, you enter the interest rate. At this point, you have substituted in all the known values of Equation 6–6, so you only need to press the NPV key to find the present value of the cash flow stream. The calculator has been programmed to find the PV of each cash flow, including CF_0, and then to sum these values to find the PV of the entire stream. To input the cash flows for this problem, enter 0 (because $CF_0 = 0$), 100, 300, 200, 200, and 1,000 in that order into the cash flow register, enter I = 6, and then press NPV to obtain the answer, $1,434.94. Appendix 6A shows the specific steps used to solve this problem with a financial calculator.

Two points should be noted. First, when dealing with the cash flow register, the calculator uses the term NPV rather than PV. The N stands for *net*, so NPV is the abbreviation for net present value, which is simply the net present value of a series of positive and negative cash flows, including CF_0. Our example has no negative cash flows, but if it did, we simply would input them with negative signs. Also, because we wanted to compute the PV, $CF_0 = 0$.

The second point to note is that consecutive cash flows that are equal (annuities) can be entered into the cash flow register more efficiently by using the function that allows you to enter the number of times the cash flow occurs (see Appendix 6A). The procedures for using the CF register vary somewhat on different calculators, so you should consult your calculator manual to determine the appropriate steps for your specific calculator. Also, note that amounts entered into the cash flow register remain in the register until they are cleared. Thus, if you had previously worked a problem with eight cash flows and then moved to a problem with only four cash flows, the calculator would assume that the last four cash flows from the first problem belonged to the second problem. Therefore, *you must be sure to clear the cash flow register before starting a new problem.*

Future Value of an Uneven Cash Flow Stream

TERMINAL VALUE
The future value of a cash flow stream.

The future value of an uneven cash flow stream, sometimes called the **terminal value,** is found by compounding each payment to the end of the stream and then summing the future values:

$$FV_n = CF_1(1 + i)^{n-1} + CF_2(1 + i)^{n-2} + \ldots + CF_n(1 + i)^0$$

$$= \sum_{t=1}^{n} CF_t(1 + i)^{n-t} = \sum_{t=1}^{n} CF_t(FVIF_{i,\, n-t})$$

6–7

The future value of our illustrative uneven cash flow stream is $1,920.27:

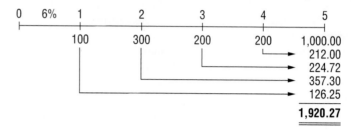

Some financial calculators have a net future value (NFV) key that, after the cash flows and interest rate have been entered into the calculator, can be used to obtain the future value of an uneven cash flow stream. In any event, it is easy enough to compound the individual cash flows to the terminal year and then to sum them to find the FV of the stream. Also, we generally are more interested in the present value of an asset's cash flow stream than in the future value because *the present value represents today's value*, which we can compare with the price of the asset. In addition, once we know its present value, we can find the future value of an uneven cash flow stream by treating the present value as a lump-sum amount and compounding it to the future period. The computation for our illustration would be as follows:

$$FV_n = PV(1 + i)^n$$

$$= \$1,434.94(1.06)^5$$

$$= \$1,434.94(FVIF_{6\%,5})$$

$$= \$1,434.94(1.3382)$$

$$= \$1,920.24 \text{ (rounding difference)}$$

Solving for i with Uneven Cash Flow Streams

It is relatively easy to solve for i *numerically* or *with the tables* when the cash flows are lump sums or annuities. However, it is extremely difficult to solve for i if the cash flows are uneven, as you will have to go through tedious trial-and-error calculations. With a financial calculator, though, it is easy to find the value of i. Simply input the CF values into the cash flow register and then press the IRR key. IRR stands for *internal rate of return*, which is the return on an investment. We will defer further discussion of this calculation for now, but we will take it up later in our discussion of capital budgeting methods in Chapter 8.

Self-Test Questions

Give two examples of financial decisions that would typically involve uneven flows of cash.

What is meant by the term *terminal value?*

Semiannual and Other Compounding Periods

ANNUAL COMPOUNDING
The arithmetic process of determining the final value of a cash flow or series of cash flows when interest is added once a year.

In our examples thus far, we have assumed that interest is compounded once a year, or annually. This is called **annual compounding.** Suppose, however, that you put $100 into a bank that states it pays a ten percent annual interest rate, but that interest is added each six months. This is called **semiannual compounding.** How much would you accumulate at the end of one year, two years, or some other period under semiannual compounding?

To illustrate semiannual compounding, assume that $100 is invested at an interest rate of ten percent for a period of three years. First, consider again what happens under *annual compounding:*

SEMIANNUAL COMPOUNDING
The arithmetic process of determining the final value of a cash flow or series of cash flows when interest is added twice a year.

1. TIME LINE, EQUATION, AND NUMERICAL SOLUTION:

```
0    10%    1         2         3
|-----------|---------|---------|
-100                           FV = ?
```

$$FV_n = PV(1 + i)^n = \$100(1.10)^3$$
$$= \$133.10$$

2. TABULAR SOLUTION:

$$FV_3 = \$100(FVIF_{10\%,3})$$
$$= \$100(1.3310)$$
$$= \$133.10$$

3. FINANCIAL CALCULATOR SOLUTION:

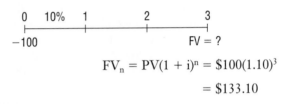

Inputs:	3	10	−100	0	?
	N	**I**	**PV**	**PMT**	**FV**
Output:					= 133.10

Now consider what happens under semiannual compounding. Here we have n = 2 × 3 = 6 semiannual periods, and you will earn I = 10%/2 = 5% every six months. Note that on all types of contracts, interest is always quoted as an annual rate, and if compounding occurs more frequently than once a year, that fact is stated, along with the rate. In our example, the quoted rate is *10 percent, compounded semiannually.* Here is how we find the FV after three years at 10 percent with semiannual compounding:

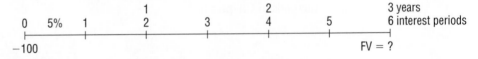

1. EQUATION AND NUMERICAL SOLUTION:

$$FV_n = PV(1 + i)^n$$
$$= \$100(1.05)^6$$
$$= \$100(1.3401)$$
$$= \$134.01$$

Here i = rate per period = (annual rate) ÷ (compounding periods per year) = 10% ÷ 2 = 5%, and n = the total number of periods = (years) × (compounding periods per year) = 3 × 2 = 6.

2. TABULAR SOLUTION:

$$FV_6 = \$100(FVIF_{5\%,\,6})$$
$$= \$100(1.3401)$$
$$= \$134.01$$

Look up FVIF for 5% and six periods in Table A–3 and complete the arithmetic.

3. FINANCIAL CALCULATOR SOLUTION:

Inputs: 6   5   −100   0   ?
           N   I   PV   PMT   FV

Output: = 134.01

Enter N = (years) × (periods per year) = 3 × 2 = 6, I = (annual rate) ÷ (periods per year) = 10/2 = 5, PV = −100, and PMT = 0, and then press FV to find the answer, $134.01 versus $133.10 under annual compounding. The FV is larger under semiannual compounding because interest on interest is being earned more frequently.

SIMPLE (QUOTED) INTEREST RATE
The contracted, or quoted, interest rate that is used to compute the interest paid per period.

Throughout the world economy, different compounding periods are used for different types of investments. For example, bank accounts generally compute interest on a daily basis; most bonds pay interest semiannually; and stocks generally pay dividends quarterly.[12] If we are to properly compare securities with different compounding periods, we need to put them on a common basis. This requires us to distinguish between the **simple** (or **quoted**) **interest rate** and the **effective annual rate (EAR)**.

EFFECTIVE ANNUAL RATE (EAR)
The annual rate of interest actually being earned, as opposed to the quoted rate, considering the compounding of interest.

The simple, or quoted, interest rate in our example is ten percent. *The effective annual rate (EAR) is defined as the rate that would produce the same ending (future) value if annual compounding had been used.* In our example, the effective annual rate is the rate that would produce an FV of $134.01 at the end of Year 3.

We can determine the effective annual rate, given the simple rate and the number of compounding periods per year, by solving this equation:

---

[12]Some banks and savings and loans even pay interest compounded continuously. Continuous compounding is discussed in Appendix 6C.

2. TABULAR SOLUTION:

$$PVA_3 = PMT \, (PVIFA_{8\%,3})$$
$$= \$100 \, (2.5771)$$
$$= \$257.71$$

3. FINANCIAL CALCULATOR SOLUTION:

Inputs:	3	8	?	−100	0
	N	I	PV	PMT	FV
Output:			= 257.71		

Now let's change the situation so that the annuity calls for payments of $50 each six months rather than $100 per year, and the rate is eight percent, compounded semiannually. Here is the cash flow time line:

CASH FLOW TIME LINE:

```
                   1         2                3 years
0   4%    1        2    3    4     5         6 6-month periods
|---------|--------|----|----|-----|---------|
PV = ?   −50     −50  −50  −50   −50       −50
```

1. NUMERICAL SOLUTION:

Find the PV of each cash flow by discounting at four percent. Treat each tick mark on the time line as a period, so there would be six periods. The PV of the annuity is $262.11 versus $257.71 under annual compounding. Solving directly, the computation is

$$PVA_6 = \$50 \left[\frac{1 - \frac{1}{(1.04)^6}}{0.04} \right]$$
$$= \$50 \, (5.2421)$$
$$= \$262.11$$

2. TABULAR SOLUTION:

$$PVA_6 = PMT(PVIFA_{4\%,6})$$
$$= \$50(5.2421)$$
$$= \$262.11$$

3. FINANCIAL CALCULATOR SOLUTION:

Inputs:	6	4	?	−50	0
	N	I	PV	PMT	FV
Output:			= 262.11		

The semiannual payments come in sooner, so they can be invested sooner, which means the $50 semiannual annuity is more valuable than the $100 annual annuity.

Self-Test Questions

What changes must you make in your calculations to determine the future value of an amount that is being compounded at eight percent semiannually versus one being compounded annually at eight percent?

Why is semiannual compounding better than annual compounding from a saver's standpoint?

What are meant by the terms *annual percentage rate*, *effective annual rate*, and *simple interest rate*?

Fractional Time Periods

In all the examples used thus far in the chapter, we have assumed that payments occur at either the beginning or the end of periods but not at some date within a period. However, we often encounter situations that require compounding or discounting over fractional periods. For example, suppose you deposited $100 in a bank that pays an effective annual return equal to ten percent. If you leave your money in the bank for nine months, or 0.75 of the year, how much would you have in your account? Problems such as this can be handled easily, but the tables generally cannot be used.

CASH FLOW TIME LINE AND EQUATION:

```
0    8%   0.25        0.50        0.75        1.00
├─────────┼───────────┼───────────┼───────────┤
-100                               FV = ?
```

$$FV_n = PV(1 + i)^n \qquad (6\text{–}1)$$

1. NUMERICAL SOLUTION:

$$FV_{0.75} = \$100(1.10)^{0.75}$$
$$= \$100(1.0741)$$
$$= \$107.41$$

2. FINANCIAL CALCULATOR SOLUTION:[16]

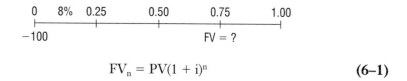

Inputs:	0.75	10	-100	0	?
	N	I	PV	PMT	FV
Output:					= 107.41

Present values, annuities, and problems where you must find interest rates or numbers of periods can all be handled with ease. Note, though, that financial calculators are essential for many fractional year problems—the tables are useless.

---

[16]Some older calculators will produce an answer of FV = 107.50. This result occurs because these calculators solve for fractional time periods using a straight-line interpolation procedure.

Self-Test Question

Why are the tables useless for fractional time periods?

Amortized Loans

AMORTIZED LOAN
A loan that is repaid in equal payments over its life.

One of the most important applications of compound interest involves loans that are paid off in installments over time. Included are automobile loans, home mortgages, student loans, and most business debt other than very short-term loans and long-term bonds. If a loan is to be repaid in equal periodic amounts (monthly, quarterly, or annually), it is said to be an **amortized loan.**[17]

To illustrate, suppose a firm borrows $15,000, and the loan is to be repaid in three equal payments at the end of each of the next three years. The lender is to receive eight percent interest on the loan balance that is outstanding at the beginning of each year. The first task is to determine the amount the firm must repay each year, or the annual payment. To find this amount, recognize that the $15,000 represents the present value of an annuity of PMT dollars per year for three years, discounted at eight percent:

CASH FLOW TIME LINE AND EQUATION:

$$
\begin{array}{ccccccc}
0 & 8\% & 1 & & 2 & & 3 \\
\vdash & & + & & + & & \dashv \\
15{,}000 & & \text{PMT} & & \text{PMT} & & \text{PMT}
\end{array}
$$

$$PVA_n = \frac{PMT}{(1+i)^1} + \frac{PMT}{(1+i)^2} + \frac{PMT}{(1+i)^3} = \sum_{t=1}^{3} \frac{PMT}{(1+i)^t}$$

$$\$15{,}000 = \sum_{t=1}^{3} \frac{PMT}{(1.08)^t}$$

Here we know everything except PMT, so we can solve the equation for PMT.

1. NUMERICAL SOLUTION:

You can solve for PMT as follows:

$$\$15{,}000 = \sum_{t=1}^{3} \frac{PMT}{(1.08)^t} = PMT\left[\sum_{t=1}^{3}\frac{1}{(1.08)^t}\right] = PMT\left[\frac{1 - \frac{1}{(1.08)^3}}{0.08}\right]$$

$$\$15{,}000 = PMT(2.2.5771)$$

$$PMT = \frac{\$15{,}000}{2.5771} = \$5{,}820.50$$

---

[17]The word *amortized* comes from the Latin *mors*, meaning "death," so an amortized loan is one that is "killed off" over time.

2. TABULAR SOLUTION:

Substitute in known values and look up PVIFA for I = 8% and n = 3 periods in Table A–2:

$$PVA_n = PMT(PVIFA_{i,n})$$

$$\$15,000 = PMT(FVIFA_{8\%,3}) = PMT(2.5771)$$

$$PMT = \frac{\$15,000}{2.5771} = \$5,820.50$$

3. FINANCIAL CALCULATOR SOLUTION:

Inputs:	3	8	15000	?	0
	N	**I**	**PV**	**PMT**	**FV**
Output:				= −5820.50	

Enter N = 3, I = 8, PV = 15000 (the firm receives the cash), and FV = 0, and then press the PMT key to find PMT = −5820.50.

Therefore, the firm must pay the lender $5,820.50 at the end of each of the next three years, and the percentage cost to the borrower, which is also the rate of return to the lender, will be 8 percent. Each payment consists partly of interest and partly of re-payment of the amount borrowed (principal). This breakdown is given in the **amortization schedule** shown in Table 6–2. The interest component is largest in the first year, and it declines as the outstanding balance of the loan decreases. For tax purposes, a business borrower reports the interest component shown in Column 3 as a deductible cost each year, while the lender reports this same amount as taxable income.

Most financial calculators are programmed to calculate amortization tables—you simply enter the input data, and then press one key to get each entry in Table 6–2. If you have a financial calculator, it is worthwhile to read the appropriate section of the manual and learn how to use its amortization feature. Appendix 6B shows the steps required to set up an amortization schedule using a financial calculator for the situation given in Table 6–2.

AMORTIZATION SCHEDULE
A schedule showing precisely how a loan will be repaid. It gives the required payment on each payment date and a breakdown of the payment, showing how much is interest and how much is repayment of principal.

	BEGINNING AMOUNT	**PAYMENT**	**INTEREST**[a]	**REPAYMENT OF PRINCIPAL**[b]	**REMAINING BALANCE**
YEAR	**(1)**	**(2)**	**(3)**	**(2) − (3) = (4)**	**(1) − (4) = (5)**
1	$15,000.00	$5,820.50	$1,200.00	$4,620.50	$10,379.50
2	10,379.50	5,820.50	830.36	4,990.14	5,389.36
3	5,389.36	5,820.50	431.15	5,389.35	0.01[c]

TABLE 6–2   Loan Amortization Schedule, 8 Percent Interest Rate

NOTES:

[a]Interest is calculated by multiplying the loan balance at the beginning of the year by the interest rate. Therefore, interest in Year 1 is $15,000(0.08) = $1,200.00; in Year 2, it is $10,379.50(0.08) = $830.36; and in Year 3, it is $5,389.36(0.08) = $431.15 (rounded).

[b]Repayment of principal is equal to the payment of $5,820.50 minus the interest charge for each year.

[c]The $0.01 Remaining Balance at the end of Year 3 results from rounding differences.

Self-Test Questions

To construct an amortization schedule, how do you determine the amount of the periodic payments?

How do you determine the amount of each payment that goes to interest and to repay the debt?

Comparison of Different Types of Interest Rates

Up to this point, we have discussed three different types of interest rates. If you will be working with relatively difficult time value problems, then it is useful to compare the three types and to know when each should be used, as we discuss next.

SIMPLE, OR QUOTED, RATE, i_{SIMPLE}
The rate quoted by borrowers and lenders that is used to determine the rate earned per compounding period (periodic rate).

1. **Simple, or quoted, rate, i_{SIMPLE}.** This is the rate that is quoted by borrowers and lenders, and it is used to determine the rate earned per compounding period (periodic rate). Practitioners in the stock, bond, lending, banking, and other markets generally express financial contracts in terms of simple rates. So if you talk with a banker, broker, mortgage lender, auto finance company, or student loan officer about rates, the simple rate is the one he or she will normally quote you. However, to be meaningful, the simple rate quotation also must include the number of compounding periods per year. For example, a bank might offer 6.5 percent, compounded annually, on CDs, or a mutual fund might offer 6 percent, compounded monthly, on its money market account.

    Simple rates can be compared with one another, *but only if the instruments being compared use the same number of compounding periods per year.* Thus, to compare a 6.5 percent annual payment CD with a six percent monthly payment money market fund, we would need to put both instruments on an effective annual rate (EAR) basis.

    Note also that the simple rate never is shown on a time line, and it is never used as an input in a financial calculator unless compounding occurs only once a year (in which case $i_{SIMPLE} = periodic\ rate = EAR$). If more frequent compounding occurs, you must use either the periodic rate or the effective annual rate as discussed below.[18]

PERIODIC RATE
The rate charged by a lender or paid by a borrower each interest period (e.g., monthly, quarterly, annually, and so on).

2. **Periodic rate.** This is the rate charged by a lender or paid by a borrower *each interest period.* It can be a rate per year, per six-month period, per quarter, per month, per day, or per any other time interval (usually one year or less). For example, a bank might charge 1 percent per month on its credit card loans, or a finance company might charge 3 percent per quarter on consumer loans. We find the periodic rate as follows:

> **6–10**
>
> $$\text{Periodic rate} = \frac{i_{SIMPLE}}{m}$$

---

[18]Some calculators have a switch that permits you to specify the number of payments per year. We find it less confusing to set this switch to 1 and then leave it there. We prefer to work with *periods* when more than one payment occurs each year because this maintains a consistency between number of periods and the periodic interest rate.

which implies that

6–11	
	i_{SIMPLE} = (Periodic rate) × (m) = APR

ANNUAL PERCENTAGE RATE, APR
The rate reported to borrowers—it is the periodic rate times the number of periods in the year; thus, interest compounding is not considered.

Here i_{SIMPLE} is the simple annual rate and m is the number of compounding periods per year. APR, which is the **annual percentage rate,** represents the periodic rate stated on an annual basis without considering interest compounding; it is i_{SIMPLE}. *The APR never is used in actual calculations; it is simply reported to borrowers.*

If there is one payment per year, or if interest is added only once a year, then m = 1 and the periodic rate is equal to the simple rate. *But, in all cases where interest is added or payments are made more frequently than annually, the periodic rate is less than the simple rate.*

The periodic rate is used for calculations in problems where two conditions hold: (a) payments occur on a regular basis more frequently than once a year, and (b) a payment is made on each compounding (or discounting) date. Thus, if you are dealing with an auto loan that requires monthly payments, with a semiannual payment bond, or with an education loan that calls for quarterly payments, then on your cash flow time line and in your calculations you would use the Periodic rate = i_{SIMPLE} ÷ m, and the appropriate number of periods would be n × m.

EFFECTIVE ANNUAL RATE, EAR
The annual rate earned or paid considering interest compounding during the year (i.e., the annual rate that equates to a given periodic rate compounded for m periods during the year).

3. **Effective annual rate, EAR.** This is the rate with which, under annual compounding (m = 1), we would obtain the same result as if we had used a given periodic rate with m compounding periods per year. As stated earlier, the EAR is found as follows:

6–8	
	$$EAR = \left(1 + \frac{i_{SIMPLE}}{m}\right)^m - 1.0$$ $$= (1 + \text{Periodic rate})^m - 1$$

To illustrate further, suppose you could borrow using either a credit card that charges 1 percent per month or a bank loan with a 12 percent quoted simple interest rate that is compounded quarterly. Which should you choose? To answer this question, the cost of each alternative must be expressed as an EAR:

$$\text{Credit card loan: EAR} = (1 + 0.01)^{12} - 1.0$$
$$= (1.01)^{12} - 1.0$$
$$= 1.126825 - 1.0$$
$$= 0.126825 = 12.6825\%.$$
$$\text{Bank loan: EAR} = (1 + 0.03)^4 - 1.0$$
$$= (1.03)^4 - 1.0$$

$$= 1.125509 - 1.0$$

$$= 0.125509 = 12.5509\%.$$

Thus, the credit card loan costs a little more than the bank loan. This result should have been intuitive to you—both loans have the same 12 percent simple rate, yet you would have to make monthly payments on the credit card versus quarterly payments under the bank loan.

Self-Test Questions

Define the *simple (or quoted) rate*, the *periodic rate*, and the *effective annual rate*.

How are the simple rate, the periodic rate, and the effective annual rate related? Can you think of a situation where all three of these rates will be the same?

Summary

Financial decisions often involve situations in which someone pays money at one point in time and receives money at some other time. Dollars that are paid or received at two different points in time are different, and this difference is recognized and accounted for by time value of money (TVM) analysis. We next summarize the types of TVM analysis and the key concepts covered in this chapter, using the data shown in Figure 6–3 to illustrate the various points. Refer to the figure constantly, and try to find in it an example of the points covered as you go through this summary.

- **Compounding** is the process of determining the **future value (FV)** of a cash flow or a series of cash flows. The compounded amount, or future value, is equal to the beginning amount plus the interest earned.

    Future value (single payment): $FV_n = PV(1 + i)^n = PV(FVIF_{i,n})$

    Example: $924.56 compounded for two years at 4 percent:

    $$FV_2 = \$924.56(1.04)^2 = \$1,000$$

- **Discounting** is the process of finding the **present value (PV)** of a future cash flow or a series of cash flows; discounting is the reciprocal (inverse) of compounding.

FIGURE 6–3	Illustration for Chapter Summary

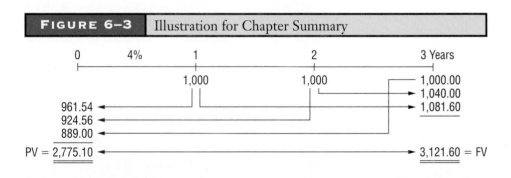

Present value (single payment): $PV = \dfrac{FV_n}{(1 + i)^n} = FV_n\left[\dfrac{1}{(1 + i)^n}\right] = FV_n(PVIF_{i,n})$

Example: $1,000 discounted back for two years at four percent:

$$PV = \dfrac{\$1,000}{(1.04)^2} = \$1,000\left[\dfrac{1}{(1.04)^2}\right] = \$1,000(0.9246) = \$924.60$$

- An **annuity** is defined as a series of equal periodic payments (PMT) for a specified number of periods.

  Future value of an annuity:
  $$FVA_n = PMT(1 + i)^0 + PMT(1 + i)^1 + \ldots + PMT(1 + i)^{n-1}$$

  $$= PMT\sum_{t=1}^{n}(1 + i)^{n-t} = PMT\left[\dfrac{(1 + i)^n - 1}{i}\right] = PMT(FVIFA_{i,n})$$

  Example: FVA of three payments of $1,000 when $i = 4\%$:

  $$FVA_3 = \$1,000(3.1216) = \$3,121.60$$

  Present value of an annuity:
  $$PVA_n = \dfrac{PMT}{(1 + i)^1} + \dfrac{PMT}{(1 + i)^2} + \ldots + \dfrac{PMT}{(1 + i)^n}$$

  $$= PMT\sum_{t=1}^{n}\left[\dfrac{1}{(1 + i)^t}\right] = PMT\left[\dfrac{1 - \frac{1}{(1 + i)^n}}{i}\right] = PMT(PVIFA_{i,n})$$

  Example: PVA of three payments of $1,000 when $i = 4\%$:

  $$PVA_3 = \$1,000(2.7751) = \$2,775.10$$

- An annuity whose payments occur at the end of each period is called an **ordinary annuity.** The preceding formulas are for ordinary annuities.
- If each payment occurs at the beginning of the period rather than at the end, then we have an **annuity due.** In Figure 6–3, the payments would be shown at Years 0, 1, and 2 rather than at Years 1, 2, and 3. The PV of each payment would be larger because each payment would be discounted back one year less; hence, the PV of the annuity would also be larger.

  Similarly, the FV of the annuity due would also be larger because each payment would be compounded for an extra year. The following formulas can be used to convert the PV and FV of an ordinary annuity to an annuity due:

  $$PVA(DUE)_n = PMT\,[(PVIFA_{i,n}) \times (1 + i)] = PMT\,[PVIFA(DUE)_{i,n}]$$

  Example: PVA of three beginning-of-year payments of $1,000 when $i = 4\%$:

  $$PVA(DUE)_3 = \$1,000\,[(2.7751)(1.04)] = \$2,886.10$$

  $$FVA(DUE)_n = PMT\,[(FVIFA_{i,n}) \times (1 + i)] = PMT\,[FVIFA(DUE)_{i,n}]$$

Example: FVA of three beginning-of-year payments of $1,000 when i = 4%:

$$\text{FVA(DUE)}_3 = \$1,000[(3.1216)(1.04)] = \$3,246.46$$

- If the cash flow time line in Figure 6–3 was extended out forever so that the $1,000 payments went on forever, we would have a **perpetuity** whose value could be found as follows:

$$\text{Value of a perpetuity} = \text{PVP} = \frac{\text{PMT}}{i} = \frac{\$1,000}{0.04} = \$25,000$$

- If the cash flows in Figure 6–3 were unequal, we could not use the annuity formulas. To find the PV or FV of an **uneven cash flow series,** find the PV or FV of each individual cash flow and then sum them. However, if some of the cash flows constitute an annuity, then the annuity formula can be used to calculate the present value of that part of the cash flow stream.
- **Financial calculators** have built-in programs that perform all the operations discussed in this chapter. It would be useful for you to buy such a calculator and to learn how to use it. Even if you do, though, it is essential that you understand the logical processes involved.
- Thus far in the summary we have assumed that payments are made and interest is earned at the end of each year, or annually. However, many contracts call for more frequent payments. For example, mortgages and auto loans call for monthly payments, and most bonds pay interest semiannually. Similarly, most banks compute interest daily. When compounding occurs more frequently than once a year, this fact must be recognized. We can use the Figure 6–3 example to illustrate the procedures. First, the following formula is used to find an **effective annual rate (EAR):**

$$\text{Effective annual rate} = \text{EAR} = \left(1 + \frac{i_{\text{SIMPLE}}}{m}\right)^m - 1.0$$

For semiannual compounding, the effective annual rate is 4.04 percent:

$$\left(1 + \frac{0.04}{2}\right)^2 - 1.0 = (1.02)^2 - 1.0 = 1.0404 - 1.0 = 0.0404 = 4.04\%.$$

This rate could then be used (with a calculator but not with the tables) to find the PV or FV of each payment in Figure 6–3.

If the $1,000 per-year payments were actually payable as $500 each six months, you would simply redraw Figure 6–3 to show 6 payments of $500 each, but you would also need to use a periodic interest rate of 4% ÷ 2 = 2% for determining the PV or FV of the payments.

- The general equation for finding the future value of a single payment for any number of compounding periods per year is

$$\text{FV}_n = \text{PV}\left(1 + \frac{i_{\text{SIMPLE}}}{m}\right)^{n \times m}$$

where

i_{SIMPLE} = Quoted interest rate.

m = Number of compounding periods per year.

n = Number of years.

■ An **amortized loan** is one that is paid off in equal payments over a specified period. An **amortization schedule** shows how much of each payment constitutes interest, how much is used to repay the debt, and the remaining balance of the loan at each point in time.

The concepts covered in this chapter will be used throughout the remainder of the book. For example, in Chapter 7 we will apply present value concepts to determine the values of stocks and bonds, and we will see that the market prices of securities are established by determining the present values of the cash flows they are expected to provide. In later chapters, the same basic concepts are applied to corporate decisions involving both expenditures on capital assets and determining the types of capital that should be used to pay for such assets.

Questions

6–1 What is an *opportunity cost rate?* How is this rate used in time value analysis, and where is it shown on a cash flow time line? Is the opportunity rate a single number that is used in all situations?

6–2 An *annuity* is defined as a series of payments of a fixed amount for a specific number of periods. Thus, $100 a year for ten years is an annuity, but $100 in Year 1, $200 in Year 2, and $400 in Years 3 through ten does *not* constitute an annuity. However, the second series *contains* an annuity. Is this statement true or false?

6–3 If a firm's earnings per share grew from $1 to $2 over a ten-year period, the total *growth* would be 100 percent, but the *annual growth rate* would be *less than* ten percent. True or false? Explain. Under what conditions would the annual growth rate *actually* be ten percent per year?

6–4 Would you rather have a savings account that pays five percent interest compounded semiannually or one that pays five percent interest compounded daily? Explain.

6–5 To find the present value of an uneven series of cash flows, you must find the PVs of the individual cash flows and then sum them. Annuity procedures can never be of use, even if some of the cash flows constitute an annuity (for example, $100 each for Years 3, 4, 5, and 6), because the entire series is not an annuity. Is this statement true or false? Explain.

6–6 The present value of a perpetuity is equal to the payment on the annuity, PMT, divided by the interest rate, i: $PVP = PMT/i$. What is the *sum*, or *future value*, of a perpetuity of PMT dollars per year? (*Hint:* The answer is infinity, but explain why.)

Self-Test Problems

(Solutions Appear in Appendix B)

key terms **ST–1** Define each of the following terms:
   a. PV; i; INT; FV_n; n; PVA_n; FVA_n; PMT; m; i_{SIMPLE}
   b. $FVIF_{i,n}$; $PVIF_{i,n}$; $FVIFA_{i,n}$; $PVIFA_{i,n}$; $FVIFA(DUE)_{i,n}$; $PVIFA(DUE)_{i,n}$
   c. Opportunity cost rate
   d. Annuity; lump-sum payment; cash flow; uneven cash flow stream
   e. Ordinary (deferred) annuity; annuity due
   f. Perpetuity; consol
   g. Outflow; inflow; cash flow time line

h. Compounding; discounting
i. Annual, semiannual, quarterly, monthly, and daily compounding
j. Effective annual rate (EAR); simple (quoted) interest rate; APR; periodic rate
k. Amortization schedule; principal component versus interest component of a payment; amortized loan
l. Terminal value

rates of return **ST–2** In the introduction to this chapter we asked whether you would prefer to invest $5,500 today and receive either $7,020 in five years or $8,126 in eight years. You should now be able to determine which investment alternative is better.

a. Based only on the return you would earn from each investment, which is better?
b. Can you think of any factors other than the expected return that might be important to consider when choosing between the two investment alternatives?

future value **ST–3** Assume that it is now January 1, 2000. On January 1, 2001, you will deposit $1,000 into a savings account that pays eight percent.

a. If the bank compounds interest annually, how much will you have in your account on January 1, 2004?
b. What would your January 1, 2004, balance be if the bank used quarterly compounding rather than annual compounding?
c. Suppose you deposited the $1,000 in four payments of $250 each on January 1 of 2001, 2002, 2003, and 2004. How much would you have in your account on January 1, 2004, based on eight percent annual compounding?
d. Suppose you deposited four equal payments in your account on January 1 of 2001, 2002, 2003, and 2004. Assuming an eight percent interest rate, how large would each of your payments have to be for you to obtain the same ending balance as you calculated in part a?

time value of money **ST–4** Assume that it is now January 1, 2000, and you will need $1,000 on January 1, 2004. Your bank compounds interest at an eight percent annual rate.

a. How much must you deposit on January 1, 2001, to have a balance of $1,000 on January 1, 2004?
b. If you want to make equal payments on each January 1 from 2001 through 2004 to accumulate the $1,000, how large must each of the four payments be?
c. If your father were to offer either to make the payments calculated in part b ($221.92) or to give you a lump sum of $750 on January 1, 2001, which would you choose?
d. If you have only $750 on January 1, 2001, what interest rate, compounded annually, would you have to earn to have the necessary $1,000 on January 1, 2004?
e. Suppose you can deposit only $186.29 each January 1 from 2001 through 2004, but you still need $1,000 on January 1, 2004. What interest rate, with annual compounding, must you seek out to achieve your goal?
f. To help you reach your $1,000 goal, your father offers to give you $400 on January 1, 2001. You will get a part-time job and make six additional payments of equal amounts each six months thereafter. If all of this money is deposited in a bank that pays eight percent, compounded semiannually, how large must each of the six payments be?
g. What is the effective annual rate being paid by the bank in part f?

effective annual rates **ST–5** Bank A pays eight percent interest, compounded quarterly, on its money market account. The managers of Bank B want the rate on its money market account to equal Bank A's effective annual rate, but interest is to be compounded on a monthly basis. What simple, or quoted, rate must Bank B set?

Problems

present and future values for different periods **6–1** Find the following values, *using the numerical solution approach*, and then work the problems using a financial calculator or the tables to check your answers. Disregard rounding errors. (*Hint:* If you are using a financial calculator, you can enter the known values and then press the appropriate key to find the unknown variable. Then, without clearing the TVM register, you can "override" the variable that changes by simply entering a new value for it and then pressing the key for the unknown variable to obtain the second answer. This procedure can be used in parts b and d, and in many other situations, to see how changes in input variables affect the output variable.)
  a. An initial $500 compounded for one year at six percent.
  b. An initial $500 compounded for two years at six percent.
  c. The present value of $500 due in one year at a discount rate of six percent.
  d. The present value of $500 due in two years at a discount rate of six percent.

present and future values for different interest rates **6–2** Use the tables or a financial calculator to find the following values. See the hint for Problem 6–1.
  a. An initial $500 compounded for ten years at six percent.
  b. An initial $500 compounded for ten years at 12 percent.
  c. The present value of $500 due in ten years at a six percent discount rate.
  d. The present value of $1,552.90 due in ten years at (1) a 12 percent discount rate and (2) a six percent rate. Give a verbal definition of the term *present value*, and illustrate it using a cash flow time line with data from this problem. As a part of your answer, explain why present values are dependent on interest rates.

time for a lump sum to double **6–3** To the closest year, how long will it take $200 to double if it is deposited and earns the following rates? (*Notes:* See the hint for Problem 6–1. You can also look up FVIF = 400/200 = 2.0 in the tables for parts a, b, and c, but figure out part d.)
  a. 7 percent.
  b. 10 percent.
  c. 18 percent.
  d. 100 percent.

future value of an annuity **6–4** Find the *future value* of the following annuities. The first payment in these annuities is made at the end of Year 1; that is, they are *ordinary annuities*. (*Note:* See the hint to Problem 6–1. Also, note that you can leave values in the TVM register, switch to "BEG," press FV, and find the FV of the *annuity due*.)
  a. $400 per year for ten years at ten percent.
  b. $200 per year for five years at five percent.
  c. $400 per year for five years at zero percent.
  d. Now rework parts a, b, and c assuming that payments are made at the beginning of each year; that is, they are *annuities due*.

present value of an annuity **6–5** Find the present value of the following ordinary annuities (see note to Problem 6–4):
  a. $400 per year for ten years at ten percent.
  b. $200 per year for five years at five percent.

c. $400 per year for five years at zero percent.

d. Now rework parts a, b, and c assuming that payments are made at the beginning of each year; that is, they are *annuities due.*

uneven cash flow stream   **6–6** Find the *present values* of the following cash flow streams under the following conditions:

YEAR	CASH STREAM A	CASH STREAM B
1	$100	$300
2	400	400
3	400	400
4	400	400
5	300	100

a. The appropriate interest rate is eight percent. (*Hint:* It is fairly easy to work this problem dealing with the individual cash flows. However, if you have a financial calculator, read the section of the manual that describes how to enter cash flows such as the ones in this problem. This will take a little time, but the investment will pay huge dividends throughout the course. Note, if you do work with the cash flow register, then you must enter $CF_0 = 0$. See Appendix 6A for an example.)

b. What is the value of each cash flow stream at a zero percent interest rate?

effective rate of interest   **6–7** Find the interest rates, or rates of return, on each of the following:

a. You *borrow* $700 and promise to pay back $749 at the end of one year.

b. You *lend* $700 and receive a promise to be paid $749 at the end of one year.

c. You borrow $85,000 and promise to pay back $201,229 at the end of ten years.

d. You borrow $9,000 and promise to make payments of $2,684.80 per year for five years.

future value of various compounding periods   **6–8** Find the amount to which $500 will grow under each of the following conditions:

a. 12 percent compounded annually for five years.

b. 12 percent compounded semiannually for five years.

c. 12 percent compounded quarterly for five years.

d. 12 percent compounded monthly for five years.

present value of various compounding periods   **6–9** Find the present value of $500 due in the future under each of the following conditions:

a. 12 percent simple rate, compounded annually, discounted back five years.

b. 12 percent simple rate, semiannual compounding, discounted back five years.

c. 12 percent simple rate, quarterly compounding, discounted back five years.

d. 12 percent simple rate, monthly compounding, discounted back one year.

FV of an annuity for various compounding periods   **6–10** Find the future values of the following ordinary annuities:

a. FV of $400 each six months for five years at a simple rate of 12 percent, compounded semiannually.

b. FV of $200 each three months for five years at a simple rate of 12 percent, compounded quarterly.

c. The annuities described in parts a and b have the same amount of money paid into them during the five-year period and both earn interest at the same simple rate, yet the annuity in part b earns $101.76 more than the one in part a over the five years. Why does this occur?

effective versus nominal interest rates

6–11 The First City Bank pays seven percent interest, compounded annually, on time deposits. The Second City Bank pays 6.5 percent interest, compounded quarterly.

a. Based on effective interest rates, in which bank would you prefer to deposit your money?

b. Could your choice of banks be influenced by the fact that you might want to withdraw your funds during the year as opposed to at the end of the year? In answering this question, assume that funds must be left on deposit during the entire compounding period in order for you to receive any interest.

amortization schedule

6–12 Lorkay Seidens Inc. just borrowed $25,000. The loan is to be repaid in equal installments at the end of each of the next five years, and the interest rate is ten percent.

a. Set up an amortization schedule for the loan.

b. How large must each annual payment be if the loan is for $50,000? Assume that the interest rate remains at ten percent and that the loan is paid off over five years.

c. How large must each payment be if the loan is for $50,000, the interest rate is ten percent, and the loan is paid off in equal installments at the end of each of the next ten years? This loan is for the same amount as the loan in part b, but the payments are spread out over twice as many periods. Why are these payments not half as large as the payments on the loan in part b?

effective rates of return

6–13 Assume that AT&T's pension fund managers are considering two alternative securities as investments: (1) Security Z (for zero intermediate year cash flows), which costs $422.41 today, pays nothing during its ten-year life, and then pays $1,000 after ten years or (2) Security B, which has a cost today of $500 and which pays $74.50 at the end of each of the next ten years.

a. What is the rate of return on each security?

b. Assume that the interest rate AT&T's pension fund managers can earn on the fund's money falls to six percent immediately after the securities are purchased and is expected to remain at that level for the next ten years. What would the price of each security change to, what would the fund's profit be on each security, and what would be the percentage profit (profit divided by cost) for each security?

c. Assuming that the cash flows for each security had to be reinvested at the new 6 percent market interest rate, (1) what would be the value attributable to each security at the end of ten years and (2) what "actual, after-the-fact" rate of return would the fund have earned on each security? (*Hint:* The "actual" rate of return is found as the interest rate that causes the PV of the compounded Year 10 amount to equal the original cost of the security.)

d. Now assume all the facts as given in parts b and c except assume that the interest rate rose to 12 percent rather than fell to six percent. What would happen to the profit figures as developed in part b and to the "actual" rates of return as determined in part c? Explain your results.

required annuity payments

6–14 A father is planning a savings program to put his daughter through college. His daughter is now 13 years old. She plans to enroll at the university in five years, and it should take her four years to complete her education. Currently, the cost per year (for everything—food, clothing, tuition, books, transportation, and so forth) is $12,500, but a five percent inflation rate in these costs is forecasted. The daughter recently received $7,500 from her grandfather's estate; this money, which is invested in a mutual fund paying eight percent interest compounded annually, will be used to help meet the costs of the daughter's education. The rest of the costs will be met by money the father will deposit in the savings account. He will make six equal deposits to the account in each year from now until his daughter starts college. These deposits will begin today and will also earn eight percent interest.

a. What will be the present value of the cost of four years of education *at the time the daughter becomes 18?* [*Hint:* Calculate the cost (at 5% inflation, or growth) for each year of her education, discount three of these costs back (at 8%) to the year in which she turns 18, then sum the four costs, including the beginning cost.]

b. What will be the value of the $7,500 that the daughter received from her grandfather's estate *when she starts college at age 18?* (*Hint:* Compound for five years at 8%.)

c. If the father is planning to make the first of six deposits today, how large must each deposit be for him to be able to put his daughter through college?

future value of a retirement fund   **6–15** As soon as she graduated from college, Kay began planning for her retirement. Her plans were to deposit $500 semiannually into an IRA (a retirement fund) beginning six months after graduation and continuing until the day she retired, which she expected to be 30 years later. Today is the day Kay retires (happy retirement). She just made the last $500 deposit into her retirement fund, and now she wants to know how much she has accumulated for her retirement. The fund earned ten percent compounded semiannually since it was established.

a. Compute the balance of the retirement fund assuming all the payments were made on time.

b. Although Kay was able to make all the $500 deposits she planned, ten years ago she had to withdraw $10,000 from the fund to pay some medical bills incurred by her mother. Compute the balance in the retirement fund based on this information.

automobile loan comparison   **6–16** Sarah is on her way to the local Chevrolet dealership to buy a Cavalier. The list, or "sticker," price of the car is $13,000. Sarah has $3,000 in her checking account that she can use as a down payment toward the purchase of a new car. Sarah has carefully evaluated her finances, and she has determined she can afford payments which *total* $2,400 per year on a loan to purchase the car. Sarah can borrow the money to purchase the car either through the dealer's "special financing package," which is advertised as 4.0% financing, or from a local bank, which has automobile loans at 12% interest. Each loan would be outstanding for a period of five years, and the payments would be made quarterly (every three months). Sarah knows the dealer's "special financing package" requires that she will have to pay the "sticker" price for the car. But if she uses the bank financing, she thinks she can negotiate with the dealer for a better price. Assume Sarah wants to pay $600 per payment, regardless of which loan she chooses, and the remainder of the purchase price will be a down payment that can be satisfied with any of the $3,000 in Sarah's checking account. Ignoring charges for taxes, tag, and title transfer, how much of a reduction in the "sticker price" must Sarah negotiate in order to make the bank financing more attractive than the dealer's "special financing package"?

required annuity payments   **6–17** Janet just graduated from a women's college in Mississippi with a degree in business administration, and she is about to start a new job with a large financial services firm based in Tampa, Florida. From reading various business publications while she was in college, Janet has concluded it probably is a good idea to begin planning for her retirement now. Even though she is only 22 years old and just beginning her career, Janet is concerned that social security will not be able to meet her needs when she retires. Fortunately for Janet, the company that hired her has created a good retirement/investment plan that permits her to make contributions every year. So Janet is now evaluating the amount she needs to contribute to satisfy her financial requirements at retirement. She has decided that she would like to take a trip as soon as her retirement begins (a reward to herself for many years of excellent work). The estimated cost of the trip, including all expenses such as meals and souvenirs, will be $120,000, and it will last for one year (no other funds will be needed during the first year of retirement). After she returns from her trip, Janet plans to settle down to enjoy her retirement. She estimates she will need $70,000 each year to be able to live comfortably and enjoy her "twilight years." The retirement/investment plan available to employees where Janet is going to work pays seven percent interest compounded annually, and it is expected this rate will continue as long as the company offers the opportunity to contribute to the fund. When she retires, Janet will have to move her retirement "nest egg" to another investment so she can withdraw money when she needs it. Her plans are to move the money to a fund that allows withdrawals at the beginning of each year; the fund is expected to pay five percent interest compounded annually. Janet expects to retire in 40 years, and, after looking at the life insurance actuarial tables, she has decided she will live another 20 years after she returns from her "retirement trip" around the world. If Janet's expectations are correct, how much must she contribute to the retirement fund to satisfy her retirement plans if she plans to make her first contribution to the fund one year from today, and the last contribution will be made on the day she retires?

Exam-Type Problems

The problems in this section are set up in such a way that they could be used as multiple-choice exam problems.

present value comparisons | **6–18** Which amount is worth more at 14 percent: $1,000 in hand today or $2,000 due in six years?

growth rates | **6–19** Martell Corporation's 2000 sales were $12 million. Sales were $6 million five years earlier (in 1995).
   a. To the nearest percentage point, at what rate have sales grown?
   b. Suppose someone calculated the sales growth for Martell Corporation in part a as follows: "Sales doubled in five years. This represents a growth of 100 percent in five years, so, dividing 100 percent by five, we find the growth rate to be 20 percent per year." Explain what is wrong with this calculation.

effective rate of return | **6–20** Krystal Magee invested $150,000 18 months ago. Currently, the investment is worth $168,925. Krystal knows the investment has paid interest *every three months (i.e., quarterly)*, but she doesn't know what the yield on her investment is. Help Krystal. Compute both the annual percentage rate (APR) *and* the effective annual rate of interest.

effective rate of interest | **6–21** Your broker offers to sell you a note for $13,250 that will pay $2,345.05 per year for ten years. If you buy the note, what rate of interest (to the closest percent) will you be earning?

effective rate of interest | **6–22** A mortgage company offers to lend you $85,000; the loan calls for payments of $8,273.59 per year for 30 years. What interest rate is the mortgage company charging you?

<table>
<tr><td align="right">required lump-sum
payment</td><td>**6–23**</td><td>To complete your last year in business school and then go through law school, you will need $10,000 per year for four years, starting next year (that is, you will need to withdraw the first $10,000 one year from today). Your rich uncle offers to put you through school, and he will deposit in a bank paying seven percent interest a sum of money that is sufficient to provide the four payments of $10,000 each. His deposit will be made today.
a. How large must the deposit be?
b. How much will be in the account immediately after you make the first withdrawal? After the last withdrawal?</td></tr>
<tr><td align="right">repaying a loan</td><td>**6–24**</td><td>Sue wants to buy a car that costs $12,000. She has arranged to borrow the total purchase price of the car from her credit union at a simple interest rate equal to 12 percent. The loan requires quarterly payments for a period of three years. If the first payment is due in three months (one quarter) after purchasing the car, what will be the amount of Sue's quarterly payments on the loan?</td></tr>
<tr><td align="right">repaying a loan</td><td>**6–25**</td><td>While Steve Bouchard was a student at the University of Florida, he borrowed $12,000 in student loans at an annual interest rate of nine percent. If Steve repays $1,500 per year, how long, to the nearest year, will it take him to repay the loan?</td></tr>
<tr><td align="right">reaching a financial goal</td><td>**6–26**</td><td>You need to accumulate $10,000. To do so, you plan to make deposits of $1,750 per year, with the first payment being made a year from today, in a bank account that pays six percent annual interest. Your last deposit will be more than $1,750 if more is needed to round out to $10,000. How many years will it take you to reach your $10,000 goal, and how large will the last deposit be?</td></tr>
<tr><td align="right">present value of a
perpetuity</td><td>**6–27**</td><td>What is the present value of a perpetuity of $100 per year if the appropriate discount rate is seven percent? If interest rates in general were to double and the appropriate discount rate rose to 14 percent, what would happen to the present value of the perpetuity?</td></tr>
<tr><td align="right">loan amortization</td><td>**6–28**</td><td>Assume that your aunt sold her house on January 1 and that she took a mortgage in the amount of $10,000 as part of the payment. The mortgage has a quoted (or simple) interest rate of ten percent, but it calls for payments every six months, beginning on June 30, and the mortgage is to be amortized over ten years. Now, one year later, your aunt must file a Form 1099 with the IRS and with the person who bought the house, informing them of the interest that was included in the two payments made during the year. (This interest will be income to your aunt and a deduction to the buyer of the house.) To the closest dollar, what is the total amount of interest that was paid during the first year?</td></tr>
<tr><td align="right">annuity withdrawals—
ordinary annuity versus
annuity due</td><td>**6–29**</td><td>Jason worked various jobs during his teenage years to save money for college. Now it is his 20th birthday, and he is about to begin his college studies at the University of South Florida. A few months ago, Jason received a scholarship that will cover all of his college tuition for a period not to exceed five years. The money he has saved will be used for living expenses while he is in college; in fact, Jason expects to use all of his savings while attending USF. The jobs he worked as a teenager allowed him to save a total of $10,000, which currently is invested at 12 percent in a financial asset that pays interest monthly. Because Jason will be a full-time student, he expects to graduate four years from today, on his 24th birthday.
a. How much can Jason withdraw every month while he is in college if the first withdrawal occurs today?
b. How much can Jason withdraw every month while he is in college if he waits until the end of this month to make the first withdrawal?</td></tr>
</table>

simple rate of return **6-30** Sue Sharpe, manager of Oaks Mall Jewelry, wants to sell on credit, giving customers three months in which to pay. However, Sue will have to borrow from her bank to carry the accounts payable. The bank will charge a simple 15 percent, but with monthly compounding. Sue wants to quote a simple rate to her customers (all of whom are expected to pay on time) that will exactly cover her financing costs. What simple annual rate should she quote to her credit customers?

Integrative Problem

time value of money analysis **6-31** Assume that you are nearing graduation and that you have applied for a job with a local bank. As part of the bank's evaluation process, you have been asked to take an examination that covers several financial analysis techniques. The first section of the test addresses time value of money analysis. See how you would do by answering the following questions:

a. Draw cash flow time lines for
   (1) a $100 lump-sum cash flow at the end of Year 2.
   (2) an ordinary annuity of $100 per year for three years.
   (3) an uneven cash flow stream of −$50, $100, $75, and $50 at the end of Years 0 through 3.
b. (1) What is the future value of an initial $100 after three years if it is invested in an account paying ten percent annual interest?
   (2) What is the present value of $100 to be received in three years if the appropriate interest rate is ten percent?
c. We sometimes need to find how long it will take a sum of money (or anything else) to grow to some specified amount. For example, if a company's sales are growing at a rate of 20 percent per year, approximately how long will it take sales to triple?
d. What is the difference between an ordinary annuity and an annuity due? What type of annuity is shown in the following cash flow time line? How would you change it to the other type of annuity?

e. (1) What is the future value of a three-year ordinary annuity of $100 if the appropriate interest rate is ten percent?
   (2) What is the present value of the annuity?
   (3) What would the future and present values be if the annuity were an annuity due?
f. What is the present value of the following uneven cash flow stream? The appropriate interest rate is ten percent, compounded annually.

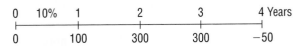

g. What annual interest rate will cause $100 to grow to $125.97 in three years?
h. (1) Will the future value be larger or smaller if we compound an initial amount more often than annually, for example, every six months, or *semiannually*, holding the stated interest rate constant? Why?

(2) Define (i) the stated, or quoted, or simple, rate, (ii) the periodic rate, and (iii) the effective annual rate (EAR).

(3) What is the effective annual rate for a simple rate of ten percent, compounded semiannually? Compounded quarterly? Compounded daily?

(4) What is the future value of $100 after three years under ten percent semiannual compounding? Quarterly compounding?

i. Will the effective annual rate ever be equal to the simple (quoted) rate? Explain.

j. (1) What is the value at the end of Year 3 of the following cash flow stream if the quoted interest rate is ten percent, compounded semiannually?

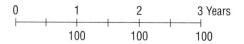

(2) What is the PV of the same stream?

(3) Is the stream an annuity?

(4) An important rule is that you should never show a simple rate on a time line or use it in calculations unless what condition holds? (*Hint:* Think of annual compounding, when $i_{SIMPLE} = EAR$.) What would be wrong with your answer to questions j (1) and j (2) if you used the simple rate 10% rather than the periodic rate $i_{SIMPLE} \div 2 = 10\% / 2 = 5\%$?

k. (1) Construct an amortization schedule for a $1,000, ten percent annual rate loan with three equal installments.

(2) What is the annual interest expense for the borrower, and the annual interest income for the lender, during Year 2?

(Parts l through o require a financial calculator.)

l. Suppose on January 1, 2000, you deposit $100 in an account that pays a simple, or quoted, interest rate of 11.33463 percent, with interest added (compounded) daily. How much will you have in your account on October 1, or after nine months?

m. Now suppose you leave your money in the bank for 21 months. Thus, on January 1, 2000, you deposit $100 in an account that pays a 12 percent effective annual interest rate. How much will be in your account on October 1, 2001?

n. Suppose someone offered to sell you a note calling for the payment of $1,000 15 months from today. They offer to sell it to you for $850. You have $850 in a bank time deposit (savings instrument) that pays a 6.76649 percent simple rate with daily compounding, which is a seven percent effective annual interest rate, and you plan to leave the money in the bank unless you buy the note. The note is not risky—you are sure it will be paid on schedule. Should you buy the note? Check the decision in three ways: By comparing

(1) your future value if you buy the note versus leaving your money in the bank.

(2) the PV of the note with your current bank investment.

(3) the EAR on the note versus that of the bank investment.

o. Suppose the note discussed in Part n had a cost of $850, but called for five quarterly payments of $190 each, with the first payment due in three months rather than $1,000 at the end of 15 months. Would it be a good investment for you?

Computer-Related Problem

Work the problem in this section only if you are using the computer problem diskette.

authorization schedule **6–32** Use the computerized model in the File C5 to solve this problem.

  a. Set up an amortization schedule for a $30,000 loan to be repaid in equal installments at the end of each of the next 20 years at an interest rate of ten percent. What is the annual payment?

  b. Set up an amortization schedule for a $60,000 loan to be repaid in 20 equal annual installments at an interest rate of ten percent. What is the annual payment?

  c. Set up an amortization schedule for a $60,000 loan to be repaid in 20 equal annual installments at an interest rate of 20 percent. What is the annual payment?

ONLINE ESSENTIALS

http://www.financialplayerscenter.com/teachme.html
Financial Player Center
Provides basic definitions and lessons relating to personal finance, including time value of money (TVM) concepts. There are also quizzes that test your knowledge about TVM concepts and calculators you can use to calculate the answers.

http://www.teachmefinance.com/   TeachMeFinance.com
Provides lessons on various subjects covered in this book. Some of the topics include time value of money, risk analysis and computations (covered in Chapter 5), stock and bond valuation (covered in the next chapter), and capital budgeting (covered in Chapters 8 and 9).

http://www.datachimp.com/   datachimp
The home page for datachimp has links to various tutorials and interactive simulations set up by the company that illustrate various finance topics. If you click on "How Finance Works" at the bottom of the home page, you will be taken to a page that provides a basic discussion of how time value of money works. A table of contents is provided on this page that allows you to visit pages that are devoted to specific topics such as future value, present value, annuities, and so on. Each page allows you to change the numerical illustration that is provided, and to see the results of your changes on a graph.

http://www.invest-faq.com/articles/analy-fut-prs-val.html
The Investment FAQ
Provides a very basic discussion of present and future value concepts along with some simple examples.

http://www.mcsba.com/   MCS Business Association
Provides pages with calculators to compute present value, future value, annuity payments, and so forth. To access these pages, go to the FINANCIAL CALCULATORS section on the home page and click on the calculation you want.

APPENDIX 6A

Computing the PV of an Uneven Cash Flow Stream Using a Financial Calculator

To compute the PV of an uneven cash flow stream using your financial calculator, you need to use the cash flow (CF) function. You should refer to the manual that came with your calculator. The steps for computing the PV of the following cash flow stream using the Texas Instruments BAII PLUS are shown here:

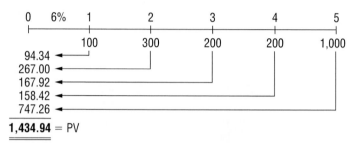

1. Enter the cash flow function by pressing the **CF** key; $CF_0 = 0$ should be displayed. Press one of the arrow keys, either **↑** or **↓**, to see if the registers are clear. If there are numbers in any of the registers, you can clear them by pressing the 2nd key, **2nd**, and then pressing **CE/C**, which has "CLR Work" written above (this is a secondary function).
2. Enter CF_0 as follows: 0 **ENTER**.
3. Enter CF_1 as follows: **↓** 100 **ENTER**. Press **↓** again, and you will see F01 = 1 displayed on the screen—the calculator is telling you that it has assumed the 100 cash flow will occur (its frequency) only once. For problems where the same cash flow occurs more than once in consecutive periods, you can enter the frequency of the CFs, and then press **ENTER** to change the F01 value (the frequency for consecutive CFs received later in a project's life can be similarly changed).
4. Enter the *remaining* CFs using one of the following approaches:

I. ENTER EACH CASH FLOW INDIVIDUALLY—DO NOT RECOGNIZE ANNUITIES	II. ENTER EQUAL CONSECUTIVE CASH FLOWS ONCE— RECOGNIZE ANNUITIES
CF_2: **↓** 300 **ENTER** **↓**	CF_2: **↓** 300 **ENTER** **↓**
CF_3: **↓** 200 **ENTER** **↓**	CF_3: **↓** 200 **ENTER** **↓** 2 **ENTER**
CF_4: **↓** 200 **ENTER** **↓**	CF_4: **↓** 1,000 **ENTER**
CF_5: **↓** 1,000 **ENTER**	

5. Once all the CFs have been entered, press **NPV**. I = 0 will appear on the display. Enter 6 and press **ENTER** **↓** **CPT** to get the answer: NPV = 1,434.9393.
6. Before you exit the cash flow register, you should clear your work; otherwise, the values you entered for the CFs will remain in the registers until they either are cleared or another value is input into the same CF location (register). To clear your work, press **2nd** **CE/C**.

APPENDIX 6B

Generating an Amortization Schedule
for a Loan Using a Financial Calculator

The following steps show you how to generate an amortization schedule using a Texas Instruments BAII PLUS. For more information or if you have a different type of calculator, refer to the manual that came with your calculator. To illustrate the process of generating an amortization schedule, let's use the example given in the chapter: A firm borrows $15,000 at eight percent, and the loan is to be repaid in three equal payments at the end of each of the next three years. In the chapter, we computed the annual payment necessary to repay the loan to be $5,820.50.

1. Enter the information for the amortized loan into the TVM registers as was described in the chapter—that is, input I/Y = 8, PV = 15000, N = 3—and press **CPT PMT**. PMT = −5,820.502711 should be displayed.
2. Enter the amortization function by pressing **2nd PV**, which has "Amort" written above (a secondary function). P1 = 1 is displayed, which indicates the starting point for the amortization schedule is the first period. Press **↓**, and P2 = 1 is displayed, which indicates the ending point for the first set of computations is the first period.
3. a. Press **↓**, and BAL = 10,379.49729 is displayed. This indicates that the remaining principal balance at the end of the first year is $10,379.50.
   b. Press **↓**, and PRN = −4,620.502711 is displayed. This indicates that the amount of principal repaid in the first period is $4,620.50.
   c. Press **↓**, and INT = −1,200 is displayed. This indicates that the amount of interest paid in the first period (year) is $1,200.
4. Press **↓ CPT**, and P1 = 2 is displayed; then press **↓**, and P2 = 2 is displayed. This information indicates that the next series of computations relate to the second payment. Follow the procedures given in Step 3:
   a. Press **↓**; display shows BAL = 5,389.354362
   b. Press **↓**; display shows PRN = −4,990.142928
   c. Press **↓**; display shows INT = −830.3597831
   These values represent the ending loan balance, the amount of principal repaid, and the amount of interest paid, respectively, for the second year.
5. Press **↓ CPT**, and P1 = 3 is displayed; then press **↓**, and P2 = 3 is displayed. This information indicates that the next series of computations relate to the third payment. Follow the procedures given in Step 3:
   a. Press **↓**; display shows BAL = −0.000000
   b. Press **↓**; display shows PRN = −5,389.354362
   c. Press **↓**; display shows INT = −431.1483489
   These values represent the ending loan balance, the amount of principal repaid, and the amount of interest paid, respectively, for the third, and final, year.

If you combine the results from Steps 3 through 5 in a table, you would find that it contains the same values given in Table 5–2. If you use a calculator to construct a complete amortization schedule, you must repeat Step 3 for each year the loan exists—that is, Step 3 must be repeated ten times for a ten-year loan. However, if you would like to know either the balance, principal repayment, or interest paid in a particular year, you need only set P1 and P2 equal to that year to display the desired values.

CHAPTER 7

Valuation Concepts

A MANAGERIAL PERSPECTIVE

On January 3, 1994, Treasury notes were selling at prices that promised investors an average return of about 5.5 percent if they were held until the year 2001. Therefore, a seven-year Treasury note with a face, or par, value equal to $10,000 that paid $275 in interest every six months had a market value equal to $10,000 on January 3, 1994. By January 3, 1995, the value of the same Treasury note was approximately $8,910. So, if you had purchased the note one year earlier, at least on paper, you would have incurred a capital loss equal to $1,090 during 1994. How could the market value of the Treasury note lose so much value in one year? The primary reason the value of this investment, as well as other debt instruments, decreased so significantly was because the Federal Reserve purposely increased interest rates six times during 1994 such that, in a single year, the return demanded by investors increased by more than 2 percent. This increase in rates caused the values of financial instruments to decrease greatly. But, even though investors who bought the seven-year Treasury notes on January 3, 1994, experienced a loss in value equal to $1,090, during the same period they received interest payments of $550 ($275 each six months); so those investors who sold their Treasury notes on January 3, 1995, lost 5.4 percent ($540 = $1,090 value loss less $550 interest received) on their original $10,000 investment. On the other hand, investors who continued to hold the Treasury notes found that their market value

had increased to $10,128 by January 4, 1999; thus, investors who sold their notes at that time would have earned an average annual return equal to about 5.7 percent. The price of the notes increased because the average market return on such investments had fallen to less than 5.0 percent.

Could investors have fared better in the stock market or in other types of investments? Probably. In 1994, according to the S&P 500 Index, the values of stocks only decreased by about 1.5 percent on average; and, after considering dividends paid by the companies, the average return earned by investors was nearly a 1.5 percent increase. Although this return was well below the return considered normal for the stock markets, an individual who invested in stocks at the beginning of 1994 and held them until January 1999 would have increased his or her investment value by more than 2.5 times, not considering dividends—according to the S&P 500 Index, the return on stocks averaged about 28 percent from 1995 through 1998. And, as we write this text in 1999, the stock market has continued to increase—the Dow Jones Industrial Average pushed above the 10,000 level for the first time in history at the end of March 1999 and by the beginning of May it was above 11,000, which translates to an increase of greater than 19 percent during the first four months of the year. At the same time, interest rates remained relatively constant, suggesting that investors had greater confidence the values of

continues

their investments would not decrease significantly if the stock markets experienced downward "adjustments" during the rest of the year.

As you read this chapter, think about why the value of the Treasury notes decreased so significantly from January 1994 to January 1995 when interest rates increased more than two percent. What happens to the value of financial assets when the returns demanded by investors change? Are bonds and stocks affected the same? Answering these questions will help you to get a basic understanding of how stocks and bonds are valued in the financial markets. Such an understanding will help you make investments decisions, including those that are critical when establishing a retirement plan. ■

In the previous chapter we examined time value of money (TVM) analysis. These TVM concepts are used by managers and investors to establish the worth of any asset whose value is derived from future cash flows, including such assets as real estate, factories, machinery, oil wells, stocks, and bonds. Now, in this chapter, we use time value of money techniques to explain how the values of assets are determined. The material covered in the chapter obviously is important to investors who want to establish the values of their investments. But knowledge of valuation is equally important to financial managers because all important corporate decisions should be analyzed in terms of how they will affect the value of the firm. Remember that in Chapter 1 we noted the goal of managerial finance is to maximize the value of the firm. Thus, it is critical that we understand the valuation process so we can determine what affects the value of the firm.

Basic Valuation

After learning about the time value of money, you should realize that the *value* of anything, whether it is a financial asset like a stock or a bond or a real asset like a building or a piece of machinery, *is based on the present value of the cash flows the asset is expected to produce in the future*. On a cash flow time line, value can be depicted as follows:

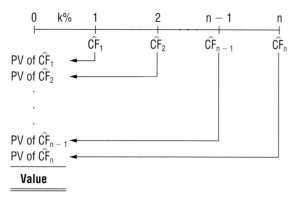

Therefore, the value of any asset can be expressed in general form as follows:

7-1

$$\text{Asset value} = V = \frac{\hat{CF}_1}{(1 + k)^1} + \frac{\hat{CF}_2}{(1 + k)^2} + \cdots + \frac{\hat{CF}_n}{(1 + k)^n}$$

Here

$\hat{CF}_t$ = The cash flow expected to be generated by the asset in period t.

k = The return investors consider appropriate for holding such an asset. This return is usually termed the *required return*, and, as we saw in Chapter 5, it is based on both economic conditions and the riskiness of the asset.

According to Equation 7-1, the value of an asset is affected by the cash flows it is expected to generate, $\hat{CF}$, and the return required by investors, k. As you can see, *the higher the expected cash flows, the greater the asset's value; also, the lower the required return, the greater the asset's value.* In the remainder of this chapter, we discuss how this general valuation concept can be applied to determine the value of various types of assets. First, we examine the valuation process for financial assets, and then we apply the process to value real assets.

Self-Test Questions

Describe the general methodology used to value any asset.

All else equal, how would an increase in an asset's expected future cash flows affect its value? What would be the impact of an increase in the required rate of return?

Valuation of Financial Assets—Bonds

Corporations raise capital in two forms—debt and equity. Our first task in this chapter is to examine the valuation process for bonds, the principal type of long-term debt.

BOND

A long-term debt instrument.

A **bond** is a long-term promissory note issued by a business or governmental unit. For example, suppose on January 3, 2000, Unilate Textiles borrowed $25 million by selling 25,000 individual bonds for $1,000 each. Unilate received the $25 million, and it promised to pay the bondholders annual interest and to repay the $25 million on a specified date.[1] The lenders were willing to give Unilate $25 million, so the value of the bond issue was $25 million. But how did the investors decide that the issue was worth $25 million? As a first step in explaining how the values of this and other bonds are determined, we need to define some terms:

---

[1]Actually, Unilate would receive some amount less than $25 million because there are costs associated with issuing the bond, such as legal fees, investment banking fees, and so forth. For our discussion here, we choose to ignore such costs to simplify the explanations. We address the topic of issuing securities and the investment banking process later in the book.

**PRINCIPAL AMOUNT,
FACE VALUE,
MATURITY VALUE,
PAR VALUE**
The amount of money the
firm borrows and
promises to repay at some
future date, often at
maturity.

1. **Principal amount, face value, maturity value, and par value.** The **principal amount** of debt generally represents the amount of money the firm borrows and promises to repay at some future date. For much debt issued by corporations, including bonds, the principal amount is repaid at maturity, so we often refer to the principal value as the **maturity value.** In addition, the principal value generally is written on the "face" of the debt instrument, or certificate, so it is also called the **face value.** Further, when the market value of debt is the same as its face value, it is said to be selling at *par*; thus the principal amount is also referred to as the **par value.** For most debt, then, *the terms principal amount, face value, maturity value, and par value refer to the same value—the amount that must be repaid by the borrower.* We use the terms interchangeably throughout the book.

   The face value of a corporate bond is usually set at $1,000, although multiples of $1,000 (for example, $5,000) are also used.

COUPON PAYMENT
The specified number of
dollars of interest paid
each period, generally each
six months, on a bond.

2. **Coupon interest rate.** The bond requires the issuer to pay a specified number of dollars of interest each year (or, more typically, each six months). When this **coupon payment,** as it is called, is divided by the par value, the result is the **coupon interest rate.** For example, Unilate's bonds have a $1,000 par value, and they pay $150 in interest each year. The bond's coupon interest is $150, so its coupon interest rate is $150/$1,000 = 15%. The $150 is the yearly "rent" on the $1,000 loan. This payment, which is fixed at the time the bond is issued, remains in force, by contract, during the life of the bond.[2]

**COUPON
INTEREST RATE**
The stated annual rate of
interest paid on a bond.

3. **Maturity date.** Bonds generally have a specified **maturity date** on which the par value must be repaid. Unilate's bonds, which were issued on January 3, 2000, will mature on January 2, 2015; thus, they had a 15-year maturity at the time they were issued. Most bonds have **original maturities** (the maturity at the time the bond is issued) of from ten to 40 years, but any maturity is legally permissible. Of course, the effective maturity of a bond declines each year after it has been issued. Thus, Unilate's bonds had a 15-year original maturity, but in 2001 they had a 14-year maturity, and so on.

MATURITY DATE
A specified date on which
the par value of a bond
must be repaid.

ORIGINAL MATURITY
The number of years to
maturity at the time a
bond is issued.

4. **Call provisions.** Often, bonds have a provision whereby the issuer can pay them off prior to maturity by "calling them in" from the investors. This feature is known as a **call provision.** If a bond is callable, and if interest rates in the economy decline, then the company can sell a new issue of low-interest-rate bonds and use the proceeds to retire the old, high-interest-rate issue, just as a homeowner can refinance a home mortgage.

CALL PROVISION
A provision in a bond
contract that gives the
issuer the right to "recall"
the bond and pay it off
under specified terms
prior to the stated
maturity date.

5. **New issues versus outstanding bonds.** As we shall see, a bond's market price is determined primarily by the cash flows it generates, or the dollar interest it pays, which depends on the coupon interest rate—the higher the coupon, other things held constant, the higher the market price of the bond. At the time a bond is issued, the coupon generally is set at a level that will cause the market price of the bond to equal its par value. If a lower coupon were set, investors

---

[2]The term *coupon payment* comes from the fact that some time ago, most bonds literally had a number of small (½- by 2-inch) dated coupons attached to them, and on the interest payment date, the owner would clip off the coupon for that date and either cash it at his or her bank or mail it to the company's paying agent, who then mailed back a check for the interest. A 30-year, semiannual bond would start with 60 coupons, whereas a five-year annual payment bond would start with only five coupons. Today most bonds are registered—no physical coupons are involved, and interest checks are mailed automatically to the registered owners of the bonds. Even so, people continue to use the terms *coupon* and *coupon interest rate* when discussing registered bonds.

simply would not be willing to pay $1,000 for the bond, while if a higher coupon were set, investors would clamor for the bond and bid its price up over $1,000. Investment bankers can judge quite precisely the coupon rate that will cause a bond to sell at its $1,000 par value.

A bond that has just been issued is known as a *new issue.* (*The Wall Street Journal* classifies a bond as a new issue for about one month after it has first been issued.) Once the bond has been on the market for a while, it is classified as an *outstanding bond,* also called a *seasoned issue.* Newly issued bonds generally sell very close to par, but the prices of outstanding bonds can vary widely from par. Coupon interest payments are constant, so when economic conditions change, a bond with a $150 coupon that sold at par when it was issued can sell for more or less than $1,000 thereafter.

The Basic Bond Valuation Model[3]

Equation 7–1 shows that the value of a financial asset is based on the cash flows expected to be generated by the asset in the future. In the case of a bond, the cash flows consist of interest payments during the life of the bond plus a return of the principal amount borrowed when the bond matures. In a cash flow time line format, here is the situation:

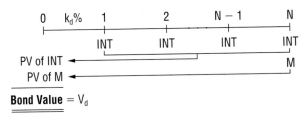

Here

k_d = The average rate of return investors require to invest in the bond. So, for the Unilate Textiles bond issue k_d = 15%. We used the term i or I to designate the interest rate in Chapter 6 because those terms are used on financial calculators, but k, with the subscript d to designate the rate on a debt security is normally used in finance.[4]

N = The number of years before the bond matures. For the Unilate bonds, N = 15. Note that N declines each year after the bond has been issued, so a bond that had a maturity of 15 years when it was issued (original maturity = 15) will have N = 14 after one year, N = 13 after two years, and so on. Note also that at this point we assume that the bond pays interest once a year, or annually, so N is measured in years. Later on, we

---

[3]In finance, the term *model* refers to an equation or set of equations designed to show how one or more variables affect some other variable. Thus, a bond valuation model shows the mathematical relationship between a bond's price and the set of variables that determine the price.

[4]The appropriate interest rate on debt securities was discussed in Chapter 2. The bond's riskiness, liquidity, and years to maturity, as well as supply and demand conditions in the capital markets, all influence the interest rate on bonds.

will deal with semiannual payment bonds, which pay interest each six months.[5]

INT = Dollars of interest paid each period = Coupon rate × Par value. In our example, INT = 0.15 × \$1,000 = \$150. In calculator terminology, PMT = INT = 150.

M = The par, or face, value of the bond = \$1,000. This amount must be paid off at maturity. In calculator terminology, FV = M = 1000.

We can now redraw the cash flow time line to show the numerical values for all variables except the bond's value:

0	15%	1	2	14	15
Value		150	150	150	150
					1,000
					1,150

Now the following general equation can be solved to find the value of any bond:

7–2

$$\text{Bond value} = V_d = \frac{INT}{(1 + k_d)^1} + \frac{INT}{(1 + k_d)^2} + \cdots + \frac{INT}{(1 + k_d)^N} + \frac{M}{(1 + k_d)^N}$$

$$= \sum_{t=1}^{n} \frac{INT}{(1 + k_d)^t} + \frac{M}{(1 + k_d)^N}$$

Notice the interest payments represent an annuity, and repayment of the par value at maturity represents a single, or lump-sum, payment. Thus, Equation 7–2 can be rewritten for use with the tables:

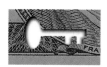

7–2a

$$V_d = INT(PVIFA_{k_d,N}) + M(PVIF_{k_d,N})$$

Inserting values for our particular bond, we have

$$V_d = \sum_{t=1}^{15} \frac{\$150}{(1.15)^t} + \frac{\$1,000}{(1.15)}$$

$$= \$150(PVIFA_{15\%,15}) + \$1,000(PVIF_{15\%,15})$$

The value of the bond can be computed by using the three procedures discussed in Chapter 6: (1) numerically, (2) using the tables, and (3) with a financial calculator.

---

[5]We should note that some bonds that have been issued either pay no interest during their lives (*zero coupon bonds*) or else pay very low coupon rates. Such bonds are sold at a discount below par, and hence they are called *original issue discount bonds*. The "interest" earned on a zero coupon bond comes at the end when the company pays off at par (\$1,000) a bond that was purchased for, say, \$321.97. The discount of \$1,000 − \$321.97 = \$678.03 substitutes for interest.

$$V_d = \$150(\text{PVIFA}_{10\%,14}) + \$1,000(\text{PVIF}_{10\%,14})$$
$$= \$150(7.3667) \qquad + \$1,000(0.2633)$$
$$= \$1,105.01 \qquad + \$263.30$$
$$= \$1,368.31$$

Thus, if k_d fell *below* the coupon rate, the bond would sell above par, or at a *premium*. With a financial calculator, just change $I = k_d$ from 15 to 10, and then press the PV key to get the answer, $1,368.33. (The calculator solution and the tabular solution differ due to rounding.)

The arithmetic of the bond value increase should be clear, but what is the logic behind it? The fact that k_d has fallen to ten percent means that if you had $1,000 to invest, you could buy new bonds like Unilate's (companies sell new bonds every day), except that these new bonds would pay $100 of interest each year rather than $150. Naturally, you would prefer $150 to $100, so you would be willing to pay more than $1,000 for Unilate Textiles' bonds to obtain its higher coupons. All investors would recognize these facts, and, as a result, the Unilate Textiles bonds would be bid up in price to $1,368.31, at which point they would provide the same rate of return to a potential investor as the new bonds—ten percent.

Assuming that interest rates remain constant at ten percent for the next 14 years, what would happen to the value of a Unilate Textiles bond? It would fall gradually from $1,368.31 at present to $1,000 at maturity, when Unilate Textiles will redeem each bond for $1,000. This point can be illustrated by calculating the value of the bond one year later, when it has 13 years remaining to maturity. With a financial calculator, merely input the values for N, I, PMT, and FV, now using $N = 13$, and press the PV key to find the value of the bond, $1,355.17. Using the tables, we have

$$V_d = \$150(\text{PVIFA}_{10\%,13}) + \$1,000(\text{PVIF}_{10\%,13})$$
$$= \$150(7.1034) \qquad + \$1,000(0.2897)$$
$$= \$1,355.21 \text{ (rounding difference)}$$

Thus, the value of the bond will have fallen from $1,368.31 to $1,355.21, or by $13.10. If you were to calculate the value of the bond at other future dates, the price would continue to fall as the maturity date is approached. At maturity, the value of the bond would have to equal $1,000 (as long as the firm does not go bankrupt).

Notice that if you purchased the bond at a price of $1,368.31 and then sold it one year later with k_d still at ten percent, you would have a capital loss of $13.10, or a total return of $150.00 − $13.10 = $136.90. Your percentage rate of return would consist of an *interest yield* (also called a *current yield*) plus a *capital gains yield*. The computations for the current yield and the capital gains yield are defined as follows:

$$\text{Current yield} = \frac{\text{INT}}{V_d}$$

$$\text{Capital gains yield} = \frac{\left(\begin{array}{c}\text{Ending}\\\text{bond value}\end{array}\right) - \left(\begin{array}{c}\text{Beginning}\\\text{bond value}\end{array}\right)}{\left(\begin{array}{c}\text{Beginning}\\\text{bond value}\end{array}\right)} = \frac{V_{d,End} - V_{d,Begin}}{V_{d,Begin}}$$

The yields for Unilate's bond after one year are as follows:

$$\text{Current yield} = \$150.00/\$1,368.31 = 0.1096 = 10.96\%$$

$$\text{Capital gains yield} = -\$13.10/\$1,368.31 = -0.0096 = \underline{-0.96\%}$$

$$\text{Total rate of return (yield)} = \$136.90/\$1,368.31 = 0.1001 \approx \underline{\underline{10.00\%}}$$

Had interest rates risen from 15 to 20 percent during the first year after issue rather than fallen, the value of the bond would have declined to $769.49:

$$V_d = \$150(\text{PVIFA}_{20\%,14}) + \$1,000(\text{PVIF}_{20\%,14})$$

$$= \$150(4.6106) \qquad + \$1,000(0.0779)$$

$$= \$691.59 \qquad\qquad + \$77.90$$

$$= \$769.49$$

In this case, the bond would sell at a *discount* of $230.51 below its par value:

$$\text{Discount} = \text{Price} - \text{Par value}$$

$$= \$769.49 - \$1,000.00$$

$$= -\$230.51$$

CURRENT YIELD
The annual interest payment on a bond divided by its current market value.

The total expected future yield on the bond would again consist of a **current yield** and a capital gains yield, but now the capital gains yield would be positive. The total yield would be 20 percent. To see this, calculate the price of the bond with 13 years left to maturity, assuming that interest rates remain at 20 percent. With a calculator, enter $N = 13, I = 20, \text{PMT} = 150$, and $\text{FV} = 1000$, and then press PV to obtain the bond's value, $773.37. Using the tables, proceed as follows:

$$V_d = \$150(\text{PVIFA}_{20\%,13}) + \$1,000(\text{PVIF}_{20\%,13})$$

$$= \$150(4.5327) \qquad + \$1,000(0.0935)$$

$$= \$773.41 \text{ (rounding difference)}$$

Notice that the capital gain for the year is the difference between the bond's value at $N=13$ and the bond's value at $N = 14$, or $773.41 - \$769.49 = \$3.92$. The current yield, capital gains yield, and total yield are calculated as follows:

$$\text{Current yield} = \$150.00/\$769.49 = 0.1949 = 19.49\%$$

$$\text{Capital gains yield} = \$3.92/\$769.49 = 0.0051 = \underline{0.51\%}$$

$$\text{Total rate of return (yield)} = \$153.92/\$769.49 = 0.2000 = \underline{\underline{20.00\%}}$$

What would happen to the value of the bond if market interest rates remain constant at 20 percent until maturity? Because the value of the bond must equal the principal, or par, amount at maturity (as long as bankruptcy does not occur), its value will gradually increase from the current price of $773.41 to its maturity value of $1,000. For example, the value of the bond would increase to $778.04 at $N = 12$, its value would be $783.65 at $N = 11$, and so forth.

Equation 7–3 is based on computations of approximate yields in the past and it does not consider the time value of money, so it should be used only to approximate a bond's yield to maturity. For the bond we are examining, the approximate yield to maturity is

$$\text{Yield to maturity} = k_d \approx \frac{\$150 + \left(\frac{\$1,000 - \$1,368.31}{14}\right)}{\left[\frac{2(\$1,368.31) + \$1,000}{3}\right]}$$

$$= \frac{\$150 + (-\$26.31)}{\$1,245.54} = 0.0993 \approx 10\%$$

Inserting interest factors for ten percent, you obtain a value equal to

$$V_d = \$150(7.3667) + \$1,000(0.2633)$$

$$= \$1,105.01 + \$263.30$$

$$= \$1,368.31$$

This calculated value is equal to the market price of the bond, so 10 percent is the bond's actual yield to maturity: $k_d = \text{YTM} = 10.0\%$.[8]

The yield to maturity is identical to the total annual rate of return discussed in the preceding section. The YTM for a bond that sells at par consists entirely of an interest yield, but if the bond sells at a price other than its par value, the YTM consists of the interest yield plus a positive or negative capital gains yield. Note also that a bond's yield to maturity changes whenever interest rates in the economy change, and this is almost daily. One who purchases a bond and holds it until it matures will receive the YTM that existed on the purchase date, but the bond's calculated YTM will change frequently between the purchase date and the maturity date.[9]

---

[8]Many years ago, bond traders all had specialized tables called *bond tables* that gave yields on bonds of different maturities selling at different premiums and discounts. Because calculators are so much more efficient (and accurate), bond tables are rarely used any more.

[9]Bonds that contain call provisions (callable bonds) are often called by the firm prior to maturity. In cases where a bond issue is called, investors do not have the opportunity to earn the yield to maturity (YTM) because the bond issue is retired before the maturity date arrives. Thus, for callable bonds, we often compute the *yield to call (YTC)* rather than the yield to maturity. The computation for the yield to call is the same as the yield to maturity, except the *call price* of the bond is substituted for the maturity (par) value, and the number of years until the bond can be called is substituted for the years to maturity. So to calculate the yield to call (YTC) we modify Equation 7–2 and solve the following equation for k_d:

$$\text{Price of bond} = \sum_{t=1}^{N_c} \frac{\text{INT}}{(1 + k_d)^t} + \frac{\text{Call price}}{(1 + k_d)^{N_C}}$$

Here N_C is the number of years until the company can call the bond; Call price is the price the company must pay in order to call the bond (it is often set equal to the par value plus one year's interest); and k_d is the yield to call (YTC). To solve for the YTC, proceed just like the solution for the yield to maturity of a bond. For example, suppose Unilate's 15 percent coupon bonds, which have a current price of $1,368.31, are callable in nine years at $1,150. The set up for computing the YTC is:

$$\$1,368.31 = \frac{\$150}{(1 + k_d)^1} + \frac{\$150}{(1 + k_d)^2} + \cdots + \frac{\$150 + \$1,150}{(1 + k_d)^9}$$

Using your calculator, you would find the solution for the yield to call is 9.78 percent.

Bond Values with Semiannual Compounding

Although some bonds pay interest annually, most actually pay interest semiannually. To evaluate semiannual payment bonds, we must modify the valuation equations the same as we did in Chapter 6 to take into consideration that interest compounding can occur more than once a year. So, Equations 7–2 and 7–2a become

7–2b

$$V_d = \sum_{t=1}^{2N} \frac{\left(\frac{INT}{2}\right)}{\left(1 + \frac{k_d}{2}\right)^t} + \frac{M}{\left(1 + \frac{k_d}{2}\right)^{2N}}$$

$$= \left(\frac{INT}{2}\right)(PVIFA_{\frac{k_d}{2}, 2N}) + M(PVIF_{\frac{k_d}{2}, 2N})$$

To illustrate, assume now that Unilate's 14-year bonds pay $75 interest each six months rather than $150 at the end of each year. Thus, each interest payment is only half as large, but there are twice as many of them. When the going (simple) rate of interest is ten percent with semiannual compounding, the value of this 14-year bond is found as follows:[10]

$$V_d = \$75(PVIFA_{5\%,28}) + \$1,000(PVIF_{5\%,28})$$

$$= \$75(14.8981) + \$1,000(0.2551)$$

$$= \$1,117.36 + \$255.10$$

$$= \$1,372.46$$

With a financial calculator, enter N = 28, I = k_d = 5, PMT = INT = 75, FV = 1000, and then press the PV key to obtain the bond's value, $1,372.45 (rounding difference). The value with semiannual interest payments is slightly higher than $1,368.31, the value when interest is paid annually. This higher value occurs because interest payments are received, and therefore can be reinvested, somewhat faster under semiannual compounding.

Students sometimes want to discount the *maturity (par) value* at ten percent over 14 years rather than at five percent over 28 six-month periods. This is incorrect. Logically, all cash flows in a given contract must be discounted at the same periodic rate, the five percent semiannual rate in this instance, because this is the opportunity rate for the investor. For consistency, bond traders must use the same discount rate for all cash flows, including the cash flow at maturity; and they do.

Interest Rate Risk on a Bond

As we saw in Chapter 2, interest rates go up and down over time. Further, changes in interest rates affect the bondholders in two ways:

---

[10]We are also assuming a change in the effective annual interest rate, from ten percent to EAR = $(1.05)^2 - 1 = 1.1025 - 1.0 = 0.1025 = 10.25\%$. Most bonds pay interest semiannually, and the rates quoted are simple rates compounded semiannually. Therefore, effective annual rates for most bonds are somewhat higher than the quoted rates, which, in effect, represent the APRs for the bonds.

INTEREST RATE PRICE RISK
The risk of changes in bond prices to which investors are exposed due to changing interest rates.

1. An increase in interest rates leads to a decline in the values of outstanding bonds. Because interest rates can rise, bondholders face the risk of losses in the values of their portfolios. This risk is called **interest rate price risk.**

2. Many bondholders, including such institutional bondholders as pension funds and life insurance companies, buy bonds to build funds for some future use. These bondholders reinvest the cash flows, which include interest payments plus repayment of principal when the bonds mature or are called. If interest rates decline, the bondholders will earn a lower rate of return on reinvested cash flows, and this will reduce the future value of their portfolios relative to the values they would have had if interest rates had not fallen. This is called **interest rate reinvestment risk.**

INTEREST RATE REINVESTMENT RISK
The risk that income from a bond portfolio will vary because cash flows have to be reinvested at current market rates.

We see, then, that any given change in interest rates has two separate effects on bondholders—it changes the current values of their portfolios (price risk), and it also changes the rates of return at which the cash flows from their portfolios can be reinvested (reinvestment risk). Note that these two risks tend to offset one another. For example, an increase in interest rates will lower the *current* value of a bond portfolio, but because the future cash flows produced by the portfolio will then be reinvested at a higher rate of return, the *future* value of the portfolio will be increased. In this section we will look at just how these two effects operate to affect bondholders' positions.[11]

Suppose you bought some of Unilate Textiles' 15 percent, 14-year bonds at a price of $1,000, and interest rates subsequently rose to 20 percent. As we saw before, the price of the bonds would fall to $769.49, so you would have a loss of $230.51 per bond.[12] Interest rates can and do rise, and rising rates cause a loss of value for bondholders. Thus, people or firms who invest in bonds are exposed to risk from changing interest rates.

Exposure to interest rate price risk is higher on bonds with long maturities than on those maturing in the near future. This point can be demonstrated by showing how the value of a one-year bond with a 15 percent coupon fluctuates with changes in k_d and then comparing these changes with Unilate's 14-year bond. The values for a one-year bond and Unilate's 14-year bond at several different market interest rates, k_d, are shown in Figure 7–3. The values for the bonds were computed assuming the coupon interest payments for the bonds occur annually. Notice how much more sensitive the price of the long-term bond is to changes in interest rates. At a 15 percent interest rate, both the long- and the short-term bonds are valued at $1,000. When rates rise to 20 percent, the long-term bond falls to $769.47, but the short-term bond falls only to $958.33.

---

[11]Actually, we will stop far short of a full examination of the effects of interest rate changes on bondholders' positions because such an examination would go well beyond the scope of the text. We can note, however, that a concept called "duration" has been developed to help fixed income investors deal with changing interest rates, and, with a properly structured portfolio (one that has the proper duration), most of the risks of changing interest rates can be eliminated because price risk and reinvestment risk can be made to exactly offset one another.

[12]You would have an *accounting* (and tax) loss only if you sold the bond; if you held it to maturity, you would not have such a loss. However, even if you did not sell, you would still have suffered a *real economic loss in an opportunity cost sense* because you would have lost the opportunity to invest at 20 percent and would be stuck with a 15 percent bond in a 20 percent market. Thus, in an economic sense "paper losses" are just as bad as realized accounting losses.

| FIGURE 7–3 | Value of Long- and Short-Term 15% Annual Coupon Rate Bonds at Different Market Interest Rates |

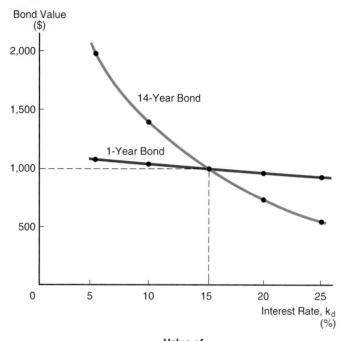

| | Value of | |
Current Market Interest Rate, k_d	1-Year Bond	14-Year Bond
5%	$1,095.24	$1,989.86
10	1,045.45	1,368.33
15	1,000.00	1,000.00
20	958.33	769.47
25	920.00	617.59

NOTE: Bond values were calculated using a financial calculator.

For bonds with similar coupons, this differential sensitivity to changes in interest rates always holds true—*the longer the maturity of the bond, the greater its price changes in response to a given change in interest rates.* Thus, even if the risk of default on two bonds is exactly the same, the one with the longer maturity is typically exposed to more price risk from a change in interest rates.[13]

The logical explanation for this difference in interest rate price risk is simple. Suppose you bought a 14-year bond that yielded 15 percent, or $150 a year. Now suppose interest rates on comparable-risk bonds rose to 20 percent. You would be stuck with

---

[13]If a ten-year bond were plotted in Figure 7–3, its curve would lie between those of the 14-year bond and the one-year bond. The curve of a one-month bond would be almost horizontal, indicating that its price would change very little in response to an interest rate change, but a perpetuity would have a very steep slope.

only $150 of interest for the next 14 years. On the other hand, had you bought a one-year bond, you would have had a low return for only one year. At the end of the year, you would get your $1,000 back, and you could then reinvest it and receive 20 percent, or $200 per year, for the next 13 years. Thus, interest rate price risk reflects the length of time one is committed to a given investment.

Although a one-year bond has less interest rate price risk than a 14-year bond, the one-year bond exposes the buyer to more interest rate reinvestment risk. Suppose you bought a one-year bond that yielded 15 percent, and then interest rates on comparable-risk bonds fell to ten percent. After one year, when you got your $1,000 back, you would have to invest it at only ten percent, so you would lose $150 − $100 = $50 in annual interest. Had you bought the 14-year bond, you would have continued to receive $150 in annual interest payments even if rates fell. If you reinvested those coupon payments, you would have to accept a lower rate of return, but you would still be much better off than if you had been holding the one-year bond.

Bond Prices in Recent Years

We know from Chapter 2 that interest rates fluctuate, and we have just seen that the prices of outstanding bonds rise and fall inversely with changes in interest rates. When interest rates fall, many firms "refinance" by issuing new, lower-cost debt and using the proceeds to repay higher-cost debt. In 1993, interest rates were low relative to the rates that existed during the previous 15 years; thus, firms that had issued higher-cost debt in earlier years refinanced much of their debt at that time. Consequently, much of the corporate debt that exists today was issued in 1993 or later.

Figure 7–4 shows what has happened to the price of the 30-year, 7¾ percent bond that Florida Power & Light (FPL) issued in 1993. Because the FPL bond was issued February 1, 1993, the prices given on the graph are for the last trading day of January in each year.

When Florida Power first issued this bond, it was worth $1,000, but on the last trading day of January 1995, it sold for only $917.50, a discount of $82.50 from its par value, because rates on similar risk bonds had increased to more than 8½ percent. As interest rates decreased, the price of FPL's bond rose such that it was selling for $1,053.75, a premium of $53.75, in 1996. At that time, the yield on similar risk bonds was approximately 7.3 percent, which was below the 7¾ percent coupon rate. By February 1999, the bond was still selling for a premium, at $1,046.25, because market yield had stayed at about 7.3 percent. As the graph shows, if the interest rates stay at the 1999 level of 7.3 percent for the remaining 24 years of the bond's life, the price of the bond will gradually decrease to its maturity value of $1,000 just before it matures in 2023.

Self-Test Questions

What is meant by the terms "new issue" debt and "seasoned issue" debt?

Explain, verbally, the following equation:

$$V_d = \sum_{t=1}^{N} \frac{INT}{(1 + k_d)^t} + \frac{M}{(1 + k_d)^N}$$

Explain what happens to the price of a bond if (1) interest rates rise above the bond's coupon rate or (2) interest rates fall below the bond's coupon rate.

| **FIGURE 7–4** | Florida Power & Light 7⅜%, 30-Year Bond: Market Value (Yield to Maturity) from 1978–1994 |

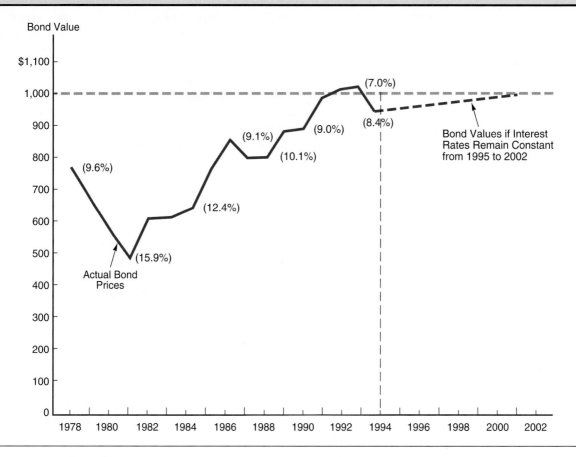

Write out a formula that can be used to calculate the discount or premium on a bond, and explain it.

Differentiate between interest rate price risk and interest rate reinvestment risk.

Differentiate between a bond's yield to maturity and its current yield.

How is the bond valuation formula shown above changed to deal with bonds that have semiannual coupons rather than annual coupons?

Valuation of Financial Assets—Equity (Stock)

Each corporation issues at least one type of stock, or equity, called *common stock*. Some corporations issue more than one type of common stock, and some issue *preferred stock* in addition to common stock. As the names imply, most equity is in the form of common stock, and preferred shareholders have preference over common shareholders when a firm distributes funds to stockholders. Dividends, as well as liquidation proceeds resulting from bankruptcy, are paid to preferred stockholders before common stockholders. But preferred stockholders generally are paid the same dividend each year, while the dividends paid to common stockholders can vary and are often dependent on current and previous earnings levels and the future growth plans of the firm. We discuss the characteristics of both common stock and preferred stock in greater detail in later chapters. For the purposes of our discussion in this section, you need to be aware that the cash flows generated by investing in preferred stock are normally constant, while the cash flows generated by common stock can be constant, but often vary from year to year.

In this section, we examine the process to value stock, both preferred and common. We begin by introducing a general stock valuation model. Then, we apply the model to three scenarios: (1) when there is no growth in dividends so the amount paid each year remains constant (like preferred dividends); (2) when dividends increase at a constant rate each year; and (3) when dividends grow at different rates.

Definitions of Terms Used in the Stock Valuation Models

Stocks provide an expected future cash flow stream, and a stock's value is found in the same manner as the values of other assets—namely, as the present value of the expected future cash flow stream. The expected cash flows consist of two elements: (1) the dividends expected in each year and (2) the price investors expect to receive when they sell the stock, which includes the return of the original investment plus a capital gain or loss.

Before we present the general stock valuation model, let's define some terms and notations we will use throughout this section.

$\hat{D}_t$ = Dividend the stockholder expects to receive at the end of Year t (pronounced "D hat t"). D_0 is the most recent dividend, which has already been paid; $\hat{D}_1$ is the next dividend expected to be paid, and it will be paid at the end of this year; $\hat{D}_2$ is the dividend expected at the end of two years; and so forth. $\hat{D}_1$ represents the first cash flow a new purchaser of the stock will receive. Note that D_0, the dividend that has just been paid, is known with certainty (thus, there is no "hat" over the D). However, all future dividends are *expected* values, so the estimate of $\hat{D}_t$ might differ among investors for some stocks.[14]

MARKET PRICE, P_0
The price at which a stock sells in the market.

P_0 = Actual **market price** of the stock today.

INTRINSIC VALUE, $\hat{P}_0$
The value of an asset that in the mind of a particular investor is justified by the facts; $\hat{P}_0$ may be different from the asset's current market value, its book value, or both.

$\hat{P}_t$ = Expected price of the stock at the end of Year t. $\hat{P}_0$ is the **intrinsic,** or *theoretical,* **value** of the stock today as seen by the particular investor doing the analysis; $\hat{P}_1$ is the price *expected* at the end of one year; and so on. Note that $\hat{P}_0$ is the intrinsic value of the stock today based on a particular investor's estimate of the stock's expected dividend stream and the riskiness of that stream. Hence, whereas P_0 is fixed and is identical for all investors because it represents the price at which the

---

[14]Stocks generally pay dividends quarterly, so theoretically we should evaluate them on a quarterly basis. However, in stock valuation, most analysts work on an annual basis because the data generally are not precise enough to warrant refinement to a quarterly model.

stock currently can be purchased in the stock market, $\hat{P}_0$ could differ among investors depending on what they feel the firm actually is worth. The caret, or "hat," is used to indicate that $\hat{P}_t$ is an estimated value. $\hat{P}_0$, the individual investor's estimate of the intrinsic value today, could be above or below P_0, the current stock price, but an investor would buy the stock only if his or her estimate of $\hat{P}_0$ were equal to or greater than P_0.

Because there are many investors in the market, there can be many values for $\hat{P}_0$. However, we can think of a group of "average," or "marginal," investors whose actions actually determine the market price. For these marginal investors, P_0 must equal $\hat{P}_0$; otherwise, a disequilibrium would exist, and buying and selling in the market would change P_0 until $P_0 = \hat{P}_0$.

GROWTH RATE, g
The expected rate of change in dividends per share.

g = Expected **growth rate** in dividends as predicted by a marginal, or average, investor. (If we assume that dividends are expected to grow at a constant rate, g is also equal to the expected rate of growth in the stock's price.) Different investors might use different g's to evaluate a firm's stock, but the market price, P_0, is set on the basis of the g estimated by marginal investors.

REQUIRED RATE OF RETURN, k_s
The minimum rate of return on a stock that stockholders consider acceptable.

k_s = Minimum acceptable, or **required, rate of return** on the stock, considering both its riskiness and the returns available on other investments. Again, this term generally relates to average investors. The determinants of k_s were discussed in detail in Chapter 5.

DIVIDEND YIELD
The expected dividend divided by the current price of a share of stock.

$\dfrac{\hat{D}_1}{P_0}$ = Expected **dividend yield** on the stock during the coming year. If the stock is expected to pay a dividend of $1 during the next 12 months, and if its current price is $10, then the expected dividend yield is $1/$10 = 0.10 = 10\%$.

CAPITAL GAINS YIELD
The change in price (capital gain) during a given year divided by the price at the beginning of the year.

$\dfrac{\hat{P}_1 - P_0}{P_0}$ = Expected **capital gains yield** on the stock during the coming year. If the stock sells for $10 today, and if it is expected to rise to $10.50 at the end of one year, then the expected capital gain is $\hat{P}_1 - P_0 =$ $10.50 - $10.00 = $0.50, and the expected capital gains yield is $0.50/$10 = 0.05 = 5\%$.

EXPECTED RATE OF RETURN, $\hat{k}_s$
The rate of return on a common stock that an individual stockholder expects to receive; equal to the expected dividend yield plus the expected capital gains yield.

$\hat{k}_s$ = **Expected rate of return** that an investor who buys the stock anticipates, or expects to receive. $\hat{k}_s$ could be above or below k_s, but one would buy the stock only if $\hat{k}_s$ was equal to or greater than k_s. $\hat{k}_s$ = expected dividend yield plus expected capital gains yield; in other words,

$$\hat{k}_s = \frac{\hat{D}_1}{P_0} + \frac{\hat{P}_1 - P_0}{P_0}$$

In our example, the expected total return = $\hat{k}_s$ = 10\% + 5\% = 15\%.

ACTUAL (REALIZED) RATE OF RETURN, $\bar{k}_s$
The rate of return on a common stock actually received by stockholders. $\bar{k}_s$ may be greater than or less than $\hat{k}_s$ and/or k_s.

$\bar{k}_s$ = **Actual,** or **realized,** *after the fact* **rate of return** (pronounced "k bar s"). You might expect to obtain a return of $\hat{k}_s$ = 14 percent if you buy IBM stock today, but if the market goes down, you might end up next year with an actual realized return that is much lower, perhaps even negative (e.g., $\bar{k}_s$ = 8\%).

Expected Dividends as the Basis for Stock Values

Remember that according to Equation 7–1 the value of any asset is the present value of the cash flows expected to be generated by the asset in the future. In our discussion of bonds, we found that the value of a bond is the present value of the interest payments over the life of the bond plus the present value of the bond's maturity (or par) value. Stock prices are likewise determined as the present value of a stream of cash flows, and the basic stock valuation equation is similar to the bond valuation equation (Equation 7–2). What are the cash flows that corporations provide to their stockholders? First, think of yourself as an investor who buys a stock with the intention of holding it (in your family) forever. In this case, all that you (and your heirs) will receive is a stream of dividends, and the value of the stock today is calculated as the present value of an infinite stream of dividends, which is depicted on a cash flow time line as follows:

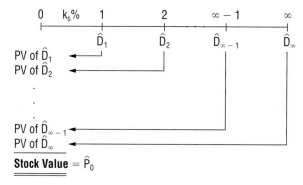

Thus, to compute the value of the stock, we must solve the following equation:

7–4

$$\text{Value of stock} = V_s = \hat{P}_0 = \text{PV of expected future dividends}$$

$$= \frac{\hat{D}_1}{(1 + k_s)^1} + \frac{\hat{D}_2}{(1 + k_s)^2} + \cdots + \frac{\hat{D}_\infty}{(1 + k_s)^\infty}$$

$$= \sum_{t=1}^{\infty} \frac{\hat{D}_t}{(1 + k_s)^t}$$

What about the more typical case, where you expect to hold the stock for a specific (finite) period and then sell it—what will be the value of $\hat{P}_0$ in this case? Unless the company is likely to be liquidated and thus to disappear, *the value of the stock is still determined by Equation 7–4.* To see this, recognize that for any individual investor, the expected cash flows consist of expected dividends plus the expected sale price of the stock. However, the sale price the current investor receives will depend on the dividends the future investor expects. Therefore, for all present and future investors in total, expected cash flows must be based on all of the expected future dividends. To put it another way, unless a firm is liquidated or sold to another concern, the cash flows it provides to its stockholders will consist only of a stream of dividends; therefore, the value of a share of its stock must be established as the present value of that expected dividend stream that will be paid throughout the life of the company.

The general validity of Equation 7–4 also can be confirmed by asking the following question: Suppose I buy a stock and expect to hold it for one year. I will receive dividends during the year plus the value $\hat{P}_1$ when I sell the stock at the end of the year. But what will determine the value of $\hat{P}_1$? The answer is that it will be determined as the present value of the dividends during Year 2 plus the stock price at the end of that year, which in turn will be determined as the present value of another set of future dividends and an even more distant stock price. This process can be continued forever, and the ultimate result is Equation 7–4.[15]

Equation 7–4 is a generalized stock valuation model in the sense that the time pattern of $\hat{D}_t$ can be anything: $\hat{D}_t$ can be rising, falling, or constant, or it can even be fluctuating randomly, and Equation 7–4 still will hold. Often, however, the projected stream of dividends follows a systematic pattern, in which case we can develop a simplified (that is, easier to apply) version of the stock valuation model expressed in Equation 7–4. In the following sections we consider the cases of zero growth, constant growth, and nonconstant growth.

Valuing Stocks with Zero Growth

ZERO-GROWTH STOCK
A common stock whose future dividends are not expected to grow at all; that is, g = 0, and $\hat{D}_1 = \hat{D}_2 = \cdots = \hat{D}_\infty$.

Suppose dividends are not expected to grow at all; instead they are expected to stay the same every year. Here we have a **zero-growth stock,** for which the dividends expected in future years are equal to some constant amount—the current dividend. That is, $\hat{D}_1 = \hat{D}_2 = \cdots = \hat{D}_\infty$. Therefore, we can drop the subscripts and the "hats" on D and rewrite Equation 7–4 as follows:

7–4a
$$\hat{P}_0 = \frac{D}{(1 + k_s)^1} + \frac{D}{(1 + k_s)^2} + \cdots + \frac{D}{(1 + k_s)^\infty}$$

As we noted in Chapter 6 in connection with the British consol bond, a security that is expected to pay a constant amount each year forever is called a perpetuity. Therefore, a *zero-growth stock is a perpetuity.*

Remember the value of any perpetuity is simply the payment amount divided by the discount rate, so the value of a zero-growth stock reduces to this formula:

7–5
$$\text{Value of zero-growth stock: } \hat{P}_0 = \frac{D}{k_s}$$

[15]We should note that investors periodically lose sight of the long-run nature of stocks as investments and forget that in order to sell a stock at a profit, one must find a buyer who will pay the higher price. If you analyzed a stock's value in accordance with Equation 7–4, concluded that the stock's market price exceeded a reasonable value, and then bought the stock anyway, then you would be following the "bigger fool" theory of investment—you think that you may be a fool to buy the stock at its excessive price, but you also think that when you get ready to sell it, you can find someone who is an even bigger fool. The bigger fool theory was widely followed in the summer of 1987, just before the stock market lost over one-third of its value in the October 1987 crash. Some believe the bigger fool theory is being followed today with the Internet, or ".com," stocks.

7-7

$$\text{Expected rate} \atop \text{of return} = {\text{Expected} \atop \text{dividend yield}} + {\text{Expected growth rate,} \atop \text{or capital gains yield}}$$

$$\hat{k}_s = \frac{\hat{D}_1}{P_0} + g$$

Thus, if you buy a stock for a price $P_0 = \$18$, and if you expect the stock to pay a dividend $\hat{D}_1 = \$1.26$ one year from now and to grow at a constant rate $g = 5\%$ in the future, then your expected rate of return will be 12 percent:

$$\hat{k}_s = \frac{\$1.26}{\$18} + 0.05 = 0.07 + 0.05 = 0.12 = 12.0\%$$

In this form, we see that $\hat{k}_s$ is the *expected total return* and that it consists of an *expected dividend yield*, $\hat{D}_1/P_0 = 7\%$, plus an *expected growth rate or capital gains yield*, $g = 5\%$.

Suppose this analysis had been conducted on January 1, 2000, so $P_0 = \$18$ is the January 1, 2000 stock price and $\hat{D}_1 = \$1.26$ is the dividend expected at the end of 2000 (December 31). What is the expected stock price at the end of 2000 (or the beginning of 2001)? We would again apply Equation 7–6, but this time we would use the expected 2001 dividend, $\hat{D}_{2001} = \hat{D}_2 = \hat{D}_1(1 + g) = \$1.26(1.05) = \$1.323$:

$$\hat{P}_1 = \frac{\hat{D}_2}{k_s - g} = \hat{P}_{1/1/01} = \frac{\hat{D}_{12/31/01}}{k_s - g} = \frac{\$1.323}{0.12 - 0.05} = \$18.90$$

Now notice that $\$18.90$ is 5 percent greater than P_0, the $\$18$ price on January 1, 2000:

$$\hat{P}_{1/1/00} = \$18.00(1.05) = \$18.90$$

Thus, we would expect to make a capital gain of $\$18.90 - \$18.00 = \$0.90$ during the year, which is a capital gains yield of five percent:

$$\text{Capital gains yield} = \frac{\text{Capital gain}}{\text{Beginning price}} = \frac{\text{Ending price} - \text{Beginning price}}{\text{Beginning price}}$$

$$= \frac{\$18.90 - \$18.00}{\$18.00} = \frac{\$0.90}{\$18.00} = 0.05 = 5.0\%$$

We could extend the analysis on out, and in each future year the expected capital gains yield would equal $g = 5\%$, the expected dividend growth rate.

Continuing, the dividend yield in 2001 could be estimated as follows:

$$\text{Dividend yield}_{2001} = \frac{\hat{D}_{12/31/01}}{P_{1/1/01}} = \frac{\$1.323}{\$18.90} = 0.07 = 7.0\%$$

The dividend yield for 2002 could also be calculated, and again it would be seven percent. Thus, for a constant growth stock, the following conditions must hold:

1. The dividend is expected to grow forever at a constant rate, g.
2. The stock price is expected to grow at this same rate.
3. The expected dividend yield is a constant.
4. The expected capital gains yield is also a constant, and it is equal to g.
5. The expected total rate of return, $\hat{k}_s$, is equal to the expected dividend yield plus the expected growth rate: $\hat{k}_s$ = dividend yield + g.

The term *expected* should be clarified—it means expected in a probabilistic sense, as the statistically expected outcome. Thus, if we say the growth rate is expected to remain constant at five percent, we mean that the best prediction for the growth rate in any future year is five percent, not that we literally expect the growth rate to be exactly equal to five percent in each future year. In this sense, the constant growth assumption is a reasonable one for many large, mature companies.

Valuing Stocks with Nonconstant Growth

NONCONSTANT GROWTH

The part of the life cycle of a firm in which growth either is much faster or much slower than that of the economy as a whole.

Firms typically go through *life* cycles. During the early part of their lives, their growth is much faster than that of the economy as a whole; then they match the economy's growth; and finally their growth is slower than that of the economy.[19] Automobile manufacturers in the 1920s and computer software firms such as Microsoft in the 1990s are examples of firms in the early part of the cycle. Other firms, such as the those in the tobacco industry or coal industry, are currently in the waning stages of their life cycles, so their growth is not keeping pace with the general economic growth (in some cases growth is negative). Firms whose growths are not about the same as the economy's growth are called **nonconstant growth** firms. Figure 7–6 illustrates nonconstant growth and also compares it with normal growth and zero growth.[20]

In the figure, the dividends of the supernormal growth (growth much greater than the economy) firm are expected to grow at a 30 percent rate for three years, after which the growth rate is expected to fall to five percent, the assumed average for the economy. The value of this firm, like any other, is the present value of its expected future dividends as determined by Equation 7–4. In the case in which $\hat{D}_t$ is growing at a constant rate, we simplified Equation 7–4 to $\hat{P}_0 = \hat{D}_1/(k_s - g)$. In the supernormal case, however, the expected growth rate is not a constant—it declines at the end of the period of supernormal growth. To find the value of such a stock, or of any nonconstant growth stock when the growth rate will eventually stabilize, we proceed in three steps:

---

[19]The concept of life cycles could be broadened to *product cycle*, which would include both small, start-up companies and large companies like IBM, which periodically introduce new products that give sales and earnings a boost. We should also mention *business cycles*, which alternately depress and boost sales and profits. The growth rate just after a major new product has been introduced, or just after a firm emerges from the depths of a recession, is likely to be much higher than the "expected long-run average growth rate," which is the proper value to use for evaluating the project.

[20]A negative growth rate indicates a declining company. A mining company whose profits are falling because of a declining ore body is an example. Someone buying such a company would expect its earnings, and consequently its dividends and stock price, to decline each year, and this would lead to capital losses rather than capital gains. Obviously, a declining company's stock price will be relatively low, and its dividend yield must be high enough to offset the expected capital loss and still produce a competitive total return. Students sometimes argue that they would not be willing to buy a stock whose price was expected to decline. However, if the annual dividends are large enough to *more than offset* the falling stock price, the stock still could provide a good return.

FIGURE 7–6	Illustrative Dividend Growth Rates

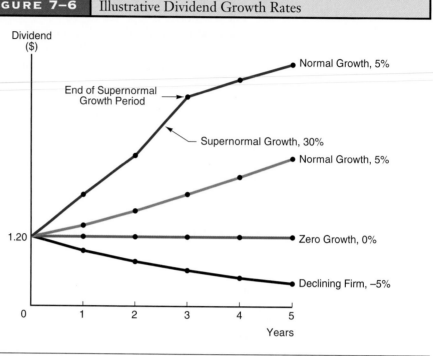

1. Compute the value of the dividends that experience nonconstant growth, and then find the PV of these dividends.
2. Using Equation 7–6, *find the price of the stock at the end of the nonconstant growth period, at which point it has become a constant growth stock*, and discount this price back to the present.
3. Add these two components to find the intrinsic value of the stock, $\hat{P}_0$.

Figure 7–7 can be used to illustrate the process for valuing nonconstant growth stocks, assuming the following five facts exist:

k_s = Stockholders' required rate of return = 12%. This rate is used to discount the cash flows.

N_s = Years of supernormal growth = 3.

g_s = Rate of growth in both earnings and dividends during the supernormal growth period = 30%. (*Note:* The growth rate during the supernormal growth period could vary from year to year. Also, there could be several different supernormal growth periods—for example, 30% for three years, then 20% for three years, and then a constant rate.) This rate is shown directly on the time line.

g_n = Rate of normal, constant growth after the supernormal period = 5%. This rate is also shown on the cash flow time line, after Year 3.

D_0 = Last (most recently paid) dividend the company paid = $1.20.

FIGURE 7-7   Process for Finding the Value of a Nonconstant Growth Stock

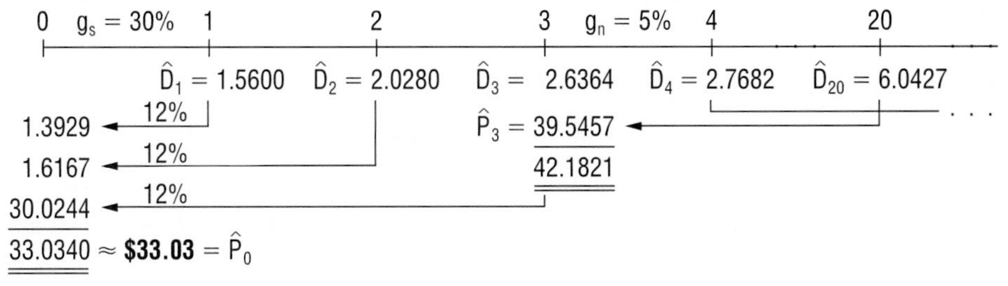

Step 1. Calculate the dividends for each year during the nonconstant growth period—$\hat{D}_t = D_0(1 + g_s)^t$:

$$\hat{D}_t = \$1.20(1.30)^1 = \$1.5600$$

$$\hat{D}_2 = \$1.20(1.30)^2 = \$2.0280$$

$$\hat{D}_3 = \$1.20(1.30)^3 = \$2.6364$$

Show these values on the cash flow time line as cash flows for Years 1 through 3.

Step 2. The price of the stock is the PV of dividends from Year 1 to infinity. So, in theory, we could continue projecting each future dividend beyond Year 3, when normal growth of five percent occurs. In other words, use $g_n = 5\%$ to compute $\hat{D}_4$, $\hat{D}_5$, and so on with $\hat{D}_3$ as the base dividend for normal growth:

$$\hat{D}_4 = \$2.6364(1.05)^1 = \$2.7682$$

$$\hat{D}_5 = \$2.6364(1.05)^2 = \$2.9066$$

$$\cdot$$
$$\cdot$$
$$\cdot$$

$$\hat{D}_{20} = \$2.6364(1.05)^{17} = \$6.0427$$

We can continue this process and then find the PV of this stream of dividends. However, we know that after $\hat{D}_3$ has been paid in Year 3, the stock becomes a constant growth stock, so we can apply the constant growth formula at that point and find $\hat{P}_3$, which is the PV of the dividends from Year 4 through infinity as evaluated in Year 3. After the Year 3 dividend has been paid, all of the future dividends will grow at a constant rate equal to 5 percent, so

$$\hat{P}_3 = \frac{\hat{D}_4}{k_s - g_n} = \frac{\$2.7682}{0.12 - 0.05} = \$39.5457$$

We show this $39.5457 on the cash flow time line as a second cash flow at Year 3. The $39.5457 is a Year 3 cash flow in the sense that the owner of the stock could sell it for $39.5457 at the end of Year 3, and also in the sense that $39.5457 is the present value equivalent of the dividend cash flows from Year 4 to infinity. Therefore, the *total cash flow* we recognize in Year 3 is the sum of $\hat{D}_3 + \hat{P}_3 = \$2.6364 + \$39.5457 = \$42.1821$.

Step 3. Now that the cash flows have been placed on the cash flow time line, we need to discount each cash flow at the required rate of return, $k_s = 12\%$. To find the present value, you either (1) compute the PVs directly, (2) use the PV tables, or (3) use the cash flow registers on your calculator. You can compute the PVs directly by dividing each cash flow by $(1.12)^t$. If you use the cash flow registers on your calculator, input $CF_0 = 0$, $CF_1 = 1.5600$, $CF_2 = 2.0280$, $CF_3 = 42.1821$, $I = 12$. The result is shown to the left below the cash flow time line.

The valuation process as diagrammed in Figure 7–7 is explained in the steps set forth below the cash flow time line. The value of the supernormal growth stock is calculated to be $33.03.

Self-Test Questions

What are the two elements of a stock's expected return?

Write out and explain the valuation model for a zero growth stock.

Write out and explain the valuation model for a constant growth stock.

How does one calculate the capital gains yield and the dividend yield of a stock?

Explain how one would find the value of a stock with nonconstant growth.

Stock Market Equilibrium

Recall from Chapter 5 that the required return on a stock, k_s, can be found using the Security Market Line (SML) equation as it was developed in our discussion of the Capital Asset Pricing Model (CAPM):

$$k_s = k_{RF} + (k_M - k_{RF})\beta_s$$

If the risk-free rate of return is 8 percent, if the market risk premium is four percent, and if Stock X has a beta of 2, then the marginal investor will require a return of 16 percent on Stock X, calculated as follows:

$$k_X = 8\% + (12\% - 8\%)\,2.0 = 16\%$$

This 16 percent required return is shown as a point on the SML in Figure 7–8.

The average investor will want to buy Stock X if the expected rate of return is more than 16 percent, will want to sell it if the expected rate of return is less than 16 percent, and will be indifferent, hence will hold but not buy or sell, if the expected rate of return is exactly 16 percent. Now suppose the investor's portfolio contains Stock X, and he or she analyzes the stock's prospects and concludes that its earnings, dividends, and price can be expected to grow at a constant rate of five percent per year. The last dividend was $D_0 = \$2.86$, so the next expected dividend is

$$\hat{D}_1 = \$2.86(1.05) = \$3.00$$

Our average investor observes that the present price of the stock, P_0, is $30. Should he or she purchase more of Stock X, sell the present holdings, or maintain the present position?

The investor can calculate Stock X's *expected rate of return* as follows:

$$\hat{k}_x = \frac{\hat{D}_1}{P_0} + g = \frac{\$3.00}{\$30.00} + 0.05 = 0.15 = 15\%$$

This value is plotted on Figure 7–8 as Point X, which is below the SML. Because the expected rate of return is less than the required return, this marginal investor would want to sell the stock, as would other holders. However, few people would want to buy at the $30 price, so the present owners would be unable to find buyers unless they cut

FIGURE 7–8	Expected and Required Returns on Stock X

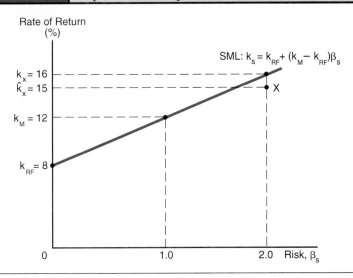

the price of the stock. Thus, the price would decline, and this decline would continue until the stock's price reached $27.27, at which point the market for this security would be in **equilibrium,** because the expected rate of return, 16 percent, would be equal to the required rate of return:

$$\hat{k}_x = \frac{\$3.00}{\$27.27} + 0.05 = 0.11 + 0.05 = 0.16 = 16\% = k_x$$

Had the stock initially sold for less than $27.27, say at $25, events would have been reversed. Investors would have wanted to buy the stock because its expected rate of return would have exceeded its required rate of return, and buy orders would have driven the stock's price up to $27.27.

To summarize, in equilibrium these two conditions must hold:

1. The expected rate of return as seen by the marginal investor must equal the required rate of return: $\hat{k}_x = k_x$.
2. The actual market price of the stock must equal its intrinsic value as estimated by the marginal investor: $P_0 = \hat{P}_0$.

Of course, some individual investors might believe that $\hat{k}_x > k_x$ and $P_0, < \hat{P}_0$, and hence they would invest most of their funds in the stock, while other investors might have an opposite view and would sell all of their shares. However, it is the marginal investor who establishes the actual market price, and for this investor, $\hat{k}_x = k_x$ and $P_0 = \hat{P}_0$. If these conditions do not hold, trading will occur until they do hold.

Changes in Equilibrium Stock Prices

Stock market prices are not constant—they undergo violent changes at times. For example, on October 19, 1987, the Dow Jones average dropped 508 points, and the average stock lost about 23 percent of its value in just one day. Some stocks lost more than half of their value that day. To see how such changes can occur, let us assume that

EQUILIBRIUM
The condition under which the expected return on a security is just equal to its required return, $\hat{k} = k$, and the price is stable.

Stock X is in equilibrium, selling at a price of $27.27 per share. If all expectations were exactly met, during the next year the price would gradually rise to $28.63, or by five percent. However, many different events could occur to cause a change in the equilibrium price of the stock. To illustrate, consider again the set of inputs used to develop Stock X's price of $27.27, along with a new set of assumed input variables:

	VARIABLE VALUE	
	ORIGINAL	NEW
Risk-free rate, k_{RF}	8%	7%
Market risk premium, $k_M - k_{RF}$	4%	3%
Stock X's beta coefficient, β_x	2.0	1.0
Stock X's expected growth rate, g_x	5%	6%
Current dividend, D_0	$ 2.86	$2.86
Price of Stock X	$27.27	?

Now give yourself a test: How would the change in each variable, by itself, affect the price, and what is your guess as to the new stock price?

Every change, taken alone, would lead to an increase in the price. The first three variables influence k_x, which declines from 16 percent to ten percent:

$$\text{Original } k_x = 8\% + 4\%(2.0) = 16\%.$$

$$\text{New } k_x = 7\% + 3\%(1.0) = 10\%.$$

Using these values, together with the new g value, we find that $\hat{P}_0$ rises from $27.27 to $75.79.[21]

$$\text{Original } \hat{P}_0 = \frac{\$2.86(1.05)}{0.16 - 0.05} = \frac{\$3.00}{0.11} = \$27.27$$

$$\text{New } \hat{P}_0 = \frac{\$2.86(1.06)}{0.10 - 0.06} = \frac{\$3.0316}{0.04} = \$75.79$$

At the new price, the expected and required rates of return will be equal:[22]

$$\hat{k}_x = \frac{\$3.0316}{\$75.79} + 0.06 = 0.10 = 10\% = k_x$$

Evidence suggests that stocks, especially those of large companies, adjust rapidly to disequilibrium situations. Consequently, equilibrium ordinarily exists for any given stock, and, in general, required and expected returns are equal. Stock prices certainly

[21]A price change of this magnitude is by no means rare. The prices of *many* stocks double or halve during a year. For example, during 1998, the stocks of Sun Microsystems and Lowe's Companies increased in value by more than 100 percent; on the other hand, the stocks of PeopleSoft and Diamond Offshore Drilling decreased in value by more than 50 percent.

[22]It should be obvious by now that *actual realized* rates of return are not necessarily equal to expected and required returns. Thus, an investor might have *expected* to receive a return of 15 percent if he or she had bought Lowe's or Diamond Offshore Drilling stock in 1998, but, after the fact, the realized return on Lowe's was far above 15 percent, whereas that on Diamond Offshore Drilling was far below.

change, sometimes violently and rapidly, but this simply reflects changing conditions and expectations. There are, of course, times when a stock continues to react for several months to a favorable or unfavorable development, but this does not signify a long adjustment period; rather, it simply illustrates that as more new pieces of information about the situation become available, the market adjusts to them. The ability of the market to adjust to new information is discussed next.

The Efficient Markets Hypothesis

EFFICIENT MARKETS HYPOTHESIS (EMH)
The hypothesis that securities are typically in equilibrium—that they are fairly priced in the sense that the price reflects all publicly available information on each security.

A body of theory called the **Efficient Markets Hypothesis (EMH)** holds (1) that stocks are always in equilibrium and (2) that it is impossible for an investor to *consistently* "beat the market." Essentially, those who believe in the EMH note that there are 100,000 or so full-time, highly trained, professional analysts and traders operating in the market, while there are fewer than 4,000 major stocks.[23] Therefore, if each analyst followed 30 stocks (which is about right, as analysts tend to specialize in the stocks in a specific industry), there would be 750 analysts following each stock. Further, these analysts work for organizations such as Citigroup, Merrill Lynch, and the like, which have billions of dollars available with which to take advantage of bargains. As a result of Securities and Exchange Commission (SEC) disclosure requirements and electronic information networks, as new information about a stock becomes available, these 750 analysts all receive and evaluate it at approximately the same time. Therefore, the price of the stock adjusts almost immediately to reflect any new developments.

Financial theorists generally define three forms, or levels, of information efficiency in the market:

1. The *weak form* of the EMH states that all information contained in past price movements is fully reflected in current market prices. Therefore, information about recent, or past, trends in stock prices is of no use in selecting stocks—the fact that a stock has risen for the past three days, for example, gives us no useful clues as to what it will do today or tomorrow. People who believe that weak-form efficiency exists also believe that "tape watchers" and "chartists" are wasting their time.[24]

2. The *semistrong form* of the EMH states that current market prices reflect all *publicly available* information. If this is true, no abnormal returns can be earned by analyzing stocks.[25] Thus, if semistrong-form efficiency exists, it does no good to pore over annual reports or other published data because market prices will have adjusted to any good or bad news contained in such reports as soon as they came out. However, insiders (say, the presidents of companies), even under semistrong-form efficiency, can still make abnormal returns on their own companies' stocks.

---

[23]There actually are many more than 4,000 stocks traded in the United States, but many of them are stocks of small firms that are traded infrequently. The 4,000 *major* stocks include those listed on both the New Stock Exchange and the American Stock Exchange, and other relatively large firms that institutional investors like pension funds and investment companies consider appropriate for their portfolios.

[24]Tape watchers are people who watch the NYSE tape, or price quotes, while chartists plot past patterns of stock price movements. Both are called "technicians," and both believe that they can see if something is happening to the stock that will cause its price to move up or down in the near future.

[25]An abnormal return is one that exceeds the return justified by the riskiness of the investment; that is, a return that plots above the SML in a graph like Figure 7–8.

3. The *strong form* of the EMH states that current market prices reflect all pertinent information, whether publicly available or privately held. If this form holds, even insiders would find it impossible to earn abnormal returns in the stock market.[26]

Many empirical studies have been conducted to test for the three forms of market efficiency. Most of these studies suggest that the stock market is indeed highly efficient in the weak form and reasonably efficient in the semistrong form, at least for the larger and more widely followed stocks. However, the strong-form EMH does not hold, so abnormal profits can be made by those who possess inside information.

What bearing does the EMH have on financial decisions? Because stock prices do seem to reflect public information, most stocks appear to be fairly valued. This does not mean that new developments could not cause a stock's price to soar or to plummet, but it does mean that stocks, in general, are fairly priced, and the prices probably are in equilibrium—it is safe to assume $\hat{k} = k$ and $P = \hat{P}$. However, there are certainly cases in which corporate insiders have information not known to outsiders.

Actual Stock Prices and Returns

Our discussion thus far has focused on expected stock prices and expected rates of return. Anyone who has ever invested in the stock market knows that there can be, and there generally are, large differences between expected and realized prices and returns.

Figure 7–9 shows how the price of an average share of stock has varied in recent years, and Figure 7–10 shows how total annual realized returns have varied. The market trend has been strongly up, but it has gone up in some years and down in others, and the stocks of individual companies have likewise gone up and down. We know from theory that expected returns as estimated by a marginal investor are always positive, but in some years, as Figure 7–10 shows, negative returns have been realized. Of course, even in bad years some individual companies do well, so the "name of the game" in security analysis is to pick the winners. Financial managers attempt to take actions that will put their companies into the winners' column, but they don't always succeed. In subsequent chapters, we will examine the actions that managers can take to increase the odds of their firms doing relatively well in the marketplace.

Self-Test Questions

When a stock is in equilibrium, what two conditions must hold?

What is the major conclusion of the Efficient Markets Hypothesis (EMH)?

What is the difference between the three forms of the EMH: (1) weak form, (2) semistrong form, and (3) strong form?

If a stock is not in equilibrium, explain how financial markets adjust to bring it into equilibrium.

---

[26]In the past, several cases of illegal insider trading have made the news headlines. These cases involved employees of several major investment banking houses and even an employee of the SEC. In a famous case, for example, Ivan Boesky admitted to making $50 million by purchasing the stock of firms he knew were about to merge. He went to jail, and he had to pay a large fine, but he helped disprove the strong-form EMH.

FIGURE 7–9	S&P 500 Index, 1970–1998

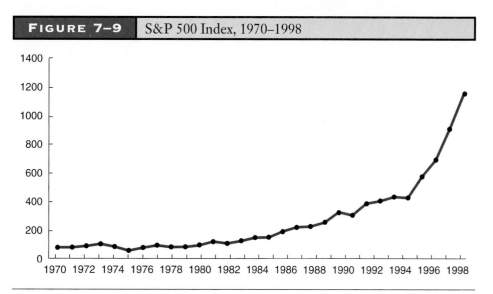

NOTE: Each data point represents the value of the S&P 500 Index on the last trading day of the year.
SOURCE: Standard & Poor's.

FIGURE 7–10	S&P 500 Index Total Returns: Capital Gain or Loss + Dividend Yield, 1970–1998

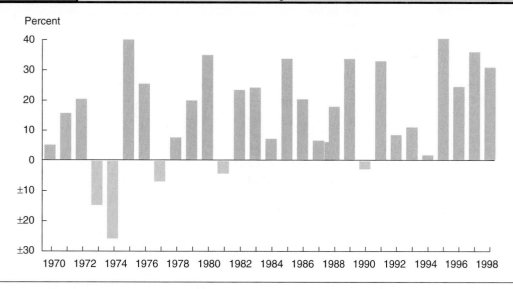

NOTE: S&P 500 data are from the last trading day of the year. Thus, total return is defined as the percent change in the S&P 500 index from the beginning of the year to the end of the year plus the annual dividend yield.
SOURCE: Standard & Poor's.

Valuation of Real (Tangible) Assets

In the previous sections, we found that the values of financial assets, bonds and stocks, are based on the present value of the future cash flows expected from the assets. Valuing real assets is no different. We need to compute the present value of the expected cash flows associated with the asset. For example, suppose Unilate Textiles is considering purchasing a machine so that it can manufacture a new line of products. After five years, the machine will be worthless because it will be used up. But during the five years Unilate uses the machine, the firm will be able to increase its net cash flows by the following amounts:

YEAR	EXPECTED CASH FLOW, $\hat{CF}_t$
1	$120,000
2	100,000
3	150,000
4	80,000
5	50,000

If Unilate wants to earn a 14 percent return on investments like this machine, what is the value of the machine to the company? To find the answer, we need to solve for the present value of the uneven cash flow stream produced by the machine. Thus, the value of this machine can be depicted as follows:

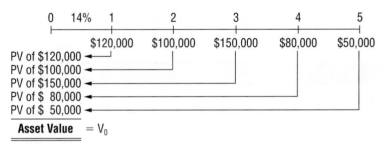

To compute the value of the machine, we simply apply Equation (7–1):

$$V_0 = \frac{\text{Present value}}{\text{of future CF}} = \frac{\$120,000}{(1.14)^1} + \frac{\$100,000}{(1.14)^2} + \frac{\$150,000}{(1.14)^3} + \frac{\$80,000}{(1.14)^4} + \frac{\$50,000}{(1.14)^5}$$

The value of the machine can be computed by using the three procedures discussed in Chapter 6: (1) numerically, (2) using the tables, and (3) with a financial calculator.

1. NUMERICAL SOLUTION:

Because the stream of cash flows is uneven (i.e., it is not an annuity), we must discount each cash flow back to the present and sum these PVs to find the machine's value:

$$V_0 = \$120,000 \times \left[\frac{1}{(1.14)^1}\right] + \$100,000 \times \left[\frac{1}{(1.14)^2}\right] + \$150,000 \times \left[\frac{1}{(1.14)^3}\right]$$

$$+ \$80,000 \times \left[\frac{1}{(1.14)^4}\right] + \$50,000 \times \left[\frac{1}{(1.14)^5}\right]$$

$$= \$105,263.16 + \$76,946.75 + \$101,245.73 + \$47,366.42 + \$25,968.43$$

$$= \$356,790.49$$

2. TABULAR SOLUTION:

Simply look up the appropriate PVIF values in Table A–1 at the end of the book, insert them into the equation, and complete the arithmetic:

$$V_0 = \$120{,}000(PVIF_{14\%,1}) + \$100{,}000(PVIF_{14\%,2}) + \$150{,}000(PVIF_{14\%,3})$$
$$+ \ \$80{,}000(PVIF_{14\%,4}) + \$50{,}000(PVIF_{14\%,5})$$
$$= \$120{,}000(0.8772) + \$100{,}000(0.7695) + \$150{,}000(0.6750)$$
$$+ \ \$80{,}000(0.5921) + \$50{,}000(0.5194) = \$356{,}802$$

There is a rounding difference that results from the fact that the tables only go to four decimal places.

3. Financial Calculator Solution:

To find the answer using your financial calculator, you must input the individual cash flows, in chronological order, into the cash flow register as we described in Chapter 6 (see Appendix 6A for instructions). According to the cash flow time line, the cash flows entered into the calculator are $CF_0 = 0$, $CF_1 = \$120{,}000$, $CF_2 = \$100{,}000$, $CF_3 = \$150{,}000$, $CF_4 = \$80{,}000$, and $CF_5 = \$50{,}000$. After entering these values, enter the required rate of return, $I = k = 14\%$. At this point, you have entered all the known information, so you only need to press the NPV key to find the present value of the cash flows. You should find the answer is $\$356{,}790.49$.

Real asset valuation is a critical concern for financial managers because they need to know whether the plant (e.g., buildings) and equipment (e.g., machines) and other long-term assets they purchase will help achieve the goal of wealth maximization. To determine how investing in a particular asset will affect the value of the firm, the financial manager must be able to determine whether the asset is worth its purchase price and if the asset will increase the firm's wealth. Although the general valuation procedures we outlined in this section can be used to value real assets, other factors often need to be considered before a final purchasing decision can be made. The process of evaluating projects and deciding which projects should be purchased is called *capital budgeting*. The capital budgeting decision-making process is crucial to the firm's success, and it is especially important if the firm is to achieve the goal of wealth maximization. Therefore, in the next two chapters we will explain in great detail the procedures firms use to make capital budgeting decisions—procedures that you can apply to make decisions when purchasing personal assets.

In this chapter we presented several equations for valuing a firm's common stock. These equations had one common element: they all assumed that the firm is currently paying a dividend. However, many small firms, even highly profitable ones whose stocks are traded in the market, have never paid a dividend. How does one value the stock of such firms? If a firm is expected to begin paying dividends in the future, we can modify the equations presented in the chapter and use them to determine the value of the stock.

A new business often expects to have very low sales during its first few years of operation as it develops its product. Then, if the product catches on, sales will grow rapidly for several years. For example, Compaq Computer Company had only three employees when it was incorporated in 1982. Its first year was devoted

continues

to product development, and 1982 sales were zero. In 1983, however, Compaq began marketing its personal computer, and its sales hit $111 million, a record first-year volume for any new firm at the time, and by 1986 Compaq was included in Fortune's 500 largest U.S. industrial firms. Obviously, Compaq has been more successful than most new businesses, but it is common for small firms to have growth rates of 100 percent, 500 percent, or even 1,000 percent during their first few years of operation.

Sales growth brings with it the need for additional assets—Compaq could not have increased its sales as it did without also increasing its assets, and asset growth requires an increase in liability and/or equity accounts. Small firms can generally obtain some bank credit, but they must maintain a reasonable balance between debt and equity. Thus, additional bank borrowings require increases in equity, and getting the equity capital needed to support growth can be difficult for small firms. They have limited access to the capital markets, and, even when they can sell common stock, the owners of small firms are reluctant to do so for fear of losing voting control. Therefore, the best source of equity for most small businesses is retained earnings, and for this reason most small firms pay no dividends during their rapid growth years. Eventually, though, successful small firms do pay dividends, and those dividends generally grow rapidly at first but slow down to a sustainable constant rate once the firm reaches maturity.

Finding the value of the stock of a small firm is the same as was described earlier in the chapter in the section about nonconstant growth companies, except, for most small firms, there might be numerous years in which no dividend payments are expected. If a small firm currently pays no dividend but is expected to pay dividends in the future, the value of its stock can be found as follows:

1. Estimate when dividends will be paid, the amount of the first dividend, the growth rate during the supernormal growth period, the length of the supernormal period, the long-run (constant) growth rate, and the rate of return required by investors.
2. Use the constant growth model to determine the price of the stock after the firm reaches a stable growth situation.
3. Set out on a time line the cash flows (dividends during the supernormal growth period and the stock price once the constant growth state is reached) and then find the present value of these cash flows. *That present value represents the value of the stock today.*

Summary

Corporate decisions should be analyzed in terms of how alternative courses of action are likely to affect the value of a firm. However, it is necessary to know how bond and stock prices are established before attempting to measure how a given decision will affect a specific firm's value. Accordingly, this chapter showed how bond and stock values are determined as well as how investors go about estimating the rates of return they expect to earn. The key concepts covered in the chapter are summarized here:

- The **value** of any asset can be found by computing the **present value of the cash flows** the asset is expected to generate during its life.
- A **bond** is a long-term promissory note issued by a business or governmental unit. The firm receives the selling price of the bond in exchange for promising to make interest payments and to repay the principal on a specified future date.
- The **value of a bond** is found as the present value of an **annuity** (the interest payments) plus the present value of a lump sum (the **principal**). The bond is evaluated at the appropriate periodic interest rate over the number of periods for which interest payments are made.

- The equation used to find the value of a bond is

$$V_d = \sum_{t=1}^{N \times m} \frac{INT}{\left(1 + \frac{k_d}{m}\right)^t} + \frac{M}{\left(1 + \frac{k_d}{m}\right)^{N \times m}}$$

$$= INT(PVIFA_{\frac{k_d}{m}, N \times m}) + M(PVIF_{\frac{k_d}{m}, N \times m})$$

  where INT is the dollar interest received each period, N represents the years to maturity, k_d is the required return on similar investments, and m equals the number of times interest is paid during the year.
- The return earned on a bond held to maturity is defined as the bond's **yield to maturity (YTM).**
- The longer the maturity of a bond, the more its price will change in response to a given change in interest rates; this is called **interest rate price risk.** Bonds with short maturities, however, expose the investor to high **interest rate reinvestment risk,** which is the risk that income will differ from what is expected because cash flows received from bonds will have to be reinvested at different interest rates.
- The **value of a share of stock** is calculated as the **present value of the stream of dividends** it is expected to provide in the future.
- A **zero-growth stock** is one whose future dividends are not expected to grow at all, while a **nonconstant growth stock** is one whose earnings and dividends are expected to grow at a rate different from the economy as a whole over some specified time period.
- Most **preferred stocks are perpetuities,** thus zero growth stocks, and the value of a share of such stocks is found as the dividend divided by the required rate of return: $P_0 = D/k_s$
- The equation used to find the **value of a constant, or normal, growth** stock is: $\hat{P}_0 = \hat{D}_1/(k_s - g)$.
- The **expected total rate of return** from a stock consists of an **expected dividend yield** plus an **expected capital gains yield.** For a constant growth firm, both the expected dividend yield and the expected capital gains yield are constant.
- The equation for $\hat{k}_s$, **the expected rate of return on a constant growth stock,** can be expressed as follows: $\hat{k}_s = \hat{D}_1/P_0 + g$.
- To find the **present value of a nonconstant growth stock,** (1) find the dividends expected during the nonconstant growth period; (2) find the price of the stock at the end of the nonconstant growth period; (3) discount the dividends and the projected price back to the present; and (4) sum these PVs to find the current expected value of the stock, $\hat{P}_0$.
- The **Efficient Markets Hypothesis (EMH)** holds that (1) stocks are always in equilibrium and (2) it is impossible for an investor to consistently "beat the market." Therefore, according to the EMH, stocks always are fairly valued ($\hat{P}_0 = P_0$), the required return on a stock is equal to its expected return ($k_s = \hat{k}_s$), and all stocks' expected returns plot on the SML.
- Differences can and do exist between expected and actual returns in the stock and bond markets—only for short-term, risk-free assets are expected and actual (or realized) returns equal.
- Like a financial asset, the value of a **real asset** is computed as the present value of the cash flows the asset is expected to provide in the future.

■ Determining the value of the stock of a **small firm** is the same as for larger companies with nonconstant growth, except small firms often do not pay dividends until later in their lives, which might be many years from the current period.

Questions

7–1 Describe how you should determine the value of an asset, whether it is a real asset or a financial asset.

7–2 Two investors are evaluating IBM's stock for possible purchase. They agree on the expected value of $\hat{D}_1$ and also on the expected future dividend growth rate. Further, they agree on the riskiness of the stock. However, one investor normally holds stocks for two years, while the other normally holds stocks for ten years. On the basis of the type of analysis done in this chapter, they should both be willing to pay the same price for IBM's stock. True or false? Explain.

7–3 A bond that pays interest forever and has no maturity date is a perpetual bond. In what respect is a perpetual bond similar to a no-growth common stock and to a share of preferred stock?

7–4 The rate of return you would get if you bought a bond and held it to its maturity date is called the bond's yield to maturity. If interest rates in the economy rise after a bond has been issued, what will happen to the bond's price and to its YTM? Does the length of time to maturity affect the extent to which a given change in interest rates will affect the bond's price?

7–5 If you buy a callable bond and interest rates decline, will the value of your bond rise by as much as it would have risen if the bond had not been callable? Explain.

7–6 If you bought a share of common stock, you would typically expect to receive dividends plus capital gains. Would you expect the distribution between dividend yield and capital gains to be influenced by the firm's decision to pay more dividends rather than to retain and reinvest more of its earnings?

7–7 How do you think the price of AT&T's stock will change if investors decide they want to earn a higher return for purchasing the stock? Assume all else remains constant. Do you think the price of AT&T's stock would change if the CEO announced that the company was going to have to pay a ten-year, $10 million fine for unfair trade practices? Explain your rationale.

7–8 How do you think valuing a real asset, such as a building, differs from valuing a financial asset, such as a stock or a bond?

Self-Test Problems

(Solutions appear in Appendix B)

key terms   **ST–1** Define each of the following terms:
   a. Bond
   b. Par value; face value; maturity value
   c. Coupon payment; coupon interest rate
   d. Premium bond; discount bond
   e. Current yield (on a bond); yield to maturity (YTM)
   f. Interest rate price risk; interest rate reinvestment risk
   g. Intrinsic value ($\hat{P}_0$); market price (P_0)

  h. Required rate of return, k_s; expected rate of return, $\hat{k}_s$; actual, or realized, rate of return, $\bar{k}_s$

  i. Capital gains yield; dividend yield; expected total return

  j. Zero-growth stock

  k. Normal, or constant, growth stock; nonconstant, growth stock

  l. Equilibrium

  m. Efficient Markets Hypothesis (EMH); forms (degrees) of EMH

stock growth rates and valuation   **ST–2** You are considering buying the stocks of two companies that operate in the same industry; they have very similar characteristics except for their dividend payout policies. Both companies are expected to earn $6 per share this year. However, Company D (for "dividend") is expected to pay out all of its earnings as dividends, while Company G (for "growth") is expected to pay out only one-third of its earnings, or $2 per share. D's stock price is $40. G and D are equally risky. Which of the following is most likely to be true?

  a. Company G will have a faster growth rate than Company D. Therefore, G's stock price should be greater than $40.

  b. Although G's growth rate should exceed D's, D's current dividend exceeds that of G, and this should cause D's price to exceed G's.

  c. An investor in Stock D will get his or her money back faster because D pays out more of its earnings as dividends. Thus, in a sense, D is like a short-term bond, and G is like a long-term bond. Therefore, if economic shifts cause k_d and k_s to increase and if the expected streams of dividends from D and G remain constant, Stocks D and G will both decline, but D's price should decline more.

  d. D's expected and required rate of return is $\hat{k}_s = k_s = 15\%$. G's expected return will be higher because of its higher expected growth rate.

  e. On the basis of the available information, the best estimate of G's growth rate is ten percent.

bond valuation   **ST–3** The Pennington Corporation issued a new series of bonds on January 1, 1980. The bonds were sold at par ($1,000), have a 12 percent coupon, and mature on December 31, 2009 (30 years after issue). Coupon payments are made semiannually (on June 30 and December 31).

  a. What was the YTM of Pennington's bonds on January 1, 1980?

  b. What was the price of the bond on January 1, 1985, five years later, assuming that the level of interest rates had fallen to ten percent?

  c. Find the current yield and capital gains yield on the bond on January 1, 1985, given the price as determined in part b.

  d. On July 1, 1999, Pennington's bonds sold for $891.64. What was the YTM at that date?

  e. What were the current yield and capital gains yield on July 1, 1999?

constant growth stock valuation   **ST–4** Ewald Company's current stock price is $36, and its last dividend was $2.40. In view of Ewald's strong financial position and its consequent low risk, its required rate of return is only 12 percent. If dividends are expected to grow at a constant rate, g, in the future, and if k_s is expected to remain at 12 percent, what is Ewald's expected stock price five years from now?

nonconstant growth stock valuation   **ST–5** Snyder Computer Chips Inc. is experiencing a period of rapid growth. Earnings and dividends are expected to grow at a rate of 15 percent during the next two years, at 13 percent in the third year, and at a constant rate of six percent thereafter. Snyder's *last* dividend was $1.15, and the required rate of return on the stock is 12 percent.

a. Calculate the value of the stock today.

b. Calculate $\hat{P}_1$ and $\hat{P}_2$.

c. Calculate the dividend yield and capital gains yield for Years 1, 2, and 3.

Problems

bond valuation

7–1 Suppose Ford Motor Company sold an issue of bonds with a ten-year maturity, a $1,000 par value, a ten percent coupon rate, and semiannual interest payments.

a. Two years after the bonds were issued, the going rate of interest on bonds such as these fell to six percent. At what price would the bonds sell?

b. Suppose that, two years after the initial offering, the going interest rate had risen to 12 percent. At what price would the bonds sell?

c. Suppose that the conditions in part a existed—that is, interest rates fell to six percent two years after the issue date. Suppose further that the interest rate remained at six percent for the next eight years. Describe what would happen to the price of the Ford Motor Company bonds over time.

perpetual bond valuation

7–2 The bonds of the Lange Corporation are perpetuities with a ten percent coupon. Bonds of this type currently yield eight percent, and their par value is $1,000.

a. What is the price of the Lange bonds?

b. Suppose interest rate levels rise to the point where such bonds now yield 12 percent. What would be the price of the Lange bonds?

c. At what price would the Lange bonds sell if the yield on these bonds was ten percent?

d. How would your answers to parts a, b, and c change if the bonds were not perpetuities but had a maturity of 20 years?

constant growth stock valuation

7–3 Your broker offers to sell you some shares of Wingler & Co. common stock that paid a dividend of $2 *yesterday*. You expect the dividend to grow at the rate of five percent per year for the next three years, and if you buy the stock you plan to hold it for three years and then sell it.

a. Find the expected dividend for each of the next three years; that is, calculate $\hat{D}_1$, $\hat{D}_2$, and $\hat{D}_3$. Note that $D_0 = \$2$.

b. Given that the appropriate discount rate is 12 percent and that the first of these dividend payments will occur one year from now, find the present value of the dividend stream; that is, calculate the PV of $\hat{D}_1$, $\hat{D}_2$, and $\hat{D}_3$, and then sum these PVs.

c. You expect the price of the stock three years from now to be $34.73; that is, you expect $\hat{P}_3$ to equal $34.73. Discounted at a 12 percent rate, what is the present value of this expected future stock price? In other words, calculate the PV of $34.73.

d. If you plan to buy the stock, hold it for three years, and then sell it for $34.73, what is the most you should pay for it?

e. Use Equation 7–6 to calculate the present value of this stock. Assume that g = 5%, and it is constant.

f. Is the value of this stock dependent upon how long you plan to hold it? In other words, if your planned holding period were two years or five years rather than three years, would this affect the value of the stock today, $\hat{P}_0$?

return on common stock

7–4 You buy a share of Damanpour Corporation stock for $21.40. You expect it to pay dividends of $1.07, $1.1449, and $1.2250 in Years 1, 2, and 3, respectively, and you expect to sell it at a price of $26.22 at the end of three years.

a. Calculate the growth rate in dividends.

b. Calculate the expected dividend yield.

c. Assuming that the calculated growth rate is expected to continue, you can add the dividend yield to the expected growth rate to get the expected total rate of return. What is this stock's expected total rate of return?

constant growth stock valuation   **7-5** Investors require a 15 percent rate of return on Goulet Company's stock ($k_s = 15\%$).

a. What will be Goulet's stock value if the previous dividend was $D_0 = \$2$ and if investors expect dividends to grow at a constant compound annual rate of (1) -5 percent, (2) 0 percent, (3) 5 percent, and (4) 10 percent?

b. Using data from part a and the constant growth model, what is the value for Goulet's stock if the required rate of return is 15 percent and the expected growth rate is (1) 15 percent or (2) 20 percent? Are these reasonable results? Explain.

c. Is it reasonable to expect that a constant growth stock would have $g > k_s$?

nonconstant growth stock valuation   **7-6** Bayboro Sails is expected to pay dividends of $2.50, $3.00, and $4.00 in the next three years—$\hat{D}_1$, $\hat{D}_2$, and $\hat{D}_3$, respectively. After three years, the dividend is expected to grow at a constant rate equal to four percent per year indefinitely. Stockholders require a return of 14% to invest in the common stock of Bayboro Sails.

a. Compute the present value of the dividends Bayboro is expected to pay over the next three years.

b. For what price should investors expect to be able to sell the common stock of Bayboro at the end of three years? (*Hint:* The dividend will grow at a constant 4 percent in Year 4, Year 5, and every year thereafter, so Equation 7-6 can be used to find $\hat{P}_3$—the appropriate dividend to use in the numerator is $\hat{D}_4$.)

c. Compute the value of Bayboro's common stock today, $\hat{P}_0$.

bond valuation   **7-7** In January of 1994, the yield on AAA rated corporate bonds averaged about five percent; by the end of the year the yield on these same bonds was about 8 percent because the Federal Reserve increased interest rates six times during the year. Assume IBM issued a ten-year, five percent coupon bond on January 1, 1994. On the same date, General Motors issued a 20-year, five percent coupon bond. Both bonds pay interest *annually*. Also assume that the market rate on similar risk bonds was five percent at the time the bonds were issued.

a. Compute the market value of each bond at the time of issue.

b. Compute the market value of each bond one year after issue if the market yield for similar risk bonds was 8 percent on January 1, 1995.

c. Compute the 1994 capital gains yield for each bond.

d. Compute the current yield for each bond in 1994.

e. Compute the total return each bond would have generated for investors in 1994.

f. If you invested in bonds at the beginning of 1994, would you have been better off to have held long-term or short-term bonds? Explain why.

g. Assume interest rates stabilize at the January 1995 rate of 8.5 percent, and they stay at this level indefinitely. What would be the price of each bond on January 1, 2000 after six years from the date of issue have passed? Describe what should happen to the prices of these bonds as they approach their maturities.

nonconstant growth stock valuation   **7-8** It is now January 1, 2000. Swink Electric Inc. has just developed a solar panel capable of generating 200 percent more electricity than any solar panel currently on the market. As a result, Swink is expected to experience a 15 percent annual growth rate for the next five years. By the end of five years, other firms will have developed comparable technology, and Swink's growth rate will slow to five percent per year indefinitely. Stockholders require a return of 12 percent on Swink's stock. The most recent annual dividend (D_0), which was paid yesterday, was $1.75 per share.

a. Calculate Swink's expected dividends for 2000, 2001, 2002, 2003, and 2004.

b. Calculate the value of the stock today, $\hat{P}_0$. Proceed by finding the present value of the dividends expected at the end of 2000, 2001, 2002, 2003, and 2004 plus the present value of the stock price that should exist at the end of 2004. The year-end 2004 stock price can be found by using the constant growth equation (Equation 7–6). Notice that to find the December 31, 2004, price, you use the dividend expected in 2005, which is five percent greater than the 2004 dividend.

c. Calculate the expected dividend yield, $\hat{D}_1/P_0$, the capital gains yield expected in 2000, and the expected total return (dividend yield plus capital gains yield) for 2000. (Assume that $\hat{P}_0 = P_0$, and recognize that the capital gains yield is equal to the total return minus the dividend yield.) Also calculate these same three yields for 2004.

d. How might an investor's tax situation affect his or her decision to purchase stocks of companies in the early stages of their lives, when they are growing rapidly, versus stocks of older, more mature firms? When does Swink's stock become "mature" in this example?

e. Suppose your boss tells you she believes that Swink's annual growth rate will be only 12 percent during the next five years and that the firm's normal growth rate will be only four percent. Without doing any calculations, what general effect would these growth-rate changes have on the price of Swink's stock?

f. Suppose your boss also tells you that she regards Swink as being quite risky and that she believes the required rate of return should be 14 percent, not 12 percent. Again without doing any calculations, how would the higher required rate of return affect the price of the stock, its capital gains yield, and its dividend yield?

supernormal growth stock valuation

7–9 Tanner Technologies Corporation (TTC) has been growing at a rate of 20 percent per year in recent years. This same growth rate is expected to last for another two years.

a. If $D_0 = \$1.60$, $k = 10\%$, and $g_n = 6\%$, what is TTC's stock worth today? What are its expected dividend yield and capital gains yield at this time?

b. Now assume that TTC's period of supernormal growth is to last another five years rather than two years. How would this affect its price, dividend yield, and capital gains yield? Answer in words only.

c. What will be TTC's dividend yield and capital gains yield once its period of supernormal growth ends? (*Hint:* These values will be the same regardless of whether you examine the case of two or five years of supernormal growth; the calculations are very easy.)

d. Of what interest to investors is the changing relationship between dividend yield and capital gains yield over time?

constant growth stock valuation

7–10 The risk-free rate of return, k_{RF}, is 11 percent; the required rate of return on the market, k_M, is 14 percent; and Gerlunice Company's stock has a beta coefficient, β, of 1.5.

a. Based on the Capital Asset pricing Model (CAPM), what should be the required return for Gerlunice Company's stock?

b. If the dividend expected during the coming year, $\hat{D}_1$, is $2.25, and if $g = 5\%$ and is constant, at what price should Gerlunice's stock sell?

c. Now suppose the Federal Reserve Board increases the money supply, causing the risk-free rate to drop to nine percent and k_M to fall to 12 percent. What would this do to the price of the stock?

d. In addition to the change in part c, suppose investors' risk aversion declines; this fact, combined with the decline in k_{RF}, causes k_M to fall to 11 percent. At what price would Gerlunice's stock sell?

e. Now suppose Gerlunice has a change in management. The new group institutes policies that increase the expected constant growth rate to 6 percent. Also, the new management stabilizes sales and profits, which causes the beta coefficient to decline from 1.5 to 1.3. Assume that k_{RF} and k_M are equal to the values in part d. After all these changes, what is Gerlunice's new equilibrium price? (Note: $\hat{D}_1$ goes to $2.27.)

beta coefficients   **7-11** Suppose Sartoris Chemical Company's management conducts a study and concludes that if Sartoris expanded its consumer products division (which is less risky than its primary business, industrial chemicals), the firm's beta would decline from 1.2 to 0.9. However, consumer products have a somewhat lower profit margin, and this would cause Sartoris's constant growth rate in earnings and dividends to fall from seven to five percent.

a. Should management make the change? Assume the following: $k_M = 12\%$; $k_{RF} = 9\%$; $D_0 = \$2$.

b. Assume all the facts as given above except the change in the beta coefficient. How low would the beta have to fall to cause the expansion to be a good one? (*Hint:* Set $\hat{P}_0$ under the new policy equal to $\hat{P}_0$ under the old one, and find the new beta that will produce this equality.)

Exam-Type Problems

The problems included in this section are set up in such a way that they could be used as multiple-choice exam problems.

bond valuation   **7-12** The Desreumaux Company has two bond issues outstanding. Both bonds pay $100 annual interest plus $1,000 at maturity. Bond L has a maturity of 15 years and Bond S a maturity of 1 year.

a. What will be the value of each of these bonds when the going rate of interest is (1) 5 percent, (2) 8 percent, and (3) 12 percent? Assume that there is only one more interest payment to be made on Bond S.

b. Why does the longer-term (15-year) bond fluctuate more when interest rates change than does the shorter-term (1-year) bond?

yield to maturity   **7-13** It is now January 1, 2000, and you are considering the purchase of an outstanding Puckett Corporation bond that was issued on January 1, 1998. The Puckett bond has a 9.5 percent annual coupon and a 30-year original maturity (it matures on December 31, 2027). Interest rates have declined since the bond was issued, and the bond now is selling at 116.575 percent of par, or $1,165.75. You want to determine the yield to maturity for this bond.

a. Use Equation 7–3 to approximate the yield to maturity for the Puckett bond in 2000.

b. What is the actual yield to maturity in 2000 for the Puckett bond?

yield to maturity

7–14 The Severn Company's bonds have four years remaining to maturity. Interest is paid annually, the bonds have a $1,000 par value, and the coupon interest rate is 9 percent.

   a. Compute the *approximate* yield to maturity for the bonds if the current market price is either (1) $829 or (2) $1,104.

   b. Would you pay $829 for one of these bonds if you thought that the appropriate rate of interest was 12 percent—that is, if k_d = 12%? Explain your answer.

rate of return for a perpetual bond

7–15 What will be the rate of return on a perpetual bond with a $1,000 par value, an 8 percent coupon rate, and a current market price of (a) $600, (b) $800, (c) $1,000, and (d) $1,500? Assume interest is paid annually.

declining growth stock valuation

7–16 McCue Mining Company's ore reserves are being depleted, so its sales are falling. Also, its pit is getting deeper each year, so its costs are rising. As a result, the company's earnings and dividends are declining at the constant rate of 5 percent per year. If D_0 = $5 and k_s = 15%, what is the value of McCue Mining's stock?

equilibrium rates of return

7–17 The beta coefficient for Stock C is β_C = 0.4, whereas that for Stock D is β_D = −0.5. (Stock D's beta is negative, indicating that its rate of return rises whenever returns on most other stocks fall. There are very few negative beta stocks, although collection agency stocks are sometimes cited as an example.)

   a. If the risk-free rate is nine percent and the expected rate of return on an average stock is 13 percent, what are the required rates of return on Stocks C and D?

   b. For Stock C, suppose the current price, P_0, is $25; the next expected dividend, $\hat{D}_1$, is $1.50; and the stock's expected constant growth rate is 4 percent. Is the stock in equilibrium? Explain, and describe what will happen if the stock is not in equilibrium.

supernormal growth stock valuation

7–18 Assume that the average firm in your company's industry is expected to grow at a constant rate of six percent, and its dividend yield is seven percent. Your company is about as risky as the average firm in the industry, but it has just successfully completed some R&D work that leads you to expect that earnings and dividends will grow at a rate of 50 percent [$\hat{D}_1$ = $D_0(1 + g)$ = $D_0(1.50)$] this year and 25 percent the following year, after which growth should match the six percent industry average rate. The last dividend paid (D_0) was $1. What is the value per share of your firm's stock?

effective annual rate

7–19 Assume that as investment manager of Florida Electric Company's pension plan (which is exempt from income taxes), you must choose between IBM bonds and AT&T preferred stock. The bonds have a $1,000 par value, they mature in 20 years, they pay $40 each six months, and they sell at a price of $897.40 per bond. The preferred stock is a perpetuity; it pays a dividend of $2 each quarter, and it sells for $95 per share. What is the effective annual rate of return (EAR) on the *higher* yielding security?

simple interest rate

7–20 Tapley Corporation's 14 percent coupon rate, semiannual payment, $1,000 par value bonds mature in 30 years. The bonds sell at a price of $1,353.54, and the yield curve is flat. Assuming that interest rates in the economy are expected to remain at their current level, what is the best estimate of Tapley's simple interest rate on *new* bonds?

nonconstant growth stock valuation

7–21 Microtech Corporation is expanding rapidly, and it currently needs to retain all of its earnings; hence, it does not pay any dividends. However, investors expect Microtech to begin paying dividends, with the first dividend of $1 coming three years from today. The dividend should grow rapidly—at a rate of 50 percent per year—during Years 4 and 5. After Year 5, the company should grow at a constant rate of eight percent per year. If the required return on the stock is 15 percent, what is the value of the stock today?

valuation of real assets   **7–22** Currently, there is so much demand for the Anderson Electric's products that the company cannot manufacture enough inventory to satisfy demand. Consequently, Anderson is considering purchasing a new machine that will increase inventory production. Anderson estimates that the new machine will generate the following net cash flows during its lifetime:

YEAR	NET CASH FLOW, $\hat{CF}_t$
1	$18,000
2	12,000
3	15,000
4	10,000
5	10,000
6	10,000

a. If Anderson normally requires a return equal to 12 percent for such projects, what is the *maximum* amount it should pay for the machine?

b. How would your answer to part a change if the appropriate rate of return is 15 percent?

Integrative Problem

valuation   **7–23** Robert Campbell and Carol Morris are senior vice presidents of the Mutual of Chicago Insurance Company. They are codirectors of the company's pension fund management division, with Campbell having responsibility for fixed income securities (primarily bonds) and Morris being responsible for equity investments. A major new client, the California League of Cities, has requested that Mutual of Chicago present an investment seminar to the mayors of the represented cities, and Campbell and Morris, who will make the actual presentation, have asked you to help them by answering the following questions:

Section I: Bond valuation   a. What are the key features of a bond?

b. How is the value of any asset whose value is based on expected future cash flows determined?

c. How is the value of a bond determined? What is the value of a 1-year, $1,000 par value bond with a ten percent annual coupon if its required rate of return is ten percent? What is the value of a similar ten-year bond?

d. (1) What would be the value of the bond described in part c if, just after it had been issued, the expected inflation rate rose by 3 percentage points, causing investors to require a 13 percent return? Would we now have a discount or a premium bond? (*Hint:* PVIF$_{13\%,1}$ = 0.8850; PVIF$_{13\%,10}$ = 0.2946; PVIFA$_{13\%,10}$ = 5.4262.)

(2) What would happen to the bond's value if inflation fell, and k_d declined to 7 percent? Would we now have a premium or a discount bond?

(3) What would happen to the value of the ten-year bond over time if the required rate of return remained at 13 percent or remained at seven percent?

e. (1) What is the yield to maturity on a ten-year, nine percent annual coupon, $1,000 par value bond that sells for $887.00? That sells for $1,134.20?

What does the fact that a bond sells at a discount or at a premium tell you about the relationship between k_d and the bond's coupon rate?

(2) What is the current yield, the capital gains yield, and the total return in each case?

f. What is interest rate price risk? Which bond in part c has more interest rate price risk, the one-year bond or the ten-year bond?

g. What is interest rate reinvestment risk? Which bond in part c has more interest rate reinvestment risk, assuming a ten-year investment horizon?

h. Redo parts c and d, assuming the bonds have semiannual rather than annual coupons. (*Hint:* $PVIF_{6.5\%,2} = 0.8817$; $PVIFA_{6.5\%,2} = 1.8206$; $PVIF_{6.5\%,20} = 0.2838$; $PVIFA_{6.5\%,20} = 11.0185$; $PVIF_{3.5\%,2} = 0.9335$; $PVIFA_{3.5\%,2} = 1.8997$; $PVIF_{3.5\%,20} = 0.5026$; $PVIFA_{3.5\%,20} = 14.2124$.)

i. Suppose you could buy, for $1,000, either a ten percent, ten-year, annual payment bond or a ten percent, ten-year, semiannual payment bond. They are equally risky. Which would you prefer? If $1,000 is the proper price for the semiannual bond, what is the proper price for the annual payment bond?

j. What is the value of a perpetual bond with an annual coupon of $100 if its required rate of return is ten percent? 13 percent? seven percent? Assess the following statement: "Because perpetual bonds match an infinite investment horizon, they have little interest rate price risk."

Section II: Stock valuation

To illustrate the common stock valuation process, Campbell and Morris have asked you to analyze the Bon Temps Company, an employment agency that supplies word processor operators and computer programmers to businesses with temporarily heavy workloads. You are to answer the following questions:

a. (1) Write out a formula that can be used to value any stock, regardless of its dividend pattern.

(2) What is a constant growth stock? How are constant growth stocks valued?

(3) What happens if the growth is constant, and $g > k_s$? Will many stocks have $g > k_s$?

b. Assume that Bon Temps has a beta coefficient of 1.2, that the risk-free rate (the yield on T-bonds) is ten percent, and that the required rate of return on the market is 15 percent. What is the required rate of return on the firm's stock?

c. Assume that Bon Temps is a constant growth company whose last dividend (D_0, which was paid yesterday) was $2.00 and whose dividend is expected to grow indefinitely at a six percent rate.

(1) What is the firm's expected dividend stream over the next three years?

(2) What is the firm's current stock price?

(3) What is the stock's expected value one year from now?

(4) What are the expected dividend yield, the capital gains yield, and the total return during the first year?

d. Now assume that the stock is currently selling at $21.20. What is the expected rate of return on the stock?

e. What would the stock price be if its dividends were expected to have zero growth?

f. Now assume that Bon Temps is expected to experience supernormal growth of 30 percent for the next three years, then to return to its long-run constant growth rate of six percent. What is the stock's value under these conditions? What is its expected dividend yield and capital gains yield in Year 1? In Year 4?

g. Suppose Bon Temps is expected to experience zero growth during the first three years and then to resume its steady-state growth of six percent in the fourth year. What is the stock's value now? What is its expected dividend yield and its capital gains yield in Year 1? In Year 4?

h. Finally, assume that Bon Temps's earnings and dividends are expected to decline by a constant six percent per year, that is, $g = -6\%$. Why would anyone be willing to buy such a stock, and at what price should it sell? What would be the dividend yield and capital gains yield in each year?

Section III: Real asset valuation

Mutual of Chicago currently is examining the possibility of purchasing a piece of equipment that will scan data into its main computer. The new scanner will eliminate the need to hire part-time help to make sure information about clients is recorded accurately and in a timely manner. After evaluating all future costs and benefits, management has determined the new scanner will generate the following cash flows during its ten-year life:

YEAR/PERIOD	EXPECTED CASH FLOW, $\hat{CF}_t$
1–3	$30,000
4–6	15,000
7	−20,000
8–10	10,000

Campbell and Morris would like you to evaluate the value of the scanner.

a. If Mutual of Chicago believes the appropriate return for investments like the scanner is 15 percent, what is the value of the scanner to the company?

b. Would you recommend the machine be purchased if its current cost is $100,000? Explain your reasoning.

c. Would the scanner be more attractive if the appropriate return was 10 percent, rather than 15 percent? Explain your answer.

Computer-Related Problem

Work the problem in this section only if you are using the computer problem diskette.

nonconstant growth stock valuation

7–24 Use the model on the computer problem diskette in the File C6 to solve this problem.

a. Refer back to Problem 7–8. Rework part e, using the computerized model to determine what Swink's expected dividends and stock price would be under the conditions given.

b. Suppose your boss tells you that she regards Swink as being quite risky and that she believes the required rate of return should be higher than the 12 percent originally specified. Rework the problem under the conditions given in part e, except change the required rate of return to (1) 13 percent, (2) 15 percent, and (3) 20 percent to determine the effects of the higher required rates of return on Swink's stock price.

http://www.finpipe.com   Financial Pipeline
Provides explanations, tutorials, and articles related to stock and bond valuation and trading. There are also exercises and examples that illustrate valuation of financial assets.

http://www.datachimp.com   datachimp
Click on "interactive bond page" to get explanations of bond yields, coupons, maturities, and so forth.

http://www.stockselector.com   StockSelector.com
There is a variety of information at this site. You can get stock and bond quotes, compute values, examine trading techniques, and so on. To value stocks and bonds, click on "calculators" in the list along the left side of the screen, and then choose which type of valuation you want.

http://www.moneypages.com   The Syndicate
Provides links to various sites that relate to stock and bond quotes, selection, and valuation. Various indices and investment news are also available at this site.

Most of the large brokerage firms have *limited* quotes and examples of valuation models available on their Web sites. At these sites, more detailed quotes, analyses, and other investment information are available only to clients. The following list provides an example:

http://www.jpmorgan.com   J. P. Morgan & Co., Incorporated
http://www.merrilllynch.com   Merrill Lynch & Co., Inc.
http://www.schwab.com   Charles Schwab & Co., Inc.
http://www.smithbarney.com   Salomon Smith Barney Inc.

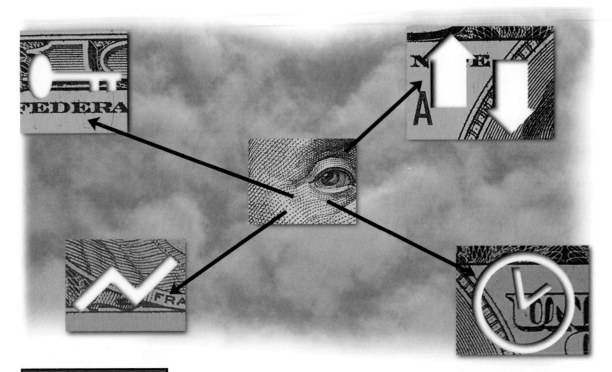

PART IV

Capital Budgeting

CHAPTER 8

Capital Budgeting Techniques

A MANAGERIAL PERSPECTIVE

After five years of planning and $3.5 billion in costs for development and for new factories and equipment, in the summer of 1990 General Motors (GM) began production of a new compact car—the Saturn. Now, nearly nine years later, it is safe to say that most people in the United States have heard of the Saturn car line. For it to have survived so long, you probably would expect that the Saturn has been a successful venture. Unfortunately for GM, however, the Saturn line has never really reached the sales necessary for the project to be considered a success. Even though consumers seem to like the Saturn concept and it has a good service reputation, annual sales (less than 300,000) have been well below the 500,000 needed for GM to begin to call the project a viable investment. Even more disturbing is the fact that Saturn sales have been declining in recent years. In 1998, for example, sales were less than 250,000, which represented the fifth straight year of falling sales and a decline of about nine percent from the previous year. Some believe GM has used the Saturn project as a loss leader to attract first-time new car buyers and as a means to satisfy federal regulations concerning the average fuel economy of the line of cars it offers. Even so, Saturn cannot survive if sales continue to decline. To try to reverse the trend, GM recently appointed Cynthia Trudell, one of its manufacturing executives, to head the Saturn division. Clearly, Trudell's first job will be to determine how to ensure Saturn's survival.

Chrysler introduced its version of a new compact car—the Neon, which is sold under the Dodge and Plymouth name—in mid-1994. The new car had a price tag that was comparable to the Ford Escort and the Saturn, but at the time it was introduced it offered extra features, including dual front air bags and a more advanced, "sportier" engine than the typical compact car. Because Chrysler used plant and equipment that it already had, only about $1.3 billion was spent to develop the Neon. For this reason, when it was introduced, most analysts believed the Neon line would be a money-making project for Chrysler. While Neon sales were fairly brisk in its early years, recently the trend has reversed, primarily because demand in the entire compact car market has declined sharply.

GM's Saturn project and Chrysler's Neon project are examples of massive capital budgeting ventures that required quite a bit of analysis and decision making before the billions of dollars required for development and implementation were spent. The principles set forth in this chapter and the next offer insights into how capital budgeting decisions such as these are made. ∎

SOURCES: Various articles available on Dow Jones Interactive® Publications Library located at http://www.wsj.com.

In the previous three chapters we showed how assets are valued and required rates of return are determined. Now we apply these concepts to investment decisions involving the fixed assets of a firm, or *capital budgeting*. Here the term *capital* refers to fixed assets used in production, while a *budget* is a plan that details projected inflows and outflows during some future period. Thus, the capital budget is an outline of planned expenditures on fixed assets, and **capital budgeting** is the process of analyzing projects and deciding which are acceptable investments and which actually should be purchased.

CAPITAL BUDGETING
The process of planning and evaluating expenditures on assets whose cash flows are expected to extend beyond one year.

Our treatment of capital budgeting is divided into two chapters. First, this chapter gives an overview and explains the basic techniques used in capital budgeting analysis. Then, in Chapter 9, we consider how the cash flows associated with capital budgeting projects are estimated and how risk is considered in capital budgeting decisions.

Importance of Capital Budgeting

A number of factors combine to make capital budgeting decisions perhaps the most important ones financial managers must make. First, the impact of capital budgeting is long-term; thus, the firm loses some decision-making flexibility when capital projects are purchased. For example, when a firm invests in an asset with a ten-year economic life, its operations are affected for ten years—the firm is "locked in" by the capital budgeting decision. Further, because asset expansion is fundamentally related to expected future sales, a decision to buy a fixed asset that is expected to last ten years involves an implicit ten-year sales forecast.

An error in the forecast of asset requirements can have serious consequences. If the firm invests too much in assets, it will incur unnecessarily heavy expenses. But if it does not spend enough on fixed assets, it might find that inefficient production and inadequate capacity lead to lost sales that are difficult, if not impossible, to recover.

Timing is also important in capital budgeting—capital assets must be ready to come "on line" when they are needed; otherwise, opportunities might be lost. For example, consider what happened to Decopot, a decorative tile manufacturer with no formal capital budgeting process. Decopot attempted to operate at full capacity as often as possible. This was not a bad idea because demand for Decopot's product and services was relatively stable. But about four years ago Decopot began to experience intermittent spurts of additional demand for its products. Decopot could not satisfy the additional demand because it did not have the capacity to produce any more products—customers had to be turned away. The spurts in demand continued, so senior management decided to add capacity to increase production so the additional orders could be filled. It took nine months to get the additional capacity ready. Finally, Decopot was ready for the increased demand the next time it arrived. Unfortunately, the "next time" never came because competitors had expanded their operations six months earlier, which allowed them to fill customers' orders when Decopot could not—many of Decopot's customers are now the competitors' customers. If Decopot had properly forecasted demand and planned its capacity requirements, it would have been able to maintain or perhaps even increase its market share; instead, its market share decreased.

Effective capital budgeting can improve both the timing of asset acquisitions and the quality of assets purchased. A firm that forecasts its needs for capital assets in advance will have an opportunity to purchase and install the assets before they are needed. Unfortunately, like Decopot, many firms do not order capital goods until they approach full capacity or are forced to replace worn-out equipment. If many firms order capital goods at the same time, backlogs result, prices increase, and firms are forced to wait for the delivery of machinery; in general, the quality of the capital goods deteriorates. If a firm foresees its needs and purchases capital assets early, it can avoid these problems.

Finally, capital budgeting is also important because the acquisition of fixed assets typically involves substantial expenditures, and before a firm can spend a large amount of money, it must have the funds available—large amounts of money are not available automatically. Therefore, a firm contemplating a major capital expenditure program must arrange its financing well in advance to be sure the funds required are available.

Self-Test Questions

Why are capital budgeting decisions so important to the success of a firm?

Why is the sales forecast a key element in a capital budgeting decision?

Generating Ideas for Capital Projects

The same general concepts that we developed for valuing financial assets are involved in capital budgeting. However, whereas a set of stocks and bonds exists in the financial markets, and investors select from this set, capital budgeting projects are created by the firm. For example, a sales representative might report that customers frequently ask for a particular product that the company does not currently produce. The sales manager then discusses the idea with the marketing research group to determine the size of the market for the proposed product. If it appears likely that a significant market does exist, cost accountants and engineers will be asked to estimate production costs. And then if it appears the product can be produced and sold at a sufficient profit, the project will be undertaken.

A firm's growth, and even its ability to remain competitive and to survive, depends on a constant flow of ideas for new products, ways to make existing products better, and ways to produce output at a lower cost. Accordingly, a well-managed firm will go to great lengths to develop good capital budgeting proposals. Some firms even provide incentives to employees to encourage suggestions that lead to beneficial investment proposals. If a firm has capable and imaginative executives and employees, and if its incentive system works properly, many ideas for capital investment will be advanced.

Because some capital investment ideas will be good and others will not, procedures must be established for evaluating the worth of such projects to the firm. Our topic in the remainder of this chapter is the evaluation of the acceptability of capital projects.

Self-Test Question

How does a firm generate ideas for capital projects?

Project Classifications

REPLACEMENT DECISIONS
Whether to purchase capital assets to take the place of existing assets to maintain or improve existing operations.

Capital budgeting decisions generally are termed either *replacement decisions* or *expansion decisions*. **Replacement decisions** involve determining whether capital projects should be purchased to take the place of (replace) existing assets that might be worn out, damaged, or obsolete. Usually the replacement projects are necessary to maintain or improve profitable operations using the existing production levels. On the other hand, if a firm is considering whether to *increase* operations by adding capital projects to existing assets that will help produce either more of its existing products or entirely new products, **expansion decisions** are made.

EXPANSION DECISIONS
Whether to purchase capital projects and add them to existing assets to *increase* existing operations.

Some of the capital budgeting decisions involve *independent projects,* while others will involve *mutually exclusive projects.* **Independent projects** are projects whose cash flows are not affected by one another, so the acceptance of one project does not affect the acceptance of the other project(s)—*all independent projects can be purchased if they all are acceptable.* For example, if Microsoft decided to purchase the NBC television network, it still could produce its computer software. On the other hand, if a capital budgeting decision involves **mutually exclusive projects,** then when one project is taken on, the others must be rejected—*only one mutually exclusive project can be purchased, even if they all are acceptable.* For example, Global Sports and Entertainment, Ltd. has a parcel of land on which it wants to build either an amusement park or a domed sports arena. The land is not large enough for both alternatives, so if Global chooses to build the amusement park, it could not build the arena, and vice versa.

INDEPENDENT PROJECTS
Projects whose cash flows are not affected by decisions made about other projects.

MUTUALLY EXCLUSIVE PROJECTS
A set of projects in which the acceptance of one project means the others cannot be accepted.

In general, relatively simple calculations, and only a few supporting documents, are required for replacement decisions, especially maintenance-type investments in profitable plants. More detailed analysis is required for cost-reduction replacements, for expansion of existing product lines, and especially for investments in new products or areas. Also, within each category projects are broken down by their dollar costs: Larger investments require both more detailed analysis and approval at a higher level within the firm. Thus, although a plant manager might be authorized to approve maintenance expenditures up to $10,000 on the basis of a relatively unsophisticated analysis, the full board of directors might have to approve decisions that involve either amounts greater than $1 million or expansions into new products or markets. Statistical data generally are lacking for new product decisions, so here judgments, as opposed to detailed cost data, are especially important.

Self-Test Question

Identify and briefly explain how capital project classification categories are used.

Similarities between Capital Budgeting and Asset Valuation

Capital budgeting decisions involve valuation of assets, or projects. Therefore, capital budgeting involves exactly the same steps used in general asset valuation, which were described in the previous two chapters:

1. Determine the cost, or purchase price, of the asset.
2. Estimate the cash flows expected from the project, including the salvage value of the asset at the end of its expected life. This is similar to estimating the future dividend or interest payment stream on a stock or bond, along with the stock's expected selling price or the bond's maturity value.
3. Evaluate the riskiness of the projected cash flows to determine the appropriate rate of return to use for computing the present value of the estimated cash flows.

For this assessment, management needs information about the probability distributions of the cash flows.

4. Compute the present value of the expected cash flows to obtain an estimate of the asset's value to the firm. This is equivalent to finding the present value of a stock's expected future dividends.

5. Compare the present value of the future expected cash flows with the initial investment, or cost, required to acquire the asset. Alternatively, the expected rate of return on the project can be calculated and compared with the rate of return considered appropriate for the project.

If an individual investor identifies and invests in a stock or bond whose true value is greater than its market price, the value of the investor's portfolio will increase. Similarly, if a firm identifies (or creates) an investment opportunity with a present value greater than its cost, the value of the firm will increase. Thus, there is a very direct link between capital budgeting and stock values: The more effective the firm's capital budgeting procedures, the higher the price of its stock.

Self-Test Questions

List the steps in the capital budgeting process, and compare them with the steps in general asset valuation.

Explain how capital budgeting is related to the wealth-maximization goal that should be pursued by the financial manager of a firm.

Capital Budgeting Evaluation Techniques

The basic methods used by businesses to evaluate projects and to decide whether they should be accepted for inclusion in the capital budget are (1) payback (PB), (2) net present value (NPV), and (3) internal rate of return (IRR). As you will see, to determine a project's acceptability using any of these three techniques, its expected cash flows are needed. However, unlike the other two, the payback method does not consider the time value of money—so we call payback a *nondiscounting technique* and NPV and IRR *discounting techniques*. We will explain how each evaluation criterion is calculated, and then we will determine how well each performs in terms of identifying those projects that will maximize the firm's stock price.

We use the tabular and time line cash flow data shown in Figure 8–1 for Project S and Project L to illustrate all the methods, and throughout this chapter we assume that the projects are equally risky. Note that the cash flows, $\hat{CF}_t$, are expected values and that they have been adjusted to reflect taxes, depreciation, salvage values, and any other changes in cash flows associated with the capital projects.[1] Also, we assume that

---

[1] Perhaps the most difficult part of the capital budgeting process is the estimation of the relevant cash flows. For simplicity, the net cash flows are treated as a given in this chapter, which allows us to focus on our main area of concern, the capital budgeting evaluation techniques. However, in Chapter 9 we discuss cash flow estimation in detail.

	FIGURE 8–1	Net Cash Flows for Project S and Project L

	EXPECTED AFTER-TAX NET CASH FLOWS, $\hat{CF}_t$	
YEAR (t)	PROJECT S	PROJECT L
0[a]	$(3,000)	$(3,000)
1	1,500	400
2	1,200	900
3	800	1,300
4	300	1,500

Project S:

0	1	2	3	4
−3,000	1,500	1,200	800	300

Project L:

0	1	2	3	4
−3,000	400	900	1,300	1,500

[a]$\hat{CF}_0$ represents the initial investment, or net cost of the project.

all cash flows occur at the end of the designated year. Incidentally, the S stands for *short* and the L for *long*: Project S is a short-term project in the sense that its cash inflows tend to come in sooner than Project L's.

Payback Period

PAYBACK PERIOD
The length of time before the original cost of an investment is recovered from the expected cash flows.

The **payback period,** defined as the expected number of years required to recover the original investment (the cost of the asset), is the simplest and, as far as we know, the oldest *formal* method used to evaluate capital budgeting projects. To compute a project's payback period, simply add up the expected cash flows for each year until the amount initially invested in the project is recovered. The total amount of time, including the fraction of a year if appropriate, that it takes to recapture the original amount invested is the payback period. The payback calculation process for both Project S and Project L is diagrammed in Figure 8–2.

The exact payback period can be found using the following formula:

8–1

$$\text{Payback} = \text{PB} = \left(\begin{array}{c}\text{Number of years before}\\\text{full recovery of}\\\text{original investment}\end{array}\right) + \left(\dfrac{\text{Uncovered cost at start of full-recovery year}}{\text{Total cash flow during full-recovery year}}\right)$$

-2 Payback Period for Project S and Project L

PROJECT S:

	0	1	2	PB$_s$	3	4
Net cash flow	−3,000	1,500	1,200		800	300
Cumulative net cash flow	−3,000	−1,500	−300		500	800

PROJECT L:

	0	1	2	3	PB$_L$	4
Net cash flow	−3,000	400	900	1,300		1,500
Cumulative net cash flow	−3,000	−2,600	−1,700	−400		1,100

The diagram in Figure 8–2 shows that the payback period for Project S is between two years and three years, so, using Equation 8–1, the exact payback period is

$$PB_s = 2 + \frac{300}{800} = 2.4 \text{ years}$$

Applying the same procedure to Project L, we find Payback$_L$ = 3.3 years.

Using payback to make capital budgeting decisions is based on the concept that it is better to recover the cost of (investment in) a project sooner rather than later. Therefore, Project S is considered better than Project L because it has a lower payback. *As a general rule, a project is considered acceptable if its payback is less than the maximum cost recovery time established by the firm.* For example, if the firm requires projects to have a payback of three years or less, Project S would be acceptable but Project L would not.

The payback method is very simple, which explains why payback traditionally has been one of the most popular capital budgeting techniques. But payback ignores the time value of money, so relying solely on this method could lead to incorrect decisions—at least if our goal is to maximize value. If a project has a payback of three years, we know how quickly the initial investment will be covered by the expected cash flows, but this information does not provide any indication of whether the return on the project is sufficient to cover the cost of the funds invested. In addition, when payback is used, the cash flows beyond the payback period are ignored. For example, even if Project L had a fifth year of cash flows equal to $50,000, its payback would remain 3.3 years, which is less desirable than the payback of 2.4 years for Project S. But, with the additional $50,000 cash flow, Project L most likely would be preferred.

NET PRESENT VALUE (NPV) METHOD
A method of evaluating capital investment proposals by finding the present value of future net cash flows, discounted at the rate of return required by the firm.

DISCOUNTED CASH FLOW (DCF) TECHNIQUES
Methods of evaluating investment proposals that employ time value of money concepts; two of these are the net present value and the internal rate of return.

Net Present Value (NPV)

To correct for the major defect of any *nondiscounting* technique—ignoring the time value of money—methods were developed to include consideration of the time value of money. One such method is the **net present value (NPV) method,** which relies on **discounted cash flow (DCF) techniques.** To implement this approach, we simply find the present value of all the future cash flows a project is expected to generate and then subtract (add a negative cash flow) its initial investment (original cost) to find the *net* benefit the firm will realize from investing in the project. *If the net benefit computed on a present value basis (that is, NPV) is positive, then the project is considered an acceptable investment.* NPV is computed using the following equation:

8–2

$$NPV = \hat{CF}_0 + \frac{\hat{CF}_1}{(1 + k)^1} + \frac{\hat{CF}_2}{(1 + k)^2} + \ldots + \frac{\hat{CF}_n}{(1 + k)^n}$$

$$= \sum_{t = 0}^{n} \frac{\hat{CF}_t}{(1 + k)^t}$$

Here $\hat{CF}_t$ is the expected net cash flow at Period t, and k is the rate of return required by the firm to invest in this project.[2] Cash outflows (expenditures on the project, such as the cost of buying equipment or building factories) are treated as negative cash flows. For Project S and Project L, only $\hat{CF}_0$ is negative, but for many large projects such as the Alaska Pipeline, an electric generating plant, or Chrysler's Neon project, outflows occur for several years before operations begin and cash flows turn positive.

At a ten percent required rate of return, Project S's NPV is $161.33:

CASH FLOW TIME LINE FOR PROJECT S:

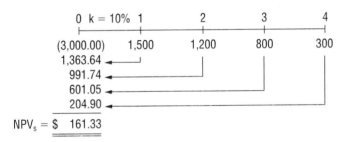

We show the regular cash flow time line as the top portion of the diagram, and then we show the solution in the bottom left portion of the diagram.

1. NUMERICAL SOLUTION:

As the lower section of the cash flow time line shows, to find the NPV, we compute the present value of each cash flow and sum the results. Using Equation 8–2, the numerical solution for the NPV for Project S is

$$PV_s = \$(3,000) + \frac{\$1,500}{(1.10)^1} + \frac{\$1,200}{(1.10)^2} + \frac{\$800}{(1.10)^3} + \frac{\$300}{(1.10)^4}$$

$$= \$(3,000) + \$1,500(0.90909) + \$1,200(0.82645) + \$800(0.75131) + \$300(0.68301)$$

$$= \$(3,000) + \quad \$1,363.64 \quad + \quad \$991.74 \quad + \quad \$601.05 \quad + \quad 204.90$$

$$= \$161.33$$

---

[2]The rate of return required by the firm generally is termed the firm's cost of capital, because it is the average rate the firm must pay for the funds used to purchase capital projects. The concept of cost of capital is discussed in Chapter 10.

Of course, if the stream of future cash flows was constant rather than nonconstant, then the future cash flow stream would represent an annuity, as we saw in Chapter 6, and our computations would be simplified.

2. Tabular Solution:

We can also write Equation 8–2 in the following form:

> **8–2a**
>
> $$NPV = \hat{CF}_0 + \hat{CF}_1(PVIF_{k,1}) + \hat{CF}_2(PVIF_{k,2}) + \ldots + \hat{CF}_n(PVIF_{k,n})$$
> $$= \hat{CF}_0 + \sum_{t=1}^{n} \hat{CF}_t(PVIF_{k,t})$$

Looking up the interest factors in Table A–1 in Appendix A, we compute NPV_S as follows:

$$NPV_S = \$(3,000) + \$1,500(0.9091) + \$1,200(0.8264) + \$800(0.7513) + \$300(0.6830)$$
$$= \$(3,000) + \quad \$1,363.65 \quad + \quad \$991.68 \quad + \quad \$601.04 \quad + \quad \$204.90$$
$$= \$161.27 \text{ (rounding difference)}$$

3. Financial Calculator Solution:

It is not hard to calculate the NPV as was done with the cash flow time line by using Equation 8–2 or 8–2a and a *regular* calculator, along with the interest rate tables. However, the most efficient way to find the NPV is with a financial calculator. Different calculators are set up somewhat differently, but they all have a section of memory called the "cash flow register" that is used for uneven cash flows such as those in Project S (as opposed to equal annuity cash flows). As we saw in Chapter 6, a solution process for Equation 8–2 is literally programmed into financial calculators, and all you have to do is enter the cash flows (being sure to observe the signs) in the order they occur, along with the value of I = k. At that point you have (in your calculator) this equation for Project S:

$$NPV_s = -3,000 + \frac{1,500}{(1.10)^1} + \frac{1,200}{(1.10)^2} + \frac{800}{(1.10)^3} + \frac{300}{(1.10)^4}$$

As you can see, the equation has one unknown, NPV. Now all you need to do is to ask the calculator to solve the equation for you, which you do by pressing the NPV key (and, on some calculators, the "compute" key). The answer, 161.33, will appear on the screen.[3]

Using the same process for Project L, we find $NPV_L = \$108.67$. On this basis, both projects should be accepted if they are independent, but Project S should be the one chosen if they are mutually exclusive.

If you look at the cash flow time line for Project S, you can see the reason it has a positive NPV is because the initial investment of $3,000 is recovered on a present

---

[3]Refer to the manual that came with your calculator to determine how the CF function is used. The steps for the Texas Instruments BAII PLUS are shown in Appendix 6A in Chapter 6.

value basis prior to the end of the project's life. In fact, if we use the payback concept developed in the previous section, we can compute how long it would take to recapture the initial outlay of $3,000 using the discounted cash flows given in the cash flow time line—the sum of the present values of the cash flows for the first three years is $2,956.43, so all of the $3,000 cost is not recovered until 3.2 years = 3 years + [($3,000 − $2,956.43)/$204.90] years. Therefore, on a present value basis, it takes 3.2 years for Project S to recover, or pay back, its original cost. This is called the **discounted payback** of Project S—it is the length of time it takes for a project's *discounted* cash flows to repay the cost of the investment. The discounted payback for Project L is 3.90 years, so Project S is more acceptable. Unlike the traditional payback computation discussed in the previous section, the discounted payback computation does consider the time value of money. *Using the discounted payback method, a project should be accepted when its discounted payback is less than its expected life* because, in such cases, the present value of the future cash flows the project is expected to generate exceeds the initial cost of the asset (initial investment)—that is, NPV > 0.

DISCOUNTED PAYBACK
The length of time it takes for a project's *discounted* cash flows to repay the cost of the investment.

Rationale for the NPV Method

The rationale for the NPV method is straightforward. An NPV of zero signifies that the project's cash flows are just sufficient to repay the invested capital and to provide the required rate of return on that capital. If a project has a positive NPV, then it generates a return that is greater than is needed to pay for funds provided by investors, and this excess return accrues solely to the firm's stockholders. Therefore, if a firm takes on a project with a positive NPV, the position of the stockholders is improved because the firm's value is greater. In our example, shareholders' wealth would increase by $161.33 if the firm takes on Project S but by only $108.67 if it takes on Project L. Viewed in this manner, it is easy to see why Project S is preferred to Project L, and it also is easy to see the logic of the NPV approach.[4]

Internal Rate of Return (IRR)

In the previous chapter, we presented procedures for finding the yield to maturity (YTM), or rate of return, on a bond—if you invest in the bond and hold it to maturity, you can expect to earn the YTM on the money you invested. Exactly the same concepts are employed in capital budgeting when the *internal rate of return method* is used. The **internal rate of return (IRR)** is the rate of return the firm expects to earn if the project is purchased; thus it is defined as the discount rate that equates the present value of a project's expected cash flows to the investment outlay, or initial cost. *As long*

INTERNAL RATE OF RETURN (IRR)
The discount rate that forces the PV of a project's expected cash flows to equal its initial cost. IRR is similar to the YTM on a bond.

---

[4]This description of the process is somewhat oversimplified. Both analysts and investors anticipate that firms will identify and accept positive NPV projects, and current stock prices reflect these expectations. Thus, stock prices react to announcements of new capital projects only to the extent that such projects were not already expected. In this sense, we can think of a firm's value as consisting of two parts: (1) the value of its existing assets and (2) the value of its "growth opportunities," or projects with positive NPVs. AT&T is a good example of this: The company has the world's largest long-distance network plus telephone manufacturing facilities, both of which provide current earnings and cash flows, and it has Bell Labs, which has the *potential* for coming up with new products in the computer/telecommunications area that could be extremely profitable. Security analysts (and investors) thus analyze AT&T as a company with a set of cash-producing assets plus a set of growth opportunities that will materialize if and only if the company can come up with a number of positive NPV projects through its capital budgeting process.

as the project's IRR, which is its expected return, is greater than the rate of return required by the firm for such an investment, the project is acceptable.

We can use the following equation to solve for a project's IRR:

8–3

$$\hat{CF}_0 + \frac{\hat{CF}_1}{(1 + IRR)^1} + \frac{\hat{CF}_2}{(1 + IRR)^2} + \ldots + \frac{\hat{CF}_n}{(1 + IRR)^n} = 0$$

$$= \sum_{t=0}^{n} \frac{\hat{CF}_t}{(1 + IRR)^t} = 0$$

For Project S, the cash flow time line for the IRR computation is as follows:

CASH FLOW TIME LINE FOR PROJECT S:

Using Equation 8–3, here is the setup for computing IRR_S:

$$-3,000 + \frac{1,500}{(1 + IRR)^1} + \frac{1,200}{(1 + IRR)^2} + \frac{800}{(1 + IRR)^3} + \frac{300}{(1 + IRR)^4} = 0$$

0	IRR = ? 1	2	3	4
(3,000)	1,500	1,200	800	300

Sum of PVs for CF_{1-4} = 3,000

NPV =   0

1 AND 2. NUMERICAL AND TABULAR SOLUTIONS:

Although it is easy to find the NPV without a financial calculator, this is *not* true of the IRR. If the cash flows are constant from year to year, then we have an annuity, and we can use annuity factors discussed in Chapter 6 to find the IRR. However, if the cash flows are not constant, as is generally the case in capital budgeting, then it is difficult to find the IRR without a financial calculator. Without a financial calculator, you basically have to solve Equation 8–3 by trial and error—try some discount rate (or corresponding PVIF factors), and see if the equation solves to zero, and if it does not, try a different discount rate until you find one that forces the equation to equal zero. The discount rate that causes the equation to equal zero is defined as the IRR. For a realistic project with a fairly long life, the trial and error approach is a tedious, time-consuming task.

3. FINANCIAL CALCULATOR SOLUTION:

Fortunately, it is easy to find IRRs with a financial calculator. You follow almost identical procedures to those used to find the NPV. First, you enter the cash flows as shown on the preceding time line into the calculator's cash flow register. In effect, you have entered the cash flows into the equation shown below the time line. Notice that we now have one unknown, IRR, or the discount rate that forces the equation to equal zero. The calculator has been programmed to solve for the IRR, and you activate this program by pressing the key labeled "IRR." Then the calculator solves for IRR and displays it on the screen. Here are the IRRs for Project S and Project L found using a financial calculator:[5]

$$IRR_S = 13.1\%$$

$$IRR_L = 11.4\%.$$

REQUIRED RATE OF RETURN, OR HURDLE RATE
The discount rate (cost of funds) that the IRR must exceed for a project to be considered acceptable.

Projects that have IRRs greater than their **required rates of return,** *or* **hurdle rates** *are acceptable investments.* For example, if the hurdle rate required by the firm is ten percent, then both Project S and Project L are acceptable. If they are mutually exclusive, Project S is more acceptable than Project L because $IRR_S > IRR_L$.

Rationale for the IRR Method

Why is a project acceptable if its IRR is greater than its required rate of return? Because the IRR on a project is its expected rate of return, and if this return exceeds the cost of the funds used to finance the project, a surplus remains after paying for the funds—this surplus accrues to the firm's stockholders. Therefore, *taking on a project whose IRR exceeds its required rate of return, or cost of funds, increases shareholders' wealth.* On the other hand, if the internal rate of return is less than the cost of funds, then taking on the project imposes a cost on current stockholders. Consider what would happen if you borrowed funds at a 15 percent interest rate to invest in the stock market, and the stocks you picked earned only 13 percent. You still have to pay the 15 percent interest, so you end up losing two percent on the investment. On the other hand, anything you earn in excess of 15 percent is yours to keep, because only 15 percent interest has to be paid to the lender. So 15 percent is your *cost of funds,* which is what you must *require* your investments to earn to break even. It is this "breakeven" characteristic that makes the IRR useful in evaluating capital projects.

Self-Test Questions

Discuss the capital budgeting techniques that were discussed in this section, and give the rationale for using each one.

What two methods always lead to the same accept/reject decision for independent projects? Explain why.

Comparison of the NPV and IRR Methods

We found the NPV for Project S is $161.33—this means that if the project is purchased, the value of the firm will increase by $161.33. The IRR for Project S is 13.1 percent—this means that if the firm purchases Project S, it will earn a 13.1 percent rate of return on its investment. We generally measure wealth in dollars, so the NPV

---

[5]To find the IRR with a Texas Instruments BAII PLUS, repeat the steps given in Appendix 6A of Chapter 6, press the **IRR** key and then press the **CPT** key. You should always get both the NPV and the IRR after entering the input data, before clearing the cash flow register.

method should be used to accomplish the goal of maximizing shareholders' wealth. In reality, using the IRR method could lead to investment decisions that increase, but do not maximize wealth. We choose to discuss the IRR method and compare it to the NPV method because many corporate executives are familiar with the meaning of IRR, it is entrenched in the corporate world, and it does have some virtues. Therefore, it is important that finance students understand the IRR method and be prepared to explain why, at times, a project with a lower IRR might be preferable to one with a higher IRR.

NPV Profiles

NET PRESENT VALUE (NPV) PROFILE
A curve showing the relationship between a project's NPV and various discount rates (required rates of return).

A graph that shows a project's NPV at various discount rates (required rates of return) is termed the project's **net present value (NPV) profile;** profiles for Project L and Project S are shown in Figure 8–3. To construct the profiles, we calculate the projects' NPVs at various discount rates, say, 0, 5, 10, 15, and 20 percent, and plot these values on a graph like that shown in Figure 8–3. The points plotted on our graph for each project are shown at the bottom of the figure.[6]

Because the IRR is defined as the discount rate at which a project's NPV equals zero, the point where its *NPV profile crosses the X axis indicates a project's internal rate of return.* NPV profiles can be very useful in project analysis, and we will use them in the remainder of the chapter.

NPVs and the Required Rate of Return

Figure 8–3 shows that the NPV profiles of both Projects L and S decline as the discount rate increases. But note that Project L has the higher NPV at low discount rates, while Project S has the higher NPV at high discount rates. And, according to the graph, $NPV_S = NPV_L = \$268$ when the discount rate, k, is equal to 8.1 percent. We call this point the **crossover rate** because, below this rate, $NPV_S < NPV_L$, and above this rate, $NPV_S > NPV_L$—that is, the NPVs cross over at 8.1 percent.[7]

CROSSOVER RATE
The discount rate at which the NPV profiles of two projects cross and, thus, at which the projects' NPVs are equal.

Figure 8–3 also indicates that Project L's NPV is "more sensitive" to changes in the discount rate than is Project S's NPV; that is, Project L's net present value profile has the steeper slope, indicating that a given change in k has a larger effect on NPV_L than on NPV_S. Project L is more sensitive to changes in k because the cash flows from Project S are received faster than those from Project L—in a payback sense, S is a short-term project, while L is a long-term project. The impact of an increase in the discount rate is much greater on distant than on near-term cash flows. To illustrate, consider the present value of $100 to be received in one year. If the $100 is discounted at ten percent, its present value is $90.91, but if it is discounted at 15 percent its present value is $86.96; so a five percentage point increase in the discount rate results in a (86.96 − 90.91)/90.91 = 4.3 percent decrease in the present value of the $100 to be received in

---

[6]Note that the NPV profiles are curved—they are *not* straight lines. Also, the NPVs approach the t = 0 cash flow (the cost of the project) as the discount rate increases without limit. The reason is that, at an infinitely high discount rate, the PV of the inflows would be zero, so NPV at k = ∞ is $\hat{CF}_0$, which in our example is −$3,000.

[7]The crossover rate is easy to calculate. Simply go back to Figure 8–1, where we first show the two projects' cash flows. Now calculate the difference in the cash flows for Project S and Project L in each year. The differences are $\hat{CF}_S - \hat{CF}_L = \$0$, +$1,100, +$300, −$500, and −$1,200, respectively. Enter these values into the cash flow register of a financial calculator, press the IRR key, and the crossover rate, 8.11, appears.

| FIGURE 8-3 | NVP Profiles for Project S and Project L |

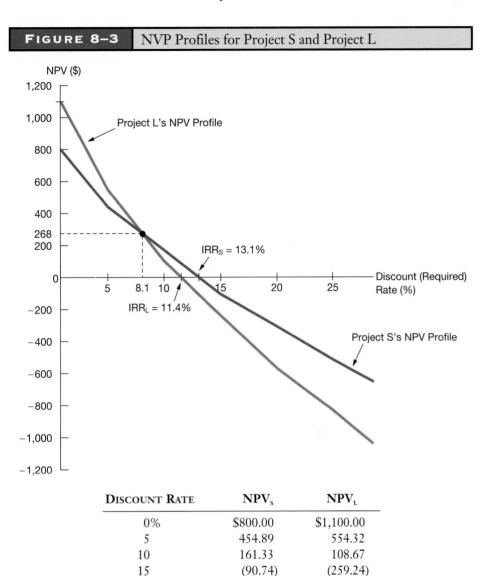

DISCOUNT RATE	NPV$_s$	NPV$_L$
0%	$800.00	$1,100.00
5	454.89	554.32
10	161.33	108.67
15	(90.74)	(259.24)
20	(309.03)	(565.97)

one year. Now consider the present value of $100 to be received in ten years. If the discount rate is ten percent, the present value of this $100 is $38.55; but if the discount rate is 15 percent, the present value of the $100 is $24.72; so a five percentage point increase in the discount rate results in a $(24.72 - 38.55)/38.55 = 35.9$ percent decrease in the present value. Thus, the farther into the future the cash flows are, the greater their sensitivity to discount rate changes. Consequently, if a project has most of its cash flows coming in the early years, its NPV will not be lowered very much if the required rate of return increases; but a project whose cash flows come later will be severely penalized by high capital costs. Accordingly, Project L, which has its largest cash flows in the later years, is hurt badly when the required rate of return is high, while Project S, which has relatively rapid cash flows, is affected less by high discount rates.

Independent Projects

Note that the internal rate of return formula, Equation 8–3, is simply the NPV formula, Equation 8–2, solved for the particular discount rate that forces the NPV to equal zero. Thus, the same basic equation is used for both methods, but in the NPV method the discount rate, k, is specified and the NPV is found, whereas in the IRR method the NPV is set equal to zero, and the interest rate that forces this equality (the IRR) is determined. Mathematically, therefore, the NPV and IRR methods will always lead to the same accept/reject decisions for independent projects: *If a project's NPV is positive, its IRR will exceed k, while if NPV is negative, k will exceed the IRR.* To see why this is so, look back at Figure 8–3, focus on Project L's profile, and note that (1) the IRR criterion for acceptance is that the required rate of return is less than (or to the left of) the IRR and (2) whenever the required rate of return is less than the IRR, its NPV is positive. Thus, at any required rate of return less than 11.4 percent, Project L will be acceptable by both the NPV and the IRR criteria, while both methods reject the project if the required rate of return is greater than 11.4 percent. Project S—and all other independent projects under consideration—could be analyzed similarly, and *in every case, if a project is acceptable using the IRR method, then the NPV method also will show it is acceptable.*

Mutually Exclusive Projects

If we assume that Project S and Project L are *mutually exclusive* rather than independent, then we can choose either Project S or Project L, or we can reject both, but we cannot invest in both. Note from Figure 8–3 that as long as the required rate of return is *greater than* the crossover rate of 8.1 percent, NPV_S is larger than NPV_L, and IRR_S also exceeds IRR_L. Therefore, if k is greater than the crossover rate of 8.1 percent, the two methods lead to the selection of the same project—Project S. However, if the required rate of return is less than 8.1 percent, the NPV method ranks Project L higher, but the IRR method suggests that Project S is better. Thus, *a conflict exists* if the required rate of return is less than the crossover rate: NPV says choose Project L over Project S, while IRR says the opposite. Which answer is correct? Logic suggests that the NPV method is better because it selects the project that adds the most to shareholder wealth.

Two basic conditions can cause NPV profiles to cross and thus lead to conflicts between NPV and IRR: (1) when *project size (or scale) differences* exist, meaning that the cost of one project is larger than that of the other, or (2) when *timing differences* exist, meaning that the timing of cash flows from the two projects differs such that most of the cash flows from one project come in the early years and most of the cash flows from the other project come in the later years, as occurs with Projects L and S.[8]

When either size or timing differences occur, the firm will have different amounts of funds to invest in the various years, depending on which of the two mutually exclusive projects it chooses. For example, if one project costs more than the other, then the firm will have more money at t = 0 to invest elsewhere if it selects the smaller project.

---

[8]Of course, it is possible for mutually exclusive projects to differ with respect to both scale and timing. Also, if mutually exclusive projects have different lives (as opposed to different cash flow patterns over a common life), this introduces further complications, and for meaningful comparisons, some mutually exclusive projects must be evaluated over a common life.

Similarly, for projects of equal size, the one with the larger early cash inflows provides more funds for reinvestment in the early years. Given this situation, the rate of return at which differential cash flows can be invested is an important consideration.

The critical issue in resolving conflicts between mutually exclusive projects is this: How useful is it to generate cash flows earlier rather than later? The value of early cash flows depends on the rate at which we can reinvest these cash flows. *The NPV method implicitly assumes that the rate at which cash flows can be reinvested is the required rate of return, whereas the IRR method implies that the firm has the opportunity to reinvest at the project's IRR.* These assumptions are inherent in the mathematics of the discounting process. The cash flows can actually be withdrawn as dividends by the stockholders and spent on pizza, but the NPV method still assumes that cash flows can be reinvested at the required rate of return, while the IRR method assumes reinvestment at the project's IRR.

Which is the better assumption—that cash flows can be reinvested at the required rate of return or that they can be reinvested at the project's IRR? To reinvest at the IRR associated with a capital project, the firm would have to be able to reinvest the project's cash flows in another project with an identical IRR—such projects generally do not continue to exist, or it is not feasible to reinvest in such projects, because competition in the investment markets drives their prices up and their IRRs down. On the other hand, at the very least, a firm could repurchase the bonds and stock it has issued to raise capital budgeting funds and thus repay some of its investors, which would be the same as investing at its required rate of return. Thus, we conclude that the *more realistic* **reinvestment rate assumption** *is the required rate of return, which is implicit in the NPV method.* This, in turn, leads us to prefer the NPV method, at least for firms willing and able to obtain capital at a cost reasonably close to their current cost of capital.

We should reiterate that *when projects are independent, the NPV and IRR methods both provide exactly the same accept/reject decision.* However, *when evaluating mutually exclusive projects,* especially those that differ in scale or timing, *the NPV method should be used to determine which project should be purchased.*

REINVESTMENT RATE ASSUMPTION
The assumption that cash flows from a project can be reinvested (1) at the cost of capital, if using the NPV method, or (2) at the internal rate of return, if using the IRR method.

Multiple IRRs

There is one other situation in which the IRR approach might not be usable—this is when projects have unconventional cash flow patterns. A project has a *conventional* cash flow pattern if it has cash outflows (costs) in one or more periods at the beginning of its life followed by a series of cash inflows. If, however, a project has a large cash outflow either sometime during or at the end of its life, then it has an *unconventional* cash flow pattern. Projects with unconventional cash flow patterns present unique difficulties when the IRR method is used, including the possibility of **multiple IRRs.**[9]

MULTIPLE IRRS
The situation in which a project has two or more IRRs.

There exists an IRR solution for each time the *direction* of the cash flows associated with a project is interrupted (i.e., inflows change to outflows, and vice versa). For example, a conventional cash flow pattern only has one net cash outflow at the beginning

---

[9]Multiple IRRs result from the manner in which Equation 8–3 must be solved to arrive at a project's IRR. The mathematical rationale and the solution to multiple IRRs will not be discussed here. Instead, we want you to be aware that multiple IRRs can exist because this possibility complicates capital budgeting evaluation using the IRR method. Some financial calculators cannot compute the IRR for projects that have unconventional cash flows because there is not a single solution. In such cases, you would have to use NPV profiles, which essentially is a trial-and-error process.

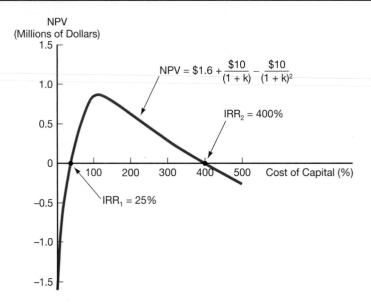

| FIGURE 8–4 | NVP Profile for Project M |

of the project's life, so the direction of the cash flows changes (is interrupted) once from negative (outflow) to positive (inflow), and there is only one IRR solution. A project with a 10-year life that has cash inflows every year except that $\hat{CF}_0 < 0$ and $\hat{CF}_5 < 0$ will have two IRR solutions because the cash flow pattern has two direction changes, or interruptions—one after the initial cost is paid and another five years later. Figure 8–4 illustrates the multiple IRR problem with a strip mining project that costs $1.6 million. The mine will produce a cash inflow of $10 million at the end of Year 1, but $10 million must be spent at the end of Year 2 to restore the land to its original condition. Two IRRs exist for this project—25 percent and 400 percent. The NPV profile for the mine shows that the project would have a positive NPV, and thus be acceptable, if the firm's required rate of return is between 25 percent and 400 percent.

Self-Test Questions

Describe how NPV profiles are constructed.

What is the crossover rate, and how does it affect the choice between mutually exclusive projects?

What two basic conditions can lead to conflicts between the NPV and IRR methods?

What is the underlying cause of conflicts between the NPV and IRR methods?

If a conflict exists, should the capital budgeting decision be made on the basis of the NPV or the IRR ranking? Why?

What is the difference between conventional and unconventional cash flow patterns?

What is the "multiple IRR problem," and what condition is necessary for its occurrence?

Practice What We Preach (Teach)

The three capital budgeting techniques presented in this chapter traditionally have been considered the most popular by corporate financial managers. Just how popular are they? Do firms use methods that help to maximize value? A study of the 1990 *Business Week* 1000 firms provides insight concerning which methods companies use to make capital budgeting decisions.* The results indicate that each of the methods discussed in this chapter is relied on to some extent to help to make final decisions about the acceptability of capital budgeting projects. About 60 percent of the companies indicated that they use the traditional payback period either as a primary or as a secondary method for capital budgeting decisions. But it appears that less than one third of the companies rely on payback as the *primary* capital budgeting technique—this represents a significant decrease from three decades ago when the number was greater than 60 percent. Nearly 90 percent of the companies responded that they use such present value techniques as net present value (NPV) and internal rate of return (IRR) either as a primary or as a secondary capital budgeting decision methodology. It is interesting to note that about 60 percent of the companies indicated that *both* NPV and IRR are the primary techniques used to make capital budgeting decisions. It seems, for the most part, that financial managers recognize these techniques provide correct decisions with respect to value maximization. The financial managers also were asked whether using IRR presented any problems, especially with regard to multiple internal rates of return and ranking differences when compared to NPV. Most of the financial managers indicated either that they had not heard of these problems or that such problems rarely occurred. In addition, it appears that most of the companies that face such problems chose to use NPV rather than IRR for their capital budgeting decisions.

In another study, the companies included in the 1990 *Fortune Magazine* directory were surveyed to determine the techniques corporations use in various financial areas of the firm, including the capital budgeting decision-making process.♦ The results,

which corroborate the findings of other studies, were compared to earlier studies to determine whether the techniques used have changed over time. The findings, as indicated in the following table, show that there has been a tendency for firms to shift toward greater use of discounted techniques such as NPV and IRR.

	FIRMS INDICATING "FREQUENT" USE OF TECHNIQUE (%)			
YEAR OF STUDY	PAYBACK	NPV	IRR	NPV OR IRR
1980	79.9%	68.1%	66.4%	86.2%
1985	75.5	82.8	79.6	89.5
1991	63.3	84.7	81.8	90.7

The results also show that firms generally do not rely on a single capital budgeting technique for evaluating projects; rather, decisions are based on information generated by more than one technique.

A more recent study corroborates the results of previous studies that firms use more than one capital budgeting method to evaluate projects.† In addition, the results indicate that more than 70 percent of the surveyed firms consider a high IRR important when deciding which capital projects to accept. And, while about 84 percent of the firms surveyed indicated that one of the methods they use to evaluate projects is NPV, only 50 percent stated that a high NPV is important for determining acceptable projects. An interesting finding of the study was that less than ten percent of the firms surveyed responded that they did not use payback to evaluate projects. In addition, the results show that nearly two thirds of the firms believe that acceptable projects should have short payback periods in addition to either high IRRs or NPVs.

For the most part, studies have shown that companies (1) use more sophisticated capital budgeting techniques today than in previous times, and (2) do not rely on a single evaluation method to make decisions about investing in capital projects. Clearly, firms still use payback period in their capital budgeting

continues

analyses. But even firms that previously relied on the traditional payback period seem to have switched to the discounted payback period. Thus, indications are that firms do use the methods we profess in finance courses such as this.

*Glenn H. Petry and James Sprow, "The Theory of Finance in the 1990s," *The Quarterly Review of Economics and Finance*, Winter 1993, 359–381.

♦Erika Gilbert and Alan Reichert, "The Practice of Financial Management among Large United States Corporations," *Financial Practice and Education*, Spring/Summer 1995, 16–23.

†Patricia Chadwell-Hatfield, Bernard Goitein, Philip Horvath, and Allen Webster, "Financial Criteria, Capital Budgeting Techniques, and Risk Analysis of Manufacturing Firms," *Journal of Applied Business Research*, Winter 1996/1997, 95–104.

Conclusions on the Capital Budgeting Decision Methods

In the previous section, we compared the NPV and IRR methods to highlight their relative strengths and weaknesses for evaluating capital projects, and in the process we probably created the impression that "sophisticated" firms should use only one method in the decision process—NPV. However, virtually all capital budgeting decisions are analyzed by computer, so it is easy to calculate and list all the decision measures: payback, discounted payback, NPV, and IRR. In making the accept/reject decision, most large, sophisticated firms such as IBM, General Electric, and General Motors calculate and consider multiple measures because each provides decision makers with a somewhat different piece of relevant information.

Payback and discounted payback provide information about both the risk and the *liquidity* of a project—a long payback means (1) that the investment dollars will be locked up for many years, hence the project is relatively illiquid, and (2) that the project's cash flows must be forecast far out into the future, hence the project is probably quite risky.[10] A good analogy for this is the bond valuation process. An investor should never compare the yields to maturity on two bonds without considering their terms to maturity because a bond's riskiness is significantly influenced by its maturity.

NPV is important because it gives a direct measure of the dollar benefit (on a present value basis) to the firm's shareholders, so we regard NPV as the best single measure of *profitability*. IRR also measures profitability, but here it is expressed as a percentage rate of return, which many decision makers, especially nonfinancial managers, seem to prefer. Further, IRR contains information concerning a project's "safety margin," which is not inherent in NPV. To illustrate, consider the following two projects: Project T costs $10,000 at t = 0 and is expected to return $16,500 at the end of one year, while Project B costs $100,000 and has an expected payoff of $115,500 after one year. At a 10 percent required rate of return, both projects have an NPV of $5,000, so by the NPV rule we should be indifferent between the two. However, Project T actually provides a much larger margin for error. Even if its realized cash inflow were almost 40 percent below the $16,500 forecast, the firm would still recover its $10,000 investment. On the other hand, if Project B's inflows fell by only 14 percent from the forecasted $115,500, the firm would not recover its investment. Further, if no inflows

---

[10]We generally define liquidity as the ability to convert an asset into cash quickly without loss of the original investment. Thus, in most cases, short-term assets are considered more liquid than long-term assets. We discuss liquidity in greater detail in Chapter 13.

were generated at all, the firm would lose only $10,000 with Project T but $100,000 if it took on Project B.

The NPV contains no information about either the "safety margin" inherent in a project's cash flow forecasts or the amount of capital at risk, but the IRR does provide "safety margin" information—Project T's IRR is a whopping 65.0 percent, while Project B's IRR is only 15.5 percent. As a result, the realized return could fall substantially for Project T, and it would still make money. Note, though, that the IRR method has a reinvestment assumption that probably is unrealistic, and it is possible for projects to have multiple IRRs. Both of these problems can be corrected using the modified IRR calculation, which is discussed in Appendix 8A.

In summary, the different methods provide different types of information to decision makers. Because it is easy to calculate them, all should be considered in the decision process. For any specific decision, more weight might be given to one method than another, but it would be foolish to ignore the information provided by any of the methods.

At this point, we should note that multinational corporations use essentially the same capital budgeting techniques that we described in this chapter. However, foreign governments, international regulatory environments, and financial and product markets in other countries pose certain challenges to U.S. firms that must make capital budgeting decisions for their foreign operations. We wait to discuss some of these challenges/differences until the next chapter.

Self-Test Questions

Describe the advantages and disadvantages of the capital budgeting methods discussed in this chapter.

Should capital budgeting decisions be made solely on the basis of a project's NPV?

The Post-Audit

POST-AUDIT
A comparison of the actual and expected results for a given capital project.

An important aspect of the capital budgeting process is the **post-audit,** which involves (1) comparing actual results with those predicted by the project's sponsors and (2) explaining why any differences occurred. For example, many firms require that the operating divisions send monthly reports for the first six months after a project goes into operation and quarterly reports thereafter, until the project's results are up to expectations. From then on, reports on the project are handled like those of other operations.

The post-audit has two main purposes:

1. **Improve forecasts.** When decision makers are forced to compare their projections to actual outcomes, there is a tendency for estimates to improve. Conscious or unconscious biases are observed and eliminated; new forecasting methods are sought as the need for them becomes apparent; and people simply tend to do everything better, including forecasting, if they know that their actions are being monitored.
2. **Improve operations.** Businesses are run by people, and people can perform at higher or lower levels of efficiency. When a divisional team has made a forecast about an investment, its members are, in a sense, putting their reputations on the line. If costs are above predicted levels, sales below expectations, and so on, executives in production, marketing, and other areas will strive to improve operations

and to bring results in line with forecasts. In a discussion related to this point, an IBM executive made this statement: "You academicians worry only about making good decisions. In business, we also worry about making decisions good."

The post-audit is not a simple process—a number of factors can cause complications. First, we must recognize that each element of the cash flow forecast is subject to uncertainty, so a percentage of all projects undertaken by any reasonably venturesome firm will necessarily go awry. This fact must be considered when appraising the performances of the operating executives who submit capital expenditure requests. Second, projects sometimes fail to meet expectations for reasons beyond the control of the operating executives and for reasons that no one could realistically be expected to anticipate. For example, the 1991–1992 recession adversely affected many projects. Third, it is often difficult to separate the operating results of one investment from those of a larger system. Although some projects stand alone and permit ready identification of costs and revenues, the actual cost savings that result from a new computer system, for example, might be very hard to measure. Fourth, it is often hard to hand out blame or praise because the executives who were actually responsible for a given decision might have moved on by the time the results of a long-term investment are known.

Because of these difficulties, some firms tend to play down the importance of the post-audit. However, observations of both businesses and governmental units suggest that the best-run and most successful organizations are the ones that put the greatest emphasis on post-audits. Accordingly, we regard the post-audit as being an extremely important element in a good capital budgeting system.

Self-Test Questions

What is done in the post-audit?

Identify several purposes of the post-audit.

What are some factors that can cause complications in the post-audit?

✳ **SMALL BUSINESS**

Capital Budgeting in the Small Firm—Part I

The allocation of capital in small firms is as important as it is in large ones. In fact, given their lack of access to the capital markets, it is often more important in the small firm because the funds necessary to correct mistakes might not be available. Also, large firms with large capital budgets generally allocate capital to numerous projects, so a mistake on one project can be offset by successes with others—large firms benefit from project diversification.

In spite of the importance of capital expenditures to small business, studies of the way capital budgeting decisions are made generally suggest that many small firms use "back-of-the-envelope" analysis, or perhaps no analysis at all. For example, when L. R. Runyon studied 214 firms with net worths of from $500,000 to $1,000,000, he found that almost 70 percent relied on either payback or some other questionable criteria; only 14 percent used a discounted cash flow analysis; and about nine percent indicated that they used no formal analysis at all. In a more recent study, Stanley Block examined 232 firms that had fewer than 1,000 employees and generated sales of less than $5 million. His results indicate that small firms have increased their use of discounted cash flow analysis for capital

continues

budgeting decision making—almost 28 percent indicated they use either NPV or IRR to evaluate capital projects. However, Block also found that nearly two thirds of the firms still use methods that do not consider the time value of money, such as the payback period. Thus, while there has been some movement in the 1990s toward increased use of appropriate capital budgeting techniques by small firms, most still rely on nondiscounted methods such as the traditional payback period. Studies of larger firms, on the other hand, generally find that most analyze capital budgeting decisions using discounted cash flow techniques. (See the Industry Practice box in this chapter.)

We are left with a puzzle. Capital budgeting is clearly important to small firms, yet these firms tend not to use the tools that have been developed to improve capital budgeting decisions. Why does this situation exist? One argument is that managers of small firms simply are not well trained; they are unsophisticated. This argument suggests that the managers would make greater use of sophisticated techniques if they understood them better. Another argument relates to the fact that management talent is a scarce resource in small firms, and managers simply cannot afford the time required to analyze projects using sophisticated methods, even if they did understand them. A third argument relates to the cost of analyzing capital projects. Some of the analyses costs are fixed, and it might not be economical to incur them if the project itself is relatively small. This argument suggests that small firms with small projects might actually be making the sensible decision when they rely on management's "gut feeling."

In their studies, both Block and Runyon also found that small firms tend to be cash oriented. They are concerned with basic survival, so they tend to look at expenditures from the standpoint of near-term effects on cash. This cash-and-survival orientation leads to a focus on a relatively short time horizon, which in turn might lead to an emphasis on the payback method. The limitations of payback are well known, but in spite of those limitations, the technique is popular in small businesses, as it gives the firm a "feel" for when the cash committed to an investment will be recovered and thus be available to repay loans or for new opportunities. Therefore, small firms that are cash oriented and have limited managerial resources might find the payback method an appealing compromise

between the need for extensive analysis on the one hand and the high costs of analysis on the other. Also, Block indicates that when a small firm borrows from a bank, it needs to show that the loan can be paid back within a particular time period, not that the project for which the funds are intended is acceptable using NPV or IRR. Interestingly, Block found that nearly 84 percent of the firms that use payback to evaluate capital projects set the minimum acceptable payback period equal to three years or less—this suggests these firms require a return greater than 30 percent for their capital projects, while large firms generally require a return less than 15 percent.

Remember from our discussion in the chapter that the single most appealing argument for the use of net present value in capital budgeting decisions is that NPV gives an explicit measure of the effect of the investment on the value of the firm: If NPV is positive, the investment will increase the value of the firm and make its owners wealthier. In small firms, however, the stock often is not traded in public markets, so its value cannot be observed. Also, for reasons of control many small business owners and managers might not want to broaden ownership by going public. It is difficult to argue for value-based techniques when the value of the firm and its required rate of return are unobservable. Furthermore, in a closely held firm the objectives of the individual owner-manager might extend beyond the firm's monetary value.

In general, we know that small firms make less extensive use of DCF techniques than do larger firms. This might be a rational decision resulting from a conscious or subconscious conclusion that the costs of sophisticated analyses outweigh their benefits; it might reflect nonmonetary goals of small businesses' owner-managers; it might reflect difficulties in estimating the values needed for DCF analysis but not payback; or it might reflect the pressures exerted by lenders, such as banks, to pay back loans within a specified period. However, nonuse of DCF methods also might reflect a weakness in many small business organizations. *We simply do not know.* We do know that small businesses must do all they can to compete effectively with big business, and to the extent that a small business fails to use DCF methods because its manager is unsophisticated or uninformed, it might be putting itself at a serious competitive disadvantage.

✷ **ETHICAL DILEMMA**

This Is a Good Investment—Be Sure the Numbers Show That It Is!

Oliver Greene is the assistant to the financial manager at Cybercomp Inc., which is a company that develops software to drive network communications for personal computers. Oliver joined Cybercomp three years ago, following graduation from college. His primary responsibility has been to evaluate capital budgeting projects and make investment recommendations to the board of directors. Oliver enjoys his job very much—he often finds himself challenged with interesting tasks, and he is paid extremely well for what he does.

Last week, Oliver started evaluating the capital projects that have been proposed for investment this year. One of the proposals is to purchase NetWare Products, a company that manufactures circuit boards, called network cards, which are required to achieve communication connectivity between personal computers. Cybercomp packages network cards with the software it sells, but it currently purchases them from another manufacturer. The proposal, which was submitted by Nadine Wilson, Cybercomp's CEO, suggests the company can reduce costs and increase profit margins by producing the network cards in-house.

Oliver barely had time to scan the proposal when he was summoned to Mrs. Wilson's office. The meeting was short and to the point. Mrs. Wilson instructed Oliver to "make the numbers for NetWare Products look good because we *want* to buy that company." She also gave Oliver an evaluation of NetWare completed two years ago by an independent appraiser that suggests NetWare might not be worth the amount Cybercomp is willing to pay. Mrs. Wilson instructed Oliver to find a way to rebut the findings of the report.

Oliver was troubled by the meeting he had with Mrs. Wilson. His gut feeling was that something was wrong. But he hadn't yet had time to carefully examine the proposal—his evaluation was very cursory, and he was far from making a final decision concerning the acceptability of the capital budgeting project that Mrs. Wilson proposed. Oliver felt like he needed much more information before forming a final recommendation.

Oliver has spent the entire day examining the appraisal report that Mrs. Wilson provided and trying to gather additional information about the proposed investment. The report contains some background information concerning NetWare's operations, but crucial financial data are missing. Further investigation into NetWare Products has produced little information. Oliver has discovered that the company's stock is closely held by a small group of investors that owns numerous businesses and that generously contributes to the local university, which happens to be Mrs. Wilson's alma mater. In addition, Oliver's secretary has informed him that the gossip around the water cooler at Cybercomp is that Mrs. Wilson and the owners of NetWare are old college buddies, and she might even have a stake in NetWare.

This morning, Mrs. Wilson called Oliver and repeated her feelings concerning the purchase of NetWare. This time she said: "We really want to purchase NetWare. Some people might not believe so, but this is a very good deal. It's your job to make the numbers work—that's why we pay you the big bucks!" As a result of the conversation, Oliver has the impression his job might be jeopardized if he doesn't make the "right" decision. This added pressure has made Oliver very tense. What should he do? What would you do if you were Oliver? Would your answer change if you knew Mrs. Wilson had recently sold much of her Cybercomp stock?

Summary

This chapter discussed the capital budgeting process, and the key concepts that were covered are listed here:

- **Capital budgeting** is the process of analyzing potential fixed asset investments. Capital budgeting decisions are probably the most important ones financial managers must make.

- The **payback period** is defined as the expected number of years required to recover a project's cost. The traditional payback method ignores cash flows beyond the payback period, and it does not consider the time value of money. The payback does, however, indicate a project's risk and liquidity because it shows how long the invested capital will be "at risk."
- The **discounted payback method** is similar to the traditional payback method except that it discounts cash flows at the project's required rate of return. Like the traditional payback, it ignores cash flows beyond the discounted payback period.
- The **net present value (NPV) method** discounts all cash flows at the project's required rate of return and then sums those cash flows. The project is acceptable if this sum, called the NPV, is positive.
- The **internal rate of return (IRR)** is defined as the discount rate that forces a project's NPV to equal zero. The project is acceptable if the IRR is greater than the project's required rate of return.
- The NPV and IRR methods make the same accept/reject decisions for **independent projects,** but if projects are **mutually exclusive,** then ranking conflicts can arise. If conflicts arise, the NPV method generally should be used. The NPV and IRR methods are both superior to the payback, but NPV is generally the single best measure of a project's profitability.
- The NPV method assumes that cash flows can be reinvested at the firm's required rate of return, while the IRR method assumes reinvestment at the project's IRR. Because **reinvestment at the required rate of return generally is a better (closer to the truth) assumption,** the NPV is superior to the IRR.
- Sophisticated managers consider several of the project evaluation measures because the **different measures provide different types of information.**
- The **post-audit** is a key element of capital budgeting. By comparing actual results with predicted results, and then determining why differences occurred, decision makers can improve both their operations and their forecasts of projects' outcomes.
- Small firms tend to use the payback method rather than a "sophisticated" method. This might be a rational decision because (1) the **cost** of a DCF analysis **might outweigh the benefits** for the project being considered, (2) the firm's **required rate of return cannot be estimated accurately,** or (3) the small business owner might be considering **nonmonetary goals.**

Although this chapter has presented the basic elements of the capital budgeting process, there are many other aspects of this crucial topic. Some of the more important ones are discussed in the next chapter.

Questions

8-1 How is a project classification scheme (for example, replacement, expansion into new markets, and so forth) used in the capital budgeting process?

8-2 Explain why the NPV of a relatively long-term project, defined as one for which a high percentage of its cash flows are expected in the distant future, is more sensitive to changes in the required rate of return than is the NPV of a short-term project.

8-3 Explain why, if two mutually exclusive projects are being compared, the short-term project might have the higher ranking under the NPV criterion if the required rate of return is high, but the long-term project might be deemed better if the required rate of return is low. Would changes in the required rate of return ever cause a change in the IRR ranking of two such projects? Explain.

8–4 In what sense is a reinvestment rate assumption embodied in the NPV and IRR methods? What is the assumed reinvestment rate of each method?

8–5 "If a firm has no mutually exclusive projects, only independent ones, and it also has both a constant required rate of return and projects with conventional cash flow patterns, then the NPV and IRR methods will always lead to identical capital budgeting decisions." Discuss this statement. What does it imply about using the IRR method in lieu of the NPV method? If each of the assumptions made in the question were changed (one by one), how would these changes affect your answer?

8–6 Are there conditions under which a firm might be better off if it were to choose a machine with a rapid payback rather than one with a larger NPV? Explain.

8–7 A firm has $100 million available for capital expenditures. It is considering investing in one of two projects; each has a cost of $100 million. Project A has an IRR of 20 percent and an NPV of $9 million. It will be terminated at the end of one year at a profit of $20 million, resulting in an immediate increase in earnings per share (EPS). Project B, which cannot be postponed, has an IRR of 30 percent and an NPV of $50 million. However, the firm's short-run EPS will be reduced if it accepts Project B because no revenues will be generated for several years.
   a. Should the short-run effects on EPS influence the choice between the two projects?
   b. How might situations like the one described here influence a firm's decision to use payback as a part of the capital budgeting process?

Self-Test Problems

(Solutions appear in Appendix B)

key terms   ST–1 Define each of the following terms:
   a. The capital budget; capital budgeting
   b. Traditional payback period; discounted payback period
   c. Independent projects; mutually exclusive projects
   d. DCF techniques; net present value (NPV) method
   e. Internal rate of return (IRR) method; IRR
   f. NPV profile; crossover rate
   g. Unconventional cash flow patterns; multiple IRRs
   h. Hurdle rate; required rate of return
   i. Reinvestment rate assumption
   j. Post-audit

project analysis   ST–2 You are a financial analyst for Damon Electronics Company. The director of capital budgeting has asked you to analyze two proposed capital investments, Projects X and Y. Each project has a cost of $10,000, and the required rate of return for each project is 12 percent. The projects' expected net cash flows are as follows:

	EXPECTED NET CASH FLOWS	
YEAR	PROJECT X	PROJECT Y
0	$(10,000)	$(10,000)
1	6,500	3,500
2	3,000	3,500
3	3,000	3,500
4	1,000	3,500

a. Calculate each project's payback period (PB), net present value (NPV), and internal rate of return (IRR).
b. Which project or projects should be accepted if they are independent?
c. Which project should be accepted if they are mutually exclusive?
d. How might a change in the required rate of return produce a conflict between the NPV and IRR rankings of these two projects? Would this conflict exist if k were 5%? (*Hint:* Plot the NPV profiles.)
e. Why does the conflict exist?

Problems

payback, NPV, and IRR calculations

8–1 Project K has a cost of $52,125, and its expected net cash inflows are $12,000 per year for eight years.
a. What is the project's payback period (to the closest year)?
b. The required rate of return for the project is 12 percent. What is the project's NPV?
c. What is the project's IRR? (*Hint:* Recognize that the project is an annuity.)
d. What is the project's discounted payback period, assuming a 12 percent required rate of return?

NPV and IRR analysis

8–2 Derek's Donuts is considering two mutually exclusive investments. The projects' expected net cash flows are as follows:

	EXPECTED NET CASH FLOWS	
YEAR	PROJECT A	PROJECT B
0	$(300)	$(405)
1	(387)	134
2	(193)	134
3	(100)	134
4	500	134
5	500	134
6	850	134
7	100	0

a. Construct NPV profiles for Projects A and B.
b. What is each project's IRR?
c. If you were told that each project's required rate of return was 12 percent, which project should be selected? If the required rate of return was 15 percent, what would be the proper choice?
d. Looking at the NPV profiles constructed in part a, what is the approximate crossover rate, and what is its significance?

timing differences

8–3 The Southwestern Oil Exploration Company is considering two mutually exclusive plans for extracting oil on property for which it has mineral rights. Both plans call for the expenditure of $12 million to drill development wells. Under Plan A, all the oil will be extracted in one year, producing a cash flow at t = 1 of $14.4 million. Under Plan B, cash flows will be $2.1 milion per year for 20 years.
a. Construct NPV profiles for Plan A and Plan B, identify each project's IRR, and indicate the approximate crossover rate of return. (To compute the exact crossover rate, see footnote 7 in the chapter.)

b. Suppose a company has a required rate of return of 12 percent, and it can get unlimited capital at that cost. Is it logical to assume that it would take on all available independent projects (of average risk) with returns greater than 12 percent? Further, if all available projects with returns greater than 12 percent have been taken on, would this mean that cash flows from past investments would have an opportunity cost of only 12 percent because all the firm could do with these cash flows would be to replace money that has a cost of 12 percent? Finally, does this imply that the required rate of return is the correct rate to assume for the reinvestment of a project's cash flows?

scale differences   **8–4** The Chaplinsky Publishing Company is considering two mutually exclusive expansion plans. Plan A calls for the expenditure of $40 million on a large-scale, integrated plant that will provide an expected cash flow stream of $6.4 million per year for 20 years. Plan B calls for the expenditure of $12 million to build a somewhat less efficient, more labor-intensive plant that has an expected cash flow stream of $2.72 million per year for 20 years. Chaplinsky's required rate of return is ten percent.

a. Calculate each project's NPV and IRR.
b. Graph the NPV profiles for Plan A and Plan B. Using the NPV profiles, approximate the crossover rate.
c. Give a logical explanation, based on reinvestment rates and opportunity costs, as to why the NPV method is better than the IRR method when the firm's required rate of return is constant at some value such as 10 percent.

Exam-Type Problems

The problems included in this section are set up in such a way that they could be used as multiple-choice exam problems.

NPVs, IRRs, and payback
for independent projects
8–5 Olsen Engineering is considering including two pieces of equipment, a truck and an overhead pulley system, in this year's capital budget. The projects are independent. The cash outlay for the truck is $22,430, and for the pulley system it is $17,100. Each piece of equipment has an estimated life of five years. The annual after-tax cash flow expected to be provided by the truck is $7,500, and for the pulley it is $5,100. The firm's required rate of return is 14 percent. Calculate the IRR, the NPV, and the payback period for each project, and indicate which project(s) should be accepted.

NPVs and IRRs for
mutually exclusive projects
8–6 Horrigan Industries must choose between a gas-powered and an electric-powered forklift truck for moving materials in its factory. Because both forklifts perform the same function, the firm will choose only one. (They are mutually exclusive investments.) The electric-powered truck will cost more, but it will be less expensive to operate; it will cost $22,000, whereas the gas-powered truck will cost $17,500. The required rate of return that applies to both investments is 12 percent. The life for both types of truck is estimated to be six years, during which time the net cash flows for the electric-powered truck will be $6,290 per year and those for the gas-powered truck will be $5,000 per year. Calculate the NPV and IRR for each type of truck, and decide which to recommend.

capital budgeting decisions   **8–7** Project S costs $15,000 and is expected to produce benefits (cash flows) of $4,500 per year for five years. Project L costs $37,500 and is expected to produce cash flows of $11,100 per year for five years.

a. Calculate the NPV, IRR, and payback period for each project, assuming a required rate of return of 14 percent.

b. If the projects are independent, which project(s) should be selected? If they are mutually exclusive projects, which project actually should be selected?

present value of costs   **8–8** The Cordell Coffee Company is evaluating the within-plant distribution system for its new roasting, grinding, and packing plant. The two alternatives are (1) a conveyor system with a high initial cost but low annual operating costs and (2) several forklift trucks, which cost less but have considerably higher operating costs. The decision to construct the plant has already been made, and the choice here will have no effect on the overall revenues of the project. The required rate of return for the plant is nine percent, and the projects' expected net costs are listed in the following table:

| | EXPECTED NET CASH FLOWS | |
YEAR	CONVEYOR	FORKLIFT
0	$(300,000)	$(120,000)
1	(66,000)	(96,000)
2	(66,000)	(96,000)
3	(66,000)	(96,000)
4	(66,000)	(96,000)
5	(66,000)	(96,000)

a. What is the present value of costs of each alternative? Which method should be chosen?

b. What is the IRR of each alternative?

NPV and IRR   **8–9** Your company is considering two mutually exclusive projects, X and Y, whose costs and cash flows are shown in the following table:

YEAR	PROJECT C	PROJECT R
1	$(14,000)	$(22,840)
2	8,000	8,000
3	6,000	8,000
4	2,000	8,000
5	3,000	8,000

The projects are equally risky, and their required rate of return is 12 percent. You must make a recommendation concerning which project should be purchased. To determine which is more appropriate, compute the NPV and IRR of each project.

NPV and IRR   **8–10** The after-tax cash flows for two mutually exclusive projects have been estimated, and the following information has been provided:

YEAR	MACHINE D	MACHINE Q
0	$(2,500)	$(2,500)
1	2,000	0
2	900	1,800
3	100	1,000
4	100	900

The company's required rate of return is 14 percent, and it can get an unlimited amount of capital at that cost. What is the IRR of the *better* project? (*Hint:* Note that the better project might not be the one with the higher IRR.)

NPV and IRR   **8–11** Diamond Hill Jewelers is considering the following independent projects:

YEAR	PROJECT Y	PROJECT Z
0	$(25,000)	$(25,000)
1	10,000	0
2	9,000	0
3	7,000	0
4	6,000	36,000

Which project(s) should be accepted if the required rate of return for the projects is ten percent? Compute the NPVs and the IRRs for both projects.

Integrative Problem

basics of capital budgeting   **8–12** Your boss, the chief financial officer (CFO) for Southern Textiles, has just handed you the estimated cash flows for two proposed projects. Project L involves adding a new item to the firm's fabric line; it would take some time to build up the market for this product, so the cash inflows would increase over time. Project S involves an add-on to an existing line, and its cash flows would decrease over time. Both projects have three-year lives because Southern is planning to introduce an entirely new fabric at that time.

Here are the net cash flow estimates (in thousands of dollars):

	EXPECTED NET CASH FLOWS	
YEAR	PROJECT L	PROJECT S
0	$(100)	$(100)
1	10	70
2	60	50
3	80	20

Depreciation, salvage values, tax effects, and so on, are all included in these cash flows.

The CFO also made subjective risk assessments of each project, and he concluded that the projects both have risk characteristics that are similar to the firm's average project. Southern's required rate of return is ten percent. You must now determine whether one or both of the projects should be accepted. Start by answering the following questions:

a. What is capital budgeting? Are there any similarities between a firm's capital budgeting decisions and an individual's investment decisions?

b. What is the difference between independent and mutually exclusive projects? Between projects with conventional cash flows and projects with unconventional cash flows?

c. (1) What is the payback period? Find the traditional paybacks for Project L and Project S.

(2) What is the rationale for the payback measure? According to the payback criterion, which project or projects should be accepted if the firm's maximum acceptable payback is two years and Project L and Project S are independent? Mutually exclusive?

(3) What is the difference between the traditional payback and the discounted payback?

(4) What are the main disadvantages of the traditional payback? Is the payback method of any real usefulness in capital budgeting decisions?

d. (1) Define the term *net present value (NPV)*. What is each project's NPV?

(2) What is the rationale behind the NPV method? According to NPV, which project or projects should be accepted if they are independent? Mutually exclusive?

(3) Would the NPVs change if the required rate of return changed?

e. (1) Define the term *internal rate of return (IRR)*. What is each project's IRR?

(2) How is the IRR on a project related to the YTM on a bond?

(3) What is the logic behind the IRR method? According to IRR, which projects should be accepted if they are independent? Mutually exclusive?

(4) Would the projects' IRRs change if the required rate of return changed? Explain.

f. (1) Draw the NPV profiles for Project L and Project S. At what discount rate do the profiles cross?

(2) Look at the NPV profile graph without referring to the actual NPVs and IRRs. Which project or projects should be accepted if they are independent? Mutually exclusive? Explain. Do your answers differ depending on the discount rate used? Explain.

g. (1) What is the underlying cause of ranking conflicts between NPV and IRR?

(2) What is the "reinvestment rate assumption," and how does it affect the NPV versus IRR conflict?

(3) Which capital budgeting method should be used when NPV and IRR give conflicting rankings? Why?

Computer-Related Problem

Work the problem in this section only if you are using the computer problem diskette.

NPV and IRR analysis   **8–13** Use the model in File C8 to solve this problem. West Coast Chemical Company (WCCC) is considering two mutually exclusive investments. The projects' expected net cash flows are as follows:

	EXPECTED NET CASH FLOWS	
YEAR	PROJECT A	PROJECT B
0	$(45,000)	$(50,000)
1	(20,000)	15,000
2	11,000	15,000
3	20,000	15,000
4	30,000	15,000
5	45,000	15,000

a. Construct NPV profiles for Projects A and B.

b. Calculate each project's IRR. Assume the required rate of return is 13 percent.

c. If the required rate of return for each project is 13 percent, which project should West Coast select? If the required rate of return is nine percent, what would be the proper choice? If the required rate of return is 15 percent, what would be the proper choice?

d. At what rate do the NPV profiles of the two projects cross?

e. Project A has a large cash flow in Year 5 associated with ending the project. WCCC's management is confident of Project A's cash flows in Years 0 to 4 but is uncertain about what its Year 5 cash flow will be. (There is no uncertainty about Project B's cash flows.) Under a worst-case scenario, Project A's Year 5 cash flow will be $40,000, whereas under a best-case scenario, the cash flow will be $50,000. Redo parts a, b, and d for each scenario, assuming a 13 percent required rate of return. If the required rate of return for each project is 13 percent, which project should be selected under each scenario?

ONLINE ESSENTIALS

http://www.teachmefinance.com   TeachMeFinance.com
Provides tutorials with examples on many finance subjects. To view the tutorial about capital budgeting, click on "Capital Budgeting" in the menu of subjects given on the left side of the screen.

http://www.studyfinance.com   *study*finance.com
This site, which is maintained by the University of Arizona, provides overviews of various finance topics, including capital budgeting. To view the overviews, go to the Overviews section and click on "Capital Budgeting."

http://www.morevalue.com   *+Value   morevalue.com*
Provides lecture notes for various finance topics. To view samples of the notes, click on Finance Channel and follow the instructions. The "full" versions of the notes are only available through purchase; but the samples give you some idea of the general subject.

http://www.cob.ohio-state.edu/~fin/resources_education/edcourse.htm
Finance Course on the Web
Provides links to finance courses taught at different universities and colleges. This site also gives a description of the sites that are linked. There are quite a few tutorials, notes, examples, and practice problems that relate to capital budgeting at the various sites.

Modified Internal Rate of Return (MIRR)

MODIFIED IRR (MIRR)
The discount rate at which the present value of a project's cost is equal to the present value of its terminal value, in which the terminal value is found as the sum of the future values of the cash inflows, compounded at the firm's required rate of return (cost of capital).

In spite of a strong academic preference for NPV, surveys indicate that most business executives prefer IRR over NPV. Apparently, managers find it intuitively more appealing to analyze investments in terms of percentage rates of return than dollars of NPV. But remember from the discussion in the chapter that the IRR method assumes the cash flows from the project are reinvested at a rate of return equal to the IRR, which we generally view as unrealistic. Given this fact, can we devise a percentage evaluator that is better than the regular IRR? The answer is yes—we can modify the IRR and make it a better indicator of relative profitability, hence better for use in capital budgeting. The new measure is called the **modified IRR,** or **MIRR,** and it is defined as follows:

8A-1

$$\text{PV costs} = \text{PV terminal value}$$

$$\sum_{t=0}^{n} \frac{COF_t}{(1+k)^t} = \frac{\sum_{t=0}^{n} CIF_t(1+k)^{n-t}}{(1+MIRR)^n}$$

$$\text{PV costs} = \frac{TV}{(1+MIRR)^n}$$

Here COF refers to cash outflows (negative numbers) and CIF refers to cash inflows (all positive numbers) associated with a project. The left term is simply the PV of the investment outlays when discounted at the project's required rate of return, k, and the numerator of the right term is the future value of the inflows, assuming that the cash inflows are reinvested at the project's required rate of return. The future value of the cash inflows is also called the *terminal value*, or TV. The discount rate that forces the PV of the TV to equal the PV of the costs is defined as the MIRR.[11]

If the investment costs are all incurred at t = 0, and if the first operating inflow occurs at t = 1, as is true for our illustrative Projects S and L (which we first presented in Figure 8–1), then this equation can be used:

8A-1a

$$\text{Cost} = \frac{TV}{(1+MIRR)^n} = \frac{\sum_{t=0}^{n} CIF_t(1+k)^{n-t}}{(1+MIRR)^n}$$

---

[11]There are several alternative definitions for the MIRR. The differences relate primarily to whether negative cash flows that occur after positive cash flows begin should be compounded and treated as part of the TV or discounted and treated as a cost. Our definition (which treats all negative cash flows as investments and thus discounts them) generally is the most appropriate procedure. For a complete discussion, see William R. McDaniel, Daniel E. McCarty, and Kenneth A. Jessell, "Discounted Cash Flow with Explicit Reinvestment Rates: Tutorial and Extension," *The Financial Review* (August 1988), 369–385.

We can illustrate the calculation with Project S:

CASH FLOW TIME LINE FOR PROJECT S:

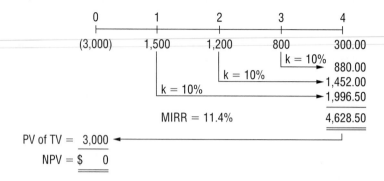

Using the cash flows as set out on the time line, first find the terminal value by compounding each cash inflow at the 10 percent required rate of return. Then, enter into your calculator PV = −3000, FV = 4628.5, and N = 4, and press the I key to find $MIRR_S = 11.4\%$. Similarly, we find $MIRR_L = 11.0\%$.

The modified IRR has a significant advantage over the traditional IRR measure. MIRR assumes that cash flows are reinvested at the required rate of return, while the traditional IRR measure assumes that cash flows are reinvested at the project's own IRR. Because reinvestment at the required rate of return (cost of funds) generally is more correct, the MIRR is a better indicator of a project's true profitability. MIRR also solves the multiple IRR problem. To illustrate, with k = 10%, the strip mine project described in the chapter has MIRR = 5.6% versus the 10 percent required rate of return, so it should be rejected. This is consistent with the decision based on the NPV method because at k = 10%, NPV = −$0.77 million.

Is MIRR as good as NPV for choosing between mutually exclusive projects? If two projects are of equal size and have the same life, then NPV and MIRR will always lead to the same project selection decision. Thus, for any projects like our Projects S and L, if $NPV_S > NPV_L$, then $MIRR_S > MIRR_L$, and the kinds of conflicts we encountered between NPV and the traditional IRR will not occur. Also, if the projects are of equal size, but differ in lives, the MIRR will always lead to the same decision as the NPV if the MIRRs are both calculated using as the terminal year the life of the longer project. (Just fill in zeros for the shorter project's missing cash flows.) However, if the projects differ in size, then conflicts can still occur. For example, if we were choosing between a large project and a small mutually exclusive one, then we might find $NPV_L > NPV_S$, but $MIRR_L < MIRR_S$.

Our conclusion is that the MIRR is superior to the regular IRR as an indicator of a project's "true" rate of return, or "expected long-term rate of return," but the NPV method is still better for choosing among competing projects that differ in size because it provides a better indicator of the extent to which each project will increase the value of the firm; thus, NPV is still the recommended approach.

Problem

MIRR and multiple rates of return

8A–1 The Upton Uranium Company is deciding whether or not it should open a strip mine, the net cost of which is $2 million. Net cash inflows are expected to be $13 million, all coming at the end of Year 1. The land must be returned to its natural state at a cost of $12 million, payable at the end of Year 2.

a. Plot the project's NPV profile. (*Hint:* Calculate NPV at k = 0%, 10%, 80%, and 450%, and possibly at other k values.)

b. Should the project be accepted if k = 10%? If k = 20%? Explain your reasoning.

c. Can you think of some other capital budgeting situations in which negative cash flows during or at the other end of the project's life might lead to multiple IRRs?

d. What is the project's MIRR at k = 10%? At k = 20%? Does the MIRR method lead to the same accept/reject decision as the NPV method?

CHAPTER 9

Project Cash Flows and Risk

A MANAGERIAL PERSPECTIVE

When RJR Nabisco canceled its smokeless cigarette project, called Premier, *The Wall Street Journal* called it "one of the most stunning new product disasters in recent history." RJR had spent more than $300 million on the product and had test marketed it for five months. The company had even built a new plant and was all set to produce smokeless cigarettes in huge quantities.

The new cigarette had two fatal flaws—it had to be lit with a special lighter and even then it was hard to light, and many, if not most, smokers didn't like the taste. In addition, it seems smokers didn't like the fact that there was no smoke to blow out or ashes to flick because Premier heated the tobacco rather than burning it. When the cigarette was introduced in 1988, these problems were well known early on, yet RJR still pumped money into the project.

What led RJR's top managers to downplay the flaws and to spend more than $300 million on a bad product? According to industry observers, many people inside the company were aware of the seriousness of the situation, but they were hesitant to voice their concerns because they did not want to offend the top managers. The top managers, meantime, were so infatuated with their "new toy" that they assumed consumers would embrace the smokeless cigarette in spite of its obvious flaws.

Interestingly, most of the top managers smoked, but none smoked the new smokeless cigarette!

At the time the Premier line was introduced, RJR was not a well-run company, even though it was entrenched in highly profitable markets and was generating billions of dollars of cash each year. The smokeless cigarette project didn't kill the company, but it did contribute to the downfall of the management team that backed the project.

Unfortunately, it seems RJR was intent on salvaging its investment in the first smokeless cigarette it introduced, so in 1996 it introduced a second smokeless cigarette called Eclipse. It invested an additional $150 million in the Eclipse brand, only to discover that it too was a flop. In fact, it lasted about the same length of time as the Premier line—just a few months.

Had RJR's top managers followed the procedures set forth in this chapter, perhaps they would not have sunk as much money into the smokeless cigarette projects. Instead, they would have discovered their original project should have been rejected because it was not expected to generate the cash flows necessary to make it a viable investment. ∎

SOURCES: Various articles available on Dow Jones Interactive® Publications Library located at http://www.wsj.com.

The basic principles of capital budgeting were covered in Chapter 8. In this chapter we examine some additional issues, including cash flow estimation and incorporating risk into the capital budgeting decision. In addition, we present some of the challenges multinational firms face when applying the capital budgeting decision-making methods we describe in both Chapter 8 and this chapter.

Cash Flow Estimation

CASH FLOW
The actual cash, as opposed to accounting net income, that a firm receives or pays during some specified period.

The most important, but also the most difficult, step in the analysis of a capital project is estimating its **cash flows**—the investment outlays and the net cash flows expected after the project is purchased. Many variables are involved in cash flow estimation, and many individuals and departments participate in the process. For example, the forecasts of unit sales and sales prices normally are made by the marketing group based on its knowledge of advertising effects, the state of the economy, competitors' reactions, and trends in consumers' tastes. Similarly, the capital outlays associated with a new product generally are determined by the engineering and product development staffs, while operating costs are estimated by cost accountants, production experts, personnel specialists, purchasing agents, and so forth.

Because it is difficult to make accurate forecasts of the costs and revenues associated with a large, complex project, forecast errors can be quite large. For example, in the 1970s, when several major oil companies decided to build the Alaska Pipeline, the original cost estimates were in the neighborhood of $700 million, but the final cost was closer to $8 billion. Similar (or even worse) miscalculations are common in forecasts of product design costs. Further, as difficult as plant and equipment costs are to estimate, sales revenues and operating costs over the life of the project generally are even more uncertain. For example, several years ago Federal Express developed an electronic delivery service system (ZapMail). It used the correct capital budgeting technique, the net present value (NPV) method, but it incorrectly estimated the project's cash flows: Projected revenues were too high and projected costs were too low; thus, virtually no one was willing to pay the price required to cover the project's costs. As a result, cash flows failed to meet the forecasted levels, and Federal Express ended up losing about $200 million on the venture. This example demonstrates a basic truth—if cash flow estimates are not reasonably accurate, any analytical technique, no matter how sophisticated, can lead to poor decisions and hence to operating losses and lower stock prices. Because of its financial strength, Federal Express was able to absorb losses on the project with no problem, but the ZapMail venture could have forced a weaker firm into bankruptcy.

The financial staff's role in the forecasting process includes (1) coordinating the efforts of the other departments, such as engineering and marketing, (2) ensuring that everyone involved with the forecast uses a consistent set of economic assumptions, and (3) making sure that no biases are inherent in the forecasts. This last point is extremely important, because division managers often become emotionally involved with pet projects or develop empire-building complexes, both of which can lead to cash flow forecasting biases that make bad projects look good—on paper. The RJR smokeless cigarette project discussed in the Managerial Perspective is an example of this problem.

It is almost impossible to overstate the difficulties one can encounter with cash flow forecasts. Also, it is difficult to overstate the importance of these forecasts. In this chapter, we will give you a sense of some of the inputs that are involved in forecasting the cash flows associated with a capital project and in minimizing forecasting errors.

Relevant Cash Flows

RELEVANT CASH FLOWS
The specific cash flows that should be considered in a capital budgeting decision.

One important element in cash flow estimation is the determination of **relevant cash flows,** which are defined as the specific set of cash flows that should be considered in the capital budgeting decision. This process can be rather difficult, but two cardinal rules can help financial analysts avoid mistakes: (1) Capital budgeting decisions must be based on *cash flows after taxes*, not accounting income, and (2) only *incremental cash flows* are relevant to the accept/reject decision. These two rules are discussed in detail in the following sections.

Cash Flow versus Accounting Income

In capital budgeting analysis, *after-tax cash flows, not accounting profits*, are used—it is cash that pays the bills and can be invested in capital projects, not profits. Cash flows and accounting profits can be very different. To illustrate, consider Table 9–1, which shows how accounting profits and cash flows are related to one another. We assume that Unilate Textiles is planning to start a new division at the end of 2000; that sales and all costs, except depreciation, represent actual cash flows and are projected to be constant over time; and that the division will use accelerated depreciation, which will cause its reported depreciation charges to decline over time.[1]

The top section of the table shows the situation in the first year of operations, 2001. Accounting profits are $7 million, but the division's net cash flow—money that is available to Unilate—is $22 million. The $7 million profit is the *return on the funds* originally invested, while the $15 million of depreciation is a *return of part of the funds* originally invested, so the $22 million cash flow consists of both a return *on* and a return *of* part of the invested capital.

The bottom part of the table shows the situation projected for 2006. Here reported profits have doubled because of the decline in depreciation, but net cash flow is down sharply because taxes have doubled. The amount of money received by the firm is represented by the cash flow figure, not the net income figure. And although accounting profits are important for some purposes, it is cash flows that are relevant for the purposes of setting a value on a project using discounted cash flow (DCF) techniques—cash flows can be reinvested to create value, profits cannot. Therefore, in capital budgeting, we are interested in net cash flows, which, in most cases, we can define as

---

[1]Depreciation procedures are discussed in detail in accounting courses, but we do provide a summary and review in Appendix 9A at the end of this chapter. The tables provided in Appendix 9A are used to calculate depreciation charges used in the chapter examples. In some instances, we simplify the depreciation assumptions in order to reduce the arithmetic. Because Congress changes depreciation procedures fairly frequently, it is always necessary to consult the latest tax regulations before developing actual capital budgeting cash flows.

TABLE 9–1	Accounting Profits versus Net Cash Flow (thousands of dollars)		
		ACCOUNTING PROFITS	**CASH FLOWS**
I. 2001 Situation			
Sales		$ 50,000	$ 50,000
Costs except depreciation		(25,000)	(25,000)
Depreciation		(15,000)	—
Net operating income or cash flow		$ 10,000	$ 25,000
Taxes based on operating income (30%)		(3,000)	(3,000)
Net income or net cash flow		$ 7,000	$ 22,000

Net cash flow = Net income plus depreciation = $7,000 + $15,000 = $22,000

II. 2006 Situation			
Sales		$ 50,000	$ 50,000
Costs except depreciation		(25,000)	(25,000)
Depreciation		(5,000)	—
Net operating income or cash flow		$ 20,000	$ 25,000
Taxes based on operating income (30%)		(6,000)	(6,000)
Net income or net cash flow		$ 14,000	$ 19,000

Net cash flow = Net income plus depreciation = $14,000 + $5,000 = $19,000

$$\text{Net cash flow} = \text{Net income} + \text{Depreciation}$$
$$= \text{Return } on \text{ capital} + \text{Return } of \text{ capital}$$

not in accounting profits per se.[2]

Incremental Cash Flows

INCREMENTAL CASH FLOW
The change in a firm's net cash flow attributable to an investment project.

In evaluating a capital project, we are concerned only with those cash flows that result directly from the decision to accept the project. These cash flows, called **incremental cash flows,** represent the changes in the firm's total cash flows that occur as a direct

[2]Actually, net cash flow should be adjusted to reflect all noncash charges, not just depreciation. However, for most projects, depreciation is by far the largest noncash charge. Also, note that Table 9–1 ignores interest charges, which would be present if the firm used debt. Most firms do use debt and hence finance part of their capital budgets with debt. Therefore, the question has been raised as to whether interest charges should be reflected in capital budgeting cash flow analysis. The consensus is that interest charges should not be dealt with explicitly in capital budgeting—rather, the effects of debt financing are reflected in the cost of capital, which is used to discount the cash flows. If interest were subtracted and cash flows were then discounted, we would be double counting the cost of debt.

result of accepting the project. To determine if a specific cash flow is considered incremental, we need to find out whether it is affected by the purchase of the project. Cash flows that will change because the project is purchased are *incremental cash flows* that need to be included in the capital budgeting evaluation; cash flows that are not affected by the purchase of the project are not relevant to the capital budgeting decision. Unfortunately, identifying the relevant cash flows for a project is not always as simple as it seems. Some special problems in determining incremental cash flows are discussed next.

Sunk Costs   Sunk costs are not incremental costs, and they should not be included in the analysis. A **sunk cost** is an outlay that has already been committed or that has already occurred and hence is not affected by the accept/reject decision under consideration. To illustrate, in 1999 Unilate Textiles considered building a distribution center in New England in an effort to increase sales in that area of the country. To help with its evaluation, Unilate hired a consulting firm to perform a site analysis and provide a feasibility study for the project; the cost was $100,000, and this amount was expensed for tax purposes. This expenditure is *not* a relevant cost that should be included in the capital budgeting evaluation of the prospective distribution center because Unilate cannot recover this money, regardless of whether the new distribution center is built.

Opportunity Costs   The second potential problem relates to **opportunity costs,** which are defined as the cash flows that could be generated from assets the firm already owns provided they are not used for the project in question. To illustrate, Unilate already owns a piece of land that is suitable for a distribution center. When evaluating the prospective center in New England, should the cost of the land be disregarded because no additional cash outlay would be required? The answer is no, because there is an opportunity cost inherent in the use of the property. In this case, the land could be sold to yield $150,000 after taxes. Use of the site for the distribution center would require forgoing this inflow, so the $150,000 must be charged as an opportunity cost against the project. Note that the proper land cost in this example is the $150,000 market-determined value, irrespective of whether Unilate originally paid $50,000 or $500,000 for the property. (What Unilate paid would, of course, have an effect on taxes and hence on the after-tax opportunity cost.)

Externalities: Effects on Other Parts of the Firm   The third potential problem involves the effects of a project on other parts of the firm; economists call these effects **externalities.** For example, Unilate does have some existing customers in New England who would use the new distribution center because its location would be more convenient than the North Carolina distribution center they have been using. The sales, and hence profits, generated by these customers would not be new to Unilate; rather, they would represent a transfer from one distribution center to another. Thus, the net revenues produced by these customers should not be treated as incremental income in the capital budgeting decision. Although they often are difficult to quantify, externalities such as these should be considered.

Shipping and Installation Costs   When a firm acquires fixed assets, it often must incur substantial costs for shipping and installing the equipment. These charges are added to the invoice price of the equipment when the total cost of the project is being

SUNK COST
A cash outlay that already has been incurred and that cannot be recovered regardless of whether the project is accepted or rejected.

OPPORTUNITY COST
The return on the best alternative use of an asset; the highest return that will not be earned if funds are invested in a particular project.

EXTERNALITIES
The effect accepting a project will have on the cash flows in other parts (areas) of the firm.

determined. Also, for depreciation purposes, the *depreciable basis* of an asset, which is the total amount that can be depreciated, includes the purchase price and any additional expenditures required to make the asset operational, including shipping and installation. Therefore, the full cost of the equipment, including shipping and installation costs, is used as the depreciable basis when depreciation charges are calculated. So if Unilate Textiles bought a computer with an invoice price of $100,000 and paid another $10,000 for shipping and installation, then the full cost of the computer, and its depreciable basis, would be $110,000.

Keep in mind that *depreciation is a noncash expense, so there is not a cash outflow associated with the recognition of depreciation expense each year.* But because depreciation is an expense, *it affects the taxable income of a firm, thus the amount of taxes paid by the firm, which is a cash flow.*

Inflation   Inflation is a fact of life, and it should be recognized in capital budgeting decisions. If expected inflation is not built into the determination of expected cash flows, then the calculated net present value and internal rate of return will be incorrect—both will be artificially low. It is easy to avoid inflation bias—simply build inflationary expectations into the cash flows used in the capital budgeting analysis. Expected inflation should be reflected in the revenue and cost figures, thus the annual net cash flow forecasts. The required rate of return does not have to be adjusted by the firm for inflation expectations because investors include such expectations when establishing the rate at which they are willing to permit the firm to use their funds. Investors decide at what rates a firm can raise funds in the capital markets, and they include an adjustment for inflation when determining the rate that is appropriate.

Self-Test Questions

Briefly explain the difference between accounting income and net cash flow. Which should be used in capital budgeting? Why?

Explain what these terms mean, and assess their relevance in capital budgeting: incremental cash flow, sunk cost, opportunity cost, externalities, shipping plus installation costs, and depreciable basis.

Explain why incremental analysis is important in capital budgeting.

How should inflation expectations be included in analysis of capital projects?

Identifying Incremental Cash Flows

Generally, when we identify the incremental cash flows associated with a capital project, we separate them according to when they occur during the life of the project. In most cases, we can classify a project's incremental cash flows as (1) cash flows that occur *only at the start* of the project's life—time period 0, (2) cash flows that *continue throughout* the project's life—time periods 1 through n, and (3) cash flows that occur *only at the end*, or the termination, of the project—time period n. We discuss these three incremental cash flow classifications and identify some of the relevant cash flows next. But keep in mind, when identifying the incremental cash flows for capital budgeting, the primary question is which cash flows will be affected by purchasing the project—if a cash flow does not change, it is not relevant for the capital budgeting analysis.

Initial Investment Outlay

The **initial investment outlay** refers to the incremental cash flows that *occur only at the start of a project's life*, $\hat{CF}_0$. The initial investment includes such cash flows as the purchase price of the new project and shipping and installation costs. If the capital budgeting decision is a *replacement decision*, the initial investment must also take into account the cash flows associated with the disposal of the old, or replaced, asset, which include any cash received or paid to scrap the old asset and any tax effects associated with the disposal.

In many cases, the addition or replacement of a capital asset has an impact on the net working capital of the firm. For example, normally, additional inventories are required to support a new operation, and expanded sales also lead to additional accounts receivable. For example, if Unilate builds the new distribution center in New England, the inventories held at that location will be *in addition to* the inventories currently held at its other distribution centers. If it is estimated the New England distribution center will require $5 million of inventory to operate normally, then Unilate must purchase an additional $5 million of inventory if the distribution center is built. This cash flow is considered part of the initial investment because the $5 million inventory increase will occur only when, and because, the distribution center opens. This inventory increase and any increase in accounts receivable resulting from the *additional* sales expected to be generated by the New England distribution must be financed. But, as we shall see later in the book, Unilate can expect its accounts payable and accruals to increase spontaneously as a result of the expanded operations, and this will reduce the net cash needed to finance inventories and receivables. The difference between the required increase in current assets and the spontaneous increase in current liabilities is the *change in net working capital*. If this change is positive, as it generally is for expansion projects like the new distribution center being considered by Unilate, then additional financing, over and above the cost of the fixed assets, is needed to fund the increase in current assets.

We should note that there are instances in which the change in net working capital associated with a capital project actually results in a decrease in the firm's current funding requirements, which frees up cash flows for investment. Usually this occurs if the project being considered is much more efficient than the existing asset(s). In any event, *the change in net working capital that results from the acceptance of a project is an incremental cash flow that must be considered in the capital budgeting analysis*. And because the changes in net working capital requirements occur at the start of the project's life, this cash flow impact is an incremental cash flow that is included as a part of the initial investment outlay.

Incremental Operating Cash Flows

Most capital projects also affect the day-to-day cash flows generated by the firm. For example, Unilate has discovered that it can reduce its total operating costs by $10 million by purchasing a new weaving machine to replace a machine it has been using for ten years. The cost reduction would result because the technological advancements of the new machine would allow Unilate to use less electricity and fewer raw materials (wool, cotton, and so on) in its manufacturing process. These cost savings, as well as any changes in depreciation expense, will affect the taxes paid by Unilate each year the new machine is in service. Thus, Unilate's normal *operating cash flows* will change if the project is accepted. We define **incremental operating cash flows** as the changes in day-to-day cash flows that result from the purchase of a capital project. The impact of incremental operating cash flows continues until the firm disposes of the asset.

In most cases, the *incremental operating cash flows* for each year can be computed directly by using the following equation:

9–1

$$\text{Incremental operating cash flow}_t = \Delta\text{Cash revenues}_t - \Delta\text{Cash expenses}_t - \Delta\text{Taxes}_t$$

$$= \Delta\text{NI}_t + \Delta\text{Depr}_t$$

$$= \Delta\text{EBT}_t \times (1 - T) + \Delta\text{Depr}_t$$

$$= (\Delta\text{S}_t - \Delta\text{OC}_t - \Delta\text{Depr}_t) \times (1 - T) + \Delta\text{Depr}_t$$

$$= (\Delta\text{S}_t - \Delta\text{OC}_t) \times (1 - T) + T(\Delta\text{Depr}_t)$$

The symbols in Equation 9–1 are defined as follows:

Δ = The Greek symbol delta, which represents the change in something.

$\Delta\text{NI}_t = \text{NI}_{t,accept} - \text{NI}_{t,reject}$ = The change in net income in period t that results from accepting the capital project; the subscript *accept* is used to indicate the firm's operations that would exist if the project is accepted, and the subscript *reject* indicates the level of operations that would exist if the project was rejected (the existing situation *without* the project).

$\Delta\text{Depr}_t = \text{Depr}_{t,accept} - \text{Depr}_{t,reject}$ = The change in depreciation expense in period t that results from accepting the project.

$\Delta\text{EBT}_t = \text{EBT}_{t,accept} - \text{EBT}_{t,reject}$ = The change in earnings before taxes in period t that results from accepting the project.

$\Delta\text{S}_t = \text{S}_{t,accept} - \text{S}_{t,reject}$ = The change in sales revenues in period t that results from accepting the project.

$\Delta\text{OC}_t = \text{OC}_{t,accept} - \text{OC}_{t,reject}$ = The change in operating costs, excluding depreciation, in period t that results from accepting the project.

T = Marginal tax rate.

TERMINAL CASH FLOW
The *net* cash flow that occurs at the end of the life of a project, including the cash flows associated with (1) the final disposal of the project and (2) returning the firm's operations to where they were before the project was accepted.

We have emphasized that depreciation is a *noncash* expense. So why is the change in depreciation expense included in the computation of incremental operating cash flow shown in Equation 9–1? The change in depreciation expense needs to be computed because, when depreciation changes, taxable income changes and so does the amount of income taxes paid; and the amount of taxes paid is a cash flow.

Terminal Cash Flow

The **terminal cash flow** occurs at the end of the life of the project, and it is associated with the final disposal of the project and returning the firm's operations to where they were before the project was accepted. Consequently, the terminal cash flow includes the salvage value, which could be either positive (selling the asset) or negative (paying for removal), and the tax impact of the disposition of the project. In addition, we generally assume the firm returns to the operating level that existed prior to the acceptance of the project; thus, any working capital accounts changes that occurred at the beginning of the project's life will be reversed at the end of its life. For example, as an expansion project's life approaches termination, inventories will be sold off and not replaced, and receivables will also be converted to cash. As these changes occur, the firm will receive an end-of-project cash flow equal to the net working capital requirement that occurred when the project was begun. Unilate expects the life of the New England distribution center to be ten years, so the inventories at that location will be reduced to zero in the tenth year. Because inventories will not have to be replenished during the last sales period, cash flows in Year 10 will increase by $5 million.

Self-Test Questions

Identify the three classifications for the incremental cash flows associated with a project, and give examples of the cash flows that would be in each category.

Why are the changes in net working capital recognized as incremental cash flows both at the beginning and the end of a project's life?

Capital Budgeting Project Evaluation

Up to this point, we have discussed several important aspects of cash flow analysis. Now we illustrate cash flow estimation for expansion projects and for replacement projects.

Expansion Projects

EXPANSION PROJECT
A project that is intended to increase sales.

Remember from Chapter 8 that an **expansion project** is one that calls for the firm to invest in new assets to *increase* sales. We illustrate an expansion project analysis with a project that is being considered by Household Energy Products (HEP), a Dallas-based technology company. HEP's research and development department has created a computerized home appliance control device that will increase a home's energy efficiency by simultaneously controlling all household appliances, large and small, the air-conditioning/heating system, the water heater, the security system, and the filtration and heating systems for pools and spas. At this point, HEP wants to decide whether it should proceed with full-scale production of the appliance control device.

HEP's marketing department plans to target sales of the appliance computer toward the owners of larger homes; the computer is cost-effective only in homes with 4,000 or more square feet of living space. The marketing vice president believes that annual sales would be 15,000 units if the units are priced at $2,000 each, so annual sales are estimated at $30 million. The engineering department has determined the firm would need no additional manufacturing or storage space; it would just need the equipment to manufacture the devices. The necessary equipment would be purchased and installed late in 2000, and it would cost $9.5 million, not including the $500,000 that would have to be paid for shipping and installation. The equipment would fall into the Modified Accelerated Cost Recovery System (MACRS) five-year class for the purposes of depreciation (see Appendix 9A for depreciation rates and an explanation of MACRS).

The project would require an initial increase in net working capital equal to $4 million, primarily because the raw materials required to produce the devices will significantly increase the amount of inventory HEP currently holds. The investment necessary to increase net working capital will be made on December 31, 2000, when the decision to manufacture the appliance control occurs. The project's estimated economic life is four years. At the end of that time, the equipment would have a market value of $2 million and a book value of $1.7 million. The production department has estimated that variable manufacturing costs would total 60 percent of sales and fixed overhead costs, excluding depreciation, would be $5 million a year. Depreciation expenses would vary from year to year in accordance with the MACRS rates. HEP's marginal tax rate is 40 percent; its cost of funds, or required rate of return, is 15 percent; and, for capital budgeting purposes, the company's policy is to assume that operating cash flows occur at the end of each year. Because manufacture of the new product would begin on January 1, 2001, the first *operating cash flows* would occur on December 31, 2001.

Analysis of the Cash Flows   The first step in the analysis is to summarize the initial investment outlays required for the project; this is done in the 2000 column of Table 9–2. For HEP's appliance control device project, the cash outlays consist of the purchase price of the needed equipment, the cost of shipping and installation, and the required investment in net working capital (NWC). Notice that these cash flows do not carry over in the years 2001 through 2004—they occur only at the start of the project. Thus, the *initial investment outlay* is $14 million.

Having estimated the investment requirements, we must now estimate the cash flows that will occur once production begins; these are set forth in the 2001 through 2004 columns of Table 9–2. The operating cash flow estimates are based on information provided by HEP's various departments. The depreciation amounts were obtained by multiplying the depreciable basis by the MACRS recovery allowance rates as set forth in the footnote to Table 9–2. As you can see, from the values given in footnote a in the table, the incremental operating cash flow differs each year only because the depreciation expense, and thus the impact depreciation has on taxes, differs each year.

The final cash flow component we need to compute is the terminal cash flow. For this computation, remember that the $4 million investment in net working capital will be recovered in 2004. Also, we need an estimate of the net cash flows from the disposal of the equipment in 2004. Table 9–3 shows the calculation of the net salvage value for the equipment. It is expected that the equipment will be sold for more than its book value, which means the company will have to pay taxes on the capital gain because, in essence, the equipment was depreciated too quickly, allowing HEP to reduce its tax liability by too much in the years 2001–2004. The book value is calculated as the depreciable basis (purchase price plus shipping and installation) minus the accumulated depreciation. The net cash flow from salvage is merely the sum of the salvage value and the tax impact resulting from the sale of the equipment, $1.88 million in this case. Thus, the *terminal cash flow* totals $5.88 million.

Notice that the total net cash flow for the year 2004 is the sum of the incremental cash flow for the year and the terminal cash flow. In the final year of a project's economic life, the firm incurs two types of cash flows—the incremental operating cash flow attributed to the project's normal operation and the terminal cash flow associated with the disposal of the project. For the appliance control device project HEP is considering, the incremental operating cash flow in 2004 is $4.68 million and the terminal cash flow is $5.88 million, so the total expected net cash flow in 2004 is $10.56 million.

TABLE 9–2	HEP Expansion Project Net Cash Flows, 2000–2004 (thousands of dollars)				
	2000	**2001**	**2002**	**2003**	**2004**
I. Initial Investment Outlay					
Cost of new asset	$(9,500)				
Shipping and installation	(500)				
Increase in net working capital	(4,000)				
Initial investment	$(14,000)				
II. Incremental Operating Cash Flow[a]					
Sales revenue		$ 30,000	$ 30,000	$ 30,000	$ 30,000
Variable costs (60% of sales)		(18,000)	(18,000)	(18,000)	(18,000)
Fixed costs		(5,000)	(5,000)	(5,000)	(5,000)
Depreciation on new equipment[b]		(2,000)	(3,200)	(1,900)	(1,200)
Earnings before taxes (EBT)		$ 5,000	$ 3,800	$ 5,100	$ 5,800
Taxes (40%)		(2,000)	(1,520)	(2,040)	(2,320)
Net income		$ 3,000	$ 2,280	$ 3,060	$ 3,480
Add back depreciation		2,000	3,200	1,900	1,200
Incremental operating cash flows		$ 5,000	$ 5,480	$ 4,960	$ 4,680
III. Terminal Cash Flow					
Return of net working capital					4,000
Net salvage value (see Table 9–3)					1,880
Terminal cash flow					$ 5,880
IV. Annual Net Cash Flow					
Total net cash flow each year	$(14,000)	$ 5,000	$ 5,480	$ 4,960	$ 10,560
Net present value (15%)	**$ 3,790**				

[a]Using Equation 9–1, the incremental operating cash flows can be computed as follows:

YEAR	INCREMENTAL OPERATING CASH FLOW COMPUTATION
2001	$5,000 = ($30,000 − $18,000 − $5,000) (1 − 0.40) + $2,000 (0.40)
2002	5,480 = (30,000 − 18,000 − 5,000) (1 − 0.40) + 3,200 (0.40)
2003	4,960 = (30,000 − 18,000 − 5,000) (1 − 0.40) + 1,900 (0.40)
2004	4,680 = (30,000 − 18,000 − 5,000) (1 − 0.40) + 1,200 (0.40)

[b]Depreciation for the new equipment was calculated using MACRS (see Appendix 9A):

YEAR	2001	2002	2003	2004
Percent depreciated	20%	32%	19%	12%

These percentages were multiplied by the depreciable basis of $10,000 to get the depreciation expense each year.

Making the Decision   A summary of the data and the computation of the project's NPV are provided with the cash flow time line that follows. The amounts are in thousands of dollars, just like in Table 9–2.

TABLE 9–3	HEP Expansion Project Net Salvage Value, 2004 (thousands of dollars)

I. Book Value of HEP's Project in 2004

Cost of new asset in 2000	$ 9,500
Shipping and installation	500
Depreciable basis of asset	$ 10,000
Depreciation from 2001–2004	
$= (0.20 + 0.32 + 0.19 + 0.12) \times \$10,000$	(8,300)
Book value in 2004	$ 1,700

II. Tax Impact of the Sale of HEP's Project in 2004

Selling price of asset in	$ 2,000
Book value of asset in	(1,700)
Gain (loss) on sale of asset	$ 300
Taxes (40%)	$ 120

III. Net Salvage Value, $\hat{CF}$, in 2004

Cash flow from sale of project	$ 2,000
Tax impact of sale	(120)
Net salvage value cash flow	$ 1,880

CASH FLOW TIME LINE FOR HEP'S APPLIANCE CONTROL DEVICE PROJECT (DOLLARS ARE IN THOUSANDS)

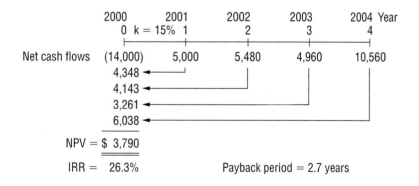

The project appears to be acceptable using the NPV and internal rate of return (IRR) methods, and it also would be acceptable if HEP required a maximum payback period of three years. Note, however, that the analysis thus far has been based on the assumption that the project has the same degree of risk as the company's average project. If the project was judged to be riskier than an average project, it would be necessary to increase the required rate of return used to compute the NPV. Later in this chapter, we will extend the evaluation of this project to include a risk analysis.

Replacement Analysis

All companies make replacement decisions. The analysis relating to replacements is the same as for expansion projects—identify the relevant cash flows, and then find the net present value of the project. But, to some extent, identifying the *incremental* cash flows associated with a replacement project is more complicated than for an expansion project because the cash flows both from the new asset *and* from the old asset must be considered. **Replacement analysis** is illustrated with another HEP example.

REPLACEMENT ANALYSIS
An analysis involving the decision of whether to replace an existing asset that is still productive with a new asset.

HEP has a lathe for trimming molded plastics that was purchased ten years ago at a cost of $7,500. The machine had an expected life of 15 years at the time it was purchased, and management originally estimated, and still believes, that the salvage value will be zero at the end of the 15-year life. The machine has been depreciated on a straight line basis; therefore, its annual depreciation charge is $500, and its present book value is $2,500 = $7,500 − 10($500).

HEP is considering the purchase of a new special-purpose machine to replace the lathe. The new machine, which can be purchased for $12,000 (including freight and installation), will reduce labor and raw materials usage sufficiently to cut annual operating costs from $7,500 to $4,000. This reduction in costs will cause before-tax profits to rise by $7,500 − $4,000 = $3,500 per year.

It is estimated that the new machine will have a useful life of five years, after which it can be sold for $2,000. The old machine's actual current market value is $1,000, which is below its $2,500 book value. If the new machine is acquired, the old lathe will be sold to another company rather than exchanged for the new machine. Net working capital requirements will increase by $1,000 if the lathe is replaced by the new machine; this increase will occur at the time of replacement. By an IRS ruling, the new machine falls into the three-year MACRS class, and because the risk associated with the new machine is considered average for HEP, the project's required rate of return is 15 percent. Should the replacement be made?

Table 9–4 shows the worksheet format HEP uses to analyze replacement projects. Determining the relevant cash flows for a *replacement decision* is more involved than for an expansion decision because we need to consider the fact that the cash flows associated with the replaced asset will not continue after the new asset is purchased—*the cash flows associated with the new asset will take the place of the cash flows associated with the old asset.* So because we want to evaluate how the acceptance of a capital budgeting project *changes* cash flows, we must compute the increase or decrease in cash flows that results from the replacement of the old asset with the new asset. Let's examine the cash flows computed in Table 9–4.

Analysis of Cash Flows   First, the initial investment outlay of $11,400 includes the cash flows associated with the cost of the new asset and the change in net working capital, which also is included in the initial investment computation for the expansion decision shown in Table 9–2. But when a replacement asset is purchased, the asset being replaced must be removed from operations. If the asset can be sold to another firm or to a scrap dealer, its disposal will generate a positive cash flow; but if the firm must pay to have the old asset removed, the cash flow will be negative. And if the firm disposes of the old asset at a value different from its book value (its purchase price less accumulated depreciation), there will be a tax effect. In our example, the old asset has a book value equal to $2,500, but it can be sold for only $1,000. So HEP will incur a capital loss equal to −$1,500 = $1,000 − $2,500 if it replaces the lathe with the new machine.

This loss will result in a tax savings equal to Capital Loss $\times$ T = $1,500 $\times$ 0.4 = $600 to account for the fact that HEP did not adequately depreciate the old asset to reflect its market value. Consequently, the disposal of the old asset will generate a positive cash flow equal to $1,600—the $1,000 selling price plus the $600 tax savings, which effectively reduces the amount of cash required to purchase the new machine and thus the initial investment outlay. Any cash flows associated with disposing of the old asset must be included in the computation of the initial investment because they affect the net amount of cash required to purchase the asset.[3]

Next, we need to compute the incremental operating cash flow each year. Section II of Table 9–4 shows these computations. The procedure is the same as before—determine how operating cash flows will change if the new machine is purchased to replace the lathe. Remember, the lathe is expected to decrease operating costs from $7,500 to $4,000, and thus increase operating profits by $3,500—less cash will have to be spent to operate the new machine. Had the replacement resulted in an increase in sales in addition to the reduction in costs (that is, if the new machine had been both larger and more efficient), then this amount would also be reported. Also, note that the $3,500 cost savings is constant over the years 2001–2005; had the annual savings been expected to change over time, this fact would have to be built into the analysis.

The change in depreciation expense must be computed to determine the impact such a change will have on the taxes paid by the firm. If the new machine is purchased, the $500 depreciation expense of the lathe (old asset) no longer will be relevant for tax purposes; instead, the depreciation expense for the new machine will be used. For example, in 2001, the depreciation expense for the new machine will be $3,960 because, according to the three-year MACRS classification, 33 percent of the cost of the new asset can be depreciated in the year it is purchased. Because HEP will dispose of the lathe if it buys the new machine, in 2001 it will replace the $500 depreciation expense associated with the lathe with the $3,960 depreciation expense associated with the new machine, and the depreciation expense will increase by $3,460 = $3,960 − $500. The computations for the remaining years are the same. Note that in 2005 the change in depreciation is negative. This results because the new machine will be fully depreciated at the end of 2004, so there is nothing left to write off in 2005; thus, if the lathe is replaced, its depreciation of $500 will be replaced by the new machine's depreciation of $0 in 2005, which is a change of −$500.

The terminal cash flow includes $1,000 for the return of net working capital, because a "normal" net working capital level will be restored at the end of the new machine's life—any additional accounts receivable created by the purchase of the new machine will be collected and any additional inventories required by the new machine will be drawn down and not replaced. The net salvage value of the new machine is $1,200—it is expected that the new machine can be sold in 2005 for $2,000, but $800 in taxes will have to be paid on the sale because the new machine will be fully

---

[3]If you think about it, the computation of the initial investment outlay for replacement decisions is similar to determining the amount you would need to purchase a new automobile to replace your old one—if the purchase price of the new car is $20,000 and the dealer is willing to give you $5,000 for your car as a trade-in, then the amount you need is only $15,000; but, if you need to pay someone to take your old car out of the garage because that is where you are going to keep the new car at night, then the total amount you need to purchase the new car actually is greater than $20,000.

TABLE 9–4 HEP Replacement Project Net Cash Flows, 2000–2005

	2000	2001	2002	2003	2004	2005
I. Initial Investment Outlay						
Cost of new asset	$(12,000)					
Change in net working capital	(1,000)					
Net cash flow from sale of old asset[a]	1,600					
Initial investment	$(11,400)					
II. Incremental Operating Cash Flows						
Δ Operating costs		$ 3,500	$ 3,500	$ 3,500	$ 3,500	$ 3,500
Δ Depreciation[b]		(3,460)	(4,900)	(1,300)	(340)	500
Δ Earnings before taxes (EBT)		40	(1,400)	2,200	3,160	4,000
Δ Taxes (40%)		(16)	560	(880)	(1,264)	(1,600)
Δ Net income		24	(840)	1,320	1,896	2,400
Add back Δ depreciation		3,460	4,900	1,300	340	(500)
Incremental operating cash flows		$ 3,484	$ 4,060	$ 2,620	$ 2,236	$ 1,900
III. Terminal Cash Flow						
Return of net working capital						$ 1,000
Net salvage value of new asset[c]						1,200
Terminal cash flow						$ 2,200
IV. Annual Net Cash Flows						
Total net cash flow each year	$(11,400)	$ 3,484	$ 4,060	$ 2,620	$ 2,236	$ 4,100
Net present value (15%)	$(261)					

continues

[a]The net present cash flow from the sale of the old (replaced) asset is computed as follows:

Selling price (market value)	$ 1,000
Subtract book value	(2,500)
Gain (loss) on sale of asset	(1,500)
Tax impact of sale of asset	600

Net cash flow from the sale of asset = $1,000 + $600 = $1,600

[b]The change in depreciation expense is computed by comparing the depreciation of the new asset with the depreciation that would have existed if the old asset was *not* replaced. The old asset has been depreciated on a straight-line basis, with 5 years of $500 depreciation remaining. The new asset will be depreciated using the rates for the 3-year MACRS class (see Appendix 9B). So the change in annual depreciation would be as follows:

YEAR	NEW ASSET DEPRECIATION	OLD ASSET DEPRECIATION		CHANGE IN DEPRECIATION
2001	$12,000 × 0.33 = $3,960	$500	=	$3,460
2002	12,000 × 0.45 = 5,400	500	=	4,900
2003	12,000 × 0.15 = 1,800	500	=	1,300
2004	12,000 × 0.07 = 840	500	=	340
2005	0	500	=	(500)
Accumulated depreciation	= $12,000			

[c]The book value of the new asset in 2005 will be zero because the entire $12,000 has been written off. So the net salvage value of the new asset in 2005 is computed as follows:

Selling price (market value)	$2,000
Subtract book value	(0)
Gain (loss) on sale of asset	2,000
Tax impact on sale of asset	(800)

Net salvage value of the new asset = $2,000 − $800 = $1,200

depreciated by the time of the sale.[4] Thus, the terminal cash flow is $2,200 = $1,000 + $1,200.

Making the Decision   A summary of the data and the computation of the project's NPV are provided with the following cash flow time line:

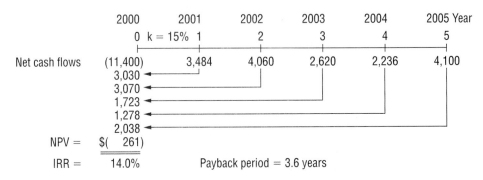

CASH FLOW TIME LINE FOR HEP'S REPLACEMENT PROJECT: (DOLLARS ARE IN THOUSANDS)

	2000	2001	2002	2003	2004	2005 Year
	0 k = 15% 1		2	3	4	5
Net cash flows	(11,400)	3,484	4,060	2,620	2,236	4,100
	3,030					
	3,070					
	1,723					
	1,278					
	2,038					
NPV =	$(261)					
IRR =	14.0%		Payback period = 3.6 years			

According to the NPV and IRR methods, HEP should not replace the lathe with the new machine.

Before we leave our discussion of replacement decisions, we should note that a replacement decision involves comparing two mutually exclusive projects: retaining the old asset versus buying a new one. To simplify matters, in our replacement example we assumed that the new machine had a life equal to the remaining life of the old machine. If, however, we were choosing between two mutually exclusive alternatives with significantly different lives, an adjustment would be necessary to make the results of the capital budgeting analysis for the two projects comparable. To attain comparability, we can either (1) use a common life for the evaluation of the two projects or (2) compute the annual annuity that could be produced from the dollar amount of the NPV of each project. Both of these procedures are described in Appendix 9B. We mention the unequal life problem here to make you aware that the evaluation of mutually exclusive projects with significantly different lives requires a slightly different analysis to ensure a correct decision is made.

Self-Test Question

Explain and differentiate between the capital budgeting analyses required for expansion projects and for replacement projects.

---

[4]In this analysis, the salvage value of the old machine is zero. However, if the old machine was expected to have a positive salvage value at the end of five years, replacing the old machine now would eliminate this cash flow. Thus, the after-tax salvage value of the old machine would represent an opportunity cost to the firm, and it would be included as a Year 5 cash outflow in the terminal cash flow section of the worksheet.

Incorporating Risk in Capital Budgeting Analysis

STAND-ALONE RISK
The risk an asset would have if it were a firm's only asset; it is measured by the variability of the asset's expected returns.

CORPORATE (WITHIN-FIRM) RISK
Risk that does not take into consideration the effects of stockholders' diversification; it is measured by a project's effect on the firm's earnings variability.

BETA (MARKET) RISK
That part of a project's risk that cannot be eliminated by diversification; it is measured by the project's beta coefficient.

To this point, we have assumed the projects being evaluated have the same risk as the projects that the firm currently possesses. However, there are three separate and distinct types of project risk that need to be examined to determine if the required rate of return used to evaluate a project should be different than the *average* required rate of the firm. The three risks are (1) the project's own **stand-alone risk,** or the risk it exhibits when evaluated alone rather than as part of a combination, or portfolio, of assets—the effect of the project on the other assets of the firm is disregarded; (2) **corporate,** or **within-firm, risk,** which is the effect a project has on the total, or overall, riskiness of the company, without considering which risk component, systematic or unsystematic, is affected—the effect the project has on the stockholders' own personal diversification is disregarded; and (3) **beta,** or **market, risk,** which is project risk assessed from the standpoint of a stockholder who holds a well-diversified portfolio. As we shall see, a particular project might have high stand-alone risk, yet taking it on might not have much effect on either the firm's risk or that of its owners because of portfolio, or diversification, effects.

Although more difficult, evaluating the risk associated with a capital budgeting project is similar to evaluating the risk of a financial asset such as a stock. Therefore, much of our discussion in this section relies on the concepts introduced in Chapter 5.

As we shall see shortly, a project's stand-alone risk is measured by the variability of the project's expected returns; its corporate risk is measured by the project's impact on the firm's earnings variability; and its beta risk is measured by the project's effect on the firm's beta coefficient. Taking on a project with a high degree of either stand-alone risk or corporate risk will not necessarily affect the firm's beta to any great extent. However, if the project has highly uncertain returns, and if those returns are highly correlated with returns on the firm's other assets and also with most other assets in the economy, the project will exhibit a high degree of all three types of risk. For example, suppose General Motors decides to undertake a major expansion to build solar-powered autos. GM is not sure how its technology will work on a mass production basis, so there are great risks in the venture—its stand-alone risk is high. Management also estimates that the project will have a higher probability of success if the economy is strong, because people will have more money to spend on the new autos. This means that the project will tend to do well if GM's other divisions also do well and to do badly if other divisions do badly. This being the case, the project will also have high corporate risk. Finally, because GM's profits are highly correlated with those of most other firms, the project's beta coefficient will also be high. Thus, this project will be risky under all three definitions of risk.

Self-Test Questions

What are the three types of project risk?

How is a project's stand-alone risk measured?

How is corporate risk measured?

How is beta risk measured?

Stand-Alone Risk

What about a project's stand-alone risk—is it of any importance to anyone? In theory, stand-alone risk should be of little or no concern, because we know diversification can eliminate some of this type of risk. However, it is of great importance for the following reasons:

1. It is easier to estimate a project's stand-alone risk than its corporate risk, and it is far easier to measure stand-alone risk than beta risk.
2. In the vast majority of cases, all three types of risk are highly correlated—if the general economy does well, so will the firm, and if the firm does well, so will most of its projects. Thus, stand-alone risk generally is a good proxy for hard-to-measure corporate and beta risk.
3. Because of Points 1 and 2, if management wants a reasonably accurate assessment of a project's riskiness, it should spend considerable effort on determining the riskiness of the project's own cash flows—that is, its stand-alone risk.

The starting point for analyzing a project's stand-alone risk involves determining the uncertainty inherent in the project's cash flows. This analysis can be handled in a number of ways, ranging from informal judgments to complex economic and statistical analyses involving large-scale computer models. To illustrate what is involved, we shall refer to Household Energy Products' appliance control computer project that we discussed earlier. Many of the individual cash flows that were shown in Table 9–2 are subject to uncertainty. For example, sales for each year were projected at 15,000 units to be sold at a net price of $2,000 per unit, or $30 million in total. Actual unit sales almost certainly would be somewhat higher or lower than 15,000, however, and also the sales price might turn out to be different from the projected $2,000 per unit. In effect, the sales quantity and the sales price estimates are expected values taken from probability distributions, as are many of the other values that were shown in Table 9–2. The distributions could be relatively "tight," reflecting small standard deviations and low risk, or they could be "flat," denoting a great deal of uncertainty about the final value of the variable in question and hence a high degree of stand-alone risk.

The nature of the individual cash flow distributions, and their correlations with one another, determine the nature of the NPV distribution and, thus, the project's stand-alone risk. We next discuss three techniques for assessing a project's stand-alone risk: (1) sensitivity analysis, (2) scenario analysis, and (3) Monte Carlo simulation.

Sensitivity Analysis

The cash flows used to determine the acceptability of a project result from forecasts of uncertain events, such as economic conditions in the future and expected demand for a product. Intuitively, then, we know the cash flow amounts used to determine the net present value of a project might be significantly different from what actually happens in the future; but those numbers represent our best, and most confident, prediction concerning the expected cash flows associated with a project. We also know that if a key input variable, such as units sold, changes, the project's NPV also will change. **Sensitivity analysis** is a technique that shows exactly how much the NPV will change in response to a given change in an input variable, other things held constant.

In a sensitivity analysis, we begin with the base case situation that was developed using the expected values for each input; next each variable is changed by specific per-

SENSITIVITY ANALYSIS
A risk analysis technique in which key variables are changed and the resulting changes in the NPV and the IRR are observed.

FIGURE 9–1	Sensitivity Analysis (thousands of dollars)

A. Unit Sales

B. Variable Cost per Unit

C. Required Rate of Return

Deviation from Base Level (%)	Net Present Value		
	Units Sold	**Variable Cost/Unit**	**Required Rate of Return**
−10	$1,735	$6,874	$4,415
0 (base case)	3,790	3,790	3,790
+10	5,846	707	3,199

centage points above and below the expected value, holding other things constant; then a new NPV is calculated for each of these values; and, finally, the set of NPVs is plotted against the variable that was changed. Figure 9–1 shows the computer project's sensitivity graphs for three of the key input variables. The table below the graphs gives the NPVs that were used to construct the graphs. The slopes of the lines in the graphs show how sensitive NPV is to changes in each of the inputs: *the steeper the slope, the more sensitive the NPV is to a change in the variable.* In the figure we see that the project's NPV is very sensitive to changes in variable costs, less sensitive to changes in unit sales, and not very sensitive at all to changes in the required rate of return. So when estimating these variables' values, HEP should take extra care to ensure the accuracy of the forecast for variable costs per unit.

If we were comparing two projects, the one with the steeper sensitivity lines would be regarded as riskier because for that project a relatively small error in estimating a variable such as unit sales would produce a large error in the project's expected NPV. Thus, sensitivity analysis can provide useful insights into the riskiness of a project.

Before we move on, two additional points about sensitivity analysis warrant attention. First, spreadsheet computer models, such as *Excel*™ or *Lotus 1-2-3*™, are ideally suited for performing sensitivity analysis. We used a spreadsheet model to conduct the analyses represented in Figure 9–1; it generated the NPVs and then drew the graphs. Second, we could have plotted all the sensitivity lines on one graph; this would have facilitated direct comparisons of the sensitivities among different input variables.

Scenario Analysis

Although sensitivity analysis probably is the most widely used risk analysis technique, it does have limitations. Consider, for example, a proposed coal mine project whose NPV is highly sensitive to changes in output, in variable costs, and in sales price. However, if a utility company has contracted to buy a fixed amount of coal at an inflation-adjusted price per ton, the mining venture might be quite safe in spite of its steep sensitivity lines. *In general, a project's stand-alone risk depends on both (1) the sensitivity of its NPV to changes in key variables and (2) the range of likely values of these variables as reflected in their probability distributions.* Because sensitivity analysis considers only the first factor, it is incomplete.

Scenario analysis is a risk analysis technique that considers both the sensitivity of NPV to changes in key variables and the likely range of variable values. In a scenario analysis, the financial analyst asks operating managers to pick a "bad" set of circumstances (low unit sales, low sales price, high variable cost per unit, high construction cost, and so on) and a "good" set. The NPVs under the bad and good conditions are then calculated and compared to the expected, or base case, NPV.

As an example, let us return to the appliance control computer project. Assume that HEP's managers are fairly confident of their estimates of all the project's cash flow variables except price and unit sales. Further, they regard a drop in sales below 10,000 units or a rise above 20,000 units as being extremely unlikely. Similarly, they expect the sales price as set in the marketplace to fall within the range of $1,500 to $2,500. Thus, 10,000 units at a price of $1,500 defines the lower bound, or the **worst-case scenario,** whereas 20,000 units at a price of $2,500 defines the upper bound, or the **best-case scenario.** Remember that the **base case** values are 15,000 units and a price of $2,000.

To carry out the scenario analysis, we use the worst-case variable values to obtain the worst-case NPV and the best-case variable values to obtain the best-case NPV.[5] We then use the result of the scenario analysis to determine the *expected* NPV, standard deviation of NPV, and the coefficient of variation. To complete these computations, we need an estimate of the probabilities of occurrence of the three scenarios, the Pr_i values. Suppose management estimates that there is a 20 percent probability of the worst case scenario occurring, a 60 percent probability of the base case, and a 20 percent probability of the best case. Of course, it is *very difficult* to estimate scenario probabilities accurately. The scenario probabilities and NPVs constitute a probability distribution of returns just like those we dealt with in Chapter 5, except that the returns are measured in dollars instead of in percentages, or rates of return.

We performed the scenario analysis using a spreadsheet model, and Table 9–5 summarizes the results of this analysis. We see that the base case (or most likely case) forecasts a positive NPV result; the worst case produces a negative NPV; and the best case results in a very large positive NPV. But the expected NPV for the project is $4.5 million and the project's coefficient of variation is 1.7. Now we can compare the project's coefficient of variation with the coefficient of variation of HEP's average project to get an idea of the relative riskiness of the appliance control computer project. HEP's

SCENARIO ANALYSIS
A risk analysis technique in which "bad" and "good" sets of financial circumstances are compared with a most likely, or base case, situation.

WORST-CASE SCENARIO
An analysis in which all of the input variables are set at their worst reasonably forecasted values.

BEST-CASE SCENARIO
An analysis in which all of the input variables are set at their best reasonably forecasted values.

BASE CASE
An analysis in which all of the input variables are set at their most likely values.

---

[5]We could have included worst- and best-case values for fixed and variable costs, income tax rates, salvage values, and so on. For illustrative purposes, we limited the changes to only two variables. Also, note that we are treating sales price and quantity as independent variables; that is, a low sales price could occur when unit sales were low, and a high sales price could be coupled with high unit sales, or vice versa. As we discuss in the next section, it is relatively easy to vary these assumptions if the facts of the situation suggest a different set of conditions.

TABLE 9–5		Scenario Analysis (dollars are in thousands, except sales price)			
Scenario	**Sales Volume (units)**	**Sales Price**	**NPV**	**Probability of Outcome (Pr_i)**	**NPV × Pr_i**
Best case	20,000	$2,500	$17,494	0.20	$3,499
Most likely case	15,000	2,000	3,790	0.60	2,274
Worst case	10,000	1,500	(6,487)	0.20	(1,297)
				1.00	Expected NPV = $4,475
					σ_{NPV} = $7,630
					CV_{NPV} = 1.7

$$\text{Expected NPV} = \sum_{i=1}^{n} Pr_i(\text{NPV}_i) = 0.20(\$17,494) + 0.60(\$3,790) + 0.20(-\$6,487) = \$4,475$$

$$\sigma_{\text{NPV}} = \sqrt{\sum_{i=1}^{n} Pr_i(\text{NPV}_i - \text{Expected NPV})^2}$$

$$= \sqrt{0.20(17,494 - \$4,475)^2 + 0.60(\$3,790 - \$4,475)^2 + 0.20(-\$6,487 - \$4,475)^2} = \$7,630$$

$$\text{CV}_{\text{NPV}} = \frac{\sigma_{\text{NPV}}}{\text{Expected NPV}} = \frac{\$7,630}{\$4,475} = 1.7$$

existing projects, on average, have a coefficient of variation of about 1.0, so, on the basis of this stand-alone risk measure, HEP's managers would conclude that the appliance computer project is riskier than the firm's "average" project.

Monte Carlo Simulation

Scenario analysis provides useful information about a project's stand-alone risk. However, it is limited in that it only considers a few discrete outcomes (NPVs) for the project, even though there really are many more possibilities. **Monte Carlo simulation,** so named because this type of analysis grew out of work on the mathematics of casino gambling, ties together sensitivities and input variable probability distributions.

Simulation is more complicated than scenario analysis because the probability distribution of each uncertain cash flow variable has to be specified. Once this has been done, a value from the probability distribution for each variable is randomly chosen to compute the project's cash flows, and then these values are used to determine the project's NPV. Simulation is usually completed using a computer because the process just described is repeated again and again, say, for 500 times, which results in 500 NPVs and a probability distribution for the project's NPV values. Thus, the output produced by simulation is a probability distribution that can be used to determine the most likely range of outcomes to be expected from a project. This provides the decision maker with a better idea of the various outcomes that are possible than is available from a point estimate of the NPV. In addition, simulation software packages can be used to estimate the probability of NPV > 0, of IRR > k, and so on. This additional information can be quite helpful in assessing the riskiness of a project.

Unfortunately, Monte Carlo simulation is not easy to apply because it is often difficult to specify the relationships, or correlations, among the uncertain cash flow

Greater Risk? Greater Return, Please.

Indications are that financial managers are quite concerned about risk when making capital budgeting decisions. A recent survey of financial managers by Glenn Petry and James Sprow* suggests that about 75 percent of companies use different required rates of return to account for risk differences when making capital budgeting decisions—only 25 percent use a single rate for all capital projects. Most of the financial managers indicated that they attempt to compute the cost of the funds used by their firms, and that rate is appropriate for determining the acceptability of projects with average risk only. For riskier projects, some of the companies adjust the expected cash flows, but most raise the rates of return required from such investments. In addition, some firms use a reduced minimum payback period to evaluate projects with above-average risk. While this approach is not common, it appears manufacturers and retailing firms are more likely to use an adjusted payback period to account for project risk than are financial service organizations, service companies, or utilities.

Other studies indicate similar results. For example, a couple of recent studies suggest that firms find risk to be an important consideration when making capital budgeting decisions; thus, the discount rate used to evaluate a project is based on the risk of the project.[†] Further, in another study, Erika Gilbert and Alan Reichert found that more than 40 percent of the firms surveyed consider the impact of a capital project on the other assets of the firm (i.e., they consider the impact on the firm's portfolio of assets).[♦]

It is interesting to note that firms generally do not attempt to use probability distributions to estimate cash flows for projects unless the outlay is extremely large. Perhaps the attitude is that it is not worth the effort to assign probabilities unless the project constitutes a major investment. When determining the terminal value of capital projects, most firms use either the expected market value or the book value of the asset at the anticipated liquidation date; in many cases, these values are expected to be the same.

In summary, it appears firms do make adjustments to the various techniques used for making capital budgeting decisions when the risks of the projects differ significantly from the average. And the most common approach for adjusting for project risk is to raise the discount rate (required rate of return) used to compute the project's net present value.

*Glenn H. Petry and James Sprow, "The Theory of Finance in the 1990s," *The Quarterly Review of Economics and Finance*, Winter 1993, 359–381.

[†]Patricia Chadwell-Hatfield, Bernard Goitein, Philip Horvath, and Allen Webster, "Financial Criteria, Capital Budgeting Techniques, and Risk Analysis of Manufacturing Firms," *Journal of Applied Business Research*, Winter 1996/1997, 95–104; and James M. Poterba and Lawrence H. Summers, "A CEO Survey of U.S. Companies' Time Horizons and Hurdle Rates," *Sloan Management Review*, Fall 1995, 43–45.

[♦]Erika Gilbert and Alan Reichert, "The Practice of Financial Management among Large United States Corporations," *Financial Practice and Education*, Spring/Summer 1995, 16–23.

variables. The problem is not insurmountable, but it is important not to underestimate the difficulty of obtaining valid estimates of probability distributions and correlations among variables. Such problems have been cited as reasons Monte Carlo simulation has not been widely used in industry.

Self-Test Questions

List three reasons why, in practice, a project's stand-alone risk is important.

Differentiate between sensitivity and scenario analyses. Why might scenario analysis be preferable to sensitivity analysis?

What is Monte Carlo simulation?

Identify some problems with (1) sensitivity analysis, (2) scenario analysis, and (3) Monte Carlo simulation.

Corporate (within-Firm) Risk

To measure corporate, or within-firm, risk, we need to determine how the capital budgeting project is related to the firm's existing assets. Remember from our discussion in Chapter 5 that two assets can be combined to reduce risk if their payoffs move in opposite directions—when the payoff from one asset falls, the payoff from the other asset rises. In reality, it is not easy to find assets with payoffs that move opposite each other. But, as we discovered in Chapter 5, as long as assets are *not* perfectly positively related (r = +1.0), some diversification, or risk reduction, can still be achieved. Many firms use this principle to reduce the risk associated with their operations—adding new projects that are not highly related to existing assets can help reduce corporate risk and reduce fluctuations associated with sales.

Corporate risk is important for three primary reasons:

1. Undiversified stockholders, including the owners of small businesses, are more concerned about corporate risk than about beta risk.
2. Empirical studies of the determinants of required rates of return (k) generally find that both beta and corporate risk affect stock prices. This suggests that investors, even those who are well diversified, consider factors other than beta risk when they establish required returns.
3. The firm's stability is important to its managers, workers, customers, suppliers, and creditors, as well as to the community in which it operates. Firms that are in serious danger of bankruptcy, or even of suffering low profits and reduced output, have difficulty attracting and retaining good managers and workers. Also, both suppliers and customers are reluctant to depend on weak firms, and such firms have difficulty borrowing money at reasonable interest rates. These factors tend to reduce risky firms' profitability and hence the prices of their stocks; thus they also make corporate risk significant.

Therefore, corporate risk is important even if a firm's stockholders are well diversified.

Self-Test Question

List three reasons why corporate risk is important.

Beta (Market) Risk

The types of risk analysis discussed thus far in the chapter provide insights into a project's risk and thus help managers make better accept/reject decisions. However, these risk measures do not take account of portfolio risk, and they do not specify whether a project should be accepted or rejected. In this section, we show how the capital asset pricing model (CAPM) can be used to help overcome those shortcomings. Of course, the CAPM has shortcomings of its own, but it nevertheless offers useful insights into risk analysis in capital budgeting.

Beta (or Market) Risk and Required Rate of Return for a Project

In Chapter 5 we developed the concept of beta, β, as a risk measure for individual stocks. From our discussion, we concluded systematic risk is the relevant risk of a stock because unsystematic, or firm-specific, risk can be reduced significantly or eliminated through diversification. This same concept can be applied to capital budgeting projects because the firm can be thought of as a composite of all the projects it has undertaken. Thus, the relevant risk of a project can be viewed as the impact it has on the firm's systematic risk. This line of reasoning leads to the conclusion that if the beta coefficient for a project, β_{proj}, can be determined, then the **project required rate of return, k_{proj},** can be found using the following form of the CAPM equation:

$$k_{proj} = k_{RF} + (k_M - k_{RF})\beta_{proj}$$

As an example, consider the case of Erie Steel Company, an integrated steel producer operating in the Great Lakes region. For simplicity, let's assume that Erie is all equity financed, so the *average* required rate of return it needs to earn on capital budgeting projects is based solely on the average return demanded by stockholders (i.e., there is no debt that might require a different return). Erie's existing beta = $\beta_{Existing}$ = 1.1; k_{RF} = 8%; and k_M = 12%. Thus, Erie's cost of equity is 12.4% = k_s = 8% + (12% − 8%)1.1, which suggests that investors should be willing to give Erie money to invest in *average risk* projects if the company expects to earn 12.4 percent or more on this money.[6] Here again, by average risk we mean projects having risk similar to the firm's existing assets.

Suppose, however, that taking on a particular project will cause a change in Erie's beta coefficient and hence change the company's required rate of return. For example, suppose Erie is considering the construction of a fleet of barges to haul iron ore, and barge operations have betas of 1.5 rather than 1.1. Because the firm itself might be regarded as a "portfolio of assets," just like the beta of any portfolio, Erie's beta is a weighted average of the betas of its individual assets. Thus, taking on the barge project will cause the overall corporate beta to rise to somewhere between the original beta of 1.1 and the barge project's beta of 1.5. The exact value of the new beta will depend on the relative size of the investment in barge operations versus Erie's other assets. If 80 percent of Erie's total funds end up in basic steel operations with a beta of 1.1 and 20 percent in the barge operations with a beta of 1.5, the new corporate beta will increase to 1.18 = 0.8(1.1) + 0.2(1.5). This increase in Erie's beta coefficient will cause its stock price to decline unless the increased beta is offset by a higher expected rate of return. Note that taking on the new project will cause the *overall* corporate required rate of return to rise from the original 12.4 percent to 12.7 percent because the new beta will be 1.18. This higher average rate can be earned only if the new project generates a return higher than the existing assets are providing. Because Erie's overall

PROJECT REQUIRED RATE OF RETURN, k_{proj}
The risk-adjusted required rate of return for an individual project.

---

[6]To simplify things somewhat, we assume at this point that the firm uses only equity capital. If debt is used, the cost of capital used must be a weighted average of the costs of debt and equity. This point is discussed at length in Chapter 10.

FIGURE 9–2	Using the Security Market Line Concept in Capital Budgeting

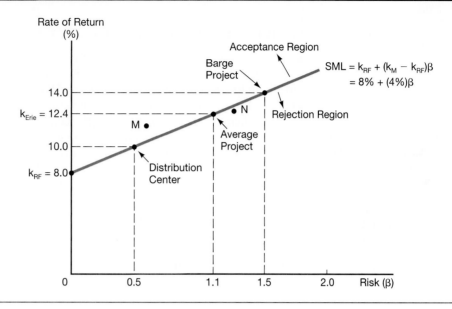

return is based on its portfolio of assets, the return required from the barge project must be sufficiently high so that, in combination with returns of the other assets, the average return is 12.7 percent; only 20 percent of the average return will be provided by the barge project. Thus, the barge project, with $\beta_{Barge} = 1.5$, should be evaluated at a 14 percent required rate of return because $k_{Barge} = 8\% + (4\%)1.5 = 14\%$. On the other hand, a low-risk project such as a new steel distribution center with a beta of only 0.5 would have a required rate of return of ten percent.

Figure 9–2 gives a graphic summary of these concepts as applied to Erie Steel. Note the following points:

1. The SML is a security market line like the one we developed in Chapter 5. It shows how investors are willing to make trade-offs between risk as measured by beta and expected returns. The higher the beta risk, the higher the rate of return needed to compensate investors for bearing this risk. The SML specifies the nature of this relationship.
2. Erie Steel initially had a beta of 1.1, so its required rate of return on average-risk investments was 12.4 percent.
3. High-risk investments such as the barge line require higher rates of return, whereas low-risk investments such as the distribution center require lower rates of return. If Erie concentrates its new investments in either high- or low-risk projects as opposed to average-risk ones, its corporate beta will either rise or fall from the current value of 1.1. Consequently, Erie's required rate of return on common stock would change from its current value of 12.4 percent.
4. If the expected rate of return on a given capital project lies *above* the SML, the expected rate of return on the project is more than enough to compensate for its risk, and the project should be accepted. Conversely, if the project's rate of

return lies *below* the SML, it should be rejected. Thus, Project M in Figure 9–2 is acceptable, whereas Project N should be rejected. N has a higher expected return than M, but the differential is not enough to offset its much higher risk.

Measuring Beta Risk for a Project

In Chapter 5, we discussed the estimation of betas for stocks, and we indicated that it is difficult to estimate *true* future betas. The estimation of project betas is even more difficult and more fraught with uncertainty. One way a firm can try to measure the beta risk of a project is to find *single-product* companies in the same line of business as the project being evaluated and then use the betas of those companies to determine the required rate of return for the project being evaluated. This technique is termed the **pure play method,** and the single-product companies that are used for comparisons are called *pure play firms.* For example, if Erie could find three existing single-product firms that operate barges, it could use the average of the betas of those firms as a proxy for the barge project's beta.

PURE PLAY METHOD
An approach used for estimating the beta of a project in which a firm identifies companies whose only business is the product in question, determines the beta for each firm, and then averages the betas to find an approximation of its own project's beta.

The pure play approach can only be used for major assets such as whole divisions, and even then it is frequently difficult to implement because it is often impossible to find pure play proxy firms. However, when IBM was considering going into personal computers, it was able to obtain data on Apple Computer and several other essentially pure play personal computer companies. This is often the case when a firm considers a major investment outside its primary field.

Self-Test Questions

What is meant by the term "average-risk project?" How could you find the required rate of return for a project with average risk, low risk, and high risk?

Complete the following sentence: An increase in a company's beta coefficient would cause its stock price to decline unless . . .

Explain why a firm should accept a given capital project if its expected rate of return lies above the SML. What if the expected rate of return lies on or below the SML?

What is the pure play method, and how is it used to estimate a project's beta?

Project Risk Conclusions

We have discussed the three types of risk normally considered in capital budgeting analysis—stand-alone risk, within-firm (or corporate) risk, and beta (or market) risk—and we have discussed ways of assessing each. However, two important questions remain: (1) Should a firm be concerned with stand-alone and corporate risk in its capital budgeting decisions, and (2) what do we do when the stand-alone or within-firm risk assessments and the beta risk assessment lead to different conclusions?

These questions do not have easy answers. From a theoretical standpoint, well-diversified investors should be concerned only with beta risk, managers should be concerned only with stock price maximization, and these two factors should lead to the conclusion that beta risk should be given virtually all the weight in capital budgeting decisions. However, if investors are not well diversified, if the CAPM does not operate exactly as theory says it should, or if measurement problems keep managers from having confidence in the CAPM approach in capital budgeting, it might be appropriate to give stand-alone and corporate risk more weight than financial theorists suggest. Note also that the CAPM ignores bankruptcy costs, even though such costs can be substantial, and that the probability of bankruptcy depends on a firm's corporate risk, not on its beta risk. Therefore, one can easily conclude that even well-diversified investors should want a firm's management to give at least some consideration to a project's corporate risk instead of concentrating entirely on beta risk.

Although it would be desirable to reconcile these problems and to measure project risk on some absolute scale, the best we can do in practice is to determine project risk in a somewhat nebulous, relative sense. For example, we can generally say with a fair degree of confidence that a particular project has more or less stand-alone risk than the firm's average project. Then, assuming that stand-alone and corporate risk are highly correlated (which is typical), the project's stand-alone risk will be a good measure of its corporate risk. Finally, assuming that beta risk and corporate risk are highly correlated (as is true for most companies), a project with more corporate risk than average will also have more beta risk, and vice versa for projects with low corporate risk.

Self-Test Questions

In theory, is it correct for a firm to be concerned with stand-alone and corporate risk in its capital budgeting decisions? Should the firm be concerned with these risks in practice?

If a project's stand-alone, corporate, and beta risk are highly correlated, would this make the task of measuring risk easier or harder? Explain.

How Project Risk Is Considered in Capital Budgeting Decisions

RISK-ADJUSTED DISCOUNT RATE
The discount rate (required rate of return) that applies to a particular risky stream of income; it is equal to the risk-free rate of interest plus a risk premium appropriate to the level of risk attached to a particular project's income stream.

Thus far, we have seen that purchasing a capital project can affect a firm's beta risk, its corporate risk, or both. We also have seen that it is extremely difficult to quantify either type of risk. In other words, although it might be possible to reach the general conclusion that one project is riskier than another, it is difficult to develop a really good *measure* of project risk. This lack of precision in measuring project risk makes it difficult to incorporate differential risk into capital budgeting decisions.

In reality, most firms incorporate project risk in capital budgeting decisions using the **risk-adjusted discount rate** approach. With this approach, the required rate of return, which is the rate at which the expected cash flows are discounted, is adjusted if the project's risk is substantially different from the average risk associated with the firm's existing assets. Therefore, average-risk projects would be discounted at the rate of return required of projects that are considered "average," or normal for the firm; above-average risk projects would be discounted at a higher-than-average rate; and below-average risk projects would be discounted at a rate below the firm's average rate of return. Unfortunately, because risk cannot be measured precisely, there is no accurate way of specifying exactly how much higher or lower these discount rates should be; given the present state of the art, *risk adjustments are necessarily judgmental and somewhat arbitrary.*

Although the process is not exact, many companies use a two-step procedure to develop risk-adjusted discount rates for use in capital budgeting. First, the overall required rate of return is established for the firm's existing assets. This process is

TABLE 9–6	Capital Budgeting Decisions Using Risk-Adjusted Discount Rates

PROJECT	PROJECT RISK	REQUIRED RETURN	ESTIMATED LIFE	INITIAL INVESTMENT OUTLAY—CF0	INCREMENTAL OPERATING CASH FLOWS— $CF_1 - CF_5$	NPV	IRR
A	Low	12%	5	$(10,000)	$2,850	$ 273.61	13.1%
B	Average	15	5	(11,000)	3,210	(239.58)	14.1
C	Average	15	5	(9,000)	2,750	218.43	16.0
D	High	20	5	(12,000)	3,825	(560.91)	17.9

PROJECT RISK CLASSIFICATION	REQUIRED RATE OF RETURN
Low	12%
Average	15
High	20

completed on a division-by-division basis for very large firms, perhaps using the CAPM. Second, all projects generally are classified into three categories—high risk, average risk, and low risk. Then, the firm or division uses the average required rate of return as the discount rate for average-risk projects, reduces the average rate by one or two percentage points when evaluating low-risk projects, and raises the average rate by several percentage points for high-risk projects. For example, if a firm's basic required rate of return is estimated to be 12 percent, an 18 percent discount rate might be used for a high-risk project and a nine percent rate for a low-risk project. Average-risk projects, which constitute about 80 percent of most capital budgets, would be evaluated at the 12 percent rate of return. Table 9–6 contains an example of the application of risk-adjusted discount rates for the evaluation of four projects. Each of the four projects has a five-year life, and each is expected to generate a constant cash flow stream during its life; therefore, each project's future cash flow pattern represents an annuity. The analysis shows that only Project A and Project C are acceptable when risk is considered. Note, though, that if the average required rate of return is used to evaluate all the projects, Project C and Project D would be considered acceptable because their IRRs are greater than 12 percent. Using the average required rate of return would lead to an incorrect decision. Thus, *if project risk is not considered in capital budgeting analysis, incorrect decisions are possible.*

Although the risk-adjusted discount rate approach is far from precise, it does at least recognize that different projects have different risks, and projects with different risks should be evaluated using different required rates of return.

Self-Test Questions

How are risk-adjusted discount rates used to incorporate project risk into the capital budget decision process?

Briefly explain the two-step process many companies use to develop risk-adjusted discount rates for use in capital budgeting.

Capital Rationing

Capital budgeting decisions are typically made on the basis of the techniques presented in Chapter 8 and applied as described in this chapter—independent projects are accepted if their NPVs are positive, and choices among mutually exclusive projects are made by selecting the one with the highest NPV. In this analysis, it is assumed that if in a particular year the firm has an especially large number of good projects, management simply will go into the financial markets and raise whatever funds are required to finance all of the acceptable projects. However, some firms do set limits on the amount of funds they are willing to raise, and, if this is done, the capital budget must also be limited. This situation is known as **capital rationing.**

CAPITAL RATIONING
A situation in which a constraint is placed on the total size of the firm's capital investment.

Elaborate and mathematically sophisticated models have been developed to help firms maximize their values when they are subject to capital rationing. However, a firm that subjects itself to capital rationing is deliberately forgoing profitable projects, and hence it is not truly maximizing its value. This point is well known, so few large, sophisticated firms ration capital today. Therefore, we shall not discuss it further, but you should know what the term *capital rationing* means.

Self-Test Questions

What is meant by the term *capital rationing?*

Why do few sophisticated firms ration capital today?

Multinational Capital Budgeting

Although the basic principles of capital budgeting analysis are the same for both domestic and foreign operations, some key differences need to be mentioned. First, cash flow estimation generally is much more complex for overseas investments. Most multinational firms set up a separate subsidiary in each foreign country in which they operate, and the relevant cash flows for these subsidiaries are the dividends and royalties **repatriated,** or returned, to the parent company. Second, these cash flows must be converted into the currency of the parent company, and thus are subject to future exchange rate changes. For example, General Motors' German subsidiary might make a profit of 150 million marks in 2000, but the value of these profits to GM will depend on the dollar-to-mark exchange rate. Third, dividends and royalties normally are taxed by both foreign and home-country governments. Furthermore, a foreign government might restrict the amount of cash that can be repatriated to the parent company, perhaps to force multinational firms to reinvest earnings in the host country or to prevent large currency outflows, which might affect the exchange rate. Whatever the host country's motivation, the result is that the parent corporation cannot use cash flows blocked in the foreign country to pay current dividends to its shareholders, nor does it have the flexibility to reinvest cash flows elsewhere in the world. Therefore, from the perspective of the parent organization, *the cash flows relevant for the analysis of a foreign investment are the cash flows that the subsidiary legally can send back to the parent.*

REPATRIATION OF EARNINGS
The process of sending cash flows from a foreign subsidiary back to the parent company.

In addition to the complexities of the cash flow analysis, *the rate of return required for a foreign project might be different than for an equivalent domestic project because foreign projects might be more or less risky.* A higher risk could arise from two primary sources—(1) exchange rate risk and (2) political risk—while a lower risk might result from international diversification.

EXCHANGE RATE RISK
The uncertainty associated with the price at which the currency from one country can be converted into the currency of another country.

Exchange rate risk reflects the inherent uncertainty about the home currency value of cash flows sent back to the parent. In other words, foreign projects have an added risk element that relates to what the basic cash flows will be worth in the parent company's home currency. The foreign currency cash flows to be turned over to the parent must be converted into U.S. dollars by translating them at *expected* future exchange rates—actual exchange rates might differ substantially from expectations.

POLITICAL RISK
The risk of expropriation (seizure) of a foreign subsidiary's assets by the host country or of unanticipated restrictions on cash flows to the parent company.

Political risk refers to any action (or the chance of such action) by a host government that reduces the value of a company's investment. It includes at one extreme the expropriation (seizure) without compensation of the subsidiary's assets; but it also includes less drastic actions that reduce the value of the parent firm's investment in the foreign subsidiary such as higher taxes, tighter repatriation or currency controls, and restrictions on prices charged. The risk of expropriation of U.S. assets abroad is small in traditionally friendly and stable countries such as Great Britain or Switzerland. However, in Latin America and Africa, for example, the risk might be substantial. Past expropriations include those of ITT and Anaconda Copper in Chile, Gulf Oil in Bolivia, Occidental Petroleum in Libya, and the assets of many companies in Iraq, Iran, and Cuba.

Generally, political risk premiums are not added to the required rate of return to adjust for this risk. If a company's management has a serious concern that a given country might expropriate foreign assets, it simply will not make significant investments in that country. Expropriation is viewed as a catastrophic or ruinous event, and managers have been shown to be extraordinarily risk averse when faced with ruinous loss possibilities. However, companies can take steps to reduce the potential loss from expropriation in three major ways: (1) by financing the subsidiary with capital raised in the country in which the asset is located, (2) by structuring operations so that the subsidiary has value only as a part of the integrated corporate system, and (3) by obtaining insurance against economic losses from expropriation from a source such as the Overseas Private Investment Corporation (OPIC). In the latter case, insurance premiums would have to be added to the project's cost.

Self-Test Questions

List some key differences in capital budgeting as applied to foreign versus domestic operations.

What are the relevant cash flows for an international investment?

Why might the required rate of return for a foreign project differ from that of an equivalent domestic project? Could it be lower?

✳ **SMALL BUSINESS**

Capital Budgeting in the Small Firm—Part II

In the "Small Business" box in Chapter 8, we concluded that, due to the somewhat different circumstances they face, small firms generally rely more heavily on nondiscounted techniques to evaluate projects than do large firms. After reading this chapter, you should be curious about how small firms incorporate risk when evaluating projects, if they do so at all.

In a recent study of firms with sales less than $5 million, Stanley Block found that more than one-half of the firms surveyed do consider risk when making

continues

capital budgeting decisions.* While this might seem somewhat surprising, as Block concludes, it is important for small firms to examine risk in their capital budgeting analysis because investment in a "bad" project is much more costly for a small firm than for a large firm that benefits from diversification in its portfolio of assets. Simply stated, in large firms, a mistake on one project can be offset by successes with others; but in small firms a capital budgeting mistake can be disastrous, even fatal.

According to the study, more than 45 percent of the small firms surveyed indicated that they use higher required rates of return to evaluate projects with higher-than-average risk; 30 percent adjust the project's cash flows; and nearly 21 percent use some type of subjective, nonquantitative risk analysis. Block discovered that about 3 percent of the firms use some type of probability analysis to incorporate risk in the capital budgeting analysis.

Block's study includes a couple of additional results that are related to the material covered in this chapter. First, he found that nearly 74 percent of the capital budgeting projects of the firms surveyed are either replacement decisions (57.6 percent) or decisions to expand existing product lines (16.3 percent); only 8 percent are decisions to expand into new products or businesses; and 18 percent of the decisions are related to safety or environmental considerations. In

addition, risk analysis is considered important by firms that plan to expand existing product lines or enter into new lines of business—more than 90 percent of the firms stated that risk analysis is part of the project evaluation in these situations. Second, Block discovered that, even though many of the respondents did not understand what the term *capital rationing* meant, nearly 93 percent do restrict the size of the capital budget, even when additional acceptable projects are available. Perhaps the reason small firms do not invest in all the acceptable projects (i.e., ration capital) is because the banks that provide them funds are more concerned with the time it takes to pay back the loan rather than whether the projects are acceptable using capital budgeting techniques such as NPV and IRR.

In general, Block's study suggests that, compared with large firms, small firms are not as well diversified with respect to the assets they hold; thus, they must be more concerned with stand-alone risk than with either corporate (within-firm) risk or beta risk when making capital budgeting decisions. Like larger firms, however, small firms find it easier to adjust the rate of return used to evaluate a project than to use one of the other techniques discussed in this chapter.

*Stanley Block, "Capital Budgeting Techniques Used by Small Business Firms in the 1990s," *The Engineering Economist*, Summer 1997, 289–302.

Summary

This chapter presented two issues in capital budgeting: cash flow estimation and evaluation and risk analysis in capital budgeting. We also provided an indication of the capital budgeting decision-making process in multinational firms. The key concepts covered are listed here:

- The most important, but also the most difficult, step in analyzing a capital budgeting project is estimating the **incremental after-tax cash flows** the project will produce.
- **Net cash flows** consist of net income plus depreciation. In determining incremental cash flows, **opportunity costs** (the cash flow forgone by using an asset) must be included, but **sunk costs** (cash outlays that have been made and that cannot be recouped) should not be included. Any **externalities** (effects of a project on other parts of the firm) should also be reflected in the analysis. In addition, **inflation** effects must be considered in project analysis. The best procedure is to build inflation directly into the cash flow estimates.

- Capital projects often require an additional investment in **net working capital (NWC).** An *increase* in NWC must be included in the Year 0 initial cash outlay and then shown as a cash inflow in the project's final year.
- **Replacement analysis** is slightly different from that for **expansion projects** because the cash flows from the old asset must be considered in replacement decisions.
- A project's **stand-alone risk** is the risk the project would have if it were the firm's only asset and if the firm's stockholders held only that one stock. Stand-alone risk is measured by the variability of the asset's expected returns, and it is often used as a proxy for both beta and corporate risk because (1) beta and corporate risk are difficult to measure and (2) the three types of risk are usually highly correlated.
- **Within-firm,** or **corporate, risk** reflects the effects of a project on the firm's risk, and it is measured by the project's effect on the firm's earnings variability. Stockholder diversification is not taken into account.
- **Beta risk** reflects the effects of a project on the risks borne by stockholders, assuming stockholders hold diversified portfolios. In theory, beta risk should be the most relevant type of risk.
- **Corporate risk** is important because it influences the firm's ability to use low-cost debt, to maintain smooth operations over time, and to avoid crises that might consume management's energy and disrupt employees, customers, suppliers, and the community.
- **Sensitivity analysis** is a technique that shows how much an output variable such as NPV will change in response to a given change in an input variable such as sales, other things held constant.
- **Scenario analysis** is a risk analysis technique in which the best- and worst-case NPVs are compared with the project's expected NPV.
- **Monte Carlo simulation** is a risk-analysis technique in which a computer is used to simulate probable future events and thus to estimate the profitability distribution and riskiness of a project.
- The **pure play method** can be used to estimate betas for large projects or for divisions.
- The **risk-adjusted discount rate** is the rate used to evaluate a particular project. The discount rate is increased for projects that are riskier than the firm's average project but is decreased for less risky projects.
- **Capital rationing** occurs when management places a constraint on the size of the firm's capital budget during a particular period.
- Investments in **international capital projects** expose the investing firm to **exchange rate risk** and **political risk.** The relevant cash flows in international capital budgeting are the dollar cash flows that can be turned over to the parent company.

Both the measurement of risk and its incorporation into capital budgeting involve judgment. It is possible to use a quantitative technique such as simulation as an aid to judgment, but in the final analysis the assessment of risk in capital budgeting is a subjective process.

Questions

9–1 Cash flows rather than accounting profits are listed in Table 9–2. What is the basis for this emphasis on cash flows as opposed to net income?

9–2 Look at Table 9–4 and answer these questions:
  a. Why is the net salvage value shown in Section III reduced for taxes?
  b. How is the change in depreciation computed?
  c. What would happen if the new machine permitted a reduction in net working capital?
  d. Why are the cost savings shown as a positive amount?

9–3 Explain why sunk costs should not be included in a capital budgeting analysis but opportunity costs and externalities should be included.

9–4 Explain how net working capital is recovered at the end of a project's life and why it is included in a capital budgeting analysis.

9–5 In general, is an explicit recognition of incremental cash flows more important in new project analysis or replacement analysis? Why?

9–6 Why is it true, in general, that a failure to adjust expected cash flows for expected inflation biases the calculated NPV downward?

9–7 Define (a) simulation analysis, (b) scenario analysis, and (c) sensitivity analysis. If AT&T were considering two investments, one calling for the expenditure of $2 million to develop a satellite communications system and the other involving the expenditure of $30,000 for a new truck, on which one would the company be more likely to use simulation analysis?

9–8 Distinguish between beta (or market) risk, within-firm (or corporate) risk, and stand-alone risk for a project being considered for inclusion in the capital budget. Which type of risk do you believe should be given the greatest weight in capital budgeting decisions? Explain.

9–9 Suppose Reading Engine Company, which has a high beta as well as a great deal of corporate risk, merged with Simplicity Patterns Inc. Simplicity's sales rise during recessions, when people are more likely to make their own clothes, and, consequently, its beta is negative but its corporate risk is relatively high. What would the merger do to the costs of capital in the consolidated company's locomotive engine division and in its patterns division?

9–10 Suppose a firm estimates its required rate of return for the coming year to be ten percent. What are reasonable required rates of return for evaluating average-risk projects, high-risk projects, and low-risk projects?

Self-Test Problems

(Solutions appear in Appendix B)

key terms   **ST–1** Define each of the following terms:
  a. Cash flow; accounting income; relevant cash flow
  b. Incremental cash flow; sunk cost; opportunity cost; externalities; inflation bias
  c. Initial investment outlay; incremental operating cash flow; terminal cash flow
  d. Change in net working capital; expansion project
  e. Salvage value
  f. Replacement analysis
  g. Stand-alone risk; within-firm risk; beta (market) risk
  h. Corporate risk
  i. Sensitivity analysis
  j. Scenario analysis

  k. Monte Carlo simulation analysis
  l. Project beta versus corporate beta
  m. Pure play method of estimating project betas
  n. Risk-adjusted discount rate; project required rate of return
  o. Capital rationing
  p. Exchange rate risk; political risk

new project analysis **ST–2** You have been asked by the president of Ellis Construction Company, head-quartered in Toledo, to evaluate the proposed acquisition of a new earthmover. The mover's basic price is $50,000, and it will cost another $10,000 to modify it for special use by Ellis Construction. Assume that the mover falls into the MACRS three-year class. (See Table 9A–2 for MACRS recovery allowance percentages.) It will be sold after three years for $20,000, and it will require an increase in net working capital (spare parts inventory) of $2,000. The earthmover purchase will have no effect on revenues, but it is expected to save Ellis $20,000 per year in before-tax operating costs, mainly labor. Ellis's marginal tax rate is 40 percent.

  a. What is the company's net initial investment outlay if it acquires the earthmover? (That is, what are the Year 0 cash flows?)
  b. What are the incremental operating cash flows in Years 1, 2, and 3?
  c. What is the terminal cash flow in Year 3?
  d. If the project's required rate of return is ten percent, should the earthmover be purchased?

replacement analysis **ST–3** The Dauten Toy Corporation currently uses an injection molding machine that was purchased two years ago. This machine is being depreciated on a straight line basis toward a $500 salvage value, and it has six years of remaining life. Its current book value is $2,600, and it can be sold for $3,000 at this time. Thus, the annual depreciation expense is ($2,600 − $500)/6 = $350 per year.

  Dauten is offered a replacement machine that has a cost of $8,000, an estimated useful life of six years, and an estimated salvage value of $800. This machine falls into the MACRS 5-year class. (See Table 9A–2 for MACRS recovery allowance percentages.) The replacement machine would permit an output expansion, so sales would rise by $1,000 per year; even so, the new machine's much greater efficiency would still cause operating expenses to decline by $1,500 per year. The new machine would require that inventories be increased by $2,000, but accounts payable would simultaneously increase by $500.

  Dauten's marginal tax rate is 40 percent, and its required rate of return is 15 percent. Should it replace the old machine?

corporate risk analysis **ST–4** The staff of Heymann Manufacturing has estimated the following net cash flows and probabilities for a new manufacturing process:

	NET CASH FLOWS		
YEAR	$P_R = 0.2$	$P_R = 0.6$	$P_R = 0.2$
0	$(100,000)	$(100,000)	$(100,000)
1	20,000	30,000	40,000
2	20,000	30,000	40,000
3	20,000	30,000	40,000
4	20,000	30,000	40,000
5	20,000	30,000	40,000
5*	0	20,000	30,000

Line 0 gives the cost of the process, Lines 1 through 5 give operating cash flows, and Line 5* contains the estimated salvage values. Heymann's required rate of return for an average risk project is ten percent.

a. Assume that the project has average risk. Find the project's expected NPV. (*Hint:* Use expected values for the net cash flow in each year.)

b. Find the best-case and worst-case NPVs. What is the probability of occurrence of the worst case if the cash flows are perfectly dependent (perfectly positively correlated) over time? If they are independent over time?

c. Assume that all the cash flows are perfectly positively correlated; that is, there are only three possible cash flow streams over time: (1) the worst case, (2) the most likely, or base, case, and (3) the best case, with probabilities of 0.2, 0.6, and 0.2, respectively. These cases are represented by each of the columns in the table. Find the expected NPV, its standard deviation, and its coefficient of variation.

d. The coefficient of variation of Heymann's average project is in the range 0.8 to 1.0. If the coefficient of variation of a project being evaluated is greater than 1.0, two percentage points are added to the firm's required rate of return. Similarly, if the coefficient of variation is less than 0.8, one percentage point is deducted from the required rate of return. What is the project's required rate of return? Should Heymann accept or reject the project?

Problems

new project analysis   **9–1** You have been asked by the president of your company to evaluate the proposed acquisition of a spectrometer for the firm's R&D department. The equipment's base price is $140,000, and it would cost another $30,000 to modify it for special use by your firm. The spectrometer, which falls into the MACRS three-year class, would be sold after three years for $60,000. (See Table 9A–2 for MACRS recovery allowance percentages.) Use of the equipment would require an increase in net working capital (spare parts inventory) of $8,000. The spectrometer would have no effect on revenues, but it is expected to save the firm $50,000 per year in before-tax operating costs, mainly labor. The firm's marginal tax rate is 40 percent.

a. What is the initial investment outlay associated with this project? (That is, what is the Year 0 net cash flow?)

b. What are the incremental operating cash flows in Years 1, 2, and 3?

c. What is the terminal cash flow in Year 3?

d. If the project's required rate of return is 12 percent, should the spectrometer be purchased?

new project analysis   **9–2** The Ewert Company is evaluating the proposed acquisition of a new milling machine. The machine's base price is $108,000, and it would cost another $12,500 to modify it for special use by the firm. The machine falls into the MACRS three-year class, and it would be sold after three years for $65,000. (See Table 9A–2 for MACRS recovery allowance percentages.) The machine would require an increase in net working capital (inventory) of $5,500. The milling machine would have no effect on revenues, but it is expected to save the firm $44,000 per year in before-tax operating costs, mainly labor. Ewert's marginal tax rate is 34 percent.

a. What is the initial investment outlay of the machine for capital budgeting purposes? (That is, what is the Year 0 net cash flow?)

    b. What are the incremental operating cash flows in Years 1, 2, and 3?

    c. What is the terminal cash flow in Year 3?

    d. If the project's required rate of return is 12 percent, should the machine be purchased?

replacement analysis   **9–3** Atlantic Control Company purchased a machine two years ago at a cost of $70,000. At that time, the machine's expected economic life was six years and its salvage value at the end of its life was estimated to be $10,000. It is being depreciated using the straight line method so that its book value at the end of six years is $10,000. In four years, however, the old machine will have a market value of $0.

    A new machine can be purchased for $80,000, including shipping and installation costs. The new machine has an economic life estimated to be four years. MACRS depreciation will be used, and the machine will be depreciated over its three-year class life rather than its five-year economic life. (See Table 9A–2 for MACRS recovery allowance percentages.) During its four-year life, the new machine will reduce cash operating expenses by $20,000 per year. Sales are not expected to change. But the new machine will require net working capital to be increased by $4,000. At the end of its useful life, the machine is estimated to have a market value of $2,500.

    The old machine can be sold today for $20,000. The firm's marginal tax rate is 40 percent. The appropriate required rate of return is ten percent.

    a. If the new machine is purchased, what is the amount of the initial investment outlay at Year 0?

    b. What incremental operating cash flows will occur at the end of Years 1 through 4 as a result of replacing the old machine?

    c. What is the terminal cash flow at the end of Year 4 if the new machine is purchased?

    d. What is the NPV of this project? Should Atlantic replace the old machine?

replacement analysis   **9–4** The Boyd Bottling Company is contemplating the replacement of one of its bottling machines with a newer and more efficient one. The old machine has a book value of $600,000 and a remaining useful life of five years. The firm does not expect to realize any return from scrapping the old machine in five years, but it can sell it now to another firm in the industry for $265,000. The old machine is being depreciated toward a zero salvage value, or by $120,000 per year, using the straight line method.

    The new machine has a purchase price of $1,175,000, an estimated useful life and MACRS class life of five years, and an estimated market value of $145,000 at the end of five years. (See Table 9A–2 for MACRS recovery allowance percentages.) It is expected to economize on electric power usage, labor, and repair costs, which will save Boyd $230,000 each year. In addition, the new machine is expected to reduce the number of defective bottles, which will save an additional $25,000 annually. The company's marginal tax rate is 40 percent and it has a 12 percent required rate of return.

    a. What initial investment outlay is required for the new machine?

    b. Calculate the annual depreciation allowances for both machines, and compute the change in the annual depreciation expense if the replacement is made.

    c. What are the incremental operating cash flows in Years 1 through 5?

    d. What is the terminal cash flow in Year 5?

    e. Should the firm purchase the new machine? Support your answer.

    f. In general, how would each of the following factors affect the investment decision, and how should each be treated?

      (1) The expected life of the existing machine decreases.

(2) The required rate of return is not constant but is increasing as Boyd adds more projects into its capital budget for the year.

risky cash flows   9–5 The Singleton Company must decide between two mutually exclusive investment projects. Each project costs $6,750 and has an expected life of three years. Annual net cash flows from each project begin one year after the initial investment is made and have the following probability distributions:

PROJECT A		PROJECT B	
PROBABILITY	NET CASH FLOWS	PROBABILITY	NET CASH FLOWS
0.2	$6,000	0.2	$ 0
0.6	6,750	0.6	6,750
0.2	7,500	0.2	18,000

Singleton has decided to evaluate the riskier project at a 12 percent rate and the less risky project at a ten percent rate.

a. What is the expected value of the annual net cash flows from each project? What is the coefficient of variation (CV_{NPV})? (*Hint:* Use Equation 5–3 from Chapter 5 to calculate the standard deviation of Project A. $\sigma_B = \$5,798$ and $CV_B = 0.76$.)

b. What is the risk-adjusted NPV of each project?

c. If it were known that Project B was negatively correlated with other cash flows of the firm whereas Project A was positively correlated, how would this knowledge affect the decision? If Project B's cash flows were negatively correlated with the gross national product (GNP), would that influence your assessment of its risk?

CAPM approach to risk adjustments   9–6 Goodtread Rubber Company has two divisions: the tire division, which manufactures tires for new autos, and the recap division, which manufactures recapping materials that are sold to independent tire recapping shops throughout the United States. Because auto manufacturing fluctuates with the general economy, the tire division's earnings contribution to Goodtread's stock price is highly correlated with returns on most other stocks. If the tire division were operated as a separate company, its beta coefficient would be about 1.5. The sales and profits of the recap division, on the other hand, tend to be countercyclical because recap sales boom when people cannot afford to buy new tires. The recap division's beta is estimated to be 0.5. Approximately 75 percent of Goodtread's corporate assets are invested in the tire division and 25 percent are invested in the recap division.

Currently, the rate of interest on Treasury securities is nine percent, and the expected rate of return on an average share of stock is 13 percent. Goodtread uses only common equity capital, so it has no debt outstanding.

a. What is the required rate of return on Goodtread's stock?

b. What discount rate should be used to evaluate capital budgeting projects? Explain your answer fully, and, in the process, illustrate your answer with a project that costs $160,000, has a ten-year life, and provides expected after-tax net cash flows of $30,000 per year.

scenario analysis   9–7 Your firm, Agrico Products, is considering the purchase of a tractor that will have a net cost of $36,000, will increase pretax operating cash flows before taking account of depreciation effects by $12,000 per year, and will be depreciated on a straight line basis to zero over five years at the rate of $7,200 per year, beginning the first year. (Annual cash flows will be $12,000 before taxes plus the tax savings that result from $7,200 of depreciation.) The board of directors is having a heated debate about whether the tractor actually will last five years. Specifically, Joan Lamm insists that she knows of some tractors that have lasted only four years. Alan Grunewald agrees with Lamm, but he argues that most tractors do give five years of service. Judy Maese says she has known some to last for as long as eight years.

Given this discussion, the board asks you to prepare a scenario analysis to ascertain the importance of the uncertainty about the tractor's life span. Assume a 40 percent marginal tax rate, a zero salvage value, and a required rate of return of ten percent. (*Hint:* Here straight line depreciation is based on the MACRS class life of the tractor and is not affected by the actual life. Also, ignore the half-year convention for this problem.)

Exam-Type Problems

The problems included in this section are set up in such a way that they could be used as multiple-choice exam problems.

replacement analysis **9–8** The Gehr Company is considering the purchase of a new machine tool to replace an obsolete one. The machine being used for the operation has both a tax book value and a market value of zero; it is in good working order, however, and will last physically for at least another ten years. The proposed replacement machine will perform the operation so much more efficiently that Gehr engineers estimate it will produce after-tax cash flows (labor savings and depreciation) of $9,000 per year. The new machine will cost $40,000 delivered and installed, and its economic life is estimated to be ten years. It has zero salvage value. The firm's required rate of return is ten percent, and its marginal tax rate is 40 percent. Should Gehr buy the new machine?

replacement analysis **9–9** Galveston Shipyards is considering the replacement of an eight-year-old riveting machine with a new one that will increase earnings before depreciation from $27,000 to $54,000 per year. The new machine will cost $82,500, and it will have an estimated life of eight years and no salvage value. The new machine will be depreciated over its five-year MACRS recovery period. (See Table 9A–2 for MACRS recovery allowance percentages.) The firm's marginal tax rate is 40 percent, and the firm's required rate of return is 12 percent. The old machine has been fully depreciated and has no salvage value. Should the old riveting machine be replaced by the new one?

risk adjustment **9–10** The risk-free rate of return is currently nine percent and the market risk premium is five percent. The beta of the project under analysis is 1.4, with expected net cash flows estimated to be $1,500 per year for five years. The required investment outlay on the project is $4,500.
  a. What is the required risk-adjusted return on the project?
  b. Should the project be accepted?

beta risk **9–11** Companioni Computer Corporation, a producer of office equipment, currently has assets of $15 million and a beta of 1.4. The risk-free rate is eight percent and the market risk premium is five percent. Companioni would like to expand into the risky home computer market. If the expansion is undertaken, Companioni would create a new division with $3.75 million in assets. The new division would have a beta of 1.8.

a. What is Companioni's current required rate of return?
b. If the expansion is undertaken, what would be the firm's new beta? What is the new overall required rate of return, and what rate of return must the home computer division produce to leave the new overall required rate of return unchanged?

Integrative Problems

9–12 Unilate Textiles is evaluating a new product, a silk/wool blended fabric. Assume that you were recently hired as assistant to the director of capital budgeting, and you must evaluate the new project.

The fabric would be produced in an unused building adjacent to Unilate's Southern Pines, North Carolina plant. Unilate owns the building, which is fully depreciated. The required equipment would cost $200,000, plus an additional $40,000 for shipping and installation. In addition, inventories would rise by $25,000, while accounts payable would go up by $5,000. All of these costs would be incurred at t = 0. By a special ruling, the machinery could be depreciated under the MACRS system as three-year property.

The project is expected to operate for four years, at which time it will be terminated. The cash inflows are assumed to begin one year after the project is undertaken, or at t = 1, and to continue out to t = 4. At the end of the project's life (t = 4), the equipment is expected to have a salvage value of $25,000.

Unit sales are expected to total 100,000 five-yard rolls per year, and the expected sales price is $2.00 per roll. Cash operating costs for the project (total operating costs less depreciation) are expected to total 60 percent of dollar sales. Unilate's marginal tax rate is 40 percent, and its required rate of return is ten percent. Tentatively, the silk/wool blend fabric project is assumed to be of equal risk to Unilate's other assets.

You have been asked to evaluate the project and to make a recommendation as to whether it should be accepted or rejected. To guide you in your analysis, your boss gave you the following set of tasks to complete:
a. Draw a cash flow time line that shows when the net cash inflows and outflows will occur, and explain how the time line can be used to help structure the analysis.
b. Unilate has a standard form that is used in the capital budgeting process; see Table IP9–1. Part of the table has been completed, but you must replace the blanks with the missing numbers. Complete the table in the following steps:
   (1) Complete the unit sales, sales price, total revenues, and operating costs excluding depreciation lines.
   (2) Complete the depreciation line.
   (3) Now complete the table down to net income and then down to net operating cash flows.
   (4) Now fill in the blanks under Year 0 and Year 4 for the initial investment outlay and the terminal cash flows and complete the cash flow time line (net $\hat{CF}$). Discuss working capital. What would have happened if the machinery were sold for less than its book value?
c. (1) Unilate uses debt in its capital structure, so some of the money used to finance the project will be debt. Given this fact, should the projected cash flows be revised to show projected interest charges? Explain.

(2) Suppose you learned that Unilate had spent $50,000 to renovate the building last year, expensing these costs. Should this cost be reflected in the analysis? Explain.

(3) Now suppose you learned that Unilate could lease its building to another party and earn $25,000 per year. Should that fact be reflected in the analysis? If so, how?

(4) Now assume that the silk/wool blend fabric project would take away profitable sales from Unilate's cotton/wool blend fabric business. Should that fact be reflected in your analysis? If so, how?

d. Disregard all the assumptions made in part c, and assume there was no alternative use for the building over the next four years. Now calculate the project's NPV, IRR, and traditional payback. Do these indicators suggest that the project should be accepted?

e. If this project had been a replacement rather than an expansion project, how would the analysis have changed? No calculations are needed; just think about the changes that would have to occur in the cash flow table.

f. Assume that inflation is expected to average five percent over the next four years, that this expectation is reflected in the required rate of return, and that inflation will increase variable costs and revenues by the same relative amount of five percent. Does it appear that inflation has been dealt with properly in the analysis? If not, what should be done, and how would the required adjustment affect the decision?

risk analysis   **9–13** Problem 9–12 contained the details of a new-project capital budgeting evaluation being conducted by Unilate Textiles. Although inflation was considered in the initial analysis, the riskiness of the project was not considered. The expected cash flows considering inflation as they were estimated in Problem 9–12 (in thousands of dollars) are given in Table IP9–2. Unilate's required rate of return is ten percent.

You have been asked to answer the following questions:

a. (1) What are the three levels, or types, of project risk that are normally considered?

(2) Which type is the most relevant?

(3) Which type is the easiest to measure?

(4) Are the three types of risk generally highly correlated?

b. (1) What is sensitivity analysis?

(2) Discuss how one would perform a sensitivity analysis on the unit sales, salvage value, and required rate of return for the project. Assume that each of these variables deviates from its base-case, or expected, value by plus and minus 10, 20, and 30 percent. How would you calculate the NPV, IRR, and the payback for each case?

(3) What is the primary weakness of sensitivity analysis? What are its primary advantages?

c. Assume that you are confident about the estimates of all the variables that affect the project's cash flows except unit sales. If product acceptance is poor, sales would be only 75,000 units a year, while a strong consumer response would produce sales of 125,000 units. In either case, cash costs would still amount to 60 percent of revenues. You believe that there is a 25 percent chance of poor acceptance, a 25 percent chance of excellent acceptance, and a 50 percent chance of average acceptance (the base case).

(1) What is the worst-case NPV? The best-case NPV?

TABLE IP9-1	Unilate's Silk/Wool Blend Project (thousands of dollars)				
	END OF YEAR				
END OF YEAR:	**0**	**1**	**2**	**3**	**4**
Unit sales (thousands)			100		
Price/unit		$ 2.00	$ 2.00		
Total revenues				$200.0	
Costs excluding depreciation			$120.0		
Depreciation				36.0	16.8
Total operating costs		$199.2	$228.0		
Earnings before taxes (EBT)				$ 44.0	
Taxes		0.3			25.3
Net income				$ 26.4	
Depreciation		79.2		36.0	
Incremental operating CF		$ 79.7			$ 54.7
Equipment cost					
Installation					
Increase in inventory					
Increase in accounts payable					
Salvage value					
Tax on salvage value					
Return of net working capital					
Cash flow time line (Net CF)	$(260.0)				$ 89.7
Cumulative CF for payback	(260.0)	(180.3)			63.0
NPV =					
IRR =					
Payback =					

    (2) Use the worst-case, most likely (or base) case, and best-case NPVs and probabilities of occurrence to find the project's expected NPV, standard deviation (σ_{NPV}), and coefficient of variation (CV_{NPV}).

d. (1) Assume that Unilate's average project has a coefficient of variation (CV_{NPV}) in the range of 1.25 to 1.75. Would the silk/wool blend fabric project be classified as high risk, average risk, or low risk? What type of risk is being measured here?

    (2) Based on common sense, how highly correlated do you think the project would be to the firm's other assets? (Give a correlation coefficient, or range of coefficients, based on your judgment.)

    (3) How would this correlation coefficient and the previously calculated σ combine to affect the project's contribution to corporate, or within-firm, risk? Explain.

e. (1) Based on your judgment, what do you think the project's correlation coefficient would be with respect to the general economy and thus with returns on "the market"?

TABLE IP9–2

		YEAR			
	0	**1**	**2**	**3**	**4**
Investment in:					
Fixed assets	$(240)				
Net working capital	(20)				
Unit sales (thousands)		100	100	100	100
Sales price (dollars)		$2.100	$ 2.205	$2.315	$2.431
Total revenues		$210.0	$ 220.5	$2.315	$243.1
Cash operating costs (60%)		(126.0)	(132.3)	(138.9)	(145.9)
Depreciation		(79.2)	(108.0)	(36.0)	(16.8)
Earnings before taxes (EBT)		$ 4.8	$(19.8)	$ 56.6	$ 80.4
Taxes (40%)		(1.9)	7.9	(22.6)	(32.2)
Net income		$ 2.9	$(11.9)	$ 34.0	$ 48.2
Plus depreciation		79.2	108.0	36.0	16.8
Net operating cash flow		$ 82.1	$ 96.1	$ 70.0	$ 65.0
Salvage value					25.0
Tax on SV (40%)					(10.0)
Recovery of NWC					20.0
Net cash flow	$(260)	$ 82.1	$ 96.1	$ 70.0	$100.0
Cumulative cash flow					
for payback:	(260.0)	(177.9)	(81.8)	(11.8)	88.2

NPV at 10% cost of capital = $15.0
IRR   = 12.6%

(2) How would correlation with the economy affect the project's market risk?

f. (1) Unilate typically adds or subtracts three percentage points to the overall required rate of return to adjust for risk. Should the project be accepted?

(2) What subjective risk factors should be considered before the final decision is made?

g. Define scenario analysis and simulation analysis, and discuss their principal advantages and disadvantages. (Note that you have already done scenario analysis in part c.)

h. (1) Assume that the risk-free rate is ten percent, the market risk premium is six percent, and the new project's beta is 1.2. What is the project's required rate of return on equity based on the CAPM?

(2) How does the project's market risk compare with the firm's overall market risk?

(3) How does the project's stand-alone risk compare with that of the firm's average project?

(4) Briefly describe how you could estimate the project's beta. How feasible do you think that procedure actually would be in this case?

(5) What are the advantages and disadvantages of focusing on a project's market risk?

Computer-Related Problem

Work the problem in this section only if you are using the computer problem diskette.

expansion project **9–14** Use the computerized model in the File C9 to work this problem. Golden State Bakers Inc. (GSB) has an opportunity to invest in a new dough machine. GSB needs more productive capacity, so the new machine will not replace an existing machine. The new machine costs $260,000 and will require modifications costing $15,000. It has an expected useful life of ten years, will be depreciated using the MACRS method over its five-year class life, and has an expected salvage value of $12,500 at the end of Year 10. (See Table 9A–2 for MACRS recovery allowance percentages.) The machine will require a $22,500 investment in net working capital. It is expected to generate additional sales revenues of $125,000 per year, but its use will also increase annual cash operating expenses by $55,000. GSB's required rate of return is ten percent and its marginal tax rate is 40 percent. The machine's book value at the end of Year 10 will be zero, so GSB will have to pay taxes on the $12,500 salvage value.

   a. What is the NPV of this expansion project? Should GSB purchase the new machine?

   b. Should GSB purchase the new machine if it is expected to be used for only five years and then sold for $31,250? (Note that the model is set up to handle a five-year life; you need only enter the new life and salvage value.)

   c. Would the machine be profitable if revenues increased by only $105,000 per year? Assume a ten-year project life and a salvage value of $12,500.

   d. Suppose that revenues rose by $125,000 but that expenses rose by $65,000. Would the machine be acceptable under these conditions? Assume a ten-year project life and a salvage value of $12,500.

ONLINE ESSENTIALS

http://csep1.phy.ornl.gov/mc/mc.html   Computational Science Education Project
This site provides an electronic book that includes an introduction to Monte Carlo simulation.

http://www.studyfinance.com   *study*finance.com
This site provides tutorials relating to capital budgeting, including how marginal cash flows are computed for replacement decisions.

http://www.teachmefinance.com   TeachMeFinance.com
This site contains tutorials related to a number of the topics covered in this chapter, including capital budgeting cash flows, probability distributions, and standard deviation.

http://www.irs.ustreas.gov   Internal Revenue Service
This site provides the Tax Code that defines depreciable assets, depreciation rates, and so on. Publication 946 defines depreciation, describes the depreciation process, gives the MACRS rates, and so forth. You can get more information by using the search function, keying in the phrase "Modified Accelerated Cost Recovery System," and then looking at the various publications.

APPENDIX 9A

Depreciation

Suppose a firm buys a milling machine for $100,000 and uses it for five years, after which it is scrapped. The cost of the goods produced by the machine each year must include a charge for using machine and reducing its value, and this charge is called *depreciation*. In this appendix we review some of the depreciation concepts covered in your accounting course.

Companies often calculate depreciation one way when figuring taxes and another way when reporting income to investors: many use the *straight line* method for stockholder reporting (or "book" purposes), but they use the fastest rate permitted by law for tax purposes.

According to the straight line method used for stockholder reporting, you normally would take the cost of the asset, subtract its estimated salvage value, and divide the net amount by the asset's useful economic life. For an asset with a five-year life that costs $100,000 and has a $12,500 salvage value, the annual straight line depreciation charge is ($100,000 − $12,500)/5 = $17,500. Note, however, as we discuss later in this appendix, that salvage value is not considered for tax depreciation purposes.

For tax purposes, Congress changes the permissible tax depreciation methods from time to time. Prior to 1954, the straight line method was required for tax purposes, but in 1954 accelerated methods (double declining balance and sum-of-years'-digits) were permitted. Then, in 1981, the old accelerated methods were replaced by a simpler procedure known as the Accelerated Cost Recovery System (ACRS). The ACRS system was changed again in 1986 as a part of the Tax Reform Act, and it is now known as the Modified Accelerated Cost Recovery System (MACRS).

Tax Depreciation Life   For tax purposes, the *entire* cost of an asset is expensed over its depreciable life. Historically, an asset's depreciable life was determined by its estimated useful economic life; it was intended that an asset would be fully depreciated at approximately the same time that it reached the end of its useful economic life. However, MACRS totally abandoned that practice and set simple guidelines that created several classes of assets, each with a more-or-less arbitrarily prescribed life called a recovery period or class life. The MACRS class life bears only a rough relationship to the expected useful economic life.

A major effect of the MACRS system has been to shorten the depreciable lives of assets, thus giving businesses larger tax deductions and thereby increasing their cash flows available for reinvestment. Table 9A–1 describes the types of property that fit into the different class life groups, and Table 9A–2 sets forth the MACRS recovery allowances (depreciation rates) for selected classes of investment property.

Consider Table 9A–1 first. The first column gives the MACRS class life, while the second column describes the types of assets that fall into each category. Property classified with lives equal to or greater that 27.5 years (real estate) must be depreciated by the straight line method, but assets classified in the other categories can be depreciated either by the accelerated method using rates shown in Table 9A–2 or by an alternate straight line method.

As we saw earlier in the chapter, higher depreciation expenses result in lower taxes, hence higher cash flows. Therefore, because a firm has the choice of using the alternate straight line rates or the accelerated rates shown in Table 9A–2, most elect to use

TABLE 9A–1	Major Classes and Asset Lives for MACRS

CLASS	TYPE OF PROPERTY
3-year	Certain special manufacturing tools.
5-year	Automobiles, light-duty trucks, computers, and certain special manufacturing equipment.
7-year	Most industrial equipment, office furniture, and fixtures.
10-year	Certain longer-lived equipment, and many water vessels.
15-year	Certain land improvement, such as shrubbery, fences, and roads; service station buildings.
20-year	Farm buildings
27.5-year	Residential rental real property such as apartment buildings.
39–year	All nonresidential real property, including commercial and industrial buildings.

TABLE 9A–2	Recovery Allowance Percentages for Personal Property

	CLASS OF INVESTMENT			
OWNERSHIP YEAR	3-YEAR	5-YEAR	7-YEAR	10-YEAR
1	33%	20%	14%	10%
2	45	32	25	18
3	15	19	17	14
4	7	12	13	12
5		11	9	9
6		6	9	7
7			9	7
8			4	7
9				7
10				6
11				3
	100%	100%	100%	100%

NOTE: These recovery allowance percentages were taken from the Internal Revenue Service Web site, which is http://www.irs.ustreas.gov. The percentages are based on the 200 percent declining balance method prescribed by MACRS, with a switch to straight line depreciation at some point in the asset's life. For example, consider the five-year recovery allowance percentages. The straight line percentage would be 20 percent per year, so the 200 percent declining balance multiplier is $2.0(20\%) = 40\% = 0.4$. However, because the half-year convention applies, the MACRS percentage for Year 1 is 20 percent. For Year 2, 80 percent of the depreciable basis remains to be depreciated, so the recovery allowance percentage is $0.40(80\%) = 32\%$, and so on. Although the tax tables carry the allowance percentages to two decimal places, we have rounded to the nearest whole number for ease of illustration.

the accelerated rates. The yearly recovery allowance, or depreciation expense, is determined by multiplying each asset's *depreciable basis* by the applicable recovery percentage shown in Table 9A–2. Calculations are discussed in the following sections.

Half-Year Convention   Under MACRS, the assumption generally is made that property is placed in service in the middle of the first year. Thus, for three-year class life property, the recovery period begins in the middle of the year the asset is placed in service and ends three years later. The effect of the *half-year convention* is to extend the recovery period out one more year, so three-year class life property is depreciated over four calendar years, five-year property is depreciated over six calendar years, and so on. This convention is incorporated into Table 9A–2's recovery allowance percentages.[7]

Depreciable Basis   The *depreciable basis* is a critical element of MACRS because each year's allowance (depreciation expense) depends jointly on the asset's depreciable basis and its MACRS class life. The depreciable basis under MACRS is equal to the purchase price of the asset plus any shipping and installation costs. The basis is not adjusted for salvage value.

Sale of a Depreciable Asset   If a depreciable asset is sold, the sale price (salvage value) minus the then-existing undepreciated book value is added to operating income and taxed at the firm's marginal tax rate. For example, suppose a firm buys a five-year class life asset for $100,000 and sells it at the end of the fourth year for $25,000. The asset's book value is equal to $100,000(0.11 + 0.06) = $17,000. Therefore, $25,000 − $17,000 = $8,000 is added to the firm's operating income and is taxed.

Depreciation Illustration   Assume that Unilate Textiles buys a $150,000 machine that falls into the MACRS five-year class life asset and places it into service on March 15, 2000. Unilate must pay an additional $30,000 for delivery and installation. Salvage value is not considered, so the machine's depreciable basis is $180,000. (Delivery and installation charges are included in the depreciable basis rather than expensed in the year incurred.) Each year's recovery allowance (tax depreciation expense) is determined by multiplying the depreciable basis by the applicable recovery allowance percentage. Thus, the depreciation expense for 2000 is 0.20($180,000) = $36,000, and for 2001 it is 0.32($180,000) = $57,600. Similarly, the depreciation expense is $34,200 for 2002, $21,600 for 2003, $19,800 for 2004, and $10,800 for 2005. The total depreciation expense over the six-year recovery period is $180,000, which is equal to the depreciable basis of the machine.

As noted previously, most firms use straight line depreciation for stockholder reporting purposes but MACRS for tax purposes. *For these firms, for capital budgeting, MACRS should be used* because in capital budgeting, we are concerned with cash flows, not reported income.

Problem

depreciation effects   **9A–1** Christina Manning, great granddaughter of the founder of Manning Tile Products and current president of the company, believes in simple, conservative

---

[7]The half-year convention also applies if the straight line alternative is used, with half of one year's depreciation taken in the first year, a full year's depreciation taken in each of the remaining years of the asset's class life, and the remaining half-year's depreciation taken in the year following the end of the class life. You should recognize that virtually all companies have computerized depreciation systems. Each asset's depreciation pattern is programmed into the system at the time of its acquisition, and the computer aggregates the depreciation allowances for all assets when the accountants close the books and prepare the financial statements and tax returns.

accounting. In keeping with her philosophy, she has decreed that the company shall use alternative straight line depreciation, based on the MACRS class lives, for all newly acquired assets. Your boss, the financial vice president and the only nonfamily officer, has asked you to develop an exhibit that shows how much this policy costs the company in terms of market value. Ms. Manning is interested in increasing the value of the firm's stock because she fears a family stockholder revolt that might remove her from office. For your exhibit, assume that the company spends $100 million each year on new capital projects, that the projects have on average a ten-year class life, that the company has a nine percent cost of debt, and that its marginal tax rate is 34 percent. (*Hint:* Show how much the total NPV of the projects in an average year would increase if Manning used the standard MACRS recovery allowances.)

APPENDIX 9B

Comparing Projects with Unequal Lives

Two procedures used to compare capital projects with unequal lives are (1) the replacement chain (common life) method and (2) the equivalent annual annuity method.

Suppose the company we followed throughout the chapter, HEP, is planning to modernize its production facilities; and, as a part of the process, it is considering either a conveyor system (Project C) or some forklift trucks (Project F) for moving materials from the parts department to the main assembly line. Both the expected net cash flows and the NPVs for these two mutually exclusive alternatives are shown in Figure 9B–1.

We see that Project C, when discounted at a 15 percent required rate of return, has the higher NPV and thus appears to be the better project, in spite of the fact that Project F has the higher IRR.

FIGURE 9B–1   Expected Net Cash Flows for Project C and Project F

PROJECT C:

	0 k = 15% 1	2	3	4	5	6
Net $\widehat{CF}_t$	(40,000) 13,000	8,000	14,000	12,000	11,000	15,000

NPV_c at 15% = $5,374
IRR_c = 19.7%

PROJECT F:

	0 k = 15% 1	2	3
Net $\widehat{CF}_t$	(20,000) 7,000	13,000	12,000

NPV_F at 15% = $3,807
IRR_F = 25.2%

Replacement Chain (Common Life) Approach   Although the analysis in Figure 9B–1 suggests that Project C should be selected, this analysis is incomplete, and the decision to choose Project C actually is incorrect. If we choose Project F, we will have the opportunity to make a similar investment in three years, and if cost and revenue conditions continue at the Figure 9B–1 levels, this second investment will also be profitable. However, if we choose Project C, we will not have this second investment opportunity. Therefore, to make a proper comparison of Projects C and F, we could apply the **replacement chain (common life) approach;** that is, we could find the NPV of Project F over a six-year period and then compare this extended NPV with the NPV of Project C over the same six years.

The NPV for Project C as calculated in Figure 9B–1 is already over the six-year common life. For Project F, however, we must expand the analysis to include the replacement of F in Year 3, resulting in the following six-year cash flow time line[8]:

	0 k = 15% 1	2	3	4	5	6
	(20,000) 7,000	13,000	12,000			
			(20,000)	7,000	13,000	12,000
Net $\hat{CF}_t$	(20,000) 7,000	13,000	(8,000)	7,000	13,000	12,000

Extended life NPV_F at 15% = $6,310

Here we make the assumption that Project F's cost and annual cash inflows will not change if the project is repeated in three years, and that HEP's required rate of return will remain at 15 percent. Project F's extended NPV is $6,310. This is the value that should be compared with Project C's NPV, $5,374. Because Project F's "true" NPV is greater than that of Project C, Project F should be selected.

Equivalent Annual Annuity Approach   Although the preceding example illustrates why an extended analysis is necessary if we are comparing mutually exclusive projects with different lives, the arithmetic is generally more complex in practice. For example, one project might have a six-year life versus a ten-year life for the other. This would require a replacement chain analysis over 30 years, the lowest common denominator of the two lives. In such a situation, it is often simpler to use a second procedure, the **equivalent annual annuity (EAA) method,** which involves three steps:

1. Find each project's NPV over its initial life. In Figure 9B–1, we found NPV_C = $5,374 and NPVF = $3,807.
2. Find the constant annuity cash flow (the equivalent annual annuity [EAA]) that has the same present value as each project's NPV. For Project F, here is the time line:

_____

[8]We also could set up Project F's extended time line as follows:

1. The Stage 1 NPV is $3,807.
2. The Stage 2 NPV is also $3,807, but this value will not accrue until Year 3, so its value today, discounted at 15 percent, is $2,503.
3. The extended life NPV is thus $3,807 + $2,503 = $6,310.

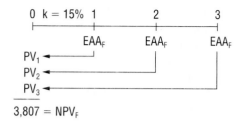

To find the value of EAA$_F$, with a financial calculator, enter $-3,807$ as the PV, I = k = 15, and N = 3, and solve for PMT. The answer, $1,667, represents the cash flow stream, which, when discounted back three years at 15 percent, has a present value equal to Project F's original NPV of $3,807. The payment figure we found, $1,667, is called the project's "equivalent annual annuity (EAA)." The EAA for Project C was found similarly to be $1,420. Thus, Project C has an NPV that is equivalent to an annuity of $1,420 per year, while Project F's NPV is equivalent to an annuity of $1,667.

3. Assuming that continuous replacements can and will be made each time a project's life ends, these EAAs will continue on out to infinity; that is, they will constitute perpetuities. Recognizing that the value of a perpetuity is V = PMT/k, we can find the net present values of the infinite EAAs of Projects C and F as follows:

$$\text{Infinite horizon NPV}_C = \$1,420/0.15 = \$ \ 9,467.$$

$$\text{Infinite horizon NPV}_F = \$1,667/0.15 = \$11,113.$$

In effect, the EAA method assumes that each project, if taken on, will be replaced each time it wears out and will provide cash flows equivalent to the calculated annuity value. The PV of this infinite annuity is then the infinite horizon NPV for the project. Because the infinite horizon NPV of F exceeds that of C, Project F should be accepted. Therefore, the EAA method leads to the same decision rule as the replacement chain method—accept Project F.

The EAA method often is easier to apply than the replacement chain method, but the replacement chain method is easier to explain to decision makers. Still, the two methods always lead to the same decision if consistent assumptions are used. Also, note that Step 3 of the EAA method is not really necessary—we could have stopped after Step 2 because the project with the higher EAA will always have the higher NPV over any common life *if the same required rate of return* is used for the projects.

When should we worry about unequal life analysis? As a general rule, the unequal life issue (1) does not arise for independent projects, but (2) can arise if mutually exclusive projects with significantly different lives are being evaluated. However, even for mutually exclusive projects, it is not always appropriate to extend the analysis to a common life. This should only be done if there is a high probability that the projects will actually be replicated beyond their initial lives.

We should note several potentially serious weaknesses inherent in this type of unequal life analysis: (1) If inflation is expected, then replacement equipment will have a higher price, and both sales prices and operating costs will probably change. Thus, the static conditions built into the analysis would be invalid. (2) Replacements that occur down the road would probably employ new technology, which in turn might change the cash flows. This factor is not built into either replacement chain analysis or the

EAA approach. (3) It is difficult enough to estimate the lives of most projects, so estimating the lives of a series of projects is often just a speculation. (4) If reasonably strong competition is present, the profitability of projects will be eroded over time, and that would reduce the need to extend the analysis beyond the projects' initial lives.

In view of these problems, no experienced financial analyst would be too concerned about comparing mutually exclusive projects with lives of, say, eight years and ten years. Given all the uncertainties in the estimation process, such projects, for all practical purposes, would be assumed to have the same life. Still, it is important to recognize that a problem does exist if mutually exclusive projects have substantially different lives. When we encounter such problems in practice, we build expected inflation or possible efficiency gains directly into the cash flow estimates and then use the replacement chain approach (but not the equivalent annual annuity method). The cash flow estimation is more complicated, but the concepts involved are exactly the same as in our example.

Problems

unequal lives **9B–1** Keenan Clothes Inc. is considering the replacement of its old, fully depreciated knitting machine. Two new models are available: Machine 190-3, which has a cost of $190,000, a three-year expected life, and after-tax cash flows (labor savings and depreciation) of $87,000 per year; and Machine 360-6, which has a cost of $360,000, a six-year life, and after-tax cash flows of $98,300 per year. Knitting machine prices are not expected to rise because inflation will be offset by cheaper components (microprocessors) used in the machines. Assume that required rate of return appropriate for evaluating the machines is 14 percent.

  a. Should the firm replace its old knitting machine, and, if so, which new machine should it use?

  b. Suppose the firm's basic patents will expire in nine years, and the company expects to go out of business at that time. Assume further that the firm depreciates its assets using the straight line method, that its marginal tax rate is 40 percent, and that the used machines can be sold at their book values. Under these circumstances, should the company replace the old machine? Explain.

unequal lives **9B–2** Zappe Airlines is considering two alternative planes. Plane A has an expected life of five years, will cost $100, and will produce net cash flows of $30 per year. Plane B has a life of ten years, will cost $132, and will produce net cash flows of $25 per year. Zappe plans to serve the route for ten years. Inflation in operating costs, airplane costs, and fares is expected to be zero, and the company's required rate of return is 12 percent. By how much would the value of the company increase if it accepted the better project (plane)? Assume all costs and cash flows are in millions of dollars.

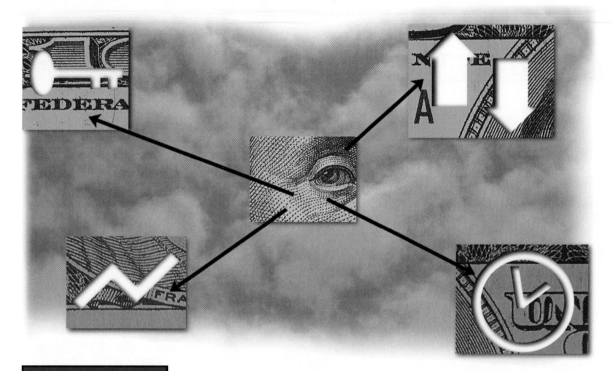

PART V

Cost of Capital, Leverage, and Dividend Policy

CHAPTER 10

The Cost of Capital

A MANAGERIAL PERSPECTIVE

A few years ago, Boomtown Inc., a small Nevada gaming company, announced its intention to purchase National Gaming, a New Jersey casino developer. According to Boomtown's management, the purpose of the acquisition was to improve liquidity and strengthen the company's financial position. But the stockholders balked at the deal, primarily because they believed the transaction would boost Boomtown's cost of capital (funds) to more than 20 percent. With such a high cost of capital, Boomtown would have difficulty finding growth opportunities (acceptable capital budgeting projects) in the future, and, quite possibly, the burden of the high financing costs eventually could force the firm into bankruptcy. Thus, Boomtown's stockholders wanted the deal blocked or restructured to reduce the impact on the company's cost of capital—the stockholders realized that a high cost of capital would be detrimental to their wealth position. And just as home buyers prefer to avoid high mortgage rates, companies should avoid using funds with high costs.

On the other side of the coin, Federated Department Stores was successful in its attempt to acquire R. H. Macy & Company in 1994. Federated, which had emerged from bankruptcy in 1992, was able to purchase Macy, which had been in bankruptcy since 1992, primarily because Citibank and Chemical Bank arranged a $2.8 billion loan package with a moderate interest rate.

The arrangement did not increase Federated's debt position much; thus, its cost of debt was not affected significantly—in fact, Federated was able to *save* about $40 million in interest with the bank arrangement compared to similar borrowing alternatives. The fact that the new capital needed for the acquisition was not expected to change Federated's existing cost of capital position was critical to the success of the deal.

Firms raise capital in the financial markets, where interest rates and other yields change continuously. We know that as interest rates change, so do the costs associated with the various types of capital. For instance, in 1994, interest rates increased dramatically while stock prices dropped, which meant that companies had to pay higher costs for using investors' funds. Since then, the trend has reversed—in 1999, for instance, interest rates were very low and the stock market reached record highs.

As you read this chapter, keep in mind that firms need funds provided by investors to take advantage of acceptable capital budgeting projects. The financial marketplace, which consists of investors like you, determines the "price" firms will have to pay for the funds they use. It is essential for us to be able to determine the "price," or the cost, of the capital used by a firm so that we know if the funds are being invested appropriately. For example, consider Boeing Company, an aircraft manufacturer, that recently revealed it has more

continues

than $2 billion invested in projects that do not generate returns at least equal to the firm's cost of capital (i.e., NPVs < 0). To improve its wealth position, Boeing plans to implement cost-cutting measures and to eliminate "wealth-destroying" projects. If successful, the price of Boeing's stock should break out of the $35 to $45 range in which it was selling at the beginning of 1999. ∎

It is vitally important that a firm knows how much it pays for the funds used to purchase assets. The average return required by the firm's investors determines how much must be paid to attract funds—it is the firm's average cost of funds, which more commonly is termed the *cost of capital.* The firm's cost of capital is very important because it represents the minimum rate of return that must be earned from investments, such as capital budgeting projects, to ensure the value of the firm does not decrease—the cost of capital is the firm's *required rate of return.* For example, if investors provide funds to a firm for an average cost of 15 percent, wealth will decrease if the funds are used to generate returns less than 15 percent, wealth will not change if exactly 15 percent is earned, and wealth will increase if returns greater than 15 percent can be generated.

In this chapter, we discuss the concept of cost of capital, how the average cost of capital is determined, and how the cost of capital is used in financial decision making. Most of the models and formulas used in this chapter are the same ones we developed in Chapter 7, where we described how stocks and bonds are valued by investors. How much it costs a firm for its funds is based on the return demanded by investors—if the return offered by the firm is not high enough, then investors will not provide sufficient funds. In other words, the rate of return an investor earns on a corporate security effectively is a cost to the firm of using those funds, so the same models are used by investors and by corporate treasurers to determine required rates of return.

Our first topic in this chapter is the logic of the weighted average cost of capital. Next, we consider the costs of the major types of capital, after which we see how the costs of the individual components of the capital structure are brought together to form a weighted average cost of capital.

The Logic of the Weighted Average Cost of Capital

It is possible to finance a firm entirely with equity funds by issuing only stock. In that case, the cost of capital used to analyze capital budgeting decisions should be the company's required return on equity. However, most firms raise a substantial portion of their funds as long-term debt, and some also use preferred stock. For these firms, their cost of capital must reflect the average cost of the various sources of long-term funds used, not just the firms' costs of equity.

Assume that Unilate Textiles has a ten percent cost of debt and a 13.7 percent cost of equity. Further, assume that Unilate has made the decision to finance next year's projects by selling debt only. The argument is sometimes made that the cost of capital for these projects is ten percent because only debt will be used to finance them. However, this position is incorrect. If Unilate finances a particular set of projects with debt, the firm will be using up some of its potential for obtaining new debt in the future. As expansion occurs in subsequent years, Unilate will at some point find it necessary to raise additional equity to prevent the debt ratio from becoming too large.

To illustrate, suppose Unilate borrows heavily at ten percent during 2001, using up its debt capacity in the process, to finance projects yielding 11.5 percent. In 2002 it has new projects available that yield 13 percent, well above the return on 2001 projects, but it cannot accept them because they would have to be financed with 13.7 percent equity money. To avoid this problem, Unilate should be viewed as an ongoing concern, and *the cost of capital used in capital budgeting should be calculated as a weighted average, or combination, of the various types of funds generally used, regardless of the specific financing used to fund a particular project.*

Self-Test Question

Why should the cost of capital used in capital budgeting be calculated as a weighted average of the various types of funds the firm generally uses, regardless of the specific financing used to fund a particular project?

Basic Definitions

CAPITAL COMPONENT
One of the types of capital used by firms to raise money.

The items on the right side of a firm's balance sheet—various types of debt, preferred stock, and common equity—are its **capital components.** Any increase in total assets must be financed by an increase in one or more of these capital components.

Capital is a necessary factor of production, and, like any other factor, it has a cost. The cost of each component is called the *component cost* of that particular type of capital; for example, if Unilate can borrow money at ten percent, its component cost of debt is ten percent.[1] Throughout this chapter we concentrate on debt, preferred stock, retained earnings, and new issues of common stock, which are the four major capital structure components. We will use the following symbols to designate specific component costs of capital:

k_d = Interest rate on the firm's debt = before-tax component cost of debt. For Unilate, k_d = 10.0%.

k_{dT} = $k_d(1 - T)$ = After-tax component cost of debt, where T is the firm's marginal tax rate. k_{dT} is the debt cost used to calculate the weighted average cost of capital. For Unilate, T = 40%, so $k_{dT} = k_d(1 - T) =$ 10.0%(1 − 0.4) = 10.0%(0.6) = 6.0%.

k_{ps} = Component cost of preferred stock. Unilate has no preferred stock at this time, but, as new funds are raised, the company plans to issue preferred stock. The cost of preferred stock, k_{ps}, will be 10.3 percent.

k_s = Component cost of retained earnings (or internal equity). It is identical to the k_s developed in Chapters 5 and 7 and defined there as the required rate of return on common stock. As we will see shortly, for Unilate, $k_s \approx 13.7\%$.

---

[1]We will see shortly that there is both a before-tax and an after-tax cost of debt; for now it is sufficient to know that ten percent is the before-tax component cost of debt.

k_e = Component cost of external equity obtained by issuing new common stock as opposed to retaining earnings. As we shall see, it is necessary to distinguish between common equity needs that can be satisfied by retained earnings and the common equity needs that are satisfied by selling new stock. This is why we distinguish between internal and external equity, k_s and k_e. Further, k_e is always greater than k_s. For Unilate, $k_e \approx 14.3\%$.

WACC = The weighted average cost of capital. In the future, when Unilate needs *new* capital to finance asset expansion, it will raise part of the new funds as debt, part as preferred stock, and part as common equity (with common equity coming either from retained earnings or from the issuance of new common stock).[2] We will calculate WACC for Unilate Textiles shortly.

CAPITAL STRUCTURE
The combination or mix of different types of capital used by a firm.

AFTER-TAX COST OF DEBT, k_{dT}
The relevant cost of new debt, taking into account the tax deductibility of interest; used to calculate the WACC.

These definitions and concepts are explained in detail in the remainder of the chapter, where we develop a marginal cost of capital (MCC) schedule that can be used in capital budgeting. Later, in the next chapter, we will extend the analysis to determine the mix of types of capital, which is termed the **capital structure,** that will minimize the firm's cost of capital and thereby maximize its value.

Self-Test Question

Identify the firm's four major capital structure components, and give their respective component cost symbols.

Cost of Debt, k_{dT}

The **after-tax cost of debt, k_{dT},** is the interest rate on debt, k_d, less the tax saving that results because interest is deductible. This is the same as k_d multiplied by $(1 - T)$, where T is the firm's marginal tax rate:

$$10\text{–}1$$

$$\text{After-tax component cost of debt} = k_{dT} = \left(\begin{array}{c}\text{Bondholders' required}\\\text{rate of return}\end{array}\right) - \left(\begin{array}{c}\text{Tax}\\\text{savings}\end{array}\right)$$
$$= k_d - k_d \times T$$
$$= k_d(1 - T)$$

In effect, the government pays part of the cost of debt because interest is deductible. Therefore, if Unilate can borrow at an interest rate of ten percent, and if it has a marginal tax rate of 40 percent, then its after-tax cost of debt is six percent:

[2]Firms try to keep their debt, preferred stock, and common equity in optimal proportions; we will learn how they establish these proportions in the next chapter. However, firms do not try to maintain any proportional relationship between the common stock and retained earnings accounts as shown on the balance sheet—for capital structure purposes, common equity is common equity, whether it comes from selling new common stock or from retaining earnings.

$$k_{dT} = k_d(1 - T) = 10.0\%(1.0 - 0.4)$$
$$= 10.0\%(0.6)$$
$$= 6.0\%$$

We use the after-tax cost of debt because the value of the firm's stock, which we want to maximize, depends on *after-tax* cash flows. Because interest is a deductible expense, it produces tax savings that reduce the net cost of debt, making the after-tax cost of debt less than the before-tax cost. We are concerned with after-tax cash flows, so after-tax rates of return are appropriate.[3]

Note that the cost of debt is the interest rate on *new* debt, not that on already outstanding debt; in other words, we are interested in the *marginal* cost of debt. Our primary concern with the cost of capital is to use it for capital budgeting decisions—for example, a decision about whether to obtain the capital needed to acquire a new machine tool. The rate at which the firm has borrowed in the past is a sunk cost, and it is irrelevant for cost of capital purposes.

In Chapter 7, we solved the following equation to find k_d, the rate of return, or yield to maturity, for a bond:

$$\text{Bond value} = \sum_{t=1}^{N} \frac{\text{INT}}{(1 + k_d)^t} + \frac{M}{(1 + k_d)^N}$$

where INT is the dollar coupon interest paid per period, M is the face value repaid at maturity, and N is the number of interest payments remaining until maturity.

Assume that Unilate is going to issue a new nine percent coupon bond in a few days. The bond has face value of $1,000, a 20-year life, and interest is paid annually. If the market price of similar risk bonds is $915, what is Unilate's k_d? The solution is set up as follows:

$$\$915 = \frac{\$90}{(1 + k_d)^1} + \frac{\$90}{(1 + k_d)^2} + \ldots + \frac{\$1,090}{(1 + k_d)^{20}}$$

Whether you use the trial-and-error method, the time value of money functions on your calculator, or the approximation equation given in Chapter 7, you should find k_d is ten percent, which is the before-tax cost of debt for this bond.[4] Unilate's marginal tax rate is 40 percent, so the after-tax cost of debt, k_{dT}, is $6.0\% = 10.0\%(1 - 0.40)$.

---

[3]The tax rate is *zero* for a firm with losses. Therefore, for a company that does not pay taxes, the cost of debt is not reduced—that is, in Equation 10–1 the tax rate equals zero, so the after-tax cost of debt is equal to the before-tax interest rate.

[4]It should also be noted that we have ignored flotation costs (the costs incurred for new issuances) on debt because nearly all debt issued by small and medium-sized firms and by many large firms is privately placed and hence has no flotation costs. However, if bonds are publicly placed and do involve flotation costs, the solution value of k_d in this formula is used as the before-tax cost of debt:

$$V_d(1 - F) = \sum_{t=1}^{N} \frac{\text{INT}}{(1 + k_d)^t} + \frac{M}{(1 + k_d)^N}$$

Here F is the percentage amount (in decimal form) of the bond flotation, or issuing, cost; N is the number of periods to maturity; INT is the dollars of interest per period; M is the maturity value of the bond; and k_d is the cost of debt adjusted to reflect flotation costs. If we assume that the bond in the example calls for annual payments, that it has a 20-year maturity, and that F = 2%, then the flotation-adjusted, before-tax cost of debt is 10.23 percent versus ten percent before the flotation adjustment.

Self-Test Questions

Why is the after-tax cost of debt rather than the before-tax cost used to calculate the weighted average cost of capital?

Is the relevant cost of debt the interest rate on already outstanding debt or that on new debt? Why?

Cost of Preferred Stock, k$_{ps}$

In Chapter 7, we found that the dividend associated with preferred stock is constant and that preferred stock has no stated maturity. Thus, a preferred dividend, which we designate D$_{ps}$, represents a perpetuity, and the component **cost of preferred stock, k$_{ps}$**, is the preferred dividend, D$_{ps}$, divided by the net issuing price, NP, or the price the firm receives after deducting the costs of issuing the stock, which are called *flotation costs:*

$$\boxed{\;10\text{–}2\;}\qquad \begin{array}{c}\text{Component cost of} \\ \text{preferred stock}\end{array} = k_{ps} = \frac{D_{ps}}{NP} = \frac{D_{ps}}{P_0 - \text{Flotation costs}}$$

COST OF PREFERRED STOCK, k$_{ps}$
The rate of return investors require on the firm's preferred stock. k$_{ps}$ is calculated as the preferred dividend, D$_{ps}$, divided by the net issuing price, NP.

For example, in the future, Unilate is going to issue preferred stock that pays a $10 dividend per share and sells for $100 per share in the market. It will cost three percent, or $3 per share, to issue the new preferred stock, so Unilate will net $97 per share. Therefore, Unilate's cost of preferred stock is 10.3 percent:

$$k_{ps} = \frac{\$10}{\$97}$$
$$= 0.103 = 10.3\%$$

No tax adjustments are made when calculating k$_{ps}$ because preferred dividends, unlike interest expense on debt, are not tax deductible, so there are no tax savings associated with the use of preferred stock.

Self-Test Questions

Does the component cost of preferred stock include or exclude flotation costs? Explain.

Is a tax adjustment made to the cost of preferred stock? Why or why not?

Cost of Retained Earnings, k$_s$

COST OF RETAINED EARNINGS, k$_s$
The rate of return required by stockholders on a firm's existing common stock.

The costs of debt and preferred stock are based on the returns investors require on these securities. Similarly, the **cost of retained earnings, k$_s$**, is the rate of return stockholders require on equity capital the firm obtains by retaining earnings that otherwise could be distributed to common stockholders as dividends.[5]

---

[5]The term *retained earnings* can be interpreted to mean either the balance sheet item "retained earnings," consisting of all the earnings retained in the business throughout its history, or the income statement item "additions to retained earnings." The income statement item is used in this chapter; for our purpose, *retained earnings* refers to that part of current earnings not paid out in dividends and hence available for reinvestment in the business this year.

TABLE 10–1	WACC and Break Points for Unilate's MCC Schedule

I. Break Points

1. $BP_{Retained\ earnings} = \$30,500,000/0.50 = \$61,000,000$
2. $\qquad BP_{Debt} = 54,000,000/0.45 = \$120,000,000$

II. Weighted Average Cost of Capital (WACC)

1. New Capital Needs: $0–$61,000,000

	BREAKDOWN OF FUNDS AT $61,000,000	WEIGHT	×	AFTER-TAX COMPONENT COST	=	WACC
Debt (10%)	$27,450,000	0.45		6.0%		2.7%
Preferred stock	3,050,000	0.05		10.3		0.5
Common equity (Retained earnings)	30,500,000	0.50		13.7		6.9
	$61,000,000	1.00				$WACC_1 = 10.1\%$

2. New Capital Needs: $61,000,001–$120,000,000

	BREAKDOWN OF FUNDS AT $120,000,000	WEIGHT	×	AFTER-TAX COMPONENT COST	=	WACC
Debt (10%)	$ 54,000,000	0.45		6.0%		2.7%
Preferred stock	6,000,000	0.05		10.3		0.5
Common equity (New stock issue)	$ 60,000,000	0.50		14.3		7.2
	$120,000,000	1.00				$WACC_2 = 10.4\%$

3. New Capital Needs: Above $120,000,000

	BREAKDOWN OF FUNDS AT $130,000,000	WEIGHT	×	AFTER-TAX COMPONENT COST	=	WACC
Debt (12%)	$ 58,000,000	0.45		7.2%		3.2%
Preferred stock	6,600,000	0.05		10.3		0.5
Common equity (New stock issue)	65,000,000	0.50		14.3		7.2
	$130,000,000	1.00				$WACC_3 = 10.9\%$

debt at a ten percent interest rate, with any additional debt costing 12 percent. This would result in a second break point in the MCC schedule, at the point where the $54 million of ten percent debt is exhausted. At what amount of total financing would the ten percent debt be used up? We know that this total financing will amount to $54 million of debt plus some amount of preferred stock and common equity. If we let BP_{Debt} represent the total financing at this second break point, then we know that 45 percent of BP_{Debt} will be debt, so

$$0.45(BP_{Debt}) = \$54\ million$$

Solving for BP$_{\text{Debt}}$, we have

$$BP_{\text{debt}} = \frac{\text{Maximum amount of 10\% debt}}{\text{Proportion of debt}}$$

$$= \frac{\$54 \text{ million}}{0.45} = \$120 \text{ million}$$

Thus, there will be another break in the MCC schedule after Unilate has raised a total of $120 million, and this second break results from an increase in the cost of debt. The higher after-tax cost of debt (7.2 percent versus 6.0 percent) will result in a higher WACC. For example, if Unilate needs $130 million for capital budgeting projects, the WACC would be 10.9 percent:

CAPITAL SOURCE	WEIGHT	AMOUNT IN MILLIONS	AFTER-TAX COMPONENT COST	WACC
Debt	0.45	$ 58.50	7.2%	3.2%
Preferred stock	0.05	6.50	10.3	0.5
Common equity	0.50	65.00	14.3	7.2
	1.00	$130.00		WACC$_3$ = 10.9%

In other words, the next dollar beyond $120 million will consist of 45¢ of 12 percent debt (7.2 percent after taxes), 5¢ of 10.3 percent preferred stock, and 50¢ of new common stock at a cost of 14.3 percent (retained earnings were used up much earlier), and this marginal dollar will have a cost of WACC$_3$ = 10.9%.

The effect of this second WACC increase is shown in Figure 10–3. Now there are two break points, one caused by using up all the retained earnings and the other by using up all the ten percent debt. With the two breaks, there are three different WACCs: WACC$_1$ = 10.1% for the first $61 million of new capital; WACC$_2$ = 10.3% in the interval between $61 million and $120 million; and WACC$_3$ = 10.9% for all new capital beyond $120 million.[10]

There could, of course, still be more break points; they would occur if the cost of debt continued to increase with more debt, if the cost of preferred stock increased at some level(s), or if the cost of common equity rose as more new common stock is

---

[10]When we use the term *weighted average cost of capital*, we are referring to the WACC, which is the cost of $1 raised partly as debt, partly as preferred stock, and partly as common equity. We could also calculate the average cost of all the capital the firm raised during a given year. For example, if Unilate raised $150 million, the first $61 million would have a cost of 10.1 percent, the next $59 million would cost 10.4 percent, and the last $30 million would cost 10.9 percent. The entire $150 million would have an average cost of

$$\left(\frac{\$61}{\$150}\right) \times (10.1\%) + \left(\frac{\$59}{\$150}\right) \times (10.4\%) + \left(\frac{\$30}{\$150}\right) \times (10.9\%) = 10.4\%$$

In general, this particular cost of capital should not be used for financial decisions—it usually has no relevance in finance. The only exception to this rule occurs when the firm is considering a very large asset that must be accepted in total or else rejected, and the capital required for it includes capital with different WACCs. For example, if Unilate were considering one $150 million project, that project should be evaluated with a 10.4 percent cost.

FIGURE 10–3	Marginal Cost of Capital Schedule for Unilate Textiles Using Retained Earnings, New Common Stock, and Higher-Cost Debt

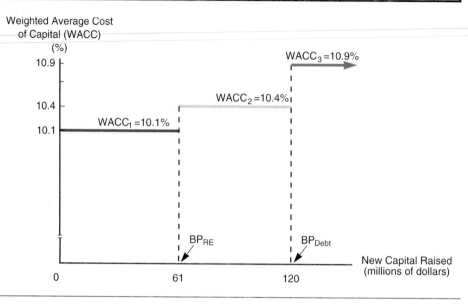

sold.[11] In general, a break point will occur whenever the cost of one of the capital components increases, and the break point can be determined by the following equation:

10–9

$$\text{Break point} = \frac{\text{Total amount of lower cost capital of a given type}}{\text{Proportion of this type of capital in the capital structure}}$$

We see, then, that numerous break points can occur. At the limit, we can even think of an MCC schedule with so many break points that it rises almost continuously beyond some given level of new financing. Such an MCC schedule is shown in Figure 10–4.

The easiest sequence for calculating MCC schedules is as follows:

1. Use Equation 10–9 to determine each point at which a break occurs. A break will occur any time the cost of one of the capital components rises. (It is possi-

---

[11]The first break point is not necessarily the point at which retained earnings are used up; it is possible for low-cost debt to be exhausted *before* retained earnings have been used up. For example, if Unilate had available only $22.5 million of ten percent debt, BP_{Debt} would occur at $50 million:

$$BP_{Debt} = \frac{\$22.5 \text{ million}}{0.45} = \$50 \text{ million}$$

Thus, the break point for debt would occur before the break point for retained earnings, which occurs at $61 million.

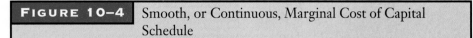

FIGURE 10–4 Smooth, or Continuous, Marginal Cost of Capital Schedule

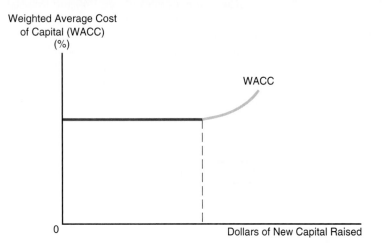

ble, however, that two capital components could both increase at the same point.) After determining the exact break points, make a list of them.

2. Determine the cost of capital for each component in the intervals between breaks.

3. Calculate the weighted averages of these component costs to obtain the WACCs in each interval, as we did in Table 10–1. The WACC is constant within each interval, but it rises at each break point.

Notice that if there are n separate breaks, there will be n + 1 different WACCs. For example, in Figure 10–3 we see two breaks and three different WACCs. Also, we should note again that a different MCC schedule would result if a different capital structure is used.

Self-Test Questions

What are break points, and why do they occur in MCC schedules? Write out and explain the equation for determining break points.

How is an MCC schedule constructed? If there are n breaks in the MCC schedule, how many different WACCs are there? Why?

Combining the MCC and Investment Opportunity Schedules

Now that we have calculated the MCC schedule, we can use it to develop a discount rate for use in the capital budgeting process—that is, *we can use the MCC schedule to find the cost of capital for determining projects' net present values (NPVs)* as discussed in Chapter 8.

To understand how the MCC schedule is used in capital budgeting, assume that Unilate Textiles has three financial executives: a financial vice president (VP), a treasurer, and a director of capital budgeting (DCB). The financial VP asks the treasurer to develop the firm's MCC schedule, and the treasurer produces the schedule shown earlier in Figure 10–3. At the same time, the financial VP asks the DCB to draw up a list of all projects that are potentially acceptable. The list shows each project's cost, projected annual net cash inflows, life, and internal rate of return (IRR). These data are presented at the bottom of Figure 10–5. For example, Project A has a cost of $39 million, it is expected to produce inflows of $9 million per year for six years, and, therefore, it has an IRR of 10.2 percent. Similarly, Project C has a cost of $36 million, it is expected to produce inflows of $10 million per year for five years, and thus it has an IRR of 12.1 percent. (NPVs cannot be shown yet because we do not yet know the marginal cost of capital.) For simplicity, we assume now that all projects are independent

FIGURE 10–5   Combining the MCC and IOS Schedules to Determine the Optimal Capital Budget

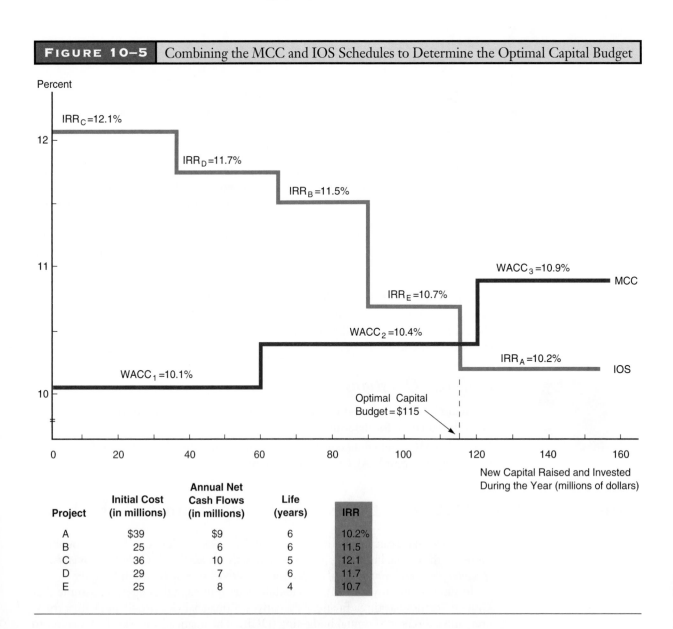

Project	Initial Cost (in millions)	Annual Net Cash Flows (in millions)	Life (years)	IRR
A	$39	$9	6	10.2%
B	25	6	6	11.5
C	36	10	5	12.1
D	29	7	6	11.7
E	25	8	4	10.7

as opposed to mutually exclusive, that they are equally risky, and that their risks are all equal to those of the firm's average existing assets.

The DCB then plots the IRR data shown at the bottom of Figure 10–5 as the **investment opportunity schedule (IOS)** shown in the graph. The IOS schedule shows, in rank order, how much money Unilate can invest at different rates of return (IRRs). Figure 10–5 also shows Unilate's MCC schedule as it was developed by the treasurer and plotted in Figure 10–3. Now consider Project C: its IRR is 12.1 percent, and it can be financed with capital that costs only 10.1 percent; consequently, it should be accepted. Recall from Chapter 8 that if a project's IRR exceeds its cost of capital, its NPV also will be positive; therefore, Project C must also be acceptable by the NPV criterion. Projects B, D, and E can be analyzed similarly; they are all acceptable because IRR > MCC = WACC and hence NPV > 0. Project A, on the other hand, should be rejected because IRR_A < MCC; hence, NPV_A < 0.

People sometimes ask this question: "If we took Project A first, it would be acceptable because its 10.2 percent return would exceed the 10.1 percent cost of money used to finance it. Why couldn't we do this?" The answer is that we are seeking, in effect, to maximize the excess of *returns over costs*, or the area that is above the WACC but below the IOS. We accomplish this by graphing (and accepting) the most profitable projects first.

Another question that sometimes arises is this: What would happen if the MCC cut through one of the projects? For example, suppose the second break point in the MCC schedule had occurred at $100 million rather than at $120 million, causing the MCC schedule to cut through Project E. Should we then accept Project E? If Project E could be accepted in part, we would take on only part of it. Otherwise, the answer would be determined by (1) finding the average cost of the funds needed to finance Project E (some of the money would cost 10.4 percent and some 10.9 percent) and (2) comparing the average cost of this money with the 10.7 percent return on the project. We should accept Project E if its return exceeds the average cost of the $25 million needed to finance it.

The preceding analysis as summarized in Figure 10–5 reveals a very important point: *The cost of capital used in the capital budgeting process as discussed in Chapters 8 and 9 actually is determined at the intersection of the IOS and MCC schedules. If the cost of capital at the intersection ($WACC_2$ = 10.4% in Figure 10–5) is used, then the firm will make correct accept/reject decisions, and its level of financing and investment will be optimal. If it uses any other rate, its capital budget will not be optimal.*

The intersection WACC as determined in Figure 10–5 should be used to find the NPVs of new projects that are about as risky as the firm's existing assets, but this corporate cost of capital should be adjusted up or down to find NPVs for projects with higher or lower risk than the average project. This point was discussed in Chapter 9 in connection with the Home Energy Products appliance control computer example.

INVESTMENT
OPPORTUNITY
SCHEDULE (IOS)

A graph of the firm's investment opportunities ranked in order of the projects' internal rates of return.

Self-Test Questions

Differentiate between the MCC and IOS schedules.

How is the corporate cost of capital, which is used to evaluate average risk projects to determine their NPVs, found?

As a general rule, should a firm's cost of capital as determined in this chapter be used to evaluate all of its capital budgeting projects? Explain.

Summary

This chapter showed how (1) the weighted average cost of capital (WACC) is computed for a firm, and (2) the MCC schedule is developed for use in the capital budgeting process. The key concepts that were covered are listed here:

- The cost of capital to be used in capital budgeting decisions is the **weighted average** of the various types of capital the firm uses, typically debt, preferred stock, and common equity.
- The **component cost of debt** is the after-tax cost of new debt. It is found by multiplying the cost of new debt by $(1 - T)$, where T is the firm's marginal tax rate: $k_{dT} = k_d(1 - T)$.
- The **component cost of preferred stock** is calculated as the preferred dividend divided by the net issuing price, where the net issuing price is the price the firm receives after deducting flotation costs: $k_{ps} = D_{ps}/[P(1 - F)] = D_{ps}/NP$.
- The **cost of common equity** is the cost of retained earnings as long as the firm has retained earnings, but the cost of equity becomes the cost of new common stock once the firm has exhausted its retained earnings.
- The **cost of retained earnings** is the rate of return required by stockholders on the firm's common stock, and it can be estimated using one of three methods: (1) the **CAPM approach**, (2) the **bond-yield-plus-risk-premium approach**, and (3) the **dividend-yield-plus-growth-rate**, or **DCF, approach.**
- To use the **CAPM approach**, (1) estimate the firm's beta, (2) multiply this beta by the market risk premium to determine the firm's risk premium, and (3) add the firm's risk premium to the risk-free rate to obtain the firm's cost of retained earnings: $k_s = k_{RF} + (k_M - k_{RF})\beta_s$.
- The **bond-yield-plus-risk-premium approach** calls for adding a risk premium of from 3 to 5 percentage points to the firm's interest rate on long-term debt: $k_s = k_d + RP$.
- To use the **discounted cash flow (DCF) approach** when constant growth exists, add the firm's expected growth rate to its expected dividend yield: $k_s = \hat{D}_1/P_0 + g$.
- The **cost of new common equity** is higher than the cost of retained earnings because the firm incurs **flotation expenses** to sell stock. To find the cost of new common equity, the stock price is first reduced by the flotation expense, then the dividend yield is calculated on the basis of the price the firm actually will receive, and finally the expected growth rate is added to this **adjusted dividend yield:** $k_e = \hat{D}_1/[P_0(1 - F)] + g$.
- Each firm has an **optimal capital structure,** defined as that mix of debt, preferred stock, and common equity that *minimizes* its **weighted average cost of capital (WACC):**

$$WACC = w_d k_{dT} + w_{ps} k_{ps} + w_e(k_s \text{ or } k_e)$$

- The **marginal cost of capital (MCC)** is defined as the cost of the last dollar of new capital that the firm raises. The MCC increases as the firm raises more and more capital during a given period. A graph of the MCC plotted against dollars raised is the **MCC schedule.**
- A **break point** occurs in the MCC schedule each time the cost of one of the capital components increases.

- The **investment opportunity schedule (IOS)** is a graph of the firm's investment opportunities, ranked in order of their internal rates of return (IRR).
- The MCC schedule is combined with the IOS schedule, and the intersection defines the **corporate cost of capital,** which is used to evaluate average-risk capital budgeting projects.
- The three equity cost estimation techniques discussed in this chapter have **serious limitations when applied to small firms,** thus increasing the need for the small-business manager to use judgment.
- The average flotation cost for small firms is much greater than for large firms. As a result, a small firm would have to earn considerably more on the same project than a large firm. Also, the capital market demands higher returns on stocks of small firms than on otherwise similar stocks of large firms—this is called the **small-firm effect.**

The concepts developed in this chapter are extended in Chapter 11, where we consider the effect of the capital structure on the cost of capital.

✳ SMALL BUSINESS

The Cost of Equity Capital for Small Firms

The three equity cost estimating techniques discussed in this chapter (DCF, bond-yield-plus-risk-premium, and CAPM) have serious limitations when applied to small firms. First, many small, rapidly growing firms do not now, and will not in the foreseeable future, pay dividends. For firms like this, the constant growth model simply is not applicable. In fact, it is difficult to imagine any dividend model that would be of practical benefit for such firms because of the difficulty of estimating dividends and growth rates. Second, the bond-yield-plus-risk-premium technique cannot be used for firms that do not have bond issues outstanding, and many small firms do not issue bonds. Third, the CAPM often is not usable because the stocks of many small firms are not traded publicly, so we cannot calculate those firms' betas. For the privately owned firm, we might use the "pure play" CAPM technique, which involves finding a firm in the same line of business with publicly held stock, estimating that firm's beta, and then using this second firm's beta as a replacement for that of the small business in question. But these "large" firms' betas would have to be subjectively modified to reflect their larger sizes and more established positions, as well as to take account of the differences in the nature of their

products and their capital structures as compared to the smaller firms.

Flotation Costs for Small Issues. We know that when external equity capital is raised, flotation costs increase the cost of equity capital beyond what it would be for internal funds. These external flotation costs are especially significant for smaller firms, and they can substantially affect capital budgeting decisions involving external equity funds. According to the latest Securities and Exchange Commission data, the average flotation costs of small common stock offerings generally are four to five times greater than those of large firms (assets greater than $50 million). Thus, small firms are at a substantial disadvantage because of the effects of flotation costs.

The Small-Firm Effect. A number of researchers have observed that portfolios of small-firm stocks have earned consistently higher average returns than those of large-firm stocks; this is called the "small-firm effect." On the surface, it would seem to be advantageous to the small firm to provide average returns in the stock market that are higher than those of large firms. In reality, this is bad news for the small firm—what the small-firm effect means is that the capital market demands higher returns on stocks of

continues

small firms than on otherwise similar stocks of large firms. Therefore, the basic cost of equity capital is higher for small firms. This compounds the high flotation cost problem noted earlier.

It might be argued that stocks of small firms are riskier than those of large ones and that this accounts for the differences in returns. However, the larger returns for small firms remain larger even after adjusting for the effects of their higher risks. Higher returns reflect higher costs of capital, so we must conclude that small firms do have higher capital costs than otherwise similar large firms. The manager of a small firm should take this factor into account when estimating the firm's cost of equity capital. In general, the cost of equity capital appears to be about four percentage points higher for small firms than for large, New York Stock Exchange firms with similar risk characteristics.

Questions

10–1 In what sense does the marginal cost of capital schedule represent a series of average costs?

10–2 The financial manager of a large national firm was overheard making the following statement: "We try to use as much retained earnings as possible for capital budgeting purposes because there is no *explicit* cost to these funds, and this allows us to invest in relatively low yielding projects that would not be feasible if we had to issue new common stock. We actually use retained earnings to invest in projects with yields below the coupon rate on our bonds." Comment on the validity of this statement.

10–3 How would each of the following affect a firm's cost of debt, k_{dT}; its cost of equity, k_s; and its weighted average cost of capital, WACC? Indicate by a plus (+), a minus (−), or a zero (0) if the factor would raise, lower, or have an indeterminate effect on the item in question. Assume other things are held constant. Be prepared to justify your answer, but recognize that some of the parts probably have no single correct answer; these questions are designed to stimulate thought and discussion.

	EFFECT ON		
	k_{dT}	k_s	WACC
a. The corporate tax rate is lowered.	____	____	____
b. The Federal Reserve tightens credit.	____	____	____
c. The firm uses more debt—that is, it increases its debt/assets ratio.	____	____	____
d. The dividend payout ratio (% of earnings paid as dividends) is increased.	____	____	____
e. The firm doubles the amount of capital it raises during the year.	____	____	____
f. The firm expands into a risky new area.	____	____	____
g. The firm merges with another firm whose earnings are countercyclical both to those of the first firm and to the stock market.	____	____	____
h. The stock market falls drastically, and the firm's stock falls along with the rest.	____	____	____

    i. Investors become more risk averse.   ____   ____   ____
    j. The firm is an electric utility with a large
        investment in nuclear plants. Several states
        propose a ban on nuclear power generation. ____   ____   ____

10–4 Suppose a firm estimates its MCC and IOS schedules for the coming year and finds that they intersect at the point ten percent, $10 million. What cost of capital should be used to evaluate average projects, high-risk projects, and low-risk projects?

Self-Test Problems

(Solutions appear in Appendix B)

key terms   **ST–1** Define each of the following terms:
    a. After-tax cost of debt, k_{dT}; capital component cost
    b. Cost of preferred stock, k_{ps}
    c. Cost of retained earnings, k_s
    d. Cost of new common equity, k_e
    e. Flotation cost, F
    f. Target capital structure; capital structure components
    g. Weighted average cost of capital, WACC
    h. Marginal cost of capital, MCC
    i. Marginal cost of capital schedule; break point, BP
    j. Investment opportunity schedule, IOS

optimal capital budget   **ST–2** Lancaster Engineering Inc. (LEI) has the following capital structure, which it considers to be optimal:

Debt	25%
Preferred stock	15
Common equity	60
	100%

LEI's expected net income this year is $34,285.72; its established dividend payout ratio is 30 percent; its marginal tax rate is 40 percent; and investors expect earnings and dividends to grow at a constant rate of nine percent in the future. LEI paid a dividend of $3.60 per share last year, and its stock currently sells at a price of $60 per share.

LEI can obtain new capital in the following ways:

Common: New common stock has a flotation cost of ten percent for up to $12,000 of new stock and 20 percent for all common stock over $12,000.

Preferred: New preferred stock with a dividend of $11 can be sold to the public at a price of $100 per share. However, flotation costs of $5 per share will be incurred for up to $7,500 of preferred stock, and flotation costs will rise to $10 per share, or ten percent, on all preferred stock over $7,500.

Debt: Up to $5,000 of debt can be sold at an interest rate of 12 percent; debt in the range of $5,001 to $10,000 must carry an interest rate of 14 percent; and all debt over $10,000 will have an interest rate of 16 percent.

LEI has the following independent investment opportunities:

Project	Cost at $t = 0$	Annual Net Cash Flow	Project Life	IRR
A	$10,000	$2,191.20	7 years	12.0%
B	10,000	3,154.42	5	17.4
C	10,000	2,170.18	8	14.2
D	20,000	3,789.48	10	13.7
E	20,000	5,427.84	6	?

a. Find the break points in the MCC schedule.
b. Determine the cost of each capital structure component.
c. Calculate the weighted average cost of capital in the interval between each break in the MCC schedule.
d. Calculate the IRR for Project E.
e. Construct a graph showing the MCC and IOS schedules.
f. Which projects should LEI accept?

Problems

cost of retained earnings   **10–1** The earnings, dividends, and stock price of Talukdar Technologies Inc. are expected to grow at seven percent per year in the future. Talukdar's common stock sells for $23 per share, its last dividend was $2.00, and the company will pay a dividend of $2.14 at the end of the current year.
  a. Using the discounted cash flow approach, what is its cost of retained earnings?
  b. If the firm's beta is 1.6, the risk-free rate is nine percent, and the average return on the market is 13 percent, what will be the firm's cost of equity using the CAPM approach?
  c. If the firm's bonds earn a return of 12 percent, what will k_s be using the bond-yield-plus-risk-premium approach? (*Hint:* Use the midpoint of the risk premium range discussed in the text.)
  d. Based on the results of parts a through c, what would you estimate Talukdar's cost of retained earnings to be?

cost of retained earnings   **10–2** The Shrieves Company's EPS was $6.50 in 1999 and $4.42 in 1994. The company pays out 40 percent of its earnings as dividends, and the stock sells for $36.
  a. Calculate the past growth rate in earnings. (*Hint:* This is a five-year growth period.)
  b. Calculate the *next* expected dividend per share, $\hat{D}_1$. [$D_0 = 0.4(\$6.50) = \$2.60$.] Assume that the past growth rate will continue.
  c. What is the cost of retained earnings, k_s, for the Shrieves Company?

break point calculations   **10–3** The Simmons Company expects earnings of $30 million next year. Its dividend payout ratio is 40 percent, and its debt/assets ratio is 60 percent. Simmons uses no preferred stock.
  a. What amount of retained earnings does Simmons expect next year?
  b. At what amount of financing will there be a break point in the MCC schedule?
  c. If Simmons can borrow $12 million at an interest rate of 11 percent, another $12 million at a rate of 12 percent, and any additional debt at a rate of 13 percent, at what points will rising debt costs cause breaks in the MCC schedule?

calculation of g and EPS **10–4** Rowell Products' stock is currently selling for $60 a share. The firm is expected to earn $5.40 per share this year and to pay a year-end dividend of $3.60.

    a. If investors require a nine percent return, what rate of growth must be expected for Rowell?

    b. If Rowell reinvests retained earnings in projects whose average return is equal to the stock's expected rate of return, what will be next year's EPS? (*Hint:* $g = b \times ROE$, where b = fraction of earnings retained.)

weighted average cost of capital **10–5** On January 1, 2000, the total assets of the Dexter Company were $270 million. The firm's present capital structure, which follows, is considered to be optimal. Assume that there is no short-term debt.

Long-term debt	$135,000,000
Common equity	135,000,000
Total liabilities and equity	$270,000,000

New bonds will have a ten percent coupon rate and will be sold at par. Common stock, currently selling at $60 a share, can be sold to net the company $54 a share. Stockholders' required rate of return is estimated to be 12 percent, consisting of a dividend yield of four percent and an expected growth rate of eight percent. (The next expected dividend is $2.40, so $2.40/$60 = 4%.) Retained earnings are estimated to be $13.5 million. The marginal tax rate is 40 percent. Assuming that all asset expansion (gross expenditures for fixed assets plus related working capital) is included in the capital budget, the dollar amount of the capital budget, ignoring depreciation, is $135 million.

    a. To maintain the present capital structure, how much of the capital budget must Dexter finance by equity?

    b. How much of the new equity funds needed will be generated internally? Externally?

    c. Calculate the cost of each of the equity components.

    d. At what level of capital expenditure will there be a break in Dexter's MCC schedule?

    e. Calculate the WACC (1) below and (2) above the break in the MCC schedule.

    f. Plot the MCC schedule. Also, draw in an IOS schedule that is consistent with both the MCC schedule and the projected capital budget. (Any IOS schedule that is consistent will do.)

weighted average cost of capital **10–6** The following tabulation gives earnings per share figures for the Brueggeman Company during the preceding ten years. The firm's common stock, 7.8 million shares outstanding, is now (January 1, 2000) selling for $65 per share, and the expected dividend at the end of the current year (2000) is 55 percent of the 1999 EPS. Because investors expect past trends to continue, g can be based on the earnings growth rate. (Note that nine years of growth are reflected in the data.)

YEAR	EPS	YEAR	EPS
1990	$3.90	1995	$5.73
1991	4.21	1996	6.19
1992	4.55	1997	6.68
1993	4.91	1998	7.22
1994	5.31	1999	7.80

The current interest rate on new debt is nine percent. The firm's marginal tax rate is 40 percent. Its capital structure, considered to be optimal, is as follows:

Debt	$104,000,000
Common equity	156,000,000
Total liabilities and equity	$260,000,000

a. Calculate Brueggeman's after-tax cost of new debt and of common equity, assuming that new equity comes only from retained earnings. Calculate the cost of equity as $k_s = \hat{D}_1/P_0 + g$.
b. Find Brueggeman's weighted average cost of capital, again assuming that no new common stock is sold and that all debt costs nine percent.
c. How much can be spent on capital investments before external equity must be sold? (Assume that retained earnings available for 2000 are 45 percent of 1999 earnings. Obtain 1999 earnings by multiplying 1999 EPS by the shares outstanding.)
d. What is Brueggeman's weighted average cost of capital (cost of funds raised in excess of the amount calculated in part c) if new common stock can be sold to the public at $65 a share to net the firm $58.50 a share? The cost of debt is constant.

optimal capital budget   **10–7** Ezzell Enterprises has the following capital structure, which it considers to be optimal under present and forecasted conditions:

Debt (long-term only)	45%
Common equity	55
Total liabilities and equity	100%

For the coming year, management expects after-tax earnings of $2.5 million. Ezzell's past dividend policy of paying out 60 percent of earnings will continue. Present commitments from its banker will allow Ezzell to borrow according to the following schedule:

LOAN AMOUNT	INTEREST RATE
$0 to $500,000	9% on this increment of debt
$500,001 to $900,000	11% on this increment of debt
$900,001 and above	13% on this increment of debt

The company's marginal tax rate is 40 percent, the current market price of its stock is $22 per share, its *last* dividend was $2.20 per share, and the expected growth rate is five percent. External equity (new common) can be sold at a flotation cost of ten percent.

Ezzell has the following investment opportunities for the next year:

PROJECT	COST	ANNUAL CASH FLOWS	PROJECT LIFE	IRR
1	$675,000	$155,401	8 years	?
2	900,000	268,484	5	15.0%
3	375,000	161,524	3	?
4	562,500	185,194	4	12.0
5	750,000	127,351	10	11.0

Management asks you to help determine which projects (if any) should be undertaken. You proceed with this analysis by answering the following questions (or performing the tasks) as posed in a logical sequence:

a. How many breaks are there in the MCC schedule? At what dollar amounts do the breaks occur, and what causes them?

b. What is the weighted average cost of capital in each of the intervals between the breaks?

c. What are the IRR values for Projects 1 and 3?

d. Graph the IOS and MCC schedules.

e. Which projects should Ezzell's management accept?

f. What assumptions about project risk are implicit in this problem? If you learned that Projects 1, 2, and 3 were of above-average risk, yet Ezzell chose the projects that you indicated in part e, how would this affect the situation?

g. The problem stated that Ezzell pays out 60 percent of its earnings as dividends. How would the analysis change if the payout ratio was changed to zero, to 100 percent, or somewhere in between? (No calculations are necessary.)

Exam-Type Problems

The problems included in this section are set up in such a way that they could be used as multiple-choice exam problems.

after-tax cost of debt   **10–8** Calculate the after-tax cost of debt under each of the following conditions:

a. Interest rate, 13 percent; tax rate, 0 percent.

b. Interest rate, 13 percent; tax rate, 20 percent.

c. Interest rate, 13 percent; tax rate, 34 percent.

after-tax cost of debt   **10–9** The McDaniel Company's financing plans for next year include the sale of long-term bonds with a ten percent coupon. The company believes it can sell the bonds at a price that will provide a yield to maturity of 12 percent. If the marginal tax rate is 34 percent, what is McDaniel's after-tax cost of debt?

cost of preferred stock   **10–10** Maness Industries plans to issue some $100 par preferred stock with an 11 percent dividend. The stock is selling on the market for $97.00, and Maness must pay flotation costs of five percent of the market price. What is the cost of the preferred stock for Maness?

cost of new common stock   **10–11** The Choi Company's next expected dividend, $\hat{D}_1$, is $3.18; its growth rate is six percent; and the stock now sells for $36. New stock can be sold to net the firm $32.40 per share.

a. What is Choi's percentage flotation cost, F?

b. What is Choi's cost of new common stock, k_e?

rate of five percent in the foreseeable future. Coleman's beta is 1.2, the yield on Treasury bonds is seven percent, and the market risk premium is estimated to be six percent. For the bond-yield-plus-risk-premium approach, the firm uses a four percentage point risk premium.

(5) Up to $300,000 of new common stock can be sold at a flotation cost of 15 percent. Above $300,000, the flotation cost would rise to 25 percent.

(6) Coleman's target capital structure is 30 percent long-term debt, ten percent preferred stock, and 60 percent common equity.

(7) The firm is forecasting retained earnings of $300,000 for the coming year.

To structure the task somewhat, Lehman has asked you to answer the following questions:

a. (1) What sources of capital should be included when you estimate Coleman's weighted average cost of capital (WACC)?

   (2) Should the component costs be figured on a before-tax or an after-tax basis? Explain.

   (3) Should the costs be historical (embedded) costs or new (marginal) costs? Explain.

b. What is the market interest rate on Coleman's debt and its component cost of debt?

c. (1) What is the firm's cost of preferred stock?

   (2) Coleman's preferred stock is riskier to investors than its debt, yet the yield to investors is lower than the yield to maturity on the debt. Does this suggest that you have made a mistake? (*Hint:* Think about taxes.)

d. (1) Why is there a cost associated with retained earnings?

   (2) What is Coleman's estimated cost of retained earnings using the CAPM approach?

   (3) Why is the Treasury bond rate a better estimate of the risk-free rate for cost of capital purposes than the Treasury bill rate?

e. What is the estimated cost of retained earnings using the discounted cash flow (DCF) approach?

f. What is the bond-yield-plus-risk-premium estimate for Coleman's cost of retained earnings?

g. What is your final estimate for k_s?

h. What is Coleman's cost for up to $300,000 of newly issued common stock, k_{e1}? What happens to the cost of equity if Coleman sells more than $300,000 of new common stock?

i. Explain in words why new common stock has a higher percentage cost than retained earnings.

j. (1) What is Coleman's overall, or weighted average, cost of capital (WACC) when retained earnings are used as the equity component?

   (2) What is the WACC after retained earnings have been exhausted and Coleman uses up to $300,000 of new common stock with a 15 percent flotation cost?

   (3) What is the WACC if more than $300,000 of new common equity is sold?

k. (1) At what amount of new investment would Coleman be forced to issue new common stock? To put it another way, what is the largest capital budget the company could support without issuing new common stock? Assume that the 30/10/60 target capital structure will be maintained.

Questions   455

(2) At what amount of new investment would Coleman be forced to issue new common stock with a 25 percent flotation cost?

(3) What is a marginal cost of capital (MCC) schedule? Construct a graph that shows Coleman's MCC schedule.

l. Coleman's director of capital budgeting has identified the following potential projects:

PROJECT	COST	LIFE	CASH FLOW	IRR
A	$700,000	5 years	$218,795	17.0%
B	500,000	5	152,705	16.0
B'	500,000	20	79,881	15.0
C	800,000	5	219,185	11.5

Projects B and B' are mutually exclusive, whereas the other projects are independent. All of the projects are equally risky.

(1) Plot the IOS schedule on the same graph that contains your MCC schedule. What is the firm's marginal cost of capital for capital budgeting purposes?

(2) What are the dollar size and the included projects in Coleman's optimal capital budget? Explain your answer fully.

(3) Would Coleman's MCC schedule remain constant at 12.8 percent beyond $2 million regardless of the amount of capital required?

(4) If WACC$_3$ had been 18.5 percent rather than 12.8 percent, but the second WACC break point had still occurred at $1,000,000, how would that have affected the analysis?

m. Suppose you learned that Coleman could raise only $200,000 of new debt at a ten percent interest rate and that new debt beyond $200,000 would have a yield to investors of 12 percent. Trace back through your work and explain how this new fact would change the situation.

Computer-Related Problem

Work the problem in this section only if you are using the computer problem diskette.

marginal cost of capital   **10-20** Use the model in the File C10 to work this problem.

a. Refer back to Problem 10-7. Now assume that the debt ratio is increased to 65 percent, causing all interest rates to rise by one percentage point, to ten percent, 12 percent, and 14 percent, and causing g to increase from five to six percent. What happens to the MCC schedule and the capital budget?

b. Assume the facts as in part a, but suppose Ezzell's marginal tax rate falls (1) to 20 percent or (2) to 0 percent. How would this affect the MCC schedule and the capital budget?

c. Ezzell's management would now like to know what the optimal capital budget would be if earnings were as high as $3.25 million or as low as $1 million. Assume a 40 percent marginal tax rate.

d. Would it be reasonable to use the model to analyze the effects of a change in the payout ratio without changing other variables?

ONLINE ESSENTIALS

http://www.teachmefinance.com   TeachMeFinance.com

This site gives a tutorial about cost of capital. The "Cost of Capital" page also includes a link to a "CAPM" page that describes the capital asset pricing model.

http://finance.yahoo.com   Yahoo!.Finance

This site provides a large amount of investment information. You can get information about the cost of capital of an individual firm by looking at its 10K or 10Q report, which contains financial information filed with the Securities and Exchange Commission. To get such reports, click on "SEC Filings" under the heading Research on the Yahoo!.Finance home page.

http://www.bondsonline.com   Bonds Online

The information provided at this site relates solely to bonds. You can get bond rates, which represent the cost of debt, for various firms. This site also provides general information and tutorials about bonds and bond price movements.

http://valuation.ibbotson.com   Ibbotson Associates Cost of Capital Center

Cost of capital data for 5,000 companies can be purchased through Ibbotson Associates. This site also provides links to other sites that have research papers, tutorials, and so on and that provide information about cost of capital and firm valuation.

CHAPTER 11

Capital Structure

In September 1990, Unisys Corporation, a manufacturer of computers and related products for commercial and defense companies, took actions to substantially reduce the amount of debt it was using to finance the firm. At the time, the debt/assets ratio of Unisys was nearly 75 percent, which was much higher than what the company felt was appropriate.

One step that was taken to change the mix of debt and equity in the firm (its capital structure) was to suspend the payment of future common stock dividends, which allowed Unisys to provide $162 million a year to repurchase, and thus reduce, debt. Unisys was able to reduce its amount of debt substantially in four years—the debt/assets ratio fell from nearly 75 percent in 1990 to just over 60 percent in 1993. The strategy to change its capital structure seemed to work, because Unisys increased its net income from a loss of a little more than $500 million in 1990 to a gain of $400 million in 1993. Unfortunately, in 1995 the company again increased its debt considerably, and its debt/assets ratio rose above 75 percent; then in 1996 and 1997, the debt/assets ratio was even higher, at about 78 percent.

Even though its actions seemed contradictory, Unisys did not abandon its goal to reduce debt. In September 1997, Lawrence A. Weinbach was appointed chairman, president, and CEO. One of his first actions was to announce that Unisys would decrease debt by $1 billion by the year 2000. True to his word, Weinbach decreased debt by more than $800 in the first four months of his tenure. It was estimated that the debt reduction saved more than $58 million annually in interest and debt-related expenses. In 1998, debt reduction actions continued such that Unisys reached its goal of a $1 billion reduction in debt about 18 months ahead of schedule. Although more improvement is needed because the debt/assets ratio hovers around 73 percent, by today (1999), the capital structure changes Unisys had made had improved both its financial strength and its profit position. In 1998, earnings per share (EPS) was $1.11, which reversed the previous trend of negative earnings, and reports of operations in the first half of 1999 indicate that Unisys would generate an EPS equal to more than $1.20 for the year.

Why did Unisys make these capital structure changes? Primarily to improve the financial position of the firm and thus improve shareholder wealth. So how has the stock been affected by the capital structure changes made since 1990? When Unisys first announced its plan, which included the suspension of dividends, the price of its common stock dropped more than 25 percent in one day and by about one-third of its value within one week—trading at just under $5 per share, the value of Unisys common stock was 76 percent lower than its high during the previous 12-month period, and 90 percent lower than its high value during the previous five years. By 1994, however,

continues

Unisys stock was selling for $11 per share; in 1998, the price was nearly $26; and in July 1999, the stock was selling for more than $41. Thus, the stock's value has rebounded substantially since 1990; it seems the stockholders realized the capital structure changes have benefited long-run stability and wealth maximization.

As you can see from the Unisys example, a firm's capital structure can affect value. As you read this chapter, keep in mind the reasons Unisys wanted to decrease the proportion of debt in its capital structure, and consider the impact a particular capital structure can have on the value of a firm. ■

In Chapter 10, when we calculated the weighted average cost of capital for use in capital budgeting, we took the capital structure weights, or the mix of securities the firm uses to finance its assets, as a given. However, if the weights are changed, the calculated cost of capital, and thus the set of acceptable projects, will also change. Further, changing the capital structure will affect the riskiness inherent in the firm's common stock, and this will affect the return demanded by stockholders, k_s, and the stock's price, P_0. Therefore, the choice of a capital structure is an important decision. In this chapter, we discuss concepts relating to capital structure decisions.

The Target Capital Structure

CAPITAL STRUCTURE
The combination of debt and equity used to finance a firm.

TARGET CAPITAL STRUCTURE
The mix of debt, preferred stock, and common equity with which the firm plans to finance its investments.

Firms can choose whatever mix of debt and equity they desire to finance their assets, subject to the willingness of investors to provide such funds. And, as we shall see, many different mixes of debt and equity, or **capital structures,** exist. In some firms, such as Chrysler Corporation, debt accounts for more than 70 percent of the financing, while other firms, like Microsoft, have little or no debt. In the next few sections, we will discuss factors that affect a firm's capital structure, and we will conclude a firm should attempt to determine what its optimal, or best, mix of financing should be. But it will become apparent that determining the exact optimal capital structure is not a science, so after analyzing a number of factors, a firm establishes a **target capital structure** it believes is optimal, and which it uses as guidance for raising funds in the future. This target might change over time as conditions vary, but at any given moment the firm's management has a specific capital structure in mind, and individual financing decisions should be consistent with this target. If the actual proportion of debt is below the target level, new funds probably will be raised by issuing debt, whereas if the proportion of debt is above the target, stock probably will be sold to bring the firm back in line with the target ratio.

Capital structure policy involves a trade-off between risk and return. Using more debt raises the riskiness of the firm's earnings stream, but a higher proportion of debt generally leads to a higher expected rate of return; and, from the concepts we discussed in Chapter 5, we know that the higher risk associated with greater debt tends to lower the stock's price. At the same time, however, the higher expected rate of return makes the stock more attractive to investors, which, in turn, ultimately increases the stock's price. Therefore, *the optimal capital structure is the one that strikes a balance between risk and return to achieve our ultimate goal of maximizing the price of the stock.*

Four primary factors influence capital structure decisions.

1. The first is the firm's *business risk*, or the riskiness that would be inherent in the firm's operations if it used no debt. The greater the firm's business risk, the lower the amount of debt that is optimal.

2. The second key factor is the firm's *tax position*. A major reason for using debt is that interest is tax deductible, which lowers the effective cost of debt. However, if much of a firm's income is already sheltered from taxes by accelerated depreciation or tax loss carryovers, its tax rate will be low, and debt will not be as advantageous as it would be to a firm with a higher effective tax rate.

3. The third important consideration is *financial flexibility*, or the ability to raise capital on reasonable terms under adverse conditions. Corporate treasurers know that a steady supply of capital is necessary for stable operations, which in turn are vital for long-run success. They also know that when money is tight in the economy, or when a firm is experiencing operating difficulties, a strong balance sheet is needed to obtain funds from suppliers of capital. Thus, it might be advantageous to issue equity to strengthen the firm's capital base and financial stability.

4. The fourth debt-determining factor has to do with *managerial attitude (conservatism or aggressiveness)* with regard to borrowing. Some managers are more aggressive than others; hence, some firms are more inclined to use debt in an effort to boost profits. This factor does not affect the optimal, or value-maximizing, capital structure, but it does influence the target capital structure a firm actually establishes.

These four points largely determine the target capital structure, but, as we shall see, operating conditions can cause the actual capital structure to vary from the target at any given time. For example, the debt/assets ratio of Unisys clearly has been much higher than its target, and the company has taken some significant corrective actions in recent years to improve its financial position. (See "A Managerial Perspective" at the beginning of this chapter.)

Self-Test Questions

What are the four factors that affect the target capital structure?

In what sense does capital structure policy involve a trade-off between risk and return?

Business and Financial Risk

When we examined risk in Chapter 5, we distinguished between *market risk*, which is measured by the firm's beta coefficient, and *total risk*, which includes both beta risk and a type of risk that can be eliminated by diversification (*firm-specific risk*). In Chapter 9 we considered how capital budgeting decisions affect the riskiness of the firm. There again we distinguished between beta risk (the effect of a project on the firm's beta) and corporate risk (the effect of the project on the firm's total risk).

Now we introduce two new dimensions of risk:

BUSINESS RISK
The risk associated with projections of a firm's future returns on assets (ROA) or returns on equity (ROE) if the firm uses no debt.

1. **Business risk** is defined as the uncertainty inherent in projections of future returns, either on assets (ROA) or on equity (ROE), if the firm uses no debt, or debt-like financing (i.e., preferred stock)—it is the risk associated with the firm's operations.

FINANCIAL RISK
The portion of
stockholders' risk, over
and above basic business
risk, resulting from the
manner in which the firm
is financed.

2. **Financial risk** is defined as the additional risk, over and above basic business risk, placed on common stockholders that results from using financing alternatives with fixed periodic payments, such as debt and preferred stock—it is the risk associated with using debt or preferred stock.

Conceptually, the firm has a certain amount of risk inherent in its production and sales operations; this is its business risk. When it uses debt, it partitions this risk and concentrates most of it on one class of investors—the common stockholders—this is its financial risk.[1] Both business risk and financial risk affect the capital structure of a firm.

Business Risk

Business risk is the single most important determinant of capital structure. To illustrate the effects of business risk, consider Bigbee Electronics Company, a firm that currently uses 100 percent equity. Figure 11–1 shows the trend in ROE from 1990 through 2000, and it gives both security analysts and Bigbee's management an idea of the degree to which ROE has varied in the past and might vary in the future. Comparing the actual results to the trend line, you can see that Bigbee's ROE has fluctuated significantly since 1990. These fluctuations in ROE were caused by many factors—booms and recessions in the national economy, successful new products introduced both by Bigbee and by its competitors, labor strikes, a fire in Bigbee's major plant, and so on. Similar events will doubtless occur in the future, and when they do, ROE will rise or fall. Further, there always is the possibility that a long-term disaster might strike, permanently depressing the company's earning power. For example, a competitor could introduce a new product that would permanently lower Bigbee's earnings.[2] This element of uncertainty about Bigbee's future ROE is the company's *basic business risk*.

Business risk varies from one industry to another and also among firms in a given industry. Further, business risk can change over time. For example, electric utilities were regarded for years as having little business risk, but a combination of events during the past couple of decades has altered their situation, producing sharp declines in ROE for some companies, and greatly increasing the industry's business risk. Today, food processors and grocery retailers frequently are cited as examples of industries with low business risk, whereas cyclical manufacturing industries, such as steel and construction, are regarded as having especially high business risk. Smaller companies, especially single-product firms, also have a relatively high degree of business risk.[3]

Business risk depends on a number of factors, the more important of which include the following:

1. Sales variability (volume and price). The more stable the unit sales (volume) and prices of a firm's products, other things held constant, the lower its business risk.

---

[1]Using preferred stock also adds to financial risk. To simplify matters somewhat, in this chapter we shall consider only debt and common equity.

[2]Two examples of "safe" industries that turned out to be risky are the railroads just before automobiles, airplanes, and trucks took away most of their business and the telegraph business just before telephones came on the scene.

[3]We have avoided any discussion of market versus company-specific risk in this section. We note now that (1) any action that increases business risk will generally increase a firm's beta coefficient, but (2) a part of business risk as we define it will generally be company-specific and hence subject to elimination through diversification by the firm's stockholders.

FIGURE 11–1	Bigbee Electronics Company: Trend in ROE, 1990–2000, and Subjective Probability Distribution in ROE, 2000

a. Trend in Return on Equity (ROE)

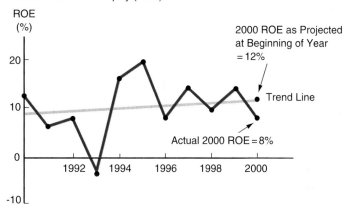

b. Subjective Probability Distribution of ROE

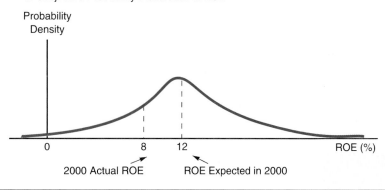

2. Input price variability. A firm whose input prices (labor, product costs, and so forth) are highly uncertain is exposed to a high degree of business risk.

3. Ability to adjust output prices for changes in input prices. Some firms have little difficulty in raising the prices of their products when input costs rise, and the greater the ability to adjust selling prices, the lower the degree of business risk. This factor is especially important during periods of high inflation.

4. The extent to which costs are fixed: operating leverage. If a high percentage of a firm's operating costs are fixed and hence do not decline when demand falls off, this increases the company's business risk. This factor is called *operating leverage*, and it was discussed at length in Chapter 4 when we described financial planning and control.

TABLE 11–2	Interest Rates for OptiCap with Different Debt/Asset Ratios

AMOUNT BORROWED[a]	DEBT/ASSETS RATIO	INTEREST RATE, k_d, ON ALL DEBT
$ 20,000	10%	8.0%
40,000	20	8.3
60,000	30	9.0
80,000	40	10.0
100,000	50	12.0
120,000	60	15.0

[a]We assume that the firm must borrow in increments of $20,000. We also assume that OptiCap is unable to borrow more than $120,000, or 60 percent of assets, because of restrictions in its corporate charter.

Now consider Table 11–3, which shows how expected EPS varies with changes in financial leverage. Section I of the table begins with a probability distribution of sales; we assume for simplicity that sales can take on only three values, $100,000, $200,000, or $300,000. In the remainder of Section I, we calculate earnings before interest and taxes (EBIT) at each of the three sales levels. Note that we assume both sales and operating costs are independent of financial leverage. Therefore, the three EBIT figures ($0, $40,000, and $80,000) will always remain the same, no matter how much debt OptiCap uses.[5]

Section II of Table 11–3, the zero-debt case, calculates OptiCap's earnings per share at each sales level under the assumption that the company continues to use no debt. Net income is divided by the 10,000 shares outstanding to obtain EPS (remember there is no preferred stock). If sales are as low as $100,000, EPS will be zero, but it will rise to $4.80 at a sales level of $300,000. The EPS at each sales level then is multiplied by the probability of that sales level and summed to calculate the expected EPS, which is $2.40. We also calculate the standard deviation of EPS and the coefficient of

---

[5]In the real world, capital structure does at times affect EBIT. First, if debt levels are excessive, the firm probably will not be able to finance at all if its earnings are low at a time when interest rates are high. This could lead to stop-start construction and research and development programs, as well as to the necessity of passing up good investment opportunities. Second, a weak financial condition (i.e., too much debt) could cause a firm to lose sales. For example, prior to the time that its huge debt forced Eastern Airlines into bankruptcy, many people refused to buy Eastern tickets because they were afraid the company would go bankrupt and leave them holding unusable tickets. Third, financially strong companies are able to bargain hard with unions as well as with their suppliers, whereas weaker ones may have to give in simply because they do not have the financial resources to carry on the fight. Finally, a company with so much debt that bankruptcy is a serious threat will have difficulty attracting and retaining managers and employees, or it will have to pay premium salaries. For all these reasons, it is not totally correct to say that a firm's financial policy has no effect on its operating income.

Note also that EBIT is dependent on operating leverage. If we were analyzing a firm with either more or less operating leverage, the top section of Table 11–3 would be quite different: fixed and variable costs would be different, and the range of EBIT over the various sales levels would be narrower if the company had lower operating leverage but wider if it had more operating leverage.

TABLE 11-3 OptiCap: EPS with Different Amounts of Financial Leverage (thousands of dollars, except per-share figures)

I. Calculation of EBIT

Probability of indicated sales	0.2	0.6	0.2
Sales	$ 100.0	$ 200.0	$ 300.0
Fixed costs	(40.0)	(40.0)	(40.0)
Variable costs (60% of sales)	(60.0)	(120.0)	(180.0)
Total costs (except interest)	$(100.0)	$(160.0)	$(220.0)
Earnings before interest and taxes (EBIT)	$ 0.0	$ 40.0	$ 80.0

II. Situation If Debt/Assets (D/A) = 0%

EBIT (from Section I)	$ 0.0	$ 40.0	$ 80.0
Less interest	(0.0)	(0.0)	(0.0)
Earnings before taxes (EBT)	$ 0.0	$ 40.0	$ 80.0
Taxes (40%)	(0.0)	(16.0)	(32.0)
Net income	$ 0.0	$ 24.0	$ 48.0
Earnings per share (EPS) on 10,000 shares[a]	$ 0.0	$ 2.40	$ 4.80
Expected EPS		$ 2.40	
Standard deviation of EPS		$ 1.52	
Coefficient of variation		0.63	

III. Situation If Debt/Assets (D/A) = 50%

EBIT (from Section I)	$ 0.0	$ 40.0	$ 80.0
Less interest (0.12 × $100,000)	(12.0)	(12.0)	(12.0)
Earnings before taxes (EBT)	$(12.0)	$ 28.0	$ 68.0
Taxes (40%; tax credit on losses)	4.8	(11.2)	(27.2)
Net income	$(7.2)	$ 16.8	$ 40.8
Earnings per share (EPS) on 5,000 shares[a]	$(1.44)	$ 3.36	$ 8.16
Expected EPS		$ 3.36	
Standard deviation of EPS		$ 3.04	
Coefficient of variation		0.90	

[a]The EPS figures can also be obtained using the following formula, in which the numerator amounts to an income statement at a given sales level laid out horizontally:

$$EPS = \frac{(Sales - Fixed\ costs - Variable\ costs - Interest)(1 - Tax\ rate)}{Shares\ outstanding} = \frac{(EBIT - I)(1 - T)}{Shares\ outstanding}$$

For example, with zero debt and Sales = $200,000, EPS is $2.40:

$$EPS_{D/A = 0} = \frac{(\$200,000 - \$40,000 - \$120,000 - 0)(0.6)}{10,000} = \$2.40$$

With 50 percent debt and Sales = $200,000, EPS is $3.36:

$$EPS_{D/A = 0.5} = \frac{(\$200,000 - \$40,000 - \$120,000 - \$12,000)(0.6)}{5,000} = \$3.36$$

The sales level at which EPS will be equal under the two financing policies, or the indifference level of sales, S_I, can be found by setting $EPS_{D/A = 0}$ equal to $EPS_{D/A = 0.5}$ and solving for S_I:

$$EPS_{D/A = 0} = \frac{(S_I - \$40,000 - 0.6S_I - 0)(0.6)}{10,000} = \frac{(S_I - \$40,000 - 0.6S_I - \$12,000)(0.6)}{5,000} = EPS_{D/A = 0.5}$$

$$S_I = \$160,000$$

By substituting this value of sales into either equation, we can find EPS_I, the earnings per share at this indifference point. In our example, $EPS_I = \$1.44$.

FIGURE 11-3 | OptiCap Relationships among Expected EPS, Risk, and Financial Leverage

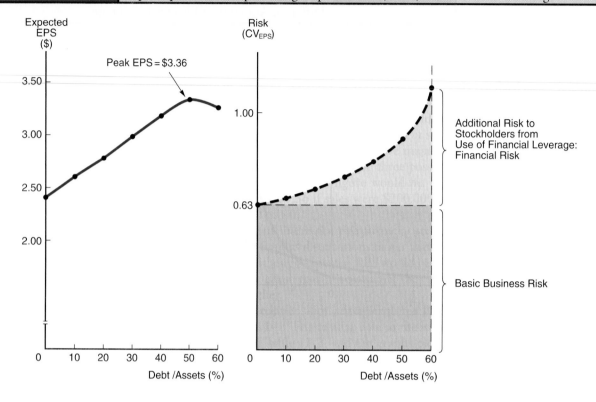

Debt/Assets Ratio	Expected EPS	Standard Deviation of EPS	Coefficient of Variation
0%[a]	$2.40[a]	$1.52[a]	0.63[a]
10	2.56	1.69	0.66
20	2.65	1.90	0.69
30	2.97	2.17	0.73
40	3.20	2.53	0.79
50[a]	3.36[a]	3.04[a]	0.90[a]
60	3.30	3.79	1.15

[a]Values for D/A = 0 and D/A = 50 percent are taken from Table 11–3. Values at other D/A ratios were calculated similarly.

This statement is demonstrated in Table 11–4, which develops OptiCap's estimated stock price and weighted average cost of capital at different debt/assets ratios. The debt cost and EPS data in Columns 2 and 3 were taken from Table 11–2 and Figure 11–3. The beta coefficients shown in Column 4 were estimated. Recall from Chapter 5 that a stock's beta measures its relative volatility compared with the volatility of an average stock. It has been demonstrated both theoretically and empirically that a firm's beta increases with its degree of financial leverage. The exact nature of this relationship for a given firm is difficult to estimate, but the values given in Column 4 do show the approximate nature of the relationship for OptiCap.

FIGURE 11-4   Earnings per Share of Stock and Debt Financing for OptiCap

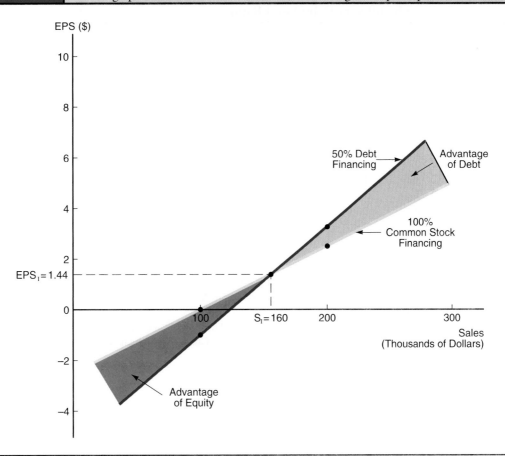

---

1. These values of the indifference level of sales, S_I and EPS_I, are the same as those obtained algebraically in Table 11–3. These relationships would be somewhat different if we did not assume that stock can be repurchased at book value.

2. We can also develop an equation to find the sales level at which EPS is the same under different degrees of financial leverage:

$$EPS_1 = \frac{S_I - F - VC - I_1}{Shares_1} = \frac{S_I - F - VC - I_2}{Shares_2} = EPS_2$$

Here, EPS_1 and EPS_2 are the EPSs at two debt levels; S_I is the sales indifference level at which $EPS_1 = EPS_2 = EPS_I$; I_1 and I_2 are interest charges at the two debt levels; $Shares_1$ and $Shares_2$ are shares outstanding at the two debt levels; F is the fixed costs; and VC = variable costs = Sales × v, where v is the variable cost percentage. Solving for S_I, we obtain this expression:

$$S_I = \left[\frac{(Shares_2)(I_1) - (Shares_1)(I_2)}{Shares_2 - Shares_1} + F \right]\left(\frac{1}{1 - v} \right)$$

In our example,

$$S_I = \left[\frac{(5,000)(0) - (10,000)(\$12,000)}{-5,000} + \$40,000 \right]\left(\frac{1}{0.4} \right)$$

$$= \$160,000$$

Assuming that the risk-free rate of return, k_{RF}, is six percent and that the required return on an average stock, k_M, is ten percent, we can use the CAPM equation to develop estimates of the required rates of return, k_s, for OptiCap as shown in Column 5.

FIGURE 11–6	Relationship between OptiCap's Capital Structure and Its EPS, Cost of Capital, and Stock Price

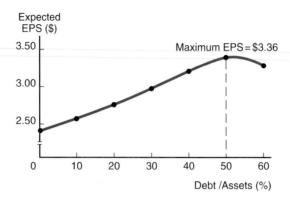

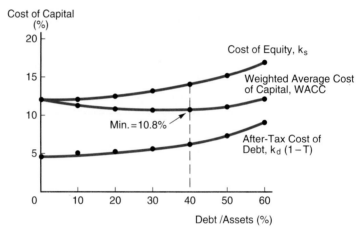

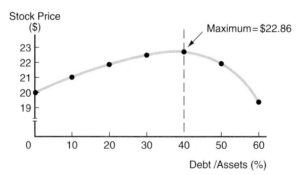

The EPS, cost of capital, and stock price data shown in Table 11–4 are plotted in Figure 11–6. As the graph shows, the debt/assets ratio that maximizes OptiCap's expected EPS is 50 percent. However, the expected stock price is maximized, and the cost of capital is minimized, at a 40 percent debt/assets ratio. Thus, *the optimal capital structure calls for 40 percent debt and 60 percent equity. Management should set its target capital structure at these ratios, and if the existing ratios are off target, it should move toward the target when new security offerings are made.*

Self-Test Questions

Explain the following statement: "Using leverage has both good and bad effects."

What does the EPS indifference point show? What occurs at sales below this point? What occurs at sales above this point?

Is the optimal capital structure the one that maximizes expected EPS? Explain.

Explain the following statement: "At the optimal capital structure, a firm has minimized its cost of capital." Do stockholders want the firm to minimize its cost of capital?

Degree of Leverage[8]

In Chapter 4 we showed that leverage, whether operating or financial, is created when a firm has fixed costs associated either with its sales and production operations or with the types of financing it uses. We also found that the two types of leverage, operating and financial, are interrelated. Therefore, if OptiCap *reduced* its operating leverage, this probably would lead to an *increase* in its optimal use of financial leverage. On the other hand, if the firm decided to *increase* its operating leverage, its optimal capital structure probably would call for *less* debt.

The theory of finance has not been developed to the point where we can actually specify simultaneously the optimal levels of operating and financial leverage. However, we can see how operating and financial leverage interact through an analysis of the *degree of leverage concept* we introduced in Chapter 4.

DEGREE OF OPERATING LEVERAGE (DOL)
The percentage change in operating income (EBIT) associated with a given percentage change in sales.

Degree of Operating Leverage (DOL)

The **degree of operating leverage (DOL)** is defined as the percentage change in operating income (that is, earnings before interest and taxes, or EBIT) associated with a given percentage change in sales. Thus, the degree of operating leverage is

11–1

$$DOL = \frac{\text{Percentage change in NOI}}{\text{Percentage change in sales}} = \frac{\left(\frac{\Delta EBIT}{EBIT}\right)}{\left(\frac{\Delta Sales}{Sales}\right)} = \frac{\left(\frac{\Delta EBIT}{EBIT}\right)}{\left(\frac{\Delta Q}{Q}\right)}$$

According to Equation 11–1, the DOL is an index number that measures the effect of a change in sales on operating income, or EBIT.

DOL for a particular level of production and sales, Q, can be computed using the following equation:

11–2

$$DOL_Q = \frac{Q(P - V)}{Q(P - V) - F}$$

---

[8]A more detailed discussion of leverage is presented in Chapter 4, and the derivations of the equations contained in this section are included in the footnotes in that chapter.

$$DTL_{S = \$200,000, \, Debt/TA = 50\%} = \frac{\$200,000 - \$120,000}{\$200,000 - \$120,000 - \$40,000 - \$12,000} = \frac{\$80,000}{\$28,000}$$

$$= 2.00 \times 1.43 = 2.86$$

We can use the degree of total leverage (DTL) to find the new earnings per share (EPS_1) for any given percentage increase in sales, proceeding as follows:

> **11–5**
>
> $$EPS_1 = EPS_0 + EPS_0[(DTL) \times (\%\Delta Sales)]$$
> $$= EPS_0[1.0 + (DTL) \times (\%\Delta Sales)]$$

For example, a 50 percent (or 0.5) increase in sales, from $200,000 to $300,000, would cause EPS_0 ($3.36 as shown in Section III of Table 11–3) to increase to $8.16:

$$EPS_1 = \$3.36[1.0 + (2.86)(0.5)] = \$3.36(2.43) = \$8.16.$$

This figure agrees with the one for EPS shown in Table 11–3.

The degree of leverage concept is useful primarily for the insights it provides regarding the joint effects of operating and financial leverage on earnings per share. The concept can be used to show management the impact of financing the firm with debt versus common stock. For example, management might find that the current capital structure is such that a ten percent decline in sales would produce a 50 percent decline in earnings, whereas with a different financing package, thus a different degree of total leverage, a ten percent sales decline would cause earnings to decline by only 20 percent. Having the alternatives stated in this manner gives decision makers a better idea of the ramifications of alternative financing plans, hence different capital structures.[10]

Self-Test Questions

Give the formula for calculating the degree of operating leverage (DOL), and explain what DOL is.

Why is the DOL different at various sales levels?

Give the formula for calculating the degree of financial leverage (DFL), and explain what this calculation means.

---

[10]The degree of leverage concept is also useful for investors. If firms in an industry are classified as to their degrees of total leverage, an investor who is optimistic about prospects for the industry might favor those firms with high leverage and vice versa if industry sales are expected to decline. However, it is very difficult to separate fixed from variable costs. Accounting statements generally do not contain this breakdown, so the analyst must make the separation in a judgmental manner. Note that costs really are fixed, variable, and "semivariable," for if times get tough enough, firms will sell off depreciable assets and thus reduce depreciation charges (a fixed cost), lay off "permanent" employees, reduce salaries of the remaining personnel, and so on. For this reason, the degree of leverage concept generally is more useful in explaining the general nature of the relationship than in developing precise numbers, and any numbers developed should be thought of as approximations rather than as exact specifications.

Give the formula for calculating the degree of total leverage (DTL), and explain what DTL is.

Why is the degree of leverage concept useful?

Liquidity and Capital Structure

There are some practical difficulties with the type of analysis described in the previous section, including the following:

1. It is virtually impossible to determine exactly how either P/E ratios or equity capitalization rates (k_s values) are affected by different degrees of financial leverage. The best we can do is make educated guesses about these relationships. Therefore, management rarely, if ever, has sufficient confidence in the type of analysis set forth in Table 11–4 and Figure 11–6 to use it as the sole determinant of the target capital structure.

2. The managers might be more or less conservative than the average stockholder, so management might set a somewhat different target capital structure than the one that would maximize the stock price. The managers of a publicly owned firm never would admit this because, unless they owned voting control, they would be removed from office very quickly. However, in view of the uncertainties about what constitutes the value-maximizing capital structure, management could always say that the target capital structure employed is, in its judgment, the value-maximizing structure, and it would be difficult to prove otherwise. Still, if management is far off target, especially on the low side, then chances are very high that some other firm or management group will take over the company, increase its leverage, and thereby raise its value.

3. Managers of large firms, especially those that provide vital services such as electricity or telephones, have a responsibility to provide continuous service; therefore, they must refrain from using leverage to the point where the firms' long-run survivals are endangered. Long-run viability might conflict with short-run stock price maximization and capital cost minimization.[11]

For all these reasons, managers are concerned about the effects of financial leverage on the risk of bankruptcy, and an analysis of this factor is therefore an important input in all capital structure decisions. Accordingly, managers give considerable weight to financial strength indicators such as the **times-interest-earned (TIE) ratio,** which, as we saw in Chapter 3, is computed by dividing earnings before interest and taxes by interest expense. Remember that the TIE ratio provides an indication of how well the firm can cover its interest payments with operating income (EBIT)—the lower this ratio, the higher the probability that a firm will default on its debt and be forced into bankruptcy.

TIMES-INTEREST-EARNED (TIE) RATIO
A ratio that measures the firm's ability to meet its annual interest obligations; calculated by dividing earnings before interest and taxes by interest charges.

---

[11]Recognizing this fact, most public service commissions require utilities to obtain the commission's approval before issuing long-term securities, and Congress has empowered the SEC to supervise the capital structures of public utility holding companies. However, in addition to concern over the firms' safety, which suggests low debt ratios, both managers and regulators recognize a need to keep all costs as low as possible, including the cost of capital. Because a firm's capital structure affects its cost of capital, regulatory commissions and utility managers try to select capital structures that will minimize the cost of capital, subject to the constraint that the firm's financial flexibility not be endangered.

SIGNAL

An action taken by a firm's
management that provides
clues to investors about
how management views
the firm's prospects.

**RESERVE BORROWING
CAPACITY**

The ability to borrow
money at a reasonable cost
when good investment
opportunities arise; firms
often use less debt than
specified by the MM
optimal capital structure
to ensure that they can
obtain debt capital later if
they need to.

have multiple financing alternatives is taken as a **signal** *that the firm's prospects as seen by its management are not bright.* This, in turn, suggests that when a mature firm announces a new stock offering, the price of its stock should decline. Empirical studies have shown that this situation does indeed exist.

What are the implications of all this for capital structure decisions? The answer is that firms should, in normal times, maintain a **reserve borrowing capacity** that can be used in the event that some especially good investment opportunities come along. *This means that firms should generally use less debt than would be suggested by the tax bene-fit/bankruptcy cost trade-off expressed in Figure 11–8.*

Signaling/asymmetric information concepts also have implications for the marginal cost of capital (MCC) curve as discussed in Chapter 10. There we saw that the weighted average cost of capital (WACC) jumped when retained earnings were exhausted and the firm was forced to sell new common stock to raise equity. The jump in the WACC, or the break in the MCC schedule, was attributed only to flotation costs. However, if the announcement of a stock sale causes a decline in the price of the stock, then k_e as measured by $k_e = \hat{D}_1/P_0 + g$ will rise because of the decline in P_0. This factor reinforces the effects of flotation costs, and perhaps it is an even more important explanation for the jump in the MCC schedule at the point at which new stock must be issued. For example, assume that $P_0 = \$10$, $\hat{D}_1 = \$1$, $g = 5\%$, and $F = 10\%$. Therefore, $k_s = 10\% + 5\% = 15\%$, and k_e, the cost of external equity, is 16.1 percent:

$$k_e = \frac{\hat{D}_1}{P_0(1 - F)} + g = \frac{\$1}{\$10(1.0 - 0.10)} + 0.05 = 0.161 = 16.1\%$$

Suppose, however, that the announcement of a stock sale causes the market price of the stock to fall from $P_0 = \$10$ to $P_0 = \$8$. This will produce an increase in the costs of both retained earnings (k_s) and external equity:

$$k_s = \frac{\hat{D}_1}{P_0} + g = \frac{\$1}{\$8} + 0.05 = 0.175 = 17.5\%$$

$$k_e = \frac{\hat{D}_1}{P_0(1 - F)} + g = \frac{\$1}{\$8(1.0 - 0.10)} + 0.05 = 0.189 = 18.9\%$$

This would, of course, have further implications for capital budgeting. Specifically, it would make it even more difficult for a marginal project to show a positive net present value (NPV) if the project required the firm to sell stock to raise capital.

If you find our discussion of capital structure theory somewhat inexact, you are not alone. In truth, no one knows how to identify precisely the optimal capital structure for a firm or how to measure precisely the effect of the firm's capital structure on either its value or its cost of capital. In real life, capital structure decisions must be made more on the basis of judgment than numerical analysis. Still, an understanding of the theoretical issues as presented here is essential to making sound judgments on capital structure issues.

Self-Test Questions

What does it mean when one hears, "The MM capital structure theory involves a trade-off between the tax benefits of debt and costs associated with actual or potential bankruptcy"?

Internal Equity First, External Equity Last

There has long been a debate concerning the relevance of financing decisions on the value of the firm. The controversy is centered around the question of whether a change in the firm's capital structure has an impact on its value. According to empirical evidence, stock prices do change when firms alter capital structures. But there still is a question as to the reason stock prices react to capital structure changes. The reactions could result because capital structure changes provide information to investors either about the firm's optimal capital structure, if one exists, or about investment opportunities, which affect the value of the firm.

A survey of *Fortune* 500 firms provides some insight into the attitudes of financial officers concerning capital structure financing decisions. According to the results, nearly 85 percent of firms reported that retained earnings was their first choice of financing long-term needs, about 15 percent indicated that debt was preferable, and none of the firms listed new equity, either common or preferred, as their first preference. Almost 40 percent of the firms said issuing new common stock would be their last choice of alternatives for raising capital. This is not surprising, considering the fact that the cost of new common equity is greater than the other sources of capital. In addition,

more than 60 percent of the firms indicated that they prefer to use debt and preferred stock to avoid diluting the ownership position of common stockholders. Other important factors that were mentioned include restrictions contained in existing debt contracts, cash flows expected from the asset to be financed, and risk.

More than 85 percent of the firms indicated that financial flexibility and long-term survival are important factors to consider when making financial decisions. About 75 percent stated that firm value, stable cash flows, and financial independence significantly influence the capital structure of a company.

The results of the survey seem to suggest that firms do not have a specific capital structure in mind when deciding how to best finance capital budgeting projects. They prefer to maintain a flexible capital structure than to operate at what might be considered a more rigid optimal position. Therefore, changes in capital structure probably should be perceived as an indication of management's desire to raise funds to acquire projects rather than an indication that management is consciously adjusting the financial make-up of the firm to maximize value.

SOURCE: J. Michael Pinegar and Lisa Wilbricht, "What Managers Think of Capital Structure Theory: A Survey," *Financial Management*, Winter 1989, 82–89.

Explain how asymmetric information and signals affect capital structure decisions. What is meant by reserve borrowing capacity, and why is it important for firms?

Variations in Capital Structures among Firms

As might be expected, wide variations in the use of financial leverage occur both across industries and among the individual firms in each industry. Table 11–5 illustrates differences for selected industries; the ranking is in descending order of common equity ratios, as shown in column 1.

Drug and industrial machinery companies do not use much debt (their common equity ratios are high); the uncertainties inherent in industries that are cyclical, oriented toward research, or subject to huge product liability suits normally render the heavy use of debt unwise. On the other hand, utilities traditionally have used large

						TIMES-	
						INTEREST-	RETURN
	COMMON	PREFERRED	TOTAL	LONG-TERM	SHORT-TERM	EARNED	ON
	EQUITY	STOCK	DEBT	DEBT	DEBT	RATIO	EQUITY
INDUSTRY	(1)	(2)	(3)	(4)	(5)	(6)	(7)
Drugs	70.1%	0.2%	29.7%	19.6%	10.1%	12.4×	23.3%
Electronics	52.8	0.3	46.9	22.1	24.8	16.3	11.2
Industrial							
machinery	51.8	0.3	47.9	31.7	16.2	11.8	13.5
Retailing	44.5	0.5	55.0	37.7	17.3	4.9	15.4
Utilities	35.6	1.8	62.6	52.6	10.0	1.7	3.5
Composite[b]	51.3	0.8	47.9	34.3	13.6	4.3	13.7

TABLE 11–5 Capital Structure Percentages, 1998: Five Industries Ranked by Common Equity Ratios[a]

[a]These ratios are based on accounting, or book values. Stated on a market value basis, the equity percentages would be higher because most stocks sell at prices that are much higher than their book values.

[b]These composite ratios include all industries, not just those listed above, except financial and professional service industries.

SOURCE: *Compustat PC Plus*, 1999.

amounts of debt, particularly long-term debt—their fixed assets make good security for mortgage bonds, and their relatively stable sales make it safe for them to carry more debt than would be true for firms with more business risk.

Particular attention should be given to the times-interest-earned (TIE) ratio because it gives a measure of how safe the debt is and how vulnerable the company is to financial distress. The TIE ratio depends on three factors: (1) the percentage of debt, (2) the interest rate on the debt, and (3) the company's profitability. Generally, the least leveraged industries, such as the drug and electronics industries, have the highest coverage ratios, whereas the utility industry, which finances heavily with debt, has a low average coverage ratio. Table 11–5 shows that companies that manufacture drugs and electronics have high average TIEs, while utilities have a very low TIE.

Wide variations in capital structures also exist among firms within given industries. For example, although the average common equity ratio in 1997 for the drug industry was 67.7 percent, Biopharmaceutics Inc.'s equity ratio was greater than 70 percent, but Matrix Pharmaceutical's equity ratio was about 15 percent. Thus, factors unique to individual firms, including managerial attitudes, play an important role in setting target capital structures.

Self-Test Question

Why do wide variations in the use of financial leverage occur both across industries and among the individual firms in each industry?

TABLE 11–6	Capital Structure Percentages for Selected Countries Ranked by Common Equity Ratios, 1995			

COUNTRY	EQUITY	TOTAL DEBT	LONG-TERM DEBT	SHORT-TERM DEBT
United Kingdom	68.3%	31.7%	N/A	N/A
United States	48.4	51.6	26.8%	24.8%
Canada	47.5	52.5	30.2	22.7
Germany	39.7	60.3	15.6	44.7
Spain	39.7	60.3	22.1	38.2
France	38.8	61.2	23.5	37.7
Japan	33.7	66.3	23.3	43.0
Italy	23.5	76.5	24.2	52.3

NOTE: The percentages were computed from financial data that were stated in domestic currency. For example, the amount of total assets for French companies was stated in francs.

SOURCE: *OECD Financial Statistics, Part 3: Non-Financial Enterprises Financial Statements*, 1996.

Capital Structures around the World

As you might expect, when we examine the capital structures of companies around the world, we find wide variations. Table 11–6 illustrates differences for selected countries; the ranking is in descending order of common equity ratios, as shown in column 1. As you can see, companies in Italy and Japan use much greater proportion of debt than companies in the United States or Canada, and companies in the United Kingdom use the lowest proportion of debt of all the countries listed. Of course, different countries use somewhat different accounting conventions, which make comparisons difficult. Still, even after adjusting for accounting differences, researchers find that Italian and Japanese firms use considerably more financial leverage than U.S. and Canadian companies. The gap among the countries has narrowed somewhat during the past couple of decades. In the early 1970s, companies in Canada and the United States had debt/assets ratios of about 40 percent and companies in Japan, and Italy had debt/assets ratios of more than 75 percent (Japanese companies averaged nearly 85 percent leverage).

Why do international differences in financial leverage exist? It seems logical to attribute the differences to dissimilar tax structures. Although the interest on corporate debt is deductible in each country, and individuals must pay taxes on interest received, both dividends and capital gains are taxed differently around the world. The tax codes in most developed countries encourage personal investing and savings more than the U.S. Tax Code. For example, Germany, Italy, and many other European countries do not tax capital gains, and in most other developed countries, including Japan, France and Canada, capital gains are not taxed unless they exceed some minimum amount. Further, in Germany and Italy, dividends are not taxed as income, and in most other countries some amount of dividends is tax-exempt. Therefore, we can make the following general conclusions: (1) From a tax standpoint, corporations should be equally inclined to use debt in most developed countries. (2) In countries where capital gains are not taxed, investors should show a preference for stocks compared to countries that have capital gains taxes. (3) Investor preferences should lead to relatively low equity capital costs in those countries that do not tax capital gains, and this, in turn, should cause firms in those countries to use significantly more equity capital than their U.S. counterparts. But, for the most part, this is exactly the opposite of the actual capital structures we observe, so differential tax laws cannot explain the observed capital structure differences.

If tax rates cannot explain the different capital structures, what might be an appropriate explanation? Another possibility relates to risk, especially bankruptcy costs. Actual bankruptcy, and even the threat of potential bankruptcy, imposes a costly burden on firms with large amounts of debt. Note, though, that the threat of bankruptcy is dependent on the probability of bankruptcy. In the United States, *equity* monitoring costs are comparatively low because corporations produce quarterly reports and must comply with relatively stringent audit requirements. These conditions are less prevalent in the other countries. On the other hand, *debt* monitoring costs probably are lower in such countries as Germany and Japan than in the United States because most of the corporate debt consists of bank loans as opposed to publicly issued bonds. More importantly, though, the banks in many European and developed Asian countries are closely linked to the corporations that borrow from them, often holding major equity positions in, and having substantial influence over, the management of the debtor firms. Given these close relationships, the banks are much more directly involved with the debtor firms' affairs, and as a result they also are more accommodating than U.S. bondholders in the event of financial distress. This, in turn, suggests that any given amount of debt gives rise to a lower threat of bankruptcy than for a U.S. firm with the same amount of business risk. Thus, an analysis of both bankruptcy costs and equity monitoring costs leads to the conclusion that U.S. firms should have more equity and less debt than firms in countries such as Japan and Germany, which is what we typically observe.

We cannot state that one financial system is better than another in the sense of making the firms in one country more efficient than those in another. However, as U.S. firms become increasingly involved in worldwide operations, they must become increasingly aware of worldwide conditions, and they must be prepared to adapt to conditions in the various countries in which they do business.

Self-Test Question

Why do international differences in financial leverage exist?

Summary

In this chapter we discussed the concept of optimal capital structure and examined the effects of financial leverage on stock prices, earnings per share, and the cost of capital. The key concepts covered are listed here:

- A firm's **optimal capital structure** is that mix of debt and equity that maximizes the price of the firm's stock. At any point in time, the firm's management has a specific **target capital structure** in mind, presumably the optimal one, although this target might change over time.
- Several factors influence a firm's capital structure decisions. These factors include the firm's (1) **business risk,** (2) **tax position,** (3) need for **financial flexibility,** and (4) **managerial conservatism or aggressiveness** toward using debt.
- **Business risk** is the uncertainty associated with projections of a firm's future returns on equity. A firm will tend to have low business risk if the demand for its products is stable, if the prices of its inputs and products remain relatively

constant, if it can adjust its prices freely when costs increase, and if a high percentage of its costs are variable and hence decrease as its output and sales decrease. Other things the same, the lower a firm's business risk, the higher its optimal debt/assets ratio.

- **Financial leverage** is the extent to which fixed-income securities (debt and preferred stock) are used in a firm's capital structure. **Financial risk** is the added risk to stockholders that results from financial leverage.

- The **EPS indifference point** is the level of sales at which EPS will be the same whether the firm uses debt or common stock financing. Equity financing will be better if the firm's sales end up below the EPS indifference point, whereas debt financing will be better at higher sales levels.

- The **degree of operating leverage (DOL)** shows how changes in sales affect operating income, whereas the **degree of financial leverage (DFL)** shows how changes in operating income affect earnings per share. The **degree of total leverage (DTL)** shows the percentage change in EPS resulting from a given percentage change in sales: DTL = DOL × DFL.

- Modigliani and Miller developed a **trade-off theory of capital structure,** where debt is useful because interest is **tax deductible,** but debt brings with it costs associated with actual or potential bankruptcy. Under MM's theory, the optimal capital structure strikes a balance between the tax benefits of debt and the costs associated with bankruptcy.

- An alternative (or, really, complementary) theory of capital structure relates to the **signals** given to investors by a firm's decision to use debt or stock to raise new capital. The use of stock is a negative signal, while using debt is a positive or at least a neutral signal. Therefore, companies try to maintain a **reserve borrowing capacity,** and this means using less debt in "normal" times than the MM trade-off theory would suggest.

- Capital structures vary widely around the world. It seems the primary reason for such variation is the **risk** associated with firms' operations and financing arrangements.

Although it is theoretically possible to determine the optimal capital structure, as a practical matter we cannot estimate this structure with precision. Accordingly, financial executives generally treat the optimal capital structure as a range—for example, 40 to 50 percent debt—rather than as a precise point, such as 45 percent. The concepts discussed in this chapter help managers understand the factors they should consider when they set the target capital structure ranges for their firms.

Questions

11-1 "One type of leverage affects both EBIT and EPS. The other type affects only EPS." Explain what this statement means.

11-2 Explain why the following statement is true: "Other things the same, firms with relatively stable sales are able to carry relatively high debt/assets ratios."

11-3 If a firm went from zero debt to successively higher levels of debt, why would you expect its stock price to first rise, then hit a peak, and then begin to decline?

11-4 Why is EBIT generally considered to be independent of financial leverage? Why might EBIT actually be influenced by financial leverage at high levels of debt?

and this year's sales are expected to be 45,000 units. Variable production costs for the expected sales under present production methods are estimated at $10,200,000, and fixed production (operating) costs at present are $1,560,000. WCC has $4,800,000 of debt outstanding at an interest rate of eight percent. There are 240,000 shares of common stock outstanding, and there is no preferred stock. The dividend payout ratio is 70 percent, and WCC is in the 40 percent marginal tax bracket.

The company is considering investing $7,200,000 in new equipment. Sales would not increase, but variable costs per unit would decline by 20 percent. Also, fixed operating costs would increase from $1,560,000 to $1,800,000. WCC could raise the required capital by borrowing $7,200,000 at ten percent or by selling 240,000 additional shares at $30 per share.

a. What would be WCC's EPS (1) under the old production process, (2) under the new process if it uses debt, and (3) under the new process if it uses common stock?

b. Calculate the DOL, DFL, and DTL under the existing setup and under the new setup with each type of financing. Assume that the expected sales level is 45,000 units, or $12,960,000.

c. At what unit sales level would WCC have the same EPS, assuming it undertakes the investment and finances it with debt or with stock? (*Hint:* $V = $ variable cost per unit $= \$8,160,000/45,000$, and EPS $= [(P \times Q - V \times Q - F - I)(1 - T)]/$Shares. Set EPS$_{Stock} =$ EPS$_{Debt}$ and solve for Q.)

d. At what unit sales level would EPS $= 0$ under the three production/financing setups—that is, under the old plan, the new plan with debt financing, and the new plan with stock financing? (*Hint:* Note that $V_{Old} = \$10,200,000/45,000$, and use the hints for part b, setting the EPS equation equal to zero.)

e. On the basis of the analysis in parts a through c, which plan is the riskiest, which has the highest expected EPS, and which would you recommend? Assume here that there is a fairly high probability of sales falling as low as 25,000 units, and determine EPS$_{Debt}$ and EPS$_{Stock}$ at that sales level to help assess the riskiness of the two financing plans.

financing alternatives   **11–4** The Strasburg Company plans to raise a net amount of $270 million to finance new equipment and working capital in early 2001. Two alternatives are being considered: Common stock can be sold to net $60 per share, or bonds yielding 12 percent can be issued. The balance sheet and income statement of the Strasburg Company prior to financing are as follows:

THE STRASBURG COMPANY:
BALANCE SHEET AS OF DECEMBER 31, 2000
(MILLIONS OF DOLLARS)

Current assets	$ 900.00	Accounts payable	$ 172.50
Net fixed assets	450.00	Notes payable to bank	255.00
		Other current liabilities	225.00
		Total current liabilities	$ 652.50
		Long-term debt (10%)	300.00
		Common stock, $3 par	60.00
		Retained earnings	337.50
Total assets	$1,350.00	Total liabilities and equity	$1,350.00

THE STRASBURG COMPANY:
INCOME STATEMENT FOR YEAR ENDED
DECEMBER 31, 2000
(MILLIONS OF DOLLARS)

Sales	$2,475.00
Operating costs	(2,227.50)
Earnings before interest and taxes (EBIT) (10%)	$ 247.50
Interest on short-term debt	(15.00)
Interest on long-term debt	(30.00)
Earnings before taxes (EBT)	$ 202.50
Taxes (40%)	(81.00)
Net income	$ 121.50

The probability distribution for annual sales is as follows:

PROBABILITY	ANNUAL SALES (MILLIONS OF DOLLARS)
0.30	$2,250
0.40	2,700
0.30	3,150

Assuming that EBIT is equal to ten percent of sales, calculate earnings per share under both the debt financing and the stock financing alternatives at each possible level of sales. Then calculate expected earnings per share and σ_{EPS} under both debt and stock financing. Also, calculate the debt ratio and the times-interest-earned (TIE) ratio at the expected sales level under each alternative. The old debt will remain outstanding. Which financing method do you recommend?

Exam-Type Problems

The problems included in this section are set up in such a way that they could be used as multiple-choice exam problems.

financial leverage effects   **11–5** The firms HL and LL are identical except for their leverage ratios and interest rates on debt. Each has $20 million in assets, earned $4 million before interest and taxes in 2000, and has a 40 percent marginal tax rate. Firm HL, however, has a leverage ratio (D/TA) of 50 percent and pays 12 percent interest on its debt, whereas LL has a 30 percent leverage ratio and pays only ten percent interest on debt.
  a. Calculate the rate of return on equity (net income/equity) for each firm.
  b. Observing that HL has a higher return on equity, LL's treasurer decides to raise the leverage ratio from 30 to 60 percent, which will increase LL's interest rate on all debt to 15 percent. Calculate the new rate of return on equity for LL.

financial leverage effects   **11–6** The Damon Company wishes to calculate next year's return on equity under different leverage ratios. Damon's total assets are $14 million, and its marginal tax rate is 40 percent. The company is able to estimate next year's earnings before interest and taxes for three possible states of the world: $4.2 million with a 0.2 probability, $2.8 million with a 0.5 probability, and $700,000 with a 0.3 probability. Calculate Damon's expected return on equity, standard deviation, and coefficient of variation for each of the following leverage ratios and evaluate the results:

LEVERAGE (DEBT/ASSETS)	INTEREST RATE
0%	—
10	9%
50	11
60	14

Integrative Problem

optimal capital structure **11–7** Assume that you have just been hired by Adams, Garitty, and Evans (AGE), a consulting firm that specializes in analyses of firms' capital structures. Your boss has asked you to examine the capital structure of Campus Deli and Sub Shop (CDSS), which is located adjacent to the campus. According to the owner, sales were $1,350,000 last year; variable costs were 60 percent of sales; and fixed costs were $40,000. Therefore, EBIT totaled $500,000. Because the university's enrollment is capped, EBIT is expected to be constant over time. Because no expansion capital is required, CDSS pays out all earnings as dividends. The management group owns about 50 percent of the stock, which is traded in the over-the-counter market.

CDSS currently has no debt—it is an all equity firm—and its 100,000 shares outstanding sell at a price of $20 per share. The firm's marginal tax rate is 40 percent. On the basis of statements made in your finance text, you believe that CDSS's shareholders would be better off if some debt financing were used. When you suggested this to your new boss, she encouraged you to pursue the idea, but to provide support for the suggestion.

You then obtained from a local investment banker the following estimates of the costs of debt and equity at different debt levels (in thousands of dollars):

AMOUNT BORROWED	k_d	k_s
$ 0	—	15.0%
250	10.0%	15.5
500	11.0	16.5
750	13.0	18.0
1,000	16.0	20.0

If the firm were recapitalized, debt would be issued, and the borrowed funds would be used to repurchase stock. Stockholders, in turn, would use funds provided by the repurchase to buy equities in other fast food companies similar to CDSS. You plan to complete your report by asking and then answering the following questions:

a. (1) What is business risk? What factors influence a firm's business risk?

(2) What is operating leverage, and how does it affect a firm's business risk?

b. (1) What is meant by the terms *financial leverage* and *financial risk*?

(2) How does financial risk differ from business risk?

c. Now, develop an example that can be presented to CDSS's management. As an illustration, consider two hypothetical firms, Firm U, with zero debt financing, and Firm L, with $10,000 of 12 percent debt. Both firms have $20,000 in total assets and a 40 percent marginal tax rate, and they face the following EBIT probability distribution for next year:

PROBABILITY	EBIT
0.25	$2,000
0.50	3,000
0.25	4,000

(1) Complete the following partial income statements and the set of ratios for Firm L.

	FIRM U			FIRM L		
Assets	$20,000	$20,000	$20,000	$20,000	$20,000	$20,000
Equity	$20,000	$20,000	$20,000	$10,000	$10,000	$10,000
Probability	0.25	0.50	0.25	0.25	0.50	0.25
Sales	$ 6,000	$ 9,000	$12,000	$ 6,000	$ 9,000	$12,000
Operating costs	(4,000)	(6,000)	(8,000)	(4,000)	(6,000)	(8,000)
Earnings before interest and taxes	$ 2,000	$ 3,000	$ 4,000	$ 2,000	$ 3,000	$ 4,000
Interest (12%)	(0)	(0)	(0)	(1,200)		(1,200)
Earnings before taxes	$ 2,000	$ 3,000	$ 4,000	$ 800	$	$ 2,800
Taxes (40%)	(800)	(1,200)	(1,600)	(320)		(1,120)
Net income	$ 1,200	$ 1,800	$ 2,400	$ 480	$	$ 1,680
ROE	6.0%	9.0%	12.0%	4.8%	%	16.8%
TIE	∞	∞	∞	1.7×	×	3.3×
Expected ROE		9.0%			10.8%	
Expected TIE		∞			2.5×	
σ_{ROE}		2.1%			4.2%	
σ_{TIE}		0×			0.6×	

(2) What does this example illustrate concerning the impact of financial leverage on expected rate of return and risk?

d. With the preceding points in mind, now consider the optimal capital structure for CDSS.

(1) To begin, define the term *optimal capital structure*.

(2) Describe briefly, without using numbers, the sequence of events that would occur if CDSS decided to change its capital structure to include more debt.

(3) Assume that shares could be repurchased at the current market price of $20 per share. Calculate CDSS's expected EPS and TIE at debt levels of $0, $250,000, $500,000, $750,000, and $1,000,000. How many shares would remain after recapitalization under each scenario?

(4) What would be the new stock price if CDSS recapitalizes with $250,000 of debt? $500,000? $750,000? $1,000,000? Recall that the payout ratio is 100 percent, so g = 0.

(5) Considering only the levels of debt discussed, what is CDSS's optimal capital structure?

(6) Is EPS maximized at the debt level that maximizes share price? Why?

(7) What is the WACC at the optimal capital structure?

e. Suppose you discovered that CDSS had more business risk than you originally estimated. Describe how this would affect the analysis. What if the firm had less business risk than originally estimated?

f. What is meant by the terms *degree of operating leverage (DOL), degree of financial leverage (DFL),* and *degree of total leverage (DTL)?* If fixed costs total $40,000 and the company uses $500,000 of debt, what are CDSS's degrees of each type of leverage? Of what practical use is the degree of leverage concept?

g. What are some factors that should be considered when establishing a firm's target capital structure?

h. Put labels on the following graph, and then discuss the graph as you might use it to explain to your boss why CDSS might want to use some debt.

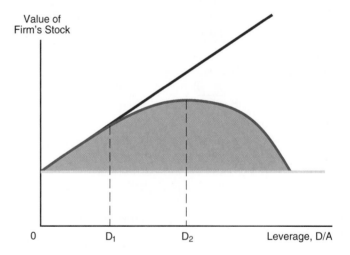

i. How does the existence of asymmetric information and signaling affect capital structure?

Computer-Related Problem

Work the problem in this section only if you are using the computer problem diskette.

effects of financial leverage　**11–8**　Use the model in File C11 to work this problem.

a. Rework Problem 11–4, assuming that the old long-term debt will not remain outstanding but, rather, that it must be refinanced at the new long-term interest rate of 12 percent. What effect does this have on the decision to refinance?

b. What would be the effect on the refinancing decision if the rate on long-term debt fell to five percent or rose to 20 percent, assuming that all long-term debt must be refinanced?

c. Which financing method would be recommended if the stock price (1) rose to $105 or (2) fell to $30? (Assume that all debt will have an interest rate of 12 percent.)

d. With $P_0 = \$60$ and $k_d = 12\%$, change the sales probability distribution to the following:

ALTERNATIVE 1		ALTERNATIVE 2	
SALES	PROBABILITY	SALES	PROBABILITY
$2,250	0.0	$ 0	0.3
2,700	1.0	2,700	0.4
3,150	0.0	7,500	0.3

What are the implications of these changes?

ONLINE ESSENTIALS

http://www.morevalue.com/themes/themes.html   +Value morevalue.com
This site provides links to news articles, lecture notes, course outlines, and so forth, that relate to various finance topics. You can get information about capital structure by entering the phrase "capital structure" in the search box and clicking on the Search key or by clicking on "Capital Structure" in the list of Themes & Topics. You can also get an outline of lecture notes by clicking on "Lecture Notes" on the left side of the screen.

http://www.olin.wustl.edu/faculty/back/general.htm
Olin School of Business spreadsheets
You can access various spreadsheets developed or compiled by Professor Kerry Black. You can download the spreadsheet labeled "Optimal Capital Structure," which allows you to change the tax rate, debt/assets ratio, and other information for a fictional company to examine the effect on the firm's stock price, expected return, and other values.

http://www.cfoeurope.com/199809g.html   CFO Europe
CFO Europe is a magazine for financial executives in European companies. This site provides the text of an article published in the magazine titled "Corporate Finance, Capital Structure, Modigliani and Miller," which gives a good summary of the views of Modigliani and Miller (MM) concerning capital structure. The article also relates the applicability of the MM theory.

http://www.irs.ustreas.gov/plain/tax_stats/soi/corp_id.html
IRS Corporate Tax Statistics: Industry Data
Balance sheet data divided by industry are available at this site. You can see how the capital structures differ among industries. You can get information about the capital structures of specific companies by visiting their respective Web sites directly.

CHAPTER 12

Dividend Policy

A MANAGERIAL PERSPECTIVE

At the beginning of Chapter 11, we described the actions Unisys Corporation, a manufacturer of computers and related products for commercial and defense companies, has taken in recent years to reduce the relative amount of debt in its capital structure. One of the first actions taken to improve the financial position of the firm was to suspend the payment of common stock dividends. This policy, which directly affected stockholders' cash receipts, has been in effect since the board of directors made the decision in September of 1990. Prior to that time, Unisys had paid a regular dividend to common stockholders for nearly 100 years. So why were dividend payments suspended? According to James Unruh, president and CEO at the time (he was replaced by Lawrence A. Weinbach in 1997), the dividend suspension was in the "best interests" of shareholders—the board felt Unisys needed to strengthen its financial condition to improve *shareholder wealth*.

Suspending the common stock dividend saved Unisys more than $162 million a year and allowed the company to use the funds to reduce debt. Unfortunately, when Unisys announced the dividend suspension, the price of its common stock dropped more than 25 percent in one day and by about one-third of its pre-announcement value within one week. Clearly, the dividend suspension was not greeted favorably by the stockholders. Since that time, however, the cash savings associated with the dividend suspension along with other actions Unisys has taken have improved the company's financial stability, and, as a result, its stock price has rebounded. The stock's market price in 1999 was greater than $41, which represented an increase of more than 720 percent since the price decline that resulted from the suspension of dividends.

As you can see from this example, a firm's dividend policy can have a significant impact on its market value. Also, from this Managerial Perspective as well as the one in Chapter 11, it should be clear that a firm's dividend policy affects its capital structure—a firm can use each dollar of earnings to finance projects internally or to pay dividends to stockholders, but not both. As you read this chapter, think about why Unisys suspended its common stock dividend. Consider the impact a particular dividend policy can have on the cash position of a firm and, more important, how a change in the policy can affect the value of a firm. ∎

DIVIDENDS
Distributions made to stockholders from the firm's earnings, whether those earnings were generated in the current period or in previous periods.

OPTIMAL DIVIDEND POLICY
The dividend policy that strikes a balance between current dividends and future growth and maximizes the firm's stock price.

We refer to the cash payments, or distributions, made to stockholders from the firm's earnings, whether those earnings were generated in the current period or in previous periods, as **dividends.** Consequently, a firm's *dividend policy* involves the decision to pay out earnings or to retain them for reinvestment in the firm. Remember that, according to the constant dividend growth model given in Chapter 7, the value of common stock can be computed as $P_0 = \hat{D}_1/(k_s - g)$. This equation shows that if the firm adopts a policy of paying out more cash dividends, $\hat{D}_1$ will rise, which will tend to increase the price of the stock. However, if cash dividends are increased, then less money will be available for reinvestment and the expected future growth rate, g, will be lowered, which will depress the price of the stock. Thus, changing the dividend has two opposing effects. *The* **optimal dividend policy** *for a firm strikes that balance between current dividends and future growth that maximizes the price of the stock.*

In this chapter, we first examine factors that affect the optimal dividend policy and the types of dividend policies generally used by firms.

Dividend Policy and Stock Value

How do dividend policy decisions affect a firm's stock price? Academic researchers have studied this question extensively for many years, and they have yet to reach definitive conclusions. On the one hand, there are those who suggest that dividend policy is *irrelevant* because they argue a firm's value should be determined by the basic earning power and business risk of the firm, in which case value depends only on the income (cash) produced, not on how the income is split between dividends and retained earnings (and hence growth).

DIVIDEND IRRELEVANCE THEORY
The theory that a firm's dividend policy has no effect on either its value or its cost of capital.

Proponents of this line of reasoning, called the **dividend irrelevance theory,** would contend that investors care *only* about the *total returns* they receive, not whether they receive those returns in the form of dividends or capital gains. Thus, *if the dividend irrelevance theory is correct, there exists no optimal dividend policy because dividend policy does not affect the value of the firm.*[1]

On the other hand, it is quite possible that investors prefer one dividend policy over another; if so, a firm's dividend policy is *relevant.* For example, it has been argued that investors prefer to receive dividends "today" because current dividend payments are more certain than the future capital gains that *might* result from investing retained earnings in growth opportunities, so k_s should decrease as the dividend payout is increased.[2]

Another factor that might cause investors to prefer a particular dividend policy is the tax effect of dividend receipts. Investors must pay taxes at the time dividends and

---

[1]The principal proponents of the *dividend irrelevance theory* are Miller and Modigliani (MM), who outlined their theory in "Dividend Policy, Growth, and the Valuation of Shares," *Journal of Business,* October 1961, 411–433. The assumptions MM made to develop their dividend irrelevance theory are similar to those they introduced in their capital structure theory mentioned in the previous chapter, which include no personal taxes, no brokerage costs, no bankruptcy, and so forth. Such assumptions are made to afford them the ability to develop a manageable theory.

[2]Myron J. Gordon, "Optimal Investment and Financing Policy," *Journal of Finance,* May 1963, 264–272, and John Lintner, "Dividends, Earnings, Leverage, Stock Prices, and the Supply of Capital to Corporations," *Review of Economics and Statistics,* August 1962, 243–269.

capital gains are received. Thus, depending on his or her tax situation, an investor might prefer either a payout of current earnings as dividends, which would be taxed in the current period, or capital gains associated with growth in stock value, which would be taxed when the stock is sold, perhaps many years in the future and perhaps at different rates than dividends. Investors who prefer to delay the impact of taxes would be willing to pay more for low payout companies than for otherwise similar high payout companies, and vice versa.

Those who believe the firm's dividend policy is relevant are proponents of the **dividend relevance theory,** which asserts dividend policy can affect the value of a firm through investors' preferences.

DIVIDEND RELEVANCE THEORY
The value of a firm is affected by its dividend policy—the optimal dividend policy is the one that maximizes the firm's value.

Self-Test Questions

Differentiate between the dividend irrelevance and dividend relevance theories.

How might taxes affect investors' preferences concerning the receipt of dividends and capital gains?

Investors and Dividend Policy

Although academic researchers have studied the dividend policy issue extensively, the issue remains unresolved; researchers at this time simply cannot tell corporate decision makers exactly how dividend policy affects stock prices and capital costs. But from the research, some views have been presented concerning investors' reactions to dividend policy changes and why firms have particular dividend policies. Three of these views are discussed in this section.

Information Content, or Signaling

If investors expect a company's dividend to increase by five percent per year, and if, in fact, the dividend is increased by five percent, then the stock price generally will not change significantly on the day the dividend increase is announced. In Wall Street parlance, such a dividend increase would be "discounted," or *anticipated,* by the market. However, if investors expect a five percent increase, but the company actually increases the dividend by 25 percent—say from $2 to $2.50—this generally would be accompanied by an increase in the price of the stock. Conversely, a less-than-expected dividend increase, or a reduction, generally would result in a price decline.

It is a well-known fact that corporations are extremely reluctant to cut dividends and, therefore, *managers do not raise dividends unless they anticipate higher, or at least stable, earnings in the future to sustain the higher dividends.* This means that a larger-than-expected dividend increase is taken by investors as a *signal* that the firm's management forecasts improved future earnings, whereas a dividend reduction signals a forecast of poor earnings. Thus, it can be argued investors' reactions to changes in dividend payments do not show that investors prefer dividends to retained earnings; rather, the stock price changes simply indicate important information is contained in dividend announcements—in effect, dividend announcements provide investors with information previously known only to management. This theory is referred to as the **information content, or signaling, hypothesis.**

INFORMATION CONTENT (SIGNALING) HYPOTHESIS
The theory that investors regard dividend changes as signals of management's earnings forecasts.

Clientele Effect

It also has been shown that it is very possible that a firm sets a particular dividend payout policy, which then attracts a *clientele* consisting of those investors who like the firm's dividend policy. For example, some stockholders, such as retired individuals, prefer current income to future capital gains, so they want the firm to pay out a higher percentage of its earnings. Other stockholders have no need for current investment income, so they favor a low payout ratio. If investors could not invest in companies with different dividend policies, it might be very expensive for them to achieve their investment goals—investors that prefer capital gains could reinvest any dividends they receive, but they first would have to pay taxes on the income. In essence, then, a **clientele effect** might exist if stockholders are attracted to companies because they have particular dividend policies. Those investors who desire current investment income can purchase shares in high-dividend-payout firms, whereas those who do not need current cash income can invest in low-payout firms. Consequently, we would expect the stock price of a firm to change if the firm changes its dividend policy, because investors will adjust their portfolios to include firms with the desired dividend policy.

CLIENTELE EFFECT
The tendency of a firm to attract the type of investor who likes its dividend policy.

Free Cash Flow Hypothesis

If it is the intent of the financial manager to maximize the value of the firm, then investors should prefer that firms pay dividends only if acceptable capital budgeting opportunities do not exist. We know that acceptable capital budgeting projects increase the value of the firm. We also know that, because flotation costs are incurred when issuing new stock, it costs a firm more to raise funds using new common equity than it does using retained earnings. So to maximize value, wherever possible a firm should use retained earnings rather than issue new common stock to finance capital budgeting projects. Thus, dividends should be paid only when *free cash flows* in excess of capital budgeting needs exist. If management does otherwise, the firm's value will not be maximized. According to the **free cash flow hypothesis,** the firm should distribute any earnings that cannot be reinvested at a rate at least as great as the investors' required rate of return, k_s (i.e., the free cash flows). Everything else equal, firms that retain *free cash flows* will have lower values than firms that distribute *free cash flows* because the firms that retain free cash flows actually decrease investors' wealth by investing in projects with IRR $< k_s$.

FREE CASH FLOW HYPOTHESIS
All else equal, firms that pay dividends from cash flows that cannot be reinvested in positive net present value projects, which are termed *free cash flows*, have higher values than firms that retain free cash flows.

The free cash flow hypothesis might help to explain why investors react differently to identical dividend changes made by similar firms. For example, a firm's stock price should not change dramatically if it reduces its dividend for the purposes of investing in capital budgeting projects with positive NPVs. On the other hand, a company that reduces its dividend simply to increase free cash flows should experience a significant decline in the market value of its stock because the dividend reduction is not in the best interests of the stockholders—in this case, an agency problem exists. Thus, the free cash flow hypothesis suggests the dividend policy can provide information about the firm's behavior with respect to wealth maximization.

Self-Test Question

Define (1) information content, (2) the clientele effect, and (3) the free cash flow hypothesis, and explain how each affects dividend policy.

Dividend Policy in Practice

We have provided some insights concerning the relevance of dividend policy and how investors might view dividend payments from firms. However, no one has been able to develop a formula that can be used to tell management specifically how a given dividend policy will affect a firm's stock price. Even so, managements still must establish dividend policies. This section discusses several alternative policies and procedures that are used in practice.

Types of Dividend Payments

The dollar amounts of dividends paid by firms follow a variety of patterns. In general, though, firms pay dividends using one of the four payout policies discussed next.

Residual Dividend Policy   In practice, dividend policy is very much influenced by investment opportunities and by the availability of funds with which to finance new investments. This fact has led to the development of a **residual dividend policy,** which states that a firm should follow these steps when deciding how much earnings should be paid out as dividends: (1) determine the optimal capital budget for the year, (2) determine the amount of capital needed to finance that budget, (3) use retained earnings to supply the equity component to the extent possible, and (4) pay dividends only if more earnings are available than are needed to support the optimal capital budget. The word *residual* means "left over," and the residual policy implies that dividends should be paid only out of "leftover" earnings.

RESIDUAL DIVIDEND POLICY

A policy in which the dividend paid is set equal to the actual earnings minus the amount of retained earnings necessary to finance the firm's optimal capital budget.

The basis of the residual policy is the fact that *investors prefer to have the firm retain and reinvest earnings rather than pay them out in dividends if the rate of return the firm can earn on reinvested earnings exceeds the rate investors, on average, can themselves obtain on other investments of comparable risk.* For example, if the corporation can reinvest retained earnings at a 14 percent rate of return, whereas the best rate the average stockholder can obtain if the earnings are passed on in the form of dividends is 12 percent, then stockholders should prefer to have the firm retain the profits.

To continue, we saw in Chapter 10 that the cost of retained earnings is an *opportunity cost* that reflects rates of return available to equity investors. If a firm's stockholders can buy other stocks of equal risk and obtain a 12 percent dividend-plus-capital-gains yield, then 12 percent is the firm's cost of retained earnings. The cost of new outside equity raised by selling common stock will be higher than 12 percent because of the costs associated with the issue.

Most firms have a target capital structure that calls for at least some debt, so new financing is done partly with debt and partly with equity. As long as the firm finances with the optimal mix of debt and equity, and as long as it uses only internally generated equity (retained earnings), its marginal cost of each new dollar of capital will be minimized. Internally generated equity is available for financing a certain amount of new investment, but beyond that amount the firm must turn to more expensive new common stock. At the point where new stock must be sold, the cost of equity, and consequently the marginal cost of capital, rises.

These concepts, which were developed in Chapter 10, are illustrated in Figure 12–1 with data from the Texas and Western (T&W) Transport Company. T&W has a marginal cost of capital (MCC) of ten percent. However, this cost rate assumes that all new equity comes from retained earnings. Therefore, MCC = 10% as long as retained earnings are available, but MCC begins to rise at the point where new stock must be sold.

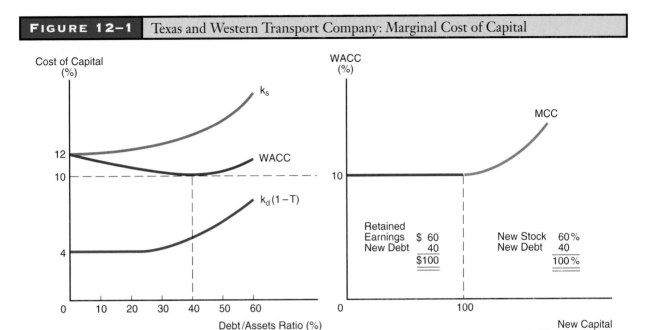

FIGURE 12-1 Texas and Western Transport Company: Marginal Cost of Capital

T&W has $60 million of net income and a 40 percent optimal debt ratio. Provided it does not pay cash dividends, T&W can make net investments (investments in addition to asset replacements financed from depreciation) of $100 million, consisting of $60 million from retained earnings plus $40 million of new debt supported by the retained earnings, at a ten percent marginal cost of capital. Therefore, its MCC is constant at ten percent up to $100 million of capital, beyond which it rises as the firm begins to use more expensive new common stock.

Suppose T&W's director of capital budgeting has determined that the optimal capital budget requires an investment equal to $70 million. The $70 million will be financed using $28 million debt ($70 million × 0.40) and $42 million in common equity ($70 million × 0.60). So the $60 million retained earnings will be more than sufficient to cover the common equity financing requirement, and the *residual* of $18 million ($60 million − $42 million) can be paid out as dividends to stockholders.

Now suppose T&W's optimal capital budget is $150 million. Should dividends be paid? Not if T&W follows the residual dividend policy. The $150 million capital budgeting needs will be financed with $60 million debt ($150 million × 0.40) and $90 million common equity ($150 million × 0.60). The common equity financing requirement of $90 million exceeds the $60 million retained earnings available, so $30 million of new common equity will have to be issued. The new, or external, common equity will have a higher cost than retained earnings, so the marginal cost of capital for T&W will be higher. Under these conditions, T&W should not pay dividends to its stockholders. If the company pays part of its earnings in dividends, the marginal cost of capital will be even higher because more common stock will have to be issued to account for the amount of retained earnings paid out as dividends. For example, if T&W pays stockholders $20 million in dividends, it still needs $90 million of common equity to satisfy the capital budgeting requirements. In this case, $70 million of

have been about 44 cents less than the close on Thursday, May 27.[4] The price of the stock actually decreased by a little more than 44 cents due to other factors, including a general market decline on that day.

PAYMENT DATE
The date on which a firm actually mails dividend checks.

4. **Payment date.** Kodak paid the common stock dividends on July 1, 1999—this is the *payment date.* Recently, many firms have started paying dividends electronically.

Dividend Reinvestment Plans

DIVIDEND REINVESTMENT PLAN (DRIP)
A plan that enables a stockholder to automatically reinvest dividends received back into the stock of the paying firm.

Most larger companies offer **dividend reinvestment plans (DRIPs),** whereby stockholders can automatically reinvest dividends received in the stock of the paying corporation.[5] There are two types of DRIPs (referred to as "drips"): (1) plans that involve only "old" stock that already is outstanding and traded in the financial markets and (2) plans that involve newly issued stock. In either case, the stockholder must pay income taxes on the amount of the dividends even though stock rather than cash is received.

Under the "old-stock" type of plan, the stockholder chooses between receiving dividend checks or having the company use the dividends to buy more stock in the corporation. If the stockholder elects reinvestment, a bank, acting as trustee, takes the total funds available for reinvestment, purchases the corporation's stock on the open market, and allocates the shares purchased to the participating stockholders' accounts on a *pro rata* basis. The transactions costs of buying shares (brokerage costs) are low because of volume purchases, so these plans benefit small stockholders who do not need cash dividends for current consumption.

The "new-stock" type of DRIP provides for dividends to be invested in newly issued stock; hence, these plans raise new capital for the firm. AT&T, Florida Power & Light, Union Carbide, and many other companies have had such plans in effect in recent years, using them to raise substantial amounts of new equity capital. No fees are charged to stockholders, and many companies offer stock at a discount of five percent

---

[4]Tax effects cause the price decline on average to be less than the full amount of the dividend. Suppose you were an investor in the 40 percent tax bracket. If you bought Kodak's stock on May 27, you would receive the dividend, but you would have to pay 40 percent of it out in taxes within one year. Thus, you would want to wait until after May 27 to buy the stock if you thought you could get it for $0.44 less per share. Your reaction, and those of others, would influence stock prices around dividend payment dates. Here is what would happen:

1. Other things held constant, a stock's price should rise during the quarter, with the daily price increase (for Kodak) equal to $0.44/90 = $0.00489. Therefore, if the price started at $70 just after its last ex-dividend date, it would rise to $70.44 on May 27.

2. In the absence of taxes, the stock's price would fall to $70 on May 28 and then start up as the next dividend accrual period began. Thus, over time, if everything else were held constant, the stock's price would follow a sawtooth pattern if it were plotted on a graph.

3. Because of taxes, the stock's price would neither rise by the full amount of the dividend nor fall by the full dividend amount when it goes ex-dividend.

4. The amount of the rise and subsequent fall would depend on the average investor's marginal tax rate.

See Edwin J. Elton and Martin J. Gruber, "Marginal Stockholder Tax Rates and the Clientele Effect," *Review of Economics and Statistics,* February 1970, 68–74, for an interesting discussion of this concept.

[5]See Richard H. Pettway and R. Phil Malone, "Automatic Dividend Reinvestment Plans," *Financial Management,* Winter 1973, 11–18, for an excellent discussion of this topic.

below the actual market price. The companies absorb these costs as a trade-off against the flotation costs that would have been incurred had they sold stock through investment bankers rather than through the dividend reinvestment plans.[6]

Self-Test Questions

Explain the logic of the residual dividend policy, the steps a firm would take to implement it, and why it is more likely to be used to establish a long-run payout target than to set the actual year-by-year payout ratio.

Describe the stable, predictable dividend policy, and give two reasons why a firm might follow such a policy.

Describe the constant payout ratio dividend policy. Why is this policy probably not as popular as a constant, or steadily increasing, dividend policy?

Explain what a low-regular-dividend-plus-extras policy is and why a firm might follow such a policy.

Why is the ex-dividend date important to investors?

Differentiate between the two types of dividend reinvestment plans.

Factors Influencing Dividend Policy

In addition to managements' beliefs concerning which dividend theory is most correct, a number of other factors are considered when a particular dividend policy is chosen. The factors firms take into account can be grouped into these four broad categories:

1. **Constraints on dividend payments.** The amount of dividends a firm can pay might be limited due to (1) debt contract restrictions, which often stipulate that no dividends can be paid unless certain financial measures, such as the times-interest-earned ratio, exceed stated minimums; (2) the fact that dividend payments cannot exceed the balance sheet item "retained earnings" (this is known as the *impairment of capital rule*, which is designed to protect creditors by prohibiting the company from distributing assets to stockholders before debtholders are paid); (3) cash availability, because cash dividends can be paid only with cash; and (4) restrictions imposed by the Internal Revenue Service (IRS) on improperly accumulated retained earnings. If the IRS can demonstrate that a firm's dividend payout ratio is being held down deliberately to help its stockholders avoid personal taxes, the firm is subject to heavy tax penalties. But this factor generally is relevant only to privately owned firms.

---

[6]One interesting aspect of DRIPs is that they are forcing corporations to reexamine their basic dividend policies. A high participation rate in a DRIP suggests that stockholders might be better off if the firm simply reduced cash dividends, as this would save stockholders some personal income taxes. Quite a few firms are surveying their stockholders to learn more about their preferences and to find out how they would react to a change in dividend policy. A more rational approach to basic dividend policy decisions might emerge from this research.

Also, it should be noted that companies either use or stop using new-stock DRIPs depending on their need for equity capital. Florida Power & Light recently stopped offering a new-stock DRIP with a five percent discount because its need for equity capital declined once it had completed a nuclear-powered generating plant.

2. **Investment opportunities.** Firms that have large numbers of acceptable capital budgeting projects generally have low dividend payout ratios, and vice versa. But if a firm can accelerate or postpone projects (flexibility), then it can adhere more closely to a target dividend policy.

3. **Alternative sources of capital.** When a firm needs to finance a given level of investment and flotation costs are high, k_e will be well above k_s, making it better to set a low payout ratio and to finance through retention rather than through sale of new common stock. Also, if the firm can adjust its debt/assets ratio without raising capital costs sharply, it can maintain a stable dollar dividend, even if earnings fluctuate, by using a variable debt/assets ratio. Another factor considered by management when making financing decisions is ownership dilution—if management is concerned about maintaining control, it might be reluctant to sell new stock; hence, the company might retain more earnings than it otherwise would.

4. **Effects of dividend policy on k_s.** The effects of dividend policy on k_s might be considered in terms of four factors: (a) stockholders' desire for current versus future income; (b) the perceived riskiness of dividends versus capital gains; (c) the tax advantage of capital gains over dividends; and (d) the information content of dividends (signaling). Because we discussed each of these factors earlier, we need only note here that the importance of each factor in terms of its effect on k_s varies from firm to firm depending on the makeup of its current and possible future stockholders.

It should be apparent from our discussions that dividend policy decisions truly are exercises in informed judgment, not decisions that can be quantified precisely. Even so, to make rational dividend decisions, financial managers must consider all of the points discussed in the preceding sections.

Self-Test Questions

Identify the four broad categories of factors that affect dividend policy.

What constraints affect dividend policy?

How do investment opportunities affect dividend policy?

How does the availability and cost of outside capital affect dividend policy?

Stock Dividends and Stock Splits

Stock dividends and stock splits are related to the firm's cash dividend policy. The rationale for stock dividends and splits can best be explained through an example. We will use Porter Electronic Controls Inc., a $700 million electronic components manufacturer, for this purpose. Since its inception, Porter's markets have been expanding, and the company has enjoyed growth in sales and earnings. Some of its earnings have been paid out in dividends, but some are also retained each year, causing earnings per share and market price per share to grow. The company began its life with only a few thousand shares outstanding, and, after some years of growth, each of Porter's shares had a very high earnings per share (EPS) and dividends per share (DPS). When a "normal" price/earnings (P/E) ratio was applied, the derived market price was so high that few people could afford to buy a "round lot" of 100 shares. This limited the demand for the stock and thus kept the total market value of the firm below what it would have been if more shares, at a lower price, had been outstanding. To correct this situation, Porter "split its stock," as described next.

Stock Splits

Although there is little empirical evidence to support the contention, there is nevertheless a widespread belief in financial circles that an *optimal, or psychological, price range* exists for stocks. "Optimal" means that if the price is within this range, the P/E ratio, hence the value of the firm, will be maximized. Many observers, including Porter's management, believe that the best range for most stocks is from $20 to $80 per share. Accordingly, if the price of Porter's stock rose to $80, management probably would declare a two-for-one **stock split,** thus doubling the number of shares outstanding, halving the earnings and dividends per share, and thereby lowering the price of the stock. Each stockholder would have more shares, but each share would be worth less. If the post-split price were $40, Porter's stockholders would be exactly as well off as they were before the split because they would have twice as many shares at half the price as before the split. However, if the price of the stock were to stabilize above $40, stockholders would be better off. Stock splits can be of any size—for example, the stock could be split 2-for-1, 3-for-1, 1½-for-1, or in any other way.[7]

> **STOCK SPLIT**
> An action taken by a firm to increase the number of shares outstanding, such as doubling the number of shares outstanding by giving each stockholder two new shares for each one formerly held.

Stock Dividends

Stock dividends are similar to stock splits in that they "divide the pie into smaller slices" without affecting the fundamental position of the current stockholders. On a five percent stock dividend, the holder of 100 shares would receive an additional five shares (without cost); on a 20 percent stock dividend, the same holder would receive 20 new shares; and so on. Again, the total number of shares is increased, so earnings, dividends, and price per share all decline.

> **STOCK DIVIDEND**
> A dividend paid in the form of additional shares of stock rather than cash.

If a firm wants to reduce the price of its stock, should it use a stock split or a stock dividend? Stock splits generally are used after a sharp price run-up to produce a large price reduction. Stock dividends typically are used on a regular annual basis to keep the stock price more or less constrained. For example, if a firm's earnings and dividends were growing at about ten percent per year, its stock price would tend to go up at about that same rate, and it would soon be outside the desired trading range. A ten percent annual stock dividend would maintain the stock price within the optimal trading range.

Balance Sheet Effects

Although the economic effects of stock splits and stock dividends are virtually identical, accountants treat them somewhat differently. On a 2-for-1 split, the shares outstanding are doubled, and the stock's par value is halved. This treatment is shown

---

[7]Reverse splits, which reduce the shares outstanding, can even be used. For instance, a company whose stock sells for $5 might employ a 1-for-5 reverse split, exchanging one new share for five old ones and raising the value of the shares to about $25, which is within the optimal range. On February 11, 1999, for example, Galaxy Foods initiated a 1-for-7 reverse split to avoid being delisted from the NASDAQ SmallCap Market.

By 1988 new competitors had entered the market, and Apple's growth was slowing down. *Value Line's* analysts estimated that Apple's revenues would grow at an annual rate of 26 percent during the period 1988 to 1993. While a growth rate of 26 percent per year was well above average, it was far below Apple's earlier growth rate of 50 percent. On the basis of these growth forecasts, Apple's board of directors met early in 1987 and declared an annual dividend of $0.24 per share. The stock price reacted favorably, so the annual dividend was raised in 1988 to $0.32, and on up to $0.48 by 1994. Unfortunately, since that time, Apple has encountered financial difficulties, primarily because of lost market share, and in 1997 dividend payments were suspended. This shows how business risk can affect dividend policy.

This story illustrates four points. First, small, rapidly growing firms generally need to retain all their earnings, and also to obtain additional capital from outside sources, to support growth. Growth requires cash, and even highly profitable companies like Apple have difficulty generating enough cash from earnings both to support rapid growth and to pay dividends. Second, as the firm matures, its growth will slow down, and its need for funds will diminish. Thus, when Apple's growth began to slow down, it no longer needed to retain all of its earnings, so it began to pay a small dividend. Third, the market recognizes that new, profitable firms often grow so fast that they must raise needed funds through new issues of common stock, and such issues can be considered indications that the firm's managers anticipate extraordinarily good investment opportunities. And fourth, business risk can have a significant effect on dividend policy; competitive conditions might impact a firm's dividend policy by affecting its cash position.

Summary

Dividend policy involves the decision to pay out earnings versus retaining them for reinvestment in the firm, and dividend policy decisions can have either favorable or unfavorable effects on the price of a firm's stock. The key concepts covered are listed here:

- The **optimal dividend policy** is that policy that strikes the exact balance between current dividends and future growth that maximizes the price of the firm's stock.
- Miller and Modigliani developed the **dividend irrelevance theory,** which holds that a firm's dividend policy has no effect either on the value of its stock or on its cost of capital.
- Those who believe in **dividend relevance** suggest that a particular dividend policy might be preferred because dividends are considered less risky than potential capital gains, taxes must be paid on dividends received in the current period, while taxes on capital gains can be deferred until the stock is sold, and so on.
- Because empirical tests of the theories have been inconclusive, *academicians simply cannot tell corporate managers precisely how a change in dividend policy will affect stock prices and capital costs.* Thus, actually determining the optimal dividend policy is often a matter of **judgment.**
- Dividend policy should reflect the existence of the **information content of dividends (signaling), the clientele effect,** and **the free cash flow effect.** The information content, or signaling, hypothesis states that investors regard dividend changes as a signal of management's forecast of future earnings. According to the clientele effect, a firm will attract investors who like the firm's dividend policy. And the free cash flow effect suggests that firms with few capital budgeting opportunities and great amounts of cash should have higher dividend payout ratios if the value maximization goal is pursued.

- In practice, most firms try to follow a policy of paying a **stable, predictable dividend.** This policy provides investors with a stable, dependable income, and it also gives investors information about management's expectations for earnings growth through signaling effects.

- Other dividend policies used include (1) the **residual dividend policy,** in which dividends are paid out of earnings left over after the capital budget has been financed; (2) the **constant payout ratio policy,** in which a constant *percentage* of earnings is targeted to be paid out; and (3) the **low-regular-dividend-plus-extras policy,** in which the firm pays a constant, low dividend that can be maintained even in bad years and then pays an extra dividend in good years.

- A **dividend reinvestment plan (DRIP)** allows stockholders to have the company automatically use their dividends to purchase additional shares of the firm's stock. DRIPs are popular with investors who do not need current income because the plans allow stockholders to acquire additional shares without incurring normal brokerage fees.

- Other factors, such as **legal constraints, investment opportunities, availability and cost of funds from other sources,** and **taxes,** are considered by managers when they establish dividend policies.

- A **stock split** is an action taken by a firm to increase the number of shares outstanding. Normally, splits reduce the price per share in proportion to the increase in shares because splits merely *divide the pie into smaller slices.* A **stock dividend** is a dividend paid in additional shares of stock rather than in cash. Both stock dividends and splits are used to keep stock prices within an "optimal," or psychological, range.

- Dividend polices differ substantially among companies in different countries. All else equal, firms pay out **greater relative amounts** of earnings as dividends **in countries that have measures that protect the rights of minority stockholders.**

- Small, rapidly growing firms generally need to **retain all their earnings** and to obtain additional capital from outside sources to support growth. As the firm matures, its growth will slow down, and its need for funds will diminish. The market recognizes that new, profitable firms often grow so fast that they simply must issue common stock and that such issues indicate that the firm's managers anticipate extraordinarily good investment opportunities.

Questions

12-1 As an investor, would you rather invest in a firm that has a policy of maintaining (a) a constant payout ratio, (b) a stable, predictable dividend per share with a target dividend growth rate, or (c) a constant regular quarterly dividend plus a year-end extra when earnings are sufficiently high or corporate investment needs sufficiently low? Explain your answer, stating how these policies would affect your required rate of return, k_s. Also, discuss how your answer might change if you were a student, a 50-year-old professional with peak earnings, or a retiree.

12-2 How would each of the following changes tend to affect the average dividend payout ratios for corporations, other things held constant? Explain your answers.
  a. An increase in the personal income tax rate.
  b. A liberalization of depreciation for federal income tax purposes—that is, faster tax write-offs.
  c. A rise in interest rates.

    d. An increase in corporate profits.

    e. A decline in corporate investment opportunities.

    f. Permission for corporations to deduct dividends for tax purposes as they now can do with interest charges.

    g. A change in the tax code so that both realized and unrealized capital gains in any year were taxed at the same rate as dividends.

12–3 Most firms would like to have their stock selling at a high P/E ratio, and they would also like to have a large number of different shareholders. Explain how stock dividends or stock splits might help achieve these goals.

12–4 What is the difference between a stock dividend and a stock split? As a stockholder, would you prefer to see your company declare a 100 percent stock dividend or a 2-for-1 split? Assume that either action is feasible.

12–5 "The cost of retained earnings is less than the cost of new outside equity capital. Consequently, it is totally irrational for a firm to sell a new issue of stock and to pay dividends during the same year." Discuss this statement.

12–6 Would it ever be rational for a firm to borrow money in order to pay dividends? Explain.

12–7 Give arguments to support both the relevance and the irrelevance of paying dividends.

12–8 One position expressed in the financial literature is that firms set their dividends as a residual after using income to support new investment.

    a. Explain what a residual dividend policy implies, illustrating your answer with a graph showing how different conditions could lead to different dividend payout ratios.

    b. Could the residual dividend policy be consistent with (1) a stable, predictable dividend policy, (2) a constant payout ratio policy, or (3) a low-regular-dividend-plus-extras policy? Answer in terms of both short-run, year-to-year consistency, and longer-run consistency.

    c. Think back to Chapter 11, where we considered the relationship between capital structure and the cost of capital. If the WACC-versus-debt-ratio plot was shaped like a sharp V, would this have a different implication for the importance of setting dividends according to the residual policy than if the plot was shaped like a shallow bowl (or a flattened U)?

Self-Test Problems

Solutions appear in Appendix B

key terms   **ST–1** Define each of the following terms:

    a. Optimal dividend policy

    b. Dividend irrelevance theory; dividend relevance theory

    c. Information content, or signaling, hypothesis; clientele effect; free cash flow hypothesis

    d. Residual dividend policy; stable, predictable dividend policy; constant payout ratio policy; low-regular-dividend-plus-extra policy

    e. Declaration date; holder-of-record date; ex-dividend date; payment date

    f. Dividend reinvestment plan (DRIP)

    g. Stock split; stock dividend

alternative dividend   **ST–2** Components Manufacturing Corporation (CMC) has an all-common-equity
policies   capital structure. It has 200,000 shares of $2 par value common stock outstand-

ing. When CMC's founder, who was also its research director and most successful inventor, retired unexpectedly to the South Pacific in late 2000, CMC was left suddenly and permanently with materially lower growth expectations and relatively few attractive new investment opportunities. Unfortunately, there was no way to replace the founder's contributions to the firm. Previously, CMC found it necessary to plow back most of its earnings to finance growth, which averaged 12 percent per year. Future growth at a five percent rate is considered realistic, but that level would call for an increase in the dividend payout. Further, it now appears that new investment projects with at least the 14 percent rate of return required by CMC's stockholders ($k_s = 14\%$) would amount to only $800,000 for 2001 in comparison to a projected $2,000,000 of net income. If the existing 20 percent dividend payout were continued, retained earnings would be $1.6 million in 2001, but, as noted, investments that yield the 14 percent cost of capital would amount to only $800,000.

The one encouraging thing is that the high earnings from existing assets are expected to continue, and net income of $2 million is still expected for 2001. Given the dramatically changed circumstances, CMC's management is reviewing the firm's dividend policy.

a. Assuming that the acceptable 2001 investment projects would be financed entirely by earnings retained during the year, calculate DPS in 2001 if CMC follows the residual dividend policy.

b. What *payout ratio* does your answer to part a imply for 2001?

c. If a 60 percent payout ratio is maintained for the foreseeable future, what is your estimate of the present market price of the common stock? How does this compare with the market price that should have prevailed under the assumptions existing just before the news about the founder's retirement? If the two values of P_0 are different, comment on why.

d. What would happen to the price of the stock if the old 20 percent payout were continued? Assume that if this payout is maintained, the average rate of return on the retained earnings will fall to 7.5 percent and the new growth rate will be

$$g = (1.0 - \text{Payout ratio})(\text{ROE})$$
$$= (1.0 - 0.2)(7.5\%) = (0.8)(7.5\%) = 6.0\%$$

Problems

stock dividend **12–1** The McLaughlin Corporation declared a six percent stock dividend. Construct a pro forma balance sheet showing the effect of this action. The stock was selling for $37.50 per share, and a condensed version of McLaughlin's balance sheet as of December 31, 2000, before the dividend, follows (in millions of dollars):

Cash	$ 112.5	Debt	$1,500
Other assets	2,887.5	Common stock (75 million shares outstanding, $1 par)	75
		Paid-in capital	300
		Retained earnings	1,125
Total assets	$3,000.0	Total liabilities and equity	$3,000

12–2 In 2000 the Sirmans Company paid dividends totaling $3.6 million on net income of $10.8 million. Sirmans had a normal year in 2000, and for the past ten years, earnings have grown at a constant rate of ten percent. However, in 2001, earnings are expected to jump to $14.4 million, and the firm expects to have profitable investment opportunities of $8.4 million. It is predicted that Sirmans will not be able to maintain the 2001 level of earnings growth—the high 2001 earnings level is attributable to an exceptionally profitable new product line introduced that year—and the company will return to its previous ten percent growth rate. Sirmans's target debt ratio is 40 percent.

a. Calculate Sirmans's total dividends for 2001 if it follows each of the following policies:
(1) Its 2001 dividend payment is set to force dividends to grow at the long-run growth rate in earnings.
(2) It continues the 2000 dividend payout ratio.
(3) It uses a pure residual dividend policy (40 percent of the $8.4 million investment is financed with debt).
(4) It employs a regular-dividend-plus-extras policy, with the regular dividend being based on the long-run growth rate and the extra dividend being set according to the residual policy.

b. Which of the preceding policies would you recommend? Restrict your choices to the ones listed, but justify your answer.

c. Assume that investors expect Sirmans to pay total dividends of $9 million in 2001 and to have the dividend grow at ten percent after 2001. The total market value of the stock is $180 million. What is the company's cost of equity?

d. What is Sirmans's long-run average return on equity? [*Hint:* g = (Retention rate) × (ROE) = (1.0 − Payout rate) × (ROE).]

e. Does a 2001 dividend of $9 million seem reasonable in view of your answers to parts c and d? If not, should the dividend be higher or lower?

12–3 Ybor City Tobacco Company has for many years enjoyed a moderate but stable growth in sales and earnings. However, cigar consumption and consequently Ybor's sales have been falling recently, primarily because of an increasing awareness of the dangers of smoking to health. Anticipating further declines in tobacco sales for the future, Ybor's management hopes eventually to move almost entirely out of the tobacco business and into a newly developed, diversified product line in growth-oriented industries. The company is especially interested in the prospects for pollution-control devices because its research department has already done much work on the problems of filtering smoke. Right now the company estimates that an investment of $15 million is necessary to purchase new facilities and to begin operations on these products, but the investment could be earning a return of about 18 percent within a short time. The only other available investment opportunity totals $6 million and is expected to return about 10.4 percent.

The company is expected to pay a $3.00 dividend on its 3 million outstanding shares, the same as its dividend last year. The directors might, however, change the dividend if there are good reasons for doing so. Total earnings after taxes for the year are expected to be $14.25 million; the common stock is currently selling for $56.25; the firm's target debt ratio (debt/assets ratio) is 45 percent; and its marginal tax rate is 40 percent. The costs of various forms of financing are as follows:

New bonds, $k_d = 11\%$. This is a before-tax rate.

New common stock sold at $56.25 per share will net $51.25.

Required rate of return on retained earnings, $k_s = 14\%$.

a. Calculate Ybor's expected payout ratio, the break point at which the marginal cost of capital (MCC) rises, and its MCC above and below the point of exhaustion of retained earnings at the current payout. (*Hint:* k_s is given, and $\hat{D}_1/P_0$ can be found. Then, knowing k_s and $\hat{D}_1/P_0$, g can be determined.)
b. How large should Ybor's capital budget be for the year?
c. What is an appropriate dividend policy for Ybor? How should the capital budget be financed?
d. How might risk factors influence Ybor's cost of capital, capital structure, and dividend policy?
e. What assumptions, if any, do your answers to the preceding parts make about investors' preferences for dividends versus capital gains (in other words, what are investors' preferences regarding the $\hat{D}_1/P_0$ and g components of k_s)?

Exam-Type Problems

The problems included in this section are set up in such a way that they could be used as multiple-choice exam problems.

external equity financing   **12-4** Northern California Heating and Cooling Inc. has a six-month backlog of orders for its patented solar heating system. To meet this demand, management plans to expand production capacity by 40 percent with a $10 million investment in plant and machinery. The firm wants to maintain a 40 percent debt/assets ratio in its capital structure; it also wants to maintain its past dividend policy of distributing 45 percent of last year's net income. In 2000, net income was $5 million. How much external equity must Northern California seek at the beginning of 2001 to expand capacity as desired?

dividend payout   **12-5** The Garlington Corporation expects next year's net income to be $15 million. The firm's debt/assets ratio currently is 40 percent. Garlington has $12 million of profitable investment opportunities, and it wishes to maintain its existing debt ratio. According to the residual dividend policy, how large should Garlington's dividend payout ratio be next year?

stock split   **12-6** After a 5-for-1 stock split, the Swensen Company paid a dividend of $0.75 per new share, which represents a nine percent increase over last year's presplit dividend. What was last year's dividend per share?

dividend payout   **12-7** The Scanlon Company's optimal capital structure calls for 50 percent debt and 50 percent common equity. The interest rate on its debt is a constant ten percent; its cost of common equity from retained earnings is 14 percent; the cost of equity from new stock is 16 percent; and its marginal tax rate is 40 percent. Scanlon has the following investment opportunities:

Project A: Cost = $5 million; IRR = 20%

Project B: Cost = $5 million; IRR = 12%

Project C: Cost = $5 million; IRR =   9%

Scanlon expects to have net income of $7,287,500. If Scanlon bases its dividends on the residual policy, what will its payout ratio be?

Integrative Problem

dividend policy   **12-8** Information Systems Inc. (ISI), which develops software for the health care industry, was founded five years ago by Donald Brown and Margaret Clark, who are still its only stockholders. ISI has now reached the stage where outside equity capital is necessary if the firm is to achieve its growth targets yet still maintain its target capital structure of 60 percent equity and 40 percent debt. Therefore, Brown and Clark have decided to take the company public. Until now, Brown and Clark have paid themselves reasonable salaries but routinely reinvested all after-tax earnings in the firm, so dividend policy has not been an issue. However, before talking with potential outside investors, they must decide on a dividend policy.

Assume that you were recently hired by Arthur Adamson & Company (AA), a national consulting firm, which has been asked to help ISI prepare for its public offering. Martha Millon, the senior AA consultant in your group, has asked you to make a presentation to Brown and Clark in which you review the theory of dividend policy and discuss the following questions:

a. (1) What is meant by the term *dividend policy*?
   (2) The terms *irrelevance* and *relevance* have been used to describe theories regarding the way dividend policy affects a firm's value. Explain what these terms mean, and briefly discuss the relevance of dividend policy.
   (3) Explain the relationships between dividend policy and (i) stock price and (ii) the cost of equity under each dividend policy theory.
   (4) What results have empirical studies of the dividend theories produced? How does all this affect what we can tell managers about dividend policy?

b. Discuss (1) the information content, or signaling, hypothesis; (2) the clientele effect; (3) the free cash flow hypothesis; and (4) their effects on dividend policy.

c. (1) Assume that ISI has an $800,000 capital budget planned for the coming year. You have determined that its present capital structure (60 percent equity and 40 percent debt) is optimal, and its net income is forecasted at $600,000. Use the residual dividend policy approach to determine ISI's total dollar dividend and payout ratio. In the process, explain what the residual dividend policy is, and use a graph to illustrate your answer. Then explain what would happen if net income were forecasted at $400,000, or at $800,000.
   (2) In general terms, how would a change in investment opportunities affect the payout ratio under the residual payment policy?
   (3) What are the advantages and disadvantages of the residual policy? (*Hint:* Don't neglect signaling and clientele effects.)

d. What are some other commonly used dividend payment policies? What are their advantages and disadvantages? Which policy is most widely used in practice?

e. What are dividend reinvestment plans (DRIPs), and how do these plans work?

f. What are stock dividends and stock splits? What are the advantages and disadvantages of stock dividends and splits? When should a stock dividend as opposed to a stock split be used?

Computer-Related Problem

Work the problem in this section only if you are using the computer problem diskette.

dividend policy and capital structure

12–9 Use the model in the File C12 to work this problem. Refer back to Problem 12–3. Assume that Ybor's management is considering a change in the firm's capital structure to include more debt; thus, management would like to analyze the effects of an increase in the debt ratio to 60 percent. The treasurer believes that such a move would cause lenders to increase the required rate of return on new bonds to 12 percent and that k_s would rise to 14.5 percent.

   a. How would this change affect the optimal capital budget?

   b. If k_s rose to 16 percent, would the low-return project be acceptable?

   c. Would the project selection be affected if the dividend was reduced to $1.88 from $3.00, still assuming $k_s = 16$ percent?

ONLINE ESSENTIALS

You can get information about the dividend policies of specific companies by visiting their Web sites directly. If you search the Web using the phrase *dividend policy*, you will find various announcements from companies that contain announcement dates, ex-dividend dates, dates of record, and so forth.

http://www.morevalue.com/themes/dividend.html
   +Value morevalue.com
   This site provides links to news articles, lecture notes, course outlines, and so forth, that relate to dividend policy, DRIPs, stock splits, and so forth. You can also get an outline of lecture notes by clicking on "Lecture Notes" on the left side of the screen.

http://www.irs.ustreas.gov/plain/tax_stats/soi/corp_id.html
   IRS Corporate Tax Statistics: Industry Data
   Income statement data divided by industry are available at this site. You can see how the dividend policies differ among industries.

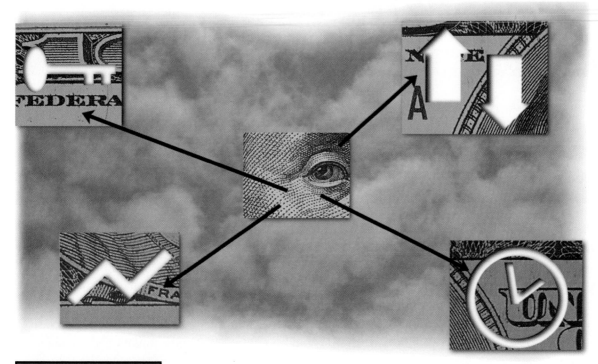

PART VI

Working Capital Management

CHAPTER 13

Working Capital Policy

In December 1993, Trans World Airlines (TWA) was labeled the best domestic airline for long flights and the second best for short flights by American business travelers. TWA received this accolade just one month after emerging from bankruptcy court. The future seemed rosy—employees had agreed to salary concessions in exchange for an equity position in the company, the airline had restructured its liabilities and lowered its cost structure, and the employees, with their new ownership position, appeared to possess a newfound motivation and concern for company success. Unfortunately, the nation's seventh largest airlines discovered that its "new lease on life" was not a long-term contract. By the summer of 1994, TWA was struggling to find ways to cover a $135 million shortfall expected for the year. Many analysts believed the company was headed toward a second, and perhaps final, bankruptcy, primarily because it was in an extremely precarious position with respect to liquidity. The company's cash reserves were not sufficient to carry TWA through the lean sales that were expected during the coming months, and analysts were very pessimistic that needed funds could be raised with a stock or bond issue or by selling off assets. Investors also recognized TWA's liquidity problems—the company's stock fell about 50 percent in less than four months. It was obvious that TWA needed to improve its liquidity position to ensure future survival. The answer for TWA has

been to reduce costs by laying off employees, by eliminating some of its flights, and by replacing outdated airplanes with more fuel-efficient ones.

TWA has emerged from its second bankruptcy, but its financial position is still very tenuous. Unforeseen circumstances, including a tragic crash and labor difficulties, and a commitment to renewing its fleet of planes have resulted in large losses in recent years. For instance, in 1996 TWA lost $285 million, and in 1997 and 1998 the losses were $110 million and $120 million, respectively. But TWA has taken actions to improve its liquidity position—recent reports from the company indicate that 1999 passenger volume has been at record levels and revenues have increased while unit costs have decreased. In addition, TWA has continued efforts to improve its short-term liquidity position by increasing its operating efficiency.

Firms strive to maintain a balance between current assets and current liabilities and between sales and each category of current assets in an effort to provide sufficient liquidity to survive to live to maximize value in the future. As long as a good balance is maintained, current liabilities can be paid on time, suppliers will continue to provide needed inventories, and companies will be able to meet sales demands. However, if the financial situation gets out of balance, liquidity problems surface and often multiply into more serious problems, perhaps even bankruptcy. As you read this chapter, consider how important liquidity,

continues

thus proper management of working capital, is to the survival of a firm. Also consider the fact that many start-up firms never make it past the first few months of business primarily because such firms do not have formal working capital policies in place. ■

Generally we divide financial management decisions into the management of assets (investments) and liabilities (sources of financing) in (1) the *long term* and (2) the *short term*. We discussed long-term decisions and analyses in the previous five chapters. In this and the next two chapters, we discuss *short-term financial management*, also termed **working capital management,** which involves management of the current assets and the current liabilities of a firm. As you read this chapter, you will realize that a firm's value cannot be maximized in the long run unless it survives the short run. In fact, the principal reason firms fail is because they are unable to meet their working capital needs. Thus, *sound working capital management is a requisite for firm survival.*

Much of a financial manager's time is devoted to working capital management, and many of you who get jobs in finance-related fields will find your first assignment on the job will involve working capital. For these reasons, working capital policy and management is an essential topic of study. In this chapter, we provide an overview of working capital policy, and the next two chapters contain discussions of how current assets and current liabilities should be managed.

WORKING CAPITAL MANAGEMENT
The management of short-term assets (investments) and liabilities (financing sources).

Working Capital Terminology

It is useful to begin the discussion of working capital policy by reviewing some basic definitions and concepts:

WORKING CAPITAL
A firm's investment in short-term assets—cash, marketable securities, inventory, and accounts receivable.

NET WORKING CAPITAL
Current assets minus current liabilities—the amount of current assets financed by long-term liabilities.

WORKING CAPITAL POLICY
Decisions regarding (1) the target levels for each current asset account and (2) how current assets will be financed.

1. The term **working capital,** sometimes called gross working capital, generally refers to current assets.
2. **Net working capital** is defined as current assets minus current liabilities.
3. The *current ratio,* which was discussed in Chapter 3, is calculated by dividing current assets by current liabilities, and it is intended to measure a firm's liquidity. However, a high current ratio does not insure that a firm will have the cash required to meet its needs. If inventories cannot be sold, or if receivables cannot be collected in a timely manner, then the apparent safety reflected in a high current ratio could be illusory.
4. The best and most comprehensive picture of a firm's liquidity position is obtained by examining its *cash budget.* The cash budget, which forecasts cash inflows and outflows, focuses on what really counts, the firm's ability to generate sufficient cash inflows to meet its required cash outflows. Cash budgeting will be discussed in the next chapter.
5. **Working capital policy** refers to the firm's basic policies regarding (a) target levels for each category of current assets and (b) how current assets will be financed.

The term *working capital* originated with the old Yankee peddler, who would load up his wagon with goods and then go off on his route to peddle his wares. The merchandise was called working capital because it was what he actually sold, or "turned over," to produce his profits. The wagon and horse were his fixed assets. He generally owned the horse and wagon, so they were financed with "equity" capital. But to buy the merchandise, he borrowed funds, which were called *working capital* loans, that had to be repaid after each trip to demonstrate to the bank that the credit was sound. If the peddler was able to repay the loan, then the bank would make another loan, and banks that followed this procedure were said to be employing sound banking practices.

We must distinguish between those current liabilities that are specifically used to finance current assets and those current liabilities that represent (1) current maturities of long-term debt; (2) financing associated with a construction program that, after the project is completed, will be funded with the proceeds of a long-term security issue; or (3) the use of short-term debt to finance fixed assets.

Table 13–1 contains balance sheets for Unilate Textiles constructed at three different dates. According to the definitions given, Unilate's December 31, 2000, working capital (current assets) was $465.0 million, and its net working capital was $335.0 million = $465.0 million − $130.0 million. Also, Unilate's year-end 2000 current ratio was 3.6.

TABLE 13–1	Unilate Textiles: Historical and Projected Balance Sheets (millions of dollars)		
	12/31/00 (HISTORICAL)	**9/30/01** (PROJECTED)	**12/31/01** (PROJECTED)
Cash and marketable securities	$ 15.0	$ 30.0	$ 16.5
Accounts receivable	180.0	251.5	198.0
Inventories	270.0	410.0	297.0
Total current assets	$465.0	$ 691.5	$511.5
Net plant and equipment	380.0	408.5	418.0
Total assets	$845.0	$1,100.0	$929.5
Accounts payable	$ 30.0	$ 90.0	$ 33.0
Accruals	60.0	100.0	66.0
Notes payable	40.0	129.0	46.8
Total current liabilities	$130.0	$ 319.0	$145.8
Long-term bonds	300.0	309.0	309.0
Total liabilities	$430.0	$ 628.0	$454.8
Common stock	130.0	159.3	159.3
Retained earnings	285.0	312.7	315.5
Total owners' equity	$415.0	$ 472.0	$474.8
Total liabilities and equity	$845.0	$1,100.0	$929.6[a]
Net working capital	$335.0	$ 372.5	$365.7
Current ratio	3.6	2.2	3.5

[a]Rounding difference. These end-of-year forecasts were derived in Appendix 4A.

What if the total current liabilities of $130 million at the end of 2000 included the current portion of long-term debt, say $10 million? This account is unaffected by changes in working capital policy because it is a function of past long-term debt financing decisions. Thus, even though we define long-term debt coming due in the next accounting period as a current liability, it is not a working capital decision variable in the current period. Similarly, if Unilate were building a new factory and initially financed the construction with a short-term loan that would be replaced later with mortgage bonds, the construction loan would not be considered part of working capital management. Although such accounts are not part of Unilate's working capital decision process, they cannot be ignored because they are *due* in the current period, and they must be taken into account when Unilate's managers construct the cash budget and assess the firm's ability to meet its current obligations (its liquidity position).

Self-Test Questions

Why is it important to properly manage short-term assets and liabilities?

Where did the term "working capital" originate?

The Requirement for External Working Capital Financing

Unilate's operations and the sale of textile products are very seasonal, typically peaking in September and October. Thus, at the end of September Unilate's inventories are significantly higher than they are at the end of the calendar year. Unilate offers significant sales incentives to wholesalers during August and September in an effort to move inventories out of its warehouses and into those of its customers; otherwise, inventories would be even higher than shown in Table 13–1. Because of this sales surge, Unilate's receivables also are much higher at the end of September than at the end of December.

Consider what is expected to happen to Unilate's current assets and current liabilities from December 31, 2000, to September 30, 2001. Current assets are expected to increase from $465.0 million to $691.5 million, or by $226.5 million. Because increases on the asset side of the balance sheet must be financed by identical increases on the liabilities and equity side, the firm must raise $226.5 million to meet the expected increase in working capital over the period. However, the higher volume of purchases, plus labor expenditures associated with increased production, will cause accounts payable and accruals to increase spontaneously by only $100 million—from $90.0 million ($30.0 million in payables plus $60.0 million in accruals) to $190.0 million ($90.0 million in payables plus $100.0 million in accruals)—during the first nine months of 2001. This leaves a projected $126.5 million = $226.5 million − $100.0 million current asset financing requirement, which Unilate expects to finance primarily by an $89.0 million increase in notes payable. Therefore, for September 30, 2001, notes payable are projected to rise to $129.0 million. Notice that from December 2000 to September 2001, Unilate's net working capital is expected to increase from $335.0 million to $372.5 million, but its current ratio is expected to fall from 3.6 to 2.2. This occurs because most, but not all, of the funds invested in current assets are expected to come from current liabilities.[1]

---

[1]Mathematically, when both the numerator and the denominator of a ratio increase by the same amount (magnitude), the value of the ratio decreases.

The fluctuations in Unilate's working capital position shown in Table 13–1 result from seasonal variations. Similar fluctuations in working capital requirements, and hence in financing needs, also occur during business cycles—working capital needs typically decline during recessions but increase during booms. For some companies, such as those involved in agricultural products, seasonal fluctuations are much greater than business cycle fluctuations, but for other companies, such as appliance or automobile manufacturers, cyclical fluctuations are larger. In the following sections we look in more detail at the requirement for working capital financing, and we examine some alternative working capital policies.

Self-Test Question

Under normal circumstances, when does the working capital position of a firm change? Explain.

The Relationships of Working Capital Accounts

It is important that you understand how the various working capital accounts are related. To illustrate the process of producing and selling inventory and the relationships between current assets and current liabilities, let's assume that you open a new textile manufacturing plant to compete with Unilate Textiles. Let's call the new business Global Cloth Products (GCP). Under normal conditions, the new plant is expected to produce and sell 50,000 units each day. Each unit, which will be sold for $14.00, has a direct production cost equal to $11.00. For simplicity, we will assume the $11.00 unit cost can be broken into two components—the cost of raw materials purchased from suppliers (cotton, wool, etc.), which is $6.50, and the cost of labor, which is $4.50—and that there are no other costs associated with the manufacture and sale of the product. GCP will purchase materials from its suppliers for credit, with cash payment due 15 days after the purchase. Likewise, GCP will allow its customers to purchase for credit, and it will require cash payment 15 days after the sale. In our illustration, we assume all GCP customers will pay for their purchases 15 days after the sales, and that GCP will pay its suppliers 15 days after purchasing raw materials. In addition, employees will be paid every 15 days (twice a month).[2] Therefore, all the cash flows associated with the production and sales functions will occur 15 days after the purchase, manufacture, and sale of the products. To simplify the illustration, we assume all cash flows will occur at the beginning of the day, before daily purchasing, producing, and selling activities begin. Thus, at the beginning of day 16 (1) inventory purchases made on the first day of business will be paid, (2) collection for the products sold on the first day of business occur, and (3) the employees will be paid for their first 15 days of work.

GCP will use $300,000 in common stock to finance the new processing plant facilities, and the raw materials purchases will be made daily and financed short term with accounts payable (owed to suppliers), wages payable (owed to employees), and short-term bank loans (notes payable). Each day, the raw materials that are purchased will be converted into finished goods and sold before the close of business.

---

[2]The 15-day period is used for simplicity because there are two 15-day periods in a 30-day month and 24 15-day periods in a 360-day year. If a 14-day period was used, the illustration would become more cumbersome.

On the first day of operations, just *prior to selling any products*, GCP will have 50,000 units in inventory at a cost of $11.00 per unit, so the inventory balance will be $550,000 = 50,000 × $11.00. The inventory cost consists of the raw materials, which amounts to $325,000 = 50,000 × $6.50 owed to suppliers, and the cost of labor, which is $225,000 = 50,000 × $4.50 owed to employees. At this point, then, the balance sheet for GCP's processing plant would be as follows:

Cash	$ 0	Accounts payable	$325,000
Accounts receivable	0	Accrued wages	225,000
Inventory	550,000	Notes payable	0
Current assets	550,000	Current liabilities	550,000
		Common Equity	300,000
Fixed assets	300,000	Retained earnings	0
Total assets	$850,000	Total liabilities and equity	$850,000

On the first day, all of the 50,000 units in inventory will be sold for $14.00 each, so the first day's sales will be $700,000 = 50,000 × $14.00. And, after the first day's sales are complete, the balance sheet will be as follows:

Cash	$ 0	Accounts payable	$ 325,000
Accounts receivable	700,000	Accrued wages	225,000
Inventory	0	Notes payable	0
Current assets	700,000	Current liabilities	550,000
		Common Equity	300,000
Fixed assets	300,000	Retained earnings	150,000
Total assets	$1,000,000	Total liabilities and equity	$1,000,000

Notice that the $150,000 profit on the first day's sales, which is the difference between the inventory cost of $550,000 and the first day's sales of $700,000, is recognized via retained earnings.[3] This shows that not all of the $700,000 in accounts receivable has to be financed because $150,000 represents the profit on the sales.

At the start of the second day, *after inventories are replenished but before daily sales begin*, the inventory balance again will be $550,000 and the balances in accounts payable and accrued wages will increase by $325,000 and $225,000, respectively. Thus, the balance sheet will be as follows:

Cash	$ 0	Accounts payable	$ 650,000
Accounts receivable	700,000	Accrued wages	450,000
Inventory	550,000	Notes payable	0
Current assets	1,250,000	Current liabilties	1,100,000
		Common Equity	300,000
Fixed assets	300,000	Retained earnings	150,000
Total assets	$1,550,000	Total liabilities and equity	$1,550,000

---

[3]In reality, profits are not posted to retained earnings each day; rather, the recognition of profits (income) occurs at the end of the fiscal period via the income summary account. We recognize the daily profits in this manner for illustrative purposes only.

When the products are sold on the second day, accounts receivable again will increase by $700,000. In fact, the balances in accounts receivable, accounts payable, wages payable, and retained earnings will continue to increase (accumulate) until cash flows affect these accounts' balances. So the balances in receivables, payables, and accrued wages will increase for a total of 15 days, while the balance in retained earnings will continue to increase until dividends are paid.

GCP neither receives nor disburses any cash until 15 days after the first day of business. At that time, GCP will have to *pay* for both the raw materials purchased on the first day of business and the wages owed to employees for the first 15 days of work. In addition, GCP will *receive* payment from those customers who purchased its products on the first day of business. So for the first 15 days of business, the balances in receivables, payables, accruals, and retained earnings continue to increase, reflecting the purchasing and selling activities of GCP prior to the receipt or payment of any cash flows. At the *end* of Day 15, therefore, the balance in each of these accounts would be as follows:

$$\text{Accounts receivable} = \$700,000 \times 15 \text{ days} = \$10,500,000$$

$$\text{Accounts payable} = \$325,000 \times 15 \text{ days} = \$ 4,875,000$$

$$\text{Accrued wages} = \$225,000 \times 15 \text{ days} = \$ 3,375,000$$

$$\text{Retained earnings} = \$150,000 \times 15 \text{ days} = \$ 2,250,000$$

And the balance sheet at the *end* of Day 15 would be as follows:

Cash	$ 0	Accounts payable	$ 4,875,000
Accounts receivable	10,500,000	Accrued wages	3,375,000
Inventory	0	Notes payable	0
Current assets	10,500,000	Current liabilities	8,250,000
		Common Equity	300,000
Fixed assets	300,000	Retained earnings	2,250,000
Total assets	$10,800,000	Total liabilities and equity	$10,800,000

At the *beginning* of Day 16, GCP must pay its employees $3,375,000 for the first 15 days of work, and it also must pay $325,000 to the suppliers for the raw materials purchased on the first day of business. But, at the same time, GCP will be paid $700,000 for the products that were sold on the first day of business. This cash receipt can be used to pay the $325,000 now due to the suppliers, which leaves only $375,000 to help pay employees' salaries. This means GCP must borrow to meet its cash obligations. If GCP uses the entire $375,000 to help pay employees' salaries, the amount that needs to be borrowed to pay the remaining wages is

$$\text{Loan amount} = \left(\begin{array}{c}\text{Payment owed} \\ \text{to suppliers}\end{array}\right) + \left(\begin{array}{c}\text{Wages owed} \\ \text{employees}\end{array}\right) - \left(\begin{array}{c}\text{Cash} \\ \text{receipts}\end{array}\right)$$

$$= [\$325,000 + \$3,375,000] - (\$700,000)$$

$$= \$3,700,000 - \$700,000 = \$3,000,000$$

If GCP borrows the funds needed from a local bank, consider what the balance sheet would look like if all of the cash flow activity occurs at the very beginning of Day 16, *prior to the daily materials purchases, inventory production, and product sales*. At this point, GCP would have (1) paid *all* of the $3,375,000 wages owed its employees, so the balance of accrued wages would equal zero; (2) paid $325,000 to its suppliers, so the balance of accounts payable would decrease by $325,000; (3) received a $700,000 payment from its customers, so the balance of accounts receivable would decrease by $700,000; and (4) borrowed $3,000,000 from a local bank to pay employees, so the balance of notes payable would increase by $3,000,000. At this point, the balance sheet would be as follows:

Cash	$ 0	Accounts payable	$ 4,550,000
Accounts receivable	9,800,000	Accrued wages	0
Inventory	0	Notes payable	3,000,000
Current assets	9,800,000	Current liabilities	7,550,000
		Common Equity	300,000
Fixed assets	300,000	Retained earnings	2,250,000
Total assets	$10,100,000	Total liabilities and equity	$10,100,000

But on Day 16, GCP must also conduct its normal daily business—raw materials must be purchased and finished goods must be manufactured and sold. Because no additional cash flows will occur on this day, the purchase of raw materials will increase accounts payable by $325,000, the use of employees to manufacture finished goods will increase accrued wages by $225,000, and credit sales will increase accounts receivable by $700,000. Consequently, at the *end of day 16*, the balance sheet will be as follows:

Cash	$ 0	Accounts payable	$ 4,875,000
Accounts receivable	10,500,000	Accrued wages	225,000
Inventory	0	Notes payable	3,000,000
Current assets	10,650,000	Current liabilities	8,100,000
		Common Equity	300,000
Fixed assets	300,000	Retained earnings	2,400,000
Total assets	$10,800,000	Total liabilities and equity	$10,800,000

At this point, the accounts payable and accounts receivable balances reflect 15 days' worth of credit activities associated with the production and sales operations that took place from Day 2 through Day 16. On the other hand, because at the beginning of the day the employees were paid the wages due them for the first 15 days of business, accrued wages include only the amount owed to employees for their work to produce inventory on Day 16. And because there have not been any cash disbursements to stockholders, the balance in retained earnings represents the profits from the products sold for all 16 days GCP has been in business—$2,400,000 = $150,000 × 16 days.

At the beginning of Day 17, GCP will pay for the materials it purchased on Day 2. It will also receive payment for the products that were sold on Day 2. This process will continue as long as the purchasing and payment patterns of both GCP and its customers do not change. So GCP will pay out $325,000 every day to pay for materials purchased 15 days earlier (a decrease in payables), but the payables balance will remain the same from this point on because GCP will also purchase on credit raw materials valuing $325,000 (an increase in payables) every day to produce the product needed for that day's sales. Therefore, the accounts payable balance will remain constant at $4,875,000. Similarly, the balance in accounts receivable will remain at $10,500,000, because each day, once this steady state has been reached, GCP will receive cash payments from customers totaling $700,000 (a decrease in receivables) at the same time $700,000 worth of products are sold for credit (an increase in receivables).

At this point, consider the cash flow position of GCP. From Day 16 on, every day, GCP will receive cash payments from its customers that total $700,000, and it will make cash payments to its suppliers that total $325,000. But the employees are paid every 15 days, not every day. Therefore, GCP can accumulate $375,000 = $700,000 − $325,000 in cash each day until employees' salaries need to be paid again. The next time employees' salaries are paid is at the beginning of Day 31, so the cash account balance will increase by $375,000 for 15 days. Therefore, on Day 31, after all cash flows except accrued wages are recognized, GCP will have a cash balance equal to $5,625,000 = $375,000 × 15 days. Accrued wages will equal $3,375,000 = $225,000 × 15 days; so, after paying its employees, GCP will still have a cash balance equal to $2,250,000. This amount represents the *total cash profit* GCP has generated during the previous 15 days of business. This amount can be used to pay off a portion of the bank loan, or it could be used to expand operations. In any event, once the balances in receivables and payables have stabilized because the daily adjustments to those accounts are offsetting, GCP actually realizes a *cash* profit of $150,000 per day.

This illustration shows that, in general, once GCP's operations have stabilized so that the credit sales and credit purchasing patterns and the collection and payment activities stay the same day after day, the balances of accounts receivable and accounts payable will remain constant—the daily increase associated with each account will be offset by the daily decrease associated the account. Therefore, once the firm's operations have stabilized and cash collections from credit sales and cash payments for credit purchases have begun, the balance in accounts receivable and accounts payable can be computed using the following equation:

13–1

$$\text{Account balance} = \begin{pmatrix} \text{Amount of} \\ \text{daily activity} \end{pmatrix} \times \begin{pmatrix} \text{Average life} \\ \text{of the account} \end{pmatrix}$$

So for accounts receivable, the balance would be the daily credit sales times the length of time each account remains outstanding—$700,000 × 15 days = $10,500,000.

The preceding scenario will occur only if GCP's expectations, including forecasted sales, come true. But what happens if GCP's forecasts are too optimistic? If GCP finds it cannot sell 50,000 units each day, its cash collections will decrease, its inventory probably will build up, and perhaps notes payable also will increase. If this pattern continues, GCP eventually might find itself in financial difficulty.

Although the illustration we used here is oversimplified, it should give you an indication of the interrelationships among the working capital accounts. It should be apparent that a decision affecting one working capital account (e.g., inventory) will have an impact on other working capital accounts (e.g., receivables and payables).

Self-Test Questions

If a firm purchases raw materials on credit, which two working capital accounts are affected? What would happen if the purchase was for cash?

Write out the equation that gives the balance in accounts receivable once cash receipts for earlier credit sales begin (assume sales/collection patterns have stabilized).

The Cash Conversion Cycle

As we noted earlier, the concept of working capital management originated with the old Yankee peddler, who would borrow to buy inventory, sell the inventory to pay off the bank loan, and then repeat the cycle. The previous section illustrates the impact of such activity on the working capital accounts of the firm. That general concept has been applied to more complex businesses, and it is useful when analyzing the effectiveness of a firm's working capital management process.

The working capital management process that Unilate Textiles faces is similar to the process we described in the previous section for GCP, and it can be summarized as follows:

1. Unilate orders and then receives the materials it needs to produce the textile products its sells. Unilate purchases from its suppliers on credit, so an account payable is created for credit purchases. Such purchases have no immediate cash flow effect because payment is not made until some later date (perhaps 20 to 30 days after purchase).
2. Labor is used to convert the materials (cotton and wool) into finished goods (cloth products, thread, etc.). However, wages are not fully paid at the time the work is done, so accrued wages build up (maybe for a period of one or two weeks).
3. The finished products are sold, but on credit; so sales create receivables, not immediate cash inflows.
4. At some point during the cycle, Unilate must pay off its accounts payable and accrued wages. *If* these payments are made before Unilate has collected cash from its receivables, a net cash outflow occurs and this outflow must be financed.
5. The cycle is completed when Unilate's receivables are collected (perhaps in 30 to 40 days). At that time, the company is in a position to pay off the credit that was used to finance production of the product, and it can then repeat the cycle.

CASH CONVERSION CYCLE
The length of time from the payment for the purchase of raw materials to manufacture a product until the collection of accounts receivable associated with the sale of the product.

The preceding steps are formalized with the **cash conversion cycle** model, which focuses on the length of time between when the company makes payments, or invests in the manufacture of inventory, and when it receives cash inflows, or realizes a cash return from its investment in production.[4] The following terms are used in the model:

1. The *inventory conversion period* is the average length of time required to convert materials into finished goods and then to sell those goods; it is the amount of time the product remains in inventory in various stages of completion. The inventory conversion period is calculated by dividing inventory by the cost of goods sold per day. For example, we can compute the inventory conversion period for Unilate Textiles using the 2000 balance sheet figures shown in Table 13–1. In 2000, Unilate sold $1,500 million of its product with a cost of goods sold equal to $1,230 million, so the inventory conversion period would be

---

[4]See Verlyn Richards and Eugene Laughlin, "A Cash Conversion Cycle Approach to Liquidity Analysis," *Financial Management*, Spring 1980, 32–38.

13-2

$$\text{Inventory conversion period} = \frac{\text{Inventory}}{\text{Cost of goods sold per day}} = \frac{\text{Inventory}}{\left(\frac{\text{Cost of goods sold}}{360}\right)}$$

$$= \frac{\$270 \text{ million}}{\left(\frac{\$1,230 \text{ million}}{360}\right)} = \frac{\$270}{\$3.417}$$

$$= 79.0 \text{ days}$$

Thus, according to its 2000 operations, it takes Unilate 79.0 days to convert materials into finished goods and then to sell those goods.

2. The *receivables collection period* is the average length of time required to convert the firm's receivables into cash—that is, to collect cash following a sale. The receivables collection period also is called the days sales outstanding (DSO), and it is calculated by dividing accounts receivable by the average credit sales per day. Because sales in 2000 equaled $1,500 million, Unilate's receivables collection period (DSO) is:

13-3

$$\text{Receivables collection period} = \text{DSO} = \frac{\text{Receivables}}{\text{Daily credit sales}} = \frac{\text{Receivables}}{\left(\frac{\text{Credit sales}}{360}\right)}$$

$$= \frac{\$180 \text{ million}}{\left(\frac{\$1,500 \text{ million}}{360}\right)} = \frac{\$180}{\$4.167}$$

$$= 43.2 \text{ days}$$

Thus, the cash payments associated with credit sales are not collected until 43.2 days after the sales.

3. The *payables deferral period* is the average length of time between the purchase of raw materials and labor and the payment of cash for them. It is computed by dividing accounts payable by the daily credit purchases. Unilate's daily cost of goods sold is $3.417 million, so the payables deferral period for Unilate would be:

13-4

$$\frac{\text{Payables}}{\text{deferral period}} = \text{DPO} = \frac{\text{Accounts payable}}{\text{Credit purchases per day}} = \frac{\text{Accounts payable}}{\left(\frac{\text{Cost of goods sold}}{360}\right)}$$

$$= \frac{\$30 \text{ million}}{\left(\frac{\$1,230 \text{ million}}{360}\right)} = \frac{\$30}{\$3.417}$$

$$= 8.8 \text{ days}$$

FIGURE 13-1	The Cash Conversion Cycle

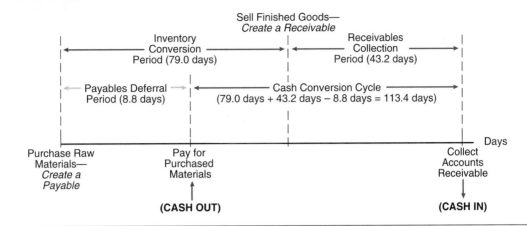

So Unilate pays its suppliers an average of 8.8 days after materials are purchased.[5]

4. The *cash conversion cycle* computation nets out the three periods just defined, resulting in a value that equals the length of time between the firm's actual cash expenditures to pay for (invest in) productive resources (materials and labor) and its own cash receipts from the sale of products (that is, the length of time between paying for labor and materials and collecting on receivables). The cash conversion cycle thus equals the average length of time a dollar is tied up in current assets.

We can now use these definitions to analyze Unilate's cash conversion cycle. First, the concept is diagrammed in Figure 13–1. Thus, the cash conversion cycle can be expressed by this equation:

$$
\begin{array}{c}
\text{13-5} \\
\begin{array}{ccc}
\text{Cash} \\
\text{conversion} = \\
\text{cycle}
\end{array}
\left(\begin{array}{c}\text{Inventory}\\\text{conversion}\\\text{period}\end{array}\right)
+
\left(\begin{array}{c}\text{Receivables}\\\text{collection}\\\text{period}\end{array}\right)
-
\left(\begin{array}{c}\text{Payables}\\\text{deferral}\\\text{period}\end{array}\right)
\end{array}
$$

$$= \quad 79.0 \text{ days} \quad + \quad 43.2 \text{ days} \quad - \quad 8.8 \text{ days}$$

$$= 113.4 \text{ days}$$

To illustrate, according to Unilate's 2000 operations, it takes an average of 79.0 days to convert raw materials (cotton, wool, etc.) into finished goods (cloth, thread, etc.) and

---

[5]The computation for the payables deferral period shown here is the traditional method used to determine the value used in the calculation of the cash conversion cycle. However, if we recognize that the intent of the computation is to determine the length of time between the purchase of raw materials and the labor used to produce inventory and the payment for these inputs, the payables deferral period might more appropriately be written to include consideration of accrued wages.

then sell them, and then it takes another 43.2 days to collect on receivables. However, 8.8 days normally elapse between receipt of raw materials and payment for them. In this case, the cash conversion cycle is 113.4 days. The *receipt* of cash from manufacturing and selling the products will be delayed by about 122 days because (1) the product will be "tied up" in inventory for 79 days and (2) the cash from the sale will not be received until about 43 days after the selling date. But the *disbursement* of cash for the raw materials purchased will be delayed by nearly 9 days because Unilate does not pay cash for the raw materials when they are purchased. So for Unilate, the net delay in cash receipts associated with an investment (cash disbursement) in inventory is 113.4 days. What does this mean to Unilate?

Given its cash conversion cycle, Unilate knows when it starts processing its textile products that it will have to finance the manufacturing and other operating costs for a 113-day period, which is nearly one-third of a year. The firm's goal should be to shorten its cash conversion cycle as much as possible without harming operations. This would improve profits because the longer the cash conversion cycle, the greater the need for external, or nonspontaneous, financing, and such financing has a cost.

The cash conversion cycle can be shortened (1) by reducing the inventory conversion period by processing and selling goods more quickly, (2) by reducing the receivables collection period by speeding up collections, or (3) by lengthening the payables deferral period by slowing down its own payments. To the extent that these actions can be taken *without harming the return* associated with the management of these accounts, they should be carried out. So when taking actions to reduce the inventory conversion period, a firm should be careful to *avoid inventory shortages* that could cause "good" customers to buy from competitors; when taking actions to speed up the collection of receivables, a firm should be careful to *maintain good relations with its "good" credit customers;* and when taking actions to lengthen the payables deferral period, a firm should be careful *not to harm its own credit reputation.*

We can illustrate the benefits of shortening the cash conversion cycle by looking again at Unilate Textiles. Suppose Unilate must spend an average of $12.30 on materials and labor to manufacture its products, which are sold for $15.00 per unit. To generate the $1,500 million sales realized in 2000, Unilate turned out 277,778 items per day. At this rate of production, it must invest $3.417 million = $12.30 × 277,778 units each day to support the manufacturing process. This investment must be financed for 113.4 days—the length of the cash conversion cycle—so the company's working capital financing needs will be $387.5 million = 113.4 × $3.417 million. If Unilate could reduce the cash conversion cycle to 93.4 days—say, by deferring payment of its accounts payable an additional 20 days or by speeding up either the production process or the collection of its receivables—it could reduce its working capital financing requirements by $68.3 million = 20 days × $3.417 million. We see, then, that actions that affect the inventory conversion period, the receivables collection period, and the payables deferral period all affect the cash conversion cycle; hence they influence the firm's need for current assets and current asset financing. You should keep the cash conversion cycle concept in mind as you go through the remainder of this chapter and the next two chapters.

Self-Test Questions

What steps are involved in estimating the cash conversion cycle?

What do the following terms mean?

a. Inventory conversion period.

   b. Receivables collection period.

   c. Payables deferral period.

What is the cash conversion cycle model? How can it be used to improve current asset management?

Working Capital Investment and Financing Policies

Working capital policy involves two basic questions: (1) What is the appropriate level for current assets, both in total and by specific accounts, and (2) how should current assets be financed?

Alternative Current Asset Investment Policies

Figure 13–2 shows three alternative policies regarding the total amount of current assets carried. Essentially, these policies differ in that different amounts of current assets are carried to support any given level of sales. The line with the steepest slope represents a **relaxed current asset investment** (or "fat cat") **policy,** where relatively large amounts of cash, marketable securities, and inventories are carried and where sales are stimulated by the use of a credit policy that provides liberal financing to customers and a corresponding high level of receivables. Conversely, with the **restricted current asset investment** (or "lean-and-mean") **policy,** the holdings of cash, securities, inventories, and receivables are minimized. The **moderate current asset investment policy** is between the two extremes.

Under conditions of certainty—when sales, costs, lead times, payment periods, and so on, are known for sure—all firms would hold only minimal levels of current assets. Any larger amounts would increase the need for external funding without a corresponding increase in profits, while any smaller holdings would involve late payments to labor and suppliers and lost sales due to inventory shortages and an overly restrictive credit policy.

However, the picture changes when uncertainty is introduced. Here the firm requires some minimum amount of cash and inventories based on expected payments, expected sales, expected order lead times, and so on, plus additional amounts, or *safety stocks*, which enable it to deal with departures from the expected values. Similarly, accounts receivable levels are determined by credit terms, and the tougher the credit terms, the lower the receivables for any given level of sales. With a restricted current asset investment policy, the firm would hold minimal levels of safety stocks for cash and inventories, and it would have a tight credit policy even though this would mean running the risk of losing sales. A restricted, lean-and-mean current asset investment policy generally provides the highest expected return on investment, but it entails the greatest risk, while the reverse is true under a relaxed policy. The moderate policy falls in between the two extremes in terms of both expected risk and return.

In terms of the cash conversion cycle, a restricted investment policy would tend to reduce the inventory conversion and receivables collection periods, which would result in a relatively short cash conversion cycle. Conversely, a relaxed policy would create higher levels of inventories and receivables, longer inventory conversion and receivables collection periods, and a relatively long cash conversion cycle. A moderate policy would produce a cash conversion cycle somewhere between the two extremes.

RELAXED CURRENT ASSET INVESTMENT POLICY
A policy under which relatively large amounts of cash and marketable securities and inventories are carried and under which sales are stimulated by a liberal credit policy that results in a high level of receivables.

RESTRICTED CURRENT ASSET INVESTMENT POLICY
A policy under which holdings of cash and marketable securities, inventories, and receivables are minimized.

MODERATE CURRENT ASSET INVESTMENT POLICY
A policy that is between the relaxed and restrictive policies.

Returning to Figure 13–3, note that we used the term *relatively* in the title for Panel b because there can be different *degrees* of aggressiveness. For example, the dashed line in Panel b could have been drawn *below* the line designating fixed assets, indicating that all of the permanent current assets and part of the fixed assets were financed with short-term credit; this would be a highly aggressive, extremely nonconservative position, and the firm would be very much subject to dangers from rising interest rates as well as to loan renewal problems. However, short-term debt often is cheaper than long-term debt, and some firms are willing to sacrifice safety for the chance of higher profits.

Conservative Approach   As shown in Panel c of Figure 13–3, the dashed line could also be drawn *above* the line designating permanent current assets, indicating that permanent capital is being used to finance all permanent asset requirements and also to meet some or all of the seasonal, temporary demands. In the situation depicted in our graph, the firm uses a small amount of short-term, nonspontaneous credit to meet its peak requirements, but it also meets a part of its seasonal needs by "storing liquidity" in the form of marketable securities during the off-season. The humps above the dashed line represent short-term financing; the troughs below the dashed line represent short-term security holdings. Panel c represents the **conservative approach,** which is a very safe current asset financing policy that generally is not as profitable as the other two approaches.

CONSERVATIVE APPROACH
A policy where all of the fixed assets, all of the permanent current assets, and some of the temporary current assets of a firm are financed with long-term capital.

Self-Test Questions

What two key issues does working capital policy involve?

What is meant by the term *current asset financing policy?*

What are three alternative current asset financing policies? Is one best?

What distinguishes *permanent current assets* from *temporary current assets?*

Which of the three alternative current asset financing policies uses the most short-term debt?

Advantages and Disadvantages of Short-Term Financing

The three possible financing policies described in the previous section were distinguished by the relative amounts of short-term debt used under each policy. The aggressive policy calls for the greatest use of short-term debt, while the conservative policy requires the least; maturity matching falls in between. Although using short-term credit generally is riskier than using long-term credit, short-term credit does have some significant advantages. The pros and cons of short-term financing are considered in this section.

Speed

A short-term loan can be obtained much faster than long-term credit. Lenders will insist on a more thorough financial examination before extending long-term credit, and the loan agreement will have to be spelled out in considerable detail because much can happen during the life of a ten- or 20-year loan. Therefore, if funds are needed in a hurry, the firm should look to short-term sources.

Flexibility

If the needs for funds are seasonal or cyclical, a firm might not want to commit itself to long-term debt for three reasons. First, the costs associated with issuing long-term debt are significantly greater than the costs of getting short-term credit. Second, some long-term debts carry expensive penalties for prepayments (paying prior to maturity). Accordingly, if a firm thinks its need for funds will diminish in the near future, it should choose short-term debt for the flexibility it provides. Third, long-term loan agreements always contain provisions, or covenants, that constrain the firm's future actions. Short-term credit agreements generally are much less onerous in this regard.

Cost of Long-Term versus Short-Term Debt

The yield curve normally is upward sloping, indicating that interest rates generally are lower on short-term than on long-term debt. Thus, under normal conditions, interest costs at the time the funds are obtained will be lower if the firm borrows on a short-term rather than on a long-term basis.

Risk of Long-Term versus Short-Term Debt

Even though short-term debt is often less expensive than long-term debt, short-term credit subjects the firm to more risk than does long-term financing. This occurs for two reasons: (1) If a firm borrows on a long-term basis, its interest costs will be relatively stable, perhaps even fixed, over time, but if it uses short-term credit, its interest expense will fluctuate widely, at times reaching quite high levels. For example, the rate banks charge large corporations for short-term debt more than tripled over a two-year period in the early 1980s, rising from 6.25 to 21 percent. Many firms that had borrowed heavily on a short-term basis simply could not meet their rising interest costs, and as a result bankruptcies hit record levels during that period. Similarly, in 1994, because the Federal Reserve increased rates six times during the year, short-term rates increased by more than 3 percent, which created a significant burden for many firms. (2) If a firm borrows heavily on a short-term basis, it could find itself unable to repay this debt, and it might be in such a weak financial position that the lender will not extend the loan; this too could force the firm into bankruptcy. Braniff Airlines failed during a credit crunch in the 1980s for this very reason.

Self-Test Questions

What are some advantages of short-term debt over long-term debt as a source of capital?

What are some disadvantages of short-term debt?

Multinational Working Capital Management

For the most part, the techniques used to manage short-term assets and liabilities in multinational corporations are the same as those used in purely domestic corporations. But multinational corporations face a far more complex task because they operate in many different business cultures, political environments, economic conditions, and so forth. In Chapter 1, we described six factors that complicate managerial finance in general in the international business arena: (1) different currency denominations,

(2) differences in economic and legal environments, (3) language differences, (4) cultural differences, (5) governmental role, and (6) political risk. Difficulties with each of these factors are more acute when managing working capital internationally because decisions made in the short run can have significant consequences on the long-run survival of the firm and such decisions are more difficult to adjust or reverse when rules and regulations and business cultures differ significantly from one business setting to another.

The results of a recent study provide some indication of how working capital policies of U.S. firms and European firms differ.[6] First, the average cash conversion cycle of European firms (about 263 days) was more than twice the average cash conversion cycle of U.S. firms (about 116 days). A possible explanation for this disparity is that European firms had much higher growth rates than their U.S. counterparts. Second, it appears from the results of the study that U.S. firms follow much more conservative working capital policies than European firms. The average current ratio and the average quick ratio proved to be significantly greater for U.S. firms than for European firms, which suggests that corporations in the United States use significantly more long-term financing alternatives than corporations in Europe (remember that when the current ratio equals to 1.0, current assets equal current liabilities). Although a more in-depth study is needed to determine why U.S. firms seem to follow more conservative working capital policies than European firms, one possible explanation might be found in the differences that are apparent in the banking systems in Europe and in the United States. In Chapter 2 we mentioned that U.S. financial institutions generally are at a competitive disadvantage in the global arena because they are subject to more restrictions and regulations than banking organizations in other countries. Foreign banks generally can branch with little or no restrictions and are allowed, in many cases, to own corporations to which they also lend funds. For these reasons, European banks often have close relationships with their debtor corporations; thus, they tend be more willing to provide short-term, risky debt than we observe in U.S. banking organizations.

In the next chapter, we discuss some of the techniques used by U.S. firms to manage short-term assets and then we give some indication of how the factors just mentioned impact on the methods used by multinational firms.

Self-Test Question

Which of the factors mentioned in this section do you think has the greatest impact on how working capital methods differ among countries?

Summary

In this chapter, we examined the relationship among working capital accounts, working capital policy, and alternative ways of financing current assets. The key concepts covered are listed here:

- **Working capital** refers to current assets, and **net working capital** is defined as current assets minus current liabilities. **Working capital policy** refers to decisions relating to the level of current assets and the way they are financed.

---

[6]Chun-Hao Chang, Krishnan Dandapani, and Arun J. Prakish, "Current Assets Policies of European Corporations: A Critical Examination," *Management International Review*, Special Issue 1995/2, 105–117.

Growth and Working Capital Needs

Working capital is the requirement that entrepreneurs most often underestimate when seeking funds to finance a new business. The entrepreneur generally plans for research and development and for the plant and equipment required for production. Working capital, however, frequently comes as a surprise to the entrepreneur, who probably expects to develop a product the market will immediately accept and for which the market will pay a substantial premium. This premium will, he or she assumes, lead to high profit margins, which will then "finance" all of the firm's other needs. As naive as this point of view seems, it nevertheless is common among founders of new businesses.

Rick was one of the founders of a new microcomputer software company that began seeking venture capital to support its products in early 2000. When speaking with a venture capitalist, who was concerned about the low level of funding being sought, Rick explained that the company's products had such a high profit margin that the company essentially would be self-financing. Rick claimed there would be no need for financing once the marketing was under way because the profits would generate more than enough cash to pay for new product development.

Sally, a venture capitalist approached by Rick, was disconcerted by Rick's reasoning. She explained to Rick that the selling price of his product would not be received fully by his company because distributors and wholesalers were involved. She also pointed out that most of the sales would be on credit, so the revenues received by his company initially would be added to accounts receivable—not received as cash—and probably not collected, on average, for about 45 to 60 days. Meanwhile, Rick would have to write checks to pay for overhead, for high research and development expenses, for a marketing staff, for advertising, and so on. So instead of cash flowing in, the firm would be, on balance, paying cash out for the first few years of its life.

Rapid growth consumes cash; it does not generate cash. Rapid growth might generate profits, but profits do not pay the bills—cash does. Consider what a firm must do to sustain a high growth rate. If it is a

manufacturer, the components of its assets include raw materials inventory, work-in-process inventory, finished goods inventory, and accounts receivable, as well as fixed assets. With the exception of fixed assets, these items all are components of gross working capital. When the firm produces a product, it makes an investment in each of these working capital items before any cash is received from collection of receivables, assuming all sales are credit sales.

Consider a small firm that finances its activities solely through the funds it generates. If the firm has a cash conversion cycle of 180 days, cash is "turned over" only twice per year. If the company earns, say, three percent on its sales dollar, it has about three percent more money available after each cash cycle than before it. With two cycles per year, about six percent more is available for investment at the end of the year than at the beginning. Thus, annual growth of approximately six percent can be supported internally; so if the company is growing at a rate of 20 percent per year, it must either obtain funds externally or face enormous pressures.

Generally, a firm can fund more rapid growth internally either by raising the profit margin or by shortening the cash conversion cycle (increasing the number of cycles per year). To raise the profit margin, the company must raise prices, cut costs, or both. Raising prices might reduce growth (because customers will be less eager to buy at higher prices), but it might also help bring growth and financial resources more into balance. Shortening the cash conversion cycle requires reducing inventory, collecting receivables more efficiently, or paying suppliers more slowly. For example, if the cash turnover changes to four times per year from two, internally fundable growth doubles (12 percent rather than six percent). Improving the cash conversion cycle and thus increasing the rate at which the firm can support growth internally reduces the firm's needs for outside funds to a more manageable level.

For the small business with serious constraints on obtaining outside funds, these discretionary policies can help bring the firm's rate of growth into balance with its ability to finance that growth. Furthermore,

continues

Exam-Type Problems

The problems included in this section are set up in such a way that they could be used as multiple-choice exam problems.

cash conversion cycle   **13–5** The Saliford Corporation has an inventory conversion period of 60 days, a receivables collection period of 36 days, and a payables deferral period of 24 days.
   a. What is the length of the firm's cash conversion cycle?
   b. If Saliford's annual sales are $3,960,000 and all sales are on credit, what is the average balance in accounts receivable?
   c. How many times per year does Saliford turn over its inventory?
   d. What would happen to Saliford's cash conversion cycle if, on average, inventories could be turned over eight times a year?

cash conversion cycle and asset turnover   **13–6** The Flamingo Corporation is trying to determine the effect of its inventory turnover ratio and days sales outstanding (DSO) on its cash flow cycle. Flamingo's 2000 sales (all on credit) were $180,000, and it earned a net profit of five percent, or $9,000. The cost of goods sold equals 85 percent of sales. Inventory was turned over eight times during the year, and the DSO, or average collection period, was 36 days. The firm had fixed assets totaling $40,000. Flamingo's payables deferral period is 30 days.
   a. Calculate Flamingo's cash conversion cycle.
   b. Assuming Flamingo holds negligible amounts of cash and marketable securities, calculate its total assets turnover and return on assets (ROA).
   c. Suppose Flamingo's managers believe that the inventory turnover can be raised to $10\times$. What would Flamingo's cash conversion cycle, total assets turnover, and ROA have been if the inventory turnover had been $10\times$ for 2000?

Integrative Problem

working capital policy and working capital financing   **13–7** Daniel Barnes, financial manager of New York Fuels (NYF), a heating oil distributor, is concerned about the company's working capital policy, and he is considering three alternative policies: (1) a *restrictive* (*lean and mean* or *tight*) policy, which calls for reducing receivables by $100,000 and inventories by $200,000; (2) a *relaxed* (*loose* or *fat cat*) policy, which calls for increasing receivables by $100,000 and inventories by $200,000; and (3) a *moderate* policy, which would mean leaving receivables and inventories at their current levels. NYF's 2000 financial statements and key ratios, plus some industry average data, are given in Table IP13–1.

   The cost of long-term debt is 12 percent versus only eight percent for short-term notes payable. Variable costs as a percentage of sales (74 percent) would not be affected by the firm's working capital policy, but fixed costs would be affected due to the storage, handling, and insurance costs associated with inventory. Here are the assumed fixed costs under the three policies:

POLICY	FIXED COSTS
Restrictive	$ 950,000
Moderate	1,000,000
Relaxed	1,100,000

TABLE IP13–1	Financial Statements and Other Data on NYF (thousands of dollars)

A. 2000 Balance Sheet

Cash and securities	$ 100	Accounts payable and accruals	$ 300
Accounts receivable	600	Notes payable (8%)	500
Inventories	1,000	Total current liabilities	$ 800
Total current assets	$1,700	Long-term debt (12%)	600
Net fixed assets	800	Common equity	1,100
Total assets	$2,500	Total liabilities and equity	$2,500

B. 2000 Income Statement

Sales	$ 5,000.00
Less: Variable costs	(3,700.00)
Fixed costs	(1,000.00)
EBIT	$ 300.00
Interest	(112.00)
Earnings before taxes	$ 188.00
Taxes (40%)	(75.20)
Net income	$ 112.80
Dividends (30% payout)	$ 33.84
Addition to retained earnings	$ 78.96

C. Key Ratios

	NYF	INDUSTRY
Profit margin	2.3%	3.0%
Return on equity	10.3%	15.0%
Days sales outstanding	43.2	30.0
Accounts receivable turnover	8.3×	12.0×
Inventory turnover	3.7	5.4
Fixed assets turnover	6.3	6.0
Total assets turnover	2.0	2.5
Debt/assets	56.0%	50.0%
Times interest earned	2.7×	4.8×
Current ratio	2.1	2.3
Quick ratio	0.9	1.3

Sales also would be affected by the policy chosen: Carrying larger inventories and using easier credit terms would stimulate sales, so sales would be highest under the relaxed policy and lowest under the restrictive policy. Also, these effects would vary depending on the strength of the economy. Here are the relationships Barnes assumes would have held in 2000:

	SALES (MILLIONS OF DOLLARS)		
STATE OF THE ECONOMY	RESTRICTIVE	MODERATE	RELAXED
Weak	$4.3	$4.5	$5.0
Average	4.7	5.0	5.5
Strong	5.3	5.5	6.0

Barnes considers the 2000 economy to be average.

You have been asked to answer the following questions to help determine NYF's optimal working capital policy:

a. How does NYF's current working capital policy as reflected in its financial statements compare with an average firm's policy? Do the differences suggest that NYF's policy is better or worse than that of the average firm in its industry?

b. Based on the 2000 ratios and financial statements, what were the company's inventory conversion period, its receivables collection period, and, assuming a 29-day payables deferral period, its cash conversion cycle? How could the cash conversion cycle concept be used to help improve the firm's working capital management?

c. Barnes has asked you to recast the 2000 financial statements, and calculate some key ratios, assuming an average economy and a restrictive (tight) working capital policy, and to check some calculations he has made. Construct these statements, and then calculate the new current ratio and return on equity (ROE). Assume that common stock is used to make the balance sheet balance, but do not get into financing feedbacks. (*Hint:* You need to change sales, fixed costs, receivables, inventories, and common equity, plus items affected by those changes, and then calculate new ratios.)

d. Barnes himself has actually analyzed the situation for each of the policies under each economic scenario; the ROEs he has calculated are shown in Table IP13–2. What are the implications of these data for the working capital policy decision?

e. The working capital policy discussion thus far has focused entirely on current assets and not at all on the current asset financing policy. How would you bring financing policy into the analysis?

TABLE IP13–2 ROEs under the Alternative Policies

	WORKING CAPITAL POLICY		
STATE OF THE ECONOMY	TIGHT	MODERATE	EASY
Weak	4.2%	3.2%	3.8%
Average	12.0	10.3	9.3
Strong	23.7	17.3	14.9
Average	13.3%	10.3%	9.3%

Computer-Related Problem

Work the problem in this section only if you are using the computer problem diskette.

working capital financing   **13–8**   Three companies—Aggressive, Moderate, and Conservative—have different working capital management policies as implied by their names. For example, Aggressive employs only minimal current assets, and it finances almost entirely with current liabilities plus equity. This restricted approach has a dual effect. It keeps total assets low, which tends to increase return on assets; but because of stock-outs and credit rejections, total sales are reduced, and because inventory is ordered more frequently and in smaller quantities, variable costs are increased. Condensed balance sheets for the three companies follow:

	AGGRESSIVE	MODERATE	CONSERVATIVE
Current assets	$225,000	$300,000	$450,000
Fixed assets	300,000	300,000	300,000
Total assets	$525,000	$600,000	$750,000
Current liabilities (cost = 12%)	$300,000	$150,000	$ 75,000
Long-term debt (cost = 10%)	0	150,000	300,000
Total debt	$300,000	$300,000	$375,000
Equity	225,000	300,000	375,000
Total liabilities and equity	$525,000	$600,000	$750,000
Current ratio	0.75	2.0	6.0

The cost of goods sold functions for the three firms are as follows:

	COST OF GOODS SOLD =	FIXED COSTS	+	VARIABLE COSTS
Aggressive:	Cost of goods sold =	$300,000	+	0.70(Sales)
Moderate:	Cost of goods sold =	$405,000	+	0.65(Sales)
Conservative:	Cost of goods sold =	$577,500	+	0.60(Sales)

Because of the working capital differences, sales for the three firms under different economic conditions are expected to vary as follows:

	AGGRESSIVE	MODERATE	CONSERVATIVE
Strong economy	$1,800,000	$1,875,000	$1,950,000
Average economy	1,350,000	1,500,000	1,725,000
Weak economy	1,050,000	1,200,000	1,575,000

a. Construct income statements for each company for strong, average, and weak economies using the following format:

> Sales
> Less: Cost of goods sold
> Earnings before interest and taxes (EBIT)
> Less: Interest expense

Earnings before taxes (EBT)
Less: Taxes (at 40%)
Net income (NI)

b. Compare the return on equity for the companies. Which company is best in a strong economy? In an average economy? In a weak economy?

c. Suppose that, with sales at the average-economy level, short-term interest rates rose to 20 percent. How would this affect the three firms?

d. Suppose that because of production slowdowns caused by inventory shortages, the aggressive company's variable cost ratio rose to 80 percent. What would happen to its ROE? Assume a short-term interest rate of 12 percent.

e. What considerations for the management of working capital are indicated by this problem?

ONLINE ESSENTIALS

http://www.tma-net.org   Treasury Management Association
This site is the home page for the Treasury Management Association, which provides access to articles published in the *TMA Journal*, results of research projects that relate to working capital and liquidity management, and links to related sites.

http://www.treasurystrat.com   Treasury Strategies
Even though Treasury Strategies is a company that provides advice about treasury management for a fee, their Web site provides links to sites with working capital management information. You are able to examine the results of various surveys the company has completed that relate to treasury and liquidity management.

http://www.treasuryandrisk.com   cfonet
Provides a variety of sources for working capital related information, including links to relevant sites, results of working capital surveys, discussions, and articles about treasury management.

http://corp.bankofamerica.com   Bank of America
Click on the box on the left of the page labeled "Global Treasury & Trade Services" to get to a page that will permit you to view newsletters, various articles, press releases, and so forth about working capital management. Many of the articles and newsletters are published by organizations other than Bank of America; thus, additional links are also provided.

CHAPTER 14

Managing Short-Term Assets

A MANAGERIAL PERSPECTIVE

Cash is the oil that lubricates the wheels of business. Without adequate oil, machines grind to a halt, and a business with inadequate cash will do likewise. However, carrying cash is expensive because cash is a nonearning asset; a firm that holds cash beyond its minimum requirements lowers its earnings potential.

Cash management is a very professional, highly refined activity. The following excerpt from PNC Bank's Web site (http://www.pncbank.com) describes its Working Cash® Receivables Advantage system and illustrates what is involved with cash management.

> PNC Bank is pleased to introduce The Working Cash Receivables Advantage, a program that adds real value to your treasury collections process. The Working Cash® Receivables Advantage makes your cash work harder through faster receipt and automated, 24-hour investment. We have combined PNC Bank's highly rated lockbox service, our PINACLE® information reporting system, and our automated investment service to deliver a comprehensive collections process to you. Each service complements the other by accelerating payment receipt, notifying you of deposits, and simplifying the daily investment process.

According to PNC's description of its Working Cash® Receivables Advantage system, lockbox arrangements are used to reduce mail delays associated with customers' payments and to accelerate the check-clearing process. The lockbox collec-tions are automated, with 24-hour processing seven days a week. In addition, once the collections are in a company's checking account, PNC Bank will help eliminate idle cash balances by automatically investing excess amounts.

> Our systems manage the investment activity through your checking account and your corresponding investment vehicle. At the end of each day, we calculate the available dollars eligible for investment. This calculation considers all daily credits (including lockbox deposits made through Working Cash® Receivables Advantage) to, and disbursements from, your account. Once the collected balance is determined, the system automatically compares the balance to a predetermined target balance. All available funds exceeding the target are swept into your overnight investment vehicle. The investment is posted as the last transaction to your checking account. You begin earning interest that same day. Funds remain invested until they are needed to cover transaction activity in your checking account. This transfer back to your checking account also occurs automatically. Because liquidity is critical in meeting daily cashflow needs, investment funds are always accessible directly through your checking account.

For some companies, the arrangement offered by PNC Bank makes good sense. However, firms sometimes go too far with their cash management systems. For example, the general practice in the securities brokerage business (until Merrill Lynch

continues

lost a major law suit and agreed to stop doing it) was to write checks to customers located east of the Mississippi on banks located on the West Coast, and vice versa. This slowed down payments on checks, deprived customers of the use of their money, and gave the brokerage firm use of billions of dollars of their customers' money for extended periods of time. According to the Securities and Exchange Commission, this practice, although it increased brokerage firms' profits by millions of dollars each year, was "inconsistent with a broker-dealer's obligation to deal fairly with its customers."

As you read this chapter, consider just how critical a firm's cash management practices really are, as well as how important it is to turn assets such as inventory and receivables into cash in a timely fashion. The lessons to be learned from this chapter apply to the cash management practices of individuals as well as to those of businesses. Maybe you will be able to take some of the ideas discussed here and apply them to your personal finances. ■

As we discovered in the previous chapter, all else equal, the riskiness of the portfolio of assets held by a firm is based on the combination of short- and long-term investments (assets) the firm makes. The relative amount that is invested in short-term assets is a function of decisions that are made concerning the management of cash and marketable securities, accounts receivable, and inventories. Of these three assets, we generally consider cash and marketable securities to be least risky, or most *liquid*. But the degree of risk can vary for either accounts receivable or inventories, depending on the general characteristics of the firm's working capital policy. For example, we generally view receivables as relatively safe assets because they represent sales the firm expects to collect in the future. But a firm with an overly aggressive, or relaxed, credit policy might have many slow payers or bad-debt customers that make its receivables extremely risky, thus fairly *illiquid*.

In this chapter, we discuss working capital management policies with respect to the current (short-term) assets of the firm. As you read the chapter, keep in mind that, although short-term assets generally are safer than long-term assets, they earn a lower rate of return. Thus, all else equal, firms that hold greater amounts of short-term assets are considered less risky than firms that hold greater amounts of long-term assets; at the same time, firms with more short-term assets earn lower returns than firms with more long-term assets. Consequently, financial managers are faced with a dilemma of whether to forgo higher returns to attain lower risk or to forgo lower risk to achieve higher returns. In general, however, we will see that some amount of short-term assets is required to maintain normal operations.

Cash Management

In Chapter 7 we discovered that value, which we want to maximize, is based on cash flows. Thus, managing cash flows is an extremely important task for a financial manager. Part of this task is determining how much cash a firm should have on hand at any time to ensure normal business operations continue uninterrupted. In this section, we discuss some of the factors that affect the amount of cash firms hold, and we describe some of the cash management techniques currently used by businesses.

For the purposes of our discussion, the term *cash* refers to the funds a firm holds that can be used for immediate disbursement—this includes the amount a firm holds in its checking account as well as the amount of actual coin and currency it holds. Cash is a "nonearning, or idle, asset" that is required to pay bills. When possible, cash should be "put to work" by investing in assets that have positive expected returns. Thus, the goal of the cash manager is to minimize the amount of cash the firm must hold for use in conducting its normal business activities, yet, at the same time, to have sufficient cash to (1) pay suppliers, (2) maintain the firm's credit rating, and (3) meet unexpected cash needs.

Firms hold cash for the following reasons:

TRANSACTIONS BALANCE
A cash balance necessary for day-to-day operations; the balance associated with routine payments and collections.

COMPENSATING BALANCE
A minimum checking account balance that a firm must maintain with a bank to help offset the costs of services such as check clearing and cash management advice.

PRECAUTIONARY BALANCES
A cash balance held in reserve for unforeseen fluctuations in cash flows.

SPECULATIVE BALANCE
A cash balance that is held to enable the firm to take advantage of any bargain purchases that might arise.

1. Cash balances are necessary in business operations because payments must be made in cash, and receipts are deposited in a cash account. Cash balances associated with routine payments and collections are known as **transactions balances.**
2. A bank often requires a firm to maintain a **compensating balance** on deposit to help offset the costs of providing services such as check clearing and cash management advice.
3. Because cash inflows and cash outflows are somewhat unpredictable, firms generally hold some cash in reserve for random, unforeseen fluctuations in cash flows. These *safety stocks* are called **precautionary balances**—the less predictable the firm's cash flows, the larger such balances should be. However, if the firm has easy access to borrowed funds—that is, if it can borrow on short notice (e.g., via a line of credit at the bank)—its need for precautionary balances is reduced.
4. Sometimes cash balances are held to enable the firm to take advantage of bargain purchases that might arise. These funds are called **speculative balances.** As with precautionary balances, though, firms that have easy access to borrowed funds are likely to rely on their ability to borrow quickly rather than to rely on cash balances for speculative purposes.

Although the cash accounts of most firms can be thought of as consisting of transactions, compensating, precautionary, and speculative balances, we cannot calculate the amount needed for each purpose, sum them, and produce a total desired cash balance because the same money often serves more than one purpose. For instance, precautionary and speculative balances can also be used to satisfy compensating balance requirements. Firms do, however, consider all four factors when establishing their target cash positions.

In addition to the four motives above, a firm maintains cash balances to preserve its credit rating by keeping its liquidity position in line with those of other firms in the industry. A strong credit rating enables the firm both to purchase goods from suppliers on favorable terms and to maintain an ample line of credit with its bank.

Self-Test Questions

Why is cash management important?

What are the motives for holding cash?

The Cash Budget

Perhaps the most critical ingredient to proper cash management is the ability to estimate the cash flows of the firm so the firm can make plans to borrow when cash is deficient or to invest when cash is in excess of what is needed. Without a doubt, financial managers will agree that the most important tool for managing cash is the cash budget (forecast). The cash budget helps management plan investment and borrowing strategies, and it also is used to provide feedback and control to improve the efficiency of cash management in the future.

The firm estimates its general needs for cash as a part of its overall budgeting, or forecasting, process. First, the firm forecasts its operating activities such as expenses and revenues for the period in question. Then, the financing and investment activities necessary to attain that level of operations must be forecasted. Such forecasts entail the construction of *pro forma* financial statements, which we discussed in Chapter 4. The information provided from the *pro forma* balance sheet and income statement is combined with projections about the delay in collecting accounts receivable, the delay in paying suppliers and employees, tax payment dates, dividend and interest payment dates, and so on. All of this information is summarized in the **cash budget,** which shows the firm's projected cash inflows and cash outflows over some specified period. Generally, firms use a monthly cash budget forecasted over the next year plus a more detailed daily or weekly cash budget for the coming month. The monthly cash budgets are used for planning purposes and the daily or weekly budgets are used for actual cash control.

CASH BUDGET
A schedule showing cash receipts, cash disbursements, and cash balances for a firm over a specified time period.

The cash budget provides much more detailed information concerning a firm's future cash flows than do the forecasted financial statements. Remember when we developed Unilate Textiles' 2001 forecasted financial statements in Chapter 4, we projected net sales to be $1,650 million and net income to be $61.0 million. Using the forecasted financial statements contained in Table 4–3 in Chapter 4, we find that the net cash flow (in millions of dollars) generated from operations in 2001 is expected to be as follows:

Net Income	$ 61.0
Add: Noncash expenses (depreciation)	55.0
Gross cash flow from operations	$116.0
Adjustments to gross cash flow:	
Increase in accounts receivable	(18.0)
Increase in inventories	(27.0)
Increase in accounts payable	3.0
Increase in accruals	6.0
Total adjustments to gross cash flow	($ 36.0)
Net cash flow from operations	$ 80.0

So in 2001, it is expected Unilate will generate $80 million cash inflow through normal production and sales operations. Much of this $80 million will be used to satisfy the financing and investment activities of the firm. Even after these activities are considered, Unilate's cash account is projected to increase by $1.5 million in 2001. Does this mean that Unilate will not have to worry about cash shortages during 2001? To answer this question, we must construct Unilate's cash budget for 2001.

To simplify the construction of Unilate's cash budget, we will only consider the last half of 2001 (July through December). Further, we will not list every cash flow that is expected to occur, but instead will focus on the operating flows. Remember that Unilate's sales peak is in September and October. All sales are made on credit with terms that allow a two percent cash discount for payments made within ten days, and, if the discount is not taken, the full amount is due in 30 days. However, like most companies, Unilate finds that some of its customers delay payment for more than 90 days. Experience has shown that payment on 20 percent of Unilate's *dollar* sales is made during the month in which the sale is made—these are the discount sales. On 70 percent of sales, payment is made during the month immediately following the month of sale, and payment is made on ten percent of sales two months or more after the initial sales. To simplify the cash budget, though, we will assume the last ten percent of sales is collected in the second month following the sale.

The costs to Unilate of cotton, wool, and other cloth-related materials average 60 percent of the sales prices of the finished products. These purchases generally are made one month before the firm expects to sell the finished products. In 2001, Unilate's suppliers have agreed to allow payment for materials to be delayed for 30 days after the purchase. Accordingly, if July sales are forecasted at $150 million, then purchases during June will amount to $90 million, and this amount actually will be paid in July.

Other cash expenses such as wage s and rent also are built into the cash budget, and Unilate must make estimated tax payments of $16 million on September 15 and $10 million on December 15, while a $20 million payment for a new plant must be made in October. Assuming that Unilate's **target, or minimum, cash balance** is $5 million and that it projects $8 million to be on hand on July 1, 2001, what will the firm's monthly cash surpluses or shortfalls be for the period from July through December?

Unilate's 2001 cash budget for July through December is presented in Table 14–1. The approach used to construct this cash budget generally is termed the **disbursements and receipts method** (also referred to as **scheduling**) because the cash disbursements and cash receipts are estimated to determine the net cash flow expected to be generated each month. The format used in Table 14–1 is quite simple—it is much like balancing a checkbook; the cash receipts are lumped into one category and the cash disbursements are lumped into another category to determine the net effect monthly cash flows have on the cash position of the firm. More detailed formats can be used, depending on how the firm prefers to present the cash budget information.

The first line of Table 14–1 gives the sales forecast for the period from May through December. These estimates are necessary to determine collections for July through December. Similarly, the second line of the table gives the credit purchases expected each month based on the sales forecasts so the monthly payments for credit purchases can be determined.

The *Cash Receipts* category shows cash collections based on credit sales originating in three months—in the current month and in the previous two months. Take a look at the collections expected in July. Remember that Unilate expects 20 percent of the dollar sales to be collected in the month of the sales, and thus to be affected by the two percent cash discount offered; 70 percent of the dollar sales will be collected one month after the sales; and the remaining ten percent of the dollar sales will be collected two months after the sales (it is assumed there are no bad debts). So in July, $29.4 million = $0.20 \times (1 - 0.02) \times \$150$ million collections will result from sales in July; $87.5 million $= 0.70 \times \$125$ million will be collected from sales that occurred in June; and, $10.0

TARGET (MINIMUM) CASH BALANCE
The minimum cash balance a firm desires to maintain in order to conduct business.

DISBURSEMENTS AND RECEIPTS METHOD (SCHEDULING)
The net cash flow is determined by estimating the cash disbursements and the cash receipts expected to be generated each period.

TABLE 14-1 Unilate Textiles: 2001 Cash Budget (millions of dollars)

	May	June	July	Aug.	Sept.	Oct.	Nov.	Dec.
Credit sales	100.0	125.0	150.0	200.0	250.0	180.0	130.0	100.0
Credit purchases = 60% of next month's sales		90.0	120.0	150.0	108.0	78.0	60.0	
Cash Receipts								
Collections from this month's sales = 0.2 × 0.98 × (current sales)			29.4	39.2	49.0	35.3	25.5	19.6
Collections from previous month's sales = 0.7 × (previous month's sales)			87.5	105.0	140.0	175.0	126.0	91.0
Collect from sales two months previously = 0.1 × (sales 2 months ago)			10.0	12.5	15.0	20.0	25.0	18.0
Total cash receipts			$126.9	$156.7	$204.0	$230.3	$176.5	$128.6
Cash Disbursements								
Payments made for credit purchases (1-month lag)			90.0	120.0	150.0	108.0	78.0	60.0
Wages and salaries (22% of monthly sales)			33.0	44.0	55.0	39.6	28.6	22.0
Rent			9.0	9.0	9.0	9.0	9.0	9.0
Other expenses			7.0	8.0	11.0	10.0	5.0	4.0
Taxes					16.0			10.0
Payment for plant construction						20.0		
Total cash disbursements			$139.0	$181.0	$241.0	$186.6	$120.6	$105.0
Net cash flow (Receipts − Disbursements)			($ 12.1)	($ 24.3)	($ 37.0)	$ 43.7	$ 55.9	$ 23.6
Beginning cash balance			$ 8.0	($ 4.1)	($ 28.4)	($ 65.4)	($ 21.7)	$ 34.2
Ending cash balance			(4.1)	(28.4)	(65.4)	(21.7)	34.2	57.8
Target (minimum) cash balance			5.0	5.0	5.0	5.0	5.0	5.0
Surplus (shortfall) cash			($ 9.1)	($ 33.4)	($ 70.4)	($ 26.7)	$ 29.2	$ 52.8

million = 0.10 × $100 million will be collected from sales that occurred in May. Thus, the total collections received in July represent 20 percent of July sales (minus the discount) plus 70 percent of June sales plus 10 percent of May sales, or $126.9 million in total.

The *Cash Disbursements* category shows payments for raw materials, wages, rent, and so on. Raw materials are purchased on credit one month before the finished goods are expected to be sold, but payments for the materials are not made until one month later (i.e., the month of the expected sales). The cost of the raw materials is expected to be 60 percent of sales. July sales are forecasted at $150 million, so Unilate will purchase $90 million of materials in June and pay for these purchases in July. Similarly, Unilate will purchase $120 million of materials in July to meet August's forecasted sales of $200 million. Additional monthly cash disbursements include employees' salaries, which equal 22 percent of monthly sales; rent, which remains constant; and other operating expenses, which vary with respect to production levels. Cash disbursements that are not expected to occur monthly include taxes (September and December) and payment for the construction of additional facilities (October).

The line labeled *Net cash flow* shows whether Unilate's operations are expected to generate positive or negative net cash flows each month. But this is only the beginning of the story. We need to examine the firm's cash position based on the cash balance existing at the beginning of the month and based on the *Target (minimum) cash balance* desired by Unilate. The bottom line provides information as to whether Unilate can expect a monthly cash surplus that can be invested temporarily in marketable securities or a monthly cash shortfall that must be financed with external, nonspontaneous sources of funds.

At the beginning of July, Unilate will have cash equal to $8 million. During July, Unilate is expected to generate a negative $12.1 million net cash flow; thus, July cash disbursements are expected to exceed cash receipts by $12.1 million (that is, deficit spending is expected). Because Unilate only has $8 million cash to begin July, the cash balance at the end of July is expected to be overdrawn by $4.1 if the firm doesn't find additional funding. To make matters worse, Unilate has a target cash balance equal to $5 million, so without any additional financing its cash balance at the end of July is expected to be $9.1 million short of its target. Therefore, Unilate must make arrangements to borrow $9.1 million in July to bring the cash account balance up to the target balance of $5 million. Assuming that this amount is indeed borrowed, loans outstanding will total $9.1 million at the end of July. (We assume that Unilate did not have any bank loans outstanding on July 1 because its beginning cash balance exceeded the target balance.)

The cash surplus or required loan balance (shortfall) is given on the bottom line of the cash budget. A positive value indicates a cash surplus, whereas a negative value (in parentheses) indicates a loan requirement. Note that the *bottom-line* surplus cash or loan requirement shown is a *cumulative amount*. Thus, Unilate must borrow $9.1 million in July; the firm has a cash shortfall during August of $24.3 million as reported on the Net cash flow line, so its total loan requirement at the end of August is $33.4 million = $9.1 million + 24.3 million, as reported on the bottom line for August. Unilate's arrangement with the bank permits it to increase its outstanding loans on a daily basis, up to a prearranged maximum, just as you could increase the amount you owe on a credit card. Unilate will use any surplus funds it generates to pay off its loans, and because the loan can be paid down at any time, on a daily basis, the firm never will have both a cash surplus and an outstanding loan balance. If Unilate actually does have a cash surplus, these funds will be invested in short-term, temporary investments.

This same procedure is used in the following months. Sales will peak in September, accompanied by increased payments for purchases, wages, and other items. Receipts

Marketable Securities

Realistically, the management of cash and marketable securities cannot be separated—management of one implies management of the other because the amount of marketable securities held by a firm depends on its short-term cash needs.

Rationale for Holding Marketable Securities

MARKETABLE SECURITIES
Securities that can be sold on short notice without loss of principal or original investment.

Marketable securities, or *near-cash* assets, are extremely liquid, short-term investments that permit the firm to earn positive returns on cash that is not needed to pay bills immediately but will be needed sometime in the near term, perhaps in a few days, weeks, or months. Although such investments typically provide much lower yields than operating assets, nearly every large firm has them. The two basic reasons for owning marketable securities are as follows:

1. Marketable securities serve as a *substitute for cash balances.* Firms often hold portfolios of marketable securities, liquidating part of the portfolio to increase the cash account when cash is needed because the *marketable securities offer a place to temporarily put cash balances to work earning a positive return.* In such situations, the marketable securities could be used as a substitute for transactions balances, for precautionary balances, for speculative balances, or for all three.
2. Marketable securities are also used as a *temporary investment* (a) to finance seasonal or cyclical operations and (b) to amass funds to meet financial requirements in the near future. For example, if the firm has a conservative financing policy as we discussed in Chapter 13, then its long-term capital will exceed its permanent assets, and marketable securities will be held when inventories and receivables are low.

Characteristics of Marketable Securities

A wide variety of securities is available to firms that choose to hold marketable securities. But the characteristics generally associated with marketable securities are as follows:

1. **Maturity.** Firms hold marketable securities in order to *temporarily* invest cash that otherwise would be idle in the short run. Therefore, marketable securities are short-term investments; often they are held only for a few days or weeks. If the cash budget indicates the funds are not needed in the foreseeable future, then longer-term investments, which generally earn higher returns, should be used.
2. **Risk.** Recall that in Chapter 2 we developed this equation for determining the nominal interest rate:

$$k_{Nom} = k^* + IP + DRP + LP + MRP$$

Here k^* is the real risk-free rate, IP is a premium for expected inflation, DRP is the default risk premium, LP is the liquidity (or marketability) risk premium, and MRP is the maturity (or interest rate) risk premium. Also, remember from Chapter 2 that the risk-free rate, k_{RF}, is equal to $k^* + IP$, and a U.S. Treasury bill comes closest to the risk-free rate. For other instruments considered appropriate as marketable securities, the default and liquidity risks are small, and the interest-rate risk is negligible. These risks are small because marketable securities mature in the short term, and the short run is less uncertain than the long run. Also, recall from Chapter 7, prices of long-term investments, such as bonds, are much more sensitive to changes in interest rates than are prices of short-term investments. In general, then, the total risk associated with a portfolio of marketable securities (short term) is less than the total risk associated with a portfolio of long-term investments.

3. **Liquidity.** We generally judge an asset's *marketability* according to how quickly and easily it can be bought and sold in the financial markets. If an asset can be sold easily on short notice for close to its original purchase price, it is said to be *liquid*. Because marketable securities are held as a *substitute* for cash and as a *temporary* investment, such instruments should be very liquid.

4. **Return (Yield).** Because the marketable securities portfolio generally is composed of highly liquid, short-term securities with low risks, the returns associated with such investments are relatively low when compared to other investments. But given the purpose of the marketable securities portfolio, treasurers should not sacrifice safety for higher rates of return.

Types of Marketable Securities

Table 14–2 lists the major types of securities available for investment, with an indication of how widely the yields on these securities have fluctuated during the past few decades. Depending on how long they will be held, the financial manager decides upon a suitable set of securities, and a suitable maturity pattern, to hold as *near-cash reserves* in the form of marketable securities. As noted in the table, long-term securities are not appropriate investments for marketable securities as we have described in this section—safety, especially maintenance of principal, should be paramount when putting together a marketable securities portfolio.

Self-Test Questions

What are the characteristics of financial instruments that are considered appropriate marketable securities?

What are some securities commonly held as marketable securities? Why are such securities held by firms?

Credit Management

If you ask financial managers whether they would prefer to sell their products for cash or for credit, you would expect them to respond by saying something like this: "*If sales levels are not affected,* cash sales are preferred because payment is certain and immediate and because the costs of granting credit and maintaining accounts receivable would be eliminated." *Ideally,* then, firms would prefer to sell for cash only. So why do firms sell for credit? The primary reason most firms offer credit sales is because their competitors offer credit. Consider what you would do if you had the opportunity to purchase the same product for the same price from two different firms, but one firm required cash payment at the time of the purchase while the other firm allowed you to pay for the product one month after the purchase without any additional cost. From which firm would you purchase? Like you, firms prefer to delay their payments, especially if there are no additional costs associated with the delay.

TABLE 14–5	Unilate Textiles: Analysis of Changing Credit Policy (millions of dollars)		
	PROJECTED 2001 REVENUES/COSTS UNDER CURRENT CREDIT POLICY	**PROJECTED 2001 REVENUES/COSTS UNDER PROPOSED CREDIT POLICY**	**INCOME EFFECT OF CREDIT POLICY CHANGE**
Gross sales[a]	$1,656.6	$1,654.6	($2.0)
Less: Cash discounts[a]	(6.6)	(6.6)	0.0
Net sales	1,650.0	1,648.0	(2.0)
Variable cost of goods sold[a]	(1,353.0)	(1,351.4)	1.6
Bad debts	(0.0)	(0.0)	0.0
Credit evaluation and collection costs	(16.0)	(17.0)	(1.0)
Receivables carrying cost	(16.3)	(13.4)	2.9
Revenues net of variable production costs and credit costs	$ 264.7	$ 266.2	$1.5
Tax impact (40%)[b]	(105.9)	(106.5)	(0.6)
After-tax revenues	$ 158.8	$ 159.7	$0.9

[a]See footnotes in Table 14–4.

[b]For this example, it is not necessary to include the tax impact because the marginal tax rate will not change under the proposed credit policy changes. Therefore, if the proposal is acceptable before taxes, it is also acceptable after taxes. This might not be the case if the marginal tax rate that applies to the proposal differs from the existing rate.

The analysis in Table 14–5 provides Unilate's managers with a vehicle for considering the impact of credit policy changes on the firm's income statement and balance sheet variables. However, a great deal of judgment must be applied to the decision because both customers' and competitors' responses to credit policy changes are very difficult to estimate. Nevertheless, this type of numerical analysis can provide a good starting point for credit policy decisions.

Self-Test Questions

What factors are included in credit policy decisions? Describe how each factor affects sales and profitability.

Define days sales outstanding (DSO). What can be learned from it? How is it affected by sales fluctuations?

What is an aging schedule? What can be learned from it? How is it affected by sales fluctuations?

Describe the procedure used to evaluate a change in credit policy.

Inventory Management

If it could, a firm would prefer to have no inventory at all because while products are in inventory they do not generate returns and they must be financed. However, most firms find it necessary to maintain inventory in some form because (1) demand cannot be predicted with certainty and (2) it takes time to transform a product into a form that is ready for sale. And while excessive inventories are costly to the firm, so are insufficient inventories because customers might purchase from competitors if products are not available when demanded, and future business could be lost.

Although inventory models are covered in depth in production management courses, it is important to understand the basics of inventory management because proper management requires coordination among the sales, purchasing, production, and finance departments. Lack of coordination among these departments, poor sales forecasts, or both, can lead to financial ruin. Therefore, in this section, we describe the concepts of inventory management.

Types of Inventory

An inventory item can be grouped into one of the following categories:

RAW MATERIALS
The inventories purchased from suppliers that ultimately will be transformed into finished goods.

WORK-IN-PROCESS
Inventory in various stages of completion; some work-in-process is at the very beginning of the production process while some is at the end of the process.

FINISHED GOODS
Inventories that have completed the production process and are ready for sale.

STOCKOUT
Occurs when a firm runs out of inventory *and* customers arrive to purchase the product.

1. **Raw materials** include new inventory items purchased from suppliers; it is the material a firm purchases to transform into finished products for sale. As long as the firm has an inventory of raw materials, delays in ordering and delivery from suppliers do not affect the production process.
2. **Work-in-process** refers to inventory items that are at various stages of the production process. If a firm has work-in-process at every stage of the production process, then it will not have to completely shut down production if a problem arises at one of the earlier stages.
3. **Finished goods** inventory represents products that are ready for sale. Firms carry finished goods to ensure that orders can be filled when they are received. If there are no finished goods, the firm has to wait for the completion of the production process before inventory can be sold; thus, demand might not be satisfied when it arrives. When a customer arrives and there is no inventory to satisfy that demand, a **stockout** exists, and the firm might lose the demand to competitors, perhaps permanently.

Optimal Inventory Level

The goal of inventory management is to provide the inventories required to sustain operations at the lowest possible cost. Thus, the first step in determining the optimal inventory level is to identify the costs involved in purchasing and maintaining inventory, and then we need to determine at what point those costs are minimized.

CARRYING COSTS
The costs associated with having inventory, which include storage costs, insurance, cost of tying up funds, depreciation costs, and so on; these costs generally increase in proportion to the average amount of inventory held.

ORDERING COSTS
The costs of placing an order; the cost of *each* order generally is fixed regardless of the average size of the inventory.

Inventory Costs   We generally classify inventory costs into three categories: those associated with carrying inventory, those associated with ordering and receiving inventory, and those associated with running short of inventory (stockouts). First, let's look at the two costs that are most directly observable—carrying costs and ordering costs.

1. **Carrying costs** include any expenses associated with having inventory, such as rent paid for the warehouse where inventory is stored and insurance on the inventory, and they generally increase in direct proportion to the average amount of inventory carried.
2. **Ordering costs** are those expenses associated with placing and receiving an order for new inventory, which include the costs of generating memos, fax

transmissions, and so forth. For the most part, the costs associated with each order are fixed regardless of the order size.[3]

If we assume that the firm knows how much total inventory it needs and sales are distributed evenly during each period, then we can combine the total carrying costs (TCC) and the total ordering costs (TOC) to find total inventory costs (TIC) as follows:

14–3

$$\begin{aligned}
\text{Total inventory costs (TIC)} &= \text{Total carrying costs} + \text{Total ordering costs} \\
&= \left(\begin{array}{c}\text{Carrying cost} \\ \text{per unit}\end{array}\right) \times \left(\begin{array}{c}\text{Average units} \\ \text{in inventory}\end{array}\right) + \left(\begin{array}{c}\text{Cost per} \\ \text{order}\end{array}\right) \times \left(\begin{array}{c}\text{Number} \\ \text{of orders}\end{array}\right) \\
&= (C \times PP) \times \left(\frac{Q}{2}\right) + O \times \left(\frac{T}{Q}\right)
\end{aligned}$$

The variables in the equation are defined as follows:

C = Carrying costs as a percent of the purchase price of each inventory item.

PP = Purchase price, or cost, per unit.

Q = Number of units purchased with each order.

T = Total demand, or number of units sold, per period.

O = Fixed costs per order.

According to Equation 14–3, the average investment in inventory depends on how frequently orders are placed and the size of each order. If we order every day, average inventory will be much smaller than if we order once a year and inventory carrying costs will be low, but the number of orders will be large and inventory ordering costs will be high. We can reduce ordering costs by ordering greater amounts less often, but then average inventory, thus the total carrying cost, will be high. This trade-off between carrying costs and ordering costs is shown in Figure 14–2. Note from the figure that there is a point where the total inventory cost (TIC) is *minimized*; this is called the **economic (optimum) ordering quantity (EOQ).**

ECONOMIC (OPTIMUM) ORDERING QUANTITY (EOQ)
The optimal quantity that should be ordered; it is this quantity that will minimize the *total inventory costs.*

The Economic Ordering Quantity (EOQ) Model   The EOQ is determined by using calculus to find the point where the slope of the TIC curve in Figure 14–2 is perfectly horizontal; thus it equals zero. The result is the following equation:

---

[3]In reality, both carrying and ordering costs can have variable and fixed cost elements, at least over certain ranges of average inventory. For example, security and utilities charges probably are fixed in the short run over a wide range of inventory levels. Similarly, labor costs in receiving inventory could be tied to the quantity received, hence could be variable. To simplify matters, we treat all carrying costs as variable and all ordering costs as fixed.

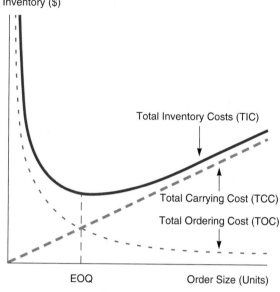

FIGURE 14–2 | Determination of the Optimal Order Quantity

Costs of Ordering and
Carrying Inventory ($)

Total Inventory Costs (TIC)

Total Carrying Cost (TCC)

Total Ordering Cost (TOC)

0   EOQ   Order Size (Units)

14–4

$$\text{Economic ordering quantity} = \text{EOQ} = \sqrt{\frac{2 \times O \times T}{C \times PP}}$$

EOQ MODEL
A formula for determining
the order quantity that
will minimize total
inventory costs:

$$\text{EOQ} = \sqrt{\frac{2 \times O \times T}{C \times PP}}$$

The primary assumptions of the **EOQ model** given by Equation 14–4 are that (1) sales are evenly distributed throughout the period examined and can be forecasted precisely, (2) orders are received when expected, and (3) the purchase price (PP) of each item in inventory is the same regardless of the quantity ordered.[4]

To illustrate the EOQ model, consider the following data supplied by Cotton Tops Inc., a distributor of custom-designed T-shirts that supplies concessionaires at Daisy World:

T = 78,000 shirts per year.

C = 25 percent of inventory value.

PP = $3.84 per shirt. (The shirts sell for $9, but this is irrelevant for our purposes here.)

O = $260 per order.

[4]The EOQ model can also be written as follows:

$$\text{EOQ} = \sqrt{\frac{2 \times O \times T}{C^*}}$$

where C* is the annual carrying cost per unit expressed in dollars.

Substituting these data into Equation 14–4, we find an EOQ of 6,500 units:

$$EOQ = \sqrt{\frac{2 \times \$260 \times 78{,}000}{0.25 \times \$3.84}}$$

$$EOQ = \sqrt{42{,}250{,}000} = 6{,}500 \text{ units}$$

If Cotton Tops orders 6,500 shirts each time it needs inventory, it will place 78,000/6,500 = 12 orders per year and carry an average inventory of 6,500/2 = 3,250 shirts. Thus, at the EOQ amount, Cotton Tops' total inventory costs would equal $6,240:

$$TIC = (C \times PP)\left(\frac{Q}{2}\right) + O\left(\frac{T}{Q}\right)$$

$$= [0.25(\$3.84)]\left(\frac{6{,}500}{2}\right) + (\$260)\left(\frac{78{,}000}{6{,}500}\right)$$

$$= \$3{,}120 + \$3{,}120$$

$$= \$6{,}240$$

Note these two points: (1) Because we assume the purchase price of each inventory item does not depend on the amount ordered, TIC does *not* include the $299,520 = 78,000($3.84) annual cost of purchasing the inventory itself. (2) As we see both in Figure 14–2 and in the numbers here, at the EOQ, total carrying cost (TCC) equals total ordering cost (TOC). This property is not unique to our Cotton Tops illustration; it always holds.

Table 14–6 contains the total inventory costs that Cotton Tops would incur at various order quantities, including the EOQ level. Note that (1) as the amount ordered increases, the total carrying costs increase but the total ordering costs decrease, and vice versa; (2) if less than the EOQ amount is ordered, then the higher ordering costs more than offset the lower carrying costs; and (3) if greater than the EOQ amount is ordered, the higher carrying costs more than offset the lower ordering costs.

EOQ Model Extensions It should be obvious that some of the assumptions necessary for the basic EOQ to hold are unrealistic. To make the model more useful, we can apply some simple extensions. First, if there is a delay between the time inventory is ordered and when it is received, the firm must reorder before it runs out of inventory. For example, if it normally takes two weeks to receive orders, then Cotton Tops should reorder when two weeks of inventory is left. Cotton Tops sells 78,000/52 = 1,500 shirts per week, so its **reorder point** is when inventory drops to 3,000 shirts. Even if Cotton Tops orders additional inventory at the appropriate reorder point, unexpected demand might cause it to run out of inventory before the new inventory is delivered. To avoid this, the firm could carry **safety stocks,** which represent additional inventory that helps guard against stockouts. The amount of safety stock a firm holds generally *increases* with (1) the uncertainty of demand forecasts, (2) the costs (in terms of lost sales and lost goodwill) that result from stockouts, and (3) the chances that delays will occur in receiving shipments. The amount of safety stock *decreases* as the cost of carrying this additional inventory increases.

Another factor a firm might need to consider when determining appropriate inventory levels is whether its suppliers offer discounts to purchase large quantities. For

REORDER POINT
The level of inventory at which an order should be placed.

SAFETY STOCKS
Additional inventory carried to guard against changes in sales rates or production/shipping delays.

TABLE 14–6	Cotton Tops, Inc.: Total Inventory Costs for Various Order Quantities				

	QUANTITY	NUMBER OF ORDERS	TOTAL ORDERING COSTS	TOTAL CARRYING COSTS	TOTAL INVENTORY COSTS
	3,000	26	$6,760	$ 1,440	$ 8,200
	5,200	15	3,900	2,496	6,396
	6,000	13	3,380	2,880	6,260
EOQ	**6,500**	**12**	**3,120**	**3,120**	**6,240**
	7,800	10	2,600	3,744	6,344
	9,750	8	2,080	4,680	6,760
	13,000	6	1,560	6,240	7,800
	78,000	1	260	37,440	37,700

T = Annual sales = 78,000 shirts
C = Carrying cost = 25 percent
PP = Purchase price = $3.84/shirt
O = Ordering cost = $260/order

example, if Cotton Tops' supplier offered a 1 percent discount for purchases equal to 13,000 units or more, the total reduction in the annual cost of purchasing inventory would be [0.01($3.84)] × 78,000 = $2,995.20. Looking in Table 14–6, we see that the total inventory cost at 13,000 units is $7,800, which is $1,560 = $7,800 − $6,240 greater than the cost at the EOQ level of 6,500 units. But the net benefit of taking advantage of the **quantity discount** is $1,435.20 = $2,995.20 − $1,560.00. Therefore, under these conditions, each time Cotton Tops orders inventory it will be more beneficial to order 13,000 units rather than the 6,500 units prescribed by the basic EOQ model.

In cases in which it is unrealistic to assume that the demand for the inventory is uniform throughout the year, the EOQ should not be applied on an annual basis. Rather, it would be more appropriate to divide the year into the seasons within which sales are relatively constant, say, the summer, the spring and fall, and the winter; then the EOQ model can be applied separately to each period.

Although we did not explicitly incorporate the extensions we mentioned here into the basic EOQ, our discussion should give you an idea of how the EOQ amount should be adjusted to determine the optimal inventory level if any of the conditions exist.

QUANTITY DISCOUNT
A discount from the purchase price offered for inventory ordered in large quantities.

Inventory Control Systems

The EOQ model can be used to help establish the proper inventory level, but inventory management also involves the establishment of an *inventory control system*. Inventory control systems run the gamut from very simple to extremely complex, depending on the size of the firm and the nature of its inventories. For example, one simple control procedure is the **red-line method**—inventory items are stocked in a bin, a red line is drawn around the inside of the bin at the level of the reorder point, and the inventory clerk places an order when the red line shows. This procedure works well for parts such as bolts in a manufacturing process or for many items in retail businesses.

RED-LINE METHOD
An inventory control procedure where a *red line* is drawn around the inside of an inventory-stocked bin to indicate the reorder point level.

can bring into a country, while tariffs, like taxes, increase the prices of products that are allowed to be imported. Both quotas and tariffs are designed to restrict the ability of foreign corporations to compete with domestic companies; at the extreme, foreign products are excluded altogether.

Another danger in certain countries is the threat of expropriation, or government takeover of the firm's local operations. If the threat of expropriation is large, inventory holdings will be minimized, and goods will be brought in only as needed. Similarly, if the operation involves extraction of raw material, processing plants might be moved offshore rather than located close to the production site.

Taxes also must be considered, and they have two effects on multinational inventory management. First, countries often impose property taxes on assets, including inventories, and when this is done, the tax is based on holdings as of a specific date, say, January 1 or March 1. Such rules make it advantageous for a multinational firm (1) to schedule production so that inventories are low on the assessment date and (2) if assessment dates vary among countries in a region, to hold safety stocks in different countries at different times during the year.

In general, then, multinational firms use techniques similar to those described in this chapter to manage current assets, but their job is more complex because business, legal, and economic environments can differ significantly from one country to another.

Self-Test Questions

What are some factors that make cash management especially complicated in a multinational corporation?

Why is granting credit especially risky in an international context?

What are some factors that make inventory management in multinational firms more complex than in purely domestic firms?

✳ **ETHICAL DILEMMA**

Money Back Guarantee, No Questions Asked

TradeSmart Inc. operates 1,200 discount electronics stores throughout the United States. TradeSmart has been quite successful in a highly competitive industry primarily because it has been able to offer brand name products at prices lower than can be found at other discount outlets. Because of its size, TradeSmart can purchase bulk inventory directly from manufacturers, and the economies of scale it derives from such purchases can be passed on to consumers in the form of lower prices.

In addition to low prices, TradeSmart offers an extremely liberal product return policy. Customers are permitted to return products for virtually any reason, and with little regard to the time period covered by

continues

manufacturers' warranties. In fact, just a few days ago, a customer returned a digital pager that was more than two years old. TradeSmart gave the customer a full refund even though the pager appeared to have been run over by a car, which, if true, clearly would have voided the manufacturer's warranty. In another instance, a customer was given a refund when he returned the camcorder he had purchased three days earlier to record his daughter's wedding festivities. The customer could not describe the camcorder's malfunction—he said "it just didn't work right." The customer refused an offer to replace the camcorder; instead, he insisted on a full refund, which he was given. The manager of the customer relations department suspected that the customer had "purchased" the camcorder intending all along to return it after his daughter's wedding. But TradeSmart's return policy does not dissuade customers from this practice. According to Ed Davidson, vice president of customer relations, TradeSmart is willing to stand behind every product it sells, regardless of the problem, because the company believes such a policy is needed to attract and keep loyal customers in such a competitive industry. The company's motto—"Customer Satisfaction Is Our Business"—is displayed prominently throughout TradeSmart stores.

With such a liberal return policy, how does TradeSmart keep its prices so low? Actually, TradeSmart ships the returned products back to the manufacturers as defective products, so the return costs are passed on to the manufacturers. According to manufacturers, only one out of every six products returned by TradeSmart actually is defective. But when the manufacturers complain about such returns as used products or products that have no mechanical problems, TradeSmart reminds them that the company does not have a service department, so its personnel are not knowledgeable concerning the technical circuitry of the products—the products are returned to the manufacturers with the customers' complaints attached. TradeSmart's inventory manager would contend that the company does not intentionally deceive or take advantage of the manufacturers' return policies and warranties. Do you agree with TradeSmart's return policy? Is it ethical? What action would you take if you were one of TradeSmart's suppliers?

Summary

In this chapter we examined methods used to manage and evaluate current assets. In addition, we provided an indication of the complexities faced by multinational firms when managing these accounts around the world. The key concepts covered in this chapter are listed here:

- The **primary goal of cash management** is to reduce the amount of cash held to the minimum necessary to conduct business.
- The **transactions balance** is the cash necessary to conduct day-to-day business, whereas the **precautionary balance** is a cash reserve held to meet random, unforeseen needs. A **compensating balance** is a minimum checking account balance that a bank requires as compensation either for services provided or as part of a loan agreement. Firms also hold **speculative balances,** which allow them to take advantage of bargain purchases.
- **Effective cash management** encompasses the proper management of cash inflows and outflows, which entails (1) synchronizing cash flows, (2) using float, (3) accelerating collections, (4) determining where and when funds will be needed and ensuring that they are available at the right place at the right time, and (5) controlling disbursements.
- **Disbursement float** is the amount of funds associated with checks written by a firm that are still in process and hence have not yet been deducted by the bank

Questions

14-1 What are principal reasons for holding cash? Can a firm estimate its target cash balance by summing the cash held to satisfy each of the reasons?

14-2 Explain how each of the following factors probably would affect a firm's target cash balance if all other factors are held constant.
   a. The firm institutes a new billing procedure that better synchronizes its cash inflows and outflows.
   b. The firm develops a new sales forecasting technique that improves its forecasts.
   c. The firm reduces its portfolio of U.S. Treasury bills.
   d. The firm arranges to use an overdraft system for its checking account.
   e. The firm borrows a large amount of money from its bank and also begins to write far more checks than it did in the past.
   f. Interest rates on Treasury bills rise from 5 percent to 10 percent.

14-3 What is a cash budget? For what purposes should cash budgets be created?

14-4 Why is a cash budget important even when there is plenty of cash in the bank?

14-5 Discuss why it is important for a financial manager to understand the concept of float in order to effectively manage the firm's cash.

14-6 Why would a lockbox plan make more sense for a firm that makes sales all over the United States than for a firm with the same volume of business that is concentrated where the corporate headquarters are located?

14-7 In general, does a firm wish to speed up or slow down collections of payments made by its customers? Why? How does the same firm wish to manage its disbursements? Why?

14-8 What does the term *liquidity* mean? Which would be more important to a firm that held a portfolio of marketable securities as precautionary balances against the possibility of losing a major lawsuit—liquidity or rate of return? Explain.

14-9 Firm A's management is very conservative whereas Firm B's is more aggressive. Is it true that, other things the same, Firm B would probably have larger holdings of marketable securities? Explain.

14-10 What are the elements of a firm's credit policy? To what extent can firms set their own credit policies as opposed to having to accept policies that are dictated by the competition?

14-11 What are aging schedules, and how can they be used to help the credit manager more effectively manage accounts receivable?

14-12 Indicate by a (+), (−), or (0) whether each of the following events would probably cause accounts receivable (A/R), sales, and profits to increase, decrease, or be affected in an indeterminate manner:

	A/R	SALES	PROFITS
a. The firm tightens its credit standards	_____	_____	_____
b. The credit terms are changed from 2/10, net 30 to 3/10, net 30	_____	_____	_____
c. The credit manager gets tough with past-due accounts	_____	_____	_____

14-13 Describe the three classifications of inventory and indicate the purpose for holding each type.

14–14 Indicate by a (+), (−), or (0) whether each of the following events would probably cause average annual inventories (the sum of the inventories held at the end of each month of the year divided by 12) to rise, fall, or be affected in an indeterminate manner:

  a. Our suppliers switch from delivering by train to air freight. _____

  b. We change from producing just in time to meet seasonal sales to steady, year-round production. (Sales peak at Christmas.) _____

  c. Competition in the markets in which we sell increases. _____

  d. The rate of general inflation increases. _____

  e. Interest rates rise; other things are constant. _____

14–15 "Every firm should use the EOQ model to determine the optimal level of inventory to maintain." Discuss the accuracy of this statement with respect to the form of the EOQ model presented in this chapter.

Self-Test Problems

(Solutions appear in Appendix B)

key terms **ST–1** Define each of the following terms:

  a. Transactions balance; compensating balance; precautionary balance; speculative balance

  b. Cash budget; target cash balance

  c. Synchronized cash flows

  d. Net float; disbursement float; collections float

  e. Mail delay; processing delay; clearing (availability) delay

  f. Lockbox arrangement; preauthorized debit; concentration banking

  g. Zero-balance account (ZBA); controlled disbursement account (CDA)

  h. Marketable securities; near-cash reserves

  i. Credit policy; credit terms; collection policy

  j. Days sales outstanding (DSO); aging schedule

  k. Carrying costs; ordering costs; total inventory costs

  l. Economic ordering quantity (EOQ); EOQ model

  m. Reorder point; safety stock; quantity discount

  n. Just-in-time system; outsourcing

float **ST–2** The Upton Company is setting up a new checking account with Howe National Bank. Upton plans to issue checks in the amount of $1 million each day and to deduct them from its own records at the close of business on the day they are written. On average, the bank will receive and clear the checks at 5 P.M. the third day after they are written; for example, a check written on Monday will be cleared on Thursday afternoon. The firm's agreement with the bank requires it to maintain a $500,000 average compensating balance; this is $250,000 greater than the cash balance the firm would otherwise have on deposit. It makes a $500,000 deposit at the time it opens the account.

  a. Assuming that the firm makes deposits at 4 P.M. each day (and the bank includes them in that day's transactions), how much must it deposit daily in order to maintain a sufficient balance once it reaches a steady state? (To do this, set up a table that shows the daily balance recorded on the company's books and the daily balance at the bank until a steady state is reached.) Indicate the required deposit on Day 1, Day 2, Day 3, if any, and each day

Collection estimates obtained from the credit and collection department are as follows: collections within the month of sale, 10 percent; collections the month following the sale, 75 percent; collections the second month following the sale, 15 percent. Payments for labor and raw materials are typically made during the month following the one in which these costs have been incurred. Total labor and raw materials costs are estimated for each month as follows:

May 2001	$ 90,000
June	90,000
July	126,000
August	882,000
September	306,000
October	234,000
November	162,000
December	90,000

General and administrative salaries will amount to approximately $27,000 a month; lease payments under long-term lease contracts will be $9,000 a month; depreciation charges will be $36,000 a month; miscellaneous expenses will be $2,700 a month; income tax payments of $63,000 will be due in both September and December; and a progress payment of $180,000 on a new design studio must be paid in October. Cash on hand on July 1 will amount to $132,000, and a minimum cash balance of $90,000 will be maintained throughout the cash budget period.

a. Prepare a monthly cash budget for the last six months of 2001.

b. Prepare an estimate of the required financing (or excess funds)—that is, the amount of money Carol's Fashion Designs will need to borrow (or will have available to invest)—for each month during that period.

c. Assume that receipts from sales come in uniformly during the month (that is, cash receipts come in at the rate of 1/30 each day), but all outflows are paid on the fifth of the month. Will this have an effect on the cash budget—in other words, would the cash budget you have prepared be valid under these assumptions? If not, what can be done to make a valid estimate of peak financing requirements? No calculations are required, although calculations can be used to illustrate the effects.

d. Carol's Fashion Designs produces on a seasonal basis, just ahead of sales. Without making any calculations, discuss how the company's current ratio and debt ratio would vary during the year assuming all financial requirements were met by short-term bank loans. Could changes in these ratios affect the firm's ability to obtain bank credit?

lockbox system   **14–4** Durst Corporation began operations five years ago as a small firm serving customers in the Denver area. However, its reputation and market area grew quickly so that today Durst has customers throughout the entire United States. Despite its broad customer base, Durst has maintained its headquarters in Denver and keeps its central billing system there. Durst's management is considering an alternative collection procedure to reduce its mail time and processing float. On average, it takes five days from the time customers mail payments until Durst is able to receive, process, and deposit them. Durst would like to set up a lockbox collection system, which it estimates would reduce the time lag from customer mailing to deposit by three days—bringing it down to two days. Durst receives an average of $1,400,000 in payments per day.

a. How many days of collection float now exist (Durst's customers' disbursement float) and what would it be under the lockbox system? What reduction in cash balances could Durst achieve by initiating the lockbox system?

b. If Durst has an opportunity cost of ten percent, how much is the lockbox system worth on an annual basis?

c. What is the maximum monthly charge Durst should pay for the lockbox system?

relaxing collection efforts   **14–5** The Pettit Corporation has annual credit sales of $2 million. Current expenses for the collection department are $30,000, bad debt losses are two percent, and the days sales outstanding is 30 days. Pettit is considering easing its collection efforts so that collection expenses will be reduced to $22,000 per year. The change is expected to increase bad debt losses to three percent and to increase the days sales outstanding to 45 days. In addition, sales are expected to increase to $2.2 million per year.

Should Pettit relax collection efforts if the opportunity cost of funds is 12 percent, the variable cost ratio is 75 percent, and its marginal tax rate is 40 percent?

easing credit terms   **14–6** Bey Technologies is considering changing its credit terms from 2/15, net 30 to 3/10, net 30 in order to speed collections. At present, 40 percent of Bey's paying customers take the two percent discount. Under the new terms, discount customers are expected to rise to 50 percent. Regardless of the credit terms, half of the customers who do not take the discount are expected to pay on time, whereas the remainder will pay ten days late. The change does not involve a relaxation of credit standards; therefore, bad debt losses are not expected to rise above their present two percent level. However, the more generous cash discount terms are expected to increase sales from $2 million to $2.6 million per year. Bey's variable cost ratio is 75 percent, the interest rate on funds invested in accounts receivable is nine percent, and the firm's marginal tax rate is 40 percent.

a. What is the days sales outstanding before and after the change?

b. Calculate the costs of the discounts taken before and after the change.

c. Calculate the dollar cost of carrying receivables before and after the change.

d. Calculate the bad debt losses before and after the change.

e. What is the incremental profit from the change in credit terms? Should Bey change its credit terms?

inventory cost   **14–7** Computer Supplies Inc. must order diskettes from its supplier in lots of one dozen boxes. Given the information provided here, complete the following table and determine the economic ordering quantity of diskettes for Computer Supplies Inc.

Annual demand: 26,000 dozen
Cost per order placed: $30.00
Carrying cost: 20%
Price per dozen: $7.80

ORDER SIZE (DOZENS)	250	500	1,000	2,000	13,000	26,000
Number of orders	____	____	____	____	____	____
Average inventory	____	____	____	____	____	____
Carrying cost	____	____	____	____	____	____
Order cost	____	____	____	____	____	____
Total cost	____	____	____	____	____	____

EOQ and inventory costs **14–8** The following inventory data have been established for the Thompson Company:

(1) Orders must be placed in multiples of 100 units.
(2) Annual sales are 338,000 units.
(3) The purchase price per unit is $6.
(4) Carrying cost is 20 percent of the purchase price of goods.
(5) Fixed order cost is $48.
(6) Three days are required for delivery.

a. What is the EOQ?
b. How many orders should Thompson place each year?
c. At what inventory level should an order be made?
d. Calculate the total cost of ordering and carrying inventories if the order quantity is (1) 4,000 units, (2) 4,800 units, or (3) 6,000 units. (4) What are the total costs if the order quantity is the EOQ?

Exam-Type Problems

The problems included in this section are set up in such a way that they could be used as multiple-choice exam problems.

computation of float **14–9** Clearwater Glass Company has examined its cash management policy, and it has found that it takes an average of five days for checks the company writes to reach its bank and thus be deducted from its checking account balance (i.e., disbursement delay, or float, is five days). On the other hand, it is an average of four days from the time Clearwater Glass receives payments from its customers until the funds are available for use at the bank (i.e., collection delay, or float, is four days). On an average day, Clearwater Glass writes checks that total $70,000, and it receives checks from customers that total $80,000.
a. Compute the disbursement float, collection float, and net float in dollars.
b. If Clearwater Glass has an opportunity cost equal to ten percent, how much would it be willing to spend each year to reduce collection delay (float) by two days? (*Hint:* Assume any funds that are freed up are invested at ten percent annually.)

receivables investment **14–10** Morrissey Industries sells on terms of 3/10, net 30. Total sales for the year are $900,000. Forty percent of the customers pay on the tenth day and take discounts; the other 60 percent pay, on average, 40 days after their purchases.
a. What is the days sales outstanding?
b. What is the average amount of receivables?
c. What would happen to average receivables if Morrissey toughened up on its collection policy with the result that all nondiscount customers paid on the 30th day?

tightening credit terms **14–11** Helen Bowers, the new credit manager of the Muscarella Corporation, was alarmed to find that Muscarella sells on credit terms of net 50 days while industry-wide credit terms have recently been lowered to net 30 days. On annual credit sales of $3 million, Muscarella currently averages 60 days' sales in accounts receivable. Bowers estimates that tightening the credit terms to 30 days would reduce annual sales to $2.6 million, but accounts receivable would drop to 35 days of sales, and the savings on investment in them should more than overcome any loss in profit.

Muscarella's variable cost ratio is 70 percent, and its marginal tax rate is 40 percent. If the interest rate on funds invested in receivables is 11 percent, should the change in credit terms be made?

cost of carrying receivables   **14–12**   The McCollough Company has a variable operating cost ratio of 70 percent, its cost of capital is ten percent, and current sales are $10,000. All of its sales are on credit, and it currently sells on terms of net 30. Its accounts receivable balance is $1,500. McCollough is considering a new credit policy with terms of net 45. Under the new policy, sales will increase to $12,000, and accounts receivable will rise to $2,500. If McCollough changes its credit policy to net 45, by how much will its cost of carrying receivables increase? Assume a 360-day year and that all customers pay on time.

EOQ   **14–13**   Green Thumb Garden Centers sells 240,000 bags of lawn fertilizer annually. The optimal safety stock (which is on hand initially) is 1,200 bags. Each bag costs Green Thumb $4, inventory carrying costs are 20 percent, and the cost of placing an order with its supplier is $25.
  a. What is the economic ordering quantity?
  b. What is the maximum inventory of fertilizer?
  c. What will Green Thumb's average inventory be?
  d. How often must the company order?

Integrative Problems

cash management   **14–14**   Ray Smith, a retired librarian, recently opened a sportsman's shop called Smitty's Sports Paradise (SSP). Smith decided at age 62 that he wasn't quite ready to stay at home, living the life of leisure. It had always been his dream to open an outdoor sportsman's shop, so his friends convinced him to go ahead. Because Smith's educational background was in literature and not in business, he hired you, a finance expert, to help him with the store's cash management. Smith is very eager to learn, so he asked you to develop a set of questions to help him understand cash management. Now answer the following questions:
  a. What is the goal of cash management?
  b. For what reasons do firms hold cash?
  c. What is meant by the terms *precautionary* and *speculative* balances?
  d. What are some specific advantages for a firm holding adequate cash balances?
  e. How can a firm synchronize its cash flows, and what good would this do?
  f. You have been going through the store's checkbook and bank balances. In the process, you discovered that SSP, on average, writes checks in the amount of $10,000 each day and that it takes about five days for these checks to clear. Also, the firm receives checks in the amount of $10,000 daily, but loses four days while they are being deposited and cleared. What is the firm's *disbursement float, collections float*, and *net float*?
  g. How can a firm speed up collections and slow down disbursements?
  h. Why would a firm hold marketable securities?
  i. What factors should a firm consider in building its marketable securities portfolio? What are some securities that should and should not be held?

credit policy   **14–15**   Ray Smith also wants you to examine his company's credit policy to determine if changes are needed because one of his employees, who graduated recently with a finance major, has recommended that the credit terms be changed from 2/10, net 30 to 3/20, net 45 and that both the credit standards and the collection policy be relaxed. According to the employee, such a change would cause sales to increase from $3.6 million to $4.0 million.

Currently, 62.5 percent of SSP's customers pay on Day 10 of the billing cycle and take the discount, 32 percent pay on Day 30, and 5.5 percent pay (on average) on Day 60. If the new credit policy is adopted, Smith thinks that 72.5 percent of customers would take the discount, ten percent would pay on Day 45, and 17.5 percent would pay late, on Day 90. Bad debt losses for both policies are expected to be trivial.

Variable operating costs are currently 75 percent of sales, the cost of funds used to carry receivables is ten percent, and its marginal tax rate is 40 percent. None of these factors would change as a result of a credit policy change.

To help decide whether to adopt the new policy, Smith has asked you to answer the following questions:

a. What variables make up a firm's credit policy? In what direction would each be changed if the credit policy were to be relaxed? How would each variable tend to affect sales, the level of receivables, and bad debt losses?

b. How are the days sales outstanding (DSO) and the average collection period (ACP) related to one another? What would the DSO be if the current credit policy is maintained? If the proposed policy is adopted?

c. What is the dollar amount of discounts granted under the current and the proposed credit policies?

d. What is the dollar cost of carrying receivables under the current and the proposed credit policies?

e. What is the expected incremental profit associated with the proposed change in credit policy? Based on the analysis, should the change be made?

f. Suppose the company makes the proposed change, but its competitors react by making changes in their own credit terms, with the net result being that gross sales remain at the $3.6 million level. What would be the impact on the company's after-tax profits?

g. (1) What does the term *monitoring accounts receivable* mean?
   (2) Why would a firm want to monitor its receivables?
   (3) How might the DSO and the aging schedule be used in this process?

EOQ model   **14–16** Now Ray Smith wants you to take a look at the company's inventory position because he thinks that inventories might be too high as a result of the manager's tendency to order in large quantities. Smith has decided to examine the situation for one key product—fly rods, which cost $320 each to purchase and prepare for sale. Annual sales of the product are 2,500 units (rods), and the annual carrying cost is ten percent of inventory value. The company has been buying 500 rods per order and placing another order when the stock on hand falls to 100 rods. Each time SSP orders, it incurs a cost equal to $64. Sales are uniform throughout the year.

a. Smith believes that the EOQ model should be used to help determine the optimal inventory situation for this product. What is the EOQ formula, and what are the key assumptions underlying this model?

b. What is the formula for total inventory costs?

c. What is the EOQ for the fly rods? What will the total inventory costs be for this product if the EOQ is produced?

d. What is SSP's added cost if it orders 500 rods rather than the EOQ quantity? What if it orders 750 rods each time?

e. Suppose it takes three days for SSP to receive its orders and package the rods before they are ready for sale. Assuming certainty in production time and usage, at what inventory level should SSP order? (Assume a 360-day year, that SSP is open every day, and that SSP orders the EOQ amount.)

f. Of course, there is uncertainty in SSP's usage rate, as well as in order delays, so the company must carry a safety stock to avoid running out of the fly rods and having to lose sales. If a safety stock of 100 rods is carried, what effect would this have on total inventory costs?

g. For most of SSP's products, inventory usage is not uniform throughout the year; rather, it follows some seasonal pattern. Could the EOQ model be used in this situation? If so, how?

h. How would these factors affect the use of the EOQ model?
   (1) "Just-in-time" (JIT) procedures.
   (2) The use of air freight for deliveries.
   (3) Computerized inventory control systems.

Computer-Related Problems

Work the problem in this section only if you are using the computer problem diskette.

cash budget   **14–17**   Use the model in File C14 to solve this problem.

a. Refer back to Problem 14–3. Suppose that by offering a two percent cash discount for paying within the month of sale, the credit manager of Carol's Fashion Designs Inc. has revised the collection percentages to 50 percent, 35 percent, and 15 percent, respectively. How will this affect the loan requirements?

b. Return the payment percentages to their base case values—ten percent, 75 percent, and 15 percent, respectively—and the discount to zero percent. Now suppose sales fall to only 70 percent of the forecasted level. Production is maintained, so cash outflows are unchanged. How does this affect Carol's Fashion Designs' financial requirements?

c. Return sales to the forecasted level (100%), and suppose collections slow down to three percent, ten percent, and 87 percent for the three months, respectively. How does this affect financial requirements? If Carol's Fashion Designs went to a cash-only sales policy, how would that affect requirements, other things held constant?

tightening credit terms   **14–18**   Use the model in File C14 to solve this problem.

a. Refer to Problem 14–11. When Bowers analyzed her proposed credit policy changes, she found that they would reduce Muscarella's profits and, therefore, should not be enacted. Bowers has reevaluated her sales estimates because all other firms in the industry have recently tightened their credit policies. She now estimates that sales would decline to only $2.8 million if she tightens the credit policy to 30 days. Would the credit policy change be profitable under these circumstances?

b. On the other hand, Bowers believes that she could tighten the credit policy to net 45 days and pick up some sales from her competitors. She estimates that sales would increase to $3.3 million and that the days sales outstanding (DSO) would fall to 50 days under this policy. What would be Muscarella's profits if Bowers enacted this change?

c. Bowers also believes that if she leaves the credit policy as it is, sales will increase to $3.4 million and the DSO will remain at 60 days. Should Bowers leave the credit policy alone or tighten it as described in either part a or part b? Which credit policy produces the largest profits for Muscarella Corporation?

ONLINE ESSENTIALS

http://onlinewbc.org/docs/finance Online Women's Business Center
This site, which is sponsored by the U.S. Small Business Administration, provides a great deal of information concerning the financial management of a small business. There is information about managing accounts receivables, cash budgeting, and so forth. Also, this site provides guides and information for financing short-term operations, which is discussed in the next chapter.

http://www.aicpa.org/members/tools/brochure/cash.htm AICPA Cash Management
This is an article posted by the American Institute of Certified Public Accountants that provides advice about cash management, including forecasting cash flows, managing disbursements, and so forth.

http://www.nacm.org National Association of Credit Management
The NACM is a professional organization that serves financial executives and employees who work in credit and financing. The site provides information about credit and financing and links to other credit associations around the world. In addition, the site has links to job opportunities in credit and financing.

http://www.effectiveinventory.com Effective Inventory Management, Inc.
This site has information and articles about inventory management, and it has links to related Web sites. The articles posted on this site give a good indication of inventory management in the real world.

CHAPTER 15

Managing Short-Term Liabilities (Financing)

A MANAGERIAL PERSPECTIVE

In April 1999, Sports Authority Inc., a sporting goods retailer, replaced its $150 million *revolving line of credit* with a $200 million credit line using the company's inventory as collateral. It was expected that the credit line would be used to support the financially ailing company's working capital needs so that it could continue short-term operations. At this time, it remains to be seen whether the credit line will improve Sports Authority's liquidity position sufficiently to keep it out of bankruptcy.

A few months earlier (at the end of 1998), the pilots of Federal Express had threatened to strike if their labor demands were not met. To ensure the company could operate without interruption in the event of a strike, Federal Express made arrangements to increase its *line of credit* by $1 billion, which doubled its existing credit line. The purpose of the additional financing was to support the alternative shipping arrangements the company had made with other airlines and trucking companies. In the end, Federal Express did not need the additional credit line; but the company prepared, just in case.

Also at the end of 1998, Netplex Group Inc., an information services company, arranged with First Union National Bank to increase its line of credit from $2 million to $6 million. The line of credit, which was secured (*pledged*) by the company's accounts receivable, was to be used to help finance working capital needs. Similarly, at about the same time, Integrated Packaging Assembly, which provides assembly and packaging services to the semiconductor industry, replaced its line of credit by selling (*factoring*) accounts receivables to its bank. The arrangement provided the company with about $2.8 million working capital financing during 1999, which was about $700,000 more than its regular line of credit. In another instance, Today's Man Inc., which operates men's clothing stores, increased its revolving line of credit from $30 million to $45 million by switching banks. The switch allowed the company to refinance some of its existing loans, reducing the financing costs by about three percent. Earlier in the year, General Credit Corporation, which provides financing for working capital, arranged a $3.6 million line of credit with Sterling National Bank. General Credit used the new line of credit to pay off a line of credit at another financial institution. By substituting one credit line for another, the company projected that it would save about $200,000 in interest each year.

As you read this chapter, think about the various sources available to companies for financing day-to-day operations, some of which are mentioned here (highlighted in italics). As you will see, the costs and availability of short-term funds can vary widely, both over time and from alternative sources. ■

In Chapter 13 we discussed the decisions the financial manager must make concerning alternative current asset financing policies. We also showed how debt maturities can affect both risk and expected returns: While short-term debt generally is riskier than long-term debt, it generally is also less expensive, and it can be obtained faster and under more flexible terms. The primary purpose of this chapter is to examine the different types of short-term credit that are available to the financial manager. We also examine the types of issues the financial manager must consider when selecting among the various types of short-term credit—that is, short-term, or current, liabilities.

Sources of Short-Term Financing

SHORT-TERM CREDIT
Any liability originally scheduled for repayment within one year.

Statements about the flexibility, cost, and riskiness of short-term debt versus long-term debt depend, to a large extent, on the type of short-term credit that actually is used. **Short-term credit** is defined as any liability *originally* scheduled for payment within one year. There are numerous sources of short-term funds, and in the following sections we describe four major types: (1) accruals, (2) accounts payable (trade credit), (3) bank loans, and (4) commercial paper. In addition, we discuss the costs of short-term funds and the factors that influence a firm's choice of a bank.

Self-Test Question

What types of liabilities are included in short-term credit?

Accruals

Firms generally pay employees on a weekly, biweekly, or monthly basis, so the balance sheet typically will show some accrued wages. Similarly, the firm's own estimated income taxes, the social security and income taxes withheld from employee payrolls, and the sales taxes collected generally are paid on a weekly, monthly, or quarterly basis, so the balance sheet typically will show some accrued taxes along with accrued wages.

ACCRUALS
Continually recurring short-term liabilities; liabilities such as wages and taxes that increase spontaneously with operations.

As we showed in Chapter 13, **accruals** increase automatically, or spontaneously, as a firm's operations expand. Further, this type of debt generally is considered "free" in the sense that no explicit interest is paid on funds raised through accruals. However, a firm ordinarily cannot control its accruals: The timing of wage payments is set by economic forces and industry custom, while tax payment dates are established by law. Thus, firms use all the accruals they can, but they have little control over the levels of these accounts.

Self-Test Questions

What types of short-term credits are classified as accruals?

What is the *explicit* cost of accruals?

How much control do financial managers have over the dollar amount of accruals?

Accounts Payable (Trade Credit)

TRADE CREDIT
The credit created when
one firm buys on credit
from another firm.

Firms generally make purchases from other firms on credit, recording the debt as an *account payable.* This type of financing, which is called **trade credit,** is the largest single category of short-term debt, representing about 40 percent of the current liabilities for the average nonfinancial corporation. The percentage is somewhat larger for smaller firms: Because small companies often do not qualify for financing from other sources, they rely especially heavily on trade credit.[1]

Trade credit is a *spontaneous* source of financing in the sense that it arises from ordinary business transactions. For example, suppose a firm makes average purchases of $2,000 a day on terms of net 30, meaning that it must pay for goods 30 days after the invoice date. As we saw in Chapter 13, on average, it will owe 30 times $2,000, or $60,000, to its suppliers. If its sales, and consequently its purchases, were to double, then its accounts payable also would double, to $120,000. So simply by growing, the firm would have spontaneously generated an additional $60,000 of financing. Similarly, if the terms under which it bought were extended from 30 to 40 days, its accounts payable would expand from $60,000 to $80,000. Thus, lengthening the credit period, as well as expanding sales and purchases, generates additional financing.

The Cost of Trade Credit

As we discussed in Chapter 14, firms that sell on credit have a *credit policy* that includes certain *terms of credit.* For example, Microchip Electronics sells on credit with terms of 2/10, net 30, which means that Microchip gives its customers a two percent discount from the invoice price if payment is made within ten days of the billing date; otherwise, if the discount is not taken, the full invoice amount is due and must be paid within 30 days of the billing date.

Note that the *true* price of the products Microchip offers is the net price, which is 98 percent of the list price, because any customer can purchase an item at a two percent "discount" as long as payment is made within ten days. Consider Personal Computer Company (PCC), which buys its memory chips from Microchip. One commonly used memory chip is listed at $100, so the true cost to PCC is $98. Now if PCC wants an additional 20 days of credit beyond the ten-day discount period, it will incur a finance charge of $2 per chip for that credit. Thus, the $100 list price can be thought of as follows:

$$\text{List price} = \$98 \text{ true price} + \$2 \text{ finance charge}$$

The question that PCC must ask before it takes the additional 20 days of credit from Microchip is whether the firm could obtain similar credit with better terms from some other lender, say a bank. In other words, could 20 days of credit be obtained for less than $2 per item?

---

[1]In a credit sale, the seller records the transaction as a receivable; the buyer, as a payable. We examined accounts receivable as an asset investment in Chapter 14. Our focus in this chapter is on accounts payable, a liability item. We might also note that if a firm's accounts payable exceed its receivables, it is said to be *receiving net trade credit,* whereas if its receivables exceed its payables, it is *extending net trade credit.* Smaller firms frequently receive net credit; larger firms generally extend it.

PCC buys an average of 44,100 memory chips from Microchip each year (assume 360 days), which, at the net or true price, amounts to an average annual purchase equal to $4,321,800, or $12,005 per day. For simplicity, assume that Microchip is PCC's only supplier. If PCC pays on the 10th day and takes the discount, its payables will average $10 \times \$12,005 = \$120,050$. Thus, PCC will receive $120,050 of credit from its only supplier, Microchip Electronics.

Now suppose PCC decides to take the additional 20 days' credit and thus must pay the finance charge. Because PCC now will pay on the 30th day, its accounts payable will increase to $30 \times \$12,005 = \$360,150$.[2] Under these circumstances, Microchip will be supplying PCC with an additional $\$240,100 = \$360,150 - \$120,050$ of credit, which PCC could use to build up its cash account, to pay off debt, to expand inventories, or even to extend more credit to its own customers and hence to increase its own accounts receivable. So it should be apparent that a firm's policy with regard to taking or not taking cash discounts can have a significant effect on its financial statements. If PCC does not take the cash discount, its accounts payable balance will be $240,100 greater than if it does take the discount ($360,150 compared to $120,050).

The additional credit offered by Microchip has a cost—PCC must pay the finance charge by forgoing the two percent discount on its purchases from Microchip. By forgoing the discount, PCC actually will pay $100 rather than $98 per chip, so its annual cost for the chips will be $\$100 \times 44,100 = \$4,410,000$ instead of $\$98 \times 44,100 = \$4,321,800$. The additional cost should be considered a finance charge for being able to keep the funds an additional 20 days. So the annual financing cost is $4,410,000 − $4,321,800 = $88,200. Dividing the $88,200 financing cost by the $240,100 in *average* annual *additional* credit, we find the implicit cost of the additional trade credit to be 36.7 percent:

$$\text{Approximate percentage cost} = \frac{\$88,200}{\$240,100} = 36.7\%$$

Should PCC take the discount, or should it wait 20 days and pay the full invoice price? If PCC can borrow from its bank (or from other sources) at an interest rate less than 36.7 percent, it should take the discount by borrowing from its bank to obtain any additional funds it needs—PCC should *not* obtain credit in the form of accounts payable by forgoing discounts if cheaper sources, such as the bank, are available.

The following equation can be used to calculate the *approximate* percentage cost, on an annual basis, of not taking cash discounts—that is, the cost of forgoing discounts:

15–1

$$\begin{array}{l}\text{Approximate cost} \\ \text{of forgoing a} \\ \text{cash discount (\%)}\end{array} = \frac{\text{Discount percent}}{100 - \left(\begin{smallmatrix}\text{Discount} \\ \text{percent}\end{smallmatrix}\right)} = \frac{360 \text{ days}}{\left(\begin{smallmatrix}\text{Total days net} \\ \text{credit is available}\end{smallmatrix}\right) - \left(\begin{smallmatrix}\text{Discount} \\ \text{period}\end{smallmatrix}\right)}$$

---

[2]A question arises here: Should accounts payable reflect gross purchases or purchases net of discounts? Although generally accepted accounting principles permit either treatment on the grounds that the difference is not material, most accountants prefer to record payables net of discounts, or at "true" prices, and then to report the higher payments that result from not taking discounts as an additional expense, called "discounts lost." *Thus, we show accounts payable net of discounts even if the company does not expect to take the discount.*

The numerator of the first term, Discount percent, is the dollar cost per $100 invoice value of forgoing (not taking) the discount, while the denominator in this term, (100 − Discount percent), represents the funds the firm has available by forgoing the discount. Thus, the first term in Equation 15–1 is the percent cost of using trade credit as a source of financing for the number of days in the credit period beyond the discount period. The denominator of the second term is the number of days of extra credit obtained by forgoing the discount; so the entire second term shows how many times each year the percent cost of the trade credit would be incurred if the firm continues this practice. To illustrate the equation, the approximate cost of not taking a discount when the terms are 2/10, net 30, is calculated as follows:

$$\begin{array}{c}\text{Approximate cost}\\\text{of forgoing}\\\text{cash discount}\end{array} = \frac{2}{100 - 2} \times \frac{360}{30 - 10} = \frac{2}{98} \times \frac{360}{20}$$

$$= 0.02041 \times 18 = 0.367 = 36.7\%$$

The approximation formula does not account for compounding, so when we use Equation 15–1 to compute the cost of forgoing a cash discount, the result actually is the *simple* annual percentage rate, or APR, we discussed in Chapter 6 (see Equation 6–11). Therefore, in effective annual interest terms, the cost of trade credit is much higher. The discount amounts to interest, and with terms of 2/10, net 30, the firm gains use of the funds for an additional 20 days, so there are 360 days ÷ 20 days = 18 "interest periods" per year. Remember that the first term in Equation 15–1, (Discount percent)/(100 − Discount percent) = 2/98 = 0.0204, is the periodic interest rate. This rate is paid 18 times each year, so, considering *compounding*, the effective annual cost (rate) of trade credit is computed as follows (see Equation 6–8 in Chapter 6):

$$\text{Effective annual rate} = (1.0204)^{18} - 1.0 = 1.439 - 1.0 = 43.9\%$$

Thus, the 36.7 percent approximate cost calculated with Equation 15–1 understates the true cost of trade credit.

Notice, that, according to Equation 15–1, the cost of trade credit *per credit period* is always the same as long as the terms of credit do not change—in our example, the cost is 2/98 = 0.0204. Therefore, the cost of using trade credit for financing can be reduced by delaying payment of accounts payable. For example, if PCC could get away with paying in 50 days rather than in the specified 30 days, then the effective credit period would become 40 days (50 days minus 10 days), the number of times during the year the discount would be lost would fall from 18 to 360/40 = 9, and the approximate cost would drop from 36.7 percent to 18.4 percent. Similarly, the effective annual rate would drop from 43.9 percent to 19.9 percent.

STRETCHING ACCOUNTS PAYABLE
The practice of deliberately paying accounts payable late.

The practice of paying trade credit beyond the credit period, or deliberately becoming a delinquent account, is called **stretching accounts payable.** In periods of excess capacity, firms might be able to get away with *stretching* because suppliers need the business. But there are consequences associated with credit delinquency, such as being branded a "slow payer"—the most serious is that credit might be cut off all together.

The cost of the additional trade credit that is incurred by not taking discounts can be worked out for other credit terms. Some illustrative costs are shown in Table 15–1. As these figures show, the cost of not taking discounts can be substantial. Incidentally, throughout the chapter, we assume that payments are made either on the *last day* for

TABLE 15–1	Comparison of the Cost of Forgoing a Cash Discount under Various Terms of Credit

	COST OF ADDITIONAL CREDIT IF THE CASH DISCOUNT IS NOT TAKEN	
CREDIT TERMS	APPROXIMATE COST	EFFECTIVE COST
1/10, net 20	36.36%	43.59%
1/10, net 30	18.18	19.83
2/10, net 20	73.47	106.95
2/10, net 30	36.73	43.86
3/15, net 45	37.11	44.12
3/10, net 100	12.37	12.96

taking discounts or on the *last day* of the net credit period, unless otherwise noted. It would be foolish to pay, say, on Day 5 or on Day 20 if the credit terms were 2/10, net 30. A firm always should pay its creditors at the last possible time under the conditions of the credit agreement, unless the benefits of early payment (lower price) are greater than the costs associated with early payment (opportunity to use the funds). You should follow the same logic—*pay your bills as late as possible without jeopardizing either your status as a good customer or your credit.* If you pay at the last possible time allowed under the payment terms (do not become delinquent), then you will get to use your funds for the maximum time and you will maintain good relationships with businesses.

Components of Trade Credit: Free versus Costly

"FREE" TRADE CREDIT
Credit received during the discount period.

COSTLY TRADE CREDIT
Credit taken in excess of "free" trade credit, whose cost is equal to the discount lost.

On the basis of the preceding discussion, trade credit can be divided into two components: (1) **"free" trade credit,** which involves credit received during the discount period and which amounts to ten days' net purchases for PCC, or $120,050, and (2) **costly trade credit,** which involves credit in excess of the free trade credit and whose cost is an implicit one based on the forgone discounts.[3] PCC could obtain $240,100, or 20 days' net purchases, of nonfree trade credit at a cost of nearly 38 percent. *Financial managers always should use the free component, but they should use the costly component only after analyzing the cost of this source of financing to make sure that it is less than the cost of funds that could be obtained from other sources.* Under the terms of trade found in most industries, the costly component will involve a relatively high percentage cost (usually greater than 25 percent), so stronger firms will take the cash discounts offered and avoid using trade credit as a source of additional financing.

As we noted earlier, firms sometimes can and do deviate from the stated credit terms, thus altering the percentage cost figures cited. For example, a California manufacturing firm that buys on terms of 2/10, net 30, makes a practice of paying in 15

---

[3]There is some question as to whether any credit is really "free," because the supplier will have a cost of carrying receivables, which must be passed on to the customer in the form of higher prices. Still, if suppliers sell on standard credit terms such as 2/10, net 30, and if the base price cannot be negotiated downward for early payment, then for all intents and purposes the 10 days of trade credit are indeed "free."

days (rather than ten days), but it still takes discounts. Its treasurer simply waits until 15 days after receipt of the goods to pay and then writes a check for the invoiced amount less the two percent discount. The company's suppliers want its business, so they tolerate this practice. Similarly, a Wisconsin firm that also buys on terms of 2/10, net 30, does not take discounts, but it pays in 60 days rather than in 30 days, thus "stretching" its trade credit. As we saw earlier, both practices reduce the cost of trade credit. Neither of these firms is "loved" by its suppliers, and neither could continue these practices in times when suppliers operate at full capacity and have order backlogs, but these practices can and do reduce the costs of trade credit to customers during times when suppliers have excess capacity.

Self-Test Questions

What is trade credit?

What is the difference between free trade credit and costly trade credit?

What is the formula for finding the approximate cost of trade credit? What is the formula for the effective annual cost (rate) of trade credit?

How does the cost of costly trade credit generally compare with the cost of other short-term sources of funds?

Short-Term Bank Loans

Commercial banks, whose loans generally appear on firms' balance sheets as notes payable, are second in importance to trade credit as a source of short-term financing.[4] The influence of banks actually is greater than it appears from the dollar amounts they lend because banks provide *nonspontaneous* funds. As a firm's financing needs increase, it specifically requests additional funds from its bank. If the request is denied, the firm might be forced to abandon attractive growth opportunities. The key features of bank loans are discussed in the following paragraphs.

Maturity

Although banks do make longer-term loans, *the bulk of their lending is on a short-term basis.* Bank loans to businesses frequently are written as 90-day notes, so the loan must be repaid or renewed at the end of 90 days. Of course, if a borrower's financial position has deteriorated, the bank might refuse to renew the loan. This can mean serious trouble for the borrower.

PROMISSORY NOTE
A document specifying the terms and conditions of a loan, including the amount, interest rate, and repayment schedule.

Promissory Note

When a bank loan is approved, the agreement is executed by signing a **promissory note.** The note specifies (1) the amount borrowed; (2) the percentage interest rate; (3) the repayment schedule, which can call for payment either as a lump sum or as a

---

[4]Although commercial banks remain the primary source of short-term loans, other sources are available. For example, in 1999 GE Capital Corporation (GECC) had several billion dollars in commercial loans outstanding. Firms such as GECC, which was initially established to finance consumers' purchases of GE's durable goods, often find business loans to be more profitable than consumer loans.

enter some of the loan arrangements we discuss here, so it is important that you have an understanding of how the cost of a loan is computed.

For any type of short-term credit, we can compute the interest rate for the *period* the funds are used with the following equation:

> **15–2**
>
> $$\text{Interest rate per period (cost)} = \frac{\text{Dollar cost of borrowing}}{\text{Amount of usable funds}}$$

In this equation, the numerator represents the dollar amount that must be paid for using the borrowed funds, which includes the interest paid, application fees, charges for commitment fees, and so forth. The denominator represents the amount of the loan that actually can be used (spent) by the borrower, which is not necessarily the same as the principal amount, or amount borrowed, because discounts or other costs might be deducted from the loan proceeds. As we will see shortly, when loan restrictions prevent the borrower from using the entire amount of the loan, the effective annual rate paid for the loan increases.

Using Equation 15–2, we can compute the effective annual rate and the annual percentage rate (APR), which we showed in Chapter 6, as follows:

> **15–3**
>
> $$\text{Effective annual rate} = \text{EAR} = (1 + \text{Interest rate per period})^{m} - 1.0$$

> **15–4**
>
> $$\text{Annual percentage rate} = \text{APR} = (\text{Interest rate per period}) \times m = i_{\text{SIMPLE}}$$

where m is the number of borrowing periods in one year (i.e., if the loan is for one month, m = 12). Remember from our discussion in Chapter 6 that the EAR incorporates interest compounding in the computation while the APR does not. Both computations measure the cost of short-term borrowing on a percentage basis.

To see the application of these equations, consider the credit terms of 2/10, net 30. If the firm does not take the cash discount, then it effectively pays $2 to borrow $98 for a 20-day period, so the cost of using the funds for an additional 20 days is

$$\text{Periodic rate} = \frac{\$2}{\$98} = 0.020408 \approx 2.041\%$$

There are m = 18 20-day periods in a 360-day year, so the *APR* associated with the trade credit is

$$\text{APR} = 0.02041 \times 18 = 0.367 = 36.7\%$$

Using Equation 15–3, the *effective annual cost (rate)* of using trade credit with these terms as a source of short-term financing is

$$\text{Effective annual rate} = (1 + 0.02041)^{18} - 1.0 = 1.439 - 1.0 = 0.439 = 43.9\%$$

These results are identical to those reported earlier both for the *approximate cost of forgoing a cash discount* and for the *effective cost of forgoing a cash discount.*

Regular, or Simple, Interest

SIMPLE INTEREST LOAN
Both the amount borrowed and the interest charged on that amount are paid at the maturity of the loan; there are no payments made before maturity.

With a **simple interest loan,** the borrower receives the **face value** of the loan (amount borrowed, or principal) and repays both the principal and the interest at maturity. For example, with a simple interest loan of $10,000 at 12 percent for one year, the borrower receives the $10,000 upon approval of the loan and pays back the $10,000 principal plus $10,000(0.12) = $1,200 in interest at maturity (one year later). The 12 percent is the quoted, or simple, interest rate. On this one-year loan, the effective annual rate also is 12 percent because the borrower pays $1,200 interest to use $10,000 for the entire year.

FACE VALUE
The amount of the loan, or the amount borrowed; also called the principal amount of the loan.

$$\text{Effective annual rate} = \left(1 + \frac{\$1,200}{\$10,000}\right)^{1} - 1 = 0.12 = 12.0\%$$

The only case in which the effective annual rate is the same as the simple interest rate is if the borrower has use of the entire face value of the loan for one full year, and the only cost associated with the loan is the interest paid on the face value. In such cases, interest compounding occurs annually. However, if the loan is for a term of less than one year, say, 90 days, then intrayear compounding should be considered. Consider the simple interest loan with the characteristics described here, except the term of the loan is 90 days. The *effective rate per period* is 0.12/4 = 0.03 = 3.0%, so $300 in interest would be paid for using $10,000 for a 90-day period, and the effective annual rate would be calculated as follows:

$$\text{Effective annual rate} = \left(1 + \frac{\$300}{\$10,000}\right)^{4} - 1 = (1 + 0.03)^{4} - 1 = 0.1255 = 12.55\%$$

The bank gets the interest sooner than under a one-year loan; hence, the effective rate is higher.

The APR for this 90-day loan is

$$\text{APR} = 0.03 \times \frac{360}{90} = 0.12 = 12.0\%$$

which is the same as the simple interest rate because the APR computation does not consider intrayear interest compounding.

DISCOUNT INTEREST LOAN
A loan in which the interest, which is calculated on the amount borrowed, is paid at the beginning of the loan period; interest is paid in advance.

Discount Interest

With a **discount interest loan,** the bank deducts the interest "up front" (*discounts* the loan) so the borrower receives less than the face value of the loan. For example, on a one-year, $10,000 discounted loan with a 12 percent quoted (simple) rate, the interest is $10,000(0.12) = $1,200, so the borrower gets to use only $10,000 − $1,200 = $8,800. The rate per period, which is one year in this case, is 13.64 percent:

$$\text{Rate per period} = \frac{0.12(\$10,000)}{\$10,000 - 0.12(\$10,000)} = \frac{0.12(\$10,000)}{\$10,000(1 - 0.12)} = \frac{\$1,200}{\$8,800}$$

$$= 0.1364 = 13.64\% = \text{Effective annual rate}$$

The effective annual rate and the APR both equal 13.64 percent because the rate per period does not have to be "annualized"—the loan has a maturity of one year. The effective annual rate for this discounted loan is considerably greater than the effective annual rate for the simple interest loan with the same quoted rate and the same maturity because the borrower does not get to "use" the entire face value of the loan. In this case, the borrower can use only 88 percent of the face value ($8,800 of the $10,000), but the dollar interest payment is computed on 100 percent of the face value rather than the amount available for use.

If the discount loan is for a period of less than one year, interest compounding must be considered to determine the effective annual rate. For example, if you borrow $10,000 at a simple rate of 12 percent, discount interest, for three months, then $m = 12/3 = 4$, and the dollar interest payment is $(0.12/4)(\$10,000) = \$300$, so the rate per period and the effective annual rate are computed as follows:

$$\text{Rate per period} = \frac{0.03(\$10,000)}{\$10,000 - 0.03(\$10,000)} = \frac{\$300}{\$10,000 - \$300}$$

$$= 0.0309 = 3.09\%$$

$$\text{Effective annual rate} = (1.0 + 0.0309)^4 - 1$$

$$= 0.1296 = 12.96\%$$

From this computation, it should be apparent that discount interest imposes less of a penalty on shorter-term loans than on longer-term loans.

The APR for this 90-day loan would be

$$\text{APR} = 0.0309 \times \frac{360}{90}$$

$$= 0.1237 = 12.37\%$$

Notice that a discounted loan represents the same situation as using trade credit as a source of short-term financing. For example, if a firm has a supplier that offers credit terms of 3/10, net 100 (very unusual terms), as Table 15–1 shows, both the effective annual rate and the APR of the trade credit would be the same as that for the 90-day discounted loan with a simple rate of 12 percent.

Installment Loans: Add-on Interest

ADD-ON INTEREST
Interest that is calculated and then added to the amount borrowed to obtain the total dollar amount to be paid back in equal installments.

Lenders often charge **add-on interest** on various types of installment loans. The term "add-on" means that the interest is calculated and then added to the amount borrowed to obtain the total dollar amount to be paid back in equal installments. To illustrate, suppose you borrow $10,000 on an add-on basis at a simple rate of 12 percent, with the loan to be repaid in 12 monthly installments. At a 12 percent add-on rate, you will pay a total interest charge of $10,000(0.12) = \$1,200$, and a total of $11,200 in twelve equal payments throughout the year. The monthly payments would be $11,200/12 = \$933.33$. Therefore, each month, you would pay $100 interest (1/12 of the total interest) and $833.33 principal repayment (1/12 of the $10,000 borrowed). Because the loan is paid off in monthly installments, you have use of the full $10,000 only for the first month, and the outstanding balance declines by $833.33 each month so that only

$833.33 in principal is due at the beginning of the last month of the loan. Thus, you are paying $1,200 for the use of only about 50 percent of the loan's face amount because the average outstanding balance of the loan is only about $5,000. Consequently, we can *approximate* the rate per period, which is one year in this case, as follows:

$$\text{Approximate rate per period} = \frac{\$1,200}{\left(\dfrac{\$10,000}{2}\right)} = 0.24 = 24.0\%$$

To determine the precise effective rate of an add-on loan, we have to apply the techniques used to compute the present value of an annuity that were discussed in Chapter 6. First, consider the situation presented here. If you want to borrow $10,000 for one year, on a monthly installment basis, beginning in one month, you would have to make 12 payments equal to $933.33. In effect, then, the bank is buying a 12-period annuity for $10,000, so the $10,000 is the present value of the annuity. The cash flow time line for this annuity would be

0	1	2	11	12
($10,000)	$933.33	$933.33	$933.33	$933.33

With a financial calculator, enter PV = −10000, PMT = 933.33, N = 12, and then press I to obtain 1.7880. However, this is a monthly rate, which, when annualized, yields[9]

$$\text{Effective annual rate} = (1 + 0.01788)^{12} - 1 = 0.237 = 23.7\%$$

Simple Interest with Compensating Balances

Compensating balances can raise the effective rate on a loan. To illustrate, suppose a firm *needs* $10,000 to pay for some equipment that it recently purchased. A bank offers to lend the company money for one year at a 12 percent simple rate, but the company must maintain a *compensating balance (CB)* equal to 20 percent of the loan amount (principal, or face value). What is the effective annual rate on the loan?

First, note that the firm needs to be able to use $10,000 to pay for the equipment. The firm might or might not already have a balance in its checking account that can be used to satisfy all or part of the compensating balance. If the firm's checking account balance is sufficient to cover the compensating balance requirement, then the amount of the loan can be $10,000 because none of this amount would have to be put aside to satisfy the compensating balance requirement. The cost of this loan would be the same as we computed in the section titled *Regular, or Simple, Interest.*

If the firm's checking account balance is *not sufficient* to cover the compensating balance requirement, it must borrow more than $10,000 because some of the funds borrowed will have to be put aside to satisfy the compensating balance requirement. In this case, the question is: How much must be borrowed so the firm will have $10,000 available for use? To answer this question, first let's compute the compensating balance requirement:

---

[9]Note that if an installment loan is paid off ahead of schedule, additional complications arise. For a discussion of this point, see Dick Bonker, "The Rule of 78," *Journal of Finance* (June 1976), 877–888.

15–5

$$\text{Compensating balance} \atop \text{requirement} = CB = \left(\begin{matrix}\text{Principal} \\ \text{amount}\end{matrix}\right) \times \left(\begin{matrix}\text{Compensating balance} \\ \text{stated as a decimal}\end{matrix}\right)$$

So *if the firm has a checking account balance equal to zero*, the amount of the borrowed funds that actually can be used is computed as follows:

15–6

$$\begin{aligned}\text{Usable funds} &= \left(\begin{matrix}\text{Principal} \\ \text{amount}\end{matrix}\right) - CB \\ &= \left(\begin{matrix}\text{Principal} \\ \text{amount}\end{matrix}\right) - \left[\left(\begin{matrix}\text{Principal} \\ \text{amount}\end{matrix}\right) \times \left(\begin{matrix}\text{CB as a} \\ \text{decimal}\end{matrix}\right)\right] \\ &= \left(\begin{matrix}\text{Principal} \\ \text{amount}\end{matrix}\right) \times \left[1 - \left(\begin{matrix}\text{CB as a} \\ \text{decimal}\end{matrix}\right)\right]\end{aligned}$$

If we know how much of the amount borrowed actually is needed as "usable funds," Equation 15–6 can be rearranged to solve for the amount that must be borrowed (principal amount) to provide the needed funds:

15–7

$$\text{Required loan} \atop \text{(principal) amount} = \frac{\text{(Amount of usable funds needed)}}{1 - \text{(CB as a decimal)}}$$

Therefore, if the firm has nothing in its checking account, it must borrow $12,500 to be able to satisfy the 20 percent compensating balance requirement and have $10,000 available to pay for the equipment:

$$\text{Required loan amount} = \frac{\$10,000}{1 - 0.20} = \$12,500$$

If the firm borrows $12,500, the compensating balance requirement would be $2,500 = $12,500(0.20), which means the firm actually could use $12,500 − $2,500 = $10,000 of the face value of the loan—the remaining $2,500 would have to be "set aside" to satisfy the compensating balance requirement. The interest paid on the loan at the end of the year will be $1,500 = $12,500(0.12). But because the firm will be able to use only $10,000 of the amount borrowed, the rate per period, which is one year, is 15 percent:

$$\begin{aligned}\text{Rate per period} &= \frac{(0.12)\$12,500}{\$12,500(1 - 0.20)} = \frac{\$1,500}{\$10,000} \\ &= \frac{0.12}{(1 - 0.20)} = \frac{0.12}{0.80} \\ &= 0.15 = 15.0\% = \text{Effective annual rate}\end{aligned}$$

If the loan has a term of 90 days rather than one year, the simple rate would be $0.12/4 = 0.03$, and the rate per period and the effective annual rate would be as follows:

$$\text{Rate per period} = \frac{(0.03)\$12,500}{\$12,500(1 - 0.20)} = \frac{\$375}{\$10,000}$$

$$= \frac{0.03}{(1 - 0.20)} = \frac{0.03}{0.80}$$

$$= 0.0375 = 3.75\%$$

$$\text{Effective annual rate} = (1 + 0.0375)^{\left(\frac{360}{90}\right)} - 1 = (1.0375)^4 - 1$$

$$= 0.1587 = 15.87\%$$

The APR for this 90-day loan would be the same as the effective rate for a one-year loan because compounding is not considered:

$$\text{APR} = \frac{\$375}{\$10,000} \times \frac{360}{90} = (.0375) \times 4 = 0.15 = 15.0\%$$

If a firm normally keeps a positive checking account balance at the lending bank, then (1) it needs to borrow less to have a specific amount of funds available for use, and (2) the effective cost of the loan will be lower. Regardless of the reason the firm maintains a positive checking account balance, we can consider that the amount in the account is available for use by the firm. For example, if our firm normally maintains a working balance equal to $1,000 in its checking account, then the amount of usable funds that has to be provided by the loan is $1,000 less than if the checking account balance was equal to zero. The numerator in Equation 15–7 can be modified easily to reflect the fact that the amount of usable funds that needs to be provided by the loan is reduced:

15–7a

$$\text{Required loan (principal) amount} = \frac{\left(\begin{array}{c}\text{Amount of} \\ \text{usable funds} \\ \text{needed}\end{array}\right) - \left(\begin{array}{c}\text{Checking} \\ \text{account} \\ \text{balance}\end{array}\right)}{1 - (\text{CB as a decimal})}$$

Thus, if the firm has a checking account balance equal to $1,000, the amount of usable funds provided by the loan needs to be $9,000 = $10,000 − $1,000, and the amount that must be borrowed to meet these needs is:

$$\text{Required loan amount} = \frac{\$10,000 - \$1,000}{1.0 - 0.20} \times \frac{\$9,000}{0.80} = \$11,250$$

If the firm borrows $11,250, the compensating balance requirement will be $2,250. The firm already has $1,000 in its checking account, so the remaining $1,250 needed company normally carries cash balances that could be used to supply all or part of the compensating balances, we would have to adjust the calculations along the lines discussed in the preceding section, and the effective annual rate would be less than 17.65 percent.

Self-Test Questions

What are some different ways banks calculate interest on loans?

What effect does a compensating balance requirement have on the effective interest rate on a loan?

Under what circumstances will the APR and the effective annual cost of a loan be equal?

Choosing a Bank

Individuals whose only contact with their bank is through the use of its checking services generally choose a bank for the convenience of its location and the competitive cost of its services. However, a business that borrows from banks must look at other criteria, and a potential borrower seeking banking relations should recognize that important differences exist among banks. Some of these differences are considered here.

Willingness to Assume Risks

Banks have different basic policies toward risk. Some banks are inclined to follow relatively conservative lending practices, while others engage in what are properly termed "creative banking practices." These policies reflect partly the personalities of officers of the bank and partly the characteristics of the bank's deposit liabilities. Thus, a bank with fluctuating deposit liabilities in a static community will tend to be a conservative lender, while a bank whose deposits are growing with little interruption might follow more liberal credit policies. Similarly, a large bank with broad diversification over geographic regions or across industries can obtain the benefit of combining and averaging risks. Thus, marginal credit risks that might be unacceptable to a small bank or a specialized bank can be pooled by a large branch banking system to reduce the overall risk of a group of marginal accounts.

Advice and Counsel

Some bank loan officers are active in providing counsel and in stimulating development loans to firms in their early and formative years. Certain banks have specialized departments that make loans to firms expected to grow and thus to become more important customers. The personnel of these departments can provide valuable counseling to customers.

Loyalty to Customers

Banks differ in the extent to which they will support the activities of borrowers in bad times. This characteristic is referred to as the degree of *loyalty* of the bank. Some banks might put great pressure on a business to liquidate its loans when the firm's outlook becomes clouded, whereas others will stand by the firm and work diligently to help it get back on its feet.

Specialization

Banks differ greatly in their degrees of loan specialization. Larger banks have separate departments that specialize in different kinds of loans—for example, real estate loans, farm loans, and commercial loans. Within these broad categories, there might be a specialization by line of business, such as steel, machinery, cattle, or textiles. The strengths of banks also are likely to reflect the nature of the business and the economic environment in which the banks operate. For example, some California banks have become specialists in lending to technology companies, while many Midwestern banks are agricultural specialists. A sound firm can obtain more creative cooperation and more active support by going to a bank that has experience and familiarity with its particular type of business. Therefore, a bank that is excellent for one firm might be unsatisfactory for another.

Maximum Loan Size

The size of a bank can be an important factor. Because the maximum loan a bank can make to any one customer is limited to 15 percent of the bank's capital accounts (capital stock plus retained earnings), it generally is not appropriate for large firms to develop borrowing relationships with small banks.

Merchant Banking

The term "merchant bank" originally was applied to banks that not only loaned depositors' money but also provided customers with equity capital and financial advice. Prior to 1933, U.S. commercial banks performed all types of merchant banking functions. However, about one-third of the U.S. banks failed during the Great Depression, in part because of these activities, so in 1933 the Glass-Steagall Act was passed in an effort to reduce banks' exposure to risk. In recent years, commercial banks have tried to get back into merchant banking, in part because their foreign competitors offer such services, and U.S. banks need to be able to compete with their foreign counterparts for multinational corporations' business. Currently, the larger banks, often through holding companies, do offer merchant banking, at least to a limited extent. This trend should continue, and, if it does, corporations will need to consider a bank's ability to provide a full range of commercial and merchant banking services when choosing a bank.

Other Services

Some banks also provide cash management services, such as those described in Chapter 14, assist with electronic funds transfers, help firms obtain foreign exchange, and the like; and the availability of such services should be taken into account when selecting a bank. Also, if the firm is a small business whose manager owns most of its stock, the bank's willingness and ability to provide trust and estate services also should be considered.

Self-Test Question

What are some of the factors that should be considered when choosing a bank?

FACTORING
The outright sale of
receivables.

Factoring, or *selling accounts receivable,* involves the purchase of accounts receivable by the lender (called a factor), generally without recourse to the borrower, which means that if the purchaser of the goods does not pay for them, the lender rather than the seller of the goods (borrower) takes the loss. Under factoring, the buyer of the goods typically is notified of the transfer and is asked to make payment directly to the lending institution. Because the factor assumes the risk of default on bad accounts, it generally carries out the credit investigation. Accordingly, factors provide not only money but also a credit department for the borrower. Incidentally, the same financial institutions that make loans against pledged receivables also serve as factors. Thus, depending on the circumstances and the wishes of the borrower, a financial institution will provide either type of receivables financing.

Procedure for Pledging Accounts Receivable   The financing of accounts receivable is initiated by a legally binding agreement between the seller of the goods and the financing institution. The agreement sets forth in detail the procedures to be followed and the legal obligations of both parties. Once the working relationship has been established, the seller periodically takes a batch of invoices to the financing institution. The lender reviews the invoices and makes credit appraisals of the buyers. Invoices of companies that do not meet the lender's credit standards are not accepted for pledging.

The financial institution seeks to protect itself at every phase of the operation. First, selection of sound invoices is one way the lender safeguards itself. Second, if the buyer of the goods does not pay the invoice, the lender still has recourse against the seller (the borrowing firm). Third, additional protection is afforded the lender because the loan generally will be less than 100 percent of the pledged receivables; for example, the lender might advance the selling firm only 75 percent of the amount of the pledged invoices. The percent advanced depends on the quality of the accounts pledged.

Procedure for Factoring Accounts Receivable   The procedures used in factoring are somewhat different from those for pledging. Again, an agreement between the seller and the factor specifies legal obligations and procedural arrangements. When the seller receives an order from a buyer, a credit approval slip is written and immediately sent to the factoring company for a credit check. If the factor approves the credit, shipment is made and the invoice is stamped to notify the buyer to make payment directly to the factoring company. If the factor does not approve the sale, the seller generally refuses to fill the order; if the sale is made anyway, the factor will not buy the account.

The factor normally performs three functions: (1) credit checking; (2) lending; and (3) risk bearing. Consider a typical factoring situation: The goods are shipped, and even though payment is not due for 30 days, the factor immediately makes funds available to the borrower (the seller of the goods). Suppose $10,000 worth of goods are shipped. Further, assume that the factoring commission for credit checking and risk bearing is $2\frac{1}{2}$ percent of the invoice price, or $250, and that the interest expense is computed at a nine percent annual rate on the invoice balance, or $75 = \$10,000 \times (0.09/360) \times 30$ days. The selling firm's accounting entry is as follows:

Cash	$ 9,175
Interest Expense	75
Factoring Commission	250
Reserve due from factor on collection account	500
Accounts receivable	$10,000

＊ **INDUSTRY PRACTICE**

"Factoring"—A Dirty Word or a Competitive Tool?

Traditionally, the word *factoring* has projected a neg-ative connotation in the business world because it was felt that a firm should sell receivables only when it was financially distressed. And companies that pur-chased other firms' receivables (called factors) were generally viewed with disdain because the rates they charged ranged from 20 percent and 35 percent or more, which seemed exorbitant. Most large, reputable banks shunned factoring because they favored the more traditional, less risky commercial lending process and because they wanted to avoid the stigma that was associated with factoring. Recently, however, banks have become more interested in factoring and have begun to offer factoring services themselves or have formed close alliances with established factoring organizations. This newfound interest has emerged for two reasons. First, there is a great deal of profit to be made in the factoring business; in the past couple of years, the volume of factored receivables has grown by more than ten percent per year. Second, and prob-ably more important, banks now view factoring as a means to establish business relationships with young, upstart companies that have substantial growth po-tentials. Such firms generally lack either suitable credit reputations or sufficient collateral to allow them to obtain traditional bank financing. But banks now view alternative financing arrangements, such as factoring, as a means to attract customers that might use the more traditional banking services in the fu-ture. Thus, banks have begun to establish business re-lationships with firms that need support for critical growth needs, hoping the firms that survive and es-tablish themselves might later begin using some of

the other services that are offered. More banks now view factoring as a way to reach future business today rather than competing for it tomorrow.

Marshall Associates, a satellite-based telecommu-nications and networking technology company that was founded in 1991, provides an example of how fac-toring can be used to establish banking relationships. After participating in government projects with major defense companies in 1993 and 1994, Marshall's cash inflows dwindled in 1995 as the government contracts ended. To generate the cash needed to keep the firm going, Marshall took the advice of its bank and sold its receivables to a factoring company (not its bank), which advanced Marshall between 75 percent and 80 percent of the face value of the factored receivables. The cash it received for its receivables helped Mar-shall keep its head above water. As Marshall's business picked up and it began generating more cash, the fac-tor was used less frequently. And, at the end of 1997, Marshall effectively returned to its bank for financing, establishing a $250,000 line of credit to provide fu-ture working capital needs. Had the bank turned its back on Marshall when the company was cash poor, either Marshall would no longer be in business today or it might have taken its business to another bank.

SOURCES: Adam Weintraub, "Factoring on the Rise as Finance Option," *City Business-Minneapolis MNCB,* January 1, 1999, and Marlon Millner, "A Matter of Factoring Money: Sterling Businessman Turned to Receivables Fi-nancing When the Bank Wouldn't Loan Him Money," *Washington Business Journal,* April 3, 1998. Both articles are from American City Business Journals Inc. and were re-trieved using the USF Virtual Library Business and Eco-nomics search.

The $500 due from the factor upon collection of the account is a reserve established by the factor to cover disputes between the seller and customers over damaged goods, goods returned by customers to the seller, and the failure to make an outright sale of goods. The reserve is paid to the selling firm when the factor collects on the account.

Factoring normally is a continuous process instead of the single cycle just described. The firm that sells the goods receives an order; it transmits this order to the factor for approval; upon approval, the firm ships the goods; the factor advances the invoice amount minus withholdings to the seller; the buyer (customer) pays the factor when payment is due; and the factor periodically remits any excess in the reserve to the seller

- **Accruals,** which are continually recurring short-term liabilities, represent free, spontaneous credit.
- **Accounts payable,** or **trade credit,** is the largest category of short-term debt. This credit arises spontaneously as a result of purchases on credit. Firms should use all the **free trade credit** they can obtain, but they should use **costly trade credit** only if it is less expensive than other forms of short-term debt. Suppliers often offer discounts to customers who pay within a stated discount period. The following equation can be used to calculate the approximate percentage cost, on an annual basis, of not taking discounts:

$$\begin{matrix} \text{Approximate cost} \\ \text{of forgoing a} \\ \text{cash discount (\%)} \end{matrix} = \frac{\text{Discount percent}}{100 - \left(\begin{smallmatrix}\text{Discount}\\\text{percent}\end{smallmatrix}\right)} = \frac{360 \text{ days}}{\left(\begin{smallmatrix}\text{Total days net}\\\text{credit is available}\end{smallmatrix}\right) - \left(\begin{smallmatrix}\text{Discount}\\\text{period}\end{smallmatrix}\right)}$$

- **Bank loans** are an important source of short-term credit. Interest on bank loans might be quoted as **simple interest, discount interest,** or **add-on interest.** The effective rate on a discount or add-on loan always exceeds the quoted simple rate. In general, the effective cost of a bank loan can be computed as follows:

$$\text{Effective annual rate} = (1 + \text{Rate per period})^m - 1.0$$

where m is the number of borrowing (compounding) periods in one year (i.e., if the loan is for one month, m = 12). The rate per period can be computed using the following equation:

$$\text{Interest rate per period (cost)} = \frac{\text{Dollar cost of borrowing}}{\text{Amount of usable funds}}$$

- When a bank loan is approved, a **promissory note** is signed. It specifies (1) the amount borrowed, (2) the percentage interest rate, (3) the repayment schedule, (4) the collateral, and (5) any other conditions to which the parties have agreed.
- Banks sometimes require borrowers to maintain **compensating balances,** which are deposit requirements set at between 10 percent and 20 percent of the loan amount. Compensating balances generally increase the effective rate of interest on bank loans.
- A **line of credit** is an understanding between the bank and the borrower indicating the maximum amount of credit the bank will extend to the borrower.
- A **revolving credit** agreement is a formal, guaranteed line of credit that involves a **commitment fee.**
- **Commercial paper** is unsecured short-term debt issued by a large, financially strong corporation. Although the cost of commercial paper is lower than the cost of bank loans, commercial paper's maturity is limited to 270 days, and it can be used only by large firms with exceptionally strong credit ratings.
- Sometimes a borrower will find it necessary to borrow on a **secured basis,** in which case the borrower pledges assets such as real estate, securities, equipment, inventories, or accounts receivable as collateral for the loan.
- Accounts receivable financing involves either *pledging* or *factoring* receivables. Under a **pledging** arrangement, the lender not only gets a claim against the receivables but also has recourse to the borrower. **Factoring** involves the purchase of accounts receivable by the lender, generally without recourse to the borrower.

- There are three primary methods of inventory financing: (1) An **inventory blanket lien** gives the lender a lien against all of the borrower's inventories. (2) A **trust receipt** is an instrument that acknowledges that goods are held in trust for the lender. (3) **Warehouse receipt** financing is an arrangement under which the lender employs a third party to exercise control over the borrower's inventory and to act as the lender's agent.
- **Pledging receivables** is especially sensible for a small firm that has customers with better credit histories than the firm itself, as this allows the firm to take advantage of the strength of its customer base.
- For small firms with limited managerial resources and limited experience in monitoring and collecting credit accounts, **factoring** might be more than worth the cost. The small firm's comparative advantage is its ability to deliver a product; the factor's advantage is its ability to provide financial and credit services.

Questions

15–1 "Firms can control their accruals within fairly wide limits; depending on the cost of accruals, financing from this source will be increased or decreased." Discuss.

15–2 Is it true that both trade credit and accruals represent a spontaneous source of capital for financing growth? Explain.

15–3 Is it true that most firms are able to obtain some free trade credit and that additional trade credit often is available, but at a cost? Explain.

15–4 The availability of bank credit often is more important to a small firm than to a large one. Why?

15–5 What kinds of firms use commercial paper? Could Mama and Papa Gus's Corner Grocery borrow using this form of credit?

15–6 Suppose a firm can obtain funds by borrowing at the prime rate or by selling commercial paper.
  a. If the prime rate is $7\frac{1}{2}$ percent, what is a reasonable estimate for the cost of commercial paper?
  b. If a substantial cost differential exists, why might a firm like this one actually borrow some of its funds in each market?

15–7 Can you think of some firms that might allow you to purchase on credit, but probably would factor your receivables account?

Self-Test Problems

(Solutions appear in Appendix B)

key terms **ST–1** Define each of the following terms:
  a. Accruals
  b. Trade credit; stretching accounts payable; free trade credit; costly trade credit
  c. Promissory note; line of credit; revolving credit agreement
  d. Prime rate
  e. Simple interest; discount interest; add-on interest
  f. Compensating balance (CB); commitment fee
  g. Commercial paper
  h. Secured loan

  i. Uniform Commercial Code

  j. Pledging receivables; factoring

  k. Recourse; without recourse

  l. Inventory blanket lien; trust receipt; warehouse receipt financing; field warehouse

receivables financing   **ST–2** The Naylor Corporation is considering two methods of raising working capital: (1) a commercial bank loan secured by accounts receivable and (2) factoring accounts receivable. Naylor's bank has agreed to lend the firm 75 percent of its average monthly accounts receivable balance of $250,000 at an annual interest rate of nine percent. The bank loan is in the form of a series of 30-day loans. The loan would be discounted, and a 20 percent compensating balance would also be required.

  A factor has agreed to purchase Naylor's accounts receivable and to advance 85 percent of the balance to the firm. The 15 percent of receivables not loaned to the firm under the factoring arrangement is held in a reserve account. The factor would charge a 3.5 percent factoring commission and annual interest of nine percent on the invoice price, less both the factoring commission and the reserve account. The monthly interest payment would be deducted from the advance. If Naylor chooses the factoring arrangement, it can eliminate its credit department and reduce operating expenses by $4,000 per month. In addition, bad debt losses of two percent of the monthly receivables will be avoided.

  a. What is the annual cost associated with each financing arrangement?

  b. Discuss some considerations other than cost that might influence management's decision between factoring and a commercial bank loan.

Problems

cash discounts   **15–1** Suppose a firm makes purchases of $3.6 million per year under terms of 2/10, net 30 and takes discounts.

  a. What is the average amount of accounts payable net of discounts? (Assume that the $3.6 million of purchases is net of discounts—that is, gross purchases are $3,673,469 and discounts are $73,469. Also, use 360 days in a year.)

  b. Is there a cost of the trade credit the firm uses?

  c. If the firm did not take discounts and it paid on time, what would be its average payables and the approximate and effective annual costs of this non-free trade credit? Assume the firm records accounts payable net of discounts.

  d. What would be its approximate and effective annual costs of not taking discounts if the firm can stretch its payments to 40 days?

trade credit versus   **15–2** Gallinger Corporation projects an increase in sales from $1.5 million to $2 million, but it needs an additional $300,000 of current assets to support this expansion. The money can be obtained from the bank at an interest rate of 13 percent, discount interest; no compensating balance is required. Alternatively, Gallinger can finance the expansion by no longer taking discounts, thus increasing accounts payable. Gallinger purchases under terms of 2/10, net 30, but it can delay payment for an *additional* 35 days—paying in 65 days and thus becoming 35 days past due—without a penalty because of its suppliers' current excess capacity problems.

  a. Based strictly on effective annual interest rate comparisons, how should Gallinger finance its expansion?

b. What additional qualitative factors should Gallinger consider before reaching a decision?

cost of bank loans **15–3** The UFSU Corporation intends to borrow $450,000 to support its short-term financing requirements during the next year. The company is evaluating its financing options at the bank where it maintains its checking account. UFSU's checking account balance, which averages $50,000, can be used to help satisfy any compensating balance requirements the bank might impose. The financing alternatives offered by the bank include the following:

Alternative 1:   A discount interest loan with a simple interest of 9¼ percent and no compensating balance requirement.

Alternative 2:   A ten percent simple interest loan that has a 15 percent compensating balance requirement.

Alternative 3:   A $1 million revolving line of credit with simple interest of 9¼ percent paid on the amount borrowed and a 1/4 percent commitment fee on the unused balance. No compensating balance is required.

a. Compute the effective cost (rate) of each financing alternative assuming UFSU *borrows* $450,000. Which alternative should UFSU use?

b. For each alternative, how much would UFSU have to borrow in order to have $450,000 available for use (to pay the firms bills)?

cost of bank loans **15–4** Gifts Galore Inc. borrowed $1.5 million from National City Bank (NCB). The loan was made at a simple annual interest rate of nine percent a year for three months. A 20 percent compensating balance requirement raised the effective interest rate because the company does not maintain a checking balance at NCB.

a. The approximate interest rate (APR) on the loan was 11.25 percent. What was the true effective rate?

b. What would be the effective cost of the loan if the note required discount interest?

c. What would be the approximate annual interest rate on the loan if National City Bank required Gifts Galore to repay the loan and interest in three equal monthly installments?

short-term financing analysis **15–5** Bankston Feed and Supply Company buys on terms of 1/10, net 30, but it has not been taking discounts and has actually been paying in 60 rather than 30 days. Bankston's balance sheet follows (thousands of dollars):

Cash	$ 50	Accounts payable[a]	$ 500
Accounts receivable	450	Notes payable	50
Inventories	750	Accruals	50
Current assets	$1,250	Current liabilities	$ 600
		Long-term debt	150
Fixed assets	750	Common equity	1,250
Total assets	$2,000	Total liabilities and equity	$2,000

[a]Stated net of discounts.

Now Bankston's suppliers are threatening to stop shipments unless the company begins making prompt payments (that is, paying in 30 days or less). The firm can borrow on a one-year note (call this a current liability) from its bank at a rate of 15 percent, discount interest, with a 20 percent compensating balance required. (Bankston's $50,000 of cash is needed for transactions; it cannot be used as part of the compensating balance.)

a. Determine what action Bankston should take by calculating (1) the cost of nonfree trade credit and (2) the cost of the bank loan.

b. Assume that Bankston forgoes discounts and then borrows the amount needed to become current on its payables from the bank. How large will the bank loan be?

c. Based on your conclusion in part a, construct a pro forma balance sheet. (*Hint:* Remember that the interest for a discount loan is paid "up front"; therefore, you will need to include an account titled "prepaid interest" under current assets.)

alternative financing   **15–6** Suntime Boats Limited estimates that because of the seasonal nature of its busi-
arrangements   ness, it will require an additional $2 million of cash for the month of July. Sun-
time Boats has the following four options available for raising the needed funds:

(1) Establish a one-year line of credit for $2 million with a commercial bank. The commitment fee will be ½ percent per year on the unused portion, and the interest charge on the used funds will be 11 percent per annum. Assume that the funds are needed only in July and that there are 30 days in July and 360 days in the year.

(2) Forgo the cash discount of 2/10, net 40 on $2 million of purchases during July.

(3) Issue $2 million of 30-day commercial paper at a 9½ percent simple annual interest rate. The total transactions fee, including the cost of a backup credit line, on using commercial paper is ½ percent of the amount of the issue.

(4) Issue $2 million of 60-day commercial paper at a nine percent per annum interest rate, plus a transactions fee of ½ percent. Because the funds are re-quired for only 30 days, the excess funds ($2 million) can be invested in 9.4 percent per annum marketable securities for the month of August. The to-tal transactions cost of purchasing and selling the marketable securities is 0.4 percent of the amount of the issue.

a. What is the *dollar* cost of each financing arrangement?

b. Is the source with the lowest expected cost necessarily the one to select? Why or why not?

factoring receivables   **15–7** Cooley Industries needs an additional $500,000, which it plans to obtain through a factoring arrangement. The factor would purchase Cooley's accounts receivable and advance the invoice amount, minus a two percent commission, on the invoices purchased each month. Cooley sells on terms of net 30 days. In addition, the factor charges a 12 percent annual interest rate on the total in-voice amount, to be deducted in advance.

a. What amount of accounts receivable must be factored to net $500,000?

b. If Cooley can reduce credit expenses by $3,500 per month and avoid bad debt losses of 2.5 percent on the factored amount, what is the total dollar cost of the factoring arrangement?

c. What would be the total cost of the factoring arrangement if Cooley's fund-ing needs rose to $750,000? Would the factoring arrangement be profitable under these circumstances?

field warehousing   **15–8** Because of crop failures last year, the San Joaquin Packing Company has no funds available to finance its canning operations during the next six months. It estimates that it will require $1,200,000 from inventory financing during the period. One alternative is to establish a six-month, $1,500,000 line of credit with terms of nine percent annual interest on the used portion, a one percent commitment fee on the unused portion, and a $300,000 compensating balance at all times. The other alternative is to use field warehouse financing. The costs of the field warehouse arrangement in this case would be a flat fee of $2,000, plus 8 percent annual interest on all outstanding credit, plus one percent of the maximum amount of credit extended.

Expected inventory levels to be financed are as follows:

MONTH	AMOUNT
July	$ 250,000
August	1,000,000
September	1,200,000
October	950,000
November	600,000
December	0

a. Calculate the cost of funds from using the line of credit. Be sure to include interest charges and commitment fees. Note that each month's borrowings will be $300,000 greater than the inventory level to be financed because of the compensating balance requirement.
b. Calculate the total cost of the field warehousing operation.
c. Compare the cost of the field warehousing arrangement to the cost of the line of credit. Which alternative should San Joaquin choose?

Exam-Type Problems

The problems included in this section are set up in such a way that they could be used as multiple-choice exam problems.

cost of trade credit   **15–9** Calculate the approximate cost of nonfree trade credit under each of following terms. Assume payment is made either on the last due date or on the discount date.
  a. 1/15, net 20.
  b. 2/10, net 60.
  c. 3/10, net 45.
  d. 2/10, net 45.
  e. 2/15, net 40.

cost of credit   **15–10 a.** If a firm buys under terms of 3/15, net 45, but actually pays on the 20th day and still takes the discount, what is the approximate cost of its nonfree trade credit?
  b. Does it receive more or less credit than it would if it paid within 15 days?

cost of bank credit   **15–11** Susan Visscher, owner of Visscher's Hardware, is negotiating with First Merchant's Bank for a $50,000, one-year loan. First Merchant's has offered Visscher the following alternatives. Calculate the effective interest rate for each alternative. Which alternative has the lowest effective interest rate?
  a. A 12 percent annual rate on a simple interest loan with no compensating balance required and interest due at the end of the year.
  b. A nine percent annual rate on a simple interest loan with a 20 percent compensating balance required and interest again due at the end of the year.
  c. An 8.75 percent annual rate on a discounted loan with a 15 percent compensating balance.

d. Interest is figured as eight percent of the $50,000 amount, payable at the end of the year, but the $50,000 is repayable in monthly installments during the year.

cost of trade credit **15–12** Howe Industries sells on terms of 2/10, net 40. Gross sales last year were $4.5 million, and accounts receivable averaged $437,500. Half of Howe's customers paid on the tenth day and took discounts. What is the cost of trade credit to Howe's nondiscount customers? (*Hint:* Calculate sales per day based on a 360-day year; then get the average receivables of discount customers; then find the DSO for the nondiscount customers.)

cost of credit **15–13** Boles Corporation needs to raise $500,000 for one year to supply capital to a new store. Boles buys from its suppliers on terms of 3/10, net 90, and it currently pays on the 10th day and takes discounts, but it could forgo discounts, pay on the 90th day, and get the needed $500,000 in the form of costly trade credit. Alternatively, Boles could borrow from its bank on a 12 percent discount interest rate basis. What is the effective annual interest rate of the lower cost source?

effective cost of short-term credit **15–14** The Meyer Company must arrange financing for its working capital requirements for the coming year. Meyer can (a) borrow from its bank on a simple interest basis (interest payable at the end of the loan) for one year at a 12 percent simple rate; (b) borrow on a three-month, renewable loan at an 11.5 percent simple rate; (c) borrow on an installment loan basis at a 6.0 percent add-on rate with 12 end-of-month payments; or (d) obtain the needed funds by no longer taking discounts and thus increasing its accounts payable. Meyer buys on terms of 1/15, net 60. What is the effective annual cost (not the approximate cost) of the least expensive type of credit, assuming 360 days per year?

Integrative Problem

short-term financing **15–15** C. Charles Smith recently was hired as president of Dellvoe Office Equipment Inc., a small manufacturer of metal office equipment. As his assistant, you have been asked to review the company's short-term financing policies and to prepare a report for Smith and the board of directors. To help you get started, Smith has prepared some questions that, when answered, will give him a better idea of the company's short-term financing policies.

a. What is short-term credit, and what are the four major sources of this credit?

b. Is there a cost to accruals, and do firms have much control over them?

c. What is trade credit?

d. Like most small companies, Dellvoe has two primary sources of short-term debt: trade credit and bank loans. One supplier, which supplies Dellvoe with $50,000 of materials a year, offers Dellvoe terms of 2/10, net 50.

　(1) What are Dellvoe's net daily purchases from this supplier?

　(2) What is the average level of Dellvoe's accounts payable to this supplier if the discount is taken? What is the average level if the discount is not taken? What are the amounts of free credit and costly credit under both discount policies?

　(3) What is the approximate cost of the costly trade credit? What is its effective annual cost?

e. In discussing a possible loan with the firm's banker, Smith has found that the bank is willing to lend Dellvoe up to $800,000 for one year at a nine percent simple, or quoted, rate. However, he forgot to ask what the specific terms would be.

(1) Assume the firm will borrow $800,000. What would be the effective interest rate if the loan were based on simple interest? If the loan had been an eight percent simple interest loan for six months rather than for a year, would that have affected the effective annual rate?

(2) What would be the effective rate if the loan were a discount interest loan? What would be the face amount of a loan large enough to net the firm $800,000 of usable funds?

(3) Assume now that the terms call for an installment (or add-on) loan with equal monthly payments. The add-on loan is for a period of one year. What would be Dellvoe's monthly payment? What would be the approximate cost of the loan? What would be the effective annual rate?

(4) Now assume that the bank charges simple interest, but it requires the firm to maintain a 20 percent compensating balance. How much must Dellvoe borrow to obtain its needed $800,000 and to meet the compensating balance requirement? What is the effective annual rate on the loan?

(5) Now assume that the bank charges discount interest of nine percent and also requires a compensating balance of 20 percent. How much must Dellvoe borrow, and what is the effective annual rate under these terms?

(6) Now assume all the conditions in part 4, that is, a 20 percent compensating balance and a nine percent simple interest loan, but assume also that Dellvoe has $100,000 of cash balances that it normally holds for transactions purposes, which can be used as part of the required compensating balance. How does this affect (i) the size of the required loan and (ii) the effective cost of the loan?

f. Dellvoe is considering using secured short-term financing. What is a secured loan? What two types of current assets can be used to secure loans?

g. What are the differences between pledging receivables and factoring receivables? Is one type generally considered better?

h. What are the differences among the three forms of inventory financing? Is one type generally considered best?

i. Dellvoe had expected a really strong market for office equipment for the year just ended, and in anticipation of strong sales, the firm increased its inventory purchases. However, sales for the last quarter of the year did not meet its expectations, and now Dellvoe finds itself short on cash. The firm expects that its cash shortage will be temporary, only lasting three months. (The inventory has been paid for and cannot be returned to suppliers. In the office equipment market, designs change nearly every two years, and Dellvoe's inventory reflects the new design changes, so its inventory is not obsolete.) Dellvoe has decided to use inventory financing to meet its short-term cash needs. It estimates that it will require $800,000 for inventory financing during this three-month period. Dellvoe has negotiated with the bank for a three-month, $1,000,000 line of credit with terms of ten percent annual interest on the used portion, a one percent commitment fee on the unused portion, and a $125,000 compensating balance at all times.

Expected inventory levels to be financed are as follows:

MONTH	AMOUNT
January	$800,000
February	500,000
March	300,000

Calculate the cost of funds from this source, including interest charges and commitment fees. (*Hint:* Each month's borrowings will be $125,000 greater than the inventory level to be financed because of the compensating balance requirement.)

Computer-Related Problem

Work the problem in this section only if you are using the computer problem diskette.

factoring receivables **15–16** Use the model in File C15 to work this problem. Refer back to Problem 15–7.
  a. Would it be to Cooley's advantage to offer to pay the factor a commission of 2.5 percent if it would lower the interest rate to 10.5 percent annually?
  b. Assume a commission of two percent and an interest rate of 12 percent. What would be the total cost of the factoring arrangement if Cooley's funding needs rose to $650,000? Would the factoring arrangement be profitable under these circumstances?

ONLINE ESSENTIALS

http://www.sba.gov/SCORE/ca/abc-boro.html   California Small Business Administration
Provides a tutorial and checklist for financing a small business.
The Small Business Administration homepage, which is located at http://www.sba.gov/, also provides a great deal of information about different types of loans available to businesses for financing current operations.

http://www.icemall.com/reports/business/68.html   Icemall—The ABC's of Borrowing
Provides a description of various types of loans, including inventory financing, businesses use to finance operations. This site also includes a worksheet for constructing a cash budget.

http://www.ideacafe.com   Idea Café
This site provides a variety of financial information for small businesses. If you click on "Financing Your Biz," you will be taken to a page that describes financing resources, how to get financing, a financing glossary, and so forth.

http://www.nfsn.com   National Financial Services Network
Provides information about both personal and commercial financing. The "Commercial Finance" page gives descriptions and definitions of the types of loans available to businesses, as well as links to related sites.

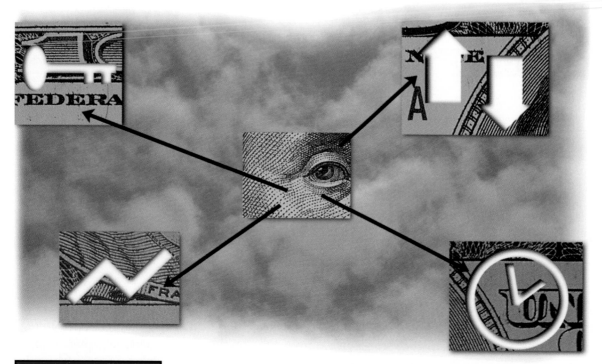

PART VII

Strategic Long-Term Financing Decisions

CHAPTER 16

Common Stock and the Investment Banking Process

A MANAGERIAL PERSPECTIVE

The initial public offering (IPO) market is very intriguing to investors, many of whom dream about "striking gold" with an IPO such as Microsoft. One share of Microsoft that was first sold to the public in March 1986 for $21 per share was worth more than $13,600 in the summer of 1999. Even though Microsoft was selling for about $95.50 per share in mid-1999, the company had split the stock eight times since the IPO such that one original share was the equivalent of 144 post-split shares. Thus, if you purchased 100 shares of stock when Microsoft originally went public, your $2,100 investment would have grown to more than $1.36 million in 1999. As investors, we all would like to find such success. But it is very difficult to find gold mines like Microsoft. Even so, IPOs have been, and will continue to be, one of the more fascinating topics in investments.

The 1990s might be best described as the era of IPOs. In 1996, IPOs hit a record amount, $49.5 billion; while in 1993 a record number of companies went public, 707. More recently, the IPO market has waned somewhat. The total dollar amount of IPOs in 1998 was a little more than $35 billion, which was about 10 percent less than in 1997. The number of new offerings (351) was the lowest since 1991, primarily because the number of small-company IPOs decreased compared with previous years.

Which IPOs have been the hottest? In the first half of the 1990s, the most popular IPOs were those associated with technologically innovative companies, especially those that developed software and produced peripheral equipment for computers. In more recent years, especially in 1998 and 1999, the most sought after IPOs are still connected with information technology, but the emphasis has been on Internet companies. For example, in 1998, more than 40 percent of the amount raised from IPOs was for Internet-based companies. Much of the remainder of the new issues came from very large offerings, each of which amounted to more than $1 billion. During the first half of 1999, the pattern in the IPO market had not changed—most new offerings were from Internet companies.

Certainly much of the appeal of the IPO market is the potential for huge gains that new issues offer. But even though IPOs offer the potential to earn significant returns, they are not the panacea many investors think. Obviously, many IPOs do very well at the time they are introduced to the market; but most of the profits are earned by company insiders and institutional investors like pension funds, not the average investor. Evidence shows that during the first five years, the value of IPOs declines by about 40 percent, and it is the average investor that generally gets hurt. For

continues

example, in 1998, BMJ Medical Management and USN Communications went public about the same date (February 3 and 4, respectively), and by the end of the year the value of each firm's stock had dropped nearly 99 percent from its original offering price (BMJ's IPO, which was offered at $7, was selling for 8¢, while USN's IPO, which was offered at $16, was selling for 19¢).

As you read this chapter, keep in mind that investment in common stock, whether an IPO or the stock from a "blue chip" company like IBM, is risky. Understanding the concepts presented in this chapter will help you avoid some of the pitfalls commonly made by naive investors, especially when investing in IPOs. Also, read the Industry Practice box for an interesting perspective into IPO trading by an individual investor. ∎

When we discussed capital structure decisions in Chapter 11, we did not spend much time on the specific characteristics of common stock or debt, nor did we discuss the process through which such securities are issued. However, these details actually are quite important. Therefore, in this and the following two chapters we will examine some of the characteristics of different equities (stock) and of the many different types of debt, and we will discuss how firms actually raise long-term capital. The focus in this chapter is on common stock.

Balance Sheet Accounts and Definitions

COMMON EQUITY
The sum of the firm's common stock, paid-in capital, and retained earnings, which equals the common stockholders' total investment in the firm stated at book value.

PAR VALUE
The nominal or face value of a stock or bond.

RETAINED EARNINGS
The balance sheet account that indicates the total amount of earnings the firm has not paid out as dividends throughout its history; these earnings have been reinvested in the firm.

An understanding of legal and accounting terminology is vital to both investors and financial managers if they are to avoid misinterpretations and possibly costly mistakes. Therefore, we begin our analysis of common stock with a discussion of accounting and legal issues. Consider first Table 16–1, which shows the **common equity** section of Unilate Textiles' balance sheet. Unilate's owners—its stockholders—have authorized management to issue a total of 40 million shares, and management has thus far actually issued (or sold) 25 million shares. Each share has a **par value** of $1; this is the minimum amount for which new shares can be issued.[1] During 2000 Unilate earned $54 million, paid $29 million in dividends, and retained $25 million. The $25 million was added to the $260 million accumulated **retained earnings** shown on the year-end 1999 balance sheet to produce the $285 million retained earnings at year-end 2000. Thus, since its inception, Unilate has retained, or plowed back, a total of $285 million. This is money that belongs to the stockholders that they could have received in the form of dividends. Instead, the stockholders chose to let management reinvest the $285 million in the business so growth could be achieved.

[1]A stock's par value is an arbitrary figure that originally indicated the minimum amount of money stockholders had put up. Today, firms generally are not required to establish a par value for their stock. Thus, Unilate Textiles could have elected to use *no-par* stock, in which case the common stock and additional paid-in capital accounts would have been consolidated under one account called *common stock*, which would show a 2000 balance of $130 million. For simplicity, in Chapter 3 we did not show the detailed breakdown of Unilate's common equity accounts. For purposes of the present discussion it is necessary to show the detail as given in Table 16–1.

TABLE 16–1	Unilate Textiles: Common Equity Accounts as of December 31 (millions of dollars, except per share data)	
	2000	**1999**
Common stock (40 million shares authorized, 25 million shares outstanding, $1 par)	$ 25.0	$ 25.0
Additional paid-in capital	105.0	105.0
Retained earnings	285.0	260.0
Total common stockholders' equity (net worth)	$415.0	$390.0
Book value per share	$16.60	$15.60

ADDITIONAL PAID-IN CAPITAL
Funds received in excess of par value when a firm issues new stock.

Now consider the $105 million **additional paid-in capital.** This account shows the difference between the stock's par value and what new stockholders paid when they bought newly issued shares. For example, in 1980, when Unilate was formed, 15 million shares were issued at par value; thus, the first balance sheet showed a zero for paid-in capital and $15 million for the common stock account. However, in 1983, to raise funds for expansion projects, Unilate issued 10 million shares at a market price of $11.50 per share—total value of the issue was $115 million. At that time, the common stock account was increased by $10 million ($1 par value for the 10 million shares issued), and the remainder of the $115 million issue value, $105 million, was added to additional paid-in capital. Unilate has not issued any more stock since 1983, so the only change in the common equity section since that time has been in retained earnings.

BOOK VALUE PER SHARE
The accounting value of a share of common stock; equal to common equity (common stock plus additional paid-in capital plus retained earnings) divided by the number of shares outstanding.

The **book value per share** shown in Table 16–1 is computed by dividing the amount of total stockholders' equity, which also is called net worth, by the number of shares outstanding. Unilate's book value per share increased in 2000 to $16.60, from $15.60 in 1999. Whenever stock is sold at a price above book value or the change in retained earnings is positive, book value will increase, and vice versa. Because book value is a historical cost amount, investors prefer that the market value of stock be greater than its book value; a stock that is selling below its book value might suggest the company is experiencing financial difficulty.

Self-Test Questions

How is book value per share calculated, and is it generally equal to the par and market values?

What differences would there be in the stockholders' equity accounts of a firm that has par value stock and one that has no-par stock?

How does the amount of earnings retained by a firm affect its common equity accounts?

Legal Rights and Privileges of Common Stockholders

The common stockholders are the owners of a corporation, and as such they have certain rights and privileges. The most important rights are discussed in this section.

Control of the Firm

The stockholders have the right to elect the firm's directors, who in turn elect the officers who manage the business. In a small firm, the major stockholder typically assumes the positions of president and chairperson of the board of directors. In a large, publicly owned firm, the managers typically have some stock, but their personal holdings are insufficient to provide voting control. Thus, the managements of most publicly owned firms can be removed by the stockholders if they decide a management team is not effective.

PROXY
A document giving one person the authority to act for another, typically the power to vote shares of common stock.

Various state and federal laws stipulate how stockholder control is to be exercised. First, corporations must hold an election of directors periodically, usually once a year, with the vote taken at the annual meeting. Frequently, one-third of the directors are elected each year for a three-year term. Each share of stock normally has one vote; thus, the owner of 1,000 shares has 1,000 votes. Stockholders can appear at the annual meeting and vote in person, but typically they transfer their right to vote to a second party by means of an instrument known as a **proxy.** Management always solicits stockholders' proxies and usually gets them. However, if earnings are poor and stockholders are dissatisfied, an outside group might solicit the proxies in an effort to overthrow management and take control of the business. This is known as a **proxy fight.**

PROXY FIGHT
An attempt by a person or group of people to gain control of a firm by getting its stockholders to grant that person or group the authority to vote their shares in order to elect a new management team.

The question of control has become a central issue in finance in recent years. The frequency of proxy fights has increased, as have attempts by one corporation to take over another by purchasing a majority of the outstanding stock. This action is called a **takeover.** Some well-known examples of past takeover battles include Kohlberg Kravis Roberts & Co.'s (KKR) acquisition of RJR Nabisco, Chevron's acquisition of Gulf Oil, and AT&T's takeover of NCR; and, more recently, the efforts of Alcoa, the world largest aluminum producer, to take over Reynolds Metals, the world's third largest producer of aluminum.

TAKEOVER
An action whereby a person or group succeeds in ousting a firm's management and taking control of the company.

Managers who do not have majority control (more than 50 percent of their firms' stock) are very much concerned about proxy fights and takeovers, and many attempt to get stockholder approval for changes in their corporate charters that would make takeovers more difficult. For example, a number of companies have gotten their stockholders to agree (1) to elect only one-third of the directors each year (rather than electing all directors each year); (2) to require 75 percent of the stockholders (rather than 50 percent) to approve a merger; and (3) to vote in a "poison pill" provision that would allow the stockholders of a firm that is taken over by another firm to buy shares in the second firm at a reduced price. The third provision makes the acquisition unattractive and, thus, wards off hostile takeover attempts. Managements seeking such changes generally cite a fear that the firm will be picked up at a bargain price, but it often appears that managers' concerns about their own positions might be an even more important consideration.

The Preemptive Right

PREEMPTIVE RIGHT
A provision in the corporate charter or bylaws that gives common stockholders the right to purchase on a *pro rata* basis new issues of common stock (or convertible securities).

Common stockholders often have the right, called the **preemptive right,** to purchase any additional shares sold by the firm. In some states the preemptive right is automatically included in every corporate charter; in others it is necessary to insert it specifically into the charter.

The purpose of the preemptive right is twofold. First, it protects the power of control of current stockholders. If it were not for this safeguard, the management of a corporation under criticism from stockholders could prevent stockholders from removing it from office by issuing a large number of additional shares and purchasing these shares itself. Management could thereby secure control of the corporation and frustrate the will of the current stockholders.

The second, and more important, reason for the preemptive right is that it protects stockholders against a dilution of value. For example, suppose 1,000 shares of common stock, each with a price of $100, were outstanding, making the total market value of the firm $100,000. If an additional 1,000 shares were sold at $50 a share, or for $50,000, this would raise the total market value of the firm to $150,000. When the total market value is divided by the new total shares outstanding, a value of $75 a share is obtained. The old stockholders thus lose $25 per share, and the new stockholders have an instant profit of $25 per share. Thus, selling common stock at a price below the market value would dilute its price and would transfer wealth from the present stockholders to those who were allowed to purchase the new shares. The preemptive right prevents such occurrences.

Self-Test Questions

Identify some actions that companies have taken to make takeovers more difficult.

What are the two primary reasons for the existence of the preemptive right?

Types of Common Stock

CLASSIFIED STOCK
Common stock that is given a special designation, such as Class A, Class B, and so forth, to meet special needs of the company.

Although most firms have only one type of common stock, in some instances **classified stock** is used to meet the special needs of the company. Generally, when special classifications of stock are used, one type is designated Class A, another Class B, and so on. Small, new companies seeking to obtain funds from outside sources frequently use different types of common stock. For example, when Genetic Concepts went public, its Class A stock was sold to the public and paid a dividend, but this stock did not have voting rights until five years after its issue. Its Class B stock, which was retained by the organizers of the company, had full voting rights for five years, but the legal terms stated that dividends could not be paid on the Class B stock until the company had established its earning power by building up retained earnings to a designated level. The use of classified stock thus enabled the public to take a position in a conservatively financed growth company without sacrificing income, while the founders retained absolute control during the crucial early stages of the firm's development. At the same time, outside investors were protected against excessive withdrawals of funds by the original owners. As is often the case in such situations, the Class B stock was called **founders' shares.**

FOUNDERS' SHARES
Stock owned by the firm's founders who have sole voting rights; this type of stock generally has restricted dividends for a specified number of years.

Note that "Class A," "Class B," and so on, have no standard meanings—one firm could designate its Class B shares as founders' shares and its Class A shares as those sold to the public, while another could reverse these designations. Still other firms could use stock classifications for entirely different purposes. For example, when General Motors acquired Hughes Aircraft for $5 billion, it paid in part with a new Class H common, GMH, which had limited voting rights and whose dividends were tied to Hughes's performance as a GM subsidiary. The reasons for the new stock were reported to be that (1) GM wanted to limit voting privileges on the new classified stock because of management's concern about a possible takeover and (2) Hughes employees wanted to be rewarded more directly on Hughes's own performance than would have been possible through regular GM stock.[2]

Self-Test Question

What are some reasons a company might use classified stock?

Evaluation of Common Stock as a Source of Funds

Thus far the chapter has covered the main characteristics of common stock. Now we will appraise stock financing both from the viewpoint of the corporation and from a social perspective.

From the Corporation's Viewpoint

The advantages and disadvantages of using common stock as a financing source are listed in this section.

Advantages   Common stock offers several advantages to the corporation:

1. Common stock does not legally obligate the firm to make payments to stockholders: Only if the company generates earnings and has no pressing internal needs for them will it pay dividends.
2. Common stock carries no fixed maturity date—it never has to be "repaid" as would a debt issue.
3. Because common stock cushions creditors against losses, the sale of common stock generally increases the creditworthiness of the firm. This in turn raises its bond rating, lowers its cost of debt, and increases its future ability to use debt.
4. If a company's prospects look bright, then common stock often can be sold on better terms than debt. Stock appeals to certain groups of investors because (a) it typically carries a higher expected total return (dividends plus capital gains) than does preferred stock or debt and (b) as a representation of the ownership of the firm, stock provides the investor with a better hedge against unanticipated inflation because common dividends tend to rise during inflationary periods.[3]

Disadvantages   Disadvantages associated with issuing common stock include the following:

---

[2]GM's deal posed a problem for the NYSE, which had a rule against listing any company's common stock if the company had any nonvoting common stock outstanding. GM made it clear that it was willing to delist if the NYSE did not change its rules. The NYSE concluded that such arrangements as GM had made were logical and were likely to be made by other companies in the future, so it changed its rules to accommodate GM.

[3]For common stock in general, the rate of increase in dividends has slightly exceeded the rate of inflation since 1970.

1. The sale of common stock gives some voting rights, and perhaps even control, to new stockholders. For this reason, additional equity financing often is avoided by managers who are concerned about maintaining control. The use of founders' shares and other classes of common stock can mitigate this problem.

2. Common stock gives new owners the right to share in the income of the firm; if profits soar, then new stockholders will share in this bonanza, whereas if debt had been used, new investors (creditors in this case) would have received only a fixed return, no matter how profitable the company had been, and existing stockholders would have received the rest.[4]

3. As we shall see, the costs of underwriting and distributing common stock usually are higher than those for debt or preferred stock. Flotation costs for common stock characteristically are higher because (a) the costs of investigating an equity security investment are higher than those for a comparable debt security and (b) stocks are riskier than debt, meaning that investors must diversify their equity holdings, so a given dollar amount of new stock must be sold to a larger number of purchasers than the same amount of debt.

4. As we saw in Chapter 11, if the firm has more equity than is called for in its optimal capital structure, the average cost of capital will be higher than necessary. Therefore, a firm would not want to sell stock if the sale caused its equity ratio (1.0 minus the debt ratio) to exceed the optimal level.

5. Under current tax laws, common stock dividends are not deductible as an expense for tax purposes, but bond interest is deductible. As we saw in Chapter 10, taxes raise the relative cost of equity as compared with debt.

From a Social Viewpoint

From a social viewpoint, common stock is a desirable form of financing because it makes businesses less vulnerable to the consequences of declines in sales and earnings. Common stock financing involves no fixed charge payments that might force a faltering firm into bankruptcy. From the standpoint of the economy as a whole, if too many firms used too much debt, business fluctuations would be amplified, and minor recessions could turn into major ones. Not long ago, when the level of leveraged mergers and buyouts was raising the aggregate debt ratio (the average debt ratio of all firms), the Federal Reserve and other authorities voiced concern over the possible dangers created by the situation, and congressional leaders debated the wisdom of social controls over corporations' use of debt. Like most important issues, this one is debatable, and the debate centers around who can better determine "appropriate" capital structures—corporate managers or government officials.[5]

---

[4]This point has given rise to an important theory: "If a firm sells a large issue of bonds, this is a signal that management expects the company to earn high profits on investments financed by the new capital and that it does not wish to share these profits with new stockholders. On the other hand, if the firm issues stock, this is a signal that its prospects are not so bright." This issue was discussed earlier in Chapters 11 and 12.

[5]When business executives hear someone say, "I'm from Washington and I'm here to help you," they generally cringe and often with good reason. On the other hand, a stable national economy does require sound businesses, and too much debt can lead to corporate instability.

Self-Test Questions

What are the major advantages and disadvantages of common stock financing?

From a social viewpoint, why is common stock a desirable form of financing?

The Market for Common Stock

CLOSELY HELD CORPORATION
A corporation that is owned by a few individuals who are typically associated with the firm's management.

PUBLICLY OWNED CORPORATION
A corporation that is owned by a relatively large number of individuals who are not actively involved in its management.

OVER-THE-COUNTER (OTC) MARKET
The network of dealers that provides for trading securities not listed on organized exchanges.

ORGANIZED SECURITY EXCHANGE
A formal organization, having a tangible physical location, that facilitates trading in designated ("listed") securities. The two major national security exchanges in the United States are the New York Stock Exchange (NYSE) and the American Stock Exchange (AMEX).

SECONDARY MARKET
The market in which "used" stocks are traded after they have been issued by corporations.

PRIMARY MARKET
The market in which firms issue new securities to raise corporate capital.

Some companies are so small that their common stocks are not actively traded; they are owned by only a few people, usually the companies' managers. Such firms are said to be *privately owned,* or **closely held, corporations,** and their stock is called closely held stock. In contrast, the stocks of most larger companies are owned by a large number of investors, most of whom are not active in management. Such companies are said to be **publicly owned corporations,** and their stock is called *publicly held stock.*

As we saw in Chapter 2, the stocks of smaller publicly owned firms are not listed on an exchange; they trade in the **over-the-counter (OTC) market,** and the companies and their stocks are said to be *unlisted.* However, larger publicly owned companies generally apply for listing on an **organized security exchange** or the NASDAQ market, and they and their stocks are said to be *listed.* As a rule, companies are first listed on a regional exchange, such as the Chicago or Midwest Exchange. As they grow, they move up to the American Stock Exchange (AMEX) and the New York Stock Exchange (NYSE). Most companies are traded in the OTC market (there are 5,000 to 8,000 actively traded stocks), but in terms of market value of both outstanding shares and daily transactions, the NYSE generates about 60 percent of the business with its listing of approximately 3,000 stocks.

Institutional investors such as pension trusts, insurance companies, and mutual funds own 45 to 50 percent of all common stocks. These institutions buy and sell fairly actively, however, so they account for more than 75 percent of all transactions. Thus, the institutional investors have a heavy influence on the prices of individual stocks.

Types of Stock Market Transactions

We can classify stock market transactions into three distinct types:

1. **Trading in the outstanding shares of established, publicly owned companies: the secondary market.** Unilate Textiles has 25 million shares of stock outstanding. If the owner of 100 shares sells his or her stock, the trade is said to have occurred in the **secondary market.** Thus, the market for outstanding shares, or used shares, is the secondary market. The company receives no new money when sales occur in this market.

2. **Additional shares sold by established, publicly owned companies: the primary market.** If Unilate decides to sell (or issue) an additional one million shares to raise new equity capital, this transaction is said to occur in the **primary market.**[6]

---

[6]Recall that Unilate has 40 million shares authorized but only 25 million outstanding; thus, it has 15 million authorized but unissued shares. If it had no authorized but unissued shares, management could increase the authorized shares by obtaining stockholders' approval, which would generally be granted without any arguments.

3. **New public offerings by privately held firms: the primary market.** When Coors Brewing Company, which was owned by the Coors family at the time, decided to sell some stock to raise capital needed for a major expansion program, it took its stock public. Whenever stock in a closely held corporation is offered to the public for the first time, the company is said to be **going public.**[7] The market for stock that has recently gone public normally is called the **initial public offering (IPO) market.**

Firms can go public without raising any additional capital. For example, the Ford Motor Company was once owned exclusively by the Ford family. When Henry Ford died, he left a substantial part of his stock to the Ford Foundation. When the foundation later sold some of this stock to the general public, the Ford Motor Company went public, even though the company raised no capital in the transaction.

A firm generally goes *public* when growth opportunities no longer can be financed solely by debt and the existing stockholder base, which generally consists of the original owners and current managers of the corporation and a few investors not actively involved in the company's management. The purpose of going public is to increase the ownership base and the funding sources available to the company so that growth opportunities can be better financed and the firm's value can be increased more than otherwise would be possible. Thus, as a firm experiences greater and greater growth and its size expands significantly, there generally is pressure to go public. Unfortunately, when a firm does go public, the red tape increases, because financial reporting and disclosure guidelines and security regulations are more restrictive for public firms than for private firms.

> **GOING PUBLIC**
> The act of selling stock to the public at large by a closely held corporation or its principal stockholders.

> **INITIAL PUBLIC OFFERING (IPO) MARKET**
> The market consisting of stocks of companies that have just gone public.

The Decision to List the Stock

To have its stock listed, a company must apply to an exchange, pay a relatively small fee, and meet the exchange's minimum requirements. These requirements relate to the size of the company's net income as well as to the number of shares outstanding and in the hands of outsiders (as opposed to the number held by insiders, who generally do not trade their stock very actively). The company also must agree to disclose certain information to the exchange; this information is designed to help the exchange track trading patterns and thus try to prevent manipulation of the stock's price.[8] The size qualifications increase as one moves from the regional exchanges to the AMEX and on

---

[7]The stock Coors offered to the public was designated Class B, and it was nonvoting. The Coors family retained the founders' shares, called Class A stock, which carried full voting privileges. The company was large enough to obtain an NYSE listing, but at that time the NYSE had a requirement that listed common stocks must have full voting rights, which precluded Coors from obtaining an NYSE listing. But in March 1999, Coors began trading on the NYSE.

[8]It is illegal for anyone to attempt to manipulate the price of a stock. Prior to the creation of the Securities and Exchange Commission (SEC) in the 1930s, syndicates would buy and sell stock back and forth at rigged prices for the purpose of deceiving the public into thinking that a particular stock was worth more or less than its true value. The exchanges, with the encouragement and support of the SEC, utilize sophisticated computer programs to help spot any irregularities that suggest manipulation. They can identify the exact day and time of each trade and the broker who executed it, and they can require the broker to disclose the name of the person for whom the trade was made. Such a system can obviously help identify manipulators. This same system also helps to identify illegal insider trading, as discussed in the next section.

	NYSE	AMEX AND REGIONAL EXCHANGES[a]	NASDAQ
Round lot (100 shares) shareholders	2,000	800	300
Number of public shares (million)	1.1	0.5	0.5
Market value of public shares ($ million)	$40	$3	$1
Net tangible assets ($ million)	$4	$4	$2
Pre-tax income ($ million)	$2.50	$0.75	$0.50

TABLE 16–2   Listing Requirements for Exchanges and NASDAQ

[a]These numbers are indicative of the listing requirements for larger regional stock exchanges, including the Chicago Stock Exchange, the Pacific Exchange, and the Philadelphia Stock Exchange. The listing requirements for smaller regional exchanges generally are not as restrictive.

to the NYSE. Table 16–2 shows some examples of the listing requirements for stock markets in the United States.

Assuming that a company qualifies, many people believe that listing is beneficial both to the company and to its stockholders. Listed companies receive a certain amount of free advertising and publicity, and the status as a listed company enhances their prestige and reputation. This might have a beneficial effect on the sales of the firm's products, and it probably is advantageous in terms of lowering the required rate of return on its common stock. Investors respond favorably to increased information, increased liquidity, and confidence that the quoted price is not being manipulated. By providing investors with these benefits in the form of listing their companies' stock, financial managers might lower their firms' costs of capital and increase the value of their stocks.

Regulation of Securities Markets

SECURITIES AND EXCHANGE COMMISSION (SEC)
The U.S. government agency that regulates the issuance and trading of stocks and bonds.

Sales of new securities, as well as operations in the secondary markets, are regulated by the **Securities and Exchange Commission (SEC)** and, to a lesser extent, by each of the 50 states. For the most part, the SEC regulations are intended to (1) ensure investors receive fair financial disclosure from publicly traded companies and (2) discourage fraudulent and misleading behavior by firms' investors, owners, and employees to manipulate stock prices. The primary elements of SEC regulation are as follows:

REGISTRATION STATEMENT
A statement of facts filed with the SEC about a company that plans to issue securities.

1. The SEC has jurisdiction over all interstate offerings of new securities to the general public in amounts of $1.5 million or more. A company wishing to issue new stock must file a **registration statement** that provides financial, legal, and technical information about the company. A **prospectus** that summarizes the information in the registration statement generally is provided to prospective investors for use in selling the securities. SEC lawyers and accountants analyze both the registration statement and the prospectus; if the information is inadequate or misleading, the SEC will delay or stop the public offering.

PROSPECTUS
A document describing a new security issue and the issuing company.

2. The SEC also regulates all national securities exchanges, and companies whose securities are listed on an exchange must file annual reports similar to the registration statement with both the SEC and the exchange.

INSIDERS
Officers, directors, major stockholders, or others who might have inside, or privileged, information on a company's operations.

3. The SEC has control over stock trades by corporate **insiders.** Officers, directors, and major stockholders must file monthly reports of changes in their holdings of the corporation's stock. Any *short-term* profits from such transactions must be handed over to the corporation.
4. The SEC has the power to prohibit manipulation by such devices as pools (aggregations of funds used to affect prices artificially) or wash sales (sales between members of the same group to record artificial transaction prices).
5. The SEC has control over the form of the proxy and the way the company uses it to solicit votes.

MARGIN REQUIREMENTS
The percentage of a security's purchase price that must be deposited by investors.

Control over the flow of credit into securities transactions is exercised by the Board of Governors of the Federal Reserve System. The Fed exercises this control through **margin requirements,** which represent the percentage of the purchase price that must be deposited (invested) by investors—the percentage that can be borrowed is equal to 100 percent less the margin requirement set by the Fed. If a great deal of margin borrowing has been going on, a decline in stock prices can result in inadequate loan coverages, which would force stock brokers to issue **margin calls,** which in turn would require investors either to put up more money or to have their margined stock sold to pay off their loans. Such forced sales would further depress the stock market and could set off a downward spiral, such as the events that took place in October 1987. The margin requirement currently is 50 percent.

MARGIN CALL
A call from a broker asking for more money to support a stock purchase loan.

BLUE SKY LAWS
State laws that prevent the sale of securities that have little or no asset backing.

States also have some control over the issuance of new securities within their boundaries. This control usually is exercised by a "corporation commissioner" or someone with a similar title. State laws relating to securities sales are called **blue sky laws** because they were put into effect to keep unscrupulous promoters from selling securities that offered the "blue sky" but that actually had little or no asset backing.

The securities industry itself realizes the importance of stable markets, sound brokerage firms, and no perception of stock manipulation. Therefore, the various exchanges work closely with the SEC to police transactions on the exchanges and to maintain the integrity and credibility of the system. Similarly, the National Association of Securities Dealers (NASD) cooperates with the SEC to police trading in the OTC market. These industry groups also cooperate with regulatory authorities to set net worth and other standards for securities firms, to develop insurance programs to protect the customers of brokerage houses, and the like.

In general, government regulation of securities trading, as well as industry self-regulation, is designed to ensure that investors receive information that is as accurate as possible, that no one artificially manipulates the market price of a given stock, and that corporate insiders do not take advantage of their position to profit in their companies' stocks at the expense of other stockholders. Neither the SEC, the state regulators, nor the industry itself can prevent investors from making foolish decisions or from having bad luck, but regulators can and do help investors obtain the best data possible for making sound investment decisions.

Self-Test Questions

Differentiate between a closely held corporation and a publicly owned corporation.

Differentiate between a listed stock and an unlisted stock.

Differentiate between the primary and secondary markets.

✳ INDUSTRY PRACTICE

So You Think You Want to Buy an IPO?

We have all heard the stories about initial public offerings (IPOs) that have increased threefold, fourfold, or even more when they first reached the market. In January 1999, for example, MarketWatch.com, a company that provides business news, went public at $17 per share. But its price was pushed up to nearly $120 before the market decided that a price around $97 per share was more appropriate. Think about the one-day return you could have made if you were able to buy MarketWatch.com at the exact time it first went public. Many individual investors do think about such extraordinary returns, and they dream about finding and being able to purchase IPOs like MarketWatch.com. But consider the experience of one individual before you "play the IPO game."

At the end of 1998, Bear Stearns Companies, an investment banker, helped take public theglobe.com, an Internet company that provides Web sites for other companies. The initial price of the IPO was set at $9 per share. The night before the offering, institutional investors subscribed (promised) to purchase 13 times the number of shares available through the IPO—purchase orders totaled more than 40 million shares even though only 3.1 million shares were scheduled to be sold. Clearly, such a large demand would force the price of the IPO to rise significantly once trading started. It did—when the IPO hit the market, the first trade was at $90 per share, ten times the offering price.

After the institutional investors placed their orders to buy large numbers of shares (most were in blocks of more than 10,000 shares), many individual investors placed smaller orders (most were for a few hundred shares). Many of the trades that were placed by the individuals were market buy orders, which instructed brokers to buy at the best possible prices *when the trades reached the stock market.* Unfortunately, most of the individuals placed their orders after the institutional investors; thus, their trades were not executed until after the price of theglobe.com had risen to above $90 per share. One investor, who had placed a market buy order for 500 shares, ended up paying $92 per share, or $46,000, for stock he had hoped to get for a little more than $9 per share, or $4,500. After his order was filled, the investor saw the price of the stock drop to $63.50, and by the time he was able to sell his 500 shares he had lost $20,000. In the end, this investor lost a substantial amount because he acted impulsively—he knew nothing about the company because he had not evaluated its viability as an investment. It seems he had ignored earlier advice from his broker to buy Dell Computer, which later more than tripled in value, so he was anxious to buy a high-tech stock and not "miss the boat" this time. This investor learned a valuable but expensive lesson, which can be summed up with an old cliche: "Look before you leap."

By the way, at the end of August 1999, theglobe.com, which went public November 13, 1998, was selling for about $11.50 per share. Its high price on opening day was $97; thus, the stock price dropped about 88 percent in a little more than nine months. The performance of this IPO was not unique—it was reported that at the end of the year about 80 percent of the 1998 IPOs were selling for less than their initial offering prices.

SOURCE: Aaron Lucchetti, "Web Tide: Initial Public Offerings Aren't the Same in Era of Internet-Stock Mania," *The Wall Street Journal*, January 19, 1999, A1.

Differentiate between a registration statement and a prospectus.

What is the primary purpose of regulating securities trading, whether it is imposed by law or self-imposed?

Financial Instruments in International Markets

For the most part, the financial securities of companies and institutions in other countries are similar to those in the United States. There are some differences, however, which we discuss in this section. Also, financial securities exist that have been created to permit investors easier access to international investments, such as *American Depository Receipts*.

American Depository Receipts

AMERICAN DEPOSITORY RECEIPTS (ADRs)
Certificates representing ownership in stocks of foreign companies, which are held in trust by a bank located in the country the stock is traded.

Foreign companies can be traded internationally through *depository receipts*, which represent shares of the underlying stocks of foreign companies. In the United States, most foreign stock is traded through **American Depository Receipts (ADRs).** ADRs are not foreign stocks; rather they are certificates created by such organizations as banks. The certificates represent ownership in stocks of foreign companies that are held in trust by a bank located in the country where the stock is traded. ADRs provide Americans the ability to invest in foreign companies with less complexity and difficulty than might otherwise be possible. Each ADR certificate represents a certain number of shares of stock of a foreign company, and it entitles the owner to receive any dividends paid by the company in U.S. dollars. In addition, ADRs are traded in the stock markets in the United States, which often are more liquid than foreign markets. All financial information, including values, is denominated in dollars and stated in English; thus, there are no problems with exchange rates and language translations.

In many cases, investors can purchase foreign securities directly. But such investments might be complicated by legal issues, the ability to take funds such as dividends out of the country, and interpretation into domestic terms. Thus, ADRs provide investors the ability to participate in the international financial markets without having to bear risks greater than those associated with the corporations in which the investments are made. The market values of ADRs move in tandem with the market values of the underlying stocks that are held in trust.

Foreign Equity Instruments

The equities of foreign companies are like those of U.S. corporations. The primary difference between stocks of foreign companies and those of American companies is that U.S. regulations provide greater protection of stockholders' rights than those of most other countries. In the international markets, equity generally is referred to as *Euro stock* or *Yankee stock*.

1. *Euro stock* refers to stock that is traded in countries other than the home country of the company, not including the United States. Thus, if the stock of a Japanese company is sold in Germany, it would be considered a Euro stock.
2. *Yankee stock* is stock issued by foreign companies that is traded in the United States. If a Japanese company sold its stock in the United States, it would be called Yankee stock in the international markets.

As the financial markets become more global and more sophisticated, the financial instruments offered both domestically and internationally will change. Already, foreign companies and governments have discovered that financial markets in the United

States provide excellent sources of funds because a great variety of financial outlets exist. As technology improves and regulations that bar or discourage foreign investing are repealed, the financial markets of other developed countries will become more prominent and new, innovative financial products will emerge.

Self-Test Questions

What is a Yankee stock?

What changes do you think will occur in the international markets during the next couple of decades?

The Investment Banking Process

INVESTMENT BANKER
An organization that underwrites and distributes new issues of securities; helps businesses and other entities obtain needed financing.

When a business (or government unit) needs to raise funds in the financial markets, it generally enlists the services of an **investment banker** (see Panel 2 in Figure 2–1). Merrill Lynch, Morgan Stanley Dean Witter, and Goldman Sachs are examples of companies that offer investment banking services. Such organizations (1) help corporations design securities with the features that are most attractive to investors given existing market conditions, (2) buy these securities from the corporations, and (3) then resell them to investors (savers). Although the securities are sold twice, this process really is one primary market transaction, with the investment banker acting as an intermediary (agent) as funds are transferred from savers to businesses.

We should note that investment banking has nothing to do with the traditional banking process as we know it—investment banking deals with the issuance of new securities, not deposits and loans. The major investment banking houses often are divisions of large financial service corporations engaged in a wide range of activities. For example, Merrill Lynch has a brokerage department that operates thousands of offices worldwide, as well as an investment banking department that helps companies issue securities, take over other companies, and the like. Merrill Lynch's brokers sell previously issued stocks as well as stocks that are issued through their investment banking departments. Thus, financial service organizations such as Merrill Lynch sell securities in both the secondary markets and the primary markets.

In this section we describe how securities are issued in the financial markets, and we explain the role of investment bankers in this process.

Raising Capital: Stage I Decisions

The firm itself makes some preliminary decisions on its own, including the following:

1. **Dollars to be raised.** How much new capital do we need?
2. **Type of securities used.** Should stock, bonds, or a combination be used? Further, if stock is to be issued, should it be offered to existing stockholders or sold directly to the general public?
3. **Competitive bid versus negotiated deal.** Should the company simply offer a block of its securities for sale to the highest bidder, or should it sit down with an investment banker and negotiate a deal? These two procedures are called *competitive bids* and *negotiated deals*. Only a handful of the largest firms on the NYSE, whose securities are already well known to the investment banking community,

TABLE 16–3	Largest Underwriters of Debt and Equity in the United States in 1998 (billions of dollars)

RANK	INVESTMENT BANKER	AMOUNT ISSUED	MARKET SHARE
1	Merrill Lynch	$ 304.1	16.7%
2	Salomon Smith Barney	225.1	12.4
3	Morgan Stanley Dean Witter	203.3	11.2
4	Goldman Sachs	191.7	10.5
5	Lehman Brothers	147.2	8.1
6	Credit Suisse First Boston	126.9	7.0
7	J. P. Morgan	89.0	4.9
8	Bear Sterns	83.2	4.6
9	Chase Manhattan	70.9	3.9
10	Donaldson, Lufkin, & Jenrette	60.6	3.3
	Others	318.3	17.5
	Total	$1,820.3	100.0%

NOTE: Rankings are based on the dollar volume of underwritings by U.S. firms managed during 1998.

SOURCE: Patrick McGeehan, "Heavyweights of Wall Street Capture Lion's Share Underwriting Fees, as Markets Take Fractious Turn," *The Wall Street Journal*, January 4, 1999, R39.

are in a position to use the competitive bid process. The investment banks would have to do a large amount of investigative work in order to bid on an issue unless they were already quite familiar with the firm, and the costs involved would be too high to make it worthwhile unless the investment bank was sure of getting the deal. Therefore, the vast majority of offerings of stocks or bonds are made on a negotiated basis.

4. **Selection of an investment banker.** Assuming the issue is to be negotiated, which investment banker should the firm use? Older firms that have "been to market" before will already have established a relationship with an investment banker, although it is easy enough to change investment bankers if the firm is dissatisfied. However, a firm that is just going public will have to choose an investment bank, and different investment banking houses are better suited for different companies. The older, larger "establishment houses" like Morgan Stanley Dean Witter deal mainly with large companies like AT&T, IBM, and Exxon. Other investment bankers specialize in more speculative issues like initial public offerings. Table 16–3 lists in ranked order the top ten investment bankers in 1998, as measured by the dollar amount of securities underwritten.

Raising Capital: Stage II Decisions

Stage II decisions, which are made jointly by the firm and its selected investment banker, include the following:

1. **Reevaluating the initial decisions.** The firm and its investment banker will reevaluate the initial decisions about the size of the issue and the type of securities to use. For example, the firm initially might have decided to raise $50 million

by selling common stock, but the investment banker might convince management that it would be better off, in view of current market conditions, to limit the stock issue to $25 million and to raise the other $25 million as debt.

UNDERWRITTEN ARRANGEMENT
Agreement for the sale of securities in which the investment bank guarantees the sale by purchasing the securities from the issuer, thus agreeing to bear any risks involved in the transaction.

2. **Best efforts or underwritten issues.** The firm and its investment banker must decide whether the investment banker will work on a best efforts basis or underwrite the issue. In an **underwritten arrangement,** the investment banker generally assures the company that the entire issue will be sold, so the investment banker bears significant risks in such an offering. With this type of arrangement, the investment banking firm typically buys the securities from the issuing firm and then sells the securities in the primary markets, hoping to make a profit. In a **best efforts arrangement,** the investment banker does not guarantee that the securities will be sold or that the company will get the cash it needs. With this type of arrangement, the investment banker does not buy the securities from the issuing firm; rather the securities are handled on a contingency basis, and the investment banker is paid a commission based on the amount of the issue that is sold. The investment banker essentially promises to exert its *best efforts* when selling the securities. With a *best efforts arrangement,* the issuing firm takes the chance the entire issue will not be sold and that all the needed funds will not be raised. For example, the very day IBM signed an *underwritten* agreement to sell $1 billion of bonds in 1979, interest rates rose sharply, and bond prices fell. IBM's investment bankers lost somewhere between $10 million and $20 million. Had the offering been on a best efforts basis, IBM would have been the loser.

BEST EFFORTS ARRANGEMENT
Agreement for the sale of securities in which the investment bank handling the transaction gives no guarantee that the securities will be sold.

3. **Issuance costs.** The investment banker's fee must be negotiated, and the firm also must estimate the other expenses it will incur in connection with the issue—lawyers' fees, accountants' costs, printing and engraving, and so on. Usually, the investment banker will buy the issue from the company at a discount below the price at which the securities are to be offered to the public, and this **underwriter's spread** covers the investment banker's costs and provides a profit.

UNDERWRITER'S SPREAD
The difference between the price at which the investment banking firm buys an issue from a company and the price at which the securities are sold in the primary market; it represents the investment banker's gross profit on the issue.

Table 16–4 gives an indication of the **flotation costs** associated with public issues of bonds, preferred stock, and common stock. As the table shows, costs as a percentage of the proceeds are higher for stocks than for bonds, and costs are also higher for small issues than for large issues. The relationship between size of issue and flotation costs is primarily due to the existence of fixed costs: certain costs must be incurred regardless of the size of the issue, so the percentage flotation cost is quite high for small issues.

FLOTATION COSTS
The costs associated with issuing new stocks or bonds.

4. **Setting the offering price.** If the company already is publicly owned, the **offering price** will be based on the existing market price of the stock or the yield on the bonds. For common stock, the most typical arrangement calls for the investment banker to buy the securities at a prescribed number of points below the closing price on the last day of registration. For example, on July 1, 2000, the stock of Unilate Textiles had a current price of $23, and it had traded between $20 and $25 a share during the previous three months. Unilate and its underwriter agreed that the investment banker would buy 5 million new shares at $1 below the closing price on the last day of registration, which was expected to be in early October. The stock actually closed at $20.50 on the day the SEC released the issue, so the company received $19.50 a share. The shares then were sold to the public at a price of $20.50. As is typical, Unilate's agreement had an escape clause that provided for the contract to be voided if the price of the stock had fallen below a predetermined figure. In the illustrative case, this "upset"

OFFERING PRICE
The price at which common stock is sold to the public.

TABLE 16–4 Costs of Flotation for Underwritten, Nonrights Offerings (Expressed as a Percentage of Gross Proceeds)

SIZE OF ISSUE (MILLIONS OF DOLLARS)	BONDS			PREFERRED STOCK			COMMON STOCK		
	UNDERWRITING COMMISSION	OTHER EXPENSES	TOTAL COSTS	UNDERWRITING COMMISSION	OTHER EXPENSES	TOTAL COSTS	UNDERWRITING COMMISSION	OTHER EXPENSES	TOTAL COSTS
Under 1.0	10.0%	4.0%	14.0%	—	—	—	13.0%	9.0%	22.0%
1.0–1.9	8.0	3.0	11.0	—	—	—	11.0	5.9	16.9
2.0–4.9	4.0	2.2	6.2	—	—	—	8.6	3.8	12.4
5.0–9.9	2.4	0.8	3.2	1.9%	0.7%	2.6%	6.3	1.9	8.2
10.0–19.9	1.2	0.7	1.9	1.4	0.4	1.8	5.1	0.9	6.0
20.0–49.9	1.0	0.4	1.4	1.4	0.3	1.7	4.1	0.5	4.6
50.0 and over	0.9	0.2	1.1	1.4	0.2	1.6	3.3	0.2	3.5

NOTES:

1. Small issues of preferred are rare, so no data on preferred issues below $5 million are given.

2. Flotation costs tend to rise somewhat when interest rates are cyclically high because when money is in relatively tight supply, the investment bankers will have a more difficult time placing issues with permanent investors. Thus, the figures shown in the table represent averages, and actual flotation costs vary somewhat over time.

SOURCES: Securities and Exchange Commission, *Cost of Flotation of Registered Equity Issues*, Washington, DC: U.S. Government Printing Office, December 1974; Richard H. Pettway, "A Note on the Flotation Costs of New Equity Capital Issues of Electric Companies," *Public Utilities Fortnightly*, March 18, 1982; Robert Hansen, "Evaluating the Costs of a New Equity Issue," *Midland Corporate Finance Journal*, Spring 1986; and informal surveys of common stock, preferred stock, and bond issues conducted by the authors.

price was set at $18.50 a share. Thus, if the closing price of the shares on the last day of registration had been $18, Unilate would have had the option of withdrawing from the agreement.

Investment bankers have an easier job if an issue is priced relatively low, but the issuer of the securities naturally wants as high a price as possible. Therefore, an inherent conflict of interest on price exists between the investment banker and the issuer. However, if the issuer is financially sophisticated and makes comparisons with similar security issues, the investment banker will be forced to price close to the market.

It is important to note that *if pressure from the new shares drives down the price of the stock, all shares outstanding, not just the new shares, will be affected.* Thus, if Unilate's stock fell from $23 to $20.50 as a result of the financing, and if the price remained at that new level, the company would incur a loss of $2.50 on each of the 25 million shares previously outstanding, or a total market value loss of $62.5 million. In a sense, that loss would be a *flotation cost* because it would be a cost associated with the new issue. However, if the company's prospects really were poorer than investors had thought, then most of the price decline eventually would have occurred anyway. On the other hand, if the company's prospects are not really all that bad (if the signal was incorrect), then over time Unilate's stock price would increase, and the company would not suffer a permanent loss of $62.5 million.

If the company is going public for the first time, it will have no established price (or demand curve), so the investment bankers will have to estimate the equilibrium price at which the stock will sell after issue. Both the Small Business box and Problem 16–2 at the end of this chapter illustrate in some detail the process involved. If the offering price is set below the true equilibrium price, the stock will rise sharply after issue, and the company and its original stockholders will have given away too many shares to raise the required capital. If the offering price is set above the true equilibrium price, either the issue will fail or, if the investment bankers succeed in selling the stock, their investment clients will be unhappy when the stock subsequently falls to its equilibrium level. Therefore, it is important that the equilibrium price be approximated as closely as possible.

Selling Procedures

Once the company and its investment bankers have decided how much money to raise, the type of securities to issue, and the basis for pricing the issue, they will prepare and file a registration statement and prospectus with the SEC. It generally takes about 20 days for the issue to be approved by the SEC. The final price of the stock (or the interest rate on a bond issue) is set at the close of business the day the issue clears the SEC, and the securities are then offered to the public the following day.

Investment bankers must pay the issuing firm within four days of the time the offering officially begins, so, typically, the investment bankers sell the stock within a day or two after the offering begins. But, on occasion investment bankers miscalculate, set the offering price too high, and are unable to move the issue. Similarly, the market might decline during the offering period, which again would force the investment bankers to reduce the price of the stock. In either instance, on an underwritten offering the firm would still receive the price that was agreed upon, and the investment bankers would have to absorb any losses that were incurred.

UNDERWRITING SYNDICATE
A syndicate of investment firms formed to spread the risk associated with the purchase and distribution of a new issue of securities.

LEAD, OR MANAGING, UNDERWRITER
The member of an underwriting syndicate that actually *manages* the distribution and sale of a new security offering.

SELLING GROUP
A group (network) of brokerage firms formed for the purpose of distributing a new issue of securities.

SHELF REGISTRATION
Securities are registered with the SEC for sale at a later date; the securities are held "on the shelf" until the sale.

Because they are exposed to large potential losses, investment bankers typically do not handle the purchase and distribution of an issue single-handedly unless it is a very small one. If the amount of money involved is large and the risk of price fluctuations substantial, an investment banker forms an **underwriting syndicate** in an effort to minimize the amount of risk each one carries. The investment banking house that sets up the deal is called the **lead,** or **managing, underwriter.**

In addition to the underwriting syndicate, on larger offerings still more investment bankers are included in a **selling group,** which handles the distribution of securities to individual investors. The selling group includes all members of the underwriting syndicate plus additional dealers who take relatively small participations (or shares of the total issue) from the syndicate members. Members of the selling group act as selling agents and receive commissions for their efforts—they do not purchase the securities, so they do not bear the same risks the underwriting syndicate does. Thus, the underwriters act as wholesalers and bear the risks associated with the issue, whereas members of the selling group act as retailers. The number of investment banking houses in a selling group depends partly on the size of the issue; for example, the one set up when Communications Satellite Corporation (Comsat) went public consisted of 385 members.

Shelf Registrations

The selling procedures described previously, including the 20-day minimum waiting period between registration with the SEC and sale of the issue, apply to most security sales. However, large, well-known public companies that issue securities frequently might file a master registration statement with the SEC and then update it with a short-form statement just prior to each individual offering. In such a case, a company could decide at 10 A.M. to sell registered securities and have the sale completed before noon. This procedure is known as **shelf registration** because in effect the company puts its new securities "on the shelf" and then sells them to investors when it thinks the market is right.

Maintenance of the Secondary Market

In the case of a large, established firm like General Motors, the investment banking firm's job is finished once it has disposed of the stock and turned the net proceeds over to the company. However, when a company is going public for the first time, the investment banker is under an obligation to maintain a market for the shares after the issue has been completed. Such stocks typically are traded in the over-the-counter market, and the lead underwriter generally agrees to "make a market" in the stock and to keep it reasonably liquid. The company wants a good market to exist for its stock, as do its stockholders. Therefore, if the investment banking house wants to do business with the company in the future, to keep its own brokerage customers happy, and to have future referral business, it will hold an inventory of the shares and help to maintain an active secondary market in the stock.

Self-Test Questions

What is the sequence of events when a firm decides to issue new securities?

What type of firm would use a shelf registration? Explain.

What is an underwriting syndicate, and why is it important in the investment banking process?

Emerging Trends

The Depository Institutions Deregulation and Monetary Control Act of 1980 had the desirable effect of increasing competition among financial institutions, which benefited both savers and borrowers, and it also slowed the decline of U.S. banks in the world markets. However, the act had several serious shortcomings, and at the time this text is being written, the financial services industry is undergoing some significant changes. In particular, limited branch banking recently has been introduced, and Congress currently is very close to repealing the Glass-Steagall Act, which prohibits commercial banks from engaging in investment banking practices.

It is unclear how the final legislation will shape up, but it is likely that U.S. banks will gain new powers to engage in security underwritings and that branching powers will be extended. However, only the strongest banks will be given these expanded powers. The result is likely to be a system of larger, stronger, and more diversified banks, yet more competition probably will exist in our financial markets. Evidence of this trend has been manifested through the merger frenzy that has occurred in the banking industry during the past few years.

Self-Test Questions

What are some important new developments that are taking place in the financial markets?

✳ ETHICAL DILEMMA

It's a "Painful" Decision—By George!

George Anderson works as an analyst for Roberts, Stephens, and Kilmer (RSK), one of the largest investment banking firms in the United States. His primary job is to analyze initial public offerings (IPOs) planned by firms that want to "go public" to determine the viability of such stock issues. RSK relies on Anderson's evaluations when negotiating with companies that want to enter the markets with IPOs, which can be very risky propositions for investment bankers.

RSK currently is handling the IPO of BioPharm, a pharmaceutical company based in Oregon. Created by a brilliant biochemist named Henry Scott, the company has developed and marketed a number of new drugs since its start in 1985. George Anderson's evaluation of BioPharm indicates that the potential for the company is tremendous, especially if its

newest drug, which offers a cure for arthritis, is approved by the Food and Drug Administration (FDA). According to Anderson's report, BioPharm has a very bright future even if the FDA does not approve the arthritis drug. BioPharm's IPO is scheduled to go to the market tomorrow at a price of $20 per share.

This morning, when he got to work and turned on his computer, Anderson discovered he had a number of E-mail messages marked urgent. The messages were sent by Rachel Raymond, a newspaper reporter from Washington, D.C., who specializes in articles about medical issues, including physician care, surgical practices, and pharmaceutical research and development. In essence, the messages indicated that an unidentified source told Raymond that within the next few days the FDA will announce BioPharm's

continues

arthritis treatment has been rejected. Anderson's repeated attempts to contact Raymond about her E-mail messages have been unsuccessful.

Because he could not get in touch with Raymond, Anderson has made inquiries throughout the day to determine the validity of Raymond's messages. The only information he has been able to verify is that William Mezina, CEO of BioPharm, has sold a significant portion of his stock holdings in the company during the past few days. Attempts to corroborate the content of Raymond's messages proved futile—sources at the FDA will not comment, and a flash fire at BioPharm has temporarily interrupted its communications systems.

At this point Anderson is beside himself because the BioPharm IPO is supposed to be distributed when the markets open tomorrow. RSK has invested considerable funds to get the IPO ready for its introduction tomorrow, and withholding the issue would cost the firm a substantial amount. But if RSK goes ahead with the issue as planned and, within a few days or weeks, the FDA announces the arthritis drug has been rejected, the per price of BioPharm's IPO certainly will plunge significantly. Even worse, if later it can be proven that RSK knew about the FDA's rejection of the arthritis drug, there could be future legal ramifications because withholding such information from stockholders might be considered fraud. What should Anderson do? Should he try to delay the IPO, even though the content of Raymond's messages is unfounded at this time?

Summary

This chapter is more descriptive than analytical, but a knowledge of the issues discussed here is essential to an understanding of finance. The key concepts covered are listed here:

- **Stockholders' equity** consists of the firm's common stock, paid-in capital (funds received in excess of the par value), and retained earnings (earnings not paid out as dividends).
- **Book value per share** is equal to stockholders' equity divided by the number of shares of stock outstanding. A stock's book value often is different from its par value and its market value.
- A **proxy** is a document that gives one person the power to act for another person, typically the power to vote shares of common stock. A **proxy fight** occurs when an outside group solicits stockholders' proxies in order to vote a new management team into office.
- Stockholders often have the right to purchase any additional shares sold by the firm. This right, called the **preemptive right,** protects the control of the present stockholders and prevents dilution of the value of their stock.
- The major **advantages of common stock financing** are as follows: (1) there is no obligation to make fixed payments; (2) common stock never matures; (3) the use of common stock increases the creditworthiness of the firm; and (4) stock often can be sold on better terms than debt.
- The major **disadvantages of common stock financing** are (1) it extends voting privileges to new stockholders; (2) new stockholders share in the firm's profits; (3) the costs of stock financing are high; (4) using stock can raise the firm's cost of capital; and (5) dividends paid on common stock are not tax deductible.
- A **closely held corporation** is one that is owned by a few individuals who typically are associated with the firm's management. A **publicly owned corporation** is one that is owned by a relatively large number of individuals who are not actively involved in its management.

- **Going public** facilitates stockholder diversification, increases liquidity of the firm's stock, makes it easier for the firm to raise capital, and establishes a value for the firm. However, reporting costs are high, operating data must be disclosed, and public ownership might make it harder for management to maintain control of the firm.
- Security markets are regulated by the **Securities and Exchange Commission (SEC).**
- Financial instruments available in the international markets are similar to those issued in the United States. But most Americans invest in foreign companies through **American Depository Receipts (ADRs),** which are certificates that represent foreign stocks held in trust, generally by a bank, in the country where the company is located.
- Stock traded internationally generally is referred to as either *Euro stock* or *Yankee Stock.* **Euro stock** is traded in countries other than the country where the company is located, except the United States, where such stock is called **Yankee stock.**
- An **investment banker** assists in the issuing of securities by helping the firm determine the size of the issue and the type of securities to be used, by establishing the selling price, by selling the issue, and, in some cases, by maintaining an after-market for the stock.
- A *small firm's stock* sold in an **initial public offering (IPO)** often increases in price immediately after issue, with the largest price increases being associated with issues where uncertainties are greatest.

✴ SMALL BUSINESS

Why Go Public for Less Than You're Worth?

For many entrepreneurs, making an initial public offering (IPO) of their company's equity is a dream come true. After years of sacrifice and hard work, the company finally is a success. The value of that sacrifice is realized by going public. Many observers are amazed that the successful entrepreneur appears willing to sell equity in his or her firm for too little money—on average, IPOs are *underpriced.*

Stocks are underpriced if they begin trading in the public markets at a price that is higher than the offering price. An example would be a stock that was sold in an IPO for $12 that begins trading immediately after the IPO for $15 to $20 per share.

This underpricing is a puzzle. The company going public, and any current shareholders of the privately owned firm who are selling as part of the public offering, receive, on average, the IPO price minus a commission or "discount" of roughly eight percent. Even if the shareholders do not sell any of their own shares in the IPO, but instead sell only the company's shares, they still are hurt by underpricing because their own-

ership in the firm is diluted more than it would have been had the shares been fully priced.

The large returns of IPOs in the public market are not caused by the companies' performance after the IPOs. They do not mean that the firms showed high earnings growth after the IPOs—the higher returns generally occur on the *first trading day.* This simply means that the IPO securities were sold at a price below their value.

Why would issuers in IPOs (i.e., selling companies) willingly sell their stocks for less than their true value? There are a number of theories to explain underpricing, but there is no widespread consensus on the reasons for underpricing. Some possible explanations are described next.

One explanation for underpricing is that the issuing companies' owners are not as knowledgeable as their underwriters; if owners have the same knowledge as underwriters, issues would be fully priced. This theory might explain some occurrences of underpricing, such as isolated instances in which an unethical underwriter

continues

(who presumably would not last long in the business) knowingly misinforms the issuer. However, some underwriters themselves have gone public, acting as their own underwriters, and they also have had substantial first-day returns due to underpricing.

A popular theory among academicians is that underpricing occurs to keep *uninformed* investors in the market. According to this theory, there are some well-informed investors who regularly watch the IPO market to identify those that are mispriced. These *informed* investors, therefore, buy only the underpriced issues. However, such informed investors do not have enough capital to buy all of the shares of any offering. On the other hand, uninformed investors tend to buy every IPO, believing significant returns will be realized. Thus, uninformed investors tend to buy a lot of stock in the overpriced or correctly priced offerings, but will obtain only a small portion of the offerings in which the informed investors are active. And unless the set of all offerings is underpriced on average, then uninformed investors would consistently lose money, they would leave the market, and the market would break down. Thus, this theory argues, the IPO market must experience general underpricing to function. Early empirical evidence is consistent with this theory.

The most popular theory with underwriters and venture capitalists is what might be called the "good taste in the mouth" theory. According to this theory, if the company underprices its issue in an IPO, investors will be more receptive to future "seasoned" issues from the same firm. Note, too, that most IPOs involve only ten to 20 percent of the stock, so the original owners still have 80 to 90 percent of the shares.

All of these theories have a similar implication: An IPO with less uncertainty concerning its value will tend to be more fully priced. This suggests that firms can prepare themselves for public offerings at higher prices by using more prestigious underwriters to issue IPOs, using reputable, visible accountants for their audits, and acquiring venture capital investment from more reputable capitalists.

The phenomenon of underpricing IPO shares remains a puzzle to finance academicians. We think we have some of the answers, but the questions are not yet settled. Meanwhile, an issuer should be aware that most IPOs are underpriced by a meaningful amount and that this underpricing is almost certainly related to the risk and uncertainty of the business. This is important information to consider when deciding when the firm should make its initial public offering.

Questions

16–1 Examine Table 16–1. Suppose Unilate Textiles sold 2 million shares, with the company netting $25 per share. Construct a statement of the equity accounts to reflect this sale.

16–2 The SEC attempts to protect investors who are purchasing newly issued securities by requiring issuers to provide relevant financial information to prospective investors. However, the SEC does not provide an opinion about the real value of the securities; hence, an investor might pay too much for some stock and consequently lose heavily. Do you think the SEC should, as a part of every new stock or bond offering, render an opinion to investors on the proper value of the securities being offered? Explain.

16–3 How do you think each of the following items would affect a company's ability to attract new capital and the flotation (issuing) costs involved in doing so?
  a. A decision to list a company's stock; the stock now trades in the over-the-counter market.
  b. A decision of a privately held company to go public.
  c. The increasing importance of institutions in the stock and bond markets.

    d. The trend toward financial conglomerates as opposed to stand-alone investment banking houses.

    e. Elimination of the preemptive right.

    f. The introduction of shelf registrations.

16–4 Before entering a formal agreement, investment bankers carefully investigate the companies whose securities they underwrite; this is especially true of the issues of firms going public for the first time. Because the bankers do not themselves plan to hold the securities but intend to sell them to others as soon as possible, why are they so concerned about making careful investigations?

16–5 It frequently is stated that the primary purpose of the preemptive right is to allow individuals to maintain their proportionate share of the ownership and control of a corporation.

    a. How important do you suppose this consideration is for the average stockholder of a firm whose shares are traded on the New York or American Stock Exchanges?

    b. Is the preemptive right likely to be of more importance to stockholders of publicly owned or closely held firms? Explain.

16–6 Why would management be interested in getting a wider distribution of its shares?

Self-Test Problem

key terms **ST–1** Define each of the following terms:

    a. Common equity; paid-in capital; retained earnings

    b. Par value; book value per share; market value per share

    c. Proxy; proxy fight; takeover

    d. Preemptive right

    e. Classified stock; founders' shares

    f. Closely held corporation; publicly owned corporation

    g. Over-the-counter (OTC) market; organized security exchange

    h. Primary market; secondary market

    i. Going public; new issue market; initial public offering (IPO)

    j. Securities and Exchange Commission (SEC); registration statement; shelf registration; blue sky laws; margin requirements; margin call; insiders

    k. Prospectus

    l. Best efforts arrangement; underwritten arrangement

    m. Underwriters' spread; flotation costs; offering price

    n. Underwriting syndicate; lead, or managing, underwriter; selling group

Problems

profit (loss) on a new stock issue **16–1** Security Brokers Inc. specializes in underwriting new issues by small firms. On a recent offering of Barenbaum Inc., the terms were as follows:

Price to public	$7.50 per share
Number of shares	3 million
Proceeds to Barenbaum	$21,000,000

The out-of-pocket expenses incurred by Security Brokers in the design and distribution of the issue were $450,000. What profit or loss would Security Brokers incur if the issue were sold to the public at an average price of

a. $7.50 per share?

b. $9.00 per share?

c. $6.00 per share?

setting the price of a new   **16-2** U-Fix-It, a small home improvement building supplier, has been successful and
issue of stock   has enjoyed a good growth trend. Now U-Fix-It is planning to go public with an issue of common stock, and it faces the problem of setting an appropriate price on the stock. The company's management and its investment bankers believe that the proper procedure is to select several similar firms with publicly traded common stock and to make relevant comparisons.

Several home improvement building suppliers are reasonably similar to U-Fix-It with respect to product mix, size, asset composition, and debt/equity proportions. Of these companies, Home Headquarters and Lows are most similar. When analyzing the following data, assume that 1995 and 2000 were reasonably normal years for all three companies—that is, these years were neither especially good nor especially bad in terms of sales, earnings, and dividends. At the time of the analysis, the risk-free rate, k_{RF}, was ten percent and the market rate, k_M, was 15 percent. Home Headquarters is listed on the AMEX and Lows on the NYSE, while U-Fix-It will be traded in the OTC market.

	HOME HEADQUARTERS	LOWS	U-FIX-IT (TOTALS)
Earnings per share			
2000	$ 3.60	$ 6.00	$ 960,000
1995	2.40	4.40	652,800
Price per share			
2000	$28.80	$52.00	—
Dividends per share			
2000	$ 1.80	$ 3.00	$ 480,000
1995	1.20	2.20	336,000
Book value per share, 2000	$24.00	$44.00	$7,200,000
Market/book ratio, 2000	120%	118%	—
Total assets, 2000	$22.4 million	$ 65.6 million	$16.0 million
Total debt, 2000	$ 9.6 million	$ 24.0 million	$ 8.8 million
Sales, 2000	$32.8 million	$112.0 million	$29.6 million

a. Assume that U-Fix-It has 100 shares of stock outstanding. Use this information to calculate earnings per share (EPS), dividends per share (DPS), and book value per share for U-Fix-It. (*Hint:* U-Fix-It's 2000 EPS = $9,600.)

b. Calculate earnings and dividend growth rates for the three companies. (*Hint:* U-Fix-It's EPS g is 8%.)

c. On the basis of your answer to part a, do you think U-Fix-It's stock would sell at a price in the same ballpark as that of Home Headquarters and Lows—that is, in the range of $25 to $100 per share?

d. Assuming that U-Fix-It's management can split the stock so that the 100 shares could be changed to 1,000 shares, 100,000 shares, or any other number, would such an action make sense in this case? Why?

e. Now assume that U-Fix-It did split its stock and has 400,000 shares. Calculate new values for EPS, DPS, and book value per share. (*Hint:* U-Fix-It's new 2000 EPS is $2.40.)

f. Return on equity (ROE) can be measured as EPS/book value per share or as total earnings/total equity. Calculate ROEs for the three companies for 2000. (*Hint:* U-Fix-It's 2000 ROE = 13.3%.)

g. Calculate dividend payout ratios for the three companies. (*Hint:* U-Fix-It's 2000 payout ratio is 50%.)

h. Calculate debt/total assets ratios for the three companies. (*Hint:* U-Fix-It's 2000 debt ratio is 55%.)

i. Calculate the P/E ratios for Home Headquarters and Lows based on 2000 data. Are these P/E ratios reasonable in view of relative growth, payout, and ROE data? If not, what other factors might explain them? (*Hint:* Home Headquarters' P/E = 8×.)

j. Now determine a range of values for U-Fix-It's stock price, with 400,000 shares outstanding, by applying Home Headquarters' and Lows' P/E ratios, price/dividends ratios, and price/book value ratios to your data for U-Fix-It. For example, one possible price for U-Fix-It's stock is (P/E Home Headquarters) × (EPS U-Fix-It) = 8 × $2.40 = $19.20 per share. Similar calculations would produce a range of prices based on both Home Headquarters' and Lows's data. (*Hint:* Our range was $19.20 to $21.60.)

k. Using the equation $k_s = \hat{D}_1/P_0 + g$, find approximate k_s values for Home Headquarters and Lows. Then use these values in the constant growth stock price model to find a price for U-Fix-It's stock. (Hint: We averaged the EPS and DPS g's for U-Fix-It.)

l. At what price do you think U-Fix-It's shares should be offered to the public? You will want to select a price that will be low enough to induce investors to buy the stock but not so low that it will rise too sharply immediately after it is issued. Think about relative growth rates, ROEs, dividend yields, and total returns ($k_s = \hat{D}_1/P_0 + g$).

Exam-Type Problems

The problems included in this section are set up in such a way that they could be used as multiple-choice exam problems.

book value per share   **16–3** Atlantic Coast Resources Company had the following balance sheet at the end of 2000:

ATLANTIC COAST RESOURCES COMPANY:
BALANCE SHEET DECEMBER 31, 2000

		Accounts payable	$ 64,400
		Notes payable	71,400
		Long-term debt	151,200
		Common stock	
		(30,000 authorized	
		20,000 shares outstanding)	364,000
		Retained earnings	336,000
Total assets	$987,000	Total liabilities and equity	$987,000

a. What is the book value per share of Atlantic's common stock?

b. Suppose the firm sold the remaining authorized shares and netted $32.55 per share from the sale. What would be the new book value per share?

underwriting and flotation expenses

16–4 The Taussig Company, whose stock price now is $30, needs to raise $15 million in common stock. Underwriters have informed Taussig's management that it must price the new issue to the public at $27.53 per share to ensure the shares will be sold. The underwriters' compensation will be seven percent of the issue price, so Taussig will net $25.60 per share. Taussig will also incur expenses in the amount of $360,000. How many shares must Taussig sell to net $15 million after underwriting and flotation expenses?

Integrative Problem

investment banking process

16–5 Gonzales Food Stores, a family-owned grocery store chain headquartered in El Paso, is considering a major expansion. The proposed expansion would require Gonzales to raise $10 million in additional capital. Because Gonzales currently has a debt ratio of 50 percent, and because the family members already have all their funds tied up in the business, the owners cannot supply any additional equity, so the company will have to sell stock to the public. However, the family wants to ensure that they retain control of the company. This would be Gonzales's first stock sale, and the owners are not sure just what would be involved. Therefore, they have asked you to research the process and to help them decide exactly how to raise the needed capital. In doing so, you should answer the following questions:

a. What are the advantages to Gonzales of financing with stock rather than bonds? What are the disadvantages of using stock?

b. Is the stock of Gonzales Food Stores currently publicly held or privately owned? Would this situation change if the stock sale were made?

c. What is classified stock? Would there be any advantage to Gonzales of designating the stock currently outstanding as "founders' shares"? What type of common stock should Gonzales sell to the public to allow the family to retain control of the business?

d. What does the term "going public" mean? What would be the advantages to the Gonzales family of having the firm go public? What would be the disadvantages?

e. What does the term "listed stock" mean? Do you think that Gonzales's stock would be listed shortly after the company goes public? If not, where would the stock trade?

f. Suppose the firm has decided to issue $10 million of Class B nonvoting stock. Now Gonzales must select an investment banker. Do you think it should select an investment banker on the basis of a competitive bid or do a negotiated deal? Explain.

g. Without doing any calculations, briefly describe of the procedures by which Gonzales and its investment banker will determine the price at which the stock will be offered to the public.

h. What is a prospectus? Why does the SEC require all firms to file registration statements and distribute prospectuses to potential stockholders before selling stock?

i. If Gonzales goes public and sells shares that the public buys at a price of $10 per share, what will be the approximate percentage cost, including both underwriting costs and other costs? Assume the company sells 1.5 million shares. Would the cost be higher or lower if the company were already publicly owned?

j. Would you recommend that Gonzales have the issue underwritten or sold on a best efforts basis? Why? What would be the difference in costs between the two procedures?

k. If some of the Gonzales family members wanted to sell some of their own shares in order to diversify at the same time the company was selling new shares to raise expansion capital, would this be feasible?

ONLINE ESSENTIALS

http://www.investorville.com   investorville
Provides information about various investment topics, including initial public offerings (IPOs), companies' earnings, research results, and so forth. This site also has an investment forum that allows participants to ask and answer questions about investing. In addition, links to related sites are provided.

http://www.secinfo.com   SEC InfoSM Securities Information
Provides information about filings with the Securities and Exchange Commission (SEC), including various financial reports, IPOs, insider trading, and so forth. There are also a variety of reports, including bankruptcy, stock sales, and financial statements, available at this site.

http://www.financialweb.com/Editorial/stockdetective   Stock Detective
This site has a great deal of information, as well as links to other sites with related information, about investments dealing primarily with stocks. You can view the "Stinky Stocks Roundup," which recommends stock that should be avoided. You can also get investment research, news reports, and so on.

http://www.ipo.com   IPO.com
Gives news, pricings, and other information about the most recent IPOs. This site also has "IPO Frequently Asked Questions" and "IPO Glossary" pages that provide basic information about the IPO process.

http://finance.yahoo.com   Yahoo!.finance
A variety of investment and financial information is available at this site. You can find research data related to earnings surprises, SEC filings, financial statements, stock splits, and so on. In addition, there are chat rooms and investment-related news articles at this location.

CHAPTER 17

Long-Term Debt

A MANAGERIAL PERSPECTIVE

During the past couple of decades, the use of debt has increased significantly in all sectors of the economy—households, businesses, and governments. The increase in business debt has been attributed primarily to the merger and acquisition frenzy that occurred in the 1980s, especially prior to 1989. Much of the merger activity was financed with debt, and some firms even "leveraged up" to make themselves less attractive takeover targets. Consequently, the average debt ratio of companies increased significantly during this era. In 1980, the average firm was financed with about 43 percent debt; by 1989, the debt ratio was more than 57 percent. The greatest increases in the issuance of corporate debt occurred from 1984 through 1988, which was also the period when there was an unprecedented number of mergers and acquisitions. Debt financing was attractive during this period because, compared to the period from 1979 to 1983, interest rates had decreased considerably and remained relatively stable.

As a result of the leveraging activity that occurred in the 1980s, more stock was taken out of the capital market than was put back in through new issues. From 1984 to 1990, a net $640 billion of stock was replaced by debt; nearly $200 billion, 7.5 percent of the outstanding equity at the time, was retired in the fourth quarter of 1988.

In the latter part of 1989, economic growth started to slow and firms began to "deleverage." The burden of servicing high amounts of debt motivated many firms to improve their cash flow positions. Stock repurchases slowed, while new stock issues increased—in 1991 and 1992 new stock issues exceeded repurchases by an average of more than $20 billion per year. Unfortunately, at this pace, it would take almost 30 years to recover the amount of equity that was converted into debt in the 1980s.

Debt ratios of companies have decreased somewhat during the 1990s, but the deleveraging effort has not significantly changed the overall debt position of the business sector. Many firms found that lower interest rates in the 1990s, especially in 1993, have helped them to reduce interest payments substantially through refinancing, which obviates the need to replace debt entirely—experts estimate that refinancing with cheaper debt has reduced annual interest on all business debt by as much as $35 billion per year. And in 1994, stocks performed poorly, making them less attractive for raising funds and more attractive for firms to repurchase. In fact, 1994 stock buybacks were the highest since the record-setting activity of the late 1980s. Although there was more money raised in the capital markets in 1998 than in any year previously, most of the activity was in the debt markets. Of the nearly $2 trillion worth of stock and bonds that were issued, more than 55 percent was debt. In fact, debt sales in 1998 reached a record. At the same time, the amount of equity decreased by more than $175 billion due to stock buybacks and corporate mergers.

continues

From recent events it appears that businesses in the United States have started to "releverage." It is unclear which direction firms will go in the future, but merger and acquisition activity is on the increase once again, and this will help sustain the current releveraging movement. In any event, it appears that many companies will experience increasing debt ratios and be saddled with servicing large amounts of debt for some time in the future. As you read this chapter, consider the positive and negative effects of debt on both businesses and our economy. ■

Different groups of investors prefer different types of securities, and investors' tastes change over time. Thus, astute financial managers offer a variety of securities, and they package their new security offerings at each point in time to appeal to the greatest possible number of potential investors. In this chapter, we consider the various types of long-term debt available to financial managers.

FUNDED DEBT
Long-term debt; "funding" means replacing short-term debt with securities of longer maturity.

Long-term debt is often called **funded debt.** When a firm "funds" its short-term debt, this means that it replaces short-term debt with securities of longer maturity. Funding does not imply that the firm places money with a trustee or other repository; it is simply part of the jargon of finance, and it means that the firm replaces short-term debt with permanent capital. Pacific Gas & Electric Company (PG&E) provides a good example of funding. PG&E has a continuous construction program, and it typically uses short-term debt to finance construction expenditures. However, once short-term debt has built up to about $100 million, the company sells a stock or bond issue, uses the proceeds to pay off (or fund) its bank loans, and starts the cycle again. There is a fixed cost involved in selling stocks or bonds that makes it quite expensive to issue small amounts of these securities. Therefore, the process used by PG&E and other companies is quite logical.

Traditional Debt Instruments

There are many types of long-term debt instruments: term loans, bonds, secured and unsecured notes, marketable and nonmarketable debt, and so on. In this section, we briefly discuss the traditional long-term debt instruments, after which we examine some important features of debt contracts and some innovations in long-term debt financing.

Term Loans

TERM LOAN
A loan, generally obtained from a bank or insurance company, on which the borrower agrees to make a series of payments consisting of interest and principal on specific dates.

A **term loan** is a contract under which a borrower agrees to make a series of interest and principal payments on specific dates to the lender. Term loans usually are negotiated directly between the borrowing firm and a financial institution—generally a bank, an insurance company, or a pension fund. Although term loans' maturities vary from two to 30 years, most are for periods in the three-year to 15-year range.[1]

---

[1]Most term loans are amortized, which means they are paid off in equal installments over the life of the loan. Amortization protects the lender against the possibility that the borrower will not make adequate provisions for the loan's retirement during the life of the loan. See Chapter 6 for a review of amortization. Also, if the interest and principal payments required under a term loan agreement are not met on schedule, the borrowing firm is said to have defaulted, and it can then be forced into bankruptcy.

Term loans have three major advantages over public offerings—*speed, flexibility,* and *low issuance costs.* Because they are negotiated directly between the lender and the borrower, formal documentation is minimized. The key provisions of a term loan can be worked out much more quickly than those for a public issue, and it is not necessary for the loan to go through the Securities and Exchange Commission registration process. A further advantage of term loans has to do with future flexibility. If a bond issue is held by many different bondholders, it is virtually impossible to obtain permission to alter the terms of the agreement, even though new economic conditions might make such changes desirable. With a term loan, the borrower generally can sit down with the lender and work out mutually agreeable modifications to the contract.

The interest rate on a term loan can be either fixed for the life of the loan or variable. If a fixed rate is used, generally it will be set close to the rate on bonds of equivalent maturity and risk. If the rate is variable, it usually will be set at a certain number of percentage points over either the prime rate, the commercial paper rate, rates on Treasury securities, or the London Inter-Bank Offered Rate (LIBOR), which is the rate of interest offered by the largest and strongest London banks on deposits of other large banks of the highest credit standing. Then, when the index rate goes up or down, so does the rate charged on the outstanding balance of the term loan. Rates might be adjusted annually, semiannually, quarterly, monthly, or on some other basis, depending on what the contract specifies. Today, most term loans made by banks have floating rates; in 1970, there were very few floating-rate term notes. With the increased volatility of interest rates in recent years, banks and other lenders have become increasingly reluctant to make long-term, fixed-rate loans.

Bonds

BOND
A long-term debt instrument.

A **bond** is a long-term contract under which a borrower agrees to make payments of interest and principal on specific dates to the holder of the bond. Although bonds traditionally have been issued with maturities of between 20 and 30 years, in recent years shorter maturities, such as seven to ten years, have been used to an increasing extent. Bonds are similar to term loans, but a bond issue generally is advertised, offered to the public, and actually sold to many different investors. Indeed, thousands of individual and institutional investors might purchase bonds when a firm sells a bond issue, whereas there usually is only one lender in the case of a term loan.[2] With bonds the interest rate generally is fixed, although in recent years there has been an increase in the use of various types of floating rate bonds. There also are a number of different types of bonds, the more important of which are discussed next.

MORTGAGE BOND
A bond backed by fixed assets. First mortgage bonds are senior in priority to claims of second mortgage bonds.

Mortgage Bonds   With a **mortgage bond,** the corporation pledges certain assets as security for the bond. To illustrate, in 2000 Scobes Corporation needed $10 million to build a major regional distribution center. Bonds in the amount of $4 million, secured by a mortgage on the property, were issued. (The remaining $6 million was financed with equity capital.) If Scobes defaults on the bonds, the bondholders can foreclose on the property and sell it to satisfy their claims.

---

[2]However, for very large term loans, 20 or more financial institutions might form a syndicate to grant the credit. Also, it should be noted that a bond issue can be sold to one lender (or to just a few); in this case, the issue is said to be "privately placed." Companies that place bonds privately do so for the same reasons that they use term loans—speed, flexibility, and low issuance costs.

If Scobes chooses to, it can issue *second mortgage bonds* secured by the same $10 million plant. In the event of liquidation, the holders of these second mortgage bonds would have a claim against the property, but only after the first mortgage bondholders had been paid off in full. Thus, second mortgages are sometimes called *junior mortgages* because they are junior in priority to the claims of *senior mortgages*, or *first mortgage bonds.*

All mortgage bonds are written subject to an *indenture*, which is a legal document that spells out in detail the rights of both the bondholders and the corporation (bond issuer). Indentures generally are "open ended," meaning that new bonds might be issued from time to time under the existing indenture. However, the amount of new bonds that can be issued almost always is limited to a specified percentage of the firm's total "bondable property," which generally includes all plant and equipment. For example, Savannah Electric Company can issue first mortgage bonds totaling up to 60 percent of its fixed assets. If its fixed assets totaled $1 billion, and if it had $500 million of first mortgage bonds outstanding, it could, by the property test, issue another $100 million of bonds (60% of $1 billion = $600 million).

DEBENTURE
A long-term bond that is not secured by a mortgage on specific property.

Debentures   A **debenture** is an unsecured bond, and as such it provides no lien against specific property as security for the obligation. Therefore, debenture holders are general creditors whose claims are protected by property not otherwise pledged. In practice, the use of debentures depends both on the nature of the firm's assets and on its general credit strength. An extremely strong company, such as IBM, will tend to use debentures; it simply does not need to put up property as security for its debt. Debentures also are issued by companies in industries in which it would not be practical to provide security through a mortgage on fixed assets. Examples of such industries are the large mail-order houses and commercial banks, which characteristically hold most of their assets in the form of inventory or loans, neither of which is satisfactory security for a mortgage bond.

SUBORDINATED DEBENTURE
A bond having a claim on assets only after the senior debt has been paid off in the event of liquidation.

Subordinated Debentures   The term *subordinate* means "below," or "inferior to," and, in the event of bankruptcy, subordinated debt has claims on assets only after senior debt has been paid off. **Subordinated debentures** might be subordinated either to designated notes payable (usually bank loans) or to all other debt. In the event of liquidation or reorganization, holders of subordinated debentures cannot be paid until all senior debt, as named in the debentures' indenture, has been paid.

CONVERTIBLE BOND
A bond that is exchangeable, at the option of the holder, for common stock of the issuing firm.

WARRANT
A long-term option to buy a stated number of shares of common stock at a specified price.

INCOME BOND
A bond that pays interest to the holder only if the interest is earned by the firm.

PUTABLE BOND
A bond that can be redeemed at the bondholder's option.

Other Types of Bonds   Several other types of bonds are used sufficiently often to warrant mention. First, **convertible bonds** are securities that are convertible into shares of common stock, at a fixed price, at the option of the bondholder. Convertibles have a lower coupon rate than nonconvertible debt, but they offer investors a chance for capital gains in exchange for the lower coupon rate. Bonds issued with **warrants** are similar to convertibles. Warrants are options that permit the holder to buy stock for a stated price, thereby providing a capital gain if the price of the stock rises. Bonds that are issued with warrants, like convertibles, carry lower coupon rates than straight bonds. **Income bonds** pay interest only when the firm has sufficient income to cover the interest payments. Thus, these securities cannot bankrupt a company, but from an investor's standpoint they are riskier than "regular" bonds. **Putable bonds** are bonds that can be turned in and exchanged for cash at the bondholder's option; generally, the option to turn in the bond can be exercised only if the firm takes some specified action,

INDEXED (PURCHASING POWER) BOND
A bond that has interest payments based on an inflation index to protect the holder from inflation.

such as being acquired by a weaker company or increasing its outstanding debt by a large amount. With an **indexed,** or **purchasing power, bond,** which is popular in countries plagued by high rates of inflation, the interest rate payment is based on an inflation index such as the consumer price index; so the interest paid rises automatically when the inflation rate rises, thus protecting the bondholders against inflation.

Self-Test Questions

What are the three major advantages that term loans have over public offerings?

Differentiate between term loans and bonds.

Differentiate between mortgage bonds and debentures.

Define convertible bonds, bonds with warrants, income bonds, putable bonds, and indexed bonds.

Why do bonds with warrants and convertible bonds have lower coupons than bonds that do not have these features?

Specific Debt Contract Features

A firm's managers are concerned with both the effective cost of debt and any restrictions in debt contracts that might limit the firm's future actions. In this section, we discuss features that could affect either the cost of the firm's debt or the firm's future flexibility.

Bond Indentures

In Chapter 1 we discussed *agency problems*, which relate to conflicts of interest among corporate stakeholders—stockholders, bondholders, and managers. Bondholders have a legitimate fear that once they lend money to a company and are "locked in" for up to 30 years, the company will take some action that is designed to benefit stockholders but that harms bondholders. For example, RJR Nabisco, when it was highly rated, sold 30-year bonds with a low coupon rate, and investors bought those bonds in spite of the low yield because of their low risk. Then, after the bonds had been sold, the company announced plans to issue a great deal more debt, increasing the expected rate of return to stockholders but also increasing the riskiness of the bonds. RJR's bonds fell 20 percent the week the announcement was made. Safeway Stores and a number of other companies have done the same thing, and their bondholders also lost heavily as the market yield on the bonds rose and drove the prices of the bonds down.

INDENTURE
A formal agreement (contract) between the issuer of a bond and the bondholders.

TRUSTEE
An official who ensures that the bondholders' interests are protected and that the terms of the indenture are carried out.

RESTRICTIVE COVENANT
A provision in a debt contract that constrains the actions of the borrower.

Investors attempt to reduce agency problems by use of legal restrictions designed to ensure, insofar as possible, that the company does nothing to cause the quality of its bonds to deteriorate after they have been issued. The **indenture** is the legal document that spells out the rights of the bondholders and the corporation. A **trustee,** usually a bank, is assigned to represent the bondholders and to make sure that the terms of the indenture are carried out. The indenture might be several hundred pages in length, and it will include **restrictive covenants** that cover such points as the conditions under which the issuer can pay off the bonds prior to maturity, the level at which the issuer's times-interest-earned ratio must be maintained if the company is to sell additional bonds, and restrictions against the payment of dividends when earnings do not meet certain specifications.

The trustee is responsible both for making sure the covenants are not violated and for taking appropriate action if they are. What constitutes "appropriate action" varies with the circumstances. It might be that to insist on immediate compliance would result in bankruptcy, which in turn might lead to large losses on the bonds. In such a case, the trustee might decide that the bondholders would be better served by giving the company a chance to work out its problems rather than by forcing it into bankruptcy.

The Securities and Exchange Commission approves indentures for publicly traded bonds and makes sure that all indenture provisions are met before allowing a company to sell new securities to the public. The indentures of many larger corporations were written back in the 1930s or 1940s, and many issues of new bonds, all covered by the same indenture, have been sold down through the years. The interest rates on the bonds, and perhaps also the maturities, will change from issue to issue, but bondholders' protection as spelled out in the indenture will be the same for all bonds of a given type.[3]

Call Provisions

CALL PROVISION
A provision in a bond contract that gives the issuer the right to redeem the bonds under specified terms prior to the normal maturity date.

Most bonds contain a **call provision,** which gives the issuing corporation the right to call the bonds for redemption. The call provision generally states that the company must pay the bondholders an amount greater than the par value for the bonds when they are called. The additional sum, which is termed a *call premium,* typically is set equal to one year's interest if the bonds are called during the first year, and the premium declines at a constant rate of INT/N each year thereafter, where INT = annual interest and N = original maturity in years. For example, the call premium on a $1,000 par value, ten-year, ten percent bond would generally be $100 if it were called during the first year, $90 during the second year (calculated by reducing the $100, or ten percent, premium by one-tenth), and so on. However, bonds usually are not callable until several years (generally five to ten) after they are issued; bonds with these *deferred calls* are said to have *call protection.*

Suppose a company sold bonds when interest rates were relatively high. Provided the issue is callable, the company could sell a new issue of low-yielding bonds if and when interest rates drop. It could then use the proceeds to retire the high-rate issue and thus reduce its interest expense. This process is called **refunding.**

REFUNDING
Retiring an existing bond issue with the proceeds of a newly issued bond.

Sinking Funds

SINKING FUND
A required annual payment designed to amortize a bond or preferred stock issue.

A **sinking fund** is a provision that facilitates the orderly retirement of a bond issue. Typically, the sinking fund provision requires the firm to retire a portion of the bond issue each year. On rare occasions the firm might be required to deposit money with a trustee, which invests the funds and then uses the accumulated sum to retire the bonds when they mature. A failure to meet the sinking fund requirement causes the bond issue to be thrown into default, which might force the company into bankruptcy. Obviously, a sinking fund can constitute a dangerous cash drain on the firm.

In most cases, the firm is given the right to handle the sinking fund in either of two ways:

1. The company can call in for redemption (at par value) a certain percentage of the bonds each year; for example, it might be able to call two percent of the total

---

[3]A firm will have different indentures for each major type of bond it issues, including its first mortgage bonds, its debentures, its convertibles, and so on.

original amount of the issue at a price of $1,000 per bond. The bonds are numbered serially, and those called for redemption are determined by a lottery administered by the trustee.

2. The company might buy the required amount of bonds on the open market.

The firm will choose the least-cost method. If interest rates have risen, causing bond prices to fall, it will buy bonds in the open market at a discount; if interest rates have fallen, it will call the bonds. Note that a call for sinking fund purposes is quite different from a refunding call as discussed previously. A sinking fund call requires no call premium, but only a small percentage of the issue normally is callable in any one year.

Self-Test Questions

How do trustees and indentures reduce agency problems for bondholders?

What are the two ways a sinking fund can be handled? Which method will be chosen by the firm if interest rates have risen? If interest rates have fallen?

What is the difference between a call for sinking fund purposes and a refunding call?

Are securities that provide for a sinking fund regarded as being riskier than those without this type of provision? Explain.

Why is a call provision so advantageous to a bond issuer? When will the issuer initiate a refunding call? Why?

Bond Innovations in the Past Few Decades

Zero (or Very Low) Coupon Bonds

ZERO COUPON BOND
A bond that pays no annual interest but is sold at a discount below par, thus providing compensation to investors in the form of capital appreciation.

Some bonds pay no interest but are offered at a substantial discount below their par values and hence provide capital appreciation rather than interest income. These securities are called **zero coupon bonds** ("*zeros*"), or *original issue discount bonds (OIDs)*. Corporations first used zeros in a major way in 1981. More recently, many large companies like IBM and JC Penney have used them to raise billions of dollars. Municipal governments also sell "zero munis," and investment bankers have in effect created zero coupon Treasury bonds by "stripping" the interest payments and selling only the right to receive principal repayment at maturity.

Not all original issue discount bonds (OIDs) have zero coupons. For example, a company might sell an issue of five-year bonds with a three percent coupon at a time when other bonds with similar ratings and maturities are yielding nine percent. If an investor purchases these bonds at a price of $762.62, the yield to maturity would be nine percent. The discount of $1,000 − $762.62 = $237.38 represents the capital appreciation the bondholder receives for holding the bond for five years. Thus, zero coupon bonds are just one type of original issue discount bond. Any nonconvertible bond whose coupon rate is set below the going market rate at the time of its issue will sell at a discount, and it will be classified as an OID bond.

OID bonds have lost favor with many individual investors in recent years. The primary reason is because the interest income that must be reported each year for tax purposes includes the dollar amount of interest actually received, which is $0 for zero coupons, plus the annual *prorated* capital appreciation. For example, the purchaser of the three percent coupon bond just mentioned actually would receive $30 interest each year. But the interest income reported for tax purposes would be $30 + ($237.38/5) = $77.48. Thus, taxes would have to be paid on prorated capital gains that would not be received for five years ($47.48 each year). For this reason, most OID bonds currently are held by institutional investors, such as insurance companies and pension funds, rather than individual investors.

Shortly after corporations began to issue zeros, investment bankers figured out a way to create zeros from U.S. Treasury bonds, which are issued only in coupon form. In 1982 Salomon Brothers (now Salomon Smith Barney) bought $1 billion of 12 percent, 30-year Treasuries. Each bond had 60 coupons worth $60 each, which represented the interest payments due every six months. Salomon then in effect clipped the coupons and placed them in 60 piles; the last pile also contained the now "stripped" bond itself, which represented a promise of $1,000 in the year 2012. These 60 piles of U.S. Treasury promises were then placed with the trust department of a bank and used as collateral for "zero coupon U.S. Treasury Trust Certificates," which are, in essence, zero coupon Treasury bonds. A pension fund that expected to need money in 2002 could have bought 20-year certificates backed by the interest the Treasury will pay in 2002. Treasury zeros are, of course, safer than corporate zeros, so they are very popular with pension fund managers.

Corporate (and municipal) zeros generally are callable at the option of the issuer, just like coupon bonds, after some stated call protection period. The call price is set at a premium over the accrued value at the time of the call. Stripped U.S. Treasury bonds (Treasury zeros) generally are not callable because the Treasury normally sells noncallable bonds. Thus, Treasury zeros are completely protected against reinvestment risk (the risk of having to invest cash flows from a bond at a lower rate because of a decline in interest rates).

Floating Rate Debt

In the early 1980s, inflation pushed interest rates up to unprecedented levels, causing sharp declines in the prices of long-term bonds. Even some supposedly "risk-free" U.S. Treasury bonds lost fully half their value, and a similar situation occurred with corporate bonds, mortgages, and other fixed-rate, long-term securities. As a result, many lenders became reluctant to lend money at fixed rates on a long-term basis, and they would do so only at extraordinarily high rates.

There normally is a *maturity risk premium* embodied in long-term interest rates; this premium is designed to offset the risk of declining bond prices if interest rates rise. Prior to the 1970s, the maturity risk premium on 30-year bonds was about one percentage point, meaning that under normal conditions, a firm might expect to pay about one percentage point more to borrow on a long-term than on a short-term basis. However, in the early 1980s, the maturity risk premium is estimated to have jumped to about three percentage points, which made long-term debt very expensive relative to short-term debt. Lenders were able and willing to lend on a short-term basis, but corporations were correctly reluctant to borrow on a short-term basis to finance long-term assets—such action is extremely dangerous. Therefore, there was a situation in which lenders did not want to lend on a long-term basis, but corporations needed long-term money. The problem was solved by the introduction of long-term, *floating rate debt*.

FLOATING RATE BOND
A bond whose interest rate fluctuates with shifts in the general level of interest rates.

A typical **floating rate bond** works as follows. The coupon rate is set for, say, the initial six-month period, after which it is adjusted every six months based on some market rate. Some corporate issues have been tied to the Treasury bond rate, while other issues have been tied to short-term rates. Many additional provisions can be included in floating rate issues; for example, some are convertible to fixed rate debt, whereas others have upper and lower limits ("caps" and "collars") on how high or low the yield can go.

Floating rate debt is advantageous to investors because the interest rate moves up if market rates rise. This causes the market value of the debt to be stabilized, and it also provides lenders such as banks with income that is better geared to their own obligations. Moreover, floating rate debt is advantageous to corporations because by using it, firms can issue debt with a long maturity without committing themselves to paying a historically high rate of interest for the entire life of the loan. Of course, if interest rates were to move even higher after a floating rate note had been signed, the borrower would have been better off issuing conventional, fixed rate debt.

Junk Bonds

Prior to the 1980s, fixed income investors such as pension funds and insurance companies generally were unwilling to buy risky bonds, so it was almost impossible for risky companies to raise capital in the public bond markets. These companies, if they could raise debt capital at all, had to do so in the term loan market, where the loan could be tailored to satisfy the lender. Then, in the late 1970s, Michael Milken of the investment banking firm Drexel Burnham Lambert, relying on historical studies that showed risky bonds yielded more than enough to compensate for their risk, began to convince certain institutional investors of the merits of purchasing risky debt. Thus was born the **junk bond,** a high-risk, high-yield bond issued to finance a leveraged buyout, a merger, or a troubled company. For example, when Ted Turner attempted to buy CBS, he planned to finance the acquisition by issuing junk bonds to CBS's stockholders in exchange for their shares. Similarly, Public Service of New Hampshire financed construction of its troubled Seabrook nuclear plant with junk bonds, and junk bonds were used in the RJR Nabisco leveraged buyout (LBOs are discussed in the next chapter). In junk bond deals, the debt ratio generally is extremely high, so the bondholders must bear as much risk as stockholders normally would. The bonds' yields reflect this fact—a coupon rate of 25 percent per annum was required to sell the Public Service of New Hampshire bonds.

The emergence of junk bonds as an important type of debt is another example of how the investment banking industry adjusts to and facilitates new developments in capital markets. In the 1980s, mergers and takeovers increased dramatically. People like T. Boone Pickens and Ted Turner thought that certain old-line, established companies were run inefficiently and were financed too conservatively, and they wanted to take these companies over and restructure them. Michael Milken and his staff at Drexel Burnham Lambert began an active campaign to persuade certain institutions (often S&Ls) to purchase high-yield bonds. Milken developed expertise in putting together deals that were attractive to the institutions yet apparently feasible in the sense that projected cash flows were sufficient to meet the required interest payments. The fact that interest on the bonds was tax deductible, combined with the much higher debt ratios of the restructured firms, also increased after-tax cash flows and helped make the deals appear feasible.

The development of junk bond financing has done as much as any single factor to reshape the U.S. financial scene. The existence of these securities led directly to the loss of independence of Gulf Oil and hundreds of other companies, and it led to major shakeups in such companies as CBS, Union Carbide, and USX (formerly U.S.

JUNK BOND
A high-risk, high-yield bond used to finance mergers, leveraged buyouts, and troubled companies.

Junk Bonds—Which Way Will the Market Go Next?

It has been more than a decade since Michael Milken, who at the time was considered the "junk bond king," was sent to jail for his role in misleading investors in the junk bond market, and the investment banking firm for which he worked, Drexel Burnham Lambert (DBL), was forced into bankruptcy as a result of its junk bond activities. When DBL dominated the junk-bond industry at the end of the 1980s, it had grown to a $200 billion business. In 1999, the junk bond market exceeded $600 billion. Clearly, then, interest in the high-yield, high-risk debt instruments that are called junk bonds has not diminished.

Donaldson Lufkin & Jenrette Incorporated (DLJ) is now considered the leader in junk bonds—the company underwrites more than 20 percent of all junk-bond issues. It is not surprising that the telecommunications industry has led all issues, with between 25 and 30 percent of the total, because there has been substantial merger activity in the industry in recent years, most of which has been financed by high-yield debt.

One reason the junk bond market has grown so much during the past decade is because the financial markets in general have performed very, very well. When the markets show a propensity to increase, investors who have not experienced significant market declines become more confident that they will gain rather than lose with their investments; thus they are more inclined to invest in riskier instruments than they normally would in an effort to reap greater rewards. One of the investments to which investors turn is the junk bond, which promises higher yields than bonds that are rated investment grade or better. But with the promise of higher returns comes higher risk.

There are signs that the higher risk associated with junk bonds will "rear its ugly head" some time soon. Even though we approach the 21st century with an expanding economy, it appears that companies and individuals in the United States have overextended themselves with respect to borrowing such that they are having difficulty making debt payments. The problem has been manifested by increases in defaults that have occurred recently. More than five percent of companies with junk bonds defaulted on interest payments from the middle of 1998 to the middle of 1999—only about four percent defaulted in all of

1998 and a little more than two percent defaulted in 1997. When all corporate debt was considered, a little more than two percent of companies defaulted during the same period, which was up from 1.3 percent in 1998 and 0.7 percent in 1997. In fact, there was $27 billion of defaulted debt in the first half of 1999, which was a record and was much greater than the $11 billion of defaults that occurred in all of 1998.

Many believe that the record defaults can be traced to the fact that the junk bond market has been somewhat lax with respect to the types of firms that have been allowed to raise funds using these financial instruments. Many of the issuing companies have shown little history of generating profits; thus, they are struggling to repay their debts as they mature. In addition, it appears that bankruptcy is no longer considered the disgrace it once was, so some firms are not as concerned about the ramifications of defaults.

To bring greater structure to the junk bond market, the Securities and Exchange Commission (SEC) recently proposed that its oversight of junk bond issues be increased. Because nearly all junk bond issues are purchased by such institutional investors as mutual funds and pension funds, which are knowledgeable professionals, many issues consist of unregistered securities for which companies are not required to file the same financial information as are companies that issue registered securities. While the SEC believes that closing the registration loophole will enhance the ability of investors to make informed decisions about junk bonds, critics believe that changing the rules will be detrimental to a market that primarily caters to start-up companies, which generally are relatively small with fewer outlets for raising funds than their larger counterparts. The future of the junk bond market could depend on which side ultimately prevails— greater regulation might curtail some junk bond issues, but it might also improve the overall quality of the junk bond market.

SOURCES: Gregory Zuckerman, "Under Boom Economy, Strain over Debt," *The Wall Street Journal*, August 8, 1999, C1; Pallavi Gogoi, "Four Men Hold Sway Over Junk-Bond World," *The Wall Street Journal*, June 15, 1999; and Michael Schroeder, "SEC Aims for Increased Junk-Bond Oversight," *The Wall Street Journal*, May 21, 1999, C19.

Steel). It also caused Drexel Burnham Lambert to leap from essentially nowhere in the 1970s to become the most profitable investment banking firm during the 1980s.

The phenomenal growth of the junk bond market was impressive but controversial. Significant risk, combined with unscrupulous dealings, created significant losses for investors. In early 1989, Drexel Burnham Lambert was forced into bankruptcy, and the so-called junk bond king, Michael Milken, eventually was sent to jail for his role in misleading investors in the junk bond market. These events badly tarnished the junk bond market, which also came under severe criticism for fueling takeover fires and adding to the cost of the S&L bailout that took place in the 1980s. Additionally, the realization that high leverage can spell trouble—as when Campeau, with $3 billion in junk financing, filed for bankruptcy in early 1990—has slowed the growth in the junk bond market. Recently, however, the junk bond market has begun to grow once again.

Self-Test Questions

Explain how the cash flows related to an issue of zero coupon bonds are determined.

What problem was solved by the introduction of long-term floating rate debt, and how is the rate on such bonds actually set?

For what purposes have junk bonds typically been used?

Bond Ratings

Since the early 1900s, bonds have been assigned quality ratings that reflect their probability of going into default. The two major rating agencies are Moody's Investors Service (Moody's) and Standard & Poor's Corporation (S&P). These agencies' rating designations are shown in Table 17–1.[4] The triple- and double-A bonds are extremely safe. Single-A and triple-B bonds are strong enough to be called **investment grade bonds,** and they are the lowest-rated bonds that many banks and other institutional investors are permitted by law to hold. Double-B and lower bonds are speculative, or junk bonds; they have a significant probability of going into default, and many financial institutions are prohibited from buying them.

INVESTMENT GRADE BONDS

Bonds rated A or triple-B; many banks and other institutional investors are permitted by law to hold only investment-grade or better bonds.

Bond Rating Criteria

Bond ratings are based on both qualitative and quantitative factors. Some of the factors considered by the bond rating agencies include the financial strength of the company as measured by various ratios, collateral provisions, seniority of the debt, restrictive covenants, provisions such as a sinking fund or a deferred call, litigation possibilities, regulation, and so on. Representatives of the rating agencies have consistently stated that no precise formula is used to set a firm's rating; all the factors listed, plus others, are taken into account, but not in a mathematically precise manner. Statistical studies have borne out this contention—researchers who have tried to predict bond ratings on the basis of quantitative data have had only limited success, indicating that the agencies use subjective judgment when establishing a firm's rating.[5]

---

[4]In the discussion to follow, reference to the S&P code is intended to imply the Moody's code as well. Thus, triple-B bonds mean both BBB and Baa bonds; double-B bonds mean both BB and Ba bonds; and so on.

[5]See Ahmed Belkaoui, *Industrial Bonds and the Rating Process* (London: Quorum Books, 1983).

TABLE 17–1	Moody's and S&P Bond Ratings							
					JUNK BONDS			
	HIGH QUALITY		**INVESTMENT GRADE**		**SUBSTANDARD**		**SPECULATIVE**	
Moody's	Aaa	Aa	A	Baa	Ba	B	Caa	C
S&P	AAA	AA	A	BBB	BB	B	CCC	D

NOTE: Both Moody's and S&P use "modifiers" for bonds rated below triple A. S&P uses a plus and minus system; thus, A+ designates the strongest A-rated bonds and A− the weakest. Moody's uses a 1, 2, or 3 designation, with 1 denoting the strongest and 3 the weakest; thus, within the double-A category, Aa1 is the best, Aa2 is average, and Aa3 is the weakest.

Importance of Bond Ratings

Bond ratings are important both to firms and to investors. First, because a bond's rating is an indicator of its default risk, the rating has a direct, measurable influence on the bond's interest rate and the firm's cost of debt. Second, most bonds are purchased by institutional investors rather than individuals, and many institutions are restricted to investment-grade securities. Thus, if a firm's bonds fall below BBB, it will have a difficult time selling new bonds because many potential purchasers will not be allowed to buy them.

As a result of their higher risk and more restricted market, lower-grade bonds have higher required rates of return, k_d, than high-grade bonds. Figure 17–1 illustrates this point. In each of the years shown on the graph, U.S. government bonds have had the lowest yields, corporate AAA have been next, and corporate BBB bonds have had the highest yields. The figure also shows that the gaps between yields on the three types of bonds vary over time, indicating that the cost differentials, or risk premiums, fluctuate from year to year. This point is highlighted in Figure 17–2, which gives the average yields on the three types of bonds and the risk premiums for AAA bonds and BBB bonds at three different time periods—April 1965, April 1982, and April 1999.[6] Note first that the risk-free rate, or vertical axis intercept, rose 8.7 percentage points from 1965 to 1982, primarily reflecting the increase in realized and anticipated inflation; the rate was only about 1.6 percent higher in 1999 than in 1965, which indicates inflation expectations were somewhat higher than in 1965 but significantly less than in 1982. Second, the slopes of the lines also have increased since 1965, indicating increases in investors' risk aversion. Thus, the penalty for having a low credit rating varies over time. Occasionally, as in 1965, the penalty is relatively small, but at other

---

[6]The term "risk premium" should to reflect only the difference in expected (and required) returns between two securities that results from differences in their risk. However, the differences between yields to maturity on different types of bonds consist of (1) a true risk premium; (2) a liquidity premium, which reflects the fact that U.S. Treasury bonds are more readily marketable than most corporate bonds; (3) a call premium, because most Treasury bonds are not callable whereas corporate bonds are; and (4) an expected loss differential, which reflects the probability of loss on the corporate bonds. As an example of the last point, suppose the yield to maturity on a BBB bond was ten percent versus seven percent on government bonds, but there was a five percent probability of total default loss on the corporate bond. In this case, the expected return on the BBB bond would be 0.95(10%) + 0.05(0%) = 9.5%, and the risk premium would be 2.5 percent, not the full three percentage point difference in "promised" yields to maturity. Because of all these points, the risk premiums given in Figure 17–2 overstate somewhat the true (but unmeasurable) risk premiums.

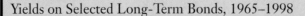

| **FIGURE 17-1** | Yields on Selected Long-Term Bonds, 1965–1998 |

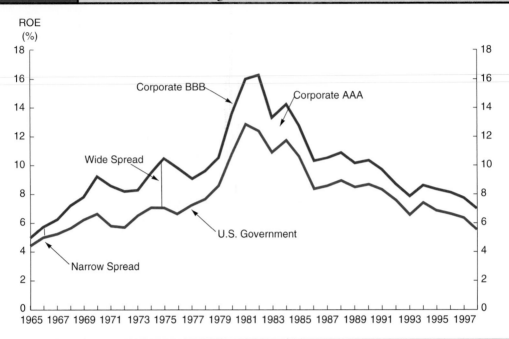

SOURCE: Federal Reserve Board; http://www.bog.frb.fed.us/Releases/H15/data.htm

NOTE: The yields are based on the annual averages of monthly yields to maturity. The yields for the government bonds are based on securities with maturities greater than ten years.

times, as in 1982, it is extremely large. These slope differences reflect investors' risk aversion. In April 1999, there was some fear of an increase in inflation, and at such times there is a "flight to quality," Treasuries are in great demand, and the premium on low-quality over high-quality bonds increases.

Changes in Ratings

Changes in a firm's bond rating affect both its ability to borrow long-term capital and the cost of that capital. Rating agencies review outstanding bonds on a periodic basis, occasionally upgrading or downgrading a bond as a result of its issuer's changed circumstances. For example, in July 1999, *Standard & Poor's CreditWeek* reported that the ratings on the debt for Transok Incorporated, a natural gas company, were lowered from AA to A−, reflecting a diminished ability to service its $173 million debt after the company was acquired by Enogex Incorporated. In the same month, S&P upgraded the unsecured debt of MCI WorldCom Incorporated because it felt that the company had successfully created an integrated, more efficient organization through the sales of nonessential businesses and reductions in operating costs that occurred since the merger that formed the company less than a year earlier.

Self-Test Questions

Name the two major rating agencies and some factors that affect bond ratings.

Why are bond ratings important both to firms and to investors?

| **FIGURE 17–2** | Relationship between Bond Ratings and Bond Yields for Selected Dates |

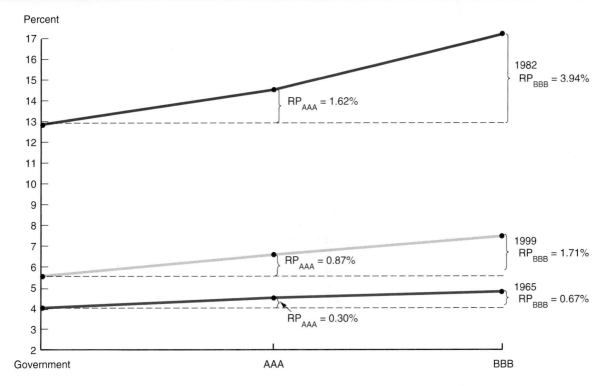

	GOVERNMENT BONDS (DEFAULT-FREE)	**AAA CORPORATE BONDS**	**BBB CORPORATE BONDS**	**RISK PREMIUMS**	
				AAA	**BBB**
	(1)	**(2)**	**(3)**	**(2) − (1)**	**(3) − (1)**
April 1965	4.14	4.44	4.81	0.30	0.67
April 1982	12.84	14.46	16.78	1.62	3.94
April 1999	5.77	6.64	7.48	0.87	1.71

SOURCE: Federal Reserve Board; http://www.bog.frb.fed.us/Releases/H15/data.htm

Rationale for Using Different Types of Securities

Why are there so many different types of long-term securities? At least a partial answer to this question might be seen in Figure 17–3, which depicts the now familiar risk/return trade-off function drawn to show the risk and the expected after-personal-tax returns for the various securities of Allied Air Products.[7] First, U.S. Treasury bills,

[7]The yields in Figure 17–3 are shown on an after-tax basis to the recipient. If yields were on a before-tax basis, those on preferred stocks would lie below those on bonds because of the tax treatment of preferreds. In essence, 70 percent of preferred dividends are tax exempt to corporations owning preferred shares, so a preferred stock with a ten percent pretax yield will have a higher after-tax return to a corporation in the 34 percent tax bracket than will a bond with a 12 percent yield.

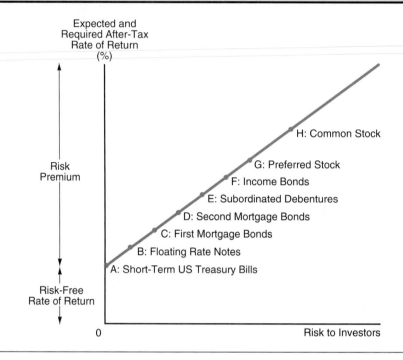

FIGURE 17–3   Allied Air Products: Risks and Returns on Different Classes of Securities

which represent the risk-free rate, are shown for reference. The lowest-risk long-term securities offered by Allied are its floating rate notes; these securities are free of interest rate risk, but they are exposed to some risk of default. The first mortgage bonds are somewhat riskier than the notes (because the bonds are exposed to interest rate risk), and they sell at a somewhat higher required and expected after-tax return. The second mortgage bonds are even riskier, so they have a still higher expected return. Subordinated debentures, income bonds, and preferred stocks are all increasingly risky, and their expected returns increase accordingly.

Why does Allied issue so many different classes of securities? Why not offer just one type of bond, plus common stock? The answer lies in the fact that different investors have different risk/return trade-off preferences, so to appeal to the broadest possible market, Allied must offer securities that attract as many different types of investors as possible. Also, different securities are more popular at different points in time, and firms tend to issue whatever is popular at the time they need money. Used wisely, a policy of selling differentiated securities to take advantage of market conditions can lower a firm's overall cost of capital below what it would be if the firm used only one class of debt.

Self-Test Questions

List the different types of securities in order of highest to lowest risk.

Why do corporations issue so many different classes of securities?

Factors Influencing Long-Term Financing Decisions

As we show in this section, many factors influence a firm's long-term financing decisions. Each factor's relative importance varies among firms at any point in time and for any given firm over time, but any company planning to raise new long-term capital should consider each of these points.

Target Capital Structure

As we discussed in Chapter 11, firms typically establish target capital structures, and one of the most important considerations in any financing decision is how the firm's actual capital structure compares to its target structure. However, few firms finance each year exactly in accordance with their target capital structures, primarily because exact adherence would increase their flotation costs. Because smaller issues of new securities have proportionally larger flotation costs, firms tend to use debt one year and stock the next.

Making fewer but larger security offerings would cause a firm's capital structure to fluctuate above and below its optimal level rather than stay right on target. However, as we discussed in Chapter 11, small fluctuations about the optimal capital structure have little effect either on a firm's cost of debt and equity or on its overall cost of capital. Also, investors would recognize that its actions were prudent and that the firm would save substantial amounts of flotation costs by financing in this manner. Therefore, even though firms do tend to finance over the long haul in accordance with their target capital structures, flotation costs have a definite influence on the specific financing decisions in any given year.

Maturity Matching

Assume that Unilate Textiles decides to float a single $13.5 million nonconvertible bond issue with a sinking fund. It must next choose a maturity for the issue, taking into consideration the shape of the yield curve, management's own expectations about future interest rates, and the maturity of the assets being financed. In the case at hand, Unilate's capital projects during the next two years consist primarily of new, automated manufacturing equipment. This equipment has an expected economic life of ten years (even though it falls into the MACRS five-year class life). Should Unilate finance the debt portion of the capital raised for this equipment with 1-year, 10-year, 20-year, or 30-year debt, or with debt of some other maturity? *One approach is to match the maturity of the liabilities with the maturity of the assets being financed.*

Note that some of the new capital for the machinery will come from common stock, which generally is considered to be a perpetual security with an infinite maturity. Of course, common stock can always be repurchased on the open market or by other means, so its effective maturity can be reduced significantly, but generally it has no maturity.

Debt maturities, however, are specified at the time of issue. If Unilate financed its capital budgets over the next two years with ten-year sinking fund bonds, it would be matching its asset and liability maturities. The cash flows resulting from the new machinery should be sufficient to make the interest and sinking fund payments on the issue, and the bonds would be retired as the machinery wore out. If Unilate used one-year debt, it would have to pay off the loan with cash flows derived from assets other than the machinery in question. If its operations were stable, the company probably could roll over the one-year debt, but if interest rates rose, then it would have to pay a higher rate. If Unilate subsequently experienced difficulties, its lenders might be hesitant to extend the loan, and the company might be unable to obtain new short-term debt at any reasonable rate. At the other extreme, if it used 20-year or 30-year debt, Unilate would still have to service the debt long after the assets purchased with the debt had been scrapped and had ceased providing cash flows, and this would worry potential lenders.

For all these reasons, one commonly used financing strategy is to match debt maturities with asset maturities. In recognition of this fact, firms do consider maturity relationships, and this factor has a major influence on the type of debt securities used.

Interest Rate Levels

Financial managers also consider interest rate levels, both absolute and relative, when making financing decisions. For example, long-term interest rates were high by historic standards in 1981 and 1982, so many managers were reluctant to issue long-term debt and thus lock in those high costs for long periods. We already know that one solution to this problem is to use long-term debt with a call provision. Callability permits the company to refund the issue should interest rates drop, as they did in 1993. But there is a cost, because firms must pay more if they make their debt callable. Alternatively, a firm might finance with short-term debt whenever long-term rates are historically high, and then, assuming that interest rates subsequently fall, sell a long-term issue to replace the short-term debt. Of course, this strategy has its risks. If interest rates climb even higher, the firm will be forced to renew the short-term debt at higher and higher rates, or to replace the short-term debt with a long-term bond that costs more than it would have cost earlier.

Forecasted Interest Rates

At a time when the interest rate on AAA corporate bonds was over 12 percent, which was high by historical standards, Exxon's investment bankers advised the company to tap the Eurodollar bond market for relatively cheap fixed rate financing.[8] At the time, Exxon could have issued its bonds in London at 0.4 percentage points *below* comparable-maturity Treasury bonds. However, one Exxon officer was quoted as cautioning, "I say so what. The absolute level of rates is too high. We would rather wait." The managers of Exxon, as well as those of many other companies, were betting that the next move in interest rates would be down.

This example illustrates that firms do base their financing decisions on expectations about future interest rates. In Exxon's case, the financial staff turned out to be correct. However, the success of such a strategy requires interest rate forecasts to be right more often than they are wrong, and it is very difficult to find someone with a long-term forecasting record better than 50–50.

The Firm's Current and Forecasted Conditions

If a firm's current financial condition is poor, its managers might be reluctant to issue new long-term debt because (1) a new bond issue probably would trigger a review by the rating agencies and (2) long-term debt issued when a firm is in poor financial condition costs more and is subject to more severe restrictive covenants than debt issued

---

[8]A *Eurodollar bond* is a bond sold outside of the United States but denominated in U.S. dollars. We discuss foreign debt later in this chapter.

from a strong position. Thus, a firm that is in a weakened condition but that is forecasting an improvement would be inclined to delay permanent financing until things improved. Conversely, a firm that is strong now but whose forecasts indicate a potentially bad time just ahead would be motivated to finance long term now rather than to wait. These scenarios imply that the capital markets are inefficient in the sense that investors do not have as much information about the firm's future as does its management. This situation undoubtedly is true at times.

The firm's earnings outlook, and the extent to which forecasted higher earnings per share are reflected in stock prices, also has an effect on the choice of securities. If a successful research and development program has just been concluded, and, consequently, management forecasts higher earnings than do most investors, the firm would not want to issue common stock. It would use debt, and then, after earnings had risen and pushed up the stock price, it would sell common stock to restore the capital structure to its target level.

Restrictions in Existing Debt Contracts

Earlier we discussed the fact that Savannah Electric has at times been restricted from issuing new first mortgage bonds by its indenture coverage requirements. This is just one example of how indenture covenants can influence a firm's financing decisions. Restrictions on the current ratio, the debt ratio, and so on, can also restrict a firm's ability to use different types of financing at a given time.

Availability of Collateral

Generally, for a particular firm, secured long-term debt will be less costly than unsecured debt. Thus, firms with large amounts of general-purpose (as opposed to specialized) fixed assets are likely to use a relatively large amount of debt, especially mortgage bonds. Additionally, each year's financing decision will be influenced by the amount of newly acquired assets that are available as security for new bonds.

Self-Test Questions

Do most firms finance each year exactly in accordance with their target capital structures? Why or why not?

Why is the matching of debt maturities with asset maturities a commonly used financing strategy?

If a firm's current financial condition is expected to improve shortly, why might its managers be reluctant to issue new long-term debt?

Which type of firm is more likely to use a relatively large amount of debt, a firm with general-purpose fixed assets or one with specialized fixed assets? Explain.

Bankruptcy and Reorganization

During recessions bankruptcies normally rise, and the recession of 1991–1992 was no exception. The 1991–1992 casualties included Pan Am, Carter Hawley Hale Stores, Continental Airlines, R. H. Macy & Company, Zale Corporation, and McCrory Corporation. Because of its importance, at least a brief discussion of bankruptcy is warranted within the chapter.

When a business becomes *insolvent*, it does not have enough cash to meet scheduled interest and principal payments—that is, the firm cannot service its debt. A decision must then be made whether to dissolve the firm through *liquidation* or to permit it to *reorganize* and thus stay alive. These issues are addressed in Chapters 7 and 11 of the federal bankruptcy statutes, and the final decision is made by a federal bankruptcy court judge.

The decision to force a firm to liquidate or to permit it to reorganize depends on whether the value of the reorganized firm is likely to be greater than the value of the firm's assets if they were sold off piecemeal. In a reorganization, a committee of unsecured creditors is appointed by the court to negotiate with management on the terms of a potential reorganization. The reorganization plan might call for a *restructuring* of the firm's debt, in which case the interest rate might be reduced, the term to maturity lengthened, or some of the debt might be exchanged for equity. The point of the restructuring is to reduce the financial charges to a level that the firm's cash flows can support. Of course, the common stockholders also have to give up something—they normally see their position eroded as a result of additional shares being given to debtholders in exchange for accepting a reduced amount of debt principal and interest. A trustee might be appointed by the court to oversee the reorganization, or the existing management might be allowed to retain control.

Liquidation occurs if the company is deemed to be too far gone to be saved—if it is worth more dead than alive. If the bankruptcy court orders a liquidation, assets are distributed as specified in Chapter 7 of the Bankruptcy Act. As a rule, proceeds are distributed to secured creditors first, then wages and taxes are paid; the remaining proceeds are distributed in order to unsecured creditors, to preferred stockholders, and finally to common stockholders, if anything is left. The priority of claims established by federal bankruptcy statutes *must* be followed when distributing the proceeds from a liquidated firm.

Self-Test Questions

When a business becomes insolvent, what two alternatives are available?

Differentiate between a liquidation and a reorganization.

In the case of liquidation, who gets paid first and who gets paid last?

Refunding Operations

A great deal of long-term debt was issued at very high interest rates during the late 1970s and early 1980s. Since then, interest rates have fallen, and the call protection periods of many bonds have expired. As a result, corporations and government units have retired old bonds and have replaced them with lower-interest rate new bonds. In fact, most long-term debt that exists today was issued in 1993 when interest rates were at historically low levels—many older debt issues were refinanced (refunded) at that time.

Bond refunding analysis is similar to capital budgeting analysis, as discussed in Chapters 8 and 9. Also, bond refunding can be compared to the process individuals go through to refinance a house—an existing debt (mortgage) with a high interest rate is replaced by a new debt (mortgage) with a lower interest rate.

The refunding decision actually involves two separate questions: (1) Would it be profitable to call an outstanding issue now and to replace it with a new issue? (2) Even if refunding currently is profitable, would it be better to call now or to postpone the refunding to a later date?

As we noted, refunding decisions are similar to capital budgeting decisions, and the net present value method is the primary tool. In essence, the costs of undertaking the refunding operation (the investment outlay) are compared to the present value of the interest that will be saved if the high-interest rate bond is called and replaced with a new, low-interest rate bond. If the net present value of refunding is positive, then the refunding should take place. The costs of the refunding operation consist primarily of the call premium on the old bond issue and the flotation costs associated with selling the new issue. The cash flow benefits consist primarily of the interest expenses that will be saved if the company replaces high-cost debt with low-cost debt. The discount rate used to find the present value of the interest savings is the after-tax cost of new debt—the interest saved is the difference between two relatively certain cash flow streams, so the difference essentially is riskless. Therefore, a low discount rate should be used, and that rate is today's after-tax cost of new debt in the market.

To illustrate the refunding decision, consider the Strasburg Communications Corporation, which has a $100 million, 13 percent, semiannual coupon bond outstanding with ten years remaining to maturity. The bond has a call provision that permits the company to retire the issue by calling in the bonds at an eight percent call premium. Investment bankers have assured Strasburg that it could issue an additional $100 million of new ten percent coupon, ten-year bonds that pay interest semiannually. Flotation costs on the new refunding issue will amount to $4,000,000. Predictions are that long-term interest rates are unlikely to fall below ten percent. Strasburg's marginal tax rate is 40 percent. Should the company refund the $100 million of 13 percent semiannual coupon bonds?

Strasburg's refunding analysis is presented in Table 17–2. Because the marginal tax rate is 40 percent, the company's after-tax cost of new debt is equal to six percent, or three percent per six-month period. And because the bonds have semiannual coupons, there will be 20 semiannual periods in the analysis.

The net present value of refunding is positive, so Strasburg should refund the old bond issue—the firm's value will be increased by $1,389,727 if the old bond is retired.

Self-Test Questions

How is bond refunding analysis similar to capital budgeting analysis?

What two questions are involved in the bond refunding decision?

What are the primary costs and the primary benefits in a bond refunding analysis?

Why is the after-tax cost of debt used as the discount rate in a bond refunding analysis?

Foreign Debt Instruments

FOREIGN DEBT
A debt instrument sold by a foreign borrower but denominated in the currency of the country in which it is sold.

Like the U.S. debt markets, the international debt markets offer a variety of instruments with many different features. In this section, we discuss a few of the more familiar types of debt that are traded internationally.

Any debt sold outside the country of the borrower is called an international debt. However, there are two important types of international debt: foreign debt and Eurodebt. **Foreign debt** is debt sold by a foreign borrower but denominated in the currency of the country in which the issue is sold. For instance, Bell Canada might need

---

TABLE 17–2 | NPV Refunding Analysis

Cost of Refunding at t = 0

Call premium on old bond (0.08 × $100 million)	$ 8,000,000
Flotation costs on new issue	4,000,000
Total initial outlay	$12,000,000

Semiannual Interest Savings Due to Refunding: t = 1 to 20
(10 years of payments twice a year)

Interest on old bond (0.065 × $100 million)	$ 6,500,000
Interest on new bond (0.050 × $100 million)	5,000,000
Interest savings per period	$ 1,500,000
Increased taxes due to lower interest payment[a] (0.40 × $1,500,000)	$ (600,000)
Net interest savings	$ 900,000

Refunding Cash Flow Time Line

				1		10 Year
Interest period	0	k = 3%	1	2		20
Initial outlay	(12,000,000)					
Interest savings	0		900,000	900,000	. . .	900,000
Net cash flow	(12,000,000)		900,000	900,000	. . .	900,000

NPV of refunding at $k_{dT}/2 = 3\%$ is $1,389,727

---

[a]Strasburg's interest expense will decrease by $1,500,000, thus taxable income will increase by $1,500,000, if the new bond is issued. Strasburg will have to pay 0.40 × $1,500,000 = $600,000 additional taxes on this increased taxable income.

U.S. dollars to finance the operations of its subsidiaries in the United States. If it decides to raise the needed capital in the domestic U.S. bond market, the bond will be underwritten by a syndicate of U.S. investment bankers, denominated in U.S. dollars, and sold to U.S. investors in accordance with SEC and applicable state regulations. Except for the foreign origin of the borrower (Canada), this bond will be indistinguishable from those issued by equivalent U.S. corporations. Because Bell Canada is a foreign corporation, however, the bond will be called a *foreign bond*. Foreign bonds generally are labeled according to the country in which they are issued. For example, if foreign bonds are issued in the United States they are called *Yankee bonds*, if they are issued in Japan they are called *Samurai bonds*, and if they are issued in England they are called *Bulldog bonds*.

EURODEBT
Debt sold in a country other than the one in whose currency the debt is denominated.

The term **Eurodebt** is used to designate any debt sold in a country other than the one in whose currency the debt is denominated. Examples include *Eurobonds*, such as a British firm's issue of pound bonds sold in France or a Ford Motor Company issue denominated in dollars and sold in Germany. The institutional arrangements by which Eurobonds are marketed are different than those for most other bond issues, with the most important distinction being a far lower level of required disclosure than normally is found for bonds issued in domestic markets, particularly in the United States. Governments tend to be less strict when regulating securities denominated in foreign currencies than they are on home-currency securities because the bonds' purchasers generally are more "sophisticated." The lower disclosure requirements result in lower total transaction costs for Eurobonds.

Eurobonds appeal to investors for several reasons. Generally, they are issued in bearer form rather than as registered bonds, so the names and nationalities of investors are not recorded. Individuals who desire anonymity, whether for privacy reasons or for tax avoidance, find Eurobonds to their liking. Similarly, most governments do not withhold taxes on interest payments associated with Eurobonds.

More than half of all Eurobonds are denominated in dollars; bonds in Japanese yen, German marks, and Dutch guilders account for most of the rest. Although centered in Europe, Eurobonds truly are international. Their underwriting syndicates include investment bankers from all parts of the world, and the bonds are sold to investors not only in Europe but also in such faraway places as Bahrain and Singapore. Until recently, Eurobonds were issued solely by multinational firms, by international financial institutions, or by national governments. Today, however, the Eurobond market also is being tapped by purely domestic U.S. firms such as electric utilities, which find that by borrowing overseas they can lower their debt costs.

Some other types of Eurodebt include the following:

1. **Eurocredits.** Eurocredits are bank loans that are denominated in the currency of a country other than where the lending bank is located. Many of these loans are very large, so the lending bank often forms a loan syndicate to help raise the needed funds and to spread out some of the risks associated with the loan.

   Interest rates on Eurocredits, as well as other short-term Eurodebt, typically are tied to a standard rate known by the acronym **LIBOR,** which stands for *London InterBank Offer Rate.* LIBOR is the rate of interest offered by the largest and strongest London banks on deposits of other large banks of the highest credit standing. In September 1999, LIBOR rates were about ½ percentage point above domestic U.S. bank rates on time deposits of the same maturity—5.04 percent for three-month CDs versus 5.53 percent for three-month LIBOR CDs.

2. **Euro-commercial paper (Euro-CP).** Euro-CP is similar to commercial paper issued in the United States. It is a short-term debt instrument issued by corporations, and it has typical maturities of one, three, and six months. The principal difference between Euro-CP and U.S. commercial paper is that there is not as much concern about the credit quality of Euro-CP issuers.

3. **Euronotes.** Euronotes, which represent medium-term debt, typically have maturities from one year to ten years. The general features of Euronotes are much like those of longer-term debt instruments like bonds. The principal amount is repaid at maturity and interest often is paid semiannually. Most foreign companies use Euronotes like they would a line of credit, continuously issuing notes to finance medium-term needs.

LIBOR
The London Interbank Offer Rate, which represents the interest rate offered by the best London banks on deposits of other large, very creditworthy banks.

Self-Test Questions

Differentiate between foreign debt and Eurodebt.

Why do Eurobonds appeal to investors?

What are Eurocredits, Euro-commercial paper, and Euronotes?

Summary

This chapter described the characteristics, advantages, and disadvantages of the major types of long-term debt securities. The key concepts covered are listed here:

- **Term loans** and **bonds** are long-term debt contracts under which a borrower agrees to make a series of interest and principal payments on specific dates to the lender. A term loan is generally sold to one lender (or a few), while a bond typically is offered to the public and sold to many different investors.
- There are many different types of bonds. They include **mortgage bonds, debentures, convertibles, bonds with warrants, income bonds, putable bonds,** and **purchasing power (indexed) bonds.** The return required on each type of bond is determined by the bond's riskiness.
- A bond's **indenture** is a legal document that spells out the rights of the bondholders and of the issuing corporation. A **trustee** is assigned to make sure that the terms of the indenture are carried out.
- A **call provision** gives the issuing corporation the right to redeem the bonds prior to maturity under specified terms, usually at a price greater than the maturity value (the difference is a **call premium**). A firm typically will call a bond and refund it if interest rates fall substantially.
- A **sinking fund** is a provision that requires the corporation to retire a portion of the bond issue each year. The purpose of the sinking fund is to provide for the orderly retirement of the issue.
- Some innovations in long-term financing that have occurred in the past few decades include **zero coupon bonds,** which pay no annual interest but are issued at a discount; **floating rate debt,** whose interest payments fluctuate with changes in the general level of interest rates; and **junk bonds,** which are high-risk, high-yield instruments issued by firms that use a great deal of financial leverage.
- Bonds are assigned **ratings** that reflect the probability of their going into default. The higher a bond's rating, the less risky it is considered, so the lower its interest rate.
- A firm's long-term financing decisions are influenced by its **target capital structure,** the **maturity of its assets,** current and forecasted **interest rate levels,** the firm's current and forecasted **financial condition, restrictions** in its existing debt contracts, and the suitability of its assets for use as collateral.
- **Bankruptcy** is an important consideration both to companies that issue debt and to investors, for it has a profound effect on all parties. **Refunding,** or paying off high-interest rate debt with new, lower-cost debt, also is an important consideration, because many firms that issued long-term debt in the early 1980s at rates of 12 percent or more now have an opportunity to refund this debt at a cost of about nine percent or less.
- The **Eurodebt** market includes any debt sold in a country other than the one in whose currency the debt is denominated. Examples of Eurodebt are **Eurobonds, Eurocredits, Euro-commercial paper,** and **Euronotes.**

Questions

17-1   What effect would each of the following items have on the interest rate a firm must pay on a new issue of long-term debt? Indicate whether each factor would tend to raise, lower, or have an indeterminate effect on the interest rate, and then explain why.

    a. The firm uses bonds rather than a term loan.

    b. The firm uses debentures rather than first mortgage bonds.

    c. The firm makes its bonds convertible into common stock.

    d. If the firm makes its debentures subordinate to its bank debt, what will the effect be on the
        (1) cost of the debentures?
        (2) cost of the bank debt?
        (3) average cost of total debt?

    e. The firm sells income bonds rather than debentures.

    f. The firm must raise $100 million, all of which will be used to construct a new plant, and it is debating the sale of first mortgage bonds or debentures. If it decides to issue $50 million of each type, as opposed to $75 million of first mortgage bonds and $25 million of debentures, how will this affect
        (1) The cost of debentures?
        (2) The cost of mortgage bonds?
        (3) The weighted average cost of the $100 million?

    g. The firm puts a call provision on its new issue of bonds.

    h. The firm includes a sinking fund on its new issue of bonds.

    i. The firm's bonds are downgraded from A to BBB.

17–2 Rank the following securities from lowest (1) to highest (9) in terms of their riskiness for an investor. All securities (except the Treasury bond) are for a given firm. If you think two or more securities are equally risky, indicate so.

    a. Income bond   _____

    b. Subordinated debentures–noncallable   _____

    c. First mortgage bond–no sinking fund   _____

    d. Common stock   _____

    e. U.S. Treasury bond   _____

    f. First mortgage bond–with sinking fund   _____

    g. Subordinated debentures–callable   _____

    h. Term loan   _____

17–3 A sinking fund can be set up in one of two ways:

    (1) The corporation makes annual payments to the trustee, who invests the proceeds in securities (frequently government bonds) and uses the accumulated total to retire the bond issue at maturity.

    (2) The trustee uses the annual payments to retire a portion of the issue each year, either calling a given percentage of the issue by a lottery and paying a specified price per bond or buying bonds on the open market, whichever is cheaper.

    Discuss the advantages and disadvantages of each procedure from the viewpoint of both the firm and its bondholders.

17–4 Draw a Security Market Line (SML) graph. Put a dot on the graph to show (approximately) where you think a particular company's bonds would lie. Now put on a dot to represent a riskier company's bonds.

Self-Test Problems

(Solutions appear in Appendix B)

key terms   **ST–1** Define each of the following terms:

    a. Funded debt

    b. Term loan; bond

    c. Mortgage bond

    d. Debenture; subordinated debenture

    e. Convertible bond; warrant; income bond; putable bond; indexed, or purchasing power, bond

    f. Indenture; restrictive covenant

    g. Trustee

    h. Call provision; sinking fund

    i. Zero coupon bond; original issue discount bond (OID)

    j. Floating rate bond

    k. Junk bond

    l. Investment grade bonds

    m. Foreign debt; Eurodebt

sinking fund   **ST–2** The Vancouver Development Company has just sold a $100 million, ten-year, 12 percent bond issue. A sinking fund will retire the issue over its life. Sinking fund payments are of equal amounts and will be made *semiannually*, and the proceeds will be used to retire bonds as the payments are made. Bonds can be called at par for sinking fund purposes, or the funds paid into the sinking fund can be used to buy bonds in the open market.

    a. How large must each semiannual sinking fund payment be?

    b. What will happen, under the conditions of the problem thus far, to the company's debt service requirements per year for this issue over time?

    c. Now suppose Vancouver Development sets up its sinking fund so that equal annual amounts, payable at the end of each year, are paid into a sinking fund trust held by a bank, with the proceeds being used to buy government bonds that pay nine percent interest. The payments, plus accumulated interest, must total $100 million at the end of ten years, and the proceeds will be used to retire the bonds at that time. How large must the annual sinking fund payment be now?

    d. What are the annual cash requirements for covering bond service costs under the trusteeship arrangement described in part c? (*Note:* Interest must be paid on Vancouver's outstanding bonds but not on bonds that have been retired.)

    e. What would have to happen to interest rates to cause the company to buy bonds on the open market rather than call them under the original sinking fund plan?

Problems

perpetual bond analysis   **17–1** In 1936 the Canadian government raised $55 million by issuing bonds at a three percent annual rate of interest. Unlike most bonds issued today, which have a specific maturity date, these bonds can remain outstanding forever; they are, in fact, perpetuities.

    At the time of issue, the Canadian government stated in the bond indenture that cash redemption was possible at face value ($100) on or after September 1966; in other words, the bonds were callable at par after September 1966. Believing that the bonds would, in fact, be called, many investors purchased these bonds in 1965 with expectations of receiving $100 in 1966 for each perpetual bond they had. In 1965 the bonds sold for $55, but a rush of buyers drove the price to just below the $100 par value by 1966. Prices fell dramatically, however, when the Canadian government announced that these perpetual bonds were indeed perpetual and would not be paid off.

The bonds' market price declined to $42 in December 1966. Because of their severe losses, hundreds of Canadian bondholders formed the Perpetual Bond Association to lobby for face value redemption of the bonds, claiming that the government had reneged on an implied promise to redeem the bonds. Government officials in Ottawa insisted that claims for face value payment were nonsense because the bonds were and always had been clearly identified as perpetuals. One Ottawa official stated, "Our job is to protect the taxpayer. Why should we pay $55 million for less than $25 million worth of bonds?"

Here are some questions relating to the Canadian issue that will test your understanding of bonds in general:

a. Would it make sense for a business firm to issue bonds like the Canadian government bonds described here? Would it matter whether the firm was a proprietorship or a corporation?

b. Suppose the U.S. government today sold $100 million each of these four types of bonds: five-year bonds, 50-year bonds, "regular" perpetuities, and Canadian-type perpetuities. Rank the bonds from the one with the lowest to the one with the highest expected interest rate. Explain your answer.

c. (1) Suppose that because of pressure by the Perpetual Bond Association, you believe that the Canadian government will redeem this particular perpetual bond issue in four years. Which course of action would be more advantageous to you if you owned the bonds: (i) sell your bonds today at $55.99 or (ii) wait four years and have them redeemed? Assume that similar-risk bonds earn nine percent today and that interest rates are expected to remain at this level for the next four years.

(2) If you had the opportunity to invest your money in bonds of similar risk, at what rate of return would you be indifferent to the choice of selling your perpetuals today or having them redeemed in four years—that is, what is the expected yield to maturity on the Canadian bonds?

d. Show mathematically the perpetuities' value if they yield 6.1 percent, pay $3 interest annually, and are considered *regular* perpetuities. Show what would happen to the price of the bonds if the going interest rate fell to two percent.

e. Are the Canadian bonds more likely to be valued as *regular* perpetuities if the going rate of interest is above or below three percent? Why?

f. Do you think the Canadian government would have taken the same action with regard to retiring the bonds if the interest rate had fallen rather than risen after they were issued?

g. Do you think the Canadian government was fair or unfair in its actions? Give the pros and cons and justify your reason for thinking that one outweighs the other. Would it matter if the bonds had been sold to "sophisticated" as opposed to "naive" investors?

zero coupon bond   17–2 Filkins Farm Equipment needs to raise $4.5 million for expansion, and its investment bankers have indicated that five-year zero coupon bonds could be sold at a price of $567.44 for each $1,000 bond. Filkins's marginal tax rate is 40 percent.

a. How many $1,000 par value zero coupon bonds would Filkins have to sell to raise the needed $4.5 million?

b. What would be the after-tax yield on the zeros (1) to an investor who is tax exempt and (2) to a taxpayer in the 31 percent marginal tax bracket?

c. What would be the after-tax cost of debt to Filkins if it decides to issue the zeros?

Exam-Type Problems

The problems included in this section are set up in such a way that they could be used as multiple-choice exam problems.

loan payment computation

17–3 Suppose a firm is setting up a term loan. What are the annual payments for a $10 million loan under the following terms:

a. eight percent, five years?

b. eight percent, ten years?

c. 14 percent, five years?

d. 14 percent, ten years?

yield to call

17–4 Six years ago The Parrish Company sold a 19-year bond issue with a 14 percent annual coupon rate and a nine percent call premium. Today Parrish called the bonds. The bonds originally were sold at their face value of $1,000. Compute the realized rate of return for investors who purchased the bonds when they were issued and who surrender them today in exchange for the call price.

EAR on zero coupon bonds

17–5 Assume that the city of Tampa sold an issue of $1,000 maturity value, tax-exempt (muni), zero coupon bonds five years ago. The bonds had a 25-year maturity when they were issued and the interest rate built into the issue was a nominal ten percent, but with semiannual compounding. The bonds are now callable at a premium of ten percent over the accrued value. What effective annual rate of return would an investor who bought the bonds when they were issued and who still owns them earn if they are called today?

17–6 The city of Gainesville issued $1,000,000 of 14 percent coupon, 30-year, semiannual payment, tax-exempt muni bonds ten years ago. The bonds had ten years of call protection, but now Gainesville can call the bonds if it chooses to do so. The call premium would be ten percent of the face amount. New 19-year, 12 percent, semiannual payment bonds can be sold at par, but flotation costs on this issue would be two percent, or $20,000. What is the net present value of the refunding? (*Hint:* Approach this problem just like the capital budgeting problems in Chapters 8 and 9.)

Integrative Problem

long-term debt financing

17–7 Hospital Development Corporation (HDC) needs $10 million to build a regional testing laboratory in Birmingham. Once the lab is completed and fully operational, which should take about five years, HDC will sell it to a health maintenance organization (HMO). HDC tentatively plans to raise the $10 million by selling five-year bonds, and its investment bankers have indicated that either regular or zero coupon bonds can be used. Regular coupon bonds would sell at par and would have annual payment coupons of 12 percent, and zero coupon bonds would also be priced to yield 12 percent annually. Either bond would be callable after three years, on the anniversary date of the issue, at a premium of six months' interest for the regular bonds or five percent over the accrued value on the call date for zero coupon bonds. HDC's marginal tax rate is 40 percent. As assistant to HDC's treasurer, you have been assigned the task of making a recommendation as to which type of bonds to issue. As part of your analysis, you have been asked to answer the following questions:

a. What is the difference between a bond and a term loan? What are the advantages of a term loan over a bond?

b. Suppose HDC issues bonds and uses the medical center (land and buildings) as collateral to secure the issue. What type of bond would this be? Suppose that instead of using secured bonds HDC had decided to sell debentures. How would this affect the interest rate that HDC would have to pay on the $10 million of debt?

c. What is a bond indenture? What are some typical provisions the bondholders would require HDC to include in its indenture?

d. HDC's bonds will be callable after three years. If the bonds were not callable, would the required interest rate be higher or lower than 12 percent? What would be the effect on the rate if the bonds were callable immediately? What are the advantages to HDC of making the bonds callable?

e. (1) Suppose HDC's indenture included a sinking fund provision that required the company to retire one-fifth of the bonds each year. Would this provision raise or lower the interest rate required on the bonds?

(2) How would the sinking fund operate?

(3) Why might HDC's investors require it to use a sinking fund?

(4) For this particular issue, would it make sense to include a sinking fund?

f. If HDC were to issue zero coupon bonds, what initial price would cause the zeros to have an annual (EAR) return of 12 percent? How many $1,000 par value zeros would HDC have to sell to raise the needed $10 million? How many regular 12 percent coupon bonds would HDC have to sell?

g. Set up a cash flow time line that shows the accrued value of the zeros at the end of Years 1 through 5, along with the annual after-tax cash flows from the zeros (1) to an investor in the 28 percent tax bracket and (2) to HDC. (*Hint:* The investor has to pay taxes on the annual accrued value increase of the bonds.)

h. What would be the after-tax yield to maturity on each type of bond to an investor in the 28 percent tax bracket? What would be the after-tax cost of debt to HDC?

i. If interest rates were to fall, causing HDC to call the bonds (either the zero or the coupon) at the end of Year 3, what would be the after-tax yield to call on each type of bond to an investor in the 28 percent tax bracket?

j. HDC is an A-rated firm. Suppose HDC's bond rating was (1) lowered to triple-B or (2) raised to double-A. Who would make these changes, and what would the changes mean? What would be the effect of these changes on the interest rate required on HDC's new long-term debt and on the market value of HDC's outstanding debt?

k. What are some of the factors a firm like HDC should consider when deciding whether to issue long-term debt, short-term debt, or equity? Why might long-term debt be HDC's best choice for this project?

l. What is meant by the terms *default, insolvent, liquidation, reorganization, bankruptcy, Chapter 11,* and *Chapter 7*?

m. In what sense is a bond refunding decision similar to a capital budgeting decision?

ONLINE ESSENTIALS

http://www.moodys.com   Moody's Investors Service
At this site, you can find recent changes in bond ratings made by Moody's, new reports related to bond issues, and credit information. In addition, this site provides an indication of how Moody's rates bonds.

http://www.bondsonline.com/index.html   Bonds Online
Provides bond quotes and news and information about both corporate and government bonds. This site also has a tutorial page that gives answers to frequently asked questions and shows the basics of bond pricing.

http://www.smartmoney.com   SmartMoney.com
This site provides a great deal of investment information, including information about stocks, bonds, and mutual funds. To get bond-related information, click on the "BONDS" tab at the top of the page. On this page, you will find current interest rates and links to information about investing in bonds, news about bonds, a bond calculator, and so forth.

http://www.publicdebt.treas.gov   Bureau of Public Debt
Provides information about public debt—municipal bonds, government bonds, and Treasury securities. This site also has current rates on various debt, tutorials, historical data, and links to related sites.

CHAPTER 18

Alternative Financing Arrangements and Corporate Restructuring

A MANAGERIAL PERSPECTIVE

The growth of convertible securities, which are debt or preferred stock issues that can be exchanged for companies' common stocks, has been extraordinary recently. For example, during the past decade, the amount of convertibles in the financial markets has grown from about $50 billion to more than $140 billion. In addition, the number of issuers and the average size of each issue has grown at a similar pace—there are about 700 companies that have issues, and those issues average more than $125 million.

Many firms use convertibles because they feel that funds can be raised more cheaply than with "straight" debt or preferred stock. For example, in 1989 MCI Corporation issued $1.3 billion of convertible bonds at rates that were significantly lower than nonconvertible debt. The price of MCI's stock never reached the point where it was attractive for investors to convert, so the bonds were called by the company in 1993 after market interest rates had dropped to historically low levels. In 1998 Amazon.com issued $1.25 billion in convertible notes that had a 4.75 percent coupon rate, which was below the rate on many Treasury notes. The debt, which matures in 2009, allowed investors to convert each $1,000 bond into 6.408 shares of common stock; thus, as long as the price of the stock was above $156 per share (its *conversion price*),

it would be worthwhile to convert the bonds into common stock. The convertible also included a call provision that allows Amazon.com to recall the bonds at a price of $1,212.60 for each $1,000 bond if the future price of the stock increases to more than $234 per share (150 percent of the conversion price). Although bondholders would get 21.26 percent more than the face value of the bonds at call, they would lose the opportunity to convert their bonds into nearly $1,500 worth of stock. By the end of April 1998, Amazon.com was selling for more than $207; thus, analysts speculated that it wouldn't be long before the bonds were called by the company. A few months later, however, Amazon.com announced earnings that were lower (more negative) than expected; thus, the stock price dropped substantially—on the day of the announcement, the stock lost about 14.6 percent of its value, while the convertible notes lost 17.8 percent during the week. As we write this book, the value of Amazon.com's stock has dropped even further—it has lost about 35 percent of its value in a four-month period at the beginning of 1999. Therefore, it seems unlikely that the company will call the bonds any time soon.

Convertibles are attractive to investors because they offer the opportunity to earn the substantial returns available with stocks, but they also offer

continues

the stability associated with debt or preferred stock. For the past decade, convertibles have generated a return equal to more than 14 percent compared to the 19 percent return provided by large stocks and the ten percent to 15 percent return associated with small stocks.

As the financial markets strengthen, convertibles gain popularity; but when the financial markets weaken, selling pressure results and convertibles lose favor with investors. Like other financial assets, convertibles are risky—most experts would caution investors not to put large portions of their investments in convertible securities but to diversify instead. Once you have read this chapter and understand the concepts presented, you should be able to make informed decisions regarding convertibles, as well as preferred stock and other hybrid securities. ■

In the two preceding chapters, we examined the use of common stock and various types of debt. In this chapter, we examine some other types of long-term financing arrangements used by financial managers. We give only fundamental descriptions of these alternative sources of financing to enlighten you about the variety of means by which a firm can raise funds. The fact is many variations and combinations of financial assets exist today, and it would take multiple volumes to describe them all. Firms often engage in "creative financing" when seeking different ways to attract investors, so you should not be surprised to see new forms of financing emerge on a continuous basis. In addition, because firms have become extremely "creative" when determining how to finance mergers and acquisitions, we briefly discuss mergers and merger activity at the end of the chapter.

The purpose of this chapter is to provide you with a basic understanding of (1) some financing techniques we have not discussed in previous chapters and (2) corporate restructuring through mergers and leveraged buyouts. If you want more in-depth discussions, you should look in either an upper-level corporate finance text or an investments text.

Preferred Stock

Preferred stock is a *hybrid* security—it is similar to bonds in some respects and to common stock in others. The hybrid nature of preferred stock becomes apparent when we try to classify it in relation to bonds and common stock. Like bonds, preferred stock has a par value. Preferred dividends also are similar to interest payments in that they generally are fixed in amount and must be paid before common stock dividends can be paid. However, if the preferred dividend is not earned, the directors can omit (or "pass") it without throwing the company into bankruptcy. So although preferred stock has a fixed payment like bonds, a failure to make this payment will not lead to bankruptcy.

Accountants classify preferred stock as equity and report it in the equity portion of the balance sheet under "preferred stock" or "preferred equity." However, financial analysts sometimes treat preferred stock as debt and sometimes as equity, depending on the type of analysis being made. If the analysis is being made by a common stockholder, the key consideration is the fact that the preferred dividend is a fixed charge that reduces the amount that can be distributed to common shareholders, so from the common stockholder's point of view preferred stock is similar to debt. Suppose, however, that the analysis is being made by a bondholder studying the firm's vulnerability to failure in the event of a decline in sales and income. If the firm's income declines, the debtholders have a prior claim to the available income ahead of preferred stockholders, and if the firm fails, debtholders have a prior claim to assets when the firm is liquidated. Thus, to a bondholder, preferred stock is similar to common equity.

From management's perspective, preferred stock lies between debt and common equity. Because failure to pay dividends on preferred stock will not force the firm into bankruptcy, preferred stock is safer to use than debt. At the same time, if the firm is highly successful, the common stockholders will not have to share that success with the preferred stockholders because preferred dividends are fixed. Remember, however, that the preferred stockholders do have a higher priority claim than the common stockholders. We see, then, that preferred stock has some of the characteristics of debt and some of the characteristics of common stock, and it is used in situations in which conditions are such that neither debt nor common stock is entirely appropriate.

Major Provisions of Preferred Stock Issues

Preferred stock has a number of features, the most important of which are discussed in the following sections. As you will see, some of the features we discuss here are also features included in debt instruments, which we discussed in the previous chapter.

Priority to Assets and Earnings   Preferred stockholders have priority over common stockholders with regard to earnings and assets. Thus, dividends must be paid on preferred stock before they can be paid on the common stock, and, in the event of bankruptcy, the claims of the preferred shareholders must be satisfied before the common stockholders receive anything. To reinforce these features, most preferred stocks have coverage requirements similar to those on bonds. These restrictions limit the amount of preferred stock a company can use, and they also require a minimum level of retained earnings before common dividends can be paid.

Par Value   Unlike common stock, preferred stock always has a par value (or its equivalent under some other name), and this value is important. First, the par value establishes the amount due the preferred stockholders in the event of liquidation. Second, the preferred dividend frequently is stated as a percentage of the par value. For example, an issue of Duke Power's preferred stock has a par value of $100 and a stated dividend of 7.8 percent of par. The same results would, of course, be produced if this issue of Duke's preferred stock simply called for an annual dividend of $7.80.

CUMULATIVE DIVIDENDS

A protective feature on preferred stock that requires preferred dividends previously not paid to be paid before any common dividends can be paid.

Cumulative Dividends   Most preferred stock provides for **cumulative dividends;** that is, any preferred dividends not paid in previous periods must be paid before common dividends can be paid. The cumulative feature is a protective device because if the preferred stock dividends were not cumulative, a firm could avoid paying preferred and common stock dividends for, say, ten years, plowing back all its earnings, and then pay a huge common stock dividend but pay only the stipulated annual dividend to the preferred stockholders. Obviously, such an action effectively would void the preferred position the preferred stockholders are supposed to have. The cumulative feature helps prevent such abuses.[1]

[1]Note, however, that compounding is absent in most cumulative plans—in other words, the unpaid preferred dividends themselves earn no return. Also, many preferred issues have a limited cumulative feature; for example, unpaid preferred dividends might accumulate for only three years.

Convertibility   Approximately 40 percent of the preferred stock that has been issued in recent years is convertible into common stock. For example, on March 25, 1999, Global Maintech issued 1,600 shares of Series C convertible preferred that can be converted into a minimum of 400 shares of common stock at the option of the preferred shareholder.

Other Provisions   Some other provisions occasionally found in preferred stocks include the following:

1. **Voting rights.** Although preferred stock is not voting stock, preferred stockholders generally are given the right to vote for directors if the company has not paid the preferred dividend for a specified period, such as ten quarters. This feature motivates management to make every effort to pay preferred dividends.
2. **Participating.** A rare type of preferred stock is one that participates with the common stock in sharing the firm's earnings. Participating preferred stocks generally work as follows: (a) the stated preferred dividend is paid—for example, $5 a share; (b) the common stock is then entitled to a dividend in an amount up to the preferred dividend; (c) if the common dividend is raised, say to $5.50, the preferred dividend must likewise be raised to $5.50.
3. **Sinking fund.** In the past (before the mid-1970s), few preferred issues had sinking funds. Today, however, most newly issued preferred stocks have sinking funds that call for the purchase and retirement of a given percentage of the preferred stock each year. If the amount is two percent, which frequently is used, the preferred issue will have an average life of 25 years and a maximum life of 50 years.
4. **Call provision.** A call provision gives the issuing corporation the right to call in the preferred stock for redemption. As in the case of bonds, call provisions generally state that the company must pay an amount greater than the par value of the preferred stock, the additional sum being termed a **call premium.** For example, Bangor Hydro-Electric Company has various issues of preferred stock outstanding, two of which are callable. The call prices on the two issues are $100 and $110. Before it was called in December 1997, Bangor had another callable preferred issue that included a sinking fund provision.
5. **Maturity.** Before the mid-1970s, most preferred stock was perpetual—it had no maturity and never needed to be paid off. Today, however, most new preferred stock has a sinking fund and thus an effective maturity date.

CALL PREMIUM
The amount in excess of par value that a company must pay when it calls a security.

Pros and Cons of Preferred Stock

As noted here, there are both advantages and disadvantages to financing with preferred stock.

Issuer's (Firm's) Viewpoint   By using preferred stock, a firm can fix its financial costs and thus keep more of the potential future profits for its existing set of common stockholders, yet still avoid the danger of bankruptcy if earnings are too low to meet these fixed charges. Also, by selling preferred stock rather than common stock, the firm avoids sharing control with new investors.

However, preferred stock does have a major disadvantage from the issuer's standpoint: It has a higher after-tax cost of capital than debt. The major reason for this higher cost is taxes: Preferred dividends are not deductible as a tax expense, whereas interest expense is deductible.[2] This makes the component cost of preferred stock much greater than that of bonds—the after-tax cost of debt is approximately two-thirds of the stated coupon rate for profitable firms, whereas the cost of preferred stock is the full percentage amount of the preferred dividend. Of course, the deductibility differential is most important for issuers that are in relatively high tax brackets. If a company pays little or no taxes because it is unprofitable or because it has a great deal of accelerated depreciation, the deductibility of interest does not make much difference. Thus, the lower a company's tax bracket, the more likely it is to issue preferred stock.

Bondholder's (Investor's) Viewpoint   In designing securities, the financial manager must consider the investor's point of view. It is sometimes asserted that preferred stock has so many disadvantages to both the issuer and the investor that it should never be issued. Nevertheless, preferred stock is being issued in substantial amounts. It provides investors with a steadier and more assured income than common stock, and it has a preference over common stock in the event of liquidation. In addition, 70 percent of the preferred dividends received by corporations are not taxable. For this reason, most preferred stock is owned by corporations.

The principal disadvantage of preferred stock from an investor's standpoint is that although preferred stockholders bear some of the ownership risks, their returns are limited. Other disadvantages are that (1) preferred stockholders have no legally enforceable right to dividends, even if a company earns a profit and (2) *for individual as opposed to corporate investors,* after-tax bond yields generally are higher than those on preferred stock, even though the preferred is riskier.

Self-Test Questions

Explain the following statement: "Preferred stock is a hybrid."

Identify and briefly explain some of the key features of preferred stock.

What are the advantages and disadvantages of preferred stock from an issuer's viewpoint?

What are the advantages and disadvantages of preferred stock from an investor's viewpoint?

Leasing

Firms generally own fixed assets and report them on their balance sheets, but it is the *use* of buildings and equipment that is important, not their ownership per se. One way of obtaining the use of assets is to buy them, but an alternative is to lease them. Prior to the 1950s, leasing generally was associated with real estate—land and buildings. Today, however, it is possible to lease virtually any kind of fixed asset, and in 1999 more

---

[2]One would think that a given firm's preferred stock would carry a higher coupon rate than its bonds because of the preferred's greater risk from the holder's viewpoint. However, 70 percent of preferred dividends received by corporate owners are exempt from income taxes, and this has made preferred stock very attractive to corporate investors. Therefore, most preferred stock is owned by corporations, and in recent years high-grade preferreds, on average, have sold on a lower-yield basis, before taxes, than high-grade bonds. On an after-tax basis, though, the yield on preferred stock generally is greater than the yield on high-grade corporate bonds.

than 25 percent of all new capital equipment acquired by businesses was leased. In fact, it is estimated that 70 percent of firms listed in the *Fortune 1000* lease some equipment.

Types of Leases

Leasing takes three different forms: (1) sale-and-leaseback arrangements, (2) operating leases, and (3) straight financial, or capital, leases.

Sale and Leaseback Under a **sale and leaseback,** a firm that owns land, buildings, or equipment sells the property and simultaneously executes an agreement to lease the property back for a particular period under specific terms. The purchaser could be an insurance company, a commercial bank, a specialized leasing company, or even an individual investor. The sale-and-leaseback plan is an alternative to taking out a mortgage loan. The firm that sells the property, or the **lessee,** immediately receives the purchase price from the buyer, or the **lessor.**[3] At the same time, the seller-lessee firm retains the use of the property just as if it had borrowed and mortgaged the property to secure the loan. Note that under a mortgage loan arrangement, the financial institution normally would receive a series of equal payments just sufficient to amortize the loan while providing a specified rate of return to the lender on the outstanding balance. Under a sale-and-leaseback arrangement, the lease payments are set up in exactly the same way; the payments are set so the investor-lessor recoups the purchase price and earns a specified rate of return on the investment.

Operating Leases **Operating leases,** sometimes called *service leases*, provide for both *financing* and *maintenance*. IBM is one of the pioneers of the operating lease contract, and computers and office copying machines, together with automobiles and trucks, are the primary types of equipment involved. Ordinarily, these leases call for the lessor to maintain and service the leased equipment, and the cost of providing maintenance is built into the lease payments.

Another important characteristic of operating leases is the fact that they frequently are *not fully amortized;* in other words, the payments required under the lease contract are not sufficient to recover the full cost of the equipment. However, the lease contract is written for a period considerably shorter than the expected economic life of the leased equipment, and the lessor expects to recover all investment costs through subsequent renewal payments, through subsequent leases to other companies (lessees), or by selling the leased equipment.

A final feature of operating leases is that they frequently contain a *cancellation clause*, which gives the lessee the right to cancel the lease before the expiration of the basic agreement. This is an important consideration for the lessee, because it means that the equipment can be returned if it is rendered obsolete by technological developments or if it no longer is needed because of a decline in the lessee's business.

Financial, or Capital, Leases **Financial leases,** sometimes called *capital leases*, are differentiated from operating leases in three respects: (1) they do *not* provide for maintenance services; (2) they are *not* cancelable; and (3) they are *fully amortized*—that is, the lessor receives rental payments that are equal to the full price of the leased equipment plus a return on the investment. In a typical financial lease arrangement, the firm

---

[3]The term *lessee* is pronounced "less-ee," not "lease-ee," and *lessor* is pronounced "less-or."

that will use the equipment (the lessee) selects the specific items it requires and negotiates the price and delivery terms with the manufacturer. The user firm then negotiates terms with a leasing company and, once the lease terms are set, arranges to have the lessor buy the equipment from the manufacturer or the distributor. When the equipment is purchased, the user firm simultaneously executes the lease agreement.

Financial leases are similar to sale-and-leaseback arrangements, except that the leased equipment is new and the lessor buys it from a manufacturer or a distributor instead of from the user-lessee. A sale and leaseback might thus be thought of as a special type of financial lease, and both sale-and-leaseback leases and financial leases are analyzed in the same manner.[4]

Financial Statement Effects

Lease payments are shown as operating expenses on a firm's income statement, but under certain conditions, neither the leased assets nor the liabilities under the lease contract appear on the firm's balance sheet. For this reason, leasing is often called **off-balance-sheet financing.** This point is illustrated in Table 18–1 by the balance sheets of two hypothetical firms, B (for Buy) and L (for Lease). Initially, the balance sheets of both firms are identical, and both have debt ratios of 50 percent. Each firm then decides to acquire fixed assets that cost $100. Firm B borrows $100 to make the purchase, so both an asset and a liability are recorded on its balance sheet, and its debt ratio is increased to 75 percent. Firm L leases the equipment, so its balance sheet is unchanged. The lease might call for fixed charges as high as or even higher than those on the loan, and the obligations assumed under the lease might be equally or more dangerous from the standpoint of financial safety, but the firm's debt ratio remains at 50 percent.

To correct this problem, the Financial Accounting Standards Board (FASB) issued **FASB #13,** which requires that for an unqualified audit report, firms that enter into financial (or capital) leases must restate their balance sheets to report leased assets as fixed assets and the present value of future lease payments as a debt. This process is called *capitalizing the lease,* and its net effect is to cause Firms B and L to have similar balance sheets, both of which will resemble the one shown for Firm B after the asset increase.[5]

The logic behind FASB #13 is as follows. If a firm signs a lease contract, its obligation to make lease payments is just as binding as if it had signed a loan agreement. The failure to make lease payments can bankrupt a firm just as surely as can the failure to make principal and interest payments on a loan. Therefore, for all intents and purposes, a financial lease is identical to a loan.[6] This being the case, when a firm signs a

OFF-BALANCE-SHEET FINANCING
Financing in which the assets and liabilities involved do not appear on the firm's balance sheet.

FASB #13
The statement of the Financial Accounting Standards Board (FASB) that details the conditions and procedures for capitalizing leases.

---

[4]For a lease transaction to qualify as a lease for *tax purposes,* and thus for the lessee to be able to deduct the lease payments, the life of the lease must not exceed 80 percent of the expected life of the asset, and the lessee cannot be permitted to buy the asset at a nominal value. These conditions are IRS requirements, and they should not be confused with the FASB requirements discussed in the next section concerning the capitalization of leases. It is important to consult lawyers and accountants to ascertain whether a prospective lease meets current IRS regulations.

[5]FASB #13, "Accounting for Leases," November 1976, spells out in detail the conditions under which leases must be capitalized and the procedures for doing so.

[6]There are, however, certain legal differences between loans and leases. For example, in a bankruptcy liquidation, the lessor is entitled to take possession of the leased asset, and, if the value of the asset is less than the required payments under the lease, the lessor can enter a claim (as a general creditor) for one year's lease payments. In a bankruptcy reorganization, the lessor receives the asset plus three years' lease payments if needed to bring the value of the asset up to the remaining investment in the lease.

Leveraged Buyouts (LBOs)

LEVERAGED BUYOUT (LBO)
A transaction in which a firm's publicly owned stock is bought up in a mostly debt-financed tender offer, and a privately owned, highly leveraged firm results.

With the extraordinary merger activity that took place in the 1980s, we witnessed a huge increase in the popularity of **leveraged buyouts,** or **LBOs.** The number and size of LBOs jumped significantly during this period. This development occurred for the same reasons that mergers and divestitures occurred—the existence of potential bargains, situations in which companies were using insufficient leverage, and the development of the junk bond market, which facilitated the use of leverage in takeovers.

LBOs can be initiated in one of two ways: (1) The firm's own managers can set up a new company whose equity comes from the managers themselves, plus some equity from pension funds and other institutions. This new company then arranges to borrow a large amount of money by selling junk bonds through an investment banking firm. With the financing arranged, the management group then makes an offer to purchase all the publicly owned shares through a tender offer. (2) A specialized LBO firm, with Kohlberg Kravis Roberts (KKR) being the best known, will identify a potential target company, go to the management, and suggest that an LBO deal be done. KKR and other LBO firms have billions of dollars of equity, most put up by pension funds and other large investors, available for the equity portion of the deals, and they arrange junk bond financing just as would a management-led group. Generally, the newly formed company will have at least 80 percent debt, and sometimes the debt ratio is as high as 98 percent. Thus, the term *leveraged* is most appropriate.

To illustrate an LBO, consider the $25 billion leveraged buyout of RJR Nabisco by KKR in 1989. RJR, a leading producer of tobacco and food products with such brands as Winston, Camel, Planters, Ritz, and Oreo, was trading at about $55 a share. Then F. Ross Johnson, RJR Nabisco's president and CEO at the time, announced a $75 per share, or $17.6 billion, offer to take the firm private. The day after the announcement, RJR's stock soared to $77.25, which indicated that investors thought that the final price would be even higher than Johnson's opening bid. A few days later, KKR offered $90 per share, or $20.6 billion, for the firm. The battle between the two bidders continued until late November, when RJR's board accepted a revised KKR bid of cash and securities worth about $109 per share, for a total value of about $25.1 billion.

Was RJR worth $25 billion, or did Henry Kravis and his partners let their egos govern their judgment? At the time the LBO was initiated, analysts believed that the deal was workable, but barely. Six years after the deal, KKR had disposed of all its interest in RJR Nabisco, and many experts called the biggest LBO of its time the biggest financial flop in history. More information about the history of KKR's ownership of RJR Nabisco is provided in the Industry Practice box in this chapter.

It is not clear if LBOs are, on balance, a good or a bad idea. Some government officials and others have stated a belief that the leverage involved might destabilize the economy. On the other hand, LBOs certainly have stimulated some lethargic managements, and that is good. Good or bad, though, LBOs have helped reshape the face of corporate America.

Self-Test Questions

Identify and briefly explain the two ways in which an LBO can be initiated.

How has the development of the junk bond market affected the use of LBOs?

Déjà Vu All Over Again?

The largest leveraged buyout (LBO) of the times was finalized February 1989 when Kohlberg Kravis Roberts & Co. (KKR), a large and powerful LBO firm, acquired RJR Nabisco for just over $25 billion. The deal evolved in October 1988, when a group headed by F. Ross Johnson, chairman of RJR Nabisco at the time, offered stockholders $75 per share in an attempt to purchase the company and take it private; the total offer was equal to nearly $18 billion. Within days, Henry Kravis and George Roberts, KKR's leaders, started a bidding war by offering $90 per share for RJR Nabisco. Ultimately KKR won the war and paid $109 per share, which was nearly twice the per share market price at the time the first buyout offer was made by Johnson. Of the $25 billion paid, only $1.35 billion represented equity invested by KKR; the rest was financed by debt and was raised primarily in the junk bond market. At the time the RJR Nabisco LBO was finalized, there was a great deal of skepticism about whether the deal would be successful. Some experts speculated that the phenomenal price paid for the RJR Nabisco LBO was the result of a battle of egos between two very powerful individuals; others believed the LBO was a good deal. In any event, the degree of financial leverage, thus the risk, associated with the LBO was substantial.

Several years after the RJR Nabisco LBO, experts dubbed the "deal of the century" the "turkey of the century." The average annual return earned by KKR on its investment in the LBO was only in the single digits range, quite a contrast to the 25 percent to 30 percent returns KKR normally sees, and well below expectations given the risk involved. According to analysts, KKR made two fundamental mistakes with the RJR Nabisco deal: (1) too much was paid for the buyout, and (2) the investment was made in the wrong industry (tobacco).

Not long after KKR put together the LBO, the junk bond market tumbled. To save RJR from insolvency, in July 1990, KKR refinanced some of the debt by infusing another $1.7 billion of equity; this increased KKR's equity position to about $3.1 billion.

Then in 1991, KKR took RJR Nabisco public with an initial public offering (IPO) of 100 million shares at a price of $11.25 per share. The stock sold by KKR represented 60 percent equity ownership in RJR Nabisco. KKR believed the funds raised through the IPO could be used to better stabilize the financial position of RJR. Unfortunately, legal and competitive battles in the tobacco industry resulted in very lackluster operating performances by RJR in the 1990s. In 1993, RJR's primary competitor, Philip Morris, started an aggressive campaign to increase its market share in the tobacco industry by significantly cutting cigarette prices and increasing advertising expenses. These actions surprised RJR, so it missed the boat and was left behind by Philip Morris—RJR's profit decreased by 50 percent in 1993. At the same time, increases in both regulation and litigation contributed to a heightened social awareness and a degree of negativism with respect to investing in tobacco companies. Consequently, tobacco stocks were shunned by many investors in the early 1990s. In the middle of 1994, RJR Nabisco stock sold for about $5 per share, less than one half its IPO price two years earlier.

On September 12, 1994, KKR made a bid to acquire Borden Inc., a large food processor, for approximately $14.25 per share. To pay for the $2 billion buyout, KKR exchanged 275 million shares of RJR Nabisco stock for Borden's stock. This move reduced KKR's ownership of RJR from 40 percent to 17.5 percent. Then, in February and March of 1995, KKR sold its remaining stake in RJR through Borden. Six years after it consummated the "deal of the century," KKR had dumped RJR Nabisco and totally removed itself from the situation. During the same period, RJR Nabisco Holdings Corporation sold to the public nearly 20 percent of Nabisco Brands, the food division of RJR Nabisco, which was a big hit in the financial markets.

During the past couple of years, Nabisco Holdings Corporation (NHC) has been divesting itself of the tobacco products divisions in the RJR Nabisco organization. In June 1999, NHC completed the process,

continues

and R.J. Reynolds Tobacco Holdings Inc. began trading as a separate company. Thus, RJR and Nabisco are back where they were in 1985 before RJR purchased Nabisco Brands; RJR is an independent tobacco company and Nabisco is an independent food company, and both are independent of KKR. After nearly 15 years, RJR and Nabisco Brands have come full circle—starting with a merger, proceeding through the biggest LBO of its time (there have been larger LBOs in more recent years), and ultimately splitting into two companies that are publicly owned once again.

Mergers

MERGER
The combination of two or more firms to form a single firm.

Mergers have taken place at a feverish pace during the past decade. The brief discussion in this section will help you understand the motivations behind all this activity.[12]

Rationale for Mergers

There are five principal reasons two or more firms are merged to form a single firm.

1. **Synergy.** The primary motivation for most mergers is to increase the value of the combined enterprise—the hope is that *synergy* exists so that the value of the company formed by the merger is greater than the sum of the values of the individual companies taken separately. Synergistic effects can arise from four sources: (a) *operating economies of scale* occur when cost reductions result from the combination of the companies; (b) *financial economies* might include a higher price/earnings ratio, a lower cost of debt, or a greater debt capacity; (c) *differential management efficiency* generally results when one firm is relatively inefficient, so the merger improves the profitability of the acquired assets; and (d) *increased market power* occurs if reduced competition exists after the merger. Operating and financial economies are socially desirable, as are mergers that increase managerial efficiency; but mergers that reduce competition are both undesirable and often illegal.[13]

---

[12]The purpose of this section is to provide you with a general understanding of mergers, the motivations for mergers, and merger activity in the United States. Merger analysis, which is the evaluation of the attractiveness of a merger, should be conducted in the same manner as capital budgeting analysis (if the present value of the cash flows expected to result from the merger exceeds the price that must be paid for the company being acquired, then the merger has a positive net present value and the acquiring firm should proceed with the acquisition). Because the very nature of the merger process is complex, we choose not to discuss the specifics of merger analysis in this section. For a detailed discussion of mergers analysis, see Chapter 21 of Eugene F. Brigham, Louis C. Gapenski, and Phillip R. Daves, *Intermediate Financial Management*, 6th ed. (Fort Worth, TX: The Dryden Press, 1999).

[13]In the 1880s and 1890s, many mergers occurred in the United States, and some of them clearly were directed toward gaining market power at the expense of competition rather than increasing operating efficiency. As a result, Congress passed a series of acts designed to ensure that mergers are not used as a method of reducing competition. Today, the principal acts include the Sherman Act (1890), the Clayton Act (1914), and the Celler Act (1950). These acts make it illegal for firms to combine in any manner if the combination will lessen competition. They are administered by the antitrust division of the Justice Department and by the Federal Trade Commission.

2. **Tax considerations.** Tax considerations have stimulated a number of mergers. For example, a firm that is highly profitable and in the highest corporate tax bracket could acquire a company with large accumulated tax losses, then use those losses to shelter its own income.[14] Similarly, a company with large losses could acquire a profitable firm. Also, tax considerations could cause mergers to be a desirable use for excess cash. For example, if a firm has a shortage of internal investment opportunities compared to its cash flows, it will have excess cash, and its options for disposing of this excess cash are to (a) pay an extra dividend, (b) invest in marketable securities, (c) repurchase its own stock, or (d) purchase another firm. If the firm pays an extra dividend, its stockholders will have to pay taxes on the distribution. Marketable securities such as Treasury bonds provide a good temporary parking place for money, but the rate of return on such securities is less than that required by stockholders. A stock repurchase might result in a capital gain for the remaining stockholders, but it could be disadvantageous if the company has to pay a high price to acquire the stock, and, if the repurchase is designed solely to avoid paying dividends, it might be challenged by the IRS. However, using surplus cash to acquire another firm has no immediate tax consequences for either the acquiring firm or its stockholders, and this fact has motivated a number of mergers.

3. **Purchase of assets below their replacement cost.** Sometimes a firm will become an acquisition candidate because the replacement value of its assets is considerably higher than its market value. For example, in the 1980s oil companies could acquire reserves more cheaply by buying out other oil companies than by exploratory drilling. This factor was a motive in Chevron's acquisition of Gulf Oil. The acquisition of Republic Steel (the sixth largest steel company) by LTV (the fourth largest) provides another example of a firm being purchased because its purchase price was less than the replacement value of its assets. LTV found that it was less costly to purchase Republic Steel for $700 million than it would have been to construct a new steel mill. At the time, Republic's stock was selling for less than one-third of its book value. However, the merger did not help LTV's inefficient operations—ultimately, the company filed for bankruptcy.

4. **Diversification.** Managers often claim that diversification helps to stabilize the firm's earnings and thus reduces corporate risk. Therefore, diversification often is given as a reason for mergers. Stabilization of earnings certainly is beneficial to a firm's employees, suppliers, and customers, but its value to stockholders and debtholders is less clear. If an investor is worried about earnings variability, he or she probably could diversify through stock purchases (investment portfolio adjustment) more easily than the firm could through acquisitions.

5. **Maintaining control.** Some mergers and takeovers are considered *hostile* because the management of the acquired firm opposes the merger. One reason for the hostility is that the managers of the acquired companies generally lose their jobs, or at least their autonomy. Therefore, managers who own less than 50 percent plus one share of the stock in their firms look to devices that will lessen the chances of their firms' being taken over. Mergers can serve as such a device. For example, when Enron was under attack, it arranged to buy Houston Natural Gas

---

[14]Mergers undertaken only to use accumulated tax losses probably would be challenged by the IRS. However, because many factors are present in any given merger, it is hard to prove that a merger was motivated only, or even primarily, by tax considerations

DEFENSIVE MERGER
A merger designed to make a company less vulnerable to a takeover.

Company, paying for Houston primarily with debt. That merger made Enron much larger and hence harder for any potential acquirer to "digest." Also, the much higher debt level resulting from the merger made it hard for any acquiring company to use debt to buy Enron. Such **defensive mergers** are difficult to defend on economic grounds. The managers involved invariably argue that synergy, not a desire to protect their own jobs, motivated the acquisition, but there can be no question that many mergers have been designed more for the benefit of managers than for stockholders.

Types of Mergers

HORIZONTAL MERGER
A combination of two firms that produce the same type of good or service.

VERTICAL MERGER
A merger between a firm and one of its suppliers or customers.

CONGENERIC MERGER
A merger of firms in the same general industry, but for which no customer or supplier relationship exists.

CONGLOMERATE MERGER
A merger of companies in totally different industries.

Economists classify mergers into four groups: (1) horizontal, (2) vertical, (3) congeneric, and (4) conglomerate. A **horizontal merger** occurs when one firm combines with another in its same line of business. For example, the acquisition of Chrysler by Daimler-Benz AG in 1998 was a horizontal merger because both firms are automobile manufacturers. An example of a **vertical merger** is a steel producer's acquisition of one of its own suppliers, such as an iron or coal mining firm. The 1993 merger of Merck & Co., a manufacturer of health care products, and Medco Containment, the largest mail-order pharmacy service, is an example of a vertical merger. Congeneric means "allied in nature or action"; hence, a **congeneric merger** involves related enterprises but not producers of the same product (horizontal) or firms in a producer-supplier relationship (vertical). Examples of congeneric mergers include Viacom's acquisitions of Paramount Communications and Blockbuster Entertainment in 1994. Viacom owns several television stations and cable systems and distributes television programming, while Paramount produces movies and other entertainment shown both on television and in theaters, and Blockbuster's principal business is the rental of movies, most of which previously have been shown in theaters. A **conglomerate merger** occurs when unrelated enterprises combine, as illustrated by Sears, Roebuck & Company acquisitions of Dean Witter Reynolds Organization Inc., a securities broker and investment banker, and Coldwell Banker & Company, a real estate firm, in 1981. (Sears has since divested itself of both firms.)

Operating economies (and also anticompetitive effects) are dependent on the type of merger involved. Vertical and horizontal mergers generally provide the greatest synergistic operating benefits, but they also are the ones most likely to be attacked by the U.S. Department of Justice. In any event, it is useful to think of these economic classifications when analyzing the feasibility of a prospective merger.

Merger Activity

Four major "merger waves" have occurred in the United States. The first was in the late 1800s, when consolidations occurred in the oil, steel, tobacco, and other basic industries. The second was in the 1920s, when the stock market boom helped financial promoters consolidate firms in a number of industries, including utilities, communications, and autos. The third was in the 1960s, when conglomerate mergers were the rage, while the fourth began in the early 1980s, and it is still going strong. Many of the recent mergers have been horizontal mergers.

The current "merger mania" has been sparked by several factors: (1) at times, the depressed level of the dollar relative to Japanese and European currencies have made U.S. companies look cheap to foreign buyers; (2) the unprecedented level of inflation that existed during the 1970s and early 1980s, which increased the replacement value of firms' assets even while a weak stock market reduced their market values; (3) the general belief among the major natural resource companies that it is cheaper to "buy reserves on Wall Street" through mergers than to explore and find them in the field; (4) attempts to ward off raiders by use of defensive mergers; (5) the development of the junk bond market, which has made it possible to use far more debt in acquisitions than had been possible earlier; and (6) the increased globalization of business, which has led to increased economies of scale and to the formation of worldwide corporations.

The statistics that describe the latest merger wave show that it ranks as the largest in history. In every year since 1995, a new record for the values of announced mergers has been set. The amount of announced mergers in 1998 was more than $1.6 trillion, which was nearly 80 percent greater than in 1997. In fact, the ten largest deals in history were announced in 1998.

Table 18–3 shows the ten largest mergers that were completed in the United States in 1998 through the beginning of 1999. As we write this text in 1999, it appears the pace and size of mergers and acquisitions established in 1998 is continuing—the volume of merger activity in the first eight months of 1999 was nearly $900 billion, which is slightly lower than the 1998 merger level at the same time. To give you an indication of the size of the mergers that are expected to be completed in 1999, in Table 18–4 we include the deals that had recently been announced but not completed at the time this book was written.

Many of the mergers in 1998 and 1999 resulted either because the acquired firms were considered undervalued or because it was felt economies of scale could produce less costly combined operations. Increased global competition and governmental reforms were the major reasons for merger activities in the telecommunications and financial services industries, which accounted for the nearly 50 percent of the 1998 mergers. Experts expect these industries and other industries, such as defense, consumer products, and natural resources, to become significantly reshaped as merger activity continues in the future.

TABLE 18–3	The Largest Mergers Completed in the United States from June 1998 through June 1999 (billions of dollars)

RANK	ACQUIRING COMPANY	TARGET COMPANY	DATE ANNOUNCED	EFFECTIVE DATE	VALUE OF THE TRANSACTION
1	Travelers Group Inc.	Citicorp	4/6/98	10/8/98	$72.56
2	NationsBank Corp.	BankAmerica Corp.	4/13/98	9/30/98	61.63
3	Vodafone Group PLC	AirTouch Communications	1/18/99	6/30/99	60.29
4	AT&T Corp.	Tele-Communications	6/24/98	3/9/99	53.59
5	British Petroleum PLC	Amoco Corp.	8/11/98	12/31/98	48.71
6	WorldCom Inc.	MCI Communications	10/1/97	9/14/98	41.91
7	Daimler-Benz AG	Chrysler Corp.	5/7/98	11/12/98	40.47
8	Norwest Corp.	Wells Fargo & Co.	6/8/98	11/2/98	34.35
9	BANC ONE Corp.	First Chicago NBD	4/13/98	10/2/98	29.62
10	Berkshire Hathaway	General Re Corp.	6/19/98	12/21/98	22.34

SOURCE: Securities Data Company Inc., 1999.

TABLE 18–4	The Largest Mergers Announced (But Not Completed) in the United States from January 1998 through June 1999 (billions of dollars)

RANK	ACQUIRING COMPANY	TARGET COMPANY	DATE ANNOUNCED	VALUE OF THE TRANSACTION
1	Exxon	Mobil	12/1/98	$78.90
2	SBC Communications	Ameritech	5/11/98	62.59
3	AT&T	MediaOne	4/22/99	60.52
4	Bell Atlantic	GTE	7/28/98	53.59
5	Qwest Communications	US West	6/14/99	48.48
6	Viacom	CBS	9/7/99	36.30
7	BP Amoco	ARCO	4/1/99	27.22
8	Fleet Financial	BankBoston	3/14/99	15.93
9	AlliedSignal	Honeywell	6/7/99	15.60
10	Qwest Communications	Frontier	6/14/99	13.62

SOURCE: Securities Data Company Inc., 1999.

Self-Test Questions

What are the four primary motives behind most mergers?

From what sources do synergistic effects arise?

How have tax considerations stimulated mergers?

Is diversification to reduce stockholder risk a valid motive for mergers? Explain.

Explain briefly the four economic classifications of mergers.

What factors have sparked the most recent *merger mania?*

✳ **SMALL BUSINESS**

Lease Financing for Small Businesses

Earlier in this chapter we saw that, under certain conditions, leasing an asset can be less costly than borrowing to purchase the asset. For the small firm, leasing often offers three additional advantages: (1) it conserves cash, (2) it makes better use of managers' time, and (3) it provides financing quickly.

Conserving Cash. Small firms often have limited cash resources. Because many leasing companies do not require the lessee to make even a small down payment, and because leases often are for longer terms and thus require lower payments than bank loans,

leasing can help the small firm conserve its cash. Leasing companies also might be willing to work with a company to design a flexible leasing package that will help the lessee preserve its cash during critical times. For example, when Surgicare of Central Jersey opened its first surgical center, the firm did not have sufficient cash to pay for the necessary equipment. Surgicare's options were to borrow at a high interest rate, to sell stock to the public (which is difficult for a start-up firm), or to lease the equipment. Surgicare's financial vice president, John Rutzel, decided to lease the

continues

needed equipment from Copelco Financial Services, a leasing company that specializes in health care equipment. Copelco allowed Surgicare to make very low payments for the first six months, slightly higher payments during the second six months, and level payments thereafter. These unique lease terms helped Surgicare survive the most critical time for a new company—the start-up phase, when cash outflows generally exceed the cash inflows for some period of time.

Freeing Managers for Other Tasks. Most small business owners find that they never have enough time to get everything done—being in charge of sales, operations, budgeting, and everything else, they are simply spread too thin. If an asset is owned, the firm must maintain it in good working condition and also keep records on its use for tax depreciation purposes. However, leasing assets frees the business's owner of these duties. First, paperwork is reduced because maintenance records, depreciation schedules, and other records do not have to be maintained on leased assets. Second, less time might have to be spent "shopping around" for the right equipment because leasing companies that generally specialize in a particular industry can often provide the manager with the

information necessary to select the needed assets. Third, because the assets can be traded in if they become obsolete, the initial choice of equipment is less critical. Fourth, the burden of servicing and repairing the equipment often can be passed on to the lessor.

Obtaining Assets Quickly and Inexpensively. Many new, small firms find that banks are unwilling to lend them money at a reasonable cost. However, because leasing companies retain the ownership of the equipment, they might be more willing to take chances with start-up firms. When Ed Lavin started Offset Printing Company, his bank would not lend him the money to purchase the necessary printing presses—the bank wanted to lend only to firms with proven track records. Lavin arranged to lease the needed presses from Eaton Financial, which also advised him on the best type of equipment to meet his needs. As Lavin's company grew, he expanded by leasing additional equipment. Thus (1) leasing allowed Lavin to go into business when his bank was unwilling to help; (2) his leasing company provided him with help in selecting equipment; and (3) the leasing company also provided additional capital to meet his expansion needs.

Summary

This chapter discussed three hybrid forms of long-term financing: (1) preferred stock, (2) leasing, and (3) option securities. We also discussed corporate restructuring. The key concepts covered are listed here:

- **Preferred stock** is a **hybrid security** having some characteristics of debt and some of equity. Equity holders view preferred stock as being similar to debt because it has a claim on the firm's earnings ahead of the claim of the common stockholders. Bondholders, however, view preferred stock as equity because debtholders have a prior claim on the firm's income and assets.

- The primary **advantages of preferred stock to the issuer** are (1) preferred dividends are limited and (2) failure to pay them will not bankrupt the firm. The primary disadvantage to the issuer is that the cost of preferred stock is higher than that of debt because preferred dividend payments are not tax deductible.

- To the **investor,** preferred stock offers the advantage of **more dependable income** than common stock, and to a corporate investor, **70 percent of such dividends are not taxable.** The principal disadvantages to the investor are that the returns are limited and the investor has no legally enforceable right to a dividend.

- **Leasing** is a means of obtaining the use of an asset without purchasing that asset. The three most important forms of leasing are (1) **sale-and-leaseback arrangements,** under which a firm sells an asset to another party and leases the asset

- back for a specified period under specific terms; (2) **operating leases,** under which the lessor both maintains and finances the asset; and (3) **financial leases,** under which the asset is fully amortized over the life of the lease, the lessor does not normally provide maintenance, and the lease is not cancelable.

- The **decision to lease or buy an asset** is made by comparing the financing costs of the two alternatives and choosing the financing method with the lower cost. All cash flows should be discounted at the after-tax cost of debt because lease analysis cash flows are relatively certain and are on an after-tax basis.

- An **option** is a contract that gives its holder the right to buy (or sell) an asset at some predetermined price within a specified period of time. Options features are used by firms to "sweeten" debt offerings.

- A **warrant** is an **option issued by a firm** that gives the holder the right to purchase a stated number of shares of stock at a specified price within a given period. A warrant will be exercised if it is about to expire and the stock price is above the exercise price.

- A **convertible security** is a bond or preferred stock that can be exchanged for common stock. When conversion occurs, debt or preferred stock is replaced with common stock, but no money changes hands.

- The **conversion** of bonds or preferred stock by their holders **does not provide additional funds** to the company, but it does result in a lower debt ratio. The **exercise of warrants does provide additional funds,** which strengthens the firm's equity position, but it still leaves the debt or preferred stock on the balance sheet. Thus, low interest rate debt remains outstanding when warrants are exercised, but the firm loses this advantage when convertibles are converted.

- A **leveraged buyout (LBO)** is a transaction in which a firm's publicly owned stock is bought up in a mostly debt-financed tender offer, and a privately owned, highly leveraged firm results. Often, the firm's own management initiates the LBO.

- The reasons **mergers** take place include (1) *synergy*, (2) *tax considerations*, (3) low *asset values*, (4) *diversification*, and (5) ownership *control*. Mergers can be classified as **horizontal, vertical, congeneric,** or **conglomerate.**

- For the small firm, leasing offers three advantages: (1) **cash is conserved,** (2) **managers' time is freed** for other tasks, and (3) **financing often can be obtained quickly** and at a relatively low cost.

Questions

18–1 For purposes of measuring a firm's leverage, should preferred stock be classified as debt or equity? Does it matter if the classification is being made by (a) the firm's management, (b) creditors, or (c) equity investors?

18–2 You are told that one corporation just issued $100 million of preferred stock and another purchased $100 million of preferred stock as an investment. You are also told that one firm has an effective tax rate of 20 percent whereas the other is in the 34 percent bracket. Which firm is more likely to have bought the preferred? Explain.

18–3 One often finds that a company's bonds have a higher before-tax yield than its preferred stock, even though the bonds are considered to be less risky than the preferred to an investor. What causes this yield differential?

18–4 Distinguish between operating leases and financial leases. Would a firm be more likely to finance a fleet of trucks or a manufacturing plant with an operating lease?

18–5 One alleged advantage of leasing voiced in the past was that it kept liabilities off the balance sheet, thus making it possible for a firm to obtain more leverage than it otherwise could have. This raised the question of whether both the lease obligation and the asset involved should be capitalized and shown on the balance sheet. Discuss the pros and cons of capitalizing leases and related assets.

18–6 Suppose there were no IRS restrictions on what constitutes a valid lease. Explain in a manner that a legislator might understand why some restrictions should be imposed.

18–7 Suppose Congress changed the tax laws in a way that (a) permitted equipment to be depreciated over a shorter period, (b) lowered corporate tax rates, and (c) reinstated the investment tax credit. Discuss how each of these changes would affect the relative use of leasing versus conventional debt in the U.S. economy.

18–8 What effect does the expected growth rate of a firm's stock price (subsequent to issue) have on its ability to raise additional funds through (a) convertibles and (b) warrants?

18–9 a. How would a firm's decision to pay out a higher percentage of its earnings as dividends affect each of the following?
   (1) The value of its long-term warrants.
   (2) The likelihood that its convertible bonds will be converted.
   (3) The likelihood that its warrants will be exercised.
   b. If you owned the warrants or convertibles of a company, would you be pleased or displeased if it raised its payout rate from 20 percent to 80 percent? Why?

18–10 Suppose a company simultaneously issues $50 million of convertible bonds with a coupon rate of nine percent and $50 million of pure bonds with a coupon rate of 12 percent. Both bonds have the same maturity. Does the fact that the convertible issue has the lower coupon rate suggest that it is less risky than the pure bond? Would you regard its cost of capital as being lower on the convertible than on the pure bond? Explain. (*Hint:* Although it might appear at first glance that the convertible's cost of capital is lower, this is not necessarily the case because the interest rate on the convertible understates its cost. Think about this.)

18–11 Describe how LBOs are used to finance mergers.

Self-Test Problems

(Solutions appear in Appendix B)

key terms   **ST–1** Define each of the following terms:
   a. Cumulative dividends
   b. Lessee; lessor
   c. Sale and leaseback; operating lease; financial lease
   d. Off-balance-sheet financing
   e. FASB #13
   f. Residual value
   g. Option; striking, or exercise, price; call option; put option
   h. Warrant; detachable warrant; stepped-up exercise price
   i. Convertible security; conversion ratio, CR
   j. Simple EPS; primary EPS; fully diluted EPS

k. Leveraged buyout (LBO)

l. Merger; synergy

lease analysis   **ST–2** The Olsen Company has decided to acquire a new truck. One alternative is to lease the truck on a four-year contract for a lease payment of $10,000 per year, with payments to be made at the beginning of each year. The lease would include maintenance. Alternatively, Olsen could purchase the truck outright for $40,000, financing with a bank loan for the net purchase price, amortized over a four-year period at an interest rate of ten percent per year, payments to be made at the end of each year. Under the borrow-to-purchase arrangement, Olsen would have to maintain the truck at a cost of $1,000 per year, payable at year-end. The truck falls into the MACRS three-year class. It has a salvage value of $10,000, which is the expected market value after four years, at which time Olsen plans to replace the truck irrespective of whether it leases or buys. Olsen has a marginal tax rate of 40 percent.

a. What is Olsen's PV cost of leasing?

b. What is Olsen's PV cost of owning? Should the truck be leased or purchased?

c. The appropriate discount rate for use in Olsen's analysis is the firm's after-tax cost of debt. Why?

d. The salvage value is the least certain cash flow in the analysis. How might Olsen incorporate the higher riskiness of this cash flow into the analysis?

Problems

balance sheet effects of leasing   **18–1** Two textile companies, Grimm Manufacturing and Wright Mills, began operations with identical balance sheets. A year later, both required additional manufacturing capacity at a cost of $200,000. Grimm obtained a five-year, $200,000 loan at an eight percent interest rate from its bank. Wright, on the other hand, decided to lease the required $200,000 capacity from American Leasing for five years; an eight percent return was built into the lease. The balance sheet for each company, before the asset increases, is as follows:

		Debt	$200,000
		Equity	200,000
Total assets	$400,000	Total liabilities and equity	$400,000

a. Show the balance sheet of each firm after the asset increase, and calculate each firm's new debt ratio. (Assume Wright's lease is kept off the balance sheet.)

b. Show how Wright's balance sheet would have looked immediately after the financing if it had capitalized the lease.

c. Would the rate of return (i) on assets and (ii) on equity be affected by the choice of financing? How?

lease analysis   **18–2** As part of its overall plant modernization and cost reduction program, the management of Teweles Textile Mills has decided to install a new automated weaving loom. In the capital budgeting analysis of this equipment, the IRR of the project was found to be 20 percent versus a project required return of 12 percent.

The loom has an invoice price of $250,000, including delivery and installation charges. The funds needed could be borrowed from the bank through a four-year amortized loan at a ten percent interest rate, with payments to be made at the *end* of each year. In the event that the loom is purchased, the manufacturer will contract to maintain and service it for a fee of $20,000 per year paid at the end of each year. The loom falls in the MACRS five-year class, and Teweles's marginal tax rate is 40 percent.

Apilado Automation Inc., maker of the loom, has offered to lease the loom to Teweles for $70,000 upon delivery and installation (at t = 0) plus four additional annual lease payments of $70,000 to be made at the ends of Years 1 through 4. (Note that there are five lease payments in total.) The lease agreement includes maintenance and servicing. Actually, the loom has an expected life of eight years, at which time its expected salvage value is zero; however, after four years, its market value is expected to equal its book value of $42,500. Teweles plans to build an entirely new plant in four years, so it has no interest in either leasing or owning the proposed loom for more than that period.

a. Should the loom be leased or purchased?

b. The salvage value clearly is the most uncertain cash flow in the analysis. Assume that the appropriate salvage value pretax discount rate is 15 percent. What would be the effect of a salvage value risk adjustment on the decision?

c. The original analysis assumed that Teweles would not need the loom after four years. Now assume that the firm will continue to use it after the lease expires. Thus, if it leased, Teweles would have to buy the asset after four years at the then existing market value, which is assumed to equal the book value. What effect would this requirement have on the basic analysis? (No numerical analysis is required; just verbalize.)

convertible bond   **18–3**   The Swift Company was planning to finance an expansion in the summer of 2001. The principal executives of the company agreed that an industrial company like theirs should finance growth by means of common stock rather than by debt. However, they believed that the price of the company's common stock did not reflect its true worth, so they decided to sell a convertible bond.

a. What conversion price should be set by the issuer? The conversion rate will be 5.0; that is, each convertible bond can be converted into five shares of common.

b. Do you think the convertible bond should include a call provision? Why or why not?

financing alternatives   **18–4**   The Cox Computer Company has grown rapidly during the past five years. Recently its commercial bank urged the company to consider increasing its permanent financing. Its bank loan under a line of credit has risen to $150,000, carrying a ten percent interest rate, and Cox has been 30 to 60 days late in paying trade creditors.

Discussions with an investment banker have resulted in the decision to raise $250,000 at this time. Investment bankers have assured Cox that the following alternatives are feasible (flotation costs will be ignored):

Alternative 1: Sell common stock at $10 per share.

Alternative 2: Sell convertible bonds at a ten percent coupon, convertible into 80 shares of common stock for each $1,000 bond (that is, the conversion price is $12.50 per share).

Alternative 3: Sell debentures with a ten percent coupon; each $1,000 bond will have 80 warrants to buy one share of common stock at $12.50.

Charles Cox, the president, owns 80 percent of Cox's common stock and wishes to maintain control of the company; 50,000 shares are outstanding. The following are summaries of Cox's latest financial statements:

Balance Sheet

		Current liabilities	$200,000
		Common stock, $1 par	50,000
		Retained earnings	25,000
Total assets	$275,000	Total liabilities and equity	$275,000

Income Statement

Sales	$550,000
All costs except interest	495,000
EBIT	$ 55,000
Interest	15,000
EBT	$ 40,000
Taxes at 40%	16,000
Net income	$ 24,000
Shares outstanding	50,000
Earnings per share	$0.48
Price/earnings ratio	18×
Market price of stock	$8.64

a. Show the new balance sheet under each alternative. For Alternatives 2 and 3, show the balance sheet after conversion of the debentures or exercise of the warrants. Assume that $150,000 of the funds raised will be used to pay off the bank loan and the rest to increase total assets.

b. Show Charles Cox's control position under each alternative, assuming that he does not purchase additional shares.

c. What is the effect on earnings per share of each alternative if it is assumed that earnings before interest and taxes will be 20 percent of total assets?

d. What will be the debt ratio under each alternative?

e. Which of the three alternatives would you recommend to Charles Cox and why?

Exam-Type Problem

The problem included in this section is set up in such a way that it could be used as a multiple-choice exam problem.

lease versus buy   **18–5** Maltese Mining Company must install $1.5 million of new machinery in its Nevada mine. It can obtain a bank loan for 100 percent of the required amount. Alternatively, a Nevada investment banking firm that represents a group of investors believes that it can arrange for a lease financing plan. Assume that the following facts apply:

(1) The equipment falls in the MACRS three-year class.

(2) Estimated maintenance expenses are $75,000 per year.

(3) Maltese's marginal tax rate is 40 percent.

(4) If the money is borrowed, the bank loan will be at a rate of 15 percent, amortized in four equal installments to be paid at the end of each year.

(5) The tentative lease terms call for end-of-year payments of $400,000 per year for four years.

(6) Under the proposed lease terms, the lessee must pay for insurance, property taxes, and maintenance.

(7) Maltese must use the equipment if it is to continue in business, so it will almost certainly want to acquire the property at the end of the lease. If it does, then under the lease terms it can purchase the machinery at its fair market value at that time. The best estimate of this market value is the $250,000 salvage value, but it could be much higher or lower under certain circumstances.

To assist management in making the proper lease-versus-buy decision, you are asked to answer the following questions.

a. Assuming that the lease can be arranged, should Maltese lease or should it borrow and buy the equipment? Explain.

b. Consider the $250,000 estimated salvage value. Is it appropriate to discount it at the same rate as the other cash flows? What about the other cash flows—are they all equally risky? (*Hint:* Riskier cash flows are normally discounted at higher rates, but when the cash flows are *costs* rather than *inflows*, the normal procedure must be reversed.)

Integrative Problem

lease analysis **18–6** Kris Crawford, capital acquisitions manager for Heath Financial Services Inc., has been asked to perform a lease-versus-buy analysis on a new stock price quotation system for Heath's Sarasota branch office. The system would receive current prices, record the information for retrieval by the branch's brokers, and display current prices in the lobby.

The equipment costs $1,200,000, and, if it is purchased, Heath could obtain a term loan for the full amount at a ten percent cost. The loan would be amortized over the four-year life of the equipment, with payments made at the end of each year. The equipment is classified as special purpose, and hence it falls into the MACRS three-year class. If the equipment is purchased, a maintenance contract must be obtained at a cost of $25,000, payable at the beginning of each year.

After four years the equipment will be sold, and Crawford's best estimate of its residual value at that time is $125,000. Because technology is changing rapidly in real-time display systems, however, the residual value is very uncertain.

As an alternative, National Leasing is willing to write a four-year lease on the equipment, including maintenance, for payments of $340,000 at the *beginning* of each year. Heath's marginal tax rate is 40 percent. Help Crawford conduct her analysis by answering the following questions:

a. (1) Why is leasing sometimes referred to as *off-balance-sheet* financing?

(2) What is the difference between a capital lease and an operating lease?

(3) What effect does leasing have on a firm's capital structure?

b. (1) What is Heath's present value cost of owning the equipment? (*Hint:* Set up a table whose bottom line is a time line that shows the net cash flows over the period t = 0 to t = 4, and then find the PV of these net cash flows, or the PV cost of owning.)

(2) Explain the rationale for the discount rate you used to find the present value.

c. (1) What is Heath's present value cost of leasing the equipment? (*Hint:* Again, construct a cash flow time line.)

(2) What is the net advantage to leasing? Does your analysis indicate that Heath should buy or lease the equipment? Explain.

d. Now assume that Crawford believes the equipment's residual value could be as low as $0 or as high as $250,000, but she stands by $125,000 as her expected value. She concludes that the residual value is riskier than the other cash flows in the analysis, and she wants to incorporate this differential risk into her analysis. Describe how this could be accomplished. What effect would it have on Heath's lease decision?

e. Crawford knows that her firm has been considering moving to a new downtown location for some time, and she is concerned that these plans might come to fruition prior to the expiration of the lease. If the move occurs, the company would obtain completely new equipment, and hence Crawford would like to include a cancellation clause in the lease contract. What effect would a cancellation clause have on the riskiness of the lease?

Computer-Related Problem

Work the problem in this section only if you are using the computer problem diskette.

lease versus buy   **18–7** Use the model in File C18 to work this problem.

a. Refer to Problem 18–5. Determine the lease payment at which Maltese would be indifferent to buying or leasing—that is, find the lease payment that equates the NPV of leasing to that of buying. (*Hint:* Use trial and error.)

b. Using the $400,000 lease payment, what would be the effect if Maltese's tax rate fell to 20 percent? What would be the effect if the tax rate fell to zero percent? What do these results suggest?

ONLINE ESSENTIALS

http://elaonline.com   Equipment Leasing Association
Click on the selection titled "About Leasing" in the menu on the left side of the page and you will go to a page that provides information, definitions, and statistics related to equipment leases. This tutorial addresses such questions as "Why Should I Lease Equipment Instead of Buy?," "Who Leases?," "How Does Leasing Work?," and so on.

http://www.investhelp.com   The Online Investor
This site provides a great deal of investment-related information, including information about initial public offerings, stock splits, and mergers. If you click on the "Mergers" selection in the menu on the left side of the page, you will go to a page that describes the most recent mergers and acquisitions, along with the terms of the deals. If you click on the "You & Your Broker" selection, you will go to a page that provides information about stocks, including preferred stocks.

http://www.moneypages.com/syndicate   The Syndicate
Provides information about many types of financial assets and investment opportunities. There are a variety of menus that allow you to get information and research data related to stocks (both common and preferred), debt, options, and so forth.

http://www.thestockgroup.com   theStockGroup
Provides the "Preferred Stock of the Month," which gives the name of, and a link to, the company chosen to have the best preferred stock for the month. The previous month's selections are also available. In addition, there are links to other investment-related sites, including the "Top 100 Investor Sites."

Mathematical Tables

TABLE A-1	Present Value of $1 Due at the End of n Periods:

EQUATION:

$$PVIF_{i,n} = \frac{1}{(1 + i)^n}$$

FINANCIAL CALCULATOR KEYS:

n	i		0	1.0
N	**I**	**PV**	**PMT**	**FV**

Table
Value

PERIOD	1%	2%	3%	4%	5%	6%	7%	8%	9%	10%
1	.9901	.9804	.9709	.9615	.9524	.9434	.9346	.9259	.9174	.9091
2	.9803	.9612	.9426	.9246	.9070	.8900	.8734	.8573	.8417	.8264
3	.9706	.9423	.9151	.8890	.8638	.8396	.8163	.7938	.7722	.7513
4	.9610	.9238	.8885	.8548	.8227	.7921	.7629	.7350	.7084	.6830
5	.9515	.9057	.8626	.8219	.7835	.7473	.7130	.6806	.6499	.6209
6	.9420	.8880	.8375	.7903	.7462	.7050	.6663	.6302	.5963	.5645
7	.9327	.8706	.8131	.7599	.7107	.6651	.6227	.5835	.5470	.5132
8	.9235	.8535	.7894	.7307	.6768	.6274	.5820	.5403	.5019	.4665
9	.9143	.8368	.7664	.7026	.6446	.5919	.5439	.5002	.4604	.4241
10	.9053	.8203	.7441	.6756	.6139	.5584	.5083	.4632	.4224	.3855
11	.8963	.8043	.7224	.6496	.5847	.5268	.4751	.4289	.3875	.3505
12	.8874	.7885	.7014	.6246	.5568	.4970	.4440	.3971	.3555	.3186
13	.8787	.7730	.6810	.6006	.5303	.4688	.4150	.3677	.3262	.2897
14	.8700	.7579	.6611	.5775	.5051	.4423	.3878	.3405	.2992	.2633
15	.8613	.7430	.6419	.5553	.4810	.4173	.3624	.3152	.2745	.2394
16	.8528	.7284	.6232	.5339	.4581	.3936	.3387	.2919	.2519	.2176
17	.8444	.7142	.6050	.5134	.4363	.3714	.3166	.2703	.2311	.1978
18	.8360	.7002	.5874	.4936	.4155	.3503	.2959	.2502	.2120	.1799
19	.8277	.6864	.5703	.4746	.3957	.3305	.2765	.2317	.1945	.1635
20	.8195	.6730	.5537	.4564	.3769	.3118	.2584	.2145	.1784	.1486
21	.8114	.6598	.5375	.4388	.3589	.2942	.2415	.1987	.1637	.1351
22	.8034	.6468	.5219	.4220	.3418	.2775	.2257	.1839	.1502	.1228
23	.7954	.6342	.5067	.4057	.3256	.2618	.2109	.1703	.1378	.1117
24	.7876	.6217	.4919	.3901	.3101	.2470	.1971	.1577	.1264	.1015
25	.7798	.6095	.4776	.3751	.2953	.2330	.1842	.1460	.1160	.0923
26	.7720	.5976	.4637	.3607	.2812	.2198	.1722	.1352	.1064	.0839
27	.7644	.5859	.4502	.3468	.2678	.2074	.1609	.1252	.0976	.0763
28	.7568	.5744	.4371	.3335	.2551	.1956	.1504	.1159	.0895	.0693
29	.7493	.5631	.4243	.3207	.2429	.1846	.1406	.1073	.0822	.0630
30	.7419	.5521	.4120	.3083	.2314	.1741	.1314	.0994	.0754	.0573
35	.7059	.5000	.3554	.2534	.1813	.1301	.0937	.0676	.0490	.0356
40	.6717	.4529	.3066	.2083	.1420	.0972	.0668	.0460	.0318	.0221
45	.6391	.4102	.2644	.1712	.1113	.0727	.0476	.0313	.0207	.0137
50	.6080	.3715	.2281	.1407	.0872	.0543	.0339	.0213	.0134	.0085
55	.5785	.3365	.1968	.1157	.0683	.0406	.0242	.0145	.0087	.0053

TABLE A-1	Continued

PERIOD	12%	14%	15%	16%	18%	20%	24%	28%	32%	36%
1	.8929	.8772	.8696	.8621	.8475	.8333	.8065	.7813	.7576	.7353
2	.7972	.7695	.7561	.7432	.7182	.6944	.6504	.6104	.5739	.5407
3	.7118	.6750	.6575	.6407	.6086	.5787	.5245	.4768	.4348	.3975
4	.6355	.5921	.5718	.5523	.5158	.4823	.4230	.3725	.3294	.2923
5	.5674	.5194	.4972	.4761	.4371	.4019	.3411	.2910	.2495	.2149
6	.5066	.4556	.4323	.4104	.3704	.3349	.2751	.2274	.1890	.1580
7	.4523	.3996	.3759	.3538	.3139	.2791	.2218	.1776	.1432	.1162
8	.4039	.3506	.3269	.3050	.2660	.2326	.1789	.1388	.1085	.0854
9	.3606	.3075	.2843	.2630	.2255	.1938	.1443	.1084	.0822	.0628
10	.3220	.2697	.2472	.2267	.1911	.1615	.1164	.0847	.0623	.0462
11	.2875	.2366	.2149	.1954	.1619	.1346	.0938	.0662	.0472	.0340
12	.2567	.2076	.1869	.1685	.1372	.1122	.0757	.0517	.0357	.0250
13	.2292	.1821	.1625	.1452	.1163	.0935	.0610	.0404	.0271	.0184
14	.2046	.1597	.1413	.1252	.0985	.0779	.0492	.0316	.0205	.0135
15	.1827	.1401	.1229	.1079	.0835	.0649	.0397	.0247	.0155	.0099
16	.1631	.1229	.1069	.0930	.0708	.0541	.0320	.0193	.0118	.0073
17	.1456	.1078	.0929	.0802	.0600	.0451	.0258	.0150	.0089	.0054
18	.1300	.0946	.0808	.0691	.0508	.0376	.0208	.0118	.0068	.0039
19	.1161	.0829	.0703	.0596	.0431	.0313	.0168	.0092	.0051	.0029
20	.1037	.0728	.0611	.0514	.0365	.0261	.0135	.0072	.0039	.0021
21	.0926	.0638	.0531	.0443	.0309	.0217	.0109	.0056	.0029	.0016
22	.0826	.0560	.0462	.0382	.0262	.0181	.0088	.0044	.0022	.0012
23	.0738	.0491	.0402	.0329	.0222	.0151	.0071	.0034	.0017	.0008
24	.0659	.0431	.0349	.0284	.0188	.0126	.0057	.0027	.0013	.0006
25	.0588	.0378	.0304	.0245	.0160	.0105	.0046	.0021	.0010	.0005
26	.0525	.0331	.0264	.0211	.0135	.0087	.0037	.0016	.0007	.0003
27	.0469	.0291	.0230	.0182	.0115	.0073	.0030	.0013	.0006	.0002
28	.0419	.0255	.0200	.0157	.0097	.0061	.0024	.0010	.0004	.0002
29	.0374	.0224	.0174	.0135	.0082	.0051	.0020	.0008	.0003	.0001
30	.0334	.0196	.0151	.0116	.0070	.0042	.0016	.0006	.0002	.0001
35	.0189	.0102	.0075	.0055	.0030	.0017	.0005	.0002	.0001	*
40	.0107	.0053	.0037	.0026	.0013	.0007	.0002	.0001	*	*
45	.0061	.0027	.0019	.0013	.0006	.0003	.0001	*	*	*
50	.0035	.0014	.0009	.0006	.0003	.0001	*	*	*	*
55	.0020	.0007	.0005	.0003	.0001	*	*	*	*	*

*The factor is zero to four decimal places.

TABLE A-2	Present Value of an Annuity of $1 per Period for n Periods:

EQUATION:

$$PVIFA_{i,n} = \sum_{t=1}^{N} \frac{1}{(1+i)^n} = \frac{1 - \dfrac{1}{(1+i)^n}}{i} = \frac{1}{i} - \frac{1}{i(1+i)^n}$$

FINANCIAL CALCULATOR KEYS:

n	i		1.0	0
N	I	PV	PMT	FV
		Table Value		

NUMBER OF PERIODS	1%	2%	3%	4%	5%	6%	7%	8%	9%
1	0.9901	0.9804	0.9709	0.9615	0.9524	0.9434	0.9346	0.9259	0.9174
2	1.9704	1.9416	1.9135	1.8861	1.8594	1.8334	1.8080	1.7833	1.7591
3	2.9410	2.8839	2.8286	2.7751	2.7232	2.6730	2.6243	2.5771	2.5313
4	3.9020	3.8077	3.7171	3.6299	3.5460	3.4651	3.3872	3.3121	3.2397
5	4.8534	4.7135	4.5797	4.4518	4.3295	4.2124	4.1002	3.9927	3.8897
6	5.7955	5.6014	5.4172	5.2421	5.0757	4.9173	4.7665	4.6229	4.4859
7	6.7282	6.4720	6.2303	6.0021	5.7864	5.5824	5.3893	5.2064	5.0330
8	7.6517	7.3255	7.0197	6.7327	6.4632	6.2098	5.9713	5.7466	5.5348
9	8.5660	8.1622	7.7861	7.4353	7.1078	6.8017	6.5152	6.2469	5.9952
10	9.4713	8.9826	8.5302	8.1109	7.7217	7.3601	7.0236	6.7101	6.4177
11	10.3676	9.7868	9.2526	8.7605	8.3064	7.8869	7.4987	7.1390	6.8052
12	11.2551	10.5753	9.9540	9.3851	8.8633	8.3838	7.9427	7.5361	7.1607
13	12.1337	11.3484	10.6350	9.9856	9.3936	8.8527	8.3577	7.9038	7.4869
14	13.0037	12.1062	11.2961	10.5631	9.8986	9.2950	8.7455	8.2442	7.7862
15	13.8651	12.8493	11.9379	11.1184	10.3797	9.7122	9.1079	8.5595	8.0607
16	14.7179	13.5777	12.5611	11.6523	10.8378	10.1059	9.4466	8.8514	8.3126
17	15.5623	14.2919	13.1661	12.1657	11.2741	10.4773	9.7632	9.1216	8.5436
18	16.3983	14.9920	13.7535	12.6593	11.6896	10.8276	10.0591	9.3719	8.7556
19	17.2260	15.6785	14.3238	13.1339	12.0853	11.1581	10.3356	9.6036	8.9501
20	18.0456	16.3514	14.8775	13.5903	12.4622	11.4699	10.5940	9.8181	9.1285
21	18.8570	17.0112	15.4150	14.0292	12.8212	11.7641	10.8355	10.0168	9.2922
22	19.6604	17.6580	15.9369	14.4511	13.1630	12.0416	11.0612	10.2007	9.4424
23	20.4558	18.2922	16.4436	14.8568	13.4886	12.3034	11.2722	10.3711	9.5802
24	21.2434	18.9139	16.9355	15.2470	13.7986	12.5504	11.4693	10.5288	9.7066
25	22.0232	19.5235	17.4131	15.6221	14.0939	12.7834	11.6536	10.6748	9.8226
26	22.7952	20.1210	17.8768	15.9828	14.3752	13.0032	11.8258	10.8100	9.9290
27	23.5596	20.7069	18.3270	16.3296	14.6430	13.2105	11.9867	10.9352	10.0266
28	24.3164	21.2813	18.7641	16.6631	14.8981	13.4062	12.1371	11.0511	10.1161
29	25.0658	21.8444	19.1885	16.9837	15.1411	13.5907	12.2777	11.1584	10.1983
30	25.8077	22.3965	19.6004	17.2920	15.3725	13.7648	12.4090	11.2578	10.2737
35	29.4086	24.9986	21.4872	18.6646	16.3742	14.4982	12.9477	11.6546	10.5668
40	32.8347	27.3555	23.1148	19.7928	17.1591	15.0463	13.3317	11.9246	10.7574
45	36.0945	29.4902	24.5187	20.7200	17.7741	15.4558	13.6055	12.1084	10.8812
50	39.1961	31.4236	25.7298	21.4822	18.2559	15.7619	13.8007	12.2335	10.9617
55	42.1472	33.1748	26.7744	22.1086	18.6335	15.9905	13.9399	12.3186	11.0140

TABLE A-2 | Continued

NUMBER OF PERIODS	10%	12%	14%	15%	16%	18%	20%	24%	28%	32%
1	0.9091	0.8929	0.8772	0.8696	0.8621	0.8475	0.8333	0.8065	0.7813	0.7576
2	1.7355	1.6901	1.6467	1.6257	1.6052	1.5656	1.5278	1.4568	1.3916	1.3315
3	2.4869	2.4018	2.3216	2.2832	2.2459	2.1743	2.1065	1.9813	1.8684	1.7663
4	3.1699	3.0373	2.9137	2.8550	2.7982	2.6901	2.5887	2.4043	2.2410	2.0957
5	3.7908	3.6048	3.4331	3.3522	3.2743	3.1272	2.9906	2.7454	2.5320	2.3452
6	4.3553	4.1114	3.8887	3.7845	3.6847	3.4976	3.3255	3.0205	2.7594	2.5342
7	4.8684	4.5638	4.2883	4.1604	4.0386	3.8115	3.6046	3.2423	2.9370	2.6775
8	5.3349	4.9676	4.6389	4.4873	4.3436	4.0776	3.8372	3.4212	3.0758	2.7860
9	5.7590	5.3282	4.9464	4.7716	4.6065	4.3030	4.0310	3.5655	3.1842	2.8681
10	6.1446	5.6502	5.2161	5.0188	4.8332	4.4941	4.1925	3.6819	3.2689	2.9304
11	6.4951	5.9377	5.4527	5.2337	5.0286	4.6560	4.3271	3.7757	3.3351	2.9776
12	6.8137	6.1944	5.6603	5.4206	5.1971	4.7932	4.4392	3.8514	3.3868	3.0133
13	7.1034	6.4235	5.8424	5.5831	5.3423	4.9095	4.5327	3.9124	3.4272	3.0404
14	7.3667	6.6282	6.0021	5.7245	5.4675	5.0081	4.6106	3.9616	3.4587	3.0609
15	7.6061	6.8109	6.1422	5.8474	5.5755	5.0916	4.6755	4.0013	3.4834	3.0764
16	7.8237	6.9740	6.2651	5.9542	5.6685	5.1624	4.7296	4.0333	3.5026	3.0882
17	8.0216	7.1196	6.3729	6.0472	5.7487	5.2223	4.7746	4.0591	3.5177	3.0971
18	8.2014	7.2497	6.4674	6.1280	5.8178	5.2732	4.8122	4.0799	3.5294	3.1039
19	8.3649	7.3658	6.5504	6.1982	5.8775	5.3162	4.8435	4.0967	3.5386	3.1090
20	8.5136	7.4694	6.6231	6.2593	5.9288	5.3527	4.8696	4.1103	3.5458	3.1129
21	8.6487	7.5620	6.6870	6.3125	5.9731	5.3837	4.8913	4.1212	3.5514	3.1158
22	8.7715	7.6446	6.7429	6.3587	6.0113	5.4099	4.9094	4.1300	3.5558	3.1180
23	8.8832	7.7184	6.7921	6.3988	6.0442	5.4321	4.9245	4.1371	3.5592	3.1197
24	8.9847	7.7843	6.8351	6.4338	6.0726	5.4509	4.9371	4.1428	3.5619	3.1210
25	9.0770	7.8431	6.8729	6.4641	6.0971	5.4669	4.9476	4.1474	3.5640	3.1220
26	9.1609	7.8957	6.9061	6.4906	6.1182	5.4804	4.9563	4.1511	3.5656	3.1227
27	9.2372	7.9426	6.9352	6.5135	6.1364	5.4919	4.9636	4.1542	3.5669	3.1233
28	9.3066	7.9844	6.9607	6.5335	6.1520	5.5016	4.9697	4.1566	3.5679	3.1237
29	9.3696	8.0218	6.9830	6.5509	6.1656	5.5098	4.9747	4.1585	3.5687	3.1240
30	9.4269	8.0552	7.0027	6.5660	6.1772	5.5168	4.9789	4.1601	3.5693	3.1242
35	9.6442	8.1755	7.0700	6.6166	6.2153	5.5386	4.9915	4.1644	3.5708	3.1248
40	9.7791	8.2438	7.1050	6.6418	6.2335	5.5482	4.9966	4.1659	3.5712	3.1250
45	9.8628	8.2825	7.1232	6.6543	6.2421	5.5523	4.9986	4.1664	3.5714	3.1250
50	9.9148	8.3045	7.1327	6.6605	6.2463	5.5541	4.9995	4.1666	3.5714	3.1250
55	9.9471	8.3170	7.1376	6.6636	6.2482	5.5549	4.9998	4.1666	3.5714	3.1250

TABLE A-3	Future Value of $1 at the End of n Periods:

EQUATION:

$FVIF_{i,n} = (1 + i)^n$

FINANCIAL CALCULATOR KEYS:

n	i	1.0	0	
N	**I**	**PV**	**PMT**	**FV**

Table
Value

PERIOD	1%	2%	3%	4%	5%	6%	7%	8%	9%	10%
1	1.0100	1.0200	1.0300	1.0400	1.0500	1.0600	1.0700	1.0800	1.0900	1.1000
2	1.0201	1.0404	1.0609	1.0816	1.1025	1.1236	1.1449	1.1664	1.1881	1.2100
3	1.0303	1.0612	1.0927	1.1249	1.1576	1.1910	1.2250	1.2597	1.2950	1.3310
4	1.0406	1.0824	1.1255	1.1699	1.2155	1.2625	1.3108	1.3605	1.4116	1.4641
5	1.0510	1.1041	1.1593	1.2167	1.2763	1.3382	1.4026	1.4693	1.5386	1.6105
6	1.0615	1.1262	1.1941	1.2653	1.3401	1.4185	1.5007	1.5869	1.6771	1.7716
7	1.0721	1.1487	1.2299	1.3159	1.4071	1.5036	1.6058	1.7138	1.8280	1.9487
8	1.0829	1.1717	1.2668	1.3686	1.4775	1.5938	1.7182	1.8509	1.9926	2.1436
9	1.0937	1.1951	1.3048	1.4233	1.5513	1.6895	1.8385	1.9990	2.1719	2.3579
10	1.1046	1.2190	1.3439	1.4802	1.6289	1.7908	1.9672	2.1589	2.3674	2.5937
11	1.1157	1.2434	1.3842	1.5395	1.7103	1.8983	2.1049	2.3316	2.5804	2.8531
12	1.1268	1.2682	1.4258	1.6010	1.7959	2.0122	2.2522	2.5182	2.8127	3.1384
13	1.1381	1.2936	1.4685	1.6651	1.8856	2.1329	2.4098	2.7196	3.0658	3.4523
14	1.1495	1.3195	1.5126	1.7317	1.9799	2.2609	2.5785	2.9372	3.3417	3.7975
15	1.1610	1.3459	1.5580	1.8009	2.0789	2.3966	2.7590	3.1722	3.6425	4.1772
16	1.1726	1.3728	1.6047	1.8730	2.1829	2.5404	2.9522	3.4259	3.9703	4.5950
17	1.1843	1.4002	1.6528	1.9479	2.2920	2.6928	3.1588	3.7000	4.3276	5.0545
18	1.1961	1.4282	1.7024	2.0258	2.4066	2.8543	3.3799	3.9960	4.7171	5.5599
19	1.2081	1.4568	1.7535	2.1068	2.5270	3.0256	3.6165	4.3157	5.1417	6.1159
20	1.2202	1.4859	1.8061	2.1911	2.6533	3.2071	3.8697	4.6610	5.6044	6.7275
21	1.2324	1.5157	1.8603	2.2788	2.7860	3.3996	4.1406	5.0338	6.1088	7.4002
22	1.2447	1.5460	1.9161	2.3699	2.9253	3.6035	4.4304	5.4365	6.6586	8.1403
23	1.2572	1.5769	1.9736	2.4647	3.0715	3.8197	4.7405	5.8715	7.2579	8.9543
24	1.2697	1.6084	2.0328	2.5633	3.2251	4.0489	5.0724	6.3412	7.9111	9.8497
25	1.2824	1.6406	2.0938	2.6658	3.3864	4.2919	5.4274	6.8485	8.6231	10.835
26	1.2953	1.6734	2.1566	2.7725	3.5557	4.5494	5.8074	7.3964	9.3992	11.918
27	1.3082	1.7069	2.2213	2.8834	3.7335	4.8223	6.2139	7.9881	10.245	13.110
28	1.3213	1.7410	2.2879	2.9987	3.9201	5.1117	6.6488	8.6271	11.167	14.421
29	1.3345	1.7758	2.3566	3.1187	4.1161	5.4184	7.1143	9.3173	12.172	15.863
30	1.3478	1.8114	2.4273	3.2434	4.3219	5.7435	7.6123	10.063	13.268	17.449
40	1.4889	2.2080	3.2620	4.8010	7.0400	10.286	14.974	21.725	31.409	45.259
50	1.6446	2.6916	4.3839	7.1067	11.467	18.420	29.457	46.902	74.358	117.39
60	1.8167	3.2810	5.8916	10.520	18.679	32.988	57.946	101.26	176.03	304.48

TABLE A-3 Continued

PERIOD	12%	14%	15%	16%	18%	20%	24%	28%	32%	36%
1	1.1200	1.1400	1.1500	1.1600	1.1800	1.2000	1.2400	1.2800	1.3200	1.3600
2	1.2544	1.2996	1.3225	1.3456	1.3924	1.4400	1.5376	1.6384	1.7424	1.8496
3	1.4049	1.4815	1.5209	1.5609	1.6430	1.7280	1.9066	2.0972	2.3000	2.5155
4	1.5735	1.6890	1.7490	1.8106	1.9388	2.0736	2.3642	2.6844	3.0360	3.4210
5	1.7623	1.9254	2.0114	2.1003	2.2878	2.4883	2.9316	3.4360	4.0075	4.6526
6	1.9738	2.1950	2.3131	2.4364	2.6996	2.9860	3.6352	4.3980	5.2899	6.3275
7	2.2107	2.5023	2.6600	2.8262	3.1855	3.5832	4.5077	5.6295	6.9826	8.6054
8	2.4760	2.8526	3.0590	3.2784	3.7589	4.2998	5.5895	7.2058	9.2170	11.703
9	2.7731	3.2519	3.5179	3.8030	4.4355	5.1598	6.9310	9.2234	12.166	15.917
10	3.1058	3.7072	4.0456	4.4114	5.2338	6.1917	8.5944	11.806	16.060	21.647
11	3.4785	4.2262	4.6524	5.1173	6.1759	7.4301	10.657	15.112	21.199	29.439
12	3.8960	4.8179	5.3503	5.9360	7.2876	8.9161	13.215	19.343	27.983	40.037
13	4.3635	5.4924	6.1528	6.8858	8.5994	10.699	16.386	24.759	36.937	54.451
14	4.8871	6.2613	7.0757	7.9875	10.147	12.839	20.319	31.691	48.757	74.053
15	5.4736	7.1379	8.1371	9.2655	11.974	15.407	25.196	40.565	64.359	100.71
16	6.1304	8.1372	9.3576	10.748	14.129	18.488	31.243	51.923	84.954	136.97
17	6.8660	9.2765	10.761	12.468	16.672	22.186	38.741	66.461	112.14	186.28
18	7.6900	10.575	12.375	14.463	19.673	26.623	48.039	85.071	148.02	253.34
19	8.6128	12.056	14.232	16.777	23.214	31.948	59.568	108.89	195.39	344.54
20	9.6463	13.743	16.367	19.461	27.393	38.338	73.864	139.38	257.92	468.57
21	10.804	15.668	18.822	22.574	32.324	46.005	91.592	178.41	340.45	637.26
22	12.100	17.861	21.645	26.186	38.142	55.206	113.57	228.36	449.39	866.67
23	13.552	20.362	24.891	30.376	45.008	66.247	140.83	292.30	593.20	1178.7
24	15.179	23.212	28.625	35.236	53.109	79.497	174.63	374.14	783.02	1603.0
25	17.000	26.462	32.919	40.874	62.669	95.396	216.54	478.90	1033.6	2180.1
26	19.040	30.167	37.857	47.414	73.949	114.48	268.51	613.00	1364.3	2964.9
27	21.325	34.390	43.535	55.000	87.260	137.37	332.95	784.64	1800.9	4032.3
28	23.884	39.204	50.066	63.800	102.97	164.84	412.86	1004.3	2377.2	5483.9
29	26.750	44.693	57.575	74.009	121.50	197.81	511.95	1285.6	3137.9	7458.1
30	29.960	50.950	66.212	85.850	143.37	237.38	634.82	1645.5	4142.1	10143.
40	93.051	188.88	267.86	378.72	750.38	1469.8	5455.9	19427.	66521.	*
50	289.00	700.23	1083.7	1670.7	3927.4	9100.4	46890.	*	*	*
60	897.60	2595.9	4384.0	7370.2	20555.	56348.	*	*	*	*

*FVIF > 99,999.

TABLE A-4	Future Value of an Annuity of $1 per Period for n Periods:

EQUATION:

$$FVIFA_{i,n} = \sum_{t=1}^{n} (1 + i)^{n-t} = \frac{(1 + i)^n - 1}{i}$$

FINANCIAL CALCULATOR KEYS:

n	i	0	1.0	
N	**I**	**PV**	**PMT**	**FV**

Table
Value

NUMBER OF PERIODS	1%	2%	3%	4%	5%	6%	7%	8%	9%	10%
1	1.0000	1.0000	1.0000	1.0000	1.0000	1.0000	1.0000	1.0000	1.0000	1.0000
2	2.0100	2.0200	2.0300	2.0400	2.0500	2.0600	2.0700	2.0800	2.0900	2.1000
3	3.0301	3.0604	3.0909	3.1216	3.1525	3.1836	3.2149	3.2464	3.2781	3.3100
4	4.0604	4.1216	4.1836	4.2465	4.3101	4.3746	4.4399	4.5061	4.5731	4.6410
5	5.1010	5.2040	5.3091	5.4163	5.5256	5.6371	5.7507	5.8666	5.9847	6.1051
6	6.1520	6.3081	6.4684	6.6330	6.8019	6.9753	7.1533	7.3359	7.5233	7.7156
7	7.2135	7.4343	7.6625	7.8983	8.1420	8.3938	8.6540	8.9228	9.2004	9.4872
8	8.2857	8.5830	8.8923	9.2142	9.5491	9.8975	10.260	10.637	11.028	11.436
9	9.3685	9.7546	10.159	10.583	11.027	11.491	11.978	12.488	13.021	13.579
10	10.462	10.950	11.464	12.006	12.578	13.181	13.816	14.487	15.193	15.937
11	11.567	12.169	12.808	13.486	14.207	14.972	15.784	16.645	17.560	18.531
12	12.683	13.412	14.192	15.026	15.917	16.870	17.888	18.977	20.141	21.384
13	13.809	14.680	15.618	16.627	17.713	18.882	20.141	21.495	22.953	24.523
14	14.947	15.974	17.086	18.292	19.599	21.015	22.550	24.215	26.019	27.975
15	16.097	17.293	18.599	20.024	21.579	23.276	25.129	27.152	29.361	31.772
16	17.258	18.639	20.157	21.825	23.657	25.673	27.888	30.324	33.003	35.950
17	18.430	20.012	21.762	23.698	25.840	28.213	30.840	33.750	36.974	40.545
18	19.615	21.412	23.414	25.645	28.132	30.906	33.999	37.450	41.301	45.599
19	20.811	22.841	25.117	27.671	30.539	33.760	37.379	41.446	46.018	51.159
20	22.019	24.297	26.870	29.778	33.066	36.786	40.995	45.762	51.160	57.275
21	23.239	25.783	28.676	31.969	35.719	39.993	44.865	50.423	56.765	64.002
22	24.472	27.299	30.537	34.248	38.505	43.392	49.006	55.457	62.873	71.403
23	25.716	28.845	32.453	36.618	41.430	46.996	53.436	60.893	69.532	79.543
24	26.973	30.422	34.426	39.083	44.502	50.816	58.177	66.765	76.790	88.497
25	28.243	32.030	36.459	41.646	47.727	54.865	63.249	73.106	84.701	98.347
26	29.526	33.671	38.553	44.312	51.113	59.156	68.676	79.954	93.324	109.18
27	30.821	35.344	40.710	47.084	54.669	63.706	74.484	87.351	102.72	121.10
28	32.129	37.051	42.931	49.968	58.403	68.528	80.698	95.339	112.97	134.21
29	33.450	38.792	45.219	52.966	62.323	73.640	87.347	103.97	124.14	148.63
30	34.785	40.568	47.575	56.085	66.439	79.058	94.461	113.28	136.31	164.49
40	48.886	60.402	75.401	95.026	120.80	154.76	199.64	259.06	337.88	442.59
50	64.463	84.579	112.80	152.67	209.35	290.34	406.53	573.77	815.08	1163.9
60	81.670	114.05	163.05	237.99	353.58	533.13	813.52	1253.2	1944.8	3034.8

TABLE A-4	Continued

NUMBER OF PERIODS	12%	14%	15%	16%	18%	20%	24%	28%	32%	36%
1	1.0000	1.0000	1.0000	1.0000	1.0000	1.0000	1.0000	1.0000	1.0000	1.0000
2	2.1200	2.1400	2.1500	2.1600	2.1800	2.2000	2.2400	2.2800	2.3200	2.3600
3	3.3744	3.4396	3.4725	3.5056	3.5724	3.6400	3.7776	3.9184	4.0624	4.2096
4	4.7793	4.9211	4.9934	5.0665	5.2154	5.3680	5.6842	6.0156	6.3624	6.7251
5	6.3528	6.6101	6.7424	6.8771	7.1542	7.4416	8.0484	8.6999	9.3983	10.146
6	8.1152	8.5355	8.7537	8.9775	9.4420	9.9299	10.980	12.136	13.406	14.799
7	10.089	10.730	11.067	11.414	12.142	12.916	14.615	16.534	18.696	21.126
8	12.300	13.233	13.727	14.240	15.327	16.499	19.123	22.163	25.678	29.732
9	14.776	16.085	16.786	17.519	19.086	20.799	24.712	29.369	34.895	41.435
10	17.549	19.337	20.304	21.321	23.521	25.959	31.643	38.593	47.062	57.352
11	20.655	23.045	24.349	25.733	28.755	32.150	40.238	50.398	63.122	78.998
12	24.133	27.271	29.002	30.850	34.931	39.581	50.895	65.510	84.320	108.44
13	28.029	32.089	34.352	36.786	42.219	48.497	64.110	84.853	112.30	148.47
14	32.393	37.581	40.505	43.672	50.818	59.196	80.496	109.61	149.24	202.93
15	37.280	43.842	47.580	51.660	60.965	72.035	100.82	141.30	198.00	276.98
16	42.753	50.980	55.717	60.925	72.939	87.442	126.01	181.87	262.36	377.69
17	48.884	59.118	65.075	71.673	87.068	105.93	157.25	233.79	347.31	514.66
18	55.750	68.394	75.836	84.141	103.74	128.12	195.99	300.25	459.45	700.94
19	63.440	78.969	88.212	98.603	123.41	154.74	244.03	385.32	607.47	954.28
20	72.052	91.025	102.44	115.38	146.63	186.69	303.60	494.21	802.86	1298.8
21	81.699	104.77	118.81	134.84	174.02	225.03	377.46	633.59	1060.8	1767.4
22	92.503	120.44	137.63	157.41	206.34	271.03	469.06	812.00	1401.2	2404.7
23	104.60	138.30	159.28	183.60	244.49	326.24	582.63	1040.4	1850.6	3271.3
24	118.16	158.66	184.17	213.98	289.49	392.48	723.46	1332.7	2443.8	4450.0
25	133.33	181.87	212.79	249.21	342.60	471.98	898.09	1706.8	3226.8	6053.0
26	150.33	208.33	245.71	290.09	405.27	567.38	1114.6	2185.7	4260.4	8233.1
27	169.37	238.50	283.57	337.50	479.22	681.85	1383.1	2798.7	5624.8	11198.0
28	190.70	272.89	327.10	392.50	566.48	819.22	1716.1	3583.3	7425.7	15230.3
29	214.58	312.09	377.17	456.30	669.45	984.07	2129.0	4587.7	9802.9	20714.2
30	241.33	356.79	434.75	530.31	790.95	1181.9	2640.9	5873.2	12941.	28172.3
40	767.09	1342.0	1779.1	2360.8	4163.2	7343.9	22729.	69377.	*	*
50	2400.0	4994.5	7217.7	10436.	21813.	45497.	*	*	*	*
60	7471.6	18535.	29220.	46058.	*	*	*	*	*	*

*FVIFA > 99,999.

APPENDIX B

Solutions to Self-Test Problems

Note: Except for Chapter 1, we do not show an answer for ST-1 problems because they are verbal rather than quantitative in nature.

Chapter 1

ST–1 Refer to the marginal glossary definitions or relevant chapter sections to check your responses.

Chapter 2

ST–2 a. Average = (6% + 7% + 8% + 9%)/4 = 30%/4 = 7.5%.

    b. $k_{\text{T-bond}} = k^* + IP = 3.0\% + 7.5\% = 10.5\%$.

    c. If the five-year T-bond rate is 11 percent, the inflation rate is expected to average approximately 11% − 3% = 8% during the next five years. Thus, the implied Year 5 inflation rate is 10 percent:

$$8\% = (6\% + 7\% + 8\% + 9\% + I_5)/5$$

$$40\% = 30\% + \text{Infl}_5$$

$$\text{Infl}_5 = 10\%.$$

ST–3	2000	2001	2002
Thompson's Taxes as a Corporation			
Income before salary and taxes	$60,000	$90,000	$110,000
Less: salary	(40,000)	(40,000)	(40,000)
Taxable income, corporate	$20,000	$50,000	$ 70,000
Total corporate tax	3,000[a]	7,500	12,500
Salary	$40,000	$40,000	$ 40,000
Less exemptions and deductions	(17,250)	(17,250)	(17,250)
Taxable personal income	$22,750	$22,750	$ 22,750
Total personal tax	3,413[b]	3,413	3,413
Combined corporate and personal tax:	$ 6,413	$10,913	$ 15,913

Thompson's Taxes as a Proprietorship

Total income	$60,000	$90,000	$110,000
Less: exemptions and deductions	(17,250)	(17,250)	(17,250)
Taxable personal income	$42,750	$72,750	$ 92,750
Tax liability of proprietorship	$ 6,413ᶜ	$14,774	$ 20,374
Advantage to being a corporation:	$ 0	$ 3,861	$ 4,461

ᵃCorporate tax in 2000 = (0.15)($20,000) = $3,000.

ᵇPersonal tax (if Thompson incorporates) in 2000 = (0.15)($22,750) = $3,413

ᶜProprietorship tax in 2000 = $42,750(0.15) = $6,413

Proprietorship tax in 2002 = $6,457.50 + ($92,750 − $43,050)(0.28) = $20,374

The corporate form of organization allows Thompson to pay the lowest taxes in each year; therefore, on the basis of taxes over the 3-year period, Thompson should incorporate his business. However, note that to get money out of the corporation so he can spend it, Thompson will have to have the corporation pay dividends, which will be taxed to Thompson, and thus he will, sometime in the future, have to pay additional taxes.

Chapter 3

ST–2 Billingsworth paid $2 in dividends and retained $2 per share. Because total retained earnings rose by $12 million, there must be 6 million shares outstanding. With a book value of $40 per share, total common equity must be $40(6 million) = $240 million. Because Billingsworth has $120 million of debt, its debt ratio must be 33.3 percent:

$$\frac{\text{Debt}}{\text{Assets}} = \frac{\text{Debt}}{\text{Debt} + \text{Equity}} = \frac{\$120 \text{ million}}{\$120 \text{ million} + \$240 \text{ million}}$$

$$= 0.333 = 33.3\%.$$

ST–3 a. In answering questions such as this, always begin by writing down the relevant definitional equations, then start filling in numbers. Note that the extra zeros indicating millions have been deleted in the calculations below.

(1) $$\text{DSO} = \frac{\text{Accounts receivable}}{\text{Sales}/360}$$

$$40 = \frac{\text{A/R}}{\$1,000/360}$$

$$\text{A/R} = 40(\$2.778) = \$111.1 \text{ million.}$$

(2) $$\text{Quick ratio} = \frac{\text{Current assets} - \text{Inventories}}{\text{Current liabilities}} = 2.0$$

$$= \frac{\text{Cash and marketable securities} + \text{A/R}}{\text{Current liabilities}} = 2.0$$

$$2.0 = \frac{\$100 + \$111.1}{\text{Current liabilities}}$$

Current liabilities = ($100 + $111.1)/2 = $105.6 million.

(3) $$\text{Current ratio} = \frac{\text{Current assets}}{\text{Current liabilities}} = 3.0$$

$$= \frac{\text{Current assets}}{\$105.6} = 3.0$$

Current assets = 3.0($105.6) = $316.7 million.

(4)   Total assets = Current assets + Fixed assets

$$= \$316.7 + \$283.5 = \$600.1 \text{ million.}$$

(5)   ROA = Profit margin × Total assets turnover

$$= \frac{\text{Net income}}{\text{Sales}} \times \frac{\text{Sales}}{\text{Total assets}}$$

$$= \frac{\$50}{\$1,000} \times \frac{\$1,000}{\$600.1}$$

$$= 0.05 \times 1.667 = 0.0833 = 8.33\%.$$

(6) $$\text{ROE} = \frac{\text{NI}}{\text{Equity}}$$

$$12.0\% = \frac{\$50}{\text{Equity}}$$

$$\text{Equity} = \frac{\$50}{0.12}$$

$$= \$416.7 \text{ million.}$$

(7)   Total assets = Total claims = $600.1 million

Current liabilities + Long-term debt + Equity = $600.1 million

$105.6 + Long-term debt + $416.7 = $600.1 million

Long-term debt = $600.1 − $105.6 − $416.7 = $77.8 million.

b. Kaiser's average sales per day were $1,000/360 = $2.8 million. Its DSO was 40, so A/R = 40($2.8) = $111.1 million. Its new DSO of 30 would cause A/R = 30($2.8) = $83.3 million. The reduction in receivables would be $111.1 − $83.3 = $27.8 million, which would equal the amount of cash generated.

(1)   New equity = Old equity − Stock bought back

$$= \$416.7 − \$27.8$$

$$= \$388.9 \text{ million.}$$

Thus,

$$\text{New ROE} = \frac{\text{Net income}}{\text{New equity}}$$

$$= \frac{\$50}{\$388.9}$$

$$= 12.86\% \text{ (versus old ROE of 12.0\%).}$$

(2) $$\text{New ROA} = \frac{\text{Net income}}{\text{Total assets} - \text{Reduction in A/R}}$$

$$= \frac{\$50}{\$600.1 - \$27.8}$$

$$= 8.74\% \text{ (versus old ROA of 8.33\%).}$$

(3) The old debt is the same as the new debt:

$$\text{Debt} = \text{Total claims} - \text{Equity}$$

$$= \$600.1 - \$416.7 = \$183.4 \text{ million.}$$

Old total assets = $600.1 million.

New total assets = Old total assets − Reduction in A/R

$$= \$600.1 - \$27.8$$

$$= \$572.3 \text{ million.}$$

Therefore,

$$\frac{\text{Debt}}{\text{Old total assets}} = \frac{\$183.4}{\$600.1} = 30.6\%,$$

while

$$\frac{\text{New debt}}{\text{New total assets}} = \frac{\$183.4}{\$572.3} = 32.0\%.$$

Chapter 4

ST–2 a. (1) Determine the variable cost per unit at present, using the following definitions and equations:

Q = units of output (sales) = 5,000.

P = average sales price per unit of output = $100.

F = fixed operating costs = $200,000.

V = variable costs per unit.

$$\text{EBIT} = P(Q) - F - V(Q)$$

$$\$50,000 = \$100(5,000) - \$200,000 - V(5,000)$$

$$5,000V = \$250,000$$

$$V = \$50.$$

(2) Determine the new EBIT level if the change is made:

$$\text{New EBIT} = P_2(Q_2) - F_2 - V_2(Q_2)$$
$$= \$95(7,000) - \$250,000 - \$40(7,000)$$
$$= \$135,000.$$

(3) Determine the incremental EBIT:

$$\Delta\text{EBIT} = \$135,000 - \$50,000 = \$85,000.$$

(4) Estimate the approximate rate of return on the new investment:

$$\Delta\text{ROA} = \frac{\Delta\text{EBIT}}{\text{Investment}} = \frac{\$85,000}{\$400,000} = 21.25\%.$$

Because the ROA exceeds Olinde's average cost of capital, this analysis suggests that Olinde should go ahead and make the investment.

b.

$$\text{DOL} = \frac{Q(P - V)}{Q(P - V) - F}$$

$$\text{DOL}_{\text{Old}} = \frac{5,000(\$100 - \$50)}{5,000(\$100 - \$50) - \$200,000} = 5.00.$$

$$\text{DOL}_{\text{New}} = \frac{7,000(\$95 - \$40)}{7,000(\$95 - \$40) - \$250,000} = 2.85.$$

This indicates that operating income will be less sensitive to changes in sales if the production process is changed; thus the change would reduce risks. However, the change would increase the breakeven point. Still, with a lower sales price, it might be easier to achieve the higher new breakeven volume.

$$\textit{Old: } Q_{\text{OpBE}} = \frac{F}{P - V} = \frac{\$200,000}{\$100 - \$50} = 4,000 \text{ units.}$$

$$\textit{New: } Q_{\text{OpBE}} = \frac{F}{P_2 - V_2} = \frac{\$250,000}{\$95 - \$40} = 4,545 \text{ units.}$$

c. The incremental ROA is:

$$\Delta\text{ROA} = \frac{\Delta\text{Profit}}{\Delta\text{Sales}} \times \frac{\Delta\text{Sales}}{\Delta\text{Assets}}$$

Using debt financing, the incremental profit associated with the investment is equal to the incremental profit found in part a minus the interest expense incurred as a result of the investment:

$$\Delta\text{Profit} = \text{New profit} - \text{Old profit} - \text{Interest}$$
$$= \$135,000 - \$50,000 - 0.08(\$400,000)$$
$$= \$53,000.$$

The incremental sales is calculated as:

$$\Delta Sales = P_2Q_2 - P_1Q_1$$

$$= \$95(7,000) - \$100(5,000)$$

$$= \$665,000 - \$500,000$$

$$= \$165,000.$$

$$ROA = \frac{\$53,000}{\$165,000} \times \frac{\$165,000}{\$400,000} = 13.25\%.$$

The return on the new equity investment still exceeds the average cost of funds, so Olinde should make the investment.

d.
$$DFL = \frac{EBIT}{EBIT - I}$$

$$DFL_{New} = \frac{\$135,000}{\$135,000 - \$32,000}$$

$$= 1.31.$$

$$EBIT_{FinBE} = \$32,000$$

Chapter 5

ST–2 a. The average rate of return for each stock is calculated by simply averaging the returns over the five-year period. The average return for each stock is 18.90 percent, calculated for Stock A as follows:

$$\bar{k}_{Avg} = (-10.00\% + 18.50\% + 38.67\% + 14.33\% + 33.00\%)/5$$

$$= 18.90\%.$$

The realized rate of return on a portfolio made up of Stock A and Stock B would be calculated by finding the average return in each year as $\bar{k}_A$(% of Stock A) + $\bar{k}_B$(% of Stock B) and then averaging these yearly returns:

YEAR	PORTFOLIO AB's RETURN, k_{AB}
1996	(6.50%)
1997	19.90
1998	41.46
1999	9.00
2000	30.65
	$\bar{k}_{Avg}$ = 18.90%

b. The standard deviation of returns is estimated, using Equation 5-3a, as follows (see Footnote 3):

$$\text{Estimated } \sigma = S = \sqrt{\frac{\sum_{t=1}^{n} (\bar{k}_t - \bar{k}_{Avg})^2}{n - 1}} \qquad (5\text{-}3a)$$

For Stock A, the estimated σ is 19.0 percent:

$$\sigma_A = \sqrt{\frac{(-10.00 - 18.9)^2 + (18.50 - 18.9)^2 + \ldots + (33.00 - 18.9)^2}{5 - 1}}$$

$$= \sqrt{\frac{1,445.92}{4}} = 19.0\%.$$

The standard deviation of returns for Stock B and for the portfolio are similarly determined, and they are as follows:

	STOCK A	STOCK B	PORTFOLIO AB
Standard deviation	19.0	19.0	18.6

c. Because the risk reduction from diversification is small (σ_{AB} falls only from 19.0 to 18.6 percent), the most likely value of the correlation coefficient is 0.9. If the correlation coefficient were -0.9, the risk reduction would be much larger. In fact, the correlation coefficient between Stocks A and B is 0.92.

d. If more randomly selected stocks were added to the portfolio, σ_p would decline to somewhere in the vicinity of 15 percent; see Figure 5–7, σ_p would remain constant only if the correlation coefficient were $+1.0$, which is most unlikely. σ_p would decline to zero only if the correlation coefficient, r, were equal to zero and a large number of stocks were added to the portfolio, or if the proper proportions were held in a two-stock portfolio with r $= -1.0$.

Chapter 6

ST–2 a. (1)

$$FV_n = PV(1 + i)^n$$

$$\$7,020 = \$5,500(1 + i)^5$$

$$FVIF_{i,5} = \frac{\$7,020}{\$5,500} = 1.2764$$

Use the Future Value of $1 table (Table A–3 in Appendix A) for 5 periods to find the interest rate corresponding to an FVIF of 1.2764. The closest value is 1.2763, which is in the 5% column: so the return is 5 percent.

To solve for the exact rate, use your calculator or solve algebraically. Using your calculator, enter N = 5, FV = 7,020, PV = −5,500, and then press the I key—you should find the result is 5.001. To solve algebraically, recognize that, according to the above computations, $(1 + i)^5 = 1.276364$ (carried to 6 places). Therefore,

$$(1 + i)^5 = 1.276364$$

$$i = (1.276364)^{1/5} = 0.05001 = 5.001\%$$

(2)
```
   0  i = ? 1     2     3     4     5     6     7     8
   ├──┼──┼──┼──┼──┼──┼──┼──┤
  -5,500                                          8,126
```

$$FV_n = PV(1 + i)^n$$

$$\$8{,}126 = \$5{,}500(1 + i)^8$$

$$FVIF_{i,8} = \frac{\$8{,}126}{\$5{,}500} = 1.4775$$

Looking in the Future Value of $1 table (Table A–3 in Appendix A) across 8 periods, we find that an FVIF of 1.4775 corresponds to 5 percent. Using your calculator or solving algebraically will yield the same result.

Because both investments yield the same return, you should be indifferent between them.

b. If you believe there is greater uncertainty about whether the 8-year investment will pay the amount expected ($8,126) than about whether the 5-year investment will pay the amount expected ($7,020), then you should prefer the shorter-term investment. We will discuss the effects of risk on value in Chapter 7.

ST–3 a.
```
  1/1/00  8%  1/1/01        1/1/02        1/1/03        1/1/04
  ├──────────┼────────────┼────────────┼────────────┤
         -1,000                                    FV = ?
```

$1,000 is being compounded for 3 years, so your balance on January 1, 2004, is $1,259.71:

$$FV_n = PV(1 + i)^n = \$1{,}000(1 + 0.08)^3 = \$1{,}259.71.$$

Alternatively, using a financial calculator, input N = 3, I = 8, PV = −1000, PMT = 0, and FV = ? FV $1,259.71.

b.
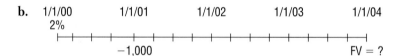

The effective annual rate for 8 percent, compounded quarterly, is

$$\text{Effective annual rate} = \left(1 + \frac{0.08}{4}\right)^4 - 1.0$$

$$= (1.02)^4 - 1.0 = 0.0824 = 8.24\%.$$

Therefore, FV = $1,000(1.0824)^3 = $1,000(1,2681) = $1,268.10. Alternatively, use FVIF for 2%, 3 × 4 = 12 periods:

$$FV_{12} = \$1{,}000(FVIF_{2\%,12}) = \$1{,}000(1.2682) = \$1{,}268.20.$$

Alternatively, using a financial calculator, input N = 12, I = 2, PV = −1000, PMT = 0, and FV = ? FV = $1,268.24.

Note that since the interest factors are carried to only four decimal places, rounding errors occur. Rounding errors also occur between calculator and tabular solutions.

c.

1/1/00	8%	1/1/01	1/1/02	1/1/03	1/1/04
		250	250	250	250
					FV = ?

As you work this problem, keep in mind that the tables assume that payments are made at the end of each period. Therefore, you may solve this problem by finding the future value of an annuity of $250 for 4 years at 8 percent:

$$FVA_4 = PMT(FVIFA_{i,n}) = \$250(4.5061) = \$1,126.53.$$

Alternatively, using a financial calculator, input N = 4, I = 8, PV = 0, PMT = −250, and FV = ? FV = $1,126.53.

d.

1/1/00	8%	1/1/01	1/1/02	1/1/03	1/1/04
		?	?	?	?
					FV = 1,259.71

N = 4; I = 8%; PV = 0; FV = $1,259.71; PMT = ?; PMT = $279.56.

$$PMT(FVIFA_{8\%,4}) = FVA_4$$

$$PMT(4.5061) = \$1,259.71$$

$$PMT = \$1,259.71/4.5061 = \$279.56.$$

Therefore, you would have to make 4 payments of $279.56 each to have a balance of $1,259.71 on January 1, 2000.

ST–4 a. Set up a time line like the one in the preceding problem:

1/1/00	8%	1/1/01	1/1/02	1/1/03	1/1/04
		PV = ?			1,000

Note that your deposit will grow for 3 years at 8 percent. The fact that it is now January 1, 2000, is irrelevant. The deposit on January 1, 2001, is the PV, and the FV is $1,000. Here is the solution:

N = 3; I = 8%; PMT = 0; FV = $1,000; PV = ?; PV = $793.83.

$$FV_3(PVIF_{8\%,3}) = PV$$

PV = $1,000(0.7938) = $793.80 = Initial deposit to accumulate $1,000.

(Difference due to rounding error.)

b.

1/1/00	8%	1/1/01	1/1/02	1/1/03	1/1/04
		PMT	PMT	PMT	PMT
					FV = 1,000

Here we are dealing with a 4-year annuity whose first payment occurs one year from today, on 1/1/01, and whose future value must equal $1,000. You should modify the time line to help visualize the situation. Here is the solution:

$$N = 4; I = 8\%; PV = 0; FV = \$1,000; PMT = ?; PMT = \$221.92.$$

$$PMT(FVIFA_{8\%,4}) = FVA_4$$

$$PMT = \frac{FVA_4}{(FVIFA_{8\%,4})}$$

$$= \frac{\$1,000}{4.5061} = \$221.92 = \begin{array}{l}\text{Payment necessary to} \\ \text{accumulate \$1,000.}\end{array}$$

c. This problem can be approached in several ways. Perhaps the simplest is to ask this question: "If I received $750 on 1/1/01 and deposited it to earn 8 percent, would I have acquired $1,000 on 1/1/04?" The answer is no:

$$FV_3 = \$750(1.08)^3 = \$944.78.$$

This indicates that you should let your father make the payments rather than accept the lump sum of $750.

  You could also compare the $750 with the PV of the payments:

$$N = 4; I = 8\%; PMT = -\$221.92; FV = 0; PV = ?; PV = \$735.03.$$

$$PMT(PVIFA_{8\%,4}) = PVA_4$$

$$\$221.92(3.3121) = \$735.02 = \begin{array}{l}\text{Present value at 1/1/96 of} \\ \text{the required payments.}\end{array}$$

(Difference due to rounding error.)

This is less than the $750 lump sum offer, so your initial reaction might be to accept the lump sum of $750. However, this would be a mistake. The problem is that when you found the $735.02 PV of the annuity, you were finding the value of the annuity *today*, on January 1, 2000. You were comparing $735.02 today with the lump sum of $750 one year from now. This is, of course, invalid. What you should have done was take the $735.02, recognize that this is the PV of an annuity as of January 1, 2000, multiply $735.02 by 1.08 to get $793.82, and compare $793.82 with the lump sum of $750. You would then take your father's offer to make the payments rather than take the lump sum on January 1, 2001. If you solved the PV for an annuity due, you would find the same answer.

d.

1/1/00	i=?	1/1/01	1/1/02	1/1/03	1/1/04

$$-750 \qquad\qquad\qquad\qquad 1{,}000$$

$N = 3$; $PV = -\$750$; $PMT = 0$; $FV = \$1{,}000$; $I = ?$; $I = 10.0642\%$.

$$PV(FVIF_{i,3}) = FV$$

$$FVIF_{i,3} = \frac{FV}{PV}$$

$$= \frac{\$1{,}000}{\$750} = 1.3333.$$

Use the Future Value of $1 table (Table A–3 in Appendix A) for 3 periods to find the interest rate corresponding to an FVIF of 1.3333. Look across the Period 3 row of the table until you come to 1.3333. The closest value is 1.3310, in the 10 percent column. Therefore, you would require an interest rate of approximately 10 percent to achieve your $1,000 goal. The exact rate required, found with a financial calculator, is 10.0642 percent. Solving directly, $i = (1.3333)^{1/3} - 1 = 10.0642\%$.

e.

1/1/00	i=?	1/1/01	1/1/02	1/1/03	1/1/04

$$186.29 \qquad 186.29 \qquad 186.29 \qquad 186.29$$
$$FV = 1{,}000$$

$N = 4$; $PV = 0$; $PMT = -\$186.29$; $FV = \$1{,}000$: $I = ?$; $I = 19.9997\%$.

$$PMT(FVIFA_{i,4}) = FVA_4$$

$$\$186.29(FVIFA_{i,4}) = \$1{,}000$$

$$FVIFA_{i,4} = \frac{\$1{,}000}{\$186.29} = 5.3680.$$

Using Table A–4 at the end of the book, we find that 5.3680 corresponds to a 20 percent interest rate. You might be able to find a borrower willing to offer you a 20 percent interest rate, but there would be some risk involved— he or she might not actually pay you your $1,000 on January 1, 2000.

f.

1/1/00	4%	1/1/01	1/1/02	1/1/03	1/1/04

$$400 \quad PMT \quad PMT \quad PMT \quad PMT \quad PMT \quad PMT$$
$$FV = 1{,}000$$

Find the future value of the original $400 deposit:

$$FV_6 = PV(FVIF_{4\%,6}) = \$400(1.2653) = \$506.12.$$

This means that on January 1, 2004, you need an additional sum of $493.88:

$$\$1{,}000.00 - \$506.12 = \$493.88.$$

This will be accumulated by making 6 equal payments that earn 8 percent compounded semiannually, or 4 percent each 6 months:

$$N = 6; I = 4\%; PV = 0; FV = \$493.88; PMT = ?; PMT = 74.46.$$

$$PMT(FVIFA_{4\%,6}) = FVA_6$$

$$PMT = \frac{FVA_6}{(FVIFA_{4\%,6})}$$

$$= \frac{\$493.88}{6.6330} = \$74.46.$$

Alternatively, using a financial calculator, input $N = 6$, $I = 4$, $PV = -400$, $FV = 1000$, and $PMT = ?$ $PMT = \$74.46$.

g. $$\text{Effective annual rate} = \left(1 + \frac{i_{SIMPLE}}{m}\right)^m - 1.0$$

$$= \left(1 + \frac{0.08}{2}\right)^2 - 1 = (1.04)^2 - 1$$

$$= 1.0816 - 1 = 0.0816 = 8.16\%.$$

ST–5 Bank A's effective annual rate is 8.24 percent:

$$\text{Effective annual rate} = \left(1 + \frac{0.08}{4}\right)^4 - 1.0$$

$$= (1.02)^4 - 1 = 1.0824 - 1$$

$$= 0.0824 = 8.24\%.$$

Now Bank B must have the same effective annual rate:

$$\left(1 + \frac{i}{12}\right)^{12} - 1.0 = 0.0824$$

$$\left(1 + \frac{i}{12}\right)^{12} = 1.0824$$

$$1 + \frac{i}{12} = (1.0824)^{1/12}$$

$$1 + \frac{i}{12} = 1.00662$$

$$\frac{i}{12} = 0.00662$$

$$i = 0.07944 = 7.94\%.$$

Thus, the two banks have different quoted rates—Bank A's quoted rate is 8 percent, while Bank B's quoted rate is 7.94 percent; however, both banks have the same effective annual rate of 8.24 percent. The difference in their quoted rates is due to the difference in compounding frequency.

Chapter 7

ST-2 a. This is not necessarily true. Because G plows back two-thirds of its earnings, its growth rate should exceed that of D, but D pays higher dividends ($6 versus $2). We cannot say which stock should have the higher price.

b. Again, we just do not know which price would be higher.

c. This is false. The changes in k_d and k_s would have a greater effect on G—its price would decline more.

d. The total expected return for D is $\hat{k}_D = \hat{D}_1/P_0 + g = 15\% + 0\% = 15\%$. The total expected return for G will have $\hat{D}_1/P_0$ less than 15 percent and g greater than 0 percent, but $\hat{k}_G$ should be neither greater nor smaller than D's total expected return, 15 percent, because the two stocks are stated to be equally risky.

e. We have eliminated a, b, c, and d, so e should be correct. On the basis of the available information, D and G should sell at about the same price, $40; thus, $\hat{k}_s = 15\%$ for both D and G. G's current dividend yield is $2/$40 = 5%. Therefore, g = 15% − 5% = 10%.

ST-3 a. Pennington's bonds were sold at par; therefore, the original YTM equaled the coupon rate of 12%.

b.
$$V_d = \sum_{t=1}^{50} \frac{\$120/2}{\left(1 + \dfrac{0.10}{2}\right)^t} + \frac{\$1,000}{\left(1 + \dfrac{0.10}{2}\right)^{50}}$$

$$= \$60(\text{PVIFA}_{5\%,50}) + \$1,000(\text{PVIF}_{5\%,50})$$

$$= \$60(18.2559) + \$1,000(0.0872)$$

$$= \$1,095.35 + \$87.20 = \$1,182.55.$$

Alternatively, with a financial calculator, input the following: N = 50, I = 5, PMT = 60, FV = 1000, and PV = ? PV = $1,182.56.

c.
$$\text{Current yield} = \text{Annual coupon payment/Price}$$

$$= \$120/\$1,182.55$$

$$= 0.1015 = 10.15\%.$$

$$\text{Capital gains yield} = \text{Total yield} - \text{Current yield}$$

$$= 10\% - 10.15\% = -0.15\%.$$

d.
$$\$891.64 = \sum_{t=1}^{21} \frac{\$60}{(1 + k_d/2)^t} + \frac{\$1,000}{(1 + k_d/2)^{21}}$$

Using Equation 7-3, the approximate YTM is:

$$\text{YTM} \approx \frac{\$60 + \left(\dfrac{\$1,000 - \$891.64}{21}\right)}{\left[\dfrac{2(\$891.64) + \$1,000}{3}\right]}$$

$$= 7.0\%$$

At $k_d = 7\%$:

$$V_d = INT(PVIFA_{7\%,21}) + M(PVIF_{7\%,21})$$

$$= \$60(10.8355) + \$1,000(0.2416)$$

$$= \$650.13 + \$241.60 = \$891.73$$

Therefore, the YTM on July 1, 1999, was $2 \times 7\% = 14\%$. Alternatively, with a financial calculator, input the following: $N = 21$, $PV = -891.64$, $PMT = 60$, $FV = 1000$, and $k_{d/2} = I = ?$ Calculator solution $= k_{d/2} = 6.97\%$; therefore, $k_d = 14.00\%$.

e.   Current yield $= \$120/\$891.64 = 13.46\%$.

Capital gains yield $= 14\% - 13.46\% = 0.54\%$

ST–4 The first step is to solve for g, the unknown variable, in the constant growth equation. Because $\hat{D}_1$ is unknown but D_0 is known, substitute $D_0(1 + g)$ as follows:

$$\hat{P}_0 = P_0 = \frac{\hat{D}_1}{k_s - g} = \frac{D_0(1 + g)}{k_s - g}$$

$$\$36 = \frac{\$2.40(1 + g)}{0.12 - g}$$

Solving for g, we find the growth rate to be 5 percent:

$$\$4.32 - \$36g = \$2.40 + \$2.40g$$

$$\$38.4g = \$1.92$$

$$g = 0.05 = 5\%.$$

The next step is to use the growth rate to project the stock price five years hence:

$$\hat{P}_5 = \frac{D_0(1 + g)^6}{k_s - g}$$

$$= \frac{\$2.40(1.05)^6}{0.12 - 0.05}$$

$$= \$45.95.$$

[Alternatively, $\hat{P}_5 = \$36(1.05)^5 = \$45.95$.]

Therefore, Ewald Company's expected stock price five years from now, $\hat{P}_5$, is $45.95.

ST–5 a. (1) Calculate the PV of the dividends paid during the supernormal growth period:

$$\hat{D}_1 = \$1.1500(1.15) = \$1.3225.$$

$$\hat{D}_2 = \$1.3225(1.15) = \$1.5209.$$

$$\hat{D}_3 = \$1.5209(1.13) = \$1.7186.$$

$$PV\hat{D} = \$1.3225(0.8929) + \$1.5209(0.7972) + \$1.7186(0.7118)$$

$$= \$1.1809 + \$1.2125 + \$1.2233$$

$$= \$3.6167 \approx \$3.62.$$

(2) Find the PV of Snyder's stock price at the end of Year 3:

$$\hat{P}_3 = \frac{\hat{D}_4}{k_s - g} = \frac{\hat{D}_3(1 + g)}{k_s - g}$$

$$= \frac{\$1.7186(1.06)}{0.12 - 0.06}$$

$$= \$30.36.$$

$$PV\,\hat{P}_3 = \$30.36(0.7118) = \$21.61.$$

(3) Sum the two components to find the value of the stock today:

$$\hat{P}_0 = \$3.62 + \$21.61 = \$25.23.$$

Alternatively, the cash flows can be placed on a time line as follows:

Enter the cash flows into the cash flow register, I = 12, and press the NPV key to obtain $P_0 = \$25.23$.

b.
$$\hat{P}_1 = \$1.5209(0.8929) + \$1.7186(0.7972) + \$30.36(0.7972)$$

$$= \$1.3580 + \$1.3701 + \$24.2030$$

$$= \$26.9311 \approx \$26.93.$$

(Calculator solution: $26.93.)

$$\hat{P}_2 = \$1.7186(0.8929) + \$30.36(0.8929)$$

$$= \$1.5345 + \$27.1084$$

$$= \$28.6429 \approx \$28.64.$$

(Calculator solution: $28.64.)

c.

YEAR	DIVIDEND YIELD	+	CAPITAL GAINS YIELD	=	TOTAL RETURN
1	$\dfrac{\$1.3225}{\$25.23} \approx 5.24\%$		$\dfrac{\$26.93 - \$25.23}{\$25.23} \approx 6.74\%$		$\approx 12\%$

YEAR	DIVIDEND YIELD	+	CAPITAL GAINS YIELD	=	TOTAL RETURN
2	$\dfrac{\$1.5209}{\$26.93} \approx 5.65\%$		$\dfrac{\$28.64 - \$26.93}{\$26.93} \approx 6.35\%$		$\approx 12\%$
3	$\dfrac{\$1.7186}{\$28.64} \approx 6.00\%$		$\dfrac{\$30.36 - \$28.64}{\$28.64} \approx 6.00\%$		$\approx 12\%$

Chapter 8

ST–2 a. *Payback:*

To determine the payback, construct the cumulative cash flows for each project:

	CUMULATIVE CASH FLOWS	
YEAR	PROJECT X	PROJECT Y
0	($10,000)	($10,000)
1	(3,500)	(6,500)
2	(500)	(3,000)
3	2,500	500
4	3,500	4,000

$$\text{Payback}_X = 2 + \frac{500}{\$3,000} = 2.17 \text{ years.}$$

$$\text{Payback}_Y = 2 + \frac{\$3,000}{\$3,500} = 2.86 \text{ years.}$$

Net present value (NPV):

$$\text{NPV}_X = -\$10,000 + \frac{\$6,500}{(1.12)^1} + \frac{\$3,000}{(1.12)^2} + \frac{\$3,000}{(1.12)^3} + \frac{\$1,000}{(1.12)^4}$$

$$= \$966.01.$$

$$\text{NPV}_Y = -\$10,000 + \frac{\$3,500}{(1.12)^1} + \frac{\$3,500}{(1.12)^2} + \frac{\$3,500}{(1.12)^3} + \frac{\$3,500}{(1.12)^4}$$

$$= \$630.72.$$

Alternatively, using a financial calculator, input the cash flows into the cash flow register, enter I = 12, and then press the NPV key to obtain $\text{NPV}_X = \$966.01$ and $\text{NPV}_Y = \$630.72$.

Internal rate of return (IRR):

To solve for each project's IRR, find the discount rates which equate each NPV to zero:

$$\text{IRR}_X = 18.0\%.$$

$$\text{IRR}_Y = 15.0\%.$$

b. The following table summarizes the project rankings by each method:

	PROJECT THAT RANKS HIGHER
Payback	X
NPV	X
IRR	X

Note that all methods rank Project X over Project Y. In addition, both projects are acceptable under the NPV and IRR criteria. Thus, both projects should be accepted if they are independent.

c. In this case, we would choose the project with the higher NPV at k = 12%, or Project X.

d. To determine the effects of changing the cost of capital, plot the NPV profiles of each project. The crossover rate occurs at about 6 to 7 percent (6.2%).

NPV PROFILES FOR PROJECTS X AND Y

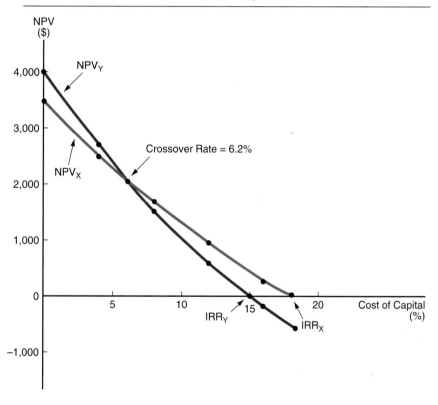

Required Rate of Return	NPV$_X$	NPV$_Y$
0%	$3,500	$4,000
4	2,545	2,705
8	1,707	1,592
12	966	631
16	307	(206)
18	5	(585)

If the firm's required rate of return is less than 6 percent, a conflict exists because $NPV_Y > NPV_X$, but $IRR_X > IRR_Y$. Therefore, if k were 5 percent, a conflict would exist.

e. The basic cause of the conflict is differing reinvestment rate assumptions between NPV and IRR. NPV assumes that cash flows can be reinvested at the cost of capital, while IRR assumes reinvestment at the (generally) higher IRR. The high reinvestment rate assumption under IRR makes early cash flows especially valuable, and hence short-term projects look better under IRR.

Chapter 9

ST–2 a. *Estimated investment outlay:*

Price	($50,000)
Modification	(10,000)
Change in net working capital	(2,000)
Total investment outlay	($62,000)

b. *Incremental operating cash flows:*

		YEAR 1	YEAR 2	YEAR 3
1.	After-tax cost savings[a]	$12,000	$12,000	$12,000
2.	Depreciation[b]	19,800	27,000	9,000
3.	Depreciation tax savings[c]	7,920	10,800	3,600
	Net cash flow (1 + 3)	$19,920	$22,800	$15,600

[a]$20,000 (1 − T).

[b]Depreciable basis = $60,000; the MACRS percentage allowances are 0.33, 0.45, and 0.15 in Years 1, 2, and 3, respectively; hence, depreciation in Year 1 = 0.33($60,000) = $19,800, and so on. There will remain $4,200, or 7 percent, undepreciated after Year 3; it would normally be taken in Year 4.

[c]Depreciation tax savings = T(Depreciation) = 0.4($19,800) = $7,920 in Year 1, and so on.

c. *Terminal cash flow:*

Salvage value	$20,000
Tax on salvage value[a]	(6,320)
Net working capital recovery	2,000
	$15,680

[a]Sales price	$20,000
Less book value	(4,200)
Taxable income	$15,800
Tax at 40%	$6,320

Book value = Depreciable basis − Accumulated depreciation
= $60,000 − $55,800 = $4,200.

d. *Project NPV:*

```
0    10%    1         2         3
├──────────┼─────────┼─────────┤
-62,000   19,920    22,800    31,280
```

$$NPV = -\$62,000 + \frac{\$19,920}{(1.10)^1} + \frac{\$22,800}{(1.10)^2} + \frac{\$31,280}{(1.10)^3}$$

$$= -\$1,547.$$

Alternatively, using a financial calculator, input the cash flows into the cash flow register, enter I = 10, and then press the NPV key to obtain NPV = −$1,547. Because the earthmover has a negative NPV, it should not be purchased.

ST-3 *First determine the initial investment outlay:*

Purchase price	($8,000)
Sale of old machine	3,000
Tax on sale of old machine	(160)[a]
Change in net working capital	(1,500)[b]
Total investment	($6,660)

---

[a]The market value is $3,000 − $2,600 = $400 above the book value. Thus, there is a $400 recapture of depreciation, and Dauten would have to pay 0.40($400) = $160 in taxes.

[b]The change in net working capital is a $2,000 increase in current assets minus a $500 increase in current liabilities, which totals to $1,500.

Now, examine the operating cash inflows:

Sales increase	$1,000
Cost decrease	1,500
Increase in pretax operating revenues	$2,500

After-tax operating revenue increase:
$$\$2,500(1 - T) = \$2,500(0.60) = \$1,500.$$

Depreciation:

YEAR	1	2	3	4	5	6
New[a]	$1,600	$2,560	$1,520	$ 960	$ 880	$ 480
Old	350	350	350	350	350	350
Change	$1,250	$2,210	$1,170	$ 610	$ 530	$ 130
Depreciation Tax savings[b]	$ 500	$ 884	$ 468	$ 244	$ 212	$ 52

---

[a]Depreciable basis = $8,000. Depreciation expense in each year equals depreciable basis times the MACRS percentage allowances of 0.20, 0.32, 0.19, 0.12, 0.11, and 0.06 in Years 1–6, respectively.

[b]Depreciation tax savings = T(ΔDepreciation) = 0.4(ΔDepreciation).

Chapter 10

ST–2 a. A break point will occur each time a low-cost type of capital is used up. We establish the break points as follows, after first noting that LEI has $24,000 of retained earnings:

$$\text{Retained earnings} = (\text{Total earnings})(1.0 - \text{Payout})$$
$$= \$34,285.72(0.7)$$
$$= \$24,000.$$

$$\text{Break point} = \frac{\text{Total amount of low-cost capital of a given type}}{\text{Proportion of this type of capital in the capital structure}}.$$

CAPITAL USED UP	BREAK POINT CALCULATION		BREAK NUMBER
Retained earnings	$BP_{RE} = \dfrac{\$24,000}{0.60}$	$= \$40,000$	2
10% flotation common	$BP_{10\%E} = \dfrac{\$24,000 + \$12,000}{0.60}$	$= \$60,000$	4
5% flotation preferred	$BP_{5\%P} = \dfrac{\$7,500}{0.15}$	$= \$50,000$	3
12% debt	$BP_{12\%D} = \dfrac{\$5,000}{0.25}$	$= \$20,000$	1
14% debt	$BP_{14\%D} = \dfrac{\$10,000}{0.25}$	$= \$40,000$	2

Summary of break points

(1) There are three common equity costs and hence two changes and, therefore, two equity-induced breaks in the MCC. There are two preferred costs and hence one preferred break. There are three debt costs and hence two debt breaks.

(2) The numbers in the third column of the table designate the sequential order of the breaks, determined after all the break points were calculated. Note that the second debt break and the break for retained earnings both occur at $40,000.

(3) The first break point occurs at $20,000, when the 12 percent debt is used up. The second break point, $40,000, results from using up both retained earnings and the 14 percent debt. The MCC curve also rises at $50,000 and $60,000, as preferred stock with a 5 percent flotation cost and common stock with a 10 percent flotation cost, respectively, are used up.

b. Component costs within indicated total capital intervals are as follows: Retained earnings (used in interval $0 to $40,000):

$$k_s = \frac{\hat{D}_1}{P_0} + g = \frac{D_0(1 + g)}{P_0} + g$$

$$= \frac{\$3.60(1.09)}{\$60} + 0.09$$

$$= 0.0654 + 0.09 \qquad = 15.54\%.$$

Common with F = 10% ($40,001 to $60,000):

$$k_e = \frac{\hat{D}_1}{P_0(1.0 - F)} + g = \frac{\$3.924}{\$60(0.9)} + 9\% \qquad = 16.27\%.$$

Common with F = 20% (over $60,000):

$$k_e = \frac{\$3.924}{\$60(0.8)} + 9\% \qquad = 17.18\%.$$

Preferred with F = 5% ($0 to $50,000):

$$k_p = \frac{D_p}{P_0 - \text{Flotation costs}} = \frac{\$11}{\$100(0.95)} \qquad = 11.58\%.$$

Preferred with F = 10% (over $50,000):

$$k_p = \frac{\$11}{\$100(0.9)} \qquad = 12.22\%.$$

Debt at k_d = 12% ($0 to $20,000):

$$k_{dT} = k_d(1 - T) = 12\%(0.6) \qquad = 7.20\%.$$

Debt at k_d = 14% ($20,001 to $40,000):

$$k_{dT} = 14\%(0.6) \qquad = 8.40\%.$$

Debt at k_d = 16% (over $40,000):

$$k_{dT} = 16\%(0.6) \qquad = 9.60\%.$$

c. WACC calculations within indicated total capital intervals:
   (1) $0 to $20,000 (debt = 7.2%, preferred = 11.58%, and retained earnings [RE] = 15.54%):

$$\text{WACC}_1 = w_d k_{dT} + w_p k_p + w_s k_s$$

$$= 0.25(7.2\%) + 0.15(11.58\%) + 0.60(15.54\%) = 12.86\%.$$

   (2) $20,001 to $40,000 (debt = 8.4%, preferred = 11.58%, and RE = 15.54%):

$$\text{WACC}_2 = 0.25(8.4\%) + 0.15(11.58\%) + 0.60(15.54\%) = 13.16\%.$$

(3) $40,001 to $50,000 (debt = 9.6%, preferred = 11.58%, and equity = 16.27%):

$$WACC_3 = 0.25(9.6\%) + 0.15(11.58\%) + 0.60(16.27\%) = 13.90\%.$$

(4) $50,001 to $60,000 (debt = 9.6%, preferred = 12.22%, and equity = 16.27%):

$$WACC_4 = 0.25(9.6\%) + 0.15(12.22\%) + 0.60(16.27\%) = 14.00\%.$$

(5) Over $60,000 (debt = 9.6%, preferred = 12.22%, and equity = 17.18%):

$$WACC_5 = 0.25(9.6\%) + 0.15(12.22\%) + 0.60(17.18\%) = 14.54\%.$$

d. IRR calculation for Project E:

$$PVIFA_{k,6} = \frac{\$20,000}{\$5,427.84} = 3.6847.$$

This is the factor for 16 percent, so $IRR_E = 16\%$.
Alternatively, N = 6, PV = −20000, PMT = 5427.84, and I = ? I = 16.00%.

e. See the graph of the MCC and IOS schedules for LEI below.

LEI: MCC and IOS Schedules

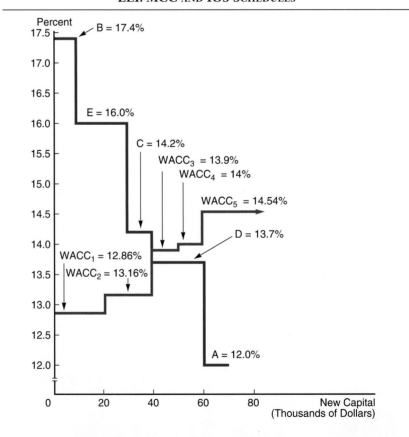

f. LEI should accept Projects B, E, and C. It should reject Projects A and D because their IRRs do not exceed the marginal costs of funds needed to finance them. The firm's capital budget would total $40,000.

Chapter 11

ST–2 a.

EBIT	$4,000,000
Interest ($2,000,000 × 0.10)	(200,000)
Earnings before taxes (EBT)	$3,800,000
Taxes (35%)	(1,330,000)
Net income	$2,470,000

EPS = $2,470,000/600,000 = $4.12.

P_0 = $4.12/0.15 = $27.47.

b.

Equity = 600,000 × ($10) = $6,000,000.

Debt = $2,000,000.

Total capital = $8,000,000.

$$\text{WACC} = w_d[k_d(1 - T)] + w_s k_s$$

$$= (2/8)[(10\%)(1 - 0.35)] + (6/8)(15\%)$$

$$= 1.63\% + 11.25\%$$

$$= 12.88\%.$$

c.

EBIT	$4,000,000
Interest ($10,000,000 × 0.12)	(1,200,000)
Earnings before taxes (EBT)	$2,800,000
Taxes (35%)	(980,000)
Net income	$1,820,000

Shares bought and retired:

$$\Delta\text{Shares} = \Delta\text{Debt}/P_0 = \$8,000,000/\$27.47 = 291,227.$$

New outstanding shares:

$$\text{Shares}_1 = \text{Shares}_0 - \Delta\text{Shares} = 600,000 - 291,227 = 308,773.$$

New EPS:

$$\text{EPS} = \$1,820,000/308,773 = \$5.89.$$

New price per share:

$$P_0 = \$5.89/0.17 = \$34.65 \text{ versus } \$27.47.$$

Therefore, Gentry should change its capital structure.

d. In this case, the company's net income would be higher by $(0.12 - 0.10)$ $(\$2,000,000)(1 - 0.35) = \$26,000$ because its interest charges would be lower. The new price would be

$$P_0 = \frac{(\$1,820,000 + \$26,000)/308,773}{0.17} = \$35.18.$$

In the first case, in which debt had to be refunded, the bondholders were compensated for the increased risk of the higher debt position. In the second case, the old bondholders were not compensated; their 10 percent coupon perpetual bonds would now be worth

$$\$100/0.12 = \$833.33,$$

or $\$1,666,667$ in total, down from the old $\$2$ million, or a loss of $\$333,333$. The stockholders would have a gain of

$$(\$35.18 - \$34.65)(308,773) = \$163,650.$$

This gain would, of course, be at the expense of the old bondholders. (There is no reason to think that bondholders' losses would exactly offset stockholders' gains.)

e.
$$TIE = \frac{EBIT}{I}.$$

$$\text{Original TIE} = \frac{\$4,000,000}{\$200,000} = 20 \text{ times.}$$

$$\text{New TIE} = \frac{\$4,000,000}{\$1,200,000} = 3.33 \text{ times.}$$

Chapter 12

ST–2 a.

Projected net income	$2,000,000
Less projected capital investments	(800,000)
Available residual	$ 1,200,000
Shares outstanding	200,000

$$DPS = \$1,200,000/200,000 \text{ shares} = \$6 = \hat{D}_1.$$

b. EPS $= \$2,000,000/200,000$ shares $= \$10$.

Payout ratio $=$ DPS/EPS $= \$6/\$10 = 60\%$, or

Total dividends/NI $= \$1,200,000/\$2,000,000 = 60\%$.

c.
$$\text{Currently, } P_0 = \frac{\hat{D}_1}{k_s - g} = \frac{\$6}{0.14 - 0.05} = \frac{\$6}{0.09} = \$66.67.$$

Under the former circumstances, $\hat{D}_1$ would be based on a 20 percent payout on $\$10$ EPS, or $\$2$. With $k_s = 14\%$ and $g = 12\%$, we solve for P_0:

$$P_0 = \frac{\hat{D}_1}{k_s - g} = \frac{\$2}{0.14 - 0.12} = \frac{\$2}{0.02} = \$100.$$

Although CMC has suffered a severe setback, its existing assets will continue to provide a good income stream. More of these earnings should now be passed on to the shareholders, as the slowed internal growth has reduced the need for funds. However, the net result is a 33 percent decrease in the value of the shares.

d. If the payout ratio were continued at 20 percent, even after internal investment opportunities had declined, the price of the stock would drop to $2/(0.14 − 0.06) = $25 rather than to $66.67. Thus, an increase in the dividend payout is consistent with maximizing shareholder wealth.

Because of the downward-sloping IOS curve, the greater the firm's level of investment, the lower the average ROE. Thus, the more money CMC retains and invests, the lower its average ROE will be. We can determine the average ROE under different conditions as follows:

Old situation (with founder active and 20 percent payout):

$$g = (1.0 − \text{Payout ratio})(\text{Average ROE})$$

$$12\% = (1.0 − 0.2)(\text{Average ROE})$$

$$\text{Average ROE} = 12\%/0.8 = 15\% > k_s = 14\%.$$

Note that the *average* ROE is 15 percent, whereas the *marginal* ROE is presumably equal to 14 percent.

New situation (with founder retired and a 60 percent payout):

$$g = 6\% = (1.0 − 0.6)(\text{ROE})$$

$$\text{ROE} = 6\%/0.4 = 15\% > k_s = 14\%.$$

This suggests that the new payout is appropriate and that the firm is taking on investments down to the point at which marginal returns are equal to the cost of capital.

Chapter 13

ST–2 a. and **b.**

**INCOME STATEMENTS FOR YEAR ENDED DECEMBER 31, 2000
(THOUSANDS OF DOLLARS)**

	VANDERHEIDEN PRESS		HERRENHOUSE PUBLISHING	
	A	B	A	B
EBIT	$ 30,000	$ 30,000	$ 30,000	$ 30,000
Interest	(12,400)	(14,400)	(10,600)	(18,600)
Taxable income	$ 17,600	$ 15,600	$ 19,400	$ 11,400
Taxes (40%)	(7,040)	(6,240)	(7,760)	(4,560)
Net income	$ 10,560	$ 9,360	$ 11,640	$ 6,840
Equity	$100,000	$100,000	$100,000	$100,000
Return on equity	10.56%	9.36%	11.64%	6.84%

The Vanderheiden Press has a higher ROE when short-term interest rates are high, whereas Herrenhouse Publishing does better when rates are lower.

c. Herrenhouse's position is riskier. First, its profits and return on equity are much more volatile than Vanderheiden's. Second, Herrenhouse must renew its large short-term loan every year, and if the renewal comes up at a time when money is very tight, when its business is depressed, or both, then Herrenhouse could be denied credit, which could put it out of business.

ST–3 THE CALGARY COMPANY: ALTERNATIVE BALANCE SHEETS

	RESTRICTED (40%)	MODERATE (50%)	RELAXED (60%)
Current assets	$1,200,000	$1,500,000	$1,800,000
Fixed assets	600,000	600,000	600,000
Total assets	$1,800,000	$2,100,000	$2,400,000
Debt	$ 900,000	$1,050,000	$1,200,000
Equity	900,000	1,050,000	1,200,000
Total liabilities and equity	$1,800,000	$2,100,000	$2,400,000

THE CALGARY COMPANY: ALTERNATIVE INCOME STATEMENTS

	RESTRICTED	MODERATE	RELAXED
Sales	$3,000,000	$3,000,000	$3,000,000
EBIT	450,000	450,000	450,000
Interest (10%)	(90,000)	(105,000)	(120,000)
Earnings before taxes (EBT)	$ 360,000	$ 345,000	$ 330,000
Taxes (40%)	(144,000)	(138,000)	(132,000)
Net income	$ 216,000	$ 207,000	$ 198,000
ROE	24.0%	19.7%	16.5%

Chapter 14

ST–2 a. First determine the balance on the firm's checkbook and the bank's records as follows:

	FIRM'S CHECKBOOK	BANK'S RECORDS
Day 1: Deposit $500,000; write check for $1,000,000	($ 500,000)	$500,000
Day 2: Write check for $1,000,000	($1,500,000)	$500,000
Day 3: Write check for $1,000,000	($2,500,000)	$500,000
Day 4: Write check for $1,000,000; deposit $1,000,000	($2,500,000)	$500,000

After Upton has reached a steady state, it must deposit $1,000,000 each day to cover the checks written three days earlier.

b. The firm has 3 days of float; not until Day 4 does the firm have to make any additional deposits.

c. As shown above, Upton should try to maintain a balance on the bank's records of $500,000. On its own books it will have a balance of *minus* $2,500,000.

ST–3 Under the current credit policy, the Boca Grande Company has no discounts, has collection expenses of $50,000, has bad debt losses of (0.02)($10,000,000) = $200,000, and has average accounts receivable of (DSO)(Average sales per day) = (30)($10,000,000/360) = $833,333. The firm's cost of carrying these receivables is (Variable cost ratio)(A/R)(Cost of capital) = (0.80)($833,333)(0.16) = $106,667. It is necessary to multiply by the variable cost ratio because the actual *investment* in receivables is less than the dollar amount of the receivables.

Proposal 1: Lengthen the credit period to net 30 so that

1. Sales increase by $1 million.
2. Discounts = $0.
3. Bad debt losses = (0.03)($11,000,000)
   = $330,000
4. DSO = 45 days on all sales.
5. New average receivables = (45)($11,000,000/360) = $1,375,000.
6. Cost of carrying receivables = (v)(k)(Average accounts receivable)
   = (0.80)(0.16)($1,375,000)
   = $176,000.
7. Collection expenses = $50,000.

Analysis of proposed change:

	INCOME STATEMENT UNDER CURRENT POLICY	EFFECT OF CHANGE	INCOME STATEMENT UNDER NEW POLICY
Gross sales	$10,000,000	+ $1,000,000	$11,000,000
Less discounts	(0)	+ (0)	(0)
Net sales	$10,000,000	+ $1,000,000	$11,000,000
Production costs (80%)	(8,000,000)	+ (800,000)	(8,800,000)
Profit before credit costs and taxes	$ 2,000,000	+ $ 200,000	$ 2,200,000
Credit-related costs			
Cost of carrying receivables	(106,667)	+ (69,333)	(176,000)
Collection expenses	(50,000)	+ (0)	(50,000)
Bad debt losses	(200,000)	+ (40,000)	(330,000)
Profit before taxes	$ 1,643,333	+ $ 667	$ 1,644,000
Federal-plus-state taxes (40%)	(657,333)	+ (267)	(657,600)
Net income	$ 986,000	+ $ 400	$ 986,400

The proposed change appears to be a good one, assuming the assumptions are correct.

Proposal 2: Shorten the credit period to net 20 so that

1. Sales decrease by $1 million.
2. Discount = $0.
3. Bad debt losses = (0.01)($9,000,000) = $90,000.
4. DSO = 22 days.
5. New average receivables = (22)($9,000,000/360) = $550,000.
6. Cost of carrying receivables = (v)(k)(Average accounts receivable)
$$= (0.80)(0.16)(\$550,000)$$
$$= \$70,400.$$
7. Collection expenses = $50,000.

Analysis of proposed change:

	INCOME STATEMENT UNDER CURRENT POLICY	EFFECT OF CHANGE	INCOME STATEMENT UNDER NEW POLICY
Gross sales	$10,000,000	($1,000,000)	$9,000,000
Less discounts	(0)	(0)	(0)
Net sales	$10,000,000	($1,000,000)	$9,000,000
Production costs (80%)	(8,000,000)	800,000	(7,200,000)
Profit before credit costs and taxes	$ 2,000,000	($ 200,000)	$1,800,000
Credit-related costs			
Cost of carrying receivables	(106,667)	36,267	(70,400)
Collection expenses	(50,000)	(0)	(50,000)
Bad debt losses	(200,000)	110,000	(90,000)
Profit before taxes	$ 1,643,333	($ 53,733)	$1,589,600
Federal-plus-state taxes (40%)	(657,333)	21,493	(635,840)
Net income	$ 986,000	($ 32,240)	$ 953,760

This change reduces net income, so it should be rejected. Boca Grande will increase profits by accepting Proposal 1 to lengthen the credit period from 25 days to 30 days, assuming all assumptions are correct. This may or may not be the *optimal*, or profit-maximizing, credit policy, but it does appear to be a movement in the right direction.

ST–2 a.
$$EOQ = \sqrt{\frac{2 \times O \times T}{C \times PP}}$$

$$= \sqrt{\frac{(2)(\$5,000)(2,600,000)}{(0.02)(\$5.00)}}$$

$$= 509,902 \text{ bushels.}$$

Because the firm must order in multiples of 2,000 bushels, it should order in quantities of 510,000 bushels.

b.   Average weekly sales = 2,600,000/52

$$= 50,000 \text{ bushels.}$$

Reorder point = 6 weeks' sales

$$= 6(50,000)$$

$$= 300,000 \text{ bushels}$$

c. Total inventory costs:

$$\text{TIC} = (\text{C})\text{PP}\left(\frac{Q}{2}\right) + \text{O}\left(\frac{T}{Q}\right)$$

$$= (0.02)(\$5)\left(\frac{510,000}{2}\right) + (\$5,000)\left(\frac{2,600,000}{510,000}\right)$$

$$= \$25,500 + \$25,490.20$$

$$= \$50,990.20$$

Chapter 15

ST–2 a. *Commercial bank loan*

Amount loaned	= (0.75)($250,000)	= $187,500
Discount	= (0.09/12)($187,500)	= (1,406)
Compensating balance	= (0.20)($187,500)	= (37,500)
Amount received		= $148,594
Interest expense	= (0.09)($187,500)	= $ 16,875
Credit department*	= ($4,000)(12)	= 48,000
Bad debts*	= (0.02)($250,000)(12)	= 60,000
Total annual costs		= $124,875

---

*The costs of the credit department and bad debts are expenses that will be incurred if a bank loan is used, but these costs will be avoided if the firm accepts the factoring arrangement.

Factoring

Amount loaned	= (0.85)($250,000)	= $212,500
Commission for period	= (0.035)($250,000)	= (8,750)
Prepaid interest	= (0.09/12)($203,750)	= (1,528)
Amount received		= $202,222
Annual commission	= ($8,750)(12)	= $105,000
Annual interest	= (0.09)($203,750)	= 18,338
Total annual costs		= $123,338

Alternatively, input the cash flows for the individual years in the cash flow register and input I = 6, then press the NPV button to arrive at the answer of ($23,036). Because the present value of the cost of leasing is less than that of owning, the truck should be leased: $23,036 − $22,038 = $998, net advantage to leasing.

c. The discount rate is based on the cost of debt because most cash flows are fixed by contract and, consequently, are relatively certain. Thus, the lease cash flows have about the same risk as the firm's debt. Also, leasing is considered to be a substitute for debt. We use an after-tax cost rate because the cash flows are stated net of taxes.

d. Olsen could increase the discount rate on the salvage value cash flow. This would increase the PV cost of owning and make leasing even more advantageous.

Answers to End-of-Chapter Problems

We present here some intermediate steps and final answers to selected end-of-chapter problems. Please note that your answer may differ slightly from ours due to rounding errors. Also, although we hope not, some of the problems may have more than one correct solution, depending upon what assumptions are made in working the problem. Finally, many of the problems involve some verbal discussion as well as numerical calculations; this verbal material is not presented here.

2–1 a. $k_1 = 9.20\%$; $k_5 = 7.20\%$.

2–3 a. 4.8%.
 b. 6.8%
 c. 5-yr bond = 7.3%

2–5 $Tax_{1999} = \$0$; Initial $tax_{2001} = \$4,500$;
 Initial $tax_{2002} = \$15,450$; Final $tax_{2002} = \$0$.

2–6 a. 2000 advantage as a corporation = \$1,456;
 2001 advantage = \$4,056;
 2002 advantage = \$5,356.

2–7 a. Personal tax = \$18,536.50
 c. IBM yield = 7.59%; choose FLA bonds.
 d. 18.18%.

2–8 a. \$13,933.50
 b. \$6,247.50

2–9 a. k_1 in Year 2 = 13%.

2–10 k_1 in Year 2 = 15%; Year 2 inflation = 11%.

2–11 a. Tax = \$61,250.
 b. Tax = \$15,600.
 c. Tax = \$4,680.

2–12 Tax = \$107,855; NI = \$222,145; Marginal tax rate = 39%; Average tax rate = 33.8%.

2–13 a. \$40
 c. \$70

2–14 Tax = \$32,156; NI = \$98,844;
 Average tax rate = 25.6%

2–15 6.0%

2–16 AT&T bonds = 8.8%.

3–2 a. Current ratio = 1.98×; DSO = 75 days;
 Total assets turnover = 1.7×;
 Debt ratio = 61.9%.

3–3 A/P = \$90,000; Inv = \$67,500;
 FA = \$160,500.

3–5 a. Quick ratio = 0.85×; DSO = 37 days;
 ROE = 13.1%; Debt ratio = 54.8%.

3–6 Net profit margin = 2%; Debt/Assets = 40%

3–7 \$262,500; 1.19×.

3–8 Sales = \$2,511,628; DSO = 37 days.

3–9 TIE = 3.5×.

3–10 ROE = 24.5%; ROA = 9.8%.

3–11 a. +5.54%.
 b. (2) +3.21%.

3–12 Total sources = $102; Net increase in cash and marketable securities = $19.

3–13 **a.** NI = $900,000; CF = $2,400,000.
b. CF = $3,000,000.

4–1 **a.** Notes payable = $31.44 million.
b. Current ratio = 2.0×; ROE = 14.2%.
c. (1) −$14.28 million.
　(2) Total assets = $147 million; Notes payable = $3.72 million.
　(3) Current ratio = 4.25×; ROE = 10.84%.

4–2 **a.** Total assets = $33,534; AFN = $2,128.
b. Notes payable = $4,228; AFN = $70; ΔInterest = $213.

4–3 **a.** DOL = 2.5×; DFL = 3.0×.

4–4 **a.** First pass AFN = $667.
b. Increase in notes payable = $51; Increase in C/S = $368.

4–5 **a.** (1) −$60,000.
b. Q_{OpBE} = 14,000.
c. (1) −1.33.

4–6 **a.** (2) $125,000.
b. Q_{OpBE} = 7,000.

4–7 **a.** $2,000.
b. DFL = 1.8.
c. $3,000.

4–8 **a.** (1) −$75,000.
　(2) $175,000.
b. Q_{OpBE} = 140,000.
c. (1) −8.3.
　(2) 15.0.
　(3) 5.0.

4–9 **a.** FC_A = $80,000; VC_A = $4.80/unit; P_A = $8.00/unit.

4–10 **a.** $480,000.
b. $18,750.

4–11 AFN = $360.

4–12 **a.** 40,000.
b. ($0.30).
c. 48,000.
d. DOL = 3.0; DFL = 1.7.

5–1 **a.** $0.5 million.

5–2 **a.** 13.5%.
b. 1.8.

c. k_F = 8% + 5.5%β_F.
d. 17.9%.

5–3 **a.** $\bar{k}_A$ = 11.30%.
c. σ_A = 20.8%; σ_p = 20.1%.

5–4 **a.** $\hat{k}_M$ = 13.5%; $\hat{k}_J$ = 11.6%.
b. σ_M = 3.85%; σ_J = 6.22%.
c. CV_M = 0.29; CV_J = 0.54.

5–5 **a.** $\hat{k}_Y$ = 14%.
b. σ_X = 12.20%.

5–6 **a.** β_B = 2.
b. k_B = 12.5%.

5–7 **a.** k_X = 15.5%.
b. (1) k_X = 16.5%.
c. (1) k_X = 18.1%.

5–8 β_{New} = 1.16.

5–9 β_p = 0.7625; k_p = 12.1%.

5–10 4.5%.

6–1 **a.** $530.
d. $445.

6–2 **a.** $895.40.
b. $1,552.90.
c. $279.20.
d. $500.03; $867.14.

6–3 **a.** ≈ 10 years.
c. ≈ 4 years.

6–4 **a.** $6,374.96.
d. (1) $7,012.46.

6–5 **a.** $2,457.84.
c. $2,000.
d. (1) $2,703.62.

6–6 **a.** Stream A: $1,251.21.

6–7 **b.** 7%.
c. 9%.
d. 15%.

6–8 **a.** $881.15.
b. $895.40.
c. $903.05.
d. $908.35.

6–9 **b.** $279.20.
c. $276.85.
d. $443.70.

6–10 **a.** $5,272.40.
b. $5,374.00.

6–11 a. 1st City = 7%; 2nd City = 6.66%.

6–12 a. PMT = $6,594.94.
  b. $13,189.87.

6–13 a. Z = 9%; B = 8%.
  b. Z = $558.39; $135.98; 32.2%;
    B = $548.33; $48.33; 9.7%.

6–14 a. $61,203.
  b. $11,020.
  c. $6,841.

6–15 a. $176,790.
  b. $150,257.

6–16 $1,901.

6–17 $4,971.

6–18 $1,000 today is worth more.

6–19 a. 15% (or 14.87%).

6–20 APR = 8.0%; EAR = 8.24%.

6–21 12%.

6–22 9%.

6–23 a. $33,872.
  b. $26,243.04 and $0.

6–24 $1,205.55.

6–25 ≈ 15 years.

6–26 5 years; $1,885.09.

6–27 $PV_{7\%}$ = $1,428.57; $PV_{14\%}$ = $714.29.

6–28 $984.88 ≈ $985.

6–29 a. $260.73.
  b. $263.34.

6–30 k_{SIMPLE} = 15.19%.

7–1 a. $1,251.26.
  b. $898.90.

7–2 a. $1,250.
  b. $833.33.
  d. At 8%, V_d = $1,196.31.

7–3 b. PV = $5.29.
  d. $30.01.

7–4 a. 7%.
  b. 5%.
  c. 12%.

7–5 a. (1) $9.50.
    (2) $13.33.
  b. (1) Undefined.

7–6 a. $7.20.
  b. $41.60.
  c. $35.28.

7–7 a. $1,000.
  b. IBM = $812.55; GM = $711.88.
  d. 5.0%.
  e. IBM return = −13.75%.

7–8 a. Dividend 2002 = $2.66.
  b. P_0 = $39.43.
  c. Dividend yield 2000 = 5.10%;
    2004 = 7.00%.

7–9 a. P_0 = $54.11.

7–10 b. P_0 = $21.43.
  c. P_0 = $26.47.
  e. P_0 = $40.54.

7–11 a. New price = $31.34.
  b. beta = 0.49865.

7–12 a. V_L at 5 percent = $1,518.97;
    V_L at 8 percent = $1,171.15;
    V_L at 12 percent = $863.79.

7–13 a. 8.02%.

7–14 a. YTM at $829 ≈ 15%.

7–15 a. 13.3%.
  b. 10%.
  c. 8%.
  d. 5.3%.

7–16 $23.75.

7–17 a. k_C = 10.6%; k_D = 7%.

7–18 $25.03.

7–19 IBM bond = 9.33%.

7–20 10.2%.

7–21 P_0 = $19.89.

7–22 a. $53,411

8–1 b. NPV = $7,486.20.
  d. DPP = 6.51 yrs.

8–2 b. IRR_A = 17.8%; IRR_B = 24.0%.

8–3 a. IRR_A = 20%; IRR_B = 16.7%;
    Crossover rate ≈ 16%.

8–4 a. NPV_A = $14,486,808;
    NPV_B = $11,156,893; IRR_A = 15.03%;
    IRR_B = 22.26%.

8–5 NPV_P = $409; IRR_P = 15%; Accept;
  NPV_T = $3,318; IRR_T = 20%; Accept.

$$E(NPV) = \sqrt{\sum_{i=1}^{n} Pr_i(NPV_i)}.$$

$$\sigma_{NPV} = \sqrt{\sum_{i=1}^{n} Pr_i[NPV_i = E(NPV)]^2}.$$

$$CV_{NPV} = \frac{\sigma_{NPV}}{E(NPV)}.$$

$$k_{proj} = k_{RF} + (k_M - k_{RF})\beta_{proj}.$$

Chapter 10

After-tax component cost of debt $= k_{dT} = k_d(1 - T).$

Component cost of preferred stock $= k_{ps} = \dfrac{D_{ps}}{NP} = \dfrac{D_{ps}}{P_0 - \text{Flotation costs}}.$

$$k_s = k_{RF} + RP = \frac{\hat{D}_1}{P_0} + g = \hat{k}_s.$$

$$k_s = k_{RF} + (k_M - k_{RF})\beta_s.$$

$$k_s = \text{Bond yield} + \text{Risk premium}.$$

$$k_e = \frac{\hat{D}_1}{P_0(1 - F)} + g = \frac{\hat{D}_1}{NP} + g.$$

$$WACC = w_d k_{dT} + w_p k_p + w_s(k_s \text{ or } k_e).$$

$$BP = \frac{\text{Total amount of lower-cost capital of a given type}}{\text{Proportion of this type of capital in the capital structure}}.$$

Chapter 11

$$EPS = \frac{(S - F - VC - I)(1 - T)}{\text{Shares outstanding}} = \frac{(EBIT - I)(1 - T)}{\text{Shares outstanding}}.$$

$$DOL_Q = \frac{Q(P - V)}{Q(P - V) - F}.$$

$$DOL_S = \frac{S - VC}{S - VC - F} = \frac{\text{Gross profit}}{EBIT}.$$

$$DFL = \frac{EBIT}{EBIT - I}.$$

$$DTL = \frac{Q(P - V)}{Q(P - V) - F - I} = \frac{S - VC}{S - VC - F - I} = \frac{\text{Gross profit}}{EBIT - I} = DOL \times DFL.$$

$$EPS_1 = EPS_0[1 + (DTL)(\%\Delta Sales)].$$

Chapter 12

$$\begin{pmatrix}\text{Dollars transferred from} \\ \text{retained earnings due to} \\ \text{stock dividend}\end{pmatrix} = \begin{pmatrix}\text{Number of} \\ \text{shares} \\ \text{outstanding}\end{pmatrix}\begin{pmatrix}\text{Stock} \\ \text{dividend as} \\ \text{a percent}\end{pmatrix}\begin{pmatrix}\text{Market} \\ \text{price of} \\ \text{the stock}\end{pmatrix}.$$

Chapter 13

$$\frac{\text{Account}}{\text{balance}} = \begin{pmatrix}\text{Amount of} \\ \text{daily activity}\end{pmatrix} \times \begin{pmatrix}\text{Average life} \\ \text{of the account}\end{pmatrix}.$$

$$\frac{\text{Inventory}}{\text{conversion period}} = \frac{\text{Inventory}}{\text{CGS}/360}.$$

$$\frac{\text{Receivables}}{\text{collection period}} = \text{DSO} = \frac{\text{Receivables}}{\text{Sales}/360}.$$

$$\frac{\text{Payables}}{\text{deferral period}} = \text{DPO} = \frac{\text{Accounts payable}}{\text{CGS}/360}.$$

$$\frac{\text{Cash conversion}}{\text{cycle}} = \frac{\text{Inventory}}{\text{conversion period}} + \frac{\text{Receivables}}{\text{collection period}} - \frac{\text{Payables}}{\text{deferral period}}.$$

Chapter 14

$$\text{Average daily sales} = \text{ADS} = \frac{\text{Annual sales}}{360} = \frac{(\text{Units sold})(\text{Sales price})}{360}.$$

$$\text{Days sales outstanding} = \text{DSO} = \frac{\text{Receivables}}{\text{ADS}}.$$

$$\text{Receivables investment} = (\text{DSO} \times \text{ADS}) \times \text{v}.$$

$$\text{Cost of carrying receivables} = [(\text{DSO})(\text{Sales}/360)(\text{v})](k_{AR}).$$

$$\text{Average inventory} = A = \frac{\text{Units per order}}{2} = \frac{Q}{2}.$$

$$\text{Total carrying cost} = \text{TCC} = (C)(PP)(A) = (C)(PP)\left(\frac{Q}{2}\right).$$

$$\text{Total ordering cost} = \text{TOC} = O\left(\frac{T}{Q}\right).$$

$$\begin{aligned}\text{Total inventory cost} = \text{TIC} &= \text{TCC} + \text{TOC} \\ &= (C)(PP)\left(\frac{Q}{2}\right) + O\left(\frac{T}{Q}\right).\end{aligned}$$

$$\text{Economic ordering quantity} = \text{EOQ} = \sqrt{\frac{2(O)(T)}{(C)(PP)}}.$$

$$\text{Reorder point} = (\text{Lead time in weeks} \times \text{Weekly usage}).$$

Chapter 15

$$\begin{array}{c}\text{Approximate cost} \\ \text{of foregoing a} \\ \text{cash discount (\%)}\end{array} = \dfrac{\text{Discount percent}}{100 - \dfrac{\text{Discount}}{\text{percent}}} \times \dfrac{360 \text{ days}}{\dfrac{\text{Total days of}}{\text{credit available}} - \dfrac{\text{Discount}}{\text{period}}}$$

$$\text{Interest rate per period} = \dfrac{\text{Dollar cost of borrowing}}{\text{Amount of usable funds}}.$$

$$\text{Effective annual rate} = \left[1 + \dfrac{i_{SIMPLE}}{m}\right]^m - 1.0 = [1 + \text{Interest rate per period}]^m - 1.0.$$

$$\text{Annual percentage rate} = APR = (\text{Interest rate per period}) \times (m) = i_{SIMPLE}.$$

$$\begin{array}{c}\text{Compensating} \\ \text{balance requirement}\end{array} = CB = \dfrac{\text{Principal}}{\text{amount}} \times \dfrac{\text{Compensating}}{\text{balance as a decimal}}$$

$$\begin{array}{c}\text{Usable funds if} \\ \text{checking is \$0}\end{array} = (\text{Principal amount}) - CB = (\text{Principal amount})(1 - \%CB).$$

$$\begin{array}{c}\text{Required loan amount} \\ \text{if checking is \$0}\end{array} = \dfrac{\text{Amount of usable funds needed}}{1 - (CB \text{ as a decimal})}.$$

$$\begin{array}{c}\text{Required loan amount} \\ \text{if checking is \$0}\end{array}\left(\begin{array}{c}\text{Discount \&} \\ \text{Compensating balance}\end{array}\right) = \dfrac{\text{Amount of usable funds needed}}{1 - \%CB - \left(\dfrac{i_{SIMPLE}}{m}\right)}.$$

$$\begin{array}{c}\text{Required loan amount for} \\ \text{a loan with a compensating} \\ \text{balance requirement} \\ \text{if checking balance is} > \$0\end{array} = \dfrac{\dfrac{\text{Amount of usable}}{\text{funds needed}} - \dfrac{\text{Checking}}{\text{account balance}}}{1 - \%CB}$$

$$\text{Approximate period rate(Add-on)} = \dfrac{\text{Interest}}{\left(\dfrac{\text{Amount received}}{2}\right)}$$

Chapter 18

$$\text{Conversion price} = P_c = \dfrac{\text{Par value of bond}}{\text{Conversion ratio}}.$$

Index

Page numbers appearing in italics refer to tables and figures.